Cosmodernism

COSMODERNISM ⊕ American Narrative,
Late Globalization, and the New Cultural Imaginary

Christian Moraru

THE UNIVERSITY OF MICHIGAN PRESS • ANN ARBOR

2014   2013   2012   2011   4   3   2   1

A CIP catalog record for this book is available from the British Library.

Library of Congress Cataloging-in-Publication Data

Moraru, Christian.
   Cosmodernism : American narrative, late globalization, and the new
cultural imaginary / Christian Moraru.
      p.   cm.
   Includes bibliographical references and index.
   ISBN 978-0-472-07129-6 (cloth : alk. paper) — ISBN 978-0-472-05129-
8 (pbk. : alk. paper)
   1. American literature—20th century—History and criticism.
2. Postmodernism (Literature)—United States.   3. Literature and
globalization—United States—History.   4. American literature—
Minority authors—History and criticism.   I. Title.
PS228.P68M66   2011
810.9'113—dc22   2010040237

To Matei Calinescu (1934–2009), in memoriam

The "in-itself" is even an absurd conception; a "constitution-in-itself" is nonsense; we possess the concept "being," "thing," only as a relational concept.

—FRIEDRICH NIETZSCHE, *The Will to Power*

In the beginning is the relation.

—MARTIN BUBER, *I and Thou*

[W]e can see ourselves because someone else has seen us first.

—PAUL AUSTER, *The Art of Hunger*

[S]elf-immuring is self-stultifying.

—CHARLES TAYLOR, *The Ethics of Authenticity*

CONTENTS

PART 3 · TRANSLATIONS

PART 4 · READINGS

PROLOGUE ⊕ TOGETHERNESS

Vingt ans après; or, No Place to Hide

> In the past ten years the Outside has greatly diminished in all its
> dimensions: geography, imagination, liberty. Transcendence has
> closed shop.
>> —ANDREI CODRESCU, *The Disappearance of the Outside*

> [O]ut is over.
>> —THOMAS L. FRIEDMAN, *The World Is Flat*

> There is no more outside.
>> —MICHAEL HARDT AND ANTONIO NEGRI, *Empire*

> [W]hat outside?
>> —JEAN-LUC NANCY, *Being Singular Plural*

"L'enfer, c'est les autres," Garcin proclaims in Sartre's 1944 play *Huis clos*
(No Exit).[1] Hell is others? How come? For one thing, the pronouncement
conveys the uneasiness the writer and modernity overall feel before "alterity." For another, Sartre insisted that he had been "misunderstood." What
his character meant, he explained, was not that our "relations with others
are tainted," "infernal" by definition, but that if these relations are
"twisted, vitiated, then the other can be to us nothing else than hell" because "the others are the most important thing within ourselves that we
can draw from to know who we are." "When we think about ourselves,
when we try to find out who we are," Sartre went on, we "use the knowledge others already have of us. We form an opinion of ourselves by means
of tools others have given us. Whatever I say about myself, an other's judgment is always contained in it. This means that if my relations with an
other are bad, I am completely dependent on this other. And then I am
truly in hell."[2]

America's Cold War private fictions and public policies stage Garcin's
ambivalence with a vengeance by acknowledging "others" yet failing to
act, or to act adequately and consistently, on this capital recognition. To be

sure, the anxieties and the indecisions, let alone the wrong decisions, do not go away after 1989. As I put the final touches on these pages twenty years thereafter, one thing is clear, though: whether "we" think of "them" as infernal or not, whether they inconvenience or soothe us, whether we grasp them through our "sympathetic imagination" like J. M. Coetzee 's Elizabeth Costello or are puzzled by them like Thomas Nagel by his bat, others' presence in American life is becoming more substantial than ever.[3] More than at any point in our past, being-in-relation, with an other, makes for the cornerstone of America and its self-perception in literature, art, and the humanities. The historically unrivaled intensity and extensity with which our relations with others recast our world and our representations of it are giving birth, I argue, to a particular way of seeing this world and ourselves in it, to a new, "cosmodern" cultural imaginary if not to a new cultural paradigm altogether—to an entire "cosmodernism." What I want to emphasize from the outset is the former rather than the latter if by paradigm we imply a distinct body of work. Granted, the two are intertwined. But what has so far emerged across fairly established discourses, genres, and complex U.S. formations such as postmodernism and ethnic literatures is not so much another canon, although this too seems to be in the offing, as a new imagination modality. This novelty is far from absolute. It is cosmodern, not modern, and in that equally reminiscent of the *post*modern. In fact, the cosmodern newness has been hesitant, slow in coming, and unabashedly redolent of prior stylistic and thematic hallmarks; cosmodernism is not only a paradigm in the making but also a "soft" one.

The onset of this paradigm nonetheless determines the last two decades as the scene of a cosmodern turn. Fundamentally shaping our present as a geocultural structure of co-presence, this turn or shift defines our age's "presentness." The post-1989 interval thus replaces the "contemporary" available in current literary-cultural periodizations. Given the history-changing significance of the Berlin Wall's fall, it is for the first time since World War II that critics may have to consider resetting the boundaries of the present. Endorsed by my book, the move would place the commencing of the contemporary—contemporary in a strong sense, if you will—no longer at the end of World War II but at the end of the Cold War, with the latter no more than the former's belated closure and with more recent events of incontestably global impact like September 11, 2001, as symptoms of the Cold War's aftermath rather than as harbingers of another, genuinely new epoch.

I submit, further, that the cosmodern lynchpin is relation itself—the concept and practices of "relationality" in narrative, theory, and other areas of post-1989 American culture. What U.S. artists and thinkers drive home with characteristic acumen after the Wall's collapse is that, as David Hollinger puts it bluntly, "there are fewer and fewer places to hide," where self and other could opt out of the mutually "defining" context of each other's proximity, influence, and inquiring gaze. Our "historical situation" in the United States and beyond in the "age of networks" is one of unparalleled panopticity, of a hitherto peerless scopic presence of individuals, groups, and cultures to one another.[4] I do share the concerns of those who associate the world's visual availability with vulnerability to surveillance, control, and military "targeting."[5] However, dicey and unevenly distributed as it is, the world's new visibility and the flows and exchanges enhancing it apace inform, for better or worse and to a formerly unmatched degree, the self's relational situatedness, its "cosmodern condition." Also a condition of knowledge, of representation and self-representation, this condition does not decouple the familial and the familiar completely. It just eats into their overlap, renders "hereness" less homey, less certain and full of certainties to the residing self and therefore correspondingly thought-provoking, rife with the questions presented by the defamiliarizing presence and beliefs of others. That is, America's location and role and the cultural meanings swirling across and around them are not simply topological but also structural or, better still, structuring. They are concurrently *in* and *of* worldly nature, actively involved in what I determine, following thinkers like Heidegger, Derrida, and Jean-Luc Nancy, as the "worlding of the world"—the world's "parts" such as people, nation-states, "spheres" (and hemispheres), "regions," "civilizations," and racial-ethnic communities coming together and being by being with each other. On this account, the meaning of U.S. culture reveals itself to the trained eye—not for the first time but with more acuity than in pre-1989 times—cosmosemiotically, in conjunction with our global era's world semantics.

This is not a case for American exceptionalism or American imperialism because, in the first place, it is not a case for what Nietzsche ridicules as "Münchhausen's audacity"—the *causa sui* delusion of "pull[ing] oneself up into existence by the hair, out of the swamp of nothingness"; I am endorsing neither the "Adamic," stand-alone American myth nor its later, self-reliantly strutting avatars.[6] Quite the contrary. While I agree with Hollinger that "the United States is not so much a model for the world as an archive of experience on which the world can draw critically," what I do in *Cosmodernism* is place, broadly speaking, the United States in "global perspective"[7] and, more narrowly, late twentieth-century and early twenty-first-century American literary, cultural, and theoretical discourse in the worldly context of the "interpersonal,"[8] where this discourse lends itself to interpretation as a fable of relatedness. I keep telling myself that if America—surely not by itself—has bestowed a particular meaning (and structure) on the globalizing world, our country, its culture, and this culture's significations cannot stand outside this meaning-making and structuring ("worlding") process either, which is another way of saying that we cannot "rely" solely on ourselves to comprehend and achieve our American selves. To be sure, the global chickens are coming home to roost. One of the biggest players in world history, the post-1989 United States is now a vibrant site for the kind of history and narratives in which Americans more and more are and read "with": with the wider world, with its stories and histories, and with these narratives' storytellers and characters. In response, students of American culture have started factoring this cultural-epistemological homecoming into their reassessments of home and of the emotions and notions that make us feel secure, at home, but also special, "unlike others"—into whatever makes us us. And so, as we wrestle with our own otherness, with the idiosyncratic landscape of domesticity, we also grapple with the location and production of "we." To grasp who we are, we struggle to figure out where we are, to locate ourselves and thus take on, anew, the "challenge of drawing" the Theophrastian "circle" of this "we."[9]

Given, on one side, the leveling thrust of globalization, and on the other, the resurgence of violent factionalisms, "clashist" views, and crude antinomies such as we/they, the West / the rest, or "McWorld"/"Jihad" not only in writers such as Samuel P. Huntington and Benjamin Barber but also in public affairs and rhetoric, there is something pressing about this challenge and the relation-grounded culture, identity, and human fellowship vision that might drive us to accept it. No doubt, globalization does, and means, various things to various people, but one of its major tendencies is to assimilate the different, the singular, and the other along with their "otherwise" and "out there." Equally ominous, antinomism of the sort invoked above reifies all these. Critics like Huntington, for instance, do allow that these days "identity at any level—personal, tribal, racial, civilizational—can only be defined in relation to an 'other,' a different person, tribe, race, or civilization," but they largely treat it as a monolith immutably opposed to analogously monolithic entities.[10] Instead, the "cosmoderns" summoned in this book hint that there is another way, neither assimilationist nor disjunctive. Here, "differential" identity does not spring from smooth, equal-to-itself sameness, and it does not reinforce "separateness," the "apartheid type of difference," either.[11] "Mov[ing] about" America and the world "with always at least two gestures[,] that of affirming 'I am like you' while persisting in her difference and that of reminding 'I am different' while unsettling every definition of otherness arrived at,"[12] this identity is, to the cosmodern mind, rationale and vehicle for a new togetherness, for a solidarity across political, ethnic, racial, religious, and other boundaries. Underwritten by concepts of concern and duty that still have to be spelled out, vaster solidarities are something that we have to foster because the problems confronting America and the world after the late 1980s place us all in relation and interaction, entangle us in a web from which it is getting harder and harder to extricate ourselves.

Those of us who buy into this picture assume, I suspect, that reciprocity, solidarity, obligation, caring for others as if one cared for one's own are the best ways to manage a condition of togetherness that not all of us have foreseen, sought, or welcomed. But this management of our world's relationality is still unethical if it proves just a "pragmatic" gambit. Ideally, it should follow from an awareness of what we owe to others *in principle*, from day one, for they have been originally constitutive to the world, and their otherness has been "there"—and thus (in) "here"—since the very beginning as a template of worldliness and thereby of selfhood itself. We shall see that thinkers like Levinas and Nancy are adamant about the a priori inscription of alterity into the self's existential-cognitive script; what we learn a posteriori from the cosmoderns' repeated surveys of the post–Cold War self-other give-and-take is that transactions of this type have never been more wide-reaching and more meaningful for who we are.

Approach, Focus, Structure

Neither the only "new thing" eager to supplant, say, postmodernism or multiculturalism nor full-blown movement or school, cosmodernism is principally (*a*) an *imaginary modality* of mapping out today's world as a cultural geography of relationality; (*b*) by the same token, a *protocol of subjectivity formation;* (*c*) an *ethical imperative* pointing to the present as much as to the future; and (*d*) a *critical algorithm* for decrypting and assembling a range of post-1989 narrative and theoretical imaginings into a reasonably coherent and, again, ahead-looking model. If the cosmoderns read the world in terms of self-other interconnectedness, this algorithm helps me read their readings and thus become the cosmoderns' voyeur, privy to their insights into the new geometry of "we." My method is not the only one applicable to the United States of the "network society" era, and I do employ it rather heuristically, but, drawing as it does from an array of methodologies and interventions, it is itself relational. It is not watertight but effective enough, so I resort to it with a fair amount of consistency. I develop it theoretically at the comparative crossroads of a Levinas-inspired ethics of selfhood, identity studies, postmodern intertextuality, and globalization scholarship's more context-oriented analysis. This approach affords, I trust, a deeper understanding of what a plethora of emblematic texts and authors mean individually as well as together in the literary and cultural history of the past two decades or so.

Which texts and authors, one might ask. If cosmodernism is just one way of trekking over the landscape of post–Cold War relationality, what I offer too is only one fashion of tracing this journey; there is a method, I would like to think, not only to how I read but also to what I choose to read. But my choices are highly representative formally and culturally, attesting to the unfolding of the cosmodern across a host of directions and genres in recent American literature and criticism. As noted earlier, the major works covered are theoretical and especially narrative, chiefly fictional: novels, short stories, romances, memoirs, and travel accounts. Without exception, my primary sources came out after the late 1980s, most of them during the past ten years. Of various ethnic and racial backgrounds, their authors are native and immigrant, mainstream and not-so-mainstream American writers, with Chang-rae Lee, Raymond Federman, Jhumpa Lahiri, Nicole Mones, Suki Kim, Azar Nafisi, Pico Iyer, Alice Randall, Don DeLillo, Karen Tei Yamashita, and John Updike the more pivotal figures. Some of them (Federman, DeLillo, Lee) have been claimed by the divergent canons of postmodernism, ethnic literature, and postcolonialism. For this reason, they have seldom if ever been treated together, all the more reason to test the cosmodern as a classification or, even better, cross-classification principle, as well as an opportunity to readdress problems the former metafictional, postmodern, ethnic, and postcolonial rubrics have left unsolved. Also, in cases such as Lee's, the cosmodern problematic shapes an author's vision from the get-go; in others (e.g., Updike), this happens much later. Some of my writers (Nafisi, Lahiri) are only now beginning to enjoy due recognition yet not necessarily under rubrics they are comfortable with, while others seem to fall completely outside established categories (Yamashita, Randall) or to fit several at once (Updike, Mones). And where names like Bharati Mukherjee are briefly discussed, others are solely mentioned even though they could have been treated in extenso alongside or in lieu of the key figures. I could have dwelled at length, for example, on Thomas Pynchon (with the 2007 novel *Against the Day* a strong contender), Richard Powers, Jonathan Franzen, or Jonathan Safran Foer rather than on DeLillo, and I could have had a separate section on cosmodern cyberpunk or on Native American literature for that matter. Likewise, Lee and Kim belong with an entire series of novelists part 1 and part 3, respectively, can only touch on; Federman makes it, also in the first part, but so could have the late Ronald Sukenick, Charles Johnson, Octavia Butler, Rebecca Goldstein, Aleksandar Hemon, Domnica Radulescu, and Gary Shteyngart, along with others across a whole spectrum of ethno-racial traditions.

A considerably theorized undertaking, this book does not propose another grand theory but a textually and contextually minded argument for cultural change in post-1989 American letters. The five parts, usually in their later sections, ground the argument in narrative analysis. The parts' initial portions, the introduction, and the epilogue nuance and historicize the basic contentions by intervening in a couple of ongoing debates so as to reframe tactically several highly charged notions including the cosmodern's neighbors: "modern," "postmodern," and "cosmopolitan." Setting up the whole presentation, the introductory segment underscores the imaginative-projective aspect of cosmodernism and makes a case for the odd term itself before working out the latter's conceptual-historical ties to "relatedness" and "otherness," on the one hand, and "late globalization," on the other. In 1848, when Karl Marx and Friedrich Engels noticed the "bourgeois" push to "establish connections everywhere,"[13] world connectivity, albeit on reduced scale and in different form, had been centuries if not millennia old. My point then is neither that global interconnectivity constitutes something new nor that the cosmoderns are the first to pick up on it. The DeLillos, the Lees, the Iyers, and the critics of their time only do so more systematically and more programmatically in response to a relationality that itself gets more world-systemic after the Cold War. This latest installment in the global saga is "late globalization" and the logic of relationality it tends to foster worldwide "ego-logical."

As a cultural-imaginary development, cosmodernism is more than a reaction to the geopolitical context. Yet, as the introduction's second section elaborates, the ecology cosmodernism wants to be sets out to critique late-global egology. What I designate by ecology is a cultural environment organized around the self's vital links to an "other" whose radical difference—whether racial or ethnic, linguistic, sex- or gender-based, and so forth—must be entertained as a possibility and cultivated in a world whose dominant thrust seems narcissistic, self-reproductive, standardizing, pushing others to reproduce "our" lifestyles and fantasies. In other words, the relatedness inherent in cosmodernism speaks to and upholds unabashedly an ethics of difference. The togetherness surfacing in cosmodern imaginings does not obtain as self and other ford the gulf of their asymmetries and contrasts (the multiculturalist pipedream of the 1960s and 1970s). It is, we discover time after time, the distinct, the singular, that makes, as Giorgio Agamben says, for the "most common" in us and thus for the basis of "real community."[14] Standing as it does on a structure of "with-ness," this community presupposes a "collegial ethic." In pursuing the ramifications of this ethic in the humanities of the past decades, particularly in the new comparatism, in global/planetary studies, and in the neocosmopolitan revival, the introduction's last section charts an epistemological shift parallel to and occasionally overlapping with the cosmodern turn.

The shift occurred, inside and outside the academy, in head-on engagement with our time's global processes and themes. Literary-cultural cosmodernism tackles these problems directly and indirectly. Even though reducing literary cosmodernism to writing "about"—let alone "on behalf of"—late globalization is abusive, the book's main divisions do plot out a road map for the cosmodern imaginary around five thematic axes that run alongside, across, or counter to staple issues, aspects, and trends of the late-global age. These axes (*a*) thematize the cosmodern as a mode of thinking about the world and its culture, about cultural perception, self-perception, and identity; (*b*) forefront, accordingly, the intersubjective-communicational, dynamic dimension of cosmodernism; and (*c*) articulate the cosmodern imaginary into five regimes of relatedness, or subimaginaries: the "idiomatic," the "onomastic," the "translational," the "readerly," and the "metabolic." These are the foci of this volume's five parts.

Exploring the linguistic facet of cosmodernism's imaginary, part 1 looks at how American cosmoderns conceive of language and the alterity it presupposes and verbalizes. As I propound in this part's first section, notable is the turn away from the classically cosmopolitan view of linguistic globalism and authority toward a multilingual, plurivocal, and more humble outlook. In this and other matters, cosmopolitanism has been universalist; cosmodernism is surprisingly idiomatic. The cosmodern self makes itself, linguistically and otherwise, as it opens itself up to the post-1989 Babel; thus, whatever this self speaks about, it speaks in tongues, other. Derrida's reflections on linguistic mastery and Doris Sommer's Derridean critique set the tone for the next two sections. These are devoted to Lee's interpellation of the ideology of nativist linguistic monopoly in his novel *Native Speaker* and to Federman's disruptions of similar "monotonies" of tongue and culture in his late fiction.

Part 2 carries on the analysis of language by taking up the representation of names and naming in recent American narrative. As I show, just as voice is unique and a *portavoce* simultaneously, a mouthpiece of others' voices, a name names the self and his or her heritage as this name names others; in fact—and this is typical of cosmodernism—the name employs those others' names to call the self and tell his or her story. Cosmodernism's "onomastic imaginary" pivots precisely on this mutual "nomination"—designation and identification—of self and other in the drama of naming. My questions here are: What makes one name oneself and those close to him or her by the name of an other from a different place or time? What kind of statement does one make "in an other's name"? What worldviews does the cross-cultural and intertextual practice of "heteronomy" unfold in the last two decades of American fiction? I provide my answers in conversation with philosophers of naming and identity such as Amin Maalouf, Alain Finkielkraut, Julia Watson, and Charles Taylor in this part's section 1, while the following three sections examine mainly "onomastic narratives" by Lahiri and Lee. Cosmodern onomastics is, I conclude, a with-ness marker, a nominal ecology.

Further expanding on the function of globally circulating words and names, languages and stories, and speakers and narrators in the cosmodern production of identity, part 3 turns to the "translational imaginary" embedded in fictional works revolving around the figure of the translator. Being, I specify in this part's beginning—having a being, being somebody—occurs, now more than ever, translationally. I also point out that critics from George Steiner to Umberto Eco and Rey Chow have shifted attention away from classical translation, which had primarily a linguistic component, to a notion as linguistic as cultural, existential, and political.

It is in this context that I seize on translation as a prime cultural modality of relatedness where, as Régis Debray reminds us, all culture is increasingly transmitted culture—that is to say, translated, relayed, and related. I close the section by theorizing cosmodern translation, that is, translation of an other's words that presents the translating self with an opportunity for "self-translation" and self-understanding. This part's remainder pursues translational cosmodernism in works by Mones and Kim.

If all translation is interpretation, reading of others and, by virtue of the same cosmodern logic, self-reading, then the translation scene is also a reading scene. Consequently, the translational and the readerly vectors of the cosmodern imaginary intersect. Focusing on the "readerly imaginary," the fourth part is part 3's natural follow-up. "Readings" is broken up into three sections. Building toward the concept of "cosmodern interpretive communities," the first theorizes the new togetherness emerging in turn-of-the-century reading practices. A modicum of reception theory helps clarify how a certain "appeal structure" (Wolfgang Iser's *Appellstruktur*) in texts read by audiences from times and places other than those where the material has been composed calls for what K. Anthony Appiah deems "cosmopolitan reading." I maintain that Appiah's notion is still fuzzy, and I use Iser's work on cultural "between-spaces" and "translatability" to detail what cosmodern "other-reading" is and how it works textually, culturally, and politically. The rest of the sections focus more closely on three representative authors: Nafisi, Iyer, and Randall.

Reading, the cosmoderns tell us, is creative and self-creative. The foray into an other's work is not merely reproductive. It is productive. Through it, the reading self produces itself, makes itself into something it has not been before. The logic of cosmodern reading and cosmodernism generally is then "metamorphic," critically transformative rather than simply iterative. It is this logic and its critique of the egological system of iterations that part 5 brings to the fore as it applies itself to the "metabolic imaginary." Drawing on Nancy and other critics of late-global cultural "incorporations," this part's section 1 approaches culture as archival-patrimonial body and, at the same time, recognizes culture's own inscription into human bodies. The segment starts out with a brief aperçu of corporeality theories, old and new, that take into consideration the world's coming together. Cosmodernism's corporeal projections and transformations further corroborate, I contend, the constitutive role of otherness inside worldly togetherness. For, as we turn to, and even into, others' bodies and bodily configurations, we come into being, get in touch with ourselves and the world. In contrast, the section's second half zeroes in on global, "metastatic" reproduction and copycat culture in DeLillo's later novels, primarily in *Underworld*, which I revisit alongside some of his recent essays to shed light on a cosmodern conception of culture that foregrounds the role the body and the discourse of physicality are assigned in the disruption of the world's redundancy. This implication segues us into this part's last portion. If the previous section looked at montage as an anti-iterative, countercultural ritual, this one analyzes the related technique of bricolage, more exactly "corporeal bricolage" and its subversive potential, with reference to Updike, Yamashita, and, again, DeLillo (*The Body Artist*).

Leaning on DeLillo one more, the epilogue asks about America's present "cultural time" in order to round off the cultural-historical definition of *Cosmodernism*'s axial concept. A series of marginalia to DeLillo's novel *Cosmopolis* and to his essay "The Power of History" clear the ground for a handful of distinctions that enable an ethical rethinking—as well as a rethinking together—of essential and interrelated categories such as alterity, temporality, history, discourse, and culture. It thus becomes, at last, possible to answer the epilogue's question in terms pointing, with some reluctance, to the aforementioned "cosmodern turn." The last pages of the concluding part limn this turn as a protracted and luminous twilight of the postmodern paradigm.

Acknowledging Others

"[T]here is no *invention* possible, whether it be philosophical or poetic, without the presence in the inventing subject of an abundance of the other," Hélène Cixous notes in an oft-quoted essay.[15] I have rediscovered the wisdom of the statement over the years spent on this project. Whatever insights and revelations this study has occasioned, they would have been impossible without the sustaining presence of others in my thoughts, on my bookshelves, and physically around me. An inquiry into the culture of indebtedness in post-1989 America, *Cosmodernism* also performs its theme. The book itself is a form of indebtedness.

I want to acknowledge first a great debt of gratitude to a number of institutions, endowments, programs, and their administrators: my academic home, University of North Carolina, Greensboro, for the several fellowships and grants awarded to me in recent years; UNCG's College of Arts and Sciences, and the College's Dean, Timothy Johnston, for his unwavering support of advanced scholarship at UNCG, in particular for my

Fall 2007 research assignment leave; UNCG's Office of Research and Economic Development; UNCG's International Programs Center, for funding my scholarly travels; also at UNCG, the English Department and its Head, Anne Wallace, for the help extended to this book all along; UNCG's Center for Critical Inquiry in the Liberal Arts for a 2007 summer stipend; my university's Library Services, the Interlibrary Loan staff, and especially Gaylor Callahan; Agnes Szarka, for help with Hungarian; and Andrew Merredith, my Spring 2009 research assistant. I am also thankful to my undergraduate and graduate students, to whom I have taught many of the works discussed in *Cosmodernism,* and to my English Department colleagues, among them Keith Cushman, Steve Yarbrough, Chris Hodgkins, Mary Ellis Gibson, Jim Evans, and Denise Baker. Karen Kilcup, Americanist of international reputation and close friend, has provided multiple and invaluable assistance to this enterprise. Phyllis Whitman Hunter, from UNCG's Department of History, has read parts of the book and offered timely comments and warm encouragement.

Outside UNCG, this undertaking has been assisted by Germany's ever-generous Alexander von Humboldt–Stiftung and by a series of universities whose hospitality and interest in my work have been nothing short of overwhelming. I mention here only Freiburg University, Germany; University of Alicante, Spain; University of Paris VIII Vincennes-Saint-Denis; University of Paris X Nanterre; University of Haute-Alsace, Mulhouse, France; John Cabot University, Rome; Bucharest University, Romania, especially its English and Literary Theory Departments; University of North Carolina, Chapel Hill and its Center for Slavic, Eurasian, and East European Studies; North Carolina State University; University of Tennessee; and Indiana University. At these and other places, hosts and colleagues have offered friendship and advice. I am pleased to acknowledge here the following individuals: Marcel Cornis-Pope, Paul Maltby, Jerome Klinkowitz, Lou Freitas Caton, Brian Richardson, Jeffrey R. Di Leo, David Herman, Amy Elias, Monika Fludernik, Jan Alber, Lourdes López Romero, Mircea Martin, Rodica Mihăilă, Mihaela Irimia, Radu Surdulescu, Ion Bogdan Lefter, and Mircea Cărtărescu. Radu Turcanu has been a great friend and host. I am also grateful to Ursula Heise for imparting her wisdom on *Kulturökologie* to me one October evening in Knoxville, Tennessee. And Henry Sussman's erudition, acumen, and kindness have provided a supreme example. Whenever students ask me about standards of intellectual and stylistic distinction in our profession, I pull out his books.

Special thanks go to the University of Michigan Press and its Acquiring

Editor, Tom Dwyer, without whose unflinching enthusiasm and expert guidance this book would not have materialized. I must also thank Marjorie Perloff, David Cowart, and Brian McHale, the Press's outside readers for their substantial, most constructive comments, and LeAnn Fields, Senior Executive Director, Alexa Ducsay, Christina Milton, and the production and marketing staff at Michigan. While I owe this book—and pretty much everything else besides—to my wife, Camelia, and my daughter, Maria, *Cosmodernism* as a whole is dedicated to Matei Calinescu, distinguished scholar of modernism and postmodernism, mentor, and friend whose warm presence and advice have meant the world to me. I miss them so much.

Cosmodernism does not reprint previously published texts properly speaking, but a few of its sections have come out, in different form, as follows: "Global Romance? Nicole Mones, Teilhard de Chardin, and the Critique of 'Planetization,'" in *Canadian Review of Comparative Literature* 29, no. 4 (December 2002): 491–518; "The Other, the Namesake: Cosmopolitan Onomastics in Chang-rae Lee's *A Gesture Life*," in *Names* 55, no. 1 (March 2007): 17–36; "Speakers and Sleepers: Chang-rae Lee's *Native Speaker*, Whitman, and the Performance of Americanness," in *College Literature* 36, no. 3 (Summer 2009): 66–91; "Cosmobabble or, Federman's Return," in *Federman's Fictions*, edited by Jeffrey R. Di Leo (forthcoming from SUNY Press). I am grateful to these journals and their editors—and once more to Jeffrey R. Di Leo—for permission to reprint modified segments of the articles, as I am to Rebecca Darlington for allowing me to use a visual reproduction of her exquisite work *Earth*, on the cover. Lastly, a note on translations: unless otherwise indicated, they are all mine.

INTRODUCTION ⊕ THE COSMODERN IMAGINARY

You wonder if everyone and everything in the world is intimately related. . . . You pluck a thread and it leads to . . . everywhere. . . . Is there a limit to relatedness?

—BHARATI MUKHERJEE, *The Tree Bride*

1. Relatedness

I am the content of a relation.

—HARUKI MURAKAMI, *Kafka on the Shore*

[O]nly by discovering ourselves already in some sense situated in the stories and tales of others . . . can we fully understand all that we presently are.

—GILES GUNN, *Beyond Solidarity*

The Relational Scene

Know thyself: what a strange paradox! Can one know oneself without also being known?

—BASARAB NICOLESCU, *Théorèmes poétiques*

We only begin to live through other people's eyes.

—MICHEL HOUELLEBECQ, *The Elementary Particles*

Once it recognizes its indebtedness . . . the subject will be able to bind with a "we" across the reference to an "Other."

—JEAN-MICHEL RABATÉ, *James Joyce*

"Meaning can happen when you least expect it," Alan Alda notes in his 2007 memoir *Things I Overheard while Talking to Myself.*[1] I agree. The "aha!" moment or place usually catches us by surprise. It may even strike us as "out of place." Why? Because it is just so, out of place and order, inordinate and ex-centric geographically, culturally, or both, displaced and perhaps *déplacé,* as the French would say; because genuine cognition entails a critical displacement, a challenge to habitual takes on things insofar as "getting it" is often not of "this" place but occurs in places remote or off the beaten path. Like identity, to whose formation it is key, understanding is not a given but a gift of an other, *"de l'Autre."*[2] If, as one of Kundera's titles assures us, "life is elsewhere," there is a good reason for that: this "elsewhere" and its "otherwise" are vital to us here.[3] Being and thinking feed off the less conspicuous proximity and seemingly less consequential immediacy of the distant, the strange, and the different. These provide the requisite, Levinasian *sortie de soi*, the "release from self-sameness," from the inherited ways and clichés poised to shape our lives and thoughts into rehearsals of previous lives and thoughts.[4] To be sure, we are and understand *with* others and their places; self-identity presupposes them.[5] "Being elsewhere," *être ailleurs*, can mark "distraction" and "absence of thought" but also the very place of being and thinking, for we come to terms with ourselves and our world *ailleurs*, "elsewhere," as Montaigne avers in his *Essays*.[6] In the heteronomous topology of understanding, the existential, the epistemological, and the ethical intertwine.[7] It is in this arena that comprehension, self-comprehension, and the self itself ultimately eventuate, relationally, in relation and thus as debt to an other. It is here that we learn about our own here and now (and their past), from others' "out there" and their "far-out" geographies, histories, and notions.

So did Alda himself. In his volume's sixth chapter, "A Passion for Reason," he recounts the kind of "relational scene" on which I dwell throughout *Cosmodernism*. A few years ago, the author reminisces, he had to travel all the way to China to "make a personal connection to [Thomas] Jefferson" and by the same token to himself as an American for whom our third president was a personification of America (65). As the actor told a roomful of Jeffersonian experts back in Monticello, a rice paddy "on the other side of the world" proved the unlikely place where, at long last, he "got" Jefferson (71).

Are we now offshoring national identity too, how we feel about who we are? Is the "making" of our innermost associations and self-revelations going the way most manufacturing jobs have? More to the point: must we connect with others and their cultures in order to connect with ourselves as Americans, Americanists, or otherwise? Must we take the route of otherness, of cultural transit and translation, to be and "find" ourselves?[8] Not entirely new, the questions are more timely today than ever. I wrote this book so I could answer them. The gist of the answers—and the core tenet of my argument—is encapsulated by Alda's realization that Yuan Long

Ping, a Chinese biologist, made him "underst[and] Jefferson for the first time" (71). Yuan did so, Alda intimates, as a "Chinese Jeffersonian" who reenacted an experiment "Jie Fu Sun" had done with rice back in his day. Following Jefferson and running similarly serious risks—the American smuggled rice out of Italy; the Chinese defied the People's Republic's "official" botany—Yuan created a high-yield rice hybrid by cross-pollinating two strains of rice.

Cross-pollination is, of course, key here, both a Jeffersonian technique and an American modus operandi, driving force of national creativity and code of Americanness on so many levels. More notably, the Chinese Jefferson, himself an incarnation of this methodology, broke the code for his American guest. In other words: it was the latter's enlightening encounter with his host that enabled Alda to relate to Jefferson, to forge the bond we normally assume we already have with those close to us, with kin, relatives, and like relations. What Yuan did and said as well as what he was—a hybrid in his own right—helped Alda and, through him, Alda's American listeners back in Virginia get a fresh grip on their individual and collective identities.

The other and the far-flung may speak to us from afar, with an accent if not in tongues, or so we may hear them and their Jie Fu Sunian whispers. But we had better pay attention to what they say because it may just unveil us to ourselves. We need not be—I for one am not—sold on a view of identity and perception thereof wholly "disembedded," "offshored," much less on the economic metaphor itself. Nor should we underestimate the formative sway of the *hic et nunc*. What we might entertain instead and what I advance here is the hypothesis of a cultural-epistemological "outsourcing" of sorts, with others and their "out-of-place" sites, images, texts, styles, ideas, and Weltanschauungen as sources of defining "parts" and junctures of a fairly distinctive protocol of identity production and self-representation. This protocol, I further suggest, is pivotal to a kind of picturing of the self and its world—to a cultural imaginary—that in the Cold War's aftermath becomes more typical of American literature, culture, and thought than at any time in their history. I call this imaginary *cosmodern* and the stories, novels, and other forms of discourse articulating it *cosmodernism*. With a terminology these pages press into service ever so often, cosmodern logic is fundamentally, systematically, and pointedly relational, turning as it does on self and other's foundational co-relationality with respect to one another. Whatever they are, both are (stand for, exist) correlatively, in relation with each other. Alda's little scene is relational—a cosmodern *Urszene*—because it decisively plays on relatedness, that is, premises the self and the self's own thematization of itself and its culture on the self-other nexus.

Cosmodern, Cosmodernism, Cosmodernity

Everything in this world is relation to an other.
—BASARAB NICOLESCU, *Théorèmes poétiques*

The unity of the world is not one: it is made of a diversity, and even disparity and opposition.... The unity of the world is nothing other than its diversity, and this, in turn, is a diversity of worlds.... the world is a multiplicity of worlds, and its unity is the mutual sharing and exposition of all its worlds—with this world.
  The sharing of the world is the law of the world. The world has nothing other; it is not subject to any authority; it does not have a sovereign. *Cosmos, nomos.* Its supreme law is within it as the multiple and mobile trace of the sharing that it is.
—JEAN-LUC NANCY, *Being Singular Plural*

Aside from the odd mention of *cosmomodernistas*—late nineteenth-century and early twentieth-century Latin American cosmopolitan *modernistas* with a knack for transgender, cross-cultural, "'self'-through-the-'other'" identity masquerade—*cosmodern, cosmodernism,* and *cosmodernity* have been absent from the lexicon of literary and cultural studies.[9] *Cosmodernity* (*cosmodernité*), however, takes center stage in the writings of Basarab Nicolescu, a mathematician, physicist, and philosopher with the French Centre National de la Recherche Scientifique. Better known in the United States after the 2002 translation of his 1996 "manifesto" *La transdisciplinarité* (Transdisciplinarity), he is the author of a number of texts where, especially since the 1994 book *Théorèmes poétiques,* he lays out a "new vision of the world."[10] This world, he proposes, must be reconceptualized as cosmos. In fact, "the resurrection of the idea of 'cosmos,'" to his mind "the most remarkable event of the twentieth-century,"[11] had already yielded a whole cosmological strain in the humanities, especially in globalization and cosmopolitan studies. Immanuel Wallerstein's own "modern world-system" comes to mind first. It adopts the framework of "cosmology"—in Wallerstein's view, "the study of the functioning of the system as a whole"—to work out a "totality" distinguished from "completeness,"[12] more broadly, a dialectical "utopistics" or future, global-scale "geocultural" configuration in which the planet's "particularisms" would restore "the universal reality of liberty and equality."[13] Worth mentioning here are also Yi-Fu Tuan's "cosmos [as] hearth,"[14] Gérard Raulet's *Critical Cosmology,* which opposes a citizenship concept of discrepant "republican" (i.e., national) traditions to Americanizing "neo-universalism,"[15] Félix Guattari's "chaosmotic," "ethico-aesthetic paradigm,"[16] and Anne Phillips's laudable effort to reconstruct multiculturalism on a "cosmic" rather than on a "discrete-cultures" model.[17] But again, neither "cosmos" nor the critical cosmologies variously built on it are without precedent. Nicolescu actually talks about the "resurrection" of the notion, and this is surely the right way to put it given not only the Greek origins of *kosmos* but also the "as above, so below" hermetic tradition of macrocosmic-microcosmic homologies of the natural and intellectual orders. Nicolescu himself revisits this line of mystic thought in a 1988 essay on Jakob Böhme and goes back to it in *Manifesto of Transdisciplinarity*'s discussion of Böhme-inspired German Romantic *Naturphilosophie*.[18] Novalis is here, as one might expect, a constant reference. Arguably, the German poet's "cosmogogy" contains Nicolescu's "cosmodernity" in a nutshell. Filtered through the numerically balanced (*arithēmtikē*) Pythagorean *harmonia,* Novalian cosmo-logism sets off both the structural parallelism of the human and cosmic (natural) spheres and the "transversal" concatenations following from this isomorphism. These cross-links make one element—be it mankind, art, the imagination and our "inner world" generally, morals, or the sphere of human values—see and regain itself with and in an other (nature, the "outer," material universe), and vice versa.[19] The mind and the body, the micro and the macro, the individual and the group, the group and other groups, human community and the world, the planet and the universe, then the arts and the sciences, the disciplines in and by which we attempt to map out this universe all reenact the principle of self-other homology, imbrication, and codependence lying at the core of this quasi-mystic, hermetic-Kabbalistic, many-layered web of symmetries.

Novalis's "cosmogogy" has something messianic to it, fancies itself a "doctrine of the future."[20] So does Nicolescu's "universal interdependence" theory.[21] As "transpersonal" as it is "transdisciplinary"—for transdisciplinarity is only the epistemological offshoot of ontological convergence—his cosmodernity is also "transnational" and "transpolitical." "Before the Eternal," he declaims, "we are all transnationals." "The transnationals do not need a piece of land to call it theirs: Earth is their land already."[22] "Capable" as it may be "to contribute to the elimination of the tensions threatening life on our planet," "a transdisciplinary culture" lies, we are told, ahead of us.[23]

Notoriously unable to deliver, this free-floating rhetoric of cosmopolitanisms ancient and modern does not sound particularly encouraging. But Nicolescu is a visionary too, a quantum physicist who harks back to Romantic natural philosophy out of scientific realism. This move's eclecticism may confuse, and the blanket ecumenism of his "trans-politism" may fare no better either. And yet two points bear making. The first pertains to cultural history and its critique: no wonder the critic turns to Romantic mysticism. He shortcuts modernity for a purpose. "Modernity," he claims, "is characterized by the binary separation subject-object." Instead, "cosmodernity" sets out to overcome "binary thought" both as mental "scheme" and "root of the new barbarianism"—this scheme has been usually behind "the annihilation of the other" (wars are "bipolar," he says).[24] Derived from the first, the second and more important point in light of my earlier hypothesis is that Nicolescu's manifesto contains the sketch of a world ethic. "The transdisciplinary ethic," he writes, "rejects any attitude that refuses dialogue and discussion. . . . Shared knowledge should lead to a shared understanding based on an absolute *respect* for the collective and individual Otherness united by our common life on one and the same Earth."[25]

Appositions: The Scandal of "We" and the New Authenticity

> Proximity as the impossible assumption of difference, impossible definition, impossible integration. Proximity as impossible appearing. But proximity!
> —EMMANUEL LEVINAS, "Proximity and Peace"

> There is nothing in the world but other people.
> —DON DELILLO, *Cosmopolis*

> [D]ifference is necessarily relational.
> —MARK C. TAYLOR, *The Moment of Complexity*

While it does not fall outside the purview of cosmodernism, "transdisciplinarity" is in Nicolescu a subset of "transpersonality," namely, of the personal, "personal identity," or "personality" of an individual or community understood as interpersonal and intercommunal, respectively. More than the critic's "trans-" and "inter-," the "with," to which my preference will go throughout, captures accurately not only the novel proximity of the self to an other and the ensuing, heretofore unparalleled exchanges in our world, but also the ethics of the relationality at play in these encounters.[26] For, insofar as the self and its group's being imply being-with and hence "requires" an "other,"[27] the self incurs an obligation and thus buys into an ethics. Relationality of this kind, then, is also an ethical concept. Grounded in this specific self-other relation, the cosmodern imaginary is ethical. Undergirding it is a strong ethos of cultural-epistemological and existential indebtedness. This is another way of saying that "we" owe it to others, but also to ourselves, to own up to how much we owe them, by behaving accordingly.

This has little to do with Baudrillard's "global debt."[28] What the authors convoked in this book recommend to a relational America that nowadays cannot but be and see itself with the world's others is that it think about, invest in, and care for this world's otherness as it would about, in, and for itself. Directly and indirectly, these writers call for a care and concern flowing from a cosmodern recharting of the world's inside/outside and self/other territories, for a "self-love" retooled to accommodate "the love for the 'other.'"[29] If the self's structure and self-thematization hinge on dealings with people who live somewhere else—Tuan's "external other"[30]—or with us here but not like "us," then such connectivity accrues a sizable ontological-cognitive debt, and this debt translates into duty: the duty "we" have to preserve and nurture the world's strange noises, concepts, and places. Yes, this preservation provides for self-preservation too. Yet it is, or should be, more than realpolitik, more than a calculated and ultimately self-interested move. It should be solidarity that reaches "'beyond solidarity,' as it were, in a space where 'self' and 'other' are no longer conceived either as opposites of one another or as complements, counterparts, or corollaries, but rather as components integral to each other's constitution." To rephrase: this should be cosmodern solidarity, solidarity that carries "us" farther than both ethno-/culturo-centric, "in-group" fellow feeling and the "out-group" camaraderie riding on the idea of an other either opposite or complementary to the self.[31] On this score, I agree with Giles Gunn and share his skepticism of arguments put forth by pragmatists like Rorty, on one side, and the universalist tradition of cosmopolitanism, on the other.

There is another side, though, which I find appealing, this time in disagreement both with Gunn and with "cultural purists": neither irreconcilably opposite nor obligatorily opposed, self and other are at once distinct and growingly *apposed* in the post–Cold War era, juxtaposed to one another into a topologically continuous yet culturally discontinuous world syntax, a sine qua non, fluid vicinity where the nearer they draw to each other as neighbors, conferees, business partners, or subjects to media stories the more visible the distinctions between them become to one another. I do take Dominique Wolton's point on *l'omniprésence de l'Autre*, yet what I see in this ubiquitousness and in the *identité culturelle relationelle* ("relational cultural identity") it is fostering worldwide is not just a test, and possibly a crisis, of "comprehension," but also a double opportunity: to discover others, no doubt, as well as ourselves.[32] The two discoveries are inseparable. The closer others stand to us in a world where "foreignness does not start at the water's edge but at the skin's," as Clifford Geertz announced not long ago, the easier it gets to figure out "at what sort of angle . . . we stand to the world."[33]

Central to *Cosmodernism* is the conviction that this self-edifying moment occurs not as self and other "iron out" their differences nor as these discrepancies and asymmetries prove superficial and our "common humanity" triumphantly shines through them, but precisely by means of such dissonances, due to them rather than despite them. In Appiah's self-described cosmopolitan ethics, cultural differences are a problem, if not *the* problem. In my account, they may well be the solution. Neither an absolute, an intellectual fetish, nor something to put up with and eventually "get over," they are the "groundless ground" on which we can and should build, as Habermas might label it, a "flexible-'we'" community across the more "entrenched" ones.[34] Inclusive of its "exteriority," in Blanchot's view, and therefore *désoeuvrée*, "inoperable" from the standpoint of a more descent-based type of communal cohesion and "effectiveness,"[35] this is, however, the kind of human association best positioned to *operate* in today's world and tackle its problems. Since the "go it alone" approach is ostensibly the wrong way to go in this world, Americans can neither opt out of this community nor *not* grow into such a community themselves. It is imperative that we do so. But doing so requires what I would label a post-multiculturalist "politics of recognition"—and with it a less conventional idea of identitarian "authenticity"[36]—whose motto is no longer the autonomist "I want to be known for what I am" but the more humbly relational "I want to be known for what or whom I am with," for, *in fine*, "I have accepted this 'co-definitional' world's 'challenge of knowing [my]self *with* others.'"[37]

Cosmodernism is post-multiculturalist to the extent that it poses being-with as a formula of authentic—because authentically self-conscious—being. "I know and am myself 'with,' because I am and am known with and by an other"; "I can bear witness, to myself and the world, because I have borne with-ness": this is the cognition, the cognition as self-cognition the cosmoderns attain and also the recognition they demand for themselves no less than for those with whom they gain this knowledge. It is in this sense that, turning the tables on traditional metaphysics of identity, Charles Taylor, James Clifford, and other critics proclaim that to be authentic is to be "relational."[38] In this sense too one could start thinking about a "theory of relational cultures," and more basically "of culture as relation,"[39] as stemming from and in turn "cultivating" relatedness. In no way, though, does the Levinasian notion that "being is relation to the other than self" render the self's being less authentic.[40] Equally important, this does not make the other's originality and uniqueness less original and unique either. If effective existentially, culturally, or cognitively, the self's being with an other trades on this other's uncompromised otherness. This is the condition of possibility of relationality, of the self's being in relation, *tout court*, of being.

That is why, as our world sets self and other side by side with historically unmatched fervor, we must at least consider the notion of a *radically distinct cultural other* who need not be, and in practice often is not, hopelessly inaccessible to us and yet, at the end of our probing day, may still prove irreducible to our approaches, conceptual grids, and overall rationality. This is what I mean in *Cosmodernism* by *other, otherness, alterity,* and their cognates: somebody with whom we inescapably are *across* an undeniable and conceivably unbridgeable cultural gap. I lay emphasis on "being-with" as much as I do on "gap," with the proviso that the latter is less and less physical while the former is more and more so: we are more and more with people who are *less* like us. This other is not as "external" to us as he or she used or seemed to be. Differently put, this other's "externality" is these days best accounted for culturally rather than physically or solely physically. The world's Yuan Long Pings reside in China and across the street, "distant" not so much geographically as ethnically, racially, linguistically, or religiously. "The Other is everywhere today," Pico Iyer brings us to speed;[41] a stranger out there or in our midst, this other may remain "strange," as Habermas also observes, by personal choice, due to our epistemological shortfalls or cultural apprehensions, and for many other reasons.

Not only must we allow for the strangeness of others philosophically. We must commit to it because it is as constitutive of them as it is of us.

This is the institutive scandal of "we," of our authenticity. Others make up the paradoxically, original ex-centricity that affords our recentering, self-identification, and self-aware identity and living. Since it is from such an extremely displaced position that we come home (and "get" it), being with our kind, with our American present and past, with our history and its meanings, in brief, with that which some deem a smooth continuum of selves and self-engendering rites, brings to light a more diverse, genuine America. "Genuine" does not signify "pure" but original along the lines of the discussion thus far, where originality denotes the original relationality or "primordial" inscription of otherness into the text and context of American selfhood.[42] The cosmoderns do not invent America's inherent heteronomy—American "culture in the plural," as Michel de Certeau says—but only report with superior method and acuity on an identity structure already there although now more bountiful and more salient than yesterday and, they predict, tomorrow more determinant than to-day.[43] "Our America" is what it is, they do not tire of pointing out, because of this complexity and richness;[44] because in it nearness and dearness are fraught with distance and more "distant" perspectives and presences; be-cause defining us has been all along a condition of liminality, life at the threshold, "being-*within* an *outside*";[45] because, reciprocally, our homes are both abodes and vicinities—the Greek *oikos*, "house," is related to the Latin *vicus*, "row of houses," and *vicinitas*—that is, the cultural-affective "oikonomy" of homeyness is shot through with the frissons of the "un-homely"; because, if you "look internally[, you] discover [the] neighbor," and this revelation is "self-transforming."[46] A "proper" America, an Amer-ica less easily "identical to itself," more mindful of what it says whenever it says "I" or "we," lends itself for Americans and Americanists alike to "dis-covery"—to "defamiliarization"—as a less familial nation and familiar notion. "Stranger" to itself and ourselves, this would be "an other Amer-ica, in the double sense of Kafka's parable [from "Investigations of a Dog"]: negatively, as cultural otherness, and ambiguously, as a set of cul-tural secrets, the other America hidden from view by interpretation."[47] Whatever cognition might arise domestically, locally, it is predicated, cos-modern artists and scholars tell us, on the "shock of recognition of the world-in-the-home" as well as of "the home-in-the-world."[48] This "world of ours" is or becomes ours because it also is a "world of others."[49] It is therefore incumbent on Americans to relate to those others and their oth-erness as such, to the *different-as-different*, along the cosmodern lines of concern and responsibility and so "give back," respond to the "gift" ethically. This strikes me as a truly apposite way of looking at the other: not as something or somebody "fitting" the "I" from afar or "befittingly" here in "my" neighborhood, an apposition or reassuring footnote to the traditional subject and hearth of American discourse and culture, but as a sovereign and one-of-a-kind entity whose "outlandish" singularity accredits mine and, for that, I must honor.

Of Allergy: Ontology, Ethics, and a Cosmodern Brief

> Subjectivity here is not that autonomous and free consciousness that thinks it can pose its questions on its own but a living entity [*une existence*] that experiences in an originary fashion [*originairement*] its derivation, its filiation, hence its finitude.
> —SYLVIANE AGACINSKI, *Critique de l'égocentrisme*

> To know is to know somebody else.
> —EVA HOFFMAN, *The Secret*

> [O]nly what does not fit in can be true.
> —THEODOR ADORNO, *Aesthetic Theory*

How can one be American? This kind of question was first asked by Montesquieu's Rica in 1721. What Rica actually wondered was, "How can one be Persian?"[50] but, as Paul Valéry commented in a famous preface to *Lettres persanes*, behind the odd interrogation lies another: "How can one be what one is?"[51] Ever since the Enlightenment, writers from Oliver Goldsmith (*The Citizen of the World*, 1760) to E. M. Cioran (*La Tentation d'exister*, 1956) have raised the broader question repeatedly.[52] The cosmoderns put it too by stressing, more than Valéry and Cioran, that what Montesquieu asked about, and in the first place, was not Persia but France, not the other but the self, yet he *had to* ask about the former in order to query the latter. We know already that the protocol of such inquiry is rarely "straightforward." The *philosophe*, and anybody mulling over being, identity, and self, for that matter, is bound to start out with the other. "Philosophy begins and ends with the question of the other," writes Mark C. Taylor, echoing Blanchot's suspicion that the most "profound" question does not concern the "One" but that which is only subsequently brought into play whenever we inquire into the One, namely, the other.[53] In keeping with the paradox of cosmodern authenticity, the question about being is, one might say, always the *other* one: the question of the other; "we" begs *that* question first. And "we" must do so, for "our" own sake. For others too are "scandalous," a "stumbling block" (cf. Gk. *skandalon*) of our anthropological cocksureness in the world, a test and a question mark (Who are they? What do they mean?) that invite self-examination (Who are we? What do we mean?).

More than a Persian for Rica, a Frenchman or Frenchwoman for Montesquieu and Valéry, an Englishman or Englishwoman for Goldsmith, or a Romanian for Cioran, for the cosmoderns the self *comes across.* It is, and appears so, obliquely, "with," a refraction of an other. But, it goes without saying, being as being-with is neither an absolute hallmark of the late twentieth century nor an exclusively cosmodern cultural "form" or insight. As an existential rite, it is coextensive to human history. As an ontological concept, it can be traced back to the existentialism of Sartre's *être-avec* and Simone de Beauvoir's "original" *Mitsein,* before them to Heidegger's *Miteinandersein* and Husserl's intersubjectivity theory from *Cartesian Meditations,* and farther back to the master-slave dialectic of Hegel's *Phenomenology of Spirit.* As one can see, I limit the concept's biography to modern and chiefly Western thought. Otherwise, being-with is, like "otherness" itself, "as primordial as human consciousness," as ancient as this consciousness's thematization in the history of philosophy, and, unfortunately, as ill-defined as any other item in philosophers' lexicon.[54] In this view, noteworthy is that ever since Descartes's cogito struck out by annulling "*l'existence d'autrui,*"[55] the other with whom the self (the "one," the "same," etc.) cannot but be has represented a "problem" to the self, a hurdle, a liability, a threat that makes the I "stand-offish," as Hegel comments, or an uncomfortable enigma.[56] In short, this other implies an adversarial correlation, an antinomian entity to cope with (à la Sartre's *L'Être et le Néant*), possibly to exclude, keep out, marginalize, or, as in Hegel, to co-opt and reduce to (my)self by "defin[ing it] according to the particular manner in which" this self "chooses to set himself up." The other is here both a restriction and a prerequisite to the subject's self-assertion; it simultaneously curbs this subject's being (confines it) and makes it possible (defines it). Indeed, in order to be "posed," the subject must be "opposed" first, that is, "opposed to the other."[57] Thus the other presents itself to the self, or the "I," Hegel concludes, as "the *negative.*"[58] In *Phenomenology of Spirit,* self-consciousness is alterity-oriented; it is "intentional," for it desires "others," and "reflexive" insofar as, in and through this desire, the "subject is discovered" while its difference (from those others, from reality, etc.) is annulled, "transfer[r]ed into identity."[59]

In her *Second Sex* Hegelian rebuttal, Beauvoir couches this negation of selfhood in terms of gender difference, but her analysis has wider bearings. What the masculine self does or is perceived as doing in the modern identitarian imagination the self at large also does. A quasi-exhaustive list of charges would run something like this:

(1) This self is "dualistic." It needs and posits an other so as to institute itself. Operating as it does via the historically known discourses and power apparatuses, this institution is also an imposition, epistemologically, culturally, and politically. It works by radically externalizing and/or internalizing this other even though otherness ties into the self's being intimately and originally and has always been part and parcel of who "I"/"we" am/are.

(2) This means that my self is heteronomous (because it is relational). It only "overlooks" this reality, tends to forget its own genetic relationality. Xenophobic, anti-Semitic, racist, jingoistic, and, according to Roland Barthes, "petit-bourgeois" culture is simply "unable to imagine the Other. If [it] comes face to face with him, [it] blinds [it]self, ignores and denies him, or else transforms [it]self into him."[60] Barthes talks about "class anthropomorphism,"[61] but I would broaden the notion to cover the cultural anthropomorphism of any culturally ingrown self or group in which "otherness is reduced to sameness."[62] On the one hand, such self or group expels the other from the domain of selfhood; on the other hand, it reduces the other to (the self) itself in the (pseudo)act of self-knowledge. Both are stratagems of negation, denial, and thus self-denial. Historically, they have played out, as Barthes alerts us, in a number of superficially conflicting ways: as outright (self)ignorance; as ideological schemes that render whole cultural epochs or directions "cover-ups" designed to cook the books of culture, that is, to conceal or make light of the debt to other cultures by filing with the national imaginary "credit reports"—from the odd article to full-fledged literary histories—that dress up intertextual acrobatics or plain borrowings as unmitigated indigenous originality; as pseudorecognition that forces the unknown into the clichés and essences customarily featured by the rhetoric of intolerance and more largely into cut-and-dried categories of intelligibility; as "agnostic" rationalization of the supposedly "exotic," "irrational," and "incomprehensible," which casts the other outside "humanity" on principle—the other is in- or subhuman, demonic, barbarian, unclean, etc.

(3) In the West, this exclusive mentality can be traced back to the Greek city-state and its setting itself off against the backdrop of "barbarian" otherness fancied as outlandish, *distinct* in space and culture, that is, incom-

patible with the local axiology of the polis and thereby im-polite and im-politic, uncouth and uncivilized, to wit, "barbarous." A barbarian, Greek historians and philosophers enlighten us, is fundamentally a non-Greek, a foreigner. Vice versa, a foreigner must be barbaric, totally different from and adverse to the native in customs and demeanor. *Alius* ("other" for Romans) is thus understood as *alienus,* "alien." The self and the barbarian other are not only distinct but also politically discordant and so liable to clash. As a nonself, the latter threatens the self by its very existence. This is how, in the dynamic of self and other as represented by the *socii* of a self-described native community, difference sets itself up as incompatibility, disjunction, contest, intolerance, and finally exclusion. It becomes so, of course, without necessarily being recognized as such. The rationale of this exclusion is reason itself, more precisely, the contrasting irrationality of the other, who is "by nature" prone to brutality, to uncouth, irrational if not utterly insane behavior (cf. the French *aliéné*). This proclivity is putatively borne out by the word's onomatopoeic root. Accordingly, the gibberish spoken by the *barbaroi* is nonsensical "bar, bar, bar" ("blah, blah, blah"), an etymology corroborated by the Sanskrit *barbara* ("stammering" *and* "non-Aryan").[63] Since presumably *phōnē barbarikē* serves no rational purpose, it provides no vehicle to logos, sense-making, communication, or cooperation either, disqualifying its speaker as *polites,* as a member of a linguistic-rational community. In brief, irrationality is both cultural diagnosis and political subterfuge, language used by the "sane," a priori civilized, and "politic" body to mark and quarantine infectious difference, to control the "pathology" of otherness.

(4) Apparently opposite to the dehumanization of the other ("they are not human like us") is the "universalization" of this other in the name and under the rubric of "our common humanity." Only the latter's traits are constantly predetermined from a privileged perspective (ours) of culture, ethnicity, religion, and so on ("they are human like us"). Historically, universalism has been just that: a "turning toward," a con-version to a *particular* version of values and criteria otherwise billed as common to us all. Magnanimous as it may sound, "identifying" with an other under the auspices of universal commonality is "inauthentic" given that "a group's self-recognition in its own models is experienced and presented in the form of an identification of the community with humanity itself."[64] In others, the group sees itself, yet not in a symmetric relation of mutual implication but in one of colonial substitution; "apposition" gives way to transposition, to

our placing in a place not ours but from which "we" evict "them." Identification does not "meet the other in [his or her] alterity," as Fred Poché urges us to do,[65] but narcissistically meets itself or its own self rather, for this is the mental process by which the self enacts its "eternal return" to itself and its assumptions.[66] Identification assimilates. It "makes similar" by making difference into an *identity simile* explicitly as it treats the different other *comme autre moi*, "*mon semblant*," as *autrui* rather than *Autre*,[67] or implicitly, by "universalizing" the other, who is supposed to become as "universal" as "us." Thus, either outside or inside humanity, the other's difference is de facto suspended, which disables the very premise of otherness. In *Humanism of the Other*, Levinas turns classical humanism on its head by demonstrating that the other is human not because "deep down" it resembles "us" (it is like "us," our semblance or *semblant*) but because it is other, strange, different. It is, the philosopher elaborates, his or her singularity that warrants his or her humanity, *as well as ours*.[68] This is as much as saying, as Levinas does in *Totality and Infinity*, that this humanity and the "fraternity" deriving from it—effective, necessary, salutary—can and must be based on that which makes us different, in-comparable and yet, by virtue of the radical distinctions between us, com-parable, etymologically, "apposable" or juxtaposable inside an ethically rather than exclusively or predominantly ethnically constituted human fellowship.[69] As critics from Sylviane Agacinski to Slavoj Žižek advise, we should be suspicious of inhuman/subhuman perceptions of the other as much as we should be of those that conceive of this other's humanity in too abstract-theoretical, "incontingent," or universalist terms. One dehumanizes by animalizing and reifying no less than by generalizing, universalizing, and, I might add, idealizing. Either way, one conveniently *allegorizes*, explains away the others—*allos* is "other," "different," "strange," and "foreign" in Greek—in terms of the same, thus refusing "to accept the other . . . in the real of his or her existence."[70] For that, "mankind" [*l'homme*] in general" and other reasonings and rationalizations of the similarly generalizing or universalizing type cannot serve as "veritable objections" to racism, chauvinism, and so forth.[71]

(5) Rationalization "de-relationalizes" the other's presence in the world and by the same movement the world itself. This explains why the cosmoderns are so keen on relationality as a counter to modern rationality's excesses. We shall notice all too frequently, cosmodern rationality is relational. In cosmodernism, *relatio* is a new, sui generis *ratio mundi*.

(6) In Western and other traditions, the other routinely serves the self-edification process. As such, it is no more than a servant, the self's sidekick in this rational/rationalist scenario whose formative-intellectual and moral components are both to be emphasized.

(7) After Hegel, "serving" is high on the agenda of this dialectic of subjection: the other is not only reduced phenomenologically and epistemologically to whatever the self is comfortable with, "feels good about," or presumes it can handle. This other is also assigned object status. Not a subject proper, it is subject but merely to objectification and thus canceled out, irrevocably "othered" as an absolute object ("thing") in no way compatible with or implicated in the life of the self. This is the "bad," undignified, "ab-ject" (not sub-ject) absolute, to which I oppose, via Levinas, a "positive" notion largely based on his *Autre,* "absolutely" other."[72] The earlier submitted hypothesis of a dramatically distinct cultural other makes allowances for strong distinctiveness while deemphasizing geographical separation and lack of commerce between self and other. In other words, the other may be culturally absolute, but he or she is not cut off from where and what I am.

(8) Critics of the reified other rightly infer that this othering does not "reciprocate," that is, does not grant this other the kind of presence "in and for himself" one normally assumes in and for oneself.[73] To an important degree, what Hegel dubs the "suspending [of] otherness" comes in modern culture from this tilted reciprocity, from grounding the self-other interface in a one-way, "self-edifying" traffic rather than in the effective mutuality logically and ethically following from the originary, constitutive nature of the other with respect to the self.[74]

(9) Overtly or covertly solipsistic, this ontology is excessively self-centered. Hostage to its own gaze and apprehensive of the actual or perceived "outside" to the point of racism and xenophobia, it can be defined as an *allergy* of being. *Allergy* too, the reader will recall, comes from the Greek *allos* and means "action against" or "rejection of the other."[75]

(10) Self-centeredness implies ontological separateness of the world's "existents." Yet it becomes clearer every day that these existents are fictions replicating a no less problematic, "vertical" representation of traditions flowing from the past straight into the future on nonintersecting tracks. We have noticed that this is also the model of multiculturalism. Instead, cosmodernism implies "transversality," culture as trans- and interculturation. This projects vertical influences as confluences, and filiations inside separate traditions "horizontally," as affiliations across traditions, shifting

away from endogenous formations (the root and, by extension, the pedigreed *Blut-und-Boden* model) toward an exogenous, "lateral," circulation-based phenomenology of cultural production and recognition (the rhizome model), "a situation in which culture will be increasingly defined in terms of the relation to some other."[76] Arguing for this definition, anthropologists from Lévi-Strauss to Geertz and Clifford have proposed an *interactional-intersectional* cultural concept according to which culture—dynamic, always in motion, running into, and overlapping with, other cultures—is a matter of roots *and* routes. Furthermore, the critics observe, even those roots, stemming from "a" place and "a" tradition as they seem to at first glance, become as they grow, if they have not been so originally, *ab origo,* a place where other places and the traditions rooted in them are rerouted, crisscross, mingle, and signify. On this account, culture is not one, "homogeneous," even though this is how it has advertised itself historically. A potpourri, a heteroclite assemblage, culture's fundamental condition is heterogeneity and fluidity. By contrast, the former model of culture "in-sists," stands for whatever it does by standing-in, by dwelling inside its carefully demarcated and nation-state-enforced paradigm. It keeps being what previous elements in its series have been, and we should remember that, after all, "standing-in" (*Inständigkeit*) is in Heidegger a sign of *Da-sein*'s "authenticity."[77] Authentic in its own way, cosmodern being ek-sists, rather, as it pushes against the repetitive "ontology of sameness."[78] As ek-sistence or ex-insistence that leaves this ontological modality of the self behind, existence grafts elements from other series onto itself in order to develop a meaning and more basically develop, grow, and be. Its ontology, then, is an "ontology of otherness," is not—cannot be—allergic, heterophobe since it depends on an other, enters in a relationship and so, Martin Buber would say, subscribes to a reciprocity.[79] This is how the self runs up an ever-outstanding debt to others. This does not mean only that its ontology has ethical consequences, but, quite the other way around, that it is premised on ethics. The primordial presence of others as others—unique, unassimilated, different—in the texture of Americanness and generally in the fabric of selfhood rests on this primacy of the ethical.

Throughout Western thought, nobody has argued this priority more persuasively than Levinas. Building principally on Buber's "innate You,"[80] Levinas refuses to accept that ethics "derives" from ontology. In the form of the "ethical relationship with th[at] other" without whom there would be no meaning and identity to being, ethics is to him "just as primary and original (*ursprünglich*) as ontology—if not more so."[81] Here, he levels a critique at the Heideggerian *Sein und Zeit,* an analysis he will expand four years later in another article, "L'ontologie est-elle fondamentale?" and then in *Totalité et infini.* In *Being and Time,* Heidegger had maintained that "The world of Da-sein is a *with-world.* Being-in is *being with* others" (112), but not before asserting that "the characteristic of encountering the *others* is, after all, oriented toward one's *own* Da-sein" (111). Consequently, Heidegger's ontology comes first, thereby ontologizing being as *self*-orientation. As Derrida glosses the Heideggerian *Letter on Humanism,* the ethical *with* derives from the question on being and so comes next, if it comes at all.[82] Some of Heidegger's commentators doubt it ever does, while still others think that it is already there but *un*ethically, as the "ontological imperialism" pinpointed by Levinas in *Totality and Infinity* (44). Accordingly, in Heidegger being-with is not genuinely relational, original. That is why the appositional language of with-ness, being-with, relatedness, and the like, which *Cosmodernism* speaks programmatically, references not so much Heidegger as Levinas's revaluation of Heidegger. As Levinas sees it, the truth of those with whom I exist in the world "proceeds," in Heidegger's view, from the "openness" of their Being and so I "comprehend" them insofar as my thought "transcends" them. "Measur[ed] . . . against the horizon whereupon it is profiled," an existent "arises upon a ground that extends beyond it, as an individual arises from a concept" (44–45). This is how, Levinas carries on, the "existing of an existent is converted into intelligibility; its independence is a surrender in radiation. To broach an existent from Being is simultaneously to let it be and to comprehend it." So the existent, the other with whom "I am" in the world, must "surrender" in the act of understanding, of conceptualization. The con*cept* holds this other captive (cf. Lat. *captum*). To size the other up is simply to seize it rationally as "reason seizes on it through the void and nothingness of existing, . . . [a]pproached from Being, from the luminous horizon where it has a silhouette, but has lost its face." The existent is an "appeal" to *my* comprehension, and comprehension "unfolds in time." But how I respond, no less than the temporality of the response, wraps exclusively around comprehending subjectivity inasmuch as understanding sanctions "the priority of *Being* over *existents*" and thus evinces the "essence of philosophy." This essence, Levinas contends, has entailed "subordinat[ing] the relation with *someone,*" an "existent" (the "ethical relation"), to "a relation with the *Being of existents,* which, impersonal, permits the apprehension, the domination of existents (a relationship of knowing), subordinates justice to freedom." And here comes the crucial part of his argument:

> If freedom denotes the mode of remaining the same in the midst of the other, knowledge, where an existent is given by interposition of impersonal Being, contains the ultimate sense of freedom. It would be opposed to justice, which involves obligations with regard to an existent that refuses to give itself, the Other, who in this sense would be an existent par excellence. In subordinating the very relation with existents to the relation with Being, Heideggerian ontology affirms the primacy of freedom over ethics. To be sure, the freedom involved in the essence of truth is not for Heidegger a principle of free will. Freedom comes from an obedience to Being: it is not man who possesses freedom; it is freedom that possesses man. But the dialectic which thus reconciles freedom and obedience in the concept of truth presupposes the primacy of the same, which marks the direction of and defines the whole of Western philosophy. (45)

"Neutralizing" the other, the "relation with Being," ontology, is not an actual relation with this other but its "reduction to the same" (45–46). Entailing "possession" and "suppression," the "thematization" and "conceptualization" of the other through a notion, research model, or whole cultural paradigm have worked historically hand in glove with the "imperialist domination" and "tyranny" (46–47) exerted by an ethnic group, political party, or state set on bringing the "irreducible Other" (47) under the jurisdiction of preexisting majorities and reflexes.

Late Globalization and the Cosmodern Double-Bind

Developments in the late 1980s and early 1990s, the end of the Cold War in particular, abated this multiply reductive logic but also gave it an unexpected lease on life inside the United States as much as outside. A watershed in recent history, the Berlin Wall's fall was, not unlike the New York City Twin Towers' on 9/11, both an American and a world event. Granted, the U.S. Marines were not its main actors, nor did it happen in our backyard. But, for one thing, America had been involved in it. For another, the Wall's collapse has been playing a deeply transformative role in American society. Like the rest of the world, the United States changed forever in or about 1989, as Virginia Woolf might have put it. Most historians concur that the 1970s and even the early 1980s had allowed only inklings of the post-1989 global setup. During those decades, episodes such as the one reported by Alda, although not entirely isolated, had been few and far between comparatively speaking and in any case hardly in tune with the prevailingly antinomian geopolitical logic of spheres, blocs, regions, and countries separated by all sorts of "curtains" and checkpoints. We may have been "together" back then, if not since day one, as Nancy says; ontologically and sociologically, this "communality," this "being-together-in-the-world," may be the human's perennial signature. But, to paraphrase the philosopher, after the Wall came down, our becoming what we have always been has itself become unprecedented in scope, pace, and obviousness, at home and abroad.[83] With another vocabulary, the period following the Cold War witnesses the coming of hypernetworked, "strong," or "late" globalization.[84]

This chapter in the age-old epos of global processes has been covered ad nauseam by an army of critics.[85] Consequently, I will refrain from rehashing the commonplaces of the Borgesian library accumulated on the topic, except to situate cosmodernism historically and thus highlight its "double-bind." To clarify, first I define the cosmodern as an emblematic *cultural modality of late globalization.* Since I allude to Fredric Jameson's definition of postmodernism as "cultural logic of late capitalism," I must next draw the reader's attention to the italicized part of the statement, where the preposition indexes a "logic" quite unlike Jameson's. Here, "of" does not denote a tight "construction" of the cosmodern by the global world but a more flexible affiliation with an originating, certainly shaping, but only partially determining context. The cosmodern is not to the global what cause is to effect, (back)stage (and script) to performance, or "base" to "superstructure." In this sense, cosmodernism is not the ism "of" late-global America. With Roland Robertson, Martin Albrow, Arjun Appadurai, John Tomlinson, and others, I too "caution against such frequently used formulations as 'the *impact* of globalization on culture' or 'the cultural consequences of globalization.'" These "phrases," the critics rightly hold, are "used casually as a reference to the way in which the connectivity and fluidity of globalization makes itself [*sic*] felt within the sphere of culture. Yet the trouble with these phrases is that, taken literally, they imply globalization to be a process which somehow has its sources and its sphere of operation *outside* of culture."[86] Allegedly at the receiving end of global realignments, culture does not bear *on* globalization but simply bears it, "globalizes," yet primarily in an intransitive sense, as a "patient" of external forces riding roughshod over it. And so where most critics employ "the culture *of* globalization" phrase as a subjective-possessive genitive, I favor a more descriptive usage, with the global as material-temporal, *less conditioning set of conditions* or arena *for,* and object *of,* culture's own globalizing impetus. I view globalization as a property or propensity of culture too, and the same goes for "culture *under* globalization," by which I acknowledge both the socioeconomic pressures on cultures to interchange and spawn polycultural blends, and the historical rubric "under" which culture comes temporally. As above, I do retain "context," but if we are to keep it, we are better off if we approach it less positivistically. Yes, global-era cultures' morphings, couplings, and significations are verifiably bound up with the global context, but, if we think of culture as context-bound, then we must also envision this context as "boundless," both less determined structurally and less deterministic in repercussions.[87] Those unwilling to do so, Tomlinson aptly opines, "betray some rather stubborn preconceptions about both the driving forces of globalization" and "the nature of 'culture' itself."[88] Bearing out this "nature," cosmodernism obtains, I argue, *in conjunction* with late globalization. "In conjunction" signifies here a certain form of association not quite loose but not strict either, one that combines reflection and critique. Cosmodernism comes to the fore against the backdrop of late globalization as a sustained reflection of, and on, global issues and concerns, a thematization more than once critical of the historical moment on which it otherwise depends.

In theory, late globalization should be a "with-world," ideally conducive to cosmodern scenarios of identity fashioning. After all, as has been pointed out, what distinguishes it from earlier globalization is its superiorly "webbed" makeup, its high connectivity. We are living, or so we hear, in a "network society" where the "production" of identity and meaning individually and collectively, in and of "our" culture, involves, indeed necessitates, recurring references to other cultures.[89] The pre-1989 global setup had been admittedly less technologized and hence less networked, more country- and region-focused, in brief, "thinner." By contrast, what comes after is "thicker": conspicuously more systemic, more technological and thus more integrated, transnational and cross-regional. Critics like Albrow and Robertson believe the transition from one to another occurs over a longer time span (1945–1990s in Albrow, 1960s–1990s in Robertson), whereas Thomas L. Friedman revisits the "1989 argument" made in *The Lexus and the Olive Tree* and remade in *Longitudes and Latitudes* to conclude that a "new whole era: Globalization 3.0" commences circa

2000.[90] In my estimation, 1989 was what Jean-Pierre Warnier would deem a true *année charnière*, a "hinge year" on which turned the doors opening, in the United States and elsewhere, onto the highly interconnected world of late globalization.[91]

A "new beginning," then? So think Albrow, Arif Dirlik, and others who, against Francis Fukuyama's "end of history" thesis, point to the globally inaugural thrust of the Cold War's end.[92] What with the downfall of the Berlin and related walls, barriers, and divisions, 1989 was the single major historical-geopolitical milestone that, at the end of the twentieth century, signaled that we meant to leave behind a divided, compartmental, cloistered world—Pierre Chaunu's *univers cloisonné*—and enter a new one, which held out the promise of experiencing itself as being-together with unrivaled pathos.[93] Thus, the post-Wall era purported to be equally postdivisional *urbi et orbi*, in Berlin and worldwide, to put an end to the East-West "bipolarity" and to the gulfs and schisms directly and indirectly derived from it.[94] On this score, Friedman's observation is not entirely off the mark: "to appreciate the far-reaching flattening [globalizing] effects of the fall of the Berlin Wall, it's always best to talk to non-Germans or non-Russians" such as Indian businesspeople *in* India, for they would explain to you how new digitizing technologies have made Bangalore into a Boston suburb.[95]

A happy "Fall," then? So it seemed and actually was for many in Central and Eastern Europe, in the former Soviet republics, around the world, and in the United States no less, for Cold War Manichaeanism had also exacted its toll on the American public imaginary, policies, and welfare. The world's "fall into relation" appeared to meet the logical, geocultural and political condition for closing the world's economic gaps and healing its historical wounds. The ensuing "postlapsarian" global certainly advertised itself as a postconflictual state of affairs of a world decreasingly apart, in which the polarizing and *disconnective* impetus of the Cold War and of modernity overall at long last took a back seat to a rationally managed worldly *connectedness* that in turn prompted people to see themselves *sub specie coniunctionis,* as embodiments of an existentially and culturally relational logic. This utopianism got resounding traction in sweeping pronouncements of the "new world order" sort made by Mikhail Gorbachev in the heyday of perestroika, then by George H. W. Bush as a prelude to Desert Storm. Both were belated echoes to the "new world" rhetoric of Woodrow Wilson's 1918 "Fourteen Points" speech, soon to be canceled out by the "new world *dis*order" counter-rhetoric of Ken Jowitt's 1992 influential book, followed by similar interventions by Zygmunt Bauman, Tzvetan Todorov, Amin Maalouf, Wallerstein, and other chroniclers of "le Nouveau Désordre mondial."[96] Suspiciously "orderly," one smacks of wishful, arguably self-interested thinking. The other presents us with a hopelessly entropic, world-scale pandemonium. One is overly institutional and simplistically centripetal, what with its late 1980s and early 1990s roll call of accomplishments: the tearing down of the Iron Curtain; the 1993 signing of the North American Free Trade Agreement (NAFTA); the 1995 consolidation of the Bretton Woods institutions and agreements through the World Trade Organization; the new initiatives of the International Monetary Fund and the World Bank; the expansion of the European Union and the North Atlantic Treaty Organization; the new nongovernmental organizations cropping up all over the world, while the older ones bolster their activities inside or outside the United Nations; the Internet and other advances in communications, commerce, finance, and afferent technologies. The other is exceedingly centrifugal, registering chiefly the regional crises and ethnic-religious conflicts that also multiply during this time following the breakup of former supranational and imperial entities such as the Eastern bloc, the USSR, and Yugoslavia. One hawks a ubiquitously nurturing relatedness and implicitly a top-down worldly coherence yet describes them in policy-oriented, abstract, impersonal terms. Dismissing relatedness altogether, the other makes a half-gesture toward bottom-up movements although they evoke little more than the violent incoherence of a "Balkanized" planet. Both world pictures are therefore macrostructural. In that, they describe the world as much as they shortchange it.

The Contest of Orders

We live today under a new world order.
The web which weaves together all things envelops our bodies,
Bathes our limbs,
In a halo of joy.
— MICHEL HOUELLEBECQ, *The Elementary Particles*

The New World Order implies the extermination of everything
different[,] integrat[ing] it into an indifferent world's order.
— JEAN BAUDRILLARD, *Fragments: Cool Memories III, 1991–1995*

My take is more modest and more ambitious at once. I do acknowledge that, a turning point in history, 1989 heralds a new world order. But this is neither of the orderly nor of the disorderly kind. It is not an order of the world per se either, a neatly unified geopolitical or economic setup. I find both grand narratives wanting, first and foremost because they miss the "micro" level, in particular the place of the individual and individual communities in the global scheme of things and principally the role played by the imagination in the production of this scheme or "order." Homologous to its subject, the cosmodern interpretation of cosmodernism's imaginary—the cosmodern critical imaginary at work here—sets out to make up for this shortcoming by refocusing the discussion on the mental picture the individuals paint of themselves, their worlds, and the world beyond. Accordingly, what I uncover is not a "totality," a fully integrated (or disintegrating) world (dis)order, much as, again, the late-global world, and America within it, is distinct from the pre-1989 world. What this study brings to light is chiefly an order of the imagination, an imaginary in the making. Or, if this is an order of the world, it is one to the extent that the world is this order's object, gets "ordered"—taken apart, reshuffled, and put back together—in combinations that are meaningful and critical, suggestive of a structural coherence and a critical scrutiny absent from the neoliberal picture of the actual planet. Both the cohesiveness and the critique draw on a consistent and individualizing wrestling with that very distinctiveness of the post-1989 United States and world, namely, with a qualitatively and quantitatively unequaled relationality. Unlike grandiose statements of the geopolitical-corporate sort, the cosmodern worldview puts this burgeoning relatedness on trial. Neither ignoring nor discounting it, cosmodernism takes note of its presence, in effect pinpoints the excessive presence *in the world* of a "macro" sort of circuitry powered by economic and military flows decided "from above," and offers in exchange an alternative vision *of the world.* This outlook boils down to a different relational model. The model does not pull us out of the webbed world's expanding material culture of relatedness. Weary of the latter's record, it only proposes that we imagine it otherwise, as I will show momentarily.

What I wish to stress first is that the imaginary redeployments of late-global life in the life of the mind are more than aerial, disembodied figments. They are anchored in history because they document historical processes, but they do so by *necessarily* touching off fictional-imaginal mechanisms that still await critical exploration. As Valéry says in the same preface to *Lettres persanes,* the order following an interval of strife, warmongering, and belligerent anxieties is also, perhaps mostly, driven by "fictional forces," takes an effort of the imagination, and it is the individual or, even better, the individuals who make this effort and bear the ensuing order's "burden."[97] To reemphasize: hardly cut off from contemporary history, this endeavor unfolds, as I say, "in conjunction" with a certain historical moment, is part of a larger imaginary "order," and as such shares in a certain logic.

Imaginary acts are neither arbitrary nor "irrational." As Gilbert Durand underscores in the critique of Western rationalism with which his 1963 study *Les structures anthropologiques de l'imaginaire* opens, these acts should not be construed as "lapses of reason" (*vacances de la raison*).[98] They have a reason of their own; to restate a previous claim, the cosmodern imaginary attests to the rebirth of modern rationality as relationality. Staking out a Kantian middle ground halfway "between image and concept," relatedness supplies the basic imaginary "structure" or "principle of classification" around which individual imaginative acts take shape.[99] In Durand, and before him in Sartre's *L'imaginaire* (1940), this scheme has a fair deal of generality to it, while the imaginative act is concrete. Tying the two together is, to borrow from Durand once more, a certain "regime," a subject matter or problematic common to a set of imaginings and distributing them along several thematic axes or "imaginaries," all of which are in turn underlain by the unifying "deep structure" of relatedness. Yet again, there is something to be said about the ontological purview of this imaginary scheme. It may not and in fact does not coincide with the "real world"'s own "scheme" or "logic." Analogous to postmodernism in "late capitalism"—*pace* Jameson—cosmodernism instantiates the "cultural logic" of "late globalization" *only up to a point.* But this has to do more with critical resistance to late globalization, with the politics and ethics of the cosmodern vision, and less with cosmodernism's being *no more* than a matter of ahistorical "vision." We talk about "things" such as postmodern buildings and apparel, about postmodern identity and society, not solely about postmodern notions, styles, and representations of things, so we can talk too, as I often will, about a cosmodern world and view of it, about a rising albeit far from fully formed "discourse" or "culture" of cosmodernism as well as about those "things" this discourse or culture imagines. In approaching the cosmodern predominantly as an imaginary configuration—in canvassing the cosmodern imaginary—I insist, then, on the ontological inscription of an imaginary that captures objects and facts undoubtedly "real," "out there." As it does so, this imaginary imagines, gives them imaginal bodies but does not quite make them up. Both reproductive and productive, mimesis and fabulation, it invents but not ex nihilo.

In so doing, it brings forth something that affects the world by submitting it to a powerful and morally imperative representation.

This means that the cosmodern imaginary is as descriptive as it is prescriptive. Against uncritically globalist projections *in the present*, this imaginary ascertains that which, in our fast-globalizing present and owing to some of this present's tendencies, has not fully surfaced yet. It is in this sense that the cosmodern is visionary and its visionarism is committed. The cosmoderns latch onto the drawbacks of late globalization as jumping-off points for a world—a "solution"—not here yet. In this sense also, cosmodern projections are "realistically" analytic, taking stock as they do of a present-day actuality, "presentifying" and lending a material body to a reality "out there" if otherwise insufficiently charted or discernible. But they are also forward-looking and occasionally utopian. In the cosmodern project, then, a down-to-earth and critical view of *this* world and a vision of a future one into which the present can be imaginatively re-presented or outimagined run side by side. Couched in narrative or critical-theoretical fictions as it may be, the cosmodern imaginary is neither hopelessly fictitious nor solely theoretical.[100]

An important premise of critics like Appadurai, "cultural realism" attracts even outspoken "new world order" skeptics. Thomas Peyser, for instance, turns to an earlier Appadurai article to drive home the point that the imagination, "a key component of the new global order," represents a "form of negotiation between sites of agency ('individuals') and globally defined fields of possibility." Therefore, says Peyser, we need "to think about novels (and other cultural productions) depicting a globalized world not simply because we can show that art is 'grounded' in social circumstance, but because novels themselves may have a crucial role to play in the very process of globalization." Thus, he concludes, the future "world-system" will "to some extent, depend upon the way the global field is imagined by those acting as agents within it" even though "we can be tolerably certain that all the imagination coupled with the best will in the world would not dissuade capital from its global quest for profit."[101] In *Modernity at Large*, Appadurai ups the ante of his cultural realism (or culturalism, as he dubs it) to propound that the imagination is absolutely *vital*, that is, important to life and part of it. To paraphrase Daniel Cohen's remarks on *la mondialisation imaginaire* ("imaginary globalization"), the point is not that the cosmodern is also an imaginary affair but rather that the cosmodern can and does insert itself into the world to "re-world" it.[102] Pertaining to the "quotidian mental work of ordinary people in many societies," cosmodern imaginings overflow the mindscapes surveyed in *Modernity at Large*.[103] The work these imaginings do spills into the structure of the quotidian with reordering consequences; it is work that sets out to be just that: work on the world, work that works over the world order. This work is a matter of urgency. Let me explain.

2. Cosmodern Environmentalism: A Code of Worldly Conduct

Il n'y a pas d'hors risque

> . . . a stage of radicalized modernity . . . where the dynamics of individualization, globalization, and risk undermine modernity and its foundations. Whatever happens, modernity gets *reflexive*, that means concerned with its unintended consequences, risks, and foundations.
> —ULRICH BECK, "Politics of Risk Society"

In Saul Bellow's 1964 novel *Herzog*, the protagonist questions the "social and ethical reasonings" of one Dr. Emmett Strawforth, who advocates a "Philosophy of Risk in the controversy over fallout, . . . chemical pesticides, contamination of ground water, etc." (49). Strawforth has little doubt that "we must adopt his Philosophy of Risk with regard to radioactivity"; after all, "life in civilized countries" rests "upon a foundation of risk." And yet "few intellectuals have grasped the social principles behind this quantitative transformation" (50). Nietzsche, John Dewey, and Alfred North Whitehead are among the better-known exceptions (51), and, drawing freely from them, Herzog's irony seems on target: the "modern condition" may well be marked by nuclear fallout rather than by Heidegger's "fall into the quotidian" (49).

In determining being as "flinging into danger" and "daring" that "risk[s]" the Heraclitean "game" of time, Heidegger stands out, however, as a prominent risk philosopher. "Being, as the venture [that] holds all beings," existence as ad-venture, and kindred notions such as will, "unprotectedness," and "care" (*Sorge*), not least the "draft" (*Bezug*) that draws all beings out of themselves and toward life's vital center, are at the heart of his ontological topology as developed particularly in his later work on poetic language.[104] Certainly less recondite, Strawforth's "philosophy," which posits that modernity is grounded in risk, is not entirely at odds

with Heidegger's. For "the foundation of risk" recalls another Heideggerian concept: the "abyss," *der Abgrund*. Heidegger plays on the word's etymology and early uses to make an important point: *der Abgrund* is
ground and absence thereof, foundationless foundation that "[i]n the age
of the world's night, must be experienced and endured."[105] This "age" is
the Hölderlinean "destitute time" measured by the modern poetry that
inspires Heidegger in "Wozu Dichter?" It is, furthermore, Heidegger's
own time in the World War II aftermath, but also Herzog's, the Romantic
and post-Romantic epoch Bellow's character studies and whose "quantitative transformations" he is teasing out. Among these changes, modernity's "foundation of risk" constitutes a fundamental if paradoxical risking of the fundament itself.

Heidegger and, replying to Strawforth, Herzog unpack the paradox
differently. Heidegger stresses the "foundational" role of risk. In his view,
the abyss is not so much bottomless, Rilkean *Urgrund*, the "pristine
ground" casting all beings into existence.[106] In Nietzsche, Heidegger, and
some of their followers, the *Abgrund* is ontologically positive. It mounts a
potentially fruitful challenge to humans as *die dürftige Zeit*, the time of
crisis and need, dares us to look into the abyss so we can learn our condition of risk. Herzog, on the other hand, seizes on risk as a negative category that endangers modern life. His position speaks to a mindset that associates risk with "negative or undesirable outcomes."[107] The objection to
Strawforth's risk philosophy is that, while putting the finger on a real issue, "lunatics" like him miss its modern scope and effects, how risk has
come to stand for modernity and its "social principles." Herzog does not
spell out the meaning of risk either, but a later missive occasions some
clarification: "our revolutions, including nuclear terror, return the metaphysical dimension to us. All practical activity has reached this culmination: everything may go now, civilization, history, meaning, nature. Everything! Now to recall Mr. Kierkegaard's question . . ."[108]

Herzog never gets to the question, but Anthony Giddens comes to the
rescue. "'Mr. Kierkegaard's question,'" he offers in *The Consequences of
Modernity*, is how "we avoid the dread of nonexistence" given that "the
possibility of global calamity prevents us from reassuring ourselves with
the assumption that the life of the species inevitably surpasses that of the
individual."[109] Now, Kierkegaard's society was less prone to all-out disas-
ters. Accordingly, Kierkegaardian "Evil" is a philosophical rather than a
technological and political category. As for Herzog, his rebuttal of Strawforth dates back to the Truman years, when people were only beginning to

fathom the risks involved in the arms race, pollution, deforestation, and the like. At that point, the "transformations" Herzog ponders had not prompted yet a qualitative change in how society was seeing itself. Sold on the ideal of unending progress, modernity was "getting ahead of itself" at a pace that was not allowing it to review its actions "observantly." Caught in its outward, "first-order observation" of the world as Heideggerian "standing-reserve," modernity was too self-absorbed to be self-observing enough and thus accede to a "second-order observation" apt to lay bare the risks embedded in the modern project.[110]

Not until the late 1980s does awareness of global-scale threats, and with it a new narrative of modernity, articulate itself fully. In the wake of the Cold War, Giddens, Ulrich Beck, Scott Lash, Barry Smart, and other sociologists start weighing the hypothesis of two modernities fairly differentiated structurally and chronologically.[111] In *Risk Society*, Beck contends that "[j]ust as modernization dissolved the structure of feudal society in the nineteenth century and produced the industrial society, modernization today is dissolving industrial society and another modernity is coming into being." "Today," namely in 1986, when *Risikogesellschaft* came out, "We are witnessing not the end but the *beginning* of modernity—that is, of a modernity *beyond* its classical industrial design."[112] What sets this modernity apart, according to Beck, is its struggle to define itself anew by assessing the "consequences" and subsequently revisiting the premises of a former modernity driven by "wealth production" (12). A new logic—the logic of risk—gets the upper hand during a later stage of modern history once "the gain in power from techno-economic 'progress' is being increasingly overshadowed by the production of risks." The latter are no longer "latent side effects" (13) but central manifestations because where a previous modernity mass-manufactured chiefly goods, the new modernity produces risks, and it does so visibly and globally. Before long, this production swings into overproduction, rendering the world a risk-saturated "system" in which space and risk become coextensive. As with Derrida's "generalized writing," the "outside" and the "inside" of risk break out of the "exorbitant," "supplemental" routine that prevents them from swapping places.[113] As there is no "outside-text," now *there is no outside-risk* either: *Il n'y a pas d'hors risque.* No place on earth is risk-free. As Beck states in *Risk Society*, risks "possess an inherent tendency towards globalization" (36). They go global, tend to make the modern world into a "risky" whole—Giddens's "risk culture"[114] or Beck's *Weltrisikogesellschaft*, "world risk society." Turning on the equation of globalization and risk, Beck's 1999 book *World Risk Society* expands *Risk Society*'s argument to underscore that "[r]isk society, fully thought through, means world risk society" (19). The strong sense of "society" must be underlined here: multiplied and amplified risks spread around the globe and so give rise to a community affected *as a whole* by them and thus forced to think collectively about them—and in this sense, and in this sense alone, one might entertain risk theorists' notion that "there are no longer 'others,'" safely outside the reach of global risks. Globalized, risks are further globalizing the planet as they spur wider and wider debates. This way, the globalization of risk not only "unifies" the earth's physical space but also brings together those who care about this unification, redefining human consciousness as "well-distributed awareness of risk *as* risk."[115] Indisputably, risks have already made us more philosophical about the "logic of wealth," "progress," Weberian rationality, and reason's workings largely. Increasingly grasped as risks rather than "accomplishments," modernity's "consequences" have been "subject to public criticism and scientific investigation" (13). Thus, "the concept of risk" appears "directly bound to the concept of reflexive modernization" and thereby to what Beck views as a "second modernity."

Culture of Risk, Culture at Risk: The "Indeterminate Cosmos" and the Egological

"[M]an's ethical relation to the other is ultimately prior to his ontological relation to himself (egology) or to the totality of things that we call the world (cosmology).
 —EMMANUEL LEVINAS AND RICHARD KEARNEY, "Dialogue with Emmanuel Levinas"

[T]he equivalent of an ethnic cleansing which would not just affect particular populations but unrelentingly pursue all forms of otherness.
 —JEAN BAUDRILLARD, *The Perfect Crime*

If modern society becomes risk society and modernity "its own theme,"[116] then what reflexive modernity ruminates is the gamble it took qua "first" modernity to evolve into what it is today. This was the gamble of rationality, a response to the "risky" world prior and seemingly external to modernity and its modernization narrative, a world reportedly still uncharted, uncontrolled, and unexploited, alluring yet unpredictable if not utterly illogical, indeterminate, "other." In the West, modernity came of age, Foucauldian historians have shown, as it "excluded" or "domesticated" this outer/other world by bringing it within the bounds of Western political authority as well as under the "reasonable" jurisdiction of Euro-Atlantic representations, taxonomies, methodologies, and epistemologies.[117] As Deborah Lupton quotes S. Reddy, "Moderns had eliminated genuine indeterminacy, or 'uncertainty,' by . . . transform[ing] a radically indeterminate cosmos into a manageable one, through the myth of calculability."[118] Driven by faith in the "'absolute control of the accidental, understood as the irruption of the unpredictable,'" the myth fueled modernity's "delirium of reason."[119]

Delirious, excessive, out-of-control rationality is hung up on controlling the world, on rationalizing and thus reproducing it in the likeness of the rationalizing self. Here the epistemological, the cultural, and the political go hand in hand one more time: this self takes (or rather gets a sense of being in) charge by ascertaining the uncertain world as a version of itself, the rational subject or, more straightforwardly, by exporting its own cultural certainties, representations, and emblems to the world. Either way, as noted earlier, this self assimilates, likens and makes similar to itself, hence "transcends"—but only to reference and validate itself, for "others" are "out there" primarily to assist with its production or to reproduce this self. Auxiliary entities, they are there "for" or "after" it, not "with it" authentically. Its ontology, much like the ultimate meaning of Heidegger's *Mitsein,* is then "egological"; the modern philosophy of being and knowledge, one may extrapolate following Levinas, constitutes "an egology."[120] More broadly, the logic of modernity as a whole is ego-logical or egotistic, catering to the self-ascertaining self and its fantasies of sameness.

The questions I must raise at this point are: What happens to this egology in late globalization? What happens, that is, to globalization as a logic of in-difference?[121] Does the post-1989 era inaugurate another, possibly less equalizing, less "allergic" modernity? The questions funnel down to a more basic one: What kind of relationality is our global society fostering?

Critics tend to agree that this society is a "rapidly developing and ever-dens[ify]ing network of interconnections and interdependences," but the agreement ends here because network linkages among people, cultures, and places can be construed "in a number of different modalities."[122] In principle, there is nothing wrong with connectivity and its thickening; yet there is everything wrong with "netocracy" that connects to exploit and disenfranchise. Networks can help people, as fax machines did in Beijing's

Tiananmen Square back in 1989 and Twitter during Iran's presidential elections twenty years later. But the networks can also enfetter us, as Yahoo! did a few years ago, when it turned over to the Chinese government records that led to the jailing of several dissidents.[123] The same networks can speed up relief assistance *and* "McDonaldization." To net buffs like Friedman, Bill Gates, Alexander Bard, and Jan Soderqvist, networks are the solution; to net skeptics à la Alain Finkielkraut, Paul Soriano, Steven Shaviro, Jameson, Žižek, and Baudrillard, they are "public enemy number one."[124]

Thus, highly networked, late globalization is, as Michael Hardt and Antonio Negri assure us, hardly "univocal," and, again, one must recognize that it does run the whole gamut, from the diversification/localization of global vectors and influences to Robertson's "glocalization" to the serialization/homogenization of local cultures.[125] Most writers pinpoint, however, the pronounced egological penchant of "homo-hegemonizing" networks, as Derrida called them.[126] These networks come into place to standardize and subsume the world to historically privileged standards. This aspect of planetary "flattening" cannot be glossed over, for, deceptively enough, it gestures to lateral, even bottom-up moves, implies challenges to extant stratifications of power, and is otherwise suggestive of democracy, fairness, increased participation, and other things of such "horizontal" nature while its actual effects may be and often are "vertical," reworking the network into a hierarchy with its command nodes, one-way channels, preferred circuits, and profit schemes. With this observation, I now circle back to the questions above and answer them: to a worrisome extent, post-1989, strong globalization means, inside and outside the United States, the strengthening of relationality as a rationalization vehicle. Insofar as it does the bidding of modern egology in forms and with intensities previously unknown, our age carries on modernity and the selfsame logic according to which, in a relation, contact, or any other kind of association, one element attempts to co-opt another. Egological for the most part, modern ontology and, arguably, modernity as a whole have gone into egological overdrive of late. In my account, Giddens's "runaway" world is a juggernaut egology in which the self's autoreproduction has stepped up courtesy of recent geopolitical shifts, financial-economic deals, and communication technologies. What is becoming progressively evident on the heels of these developments is how, within a world risk society determined as commonality of risks, the *risks of commonality* are getting higher and higher, in other words, how in a world risk culture, cultural diversity, and ultimately culture itself, is at risk.

As the philosophers of being-with teach us, "communality" is a primordial condition and aspiration of the human. Only, in the "shrinking" world of the last two decades communality of time and space has translated apace into commonality of culture. The new proximity of self and other has often resulted in their equivalence, symmetry, and identity. Available to "us" as never before, "they" are becoming more and more like us in the global panopticon. The Walls have fallen and the Windows have opened to "flatten" the world, level the playing field, and "empower" all "communities."[127] In this cheerful survey of the late-global landscape, the "power of globalization" and power broadly are thus seized on *in abstracto* as *access to an other*, namely, "as the inexorable integration of markets, transportation systems, and communication systems to a degree never witnessed before—in a way that is enabling corporations, countries, and individuals to reach around the world farther, faster, deeper, and cheaper than ever before, and in a way that is enabling the world to reach into corporations, countries, and individuals farther, faster, deeper, and cheaper than ever before."[128] An abundance of evidence points, though, to the frequently disempowering upshots of upgraded and generalized access. More than once, reaching across previously impermeable borders has had assimilative, "rationalizing" effects on those we wished to reach. In this respect, what bears noting is the asymmetrical structure of said symmetry: indeed, "we" still have to become like "them." This lopsidedness of the world, of the world in the United States and the United States in the world, "we" must assume and think through given the lead role the United States has played in the advent of late globalization.

Coping with this worldly unevenness requires confronting the global condition of cultural risk, namely, the ongoing *relational depletion* of the world. The statement may puzzle the reader who will recall that I have been associating late globalization with an *influx* of relationality into the world. To make myself clear, I will say first that what I am taking about is a risk and an impending crisis that pertain to cultural diversity viewed as a mark of others' presence in our common world. This presence is original and vital to the world, is its inherently relational makeup. An ethical a priori and hence, Levinas reminds us, an ontological *datum*, this constitution constitutes the world, sets in train its history and makes those in it ("us" too) what they are. As such, this type of relationality should be celebrated. But there is another type, which gets into high gear after 1989. Of a more corporate, managerial, and "macro" "order," this sweepingly assimilationist, self-reproductive relationality runs counter to and threatens to eradicate the ethical kind and with it, Baudrillard fears in his late works, the alterity on which this form of relationality is premised and which in turn affords us a world. This threat is real and signals a crisis—a crisis of rationality, of rationality as modernity's egological rationale and distinctive cultural procedure. Therefore, it is not evident at all that modernity in general and modern reason in particular can overcome this crisis, as Bellow's hero, Beck, and Giddens think. "Reason exists!" Herzog exclaims. "Belief based on reason" is the antidote to "the disorder of the world."[129] This "ordering around" of the world, this "rationalization" of risks, testifies to a "commitment to reason in the name of reason" about whose "circularity" none of them has any qualms.[130] Their position is basically "that we do not have *enough* reason (*Vernunft*) to live and act in a global age of manufactured uncertainties."[131]

Egology into Ecology

> [T]o think relationally presupposes a recognition of difference.
> —PHILLIP E. WEGNER, "Soldierboys for Peace"

There is no shortage of *Vernunft,* the cosmoderns reply. There is actually too much of it, and this surplus has been driving modernity's post–Cold War fast-forward egology. What we need instead, they hint, is what I call an *ecology* of relations, that is, another way of thinking about being in the world and, more broadly, about being: with oneself, with others both like and unlike oneself, with one's country and with the world beyond. The cosmodern imaginary traces a complex move, half in progress, half still ahead of us, a shift away from an egological to an ecological modernity or cosmodernity; from a modernity that has grounded, even in its postmodern afterglow, most of its endeavors to pull the world together, map it out, and treat its "disorders," in a self-centered and self-centering relationality, in connections that assimilate and make uniform, to a modernity in dramatic and urgent search for what Finkielkraut and Soriano call "connective reason";[132] from a modernity of cultural-epistemological tactics, concepts, and rationalizing modules that make scant provisions for others and their otherness, to a genuinely "considerate" cosmodernity.

Marking the transition from self-centered and self-centering—egological—modernity, from *relationality as rationality,* to an other-oriented modernity and modern rationale, to a *rationality as relationality* and to being understood as a relationally "authentic" formation and thereby as obligation to an other, this consideration or concern entails postrational "reflexivity," a critique of the linking setups and strategies that, under the guise of progress, predicate their sociocultural, economic, and geopolitical arrangements on serialization of "alien," "foreign," or "exotic" singularities and thus damage cultural environments. This is a cultural critique and more broadly a way of conceiving the world and of being in it that emulate Levinas's ethical departure from Heidegger's *Da-sein.* That is to say, this is an effort to found comprehension, representation, and behavior not on a relation with the Heideggerian Being looming high in the background of our dealings with the world and on the ontology ingrained in that self-referencing presence but on "conversational" commerce with an other, on the face-to-face as pre-face to understanding. This is con-versation, not conversion. The self turns to an other not to convert that other, or him- or herself for that matter, but *in order to be,* thus acknowledging that which warrants his or her own being; self and other may converge *on* certain subjects (on which they may otherwise disagree), but they do not merge into a single subjectivity. This is, at last, the only "non-allergic relation with alterity," for it does not flow from, nor is geared to confirm, the self, its ideas, or historical incorporations.[133] If Heideggerian ontology and ontology at large are an "ontology of sameness," an egology, the cosmodern imaginary is an ecology.

What I mean by ecology is *cultural ecology.* Around since the 1950s, this umbrella term has been tacked recently to a direction in environmental studies that approaches landscape as a "bioculturally collaborative project,"[134] a site where local traditions of "language and knowledg[e] both shape and are shaped by" the natural settings "in which the culture exists."[135] Retaining the correlative ("collaborative") aspect, I limit its investigation to culture while ascertaining that the cultural, the topological—culture's shared topology or space—and the ethical—an obligation following from "proximal" living under late globalization—dovetail, in other words, that cultural analysis of the cosmodern stripe leads logically (eco-logically, I am tempted to say) to an ethics. I do not ignore natural habitat either, nor do I buy into a hard-and-fast nature-culture distinction. But the environments I am scouting are by and large cultural, and, alongside a number of authors, from Hubert Zapf—whose *kulturelle Ökologie* has been making inroads in Germany since 2002—and Ursula Heise to Joseph Tabbi, Michael Wutz, and Henry Sussman, I argue for a certain cultural environmentalism.[136] It is from such a culturally environmental standpoint that I claim that the world is at risk. As we will learn throughout, the world's relational equilibrium is being jeopardized by egological trends, to which I oppose an ecologically minded picture of the world. This picture is ecological not because it features nature, although it often does, but because it challenges the egotistic penchant of late globalization. In response, and this time around against recent interventions by cultural ecologists, I suggest that we think of culture's well-being in terms of an "ecological" balance understood as co-presence, co-implication, and co-responsibility of self and his or her "cultural other," in short, as ethical relatedness.[137]

This correlation runs deeper than the classically environmental, human-natural nexus. For in the cosmoderns' view, otherness may be distinct from the self but is neither isolated nor external to it. Not just environment or background to the self's figure, otherness authenticates selfhood in the sense specified above, participates massively and originally—from the moment of origination—in the self's production, performance, and auto-conceptualization. The ecological is thus deeply correlative. It acknowledges and thrives on others' presence and stories. The egological is illusorily self-referencing and self-relative; it stands as its own, superficially self-sufficient relation, relative (kin), and explanatory narrative (myth). An egological self is therefore quite inconceivable. More exactly, its authenticity is. On this account, this co-relationality cuts both ways: it is as significant to others and their own selves "out there" in Rica's Persia and Yuan Long Ping's China, as much as it is to those "from around here" who have a hard time seeing themselves "with," that is, either as shaped by others' perceptions and stories or, conversely, as shaping those perceptions, stories, and the identities behind them. At the dawn of the third millennium, U.S. literature and culture attest to a deepening awareness of this mutually fashioning process. Acuter than ever before in our history, this awareness is ethical—marks out a distinctly ethical project in post–Cold War America—in that it bears witness both to our indebtedness to others, to what others have done for us, and to what we have done *unto* them. Furthermore, as suggested earlier, this testimonial entails a moral stance insofar as such a recognition lays out explicitly or implicitly what we ought to do (or *not* to do) to honor that debt. The latter injunction is no less important given the asymmetry of identity-fashioning co-relationality, what with Western culture and U.S. media popular culture in particular aggressively reproducing themselves across and at times at the expense of selves "other" worldwide. As a critic of contemporary American literature and culture, I cannot overstate this enough: not only does this tendency threaten to remake other presences and cultural practices into similes and echoes of our domineering selves and worldviews; it also denies these selves to ourselves by inscribing us into expansionist-assimilationist scripts of identity where others are there to reflect our self-gratifying gaze back to us.

"Only the 'with'": "Globe," *mundus,* and the Ethos of Collegiality

[P]roximity is responsibility for the Other.
　　—EMMANUEL LEVINAS, "Ideology and Idealism"

Evolving cultures infer Relation, the overstepping that grounds their unity-diversity.
　　—ÉDOUARD GLISSANT, *Poetics of Relation*

The only empire we can have is an empire of personal relationships.
　　—ROBERT KAPLAN, *The Diane Rehm Show,* NPR,
　　　September 5, 2007

The cosmodern ecosystem of culture, that which Nicolescu and others refer to as our "one and the same Earth," is ethical to the extent that it faces up to the geocultural predicament of the late-global world: a shrinking space more and more finite every day, this world nevertheless must accommodate infinitely ("absolutely") the infinity or infinities of those with whom we share this space. Therefore, the cosmodern imaginary seizes on the world as an ever-imperfect, self-deferring totality, a "one world" that appears as such to itself and its inhabitants only physically because otherwise it is and must be a world of many worlds: not an all-encompassing "globe" but a *mundus.*[138] Along these lines, in Derrida's view, globalization is neither taking nor should take place.[139] If all there is to the globalizing world is its "incorporation," its corporatist one-becoming as "globe," as integrative geometry of cash and data, then globalization must be resisted. Yet Derrida himself suspects, as I do, that the planet's coming together—the world's "worlding" into one world—means more than the globalizing of the world into a globe; it also means *mondialization,* worlding of the world as *mundus,* a process susceptible of rescuing the Earth's ontological and cultural wealth.

Unlike his English translators, Derrida insisted repeatedly on this distinction between English globalization and French *mondialisation,* and it is worth recalling that he did so first in a commentary on Nancy's 1992 book *Le sens du monde* (The Sense of the World), an early gloss Derrida would develop in 2000 into a whole book, *Le toucher—Jean-Luc Nancy* (On Touching—Jean-Luc Nancy). The distinction may carry a French bias but is hardly specious. If "globalization"—its world and word alike—connotes universal translation resulting in a worldly "transparency" without "remainder," in a "global idiom" short on nuances, mondialization remains, according to Nancy, "untranslatable." Thus, it foregrounds, as *Cosmodernism*'s part 3 will expatiate, the simultaneous difficulty and urgency of translation today more than ever.[140] For, in mondializing, the world does not stop being an arcane *monde* that shows its many faces and addresses us in its many tongues, "springing forth," Nancy writes in *Being Singular Plural,* "as a properly incongruous incongruity" that exists as long as it keeps calling for dialogue and exchange.[141] Unlike globalization, which implies an undifferentiated, "compact result," mondialization suggests a process leading to a "'world' as a space of possible meaning for the whole of human relations."[142] This space is not (a) given; it gives itself, creates and re-creates itself as it keeps blossoming out into a "multiplicity of worlds."[143]

Cosmodern ecology is mapped onto and further enhances this topology. Where late globalization's egology sees the world as a "flat form" resting on an equalizing plat-form (Windows? English? neoliberalism?) that it ceaselessly falls back on, "there is" this sort of "foundation" neither to the cosmodern visualization of the globe as mundus nor to mondialization-style globalization. There is instead, Nancy explains, "only the 'with'"; there is "proximity" (topology, space) "and its distancing" (cultural difference between entities existing at close quarters); there is "the strange familiarity of all the worlds in the world" in which each finds in the "encounter with another's horizon" its most "appropriate horizon" of living, understanding, and self-understanding.[144] Promoting "the general equivalence of all meaningful forms [*formes de sens*] in an infinite uniformity," capital's "un-reason" (*sans-raison*) consumes the world of "singularities," the world as world. For it is those singularities, the unique, the one-of-a-kind, the a-serial—in brief, the *cultural* and its worldly embodiments, the planet's cultures—that make up the worldliness of the world, that plurality defying integration into a "uni-totality" (*unitotalité*).[145] According to Nancy, the modernity that lives on in and as late globalization has its other (meaning) in relation to that other-worldly entity (God). In that sense, the modernity imagined by the cosmoderns, cosmodernity, no longer has a sense but *is* one, produces one actively and continuously. This posttranscendental meaning turns on how the "existents" *in* the world "are-to" or "are-toward" one another.[146] Because of that, this meaning is not just a matter of ontology or topology, but also a matter of justice and ethics. What, how, and where we are *obligates*. Next to "them" more than we have ever been, "we" are responsible to and for them, more specifically, to and for what makes them other to us rather than others like us.

Critics from Alain Badiou to Masao Miyoshi have argued for a "postdifference" ethics allegedly better prepared to stave off "identitarianism" by doing away with otherness altogether.[147] This critic is reluctant to join them. I do not underplay the threat of "essentializing" and "parochializing" identitarianism, but the larger issue here is identity itself. It cannot obtain outside difference, that is, outside exchanges, barterings, and translations among distinct identities. Moreover, once we grant this differential genealogy of being and visualize our "common ground" as Levinasian "relationship in difference," we must also abide by this vision both conceptually—and this may well take care of "essence" as concept—and ethically, at the level of understanding how things in the world come to be what they are, all identitarian and schismatic rhetoric aside, as well as at the level of how things are still not what they should be and where, against a Baudrillardian, "indifferent world," assenting to an eco-logic of difference no longer leaves us the option of "indifference."[148]

The cosmodern world's "incongruity" and "discrepant" constitution itself should thus appear as something to recognize and strive for, to foster in the world as well as to project into it imaginatively. This is a desideratum of mundaneity, of our mundane "praxis" or being in the world.[149] In keeping with what the world consists in intrinsically—a relatedness domain where, as Derrida insists in one of his anti-Hegelian rebuttals, a relation *is* possible but in it the other must remain other, not effaced by the same[150]—this imagining of the world sets itself up as a visionary bulwark against the assaults on the world's worldly catalog of nonpareil presences, events, and meanings, against the un-worldly (*immonde*),[151] "foul and festering 'immundity'" of flattening globalization.[152] Seeking to provide an *alter* (to this) globalization, Nancy and Derrida's "cosmondialization" implies an ethics, mundane exchanges that reach beyond fashionable (*mondaine*) and often isolationist *alterglobalisme* to reinforce the world as *mundus*, as domain of a necessarily "conjunctive" ontology. Whatever and wherever we are in this world, we are with others because, a character of DeLillo avers, there is nothing in it *but* others. What cosmoderns like Nancy and DeLillo do is redraw the picture of the world along these "alternate" lines and thus pose an other to corporatist late globalization quite literally: not only do they see the world as *mundus,* as a being-with realm; they also set off the "singularity," the otherness on which this relatedness is predicated.

"Oedipus *is* how he is related to others," Stephen R. Yarbrough reflects in his "inventive intercourse" theory.[153] We all are, and *authentically* so, to the extent that we are in this intercourse, "in relation to certain interlocutors." Indeed, "a self exists" solely within "webs of interlocution," in a raucously Borgesian-Bakhtinian "world of others' words."[154] It is in this other-world that the self comes about, in exchanges with others and their locutions, with their words and stories. Not only is the self carved out narratively, by narratives, as philosophers like Jerome Bruner and Alasdair MacIntyre underscore, but this self is also fashioned by those behind the narratives because a narrative "relates" or is a "relation" twice: it both conveys information, relates or relays a meaning *to* me, and connects, relates me to the narrative's source or author. As Michael Holquist comments on Bakhtin's dynamic of author/hero, reader/author, and self/other, the writer, that other whom I am reading, becomes who he or she is (an author) "only in the event of the artwork, only as he [or she] can be perceived or shown to be a function of the relation" between himself/herself and his/her own other, myself, the reader.[155] But this dialogism cuts both ways. On the one hand, it sets up, as Holquist says, a tie into the future, with me, the work's reader. On the other, this connection only restages the work's intertextual link to its past. According to Bakhtin and the long line of critics drawing on his utterance theory, whenever I read somebody's story, I respond to a response, to a text already articulated with another prior to it. Without that response, without that reading, there would have been no writing, no story for me to read to begin with. This "architectonics of answerability" carries into my reading of this story as well as into any stories I might tell or write myself. If not literally told or written by others, people's own stories, with all that these stories comprise and disclose, are in this sense made possible by those others. From Sophocles's tragic hero to the *M*A*S*H* comedian, our greatest revelations have come from such others, in the "space of relation," as Derrida writes apropos of Édouard Glissant's *Poétique de la relation.*[156]

Glissant's is a *poétique,* a "poetics." My "poetics"—the anatomy of post–Cold War relational imaginary—is simultaneously if not in the first place a *po-éthique,* a *poethics.* The analytical is here entwined with the ethical, much as in cosmodernism itself. Discernable in the cosmodern survey of the latticework-like world or interlocutions and interpellations after 1989 is a particular ethos of relatedness. The cosmoderns home in both on what makes this world uniquely, indispensably, and thus desirably relational, and on what makes it insufficiently or worrisomely relational, on how the networks into which our words and lives are stitched threaten those from whom we need to hear in order to speak and be. Spelled out or implied in the cosmodern canvas of contacts, webs, and grids is a *relational etiquette* containing specific stipulations on treating those outside our immediate circle of relatives and relations. If in the history of ethics and in history generally, ethics, a particular ethos, has been bound up with a certain ethnos, has reflected the beliefs of an ethnicity and by extension of any group that saw itself as a community "organically" held together by descent, homeland, language, race, and so on, this etiquette is postethnic. My point is not that the cosmoderns simply deem ethnicity an "invention," nor that they think it is high time we moved "beyond" it.[157] Or, more accurately, if a move of this nature would have to be contemplated sooner or later, what they advise at present is, it seems to me, a move *across* ethnic and other locally-biologically constituted or self-represented memberships. I have italicized the preposition deliberately so as to underline this move's complexity. "More respectful" than dismissive of ethnicity, this cross-sectional move made by post- and "interethnic" critics from Hollinger to Frederick Luis Aldama and Caroline Rody takes ethnic identity seriously by dissecting its aggregate meanings to reach farther across to identities who presumably do not share them. In forefronting indigeneity as "globally disseminated material" and ethnicity as interethnic scenario, this cultural anatomy opens the local and the ethnic up and to the world, screens the ethnic and native self for that uncommonly configured plurality or authenticity likely to build a bridge to others and their places.[158]

Conceptualized as a Simmelian bridge that "unifies," or, more appropriately, draws together "separateness," difference-loaded proximity is vertiginously becoming a matrix of worldliness, the "form" in which our world comes about and presents itself.[159] To repeat: the very bedrock of worldliness, this form or domain of with-ness where distinctions rub up against each other to set forth no less distinct selves has always been there.

In designing new proximal sites and technologies, late globalization builds this proximity up, renders it more pervasive and more noticeable, but also jeopardizes it. There is, accordingly, a sense of worldwide import *and* instability to it, both captured by the cosmodern worldview. To the cosmoderns, one thing is certain: this proximity, this self-other syntax on which the semantics of selfhood depends so much, is irreversibly "post-autonomous."[160] Not so certain, however, are the cultural ramifications of this juxtaposition, that is, whether proximity in space might or might not result in proximity or, worse, identity of structure or meaning. What we need to ask ourselves, then, is this: At the same limit, in the same place where we "become ourselves under the gaze of the 'Other,'" can we honor *our own heritage* by repaying our debt?[161] Can we, that is, "mak[e] the immense effort to *know* [him or her] in [his or her] own embeddedness, not as objec[t] of [our] own unique gaze"?[162] As "the enormously distant" gets "enormously close," can we ensure it does so "without becoming any less far away"?[163] What makes these questions cosmodern is their instancy and recurrence but also their ethical weight, a certain implied obligation toward others. As the cosmoderns suggest, the exponentially intensifying self-other co-presence in the mundane neighborhood of the new millennium demands a certain conduct in venues where the interlocution drama is being played out, where we must listen in order to speak, and where we all must be with others in order to be.

Commenting on an essay of Wassily Kandinsky, Beck calls 1989 "the year of And."[164] Brutally interjectory, a censorious interruption of worldly colloquy, the Wall embodied modernity's defining caesura. But did the Wall's toppling end Kandinsky's "either-or" age? Admittedly, we are now closer to one another, in each other's face. However, that does not necessarily mean that we abide by the imperative of the Levinasian face-to-face. We do see ourselves with others on TV, at the mall, in airport terminals, "in person" and possibly less impersonally than before. We surely are "and" as others alongside us are too. But are we truly "with"? Is the new planetary "mobility" undoing what an older mobility and resulting "atomizing" urbanization have done to "the more intense, face-to-face relations [of] earlier times"?[165] Our awareness of others' adjacency to us does not guarantee that we also recognize their actual otherness and right to be part—*as such*, as other to us as we are to them—of the paratactic and-structure of the world. Until we reach this "other" recognition, we are stuck in the Cold War disjunctive mode where "the others exist," as a character in DeLillo's

2007 novel *Falling Man* "philosoph[izes,]" "only to the degree that they fill the roles we have designed for them."[166]

The "philosopher" is Amir, a 9/11 hijacker, but *Falling Man*, with *Underworld*, *Cosmopolis*, and *Point Omega* among the most sensitive fictional barometers of the post–Cold War climate, makes it clear that not only terrorism—not only terror of the terrorist kind—espouses this egology. For this is what we are ultimately talking about: egology, subordination of others to the self's preordained reasonings and rationalizations. After all, Kandinsky's either-or has been an "either" rather than an "or," not a fair contest of alternatives but a rigged game in a field tilted to the advantage of certain self-perpetuating nuclei of economic and cultural capital. The cosmoderns' suspicion is that the game has changed superficially after the official dismantling of the Iron Curtain, and so the inflationary "and" talk papers over rifts and hypotactic relations of a new sort. The "*whirlpool of reduction*," as Kundera described the Cold War world, may in fact spin faster.[167] In it, others, and with them we all, remain at risk.

Some consider otherness itself—the uncharted, the unknown, the unexpected—a risk to factor in and contain. To them, otherness, qualified racially, ethnically, religiously, or geographically, threatens intrinsically, is a subject as threat only, as it becomes subject to "our" apprehensions and reductions.[168] Turning the tables on this notion, philosophers like Derrida advise that we take "the risk of the other" ourselves. This is, he notes, "the risk of being wrongly understood, wrongly interpreted, sanctified, demonized, or else interrupted point-blank," and at the same time the "risk," or the chance, that "discourse can be driven off its" predictable "course, to inaugurate a dialogue where nothing was planned" in advance by reason's unquestioned "master[y]."[169] Knowledge, self-knowledge, and their discourse ultimately coalesce in this dialogue with others, without preconditions and prerogatives of mastery. Instead, the dialogue, the colloquy, postulates the with-ness of self and other's collocation, an ease and a closeness in space and discourse alike, a familiar tone and equal treatment—in brief, a *collegiality*.[170]

3. With-ness and the Epistemological Imaginary

... the return to world culture ...

—STEPHEN GREENBLATT, "Racial Memory and
Literary History"

> Literature and literary studies now have one basis and goal: to nurture our common bonds to the planet—to replace the imaginaries of exclusionary familialism, communitarianism, nationhood, ethnic culture, regionalism, "globalization," or even humanism, with the ideal of planetarianism. Once we accept this planet-based totality, we might for once agree in humility to devise a way to share with all the rest our only true public space and resources.
>
> —MASAO MIYOSHI, "Turn to the Planet: Literature, Diversity, and Totality"

Collegiality, Episteme, Cultural History

> . . . conceiv[ing] of the *Other* in the time of our own thought.
> —MICHEL FOUCAULT, *The Archaeology of Knowledge*

Steadily gaining ground after the Cold War, this collegiality is a *conviviality* organizing life in late globalization on a couple of intersecting levels beginning with existence itself at its most basic. To live and be "alive" (cf. Lat. *vivus*), the cosmoderns report, is to live-with (*con-vivere*). Life is convivial. To revive an old word, it posits the other as my sine qua non *convive*. I must be with him or her in order to be, for his or her presence affords worldly with-ness, a mundaneity structure on whose existence rests my own. This structure is a cultural-existential form, an ethos, and an epistemological operator shaping everyday situations, cultural-aesthetic expression, morality, and intellectual-scholarly pursuits, respectively. It is, first, a form or material format of living insofar as it conveys how I am "with" an other in the late-global universe: I am in an unremittingly widening *geography of legibility* that more and more demands collaborative effort. Second, this structure is an ethos to the degree this reading-with, this joint venture in mundane legibility, calls on me to treat those I am and read with accordingly, as colleagues and peers. They have joined me, this ethos implies, in a partnership of equal footing, of fairness, empathy, and care. In a way, however, collegiality is a moral law already inscribed in the mundane joint venture of legibility. After all, this is what *colleague* meant originally, the person I read with (cf. Lat. *con-legere*). In today's highly "proximal" world, though, the colleague is more than an assistant or optional addition to what I already do or am. He or she makes my reading, my explorations, my discourse, and the identity coagulating in them possible. I read and am "with" so I can read, understand, and ultimately be, and because this kind of reading, understanding, and being is so vital to me, it behooves me to adopt legibility, the reading-with, not only as a form of life and culture but also as a responsibility. Arising from co-reading-induced togetherness, collegiality presupposes, I must realize, a duty, lays down the with-ness law: *legere* refers to "reading," *lectura*, as well as to "law," *lex*. I "put together" my world picture and identity with an other, with my colleague, which brings me under the authority of collegiality as an ethical mode of being together, as law. This law "reads" ("legislates") that self and other cannot go on reading— and simply cannot go on—if, as they are and read with one another, face to face, are not careful not to deface each other, not to disfigure each other's figures and meanings.

Third, this structure of with-ness underlies the epistemological imaginary incrementally orienting the last twenty-odd years of U.S. intellectual history.[171] Whether we think of how American academics and humanists generally interpret the world, of their worldview, as part and parcel of, or as running parallel to, the imaginary at work in literature and the arts, whether, in other words, we extend or not the cosmodern cultural imaginary concept beyond fictional representation to scientific or analytic representation, I propose that around the late 1980s the copulative "with" nexus becomes the guiding episteme in a significant portion of the humanities. Should we identify this episteme as cosmodern? The answer is not terribly important, I think, and I am no keener on cosmodernism's clearly demarcated "epochality"; although I turn to the epoch-making outcomes of the "cosmodern turn" in my epilogue, I am a stickler neither for critical terminologies nor for neat chronologies of cultural history, including vocabularies and timelines recentered on the cosmodern. All the same, I cannot not take notice of the abrupt rise of the paradigm-altering impact of the relational episteme in a range of intellectual conversations and rhetorics after the mid-late 1980s. This means several things:

(1) The critics and researchers participating in these debates are increasingly sensitive to the thematics of relatedness.

(2) They employ this relatedness itself to interpret the world. No matter what they look at, they see it in culturally comparative terms, as involving the self-other correlation one way or the other. In cosmodernism's scholarly imaginary, much as in cosmodernism's cultural imaginary overall, collegiality is at once focus and methodology.

(3) Collegiality also marks research disciplinarily, institutionally, culturally, and geopolitically in that it is ever more collaborative across disciplines, locations, and languages. Many of "us" have been raising some im-

portant questions with others for a while now and with a growing feeling that the most viable answers, the best decisions and rules (cf. Gk. *nomoi*) to adopt are *heteronomous*, shaped by the presence and input of those others (*heteroi*). Germane to the connective makeup of the world itself, the "solution" seems thus no less connective, depends on self and other's capacity to see themselves "in this together." This consciousness of the late-global situation suggests that the key to our problems—scientific but also political, ecological, and so on—may well be built into the problems themselves, more exactly, in that which the problems are problems of.

(4) In other words, the "collegial" episteme both reproduces and fashions the worlded world, is a politics. In laboratories, libraries, chat rooms, and elsewhere, the cosmodern imaginary does not just "reflect" the relationality-saturated *mundus* "out there." No mere descriptive reaction but action too, this sort of reflection is not solely reflective but also productive in that it further thickens these relations as it relates self and other and draws them together into a worldly expanding partnership of problem-solving and reflexiveness.

(5) In this sense, the consciousness or awareness of a with-world—our turn-of-the-century "world consciousness"—leads to a with-consciousness, internalizes the collegiality of with-being as worldview as well as epistemological procedure or "hermeneutic" reflective of relatedness not only because it reflects on relations but also because it itself is of a relational kind.[172]

(6) Accordingly, the highly selective bird's-eye view of the American scholarly or epistemological imaginary that I provide in the remainder of this introduction has a necessarily comparative component. Epistemologically speaking, *comparaison* est *raison*—cross-cultural comparison of things, their consideration "together," side by side (cf. Lat. *comparo*), is or certainly becomes in the 1990s cosmodernism's very raison d'être. *Apposition is apposite*, the cosmoderns—critics and novelists—profess.

(7) This observation translates historically into additional "paradigmatic" caution. That is to say, much as the U.S. cosmodern imaginary cannot be dealt with apart from regroupings elsewhere, in other places and discursive formations, it cannot be grasped in isolation from pre-1989 domestic processes either. While, also in the epilogue, I will not shy away from "telling time" in and for today's American culture, namely, from placing this culture in a certain evolutionary narrative, I will not assume that the same narrative is in play in domestic politics and geopolitics, in economic, military, and diplomatic history, in the history, or histories rather, of the arts and sciences, and so forth.

The literary-cultural humanities, my focus below, are a case in point. Not unlike some of the writers treated in *Cosmodernism,* a good number of influential voices in theory, criticism, and cultural studies, in comparative analysis (especially in "new comparatism"), in philosophy (chiefly in ethics), in psychoanalysis (primarily among the "Champ lacanien" group members), in political science, economics, sociology (principally in risk sociology and "actor-network-theory"), and in geography are relevant to the cosmodern problematic—and, in a way, "cosmodern"—from the beginning of their careers (Nancy, Agacinski, Guy Scarpetta, Paul Gilroy, Marc C. Taylor, Hollinger). Others become so later (Derrida, Todorov, Habermas, Kristeva) as they turn to cosmopolitan, "postnational," global, planetary, and "other" issues years before the Cold War is officially over. Similarly, many have been associated with older directions such as postmodernism (Baudrillard), postcolonialism (Gayatri Chakravorty Spivak, Bhabha, Appiah), poststructuralism, and deconstruction (Deleuze and Guattari, J. Hillis Miller). Others take the lead right before and after 1989 in fields such as comparative and translation scholarship (Henry Sussman, Timothy J. Reiss, Eugene Eoyang, Rey Chow, Yunte Huang, Zhang Longxi, Emily Apter, Lawrence Venuti, Michael Cronin); cosmopolitanism, world governance, sovereignty, and human rights (Bruce Robbins, Pheng Cheah, Danilo Zolo, Derek Heater, Seyla Benhabib, Will Kymlicka, Daniele Archibugi, José María Rosales, María José Fariñas Dulce, Timothy Brennan, Amanda Anderson, Kok-Chor Tan, Volker Heins, Camilla Fojas, and many more); "cosmocultural," "geocritical," and "planetary" analysis (Franco Moretti, Yi-Fu Tuan, Raulet, Bertrand Westphal, Wai Chee Dimock, Lawrence Buell, Ursula Heise); global, world-system, "network society," and "empire" studies of various persuasions and foci (Manuel Castells, Appadurai, Alexander R. Galloway and Eugene Thacker, Steven Shaviro, Hardt and Negri, Amy Kaplan, Robertson, Albrow, David Held, Frederick Buell). Further, some of these are, I suspect, relatively comfortable with the disciplinary tags usually attached to their interventions: Beck and Jacques Demorgon (sociology), Peter Singer and Appiah again (ethics). Others, such as Žižek, Badiou, and Agamben, await classifications less nebulous than "philosophy." And critics like Charles Taylor, Hollinger, Werner Sollors, Benedict Anderson, Henry Louis Gates, Jr., Charles Johnson, Stuart Hall, Aiwa Ong, John Carlos Rowe, Clifford, and Gunn, who broke new ground in race, ethnicity, citizenship, community, ethnography, and multicultural studies ten or twenty years ago, in hindsight appear even more forward-looking. Further, one discovers that issues such as those brought up in *Cosmodernism* have rekindled interest in a number of classics, ancient and modern, in philosophy (Stoicism, Spinoza, Husserl, Buber, Levinas), hermeneutics (Gadamer and Ricoeur), psychoanalysis (Lacan), sociology (Ferdinand Tönnies and Simmel), the history of ideas and ideologies (Julien Benda and, closer to us, George Steiner, Stephen Toulmin, and Peter Coulmas), anthropology (Geertz), literary-cultural and discourse studies (Bakhtin), justice theory (John Rawls and his "law of people"), history and political economy (Wallerstein and, via his work, Fernand Braudel and the *Annales*).

To sum up: a shift has been underway in the U.S. human sciences over the last twenty to twenty-five years. Concomitant and isomorphic to recent reorientations in literature, the shift has touched off the progressive albeit uneven legitimizing and academic-intellectual institutionalization of the with-ness episteme. Also analogously to the literary history of the past quarter of century, the directions and works cataloged in what follows fit the cosmodern bill only in part. Anticipative rather than unequivocally indicative of a cosmodern imaginary, they make for a cosmodern symptomatology on the rise in the post-mid-1980s humanities and, in hindsight, afford a genealogy of cosmodernism that traces its object back to occurrences both like and unlike those for which they have paved the way. What I sketch out, then, is primarily a *pre*history of the scholarly cosmodern. Likewise, while doing justice to the headway of the cosmodern imaginary across a broad, thematic-disciplinary spectrum during this period, the interventions mentioned here make up a patently incomplete list. It is, however, a tactical incompletion; the list narrows down the foregoing wide-sweeping considerations and enumerations to those more akin to *Cosmodernism*'s own critical method—to cosmodernism *as* a critical method.

Fragments of an Interdisciplinary Genealogy

> The city that you live in is the world.
> —MARCUS AURELIUS, *Meditations*

> The study of world literature might be the study of the way in
> which cultures recognize themselves through their projections of
> otherness.
> —HOMI BHABHA, *The Location of Culture*

(1) *New Comparatism.* "The globalization of literary studies," Greenblatt notes, "is not principally a phenomenon of the Internet or Apex fares or

the spread of English on the wings of international capitalism." In his opinion, these are

> significant factors in enabling us to return to world culture, for the digitization of literary resources, the ease with which we can access newspapers and reviews from every continent, the rise of international discussion groups in multiple languages all pull us away from national and ethnic exclusivity. It is easy enough to confuse globalization with American triumphalism and an insurgent English-language parochialism. But world culture does not depend on recent events or on the current strength of the English language. A vital global cultural discourse is ancient; only the increasingly settled and bureaucratized nature of academic institutions in the nineteenth and early twentieth centuries, conjoined with a nasty intensification of ethnocentrism, racism, and nationalism, produced the temporary illusion of sedentary, indigenous literary cultures making sporadic and half-hearted ventures toward the margins. The reality, for most of the past as once again for the present, is more about nomads than natives.[173]

"The enterprise of tracking the restless and often unpredictable movements" of fantasies, symbols, and aesthetic forms—Greenblatt's "mobility studies," to which a journal like *PMLA* devotes its entire January 2002 issue—is, we are also informed, "still in its early stages,"[174] even though in 1878 it became already clear to observers like Nietzsche that, as a result of the modern "unrest," "whirling flow of men," and "polyphony of strivings," we had already entered "the age of comparisons."[175] "Comparison" was key to Nietzsche back then and is even more so today to a New Historian like Greenblatt, for whom movement usually becomes meaningful and therefore intelligible when one reads the moving objects and their movers along with other classes of objects co-present *inside* the same cultural-historical unit (period, epoch, "the long eighteenth century") or across units within *a* national tradition or cluster of traditions. One could view, actually, the cross-unit tack as a sort of diachronic equivalent to or historical projection of Gilbert Ryle's and Geertz's synchronic "thick description," which has been so instrumental to the New Historicism's effectiveness as an analytic tool operating, again, *within* particular cultures.[176] One could argue, though, as I am here, that late-global world's thick "connectional" makeup calls for another projection of the thickly descriptive model, this time *across* cultures and the national entities they are usually associated with. The age of worlding cultures requires both "a willingness to be open to comparative cultural study," as Charles Taylor points out in "The Politics of Recognition," and a methodologically committed, "collegial" "new comparatism."[177]

Prior to late globalization's 1989 formal arrival as historical phenomenon and subject of "global studies," comparative literature had focused on regions rather than on truly global developments and had done so in fashions admittedly "culturocentric" and "monist." This lessened its appeal in the U.S. academy of the mid-1980s, when postmodern, postcolonial, and cultural studies of various stripes started challenging "old comparatism" with surveys of cultural liminality dwelling more and more systematically on the border trope and its variations: "contact zones," "borderlands," "border-crossing," "transcultural frontiers," and so forth. Still regional in scope initially, this critical cartography of unstable boundaries, flowing discourses, "liquid" modernities (Bauman) and "border modernisms" (Christopher Schedler) incrementally opened out, after the "transnational turn in literary studies" (Paul Jay), with: "transversal" forays into diasporic, "hemispheric" (Ralph Bauer), transatlantic (Gilroy), "transpacific," "trans-American," and related "displacements" (Caren Kaplan, Yunte Huang) and "continental drifts" (Apter); with "new translational" (Clifford) and "transnational cultural studies" (to quote *Public Culture*'s subtitle); and with related excursions into the "trans- and multilingual" (Steven G. Kellman, Brian Lennon), "transnational" (Rob Wilson and Wimal Dissanayake), and "global imaginary" (Manfred B. Steger), which paved the way to even more markedly supraregional projects from Jameson's "geopolitical aesthetic" to Dominique Moïsi's affective geopolitics (*géopolitique de l'émotion*) and from the "anti-geopolitics" authors anthologized by Gearóid Ó Tuathail, Simon Dalby, and Paul Routledge to Laura Doyle and Laura Winkiel's "geomodernisms" and Westphal's "geocriticism."[178]

This is the context in which a "new comparatism" comes along following the publication of the famous "Bernheimer Report." Written in 1993 and subtitled "Comparative Literature at the Turn of the Century," the report is the centerpiece of the 1995 anthology *Comparative Literature in the Age of Multiculturalism*.[179] The contributors acknowledge cultural diversity and globalization, on the one hand, and cultural and global studies, on the other, as the primary historical and discursive formations pressuring, from outside and inside the academy, comparative literature to attune itself to the changing world. As underscored both in the report and in "Comparative Literature and Global Citizenship," Mary Louise Pratt's response, in the

United States "comparative literature . . . seems to have been founded by a rhetoric of vigilance associated with the Cold War."[180] This was, we saw, a disjunct-worlds rhetoric. What Pratt and others have urged, what the 2004 "Saussy Report" on the discipline once more recommends, and what masterful undertakings such as Marcel Cornis-Pope's 2001 *Narrative Innovation and Cultural Rewriting in the Cold War Era and After* accomplish is, as the title of Haun Saussy's equivalent to the Bernheimer collection puts it, "comparative literature in an age of globalization": a postantinomian, conjunctive, or relational comparatism apt to locate the examined works in their world "net-works."[181] To turn Reingard Nethersole's phrase on its head, such networks are not simply "texts without contexts" but precisely contexts or contextualizing domains in which texts, literary or otherwise, bring out their profound textuality, their Barthesian, "textile" nature, becoming what they are as they are woven into other similar "materials" of the world's web of images, sounds, and emotions.[182] This web is setting up the world's cultural mundaneity as these materials' clarifying, if not "absolute," hermeneutic horizon, providing an analytic framework within which analysis, no matter how specialized in terms of either object of objective, cannot but feature a large-scale comparison component. It is in this direction that comparative studies and literary and cultural studies generally have been slowly but clearly advancing since the 1990s.[183] This interest in the worlded texts, icons, and tunes of the "welded"—*weltet*—world has been breathing new life into Goethean *Weltliteratur* by retooling it as *Weltetliteratur,* so to speak. "Eurocentric" in its "roots" and itself "frequently misunderstood," Goethe's "world literature" has nevertheless proved useful to a host of scholars from Hendrik Birus and Pascale Casanova to Rey Chow, Lois Parkinson Zamora, David Damrosch, Kate McInturff, and other post-Eurocentric comparatists. The conclusion they have reached is that because literature is getting "*immanently* global, that is, . . . individual works are increasingly informed and constituted by social, political, and even linguistic trends that are not limited to a single nation or region," "it has become increasingly difficult to regard contemporary texts as simply the products of, for example, German, Nigerian, or Chinese writers, or even European, African, and Asian authors. With the globalization of the world economy, a true world literature, which is to say a *global* literature, is being created."[184] On this account, American and any literary history must be re-created—a "literary history in," and for, "the global age."[185]

"Global" literature may be on its way, but its advent does not strike everybody as either imminent or desirable. What has arrived, though, and what I personally welcome eight decades or so after Randolph Bourne's visionary 1916 "Trans-national America" is a new way of approaching late-global literature, in this case American, as a dramatization of world withness. For "new comparatists" and in particular for "comparative American studies" practitioners such as Rowe, Priscilla Wald, Jonathan Arac, Wai Chee Dimock, Lawrence Buell, Thomas Lutz, Philip Joseph, Paul Giles, Cyrus A. K. Patell, Hubert Zapf, Robert A. Gross, Ursula Heise, and others who are "rediscovering American Studies," including studies of "American regionalism," in "a wider world" and "deeper" temporality[186]—"American literature as world literature," with the title of Dimock and Buell's 2007 landmark collection[187]—this boils down to planetary, crisscrossing histories and literary-cultural intertextuality. They read U.S. works, authors, and trends with international works, authors, and trends in world context. In their research, inquiry within and across disciplinary and geocultural areas follows relational procedures of greater and greater sweep. More and more, these critics make sense of their objects in relation with other objects and sense-making attempts elsewhere and suspect that their take on things risks missing something essential if it does not put those things in the ever more ecumenical perspectives of the "Americas," the "Transatlantic," the "Pacific Rim," the "Global South," and the global world altogether. Accordingly, critical consciousness is becoming a consciousness of world-scale macroconnectivity, of the relation in which the object is with other comparable objects not "here" with it—or, if those objects are "here" now, they came, the same consciousness realizes, from somewhere else. Interpretive effectiveness used to be chiefly a function of the critic's *archaeological* imagination, of his or her dexterity in linking up the object's symbolic appearance or surface and a meaning-laden depth. Now it rides at least as much on critics' *arachnological* world imagination, that is, on their capacity to imagine a text, place, or event as a *relatum* enmeshed in the worldly web of links and ties. Critical "dissociations" currently hinge on the ability to draw forth the "associations," the *relationes* the *relata* are in globally, another indication that relationality is the post-1989 world's rising logic. An exercise in ecumenical relationality, comparison is, let me reiterate, rapidly turning into a leading critical rationality. I do buy into this critical rationality even though my book does not do comparative analysis consistently. While I do read Randall "with" Alexander Pushkin and Iyer "with" the Sufi poets, I do not read (though I could) DeLillo "with," say, the later Salman Rushdie or Michel Houellebecq.[188] Instead, I screen DeLillo's work for the very thematic of worldly with-ness. I tease out his novels' structural comparatism, which, we shall learn in part 5, consists in a sobering assessment of late-global collegiality. I draw, then, a somewhat tentative distinction between, on the one hand, the *ecumene*—the "inhabited world," the "world" in its entirety (cf. Gk. *oikoumenē*)—as a geopolitical focus of a comparatism keen on relations among different texts and, on the other hand, the ecumenical, or the relational, as both "with" theme inside texts and critical method for this theme's reading.

As is well known, the ecumene is a venerable notion. Reaching as far as Heraclitus and the other Greek philosophers who first took on the "task to conceptualize the unity of the world,"[189] its roots are associated with the Stoics' view of humankind as "one great world society."[190] Having exerted a lasting influence from Zeno of Citium (333–263 BC) and Saint Paul's theological universalism—recently rediscovered as a "teacher for today" by authorities from Derrida, Agamben, Badiou, and Wolfgang Feneberg to Pope Benedict XVI[191]—through Augustine, late-medieval humanism, the Enlightenment's humanitarianism and rationalism, and Kant's dreams of a "civil commonwealth . . . of mankind"[192] all the way to twentieth-century international modernism and political internationalism, the ecumene makes a spectacular comeback after 1989 following a series of interrelated developments in the humanities. Very succinctly, I review here only those immediately pertinent to my discussion.

(2) *Global Literary-Cultural Studies.* The first is what on another occasion I called "the global turn in critical theory."[193] "[H]ard" as it may be "to disentangle colonialism, anti-colonialism, postcolonialism and globalism from one another,"[194] one could argue that with critics like Appiah, Bhabha, Gilroy, Appadurai, Frederick Buell, Stuart Hall, and Spivak (I am thinking mainly of her 1999 *Critique of the Postcolonial Reason* and the 2003 book *Death of a Discipline,* especially its "Planetarity" chapter),[195] a worldly model of generalized *différance,* "in-betweenness," hybridization, "transculturality," nomadism, and diasporic condition starts challenging postcolonial studies' classical "dichotomism" metropolis-colony, center-periphery, colonizer-colonized, and so on. Analogous to and in some regards bound up with the Cold War antinomian paradigm, the latter was essentially reactive; the former opens up interactive possibilities while enabling colonized / "Third World" people to carry on their decolonizing struggles and fight off late globalization's neocolonial bent. A number of critics remain wedded to the traditional postcolonial approach in the Fanon-Said line; others, from Habermas to Azade Seyhan, attend to the dynamic of the postcolonial and

the global in terms attesting to a collective effort to account for the ongoing "postcolonial fusions" and "transitions" by moving beyond the nation and its centrality in debates so far;[196] still others, convinced that the "category" of globalization has by the early 1990s "displac[ed] postcolonialism and its twin, postmodernism,"[197] have adopted the global framework altogether with such an enthusiasm that, some say, "the term *globalization*" has already become "nearly as abused as *postcoloniality.*"[198]

I will not break my earlier promise not to belabor the topoi of the globalization bibliography if I invite the reader to overcome globalbabble fatigue and consider the "globe," in the sense described earlier, as the cause of this abuse. "Speaking of the 'globalization of culture' is" indeed "abusive"[199] as long as we think simplistically of the world as (Americanizing) one-culture. Arguably, some do, even though few of them are "global enthusiasts." Working largely in the world-system tradition, they operate, we might say, with a "strongly" ecumenical paradigm. Robertson, Tomlinson, Albrow, John Street, Barrie Axford, and Nick Stevenson, on the other hand, are partial to a "softer" version of mundane, pluricentric, and highly "diversal" ecumenism. With Jameson, they all decry late globalization's "standardization"[200] threats, but fewer allow, as I do in *Cosmodernism*, for critical engagements with them. This engagement is crucial. In it, we engage with the world and ourselves at once not just because "transnational mobility is Americanism in disguise" and so what goes places and globalizes in the "world out there" is primarily American culture[201]—a thought that should not be dismissed summarily either—but also because, as "global American studies" of literature and culture have shown more and more compellingly since the early 1990s, the world is here, in and with "us," and has made and is still making us who we are.[202]

(3) *Neocosmopolitanism.* The second ecumenical development is the late-1990s cosmopolitan revival. Scarpetta's intellectually robust *Éloge du cosmopolitisme* (1981) was no trendsetter, however. His audience was still to come, and it did a few years later, first for Stephen Toulmin, then for Heater, Brennan, Robbins, Appiah, Hollinger, Derrida, Benhabib, Beck, Jason D. Hill, Amanda Anderson, Margaret J. Jacob, Rebecca Walkowitz, Jessica Brennan, Angela Taraborrelli, Sigrid Thielking, Francis Cheneval, Ursula Heise, Nicolas Di Méo, and many others behind the cosmopolitan studies boom.[203] So was there a cosmopolitan turn too? Or was it just an upshot of the global shift?

Hoping to sort out the global chicken and cosmopolitan egg, some critics refer to "cosmopolitan" cultural-aesthetic practices (which may or may not include consumption) and political philosophies, setting aside the "global" terminology to talk about material production and its economy, finance, trade, labor aspects, and transnational corporations. Along the lines of a division of which many, myself included, have grown weary, cosmopolitanism is to globalization what superstructure is to base; along similar lines, cosmopolites need not (although they often do) leave their separate locations to converge on common interests, hobbies, and lifestyles, whereas jet-setting bankers and Nike CEOs fly out of central, highly integrated quarters to further integrate the world by wrapping it around their corporate fantasies of universal interchange. Cosmopolitanism is, the argument goes, adamant about difference and in that, appearances notwithstanding, centrifugal. Catering to an "established centrality,"[204] globalization is manifestly centripetal and demonstrably de-differentiating in its worldwide effects.

I am all for heuristic simplifications, and this one is as helpful as any. Before accepting it, however, we should remember that the ecumene is not only the Greek word but also the world envisioned and conquered by the Greeks in the mid-fourth century BC. With Alexander the Great's campaigns, the ecumene becomes both outcome *and* vehicle of Hellenization, and, ironically enough, it has remained so in the only "history of cosmopolitanism" available, Coulmas's 1990 *Weltbürger: Geschichte einer Menschheitssehnsucht*, which, despite the occasional references to Alexander's "Hellenizing" cosmopolitanism, to his "national[ist] universalism," and to Western cosmopolitanism's "Eurocentrism," is Eurocentric if not Hellenocentric. The historian takes Plutarch's point that the Macedonian made Zeno's dream of "cosmopolitanism" come true," but the "universalism" of this "idea" no less than of the imperial enterprise the idea fueled are glossed over.[205] Classical cosmopolitanism *is* universalist, but, despite what the old Stoics, eighteenth-century philosophes, or Benda's "bona fide," pre-*Volksgeist*-era *clercs* may say about slaves, women, and foreigners, this universalism has repeatedly issued empires an expansionist carte blanche. Alexander's ideal of doing away with the distinction between Greek and "barbarian" and, centuries later, Marcus Aurelius's desire to abolish the "difference between here and there" were more than idealistic will-o'-the-wisps.[206] Research has shown which the privileged terms were, that is, what "cultural hybridity," "religious syncretism," "linguistic creolization," and other cross- and multicultural formations actually meant and what the wiping out of difference came down to in imperial history.

With this history, cosmopolitanism has been complicitous. Generation after generation of Western thinkers and artists have drawn the Stoic concentric circles of belonging, with "we" natively and "naturally" at the center—the ecumenical world's omphalos—bound by blood and birthplace but also by our self-assigned task of pacifying, civilizing, democratizing, and otherwise rationalizing people elsewhere. This is, then, cosmopolitanism's perennial quandary: while it pegs the inner circles as narrow, provincial, and sectarian, it remains trapped inside them. Not only that, but it enlarges and drags them all over the planet, enveloping the global ecumene in those culturocentric *doxes* and *parti pris* that cosmopolites vow to leave behind. In short, under its universalist rhetoric of "immutable" and "common" human values,[207] cosmopolitanism has often been an extrapolation, an egology. In it, a colonization of sorts is going on not only as economic and cultural globalization but also under the guise of self-styled cosmopolitan critiques thereof. Of course, if we define the cosmopolite as the person who acquires an education through, knowledge of, taste for, and is otherwise formed by texts, values, and proclivities either alien or only considered alien to those inherited by background (native country, language, descent, religion, etc.), in brief, as the person who comes to be what he or she is through exposure to the discourse of others, then we should admit that cultural-aesthetic cosmopolitanism participates in the Westernization of the world less or less directly than, say, Jesuit missionarism. Common sense asks that we distinguish between the influence of a cosmopolitan movement like the European avant-garde on the *négritude* proponent Aimé Césaire and the impact of Christian missionaries on African religions. Besides, a strong case can be made, and has been made, for a broadly polycultural, antimetropolitan strain *within* European modernism. But overall, cosmopolitanism's professed universalism and internationalism prove lopsided or "one-sided," wedded to the Eurocentric, colonizing, and leveling underbelly of modern rationality, and socially exclusive rather than inclusive. In spite of its declared intentions, cosmopolitanism rarely manages to derail geocultural processes whose fundamental premises it shares. For this reason, critics from Brennan to Rowe have not refrained from calling today's cosmopolitans "neoimperialist,"[208] and for the same reason Peter Van der Veer thinks it is ironic "to see" cosmopolitanism "celebrat[ed] in some post-colonial writing without any critical reflection on the genealogy of the concept."[209] To be sure, rigorous historical analysis cannot miss the *mutual reinforcement* of cosmopolitanism and colonialism. While the former served more than once as the metropolis's cultural arm, the latter, Coulmas himself concedes, fostered the "conditions necessary to cosmopolitanism's development on a global scale."[210]

"Development" is misleading, though, if, as we learn from the same source, "the content of cosmopolitan thought does not change" after Saint Paul, Augustine, and the spiritual founding of "Christopolis."[211] Note that Christopolis was to *kosmopolis* what Christian was to fourth-century BC Cynic philosopher Diogenes of Sinope's *kosmopolites* ("citizen of the world").[212] As a rationalist-universalist—and thus "Greek," Euro-centered—philosophy of the human and project of global scope, cosmopolitanism becomes also "catholic," *katholikos* ("universal") in a Catholic and more broadly Christian sense and, in its dominant texts and geopolitical embodiments, remains so throughout its multimillennial career in spite of successful attempts to uncover cosmopolitan traditions in non-Christian and non-Western cultures.[213] I share critics' reluctance to "specif[y] cosmopolitism positively and definitely"—hence their talk of cosmopolitanism*s* instead of cosmopolitanism[214]—and I do appreciate the insistence with which Mitchell Cohen, Bruce Ackerman, Walter Mignolo, Jeremy Waldron, Pratap Bhanu Mehta, Ali Rattansi, Gita Rajan, Shailja Sharma, Jigna Desai, Philip Leonard, Stuart Hall, Appiah, Cronin, Kristeva, Robbins, and others have argued for "vernacular cosmopolitanism, rooted cosmopolitanism, critical cosmopolitanism, comparative cosmopolitanism, national cosmopolitanism, discrepant cosmopolitanism, situated cosmopolitanism, . . . actually existing cosmopolitanism," not to mention more intricate, theoretical-terminological reformations such as "cosmopolitan patriotism, cosmopolitan nationalism, cosmopolitan democracy and cosmopolitan post-colonialism."[215]

There is an ironic undertow to Hollinger's roll call, but the irony is not always warranted. I am quite willing to allow, in fact, that belittling such post–Cold War endeavors to query, retool, and diversify the Stoic-Enlightenment-based cosmopolitan paradigm around diversity itself and attendant "soft" "micro-cosmopolitanisms" would definitely be an "uncosmopolitan thing to do."[216] After all, the questions raised by neocosmopolitan critics are both capital and timely: What does it mean to be a cosmopolite these days? If it no longer means only a white, male, uppercrust Western affair, then what kind or kinds of cosmopolitanism become prevalent, necessary, or obsolete after 1989? The Cynics' and Stoics' world citizenship? The rational-Kantian cosmopolitanism of the Enlightenment? The modernist-aesthetic cosmopolitanism of the late nineteenth and early twentieth centuries, in the James-Wilde-Pound-Joyce-Stein—"lost generation"—"Vienna Circle" line? Non-Western—or not Western-only—postmetropolitan, religion-, ethnicity-, and profession-based cosmopolitanisms such as those of new Pan-Islamism or of collectivities and sodalities of nomads, migrant laborers, peacekeepers, charity workers, academics, activists, refugees, exiles, pilgrims, and NGO personnel perhaps? Would any of these respond to the conditions and priorities of late globalization? Assuming they would, would they also "salvage the concept" from "its associations with class and Western privilege by demonstrating the existence of a sort of popular, non-Western or nonelite cosmopolitanism"?[217] Suppose they did, would the critique built into such a rescue operation be also critical—as it should be—of the overt anticosmopolitanism of various fundamentalisms, nationalisms, racisms, anti-Semitisms, and dictatorial regimes far left and far right?

Some of the answers have been clear, others less so. Some have furthered cosmopolitan conversations vigorously in the ecological direction of cosmodern with-ness; others have not gone beyond abstract gestures toward "difference"; and others have merely occasioned a range of reentrenchments. Instructive is, in this regard, the "patriotism and cosmopolitanism" debate. Prefaced by the Rorty-Geertz cosmopolitanism-ethnocentrism exchange, to which Rorty appended, in the first volume of *Objectivism, Relativism, Truth* (1990), a relevant reply to Lyotard, the dispute reignited with Martha Nussbaum's well-attended "forum" *For Love of Country* (1996, 2002), then with Rorty's *Achieving Our Country* (1998), and with related interventions by Robbins, Appiah, Judith Butler, Amartya Sen, Charles Taylor, and Hilary Putnam, to name just a few. Ignoring prompts to avail themselves of a "postnational imaginary" (Appadurai) or, in Beck's formulation, of a "cosmopolitan," "alternative imagination . . . of ways of life and rationalities" that, unlike the "national," "monological imagination," does not ward off "the otherness of the other," most participants in this discussion of broad and abstract philosophical-ethical brushstrokes have balked at the prospect of a "future" patriotism decoupled from the national.[218] To many, the issue appeared to be, to quote Nussbaum's subtitle, how to push the "limits" of *our* "patriotism" so as to either benevolently include "others" or make some vague case for a responsibility to the welfare of the "world out there," thus only reinforcing the inside/outside, here/there, we/they, particular/general, and associated divides that had seemed to bother everybody to begin with. It turns out, some if not all of these antinomies live on not only in the unabashed if "pragmatic" communalism of Rorty but also under the universalist-humanist veneer of the cosmopolitanism of critics like Appiah, Hollinger, and Nussbaum, and in postcolonial retrofittings of the cosmopolitan à la Mignolo's "critical cosmopolitanism."[219]

(4) *Wo Narziss war, soll das Andere werden: "Other" Studies and the Return to Ethics.* To recapitulate: uncoordinated and often contradictory as they are, these intra- and cross-disciplinary evolutions do trace out the consolidation of a gradually distinct and historically characteristic analytic imaginary around the episteme of with-ness in the U.S. humanities after the Cold War. These mutations are no tectonic shakeups. As with cosmodernism and its own relation to pre-1989 cultural and scholarly styles, themes, and approaches, both continuities and discontinuities are in play; here as elsewhere, clean and sudden breaks with the past are critical fictions. A case in point, what has been described as a recent ethical upsweep in literary-cultural studies has not only been slow in coming but goes all the way back to earlier works on reading by Wayne C. Booth, Paul de Man, and J. Hillis Miller, to reframe, around 1989 and in reply to the world's ecumenical "fall into relation," its issues around the pressing and sticky thematics of "otherness." Lacanian psychoanalysis, postcolonialism, and the marked "ethical turn" in Derrida's work, in poststructuralism generally under the enduring influence of Levinas, and in philosophy overall are more and more giving pride of place to the "other," in a retrospectively coherent attempt to rethink its place in the topology of selfhood. The cosmodern analytic of American identity at the dawn of the new millennium owes a great deal to this return to the ethical and its sustained explorations of cultural alterity. As pointed out previously, concerns and interrogations of otherness have their own, time-honored history, which one cannot ignore either. But ethics *as* an ethics of otherness takes on a new meaning given late globalization's egological logic, becoming after 1989 a matter of intellectual urgency. Nor were the developments surveyed above opaque to this urgency. They do sense it and propose solutions, not all of which are throwbacks to Cold War and early-postcolonial disjunctions, as Charles Johnson's and Gilroy's works on race demonstrate. However, beginning with the 1990s, critics and philosophers apply themselves to the problem at hand with an acute sense that, more than subject matter and more than ever in history, this is an immediate, all-present, and equally important issue, a *defining* fact of life for individuals and communities alike. It is certainly not the first time that "others" have been taken notice

of and cast in cultural, historical, psychological, or philosophical accounts of selfhood; it is that the epistemological role these others and their problematic play in such accounts is now incontestably beyond compare.

What I mean is that a hitherto unparalleled number of "our" questions *and* answers have become, as already suggested in these pages, heteronomous. Today more than ever, putting and answering these questions entail asking and thinking about others, which is what I had in mind when I determined otherness as "defining"—definitional or, as I said earlier, co-definitional—with respect to America and Americanness. The other's *appositionality* in our world represents, in summation, "the way the world is"—again, now more than at any previous stage—and also a way if not *the* way to make sense of this world; it is indeed a "fact" of life, a tool for understanding, and, I have been arguing, an ethical injunction. For, the other I am with is not just a cultural-ontological "supplement" of which I need to be "tolerant," a newcomer, a newly arrived, or a neighbor who has recently moved in. His or her juxtaposition to me is not additional but foundational. Because of that, it also explains, and obligates. This "human proximity," Levinas reflects, is an "ethical order." It "gives rise to or calls for the order of objectivity, truth, and knowledge"; what we learn from it is the truth broadly and, part and parcel of it, the particular truth of our indebtedness to others.[220] Following from the necessary reframing of the self's anatomy as a with-ness inquiry is what I would label the "American alibi": the American, what I am or we are, is indeed an *alibi*, etymologically "elsewhere." My or our identity is not—or not only or where—what I or we think it is. Instead, it dovetails and overlaps with other identities. It is organized by their presence and is illuminated by their places, histories, and intuitions.

In recent cultural history, this cosmodern creed goes back to or intersects with a whole set of fields, subfields, and pursuits in which the modernist, Cold War self-other split is reimagined through a topology and an ethic of co-presence, co-participation, co-dependence, and shared spatiality. I will mention here only early 1990s "postmodern theory" broadly conceived and related reconstructions of cultural studies around the category of otherness;[221] Levinasian and non-Levinasian initiatives in "heterological"-intersubjective ethics and "ethical criticism"[222] from the late Derrida, Certeau, Thomas Docherty, Julian Pefanis, Peter Dews, Habermas, Adam Zachary Newton, Mark C. Taylor, Tobin Siebers, Rey Chow, Simon Critchley, Ricouer, Badiou, and Butler's later work to Peter Singer, T. M. Scanlon, Crystal Parikh, and especially Appiah's "cosmopolita[n] ethics in a world of strangers" and Charles Taylor's *The Ethics of Authenticity*;[223] more narrowly focused studies of otherness and Levinasian applications to reading and interpretation in works by Robert Eaglestone, Sussman, Jill Robbins, J. Hillis Miller—with his 2001 book *Others* a leading title in this series—François de Singly, Patrick McGee, Linda Bolton, Lauren Rusk, Irigaray, Kristeva, Anindita Niyogi Balslev (and her exchange with Rorty on "cultural otherness"), and W. Lawrence Hogue's "planetary" reframing of U.S. postmodernism; and countless collective projects on "others" and "our" "encounters" with "them" as "neighbors," "strangers," "exiles," "aliens," "foreigners," "outsiders," or "guests"—hence the growing popularity of the "empathy" concept and the upsurge in studies of hospitality and topo-cultural proximity following energizing initiatives by Derrida, Miller, Sussman, Žižek, Butler, Marc Augé, Edward W. Soja, Rei Terada, and their followers.[224]

What have all these interrogations, pursuits, and refocalizations accomplished, one might wonder? Quite a few things, actually, but here I single out only three. First, in a sense—a sense in which, Freud rightly thought, the human takes its own measure—they have worked toward displacing "our" ignorance, that is, toward returning the "I" to its intellectual and moral dignity by allowing him or her to see things usually hiding in the shadow of his or her egocentrism. Of course, I am paraphrasing Freud. What he talks about is the epistemological contest of the id and the ego; what I am talking about is an ego that becomes so, an actual, "authentic" ego as it learns, questions itself, and thus gives up its narcissistic delusions and egological "culturocentrism" in the radiant adjacency of others, of their books, and thoughts. Second, if there is something to be learned from the nearness mapped out by this kind of work, that is because the "common ground" of learning is, as Levinas assures us, a theater of difference. A relationship does form here, these critics and philosophers intimate. It is necessary, but, as Levinas also insists, it is necessarily a "relationship in difference," which relationship, because it is one, "signifies a nonindifference."[225] It concerns "us" more deeply than we might think. By giving us to ourselves, with-ness obliges, and so should we. Third, in reading late-twentieth- and early-twenty-first-century America as a drama of with-ness, the cosmoderns oblige as well. Inevitably sketchy, this pageant of trends, intellectual exploits, and scholarly moments instrumental or simply parallel to cosmodernism is not only cosmodernism's unauthorized biography or, as I say, its prehistory but also a historicized argument for a cosmodern ethics.

PART 1 ⊕ IDIOMATICS

1. Cosmodernism and Vernacularism

Ventriloquy
is the mother tongue.
    —BOB PERELMAN, *The Marginalization of Poetry:*
    Language Writing and Literary History

The "New Linguistic Order" and the Murmur of Foreignness

This is what one finds in the living voice, i.e., a plurality of the
voice that is granted by the voice of the other.
    —JAMES RISSER, "The Voice of the Other in
    Gadamer's Hermeneutics"

One never gets out of Babel.
    —SYLVIANE AGACINSKI, *Critique de l'égocentrisme*

With-ness predates. It sows the seeds. Nowhere, the cosmoderns tell us, is
this more apparent than in how we use and picture language, in our
speech acts and in our linguistic imaginary. In our most private solilo-
quies and in our mother tongue, "we" rub shoulders with "them"; we are
in colloquy. We must be, in order to speak, and as we do so we call up and
give voice to those other voices buried inside ours. Speaking is evocation,
vocalization of a heteroclite chorale. In a sense, language is, like writing,
"the destruction of every voice, of every point of origin," as Barthes
wrote.[1] Yet in another, language is not revocation of voice but copiously
evocative of it, does not suspend it but reveals its Bakhtinian "multi-
voicedness."

This polyphony of grammar, lexicon, and tone marks not only literature but all language. Adding to the genetic stratification of British English, a polylogue of "Englishes"—accents and "barbarianisms," regional, professional, and argotic variations, Ebonics, Spanglish, and Creole inflections—nests inside American English. Louder and louder, this boisterous Babel singsongs America, affords us a language and with it a sense of belonging. The "New Linguistic Order" we reportedly stepped into at the end of the Cold War should then demand not only that we respect and possibly learn foreign idioms—"Love Thy Neighbor's Language"[2]—but also that we honor the murmur of foreignness inside, the "always-prior other within monolingual diction."[3] For, recent American writers point out, the Babel world and the English Babel are two faces of the same coin and undergo the same crisis. At home and abroad, this "New Linguistic Order" crisis is just that, a crisis of order of self and other, "major" and "minor" languages, "standard" and "non-standard" speech, more generally of the standards of and the standings in the global and national communities into which people are speaking their way day in and day out. Increasingly overlapping, the domestic and world orders of language are more and more "ordered" by "disharmonious" appositions of voices and tones, pronunciations and sociocultural pronouncements, linguistic identities and national identifications. At the same time, this rich dissonance is disciplined States-side by "English-only" regulatory measures and overseas by regularizing developments such as the dying out of smaller languages and dialects and the expansion of English as lingua franca across countries, media, and discourses.

Reacting on one side to the revival of linguistic nationalism and on the other to the rise of English to international hegemony, the American cosmoderns reaffirm the heterology of the logos. They listen for the strangeness that renders language familiar to us, "ours," for the many voices that, in the individual voice, warrant communication across and inside national idioms. In part 3, we will see how the plurilingual Babel both challenges human fellowship and fosters it in translation. Here, I focus on critics and fiction writers who have dwelled on the Babel of sounds, variations, and possibilities intrinsic to English (English and French, in Federman) to set forth, in a similar vein, a "conception of Babel, of linguistic heterogeneity, not as an obstacle to national unity that throws us into confusion and misunderstanding but as a resource for a less conflicted society within and for more secure relations with other societies."[4] If, as these authors stress, English is just one room in the Babel house of being, this Babel too is in English. Far from "confusing"—the "tower of Babel," Dante reminds us, "is interpreted Tower of Confusion"[5]—it lays the foundation of clarity and thus institutes expression, warrants our fluency as English speakers. As the cosmoderns offer, a radical critique of linguistic imperialism might find its footing in a relational concept of national language "without nationalism" in which "they" accommodate "us."[6] Cosmodernism views our native language as accommodation that we have received so that we can extend it to others, Babel-like English that should make us "comfortable" with its further modulations by "nonnative" speakers. Derrida is on the mark: the question of language is the question of dwelling and hospitality.[7] He is also right to observe that the answer to the question is aporetic insofar as the English we speak and the linguistic-political territory we thereby claim have, as it were, already been spoken for, not entirely, of course, but just enough *so we can raise these very claims.*[8] Because, as J. Hillis Miller and, again, Derrida have shown, we are at once hosts and guests, speaking is always-already sharing, trading on those discontinuities of language, nationality, and culture inside one language, nationality, and culture, on that manifold Babel the monoglot never leaves.

Language, Ownership, and the "Monolingualism of the Other"

> [A] language does not belong exclusively to a particular people. Arrived from elsewhere, other voices can alter its course, and the same voices, as they change the language, can also enrich it.
> —PASCAL BRUCKNER, *Le Vertige de Babel:*
> *Cosmopolitisme ou mondialisme*

Linguistic mastery does exist—our command of language can be "masterful"—but it is rhetorical at most, a matter of skill instead of control or ownership of language. Beware our "appropriative madness."[9] We may have been born into American English and subsequently may acquire a "native" command thereof. But this acquisition is not "appropriation." We do not own our own language. We owe it to others, in fact. To say "I," we plunge into their words, in alterity. We are not "engineers" but "bricoleurs" working with the "already-there": we find "our voice" in an act of vocal bricolage, in ventriloquism.[10] Accordingly, speech acts do not enact "possession" (owning) but an indebtedness (owing). Arrived belatedly in a space already plural, we will never own that plurality but further it, will never define its "standards" but only perform and thus tweak and multiply them, complicating and expanding the putative oneness of language into the ever-receding horizon of the idiomatic and the vernacular. Far from buying into the preset synonymy of citizenship, nativity, and native standards on the one hand, and English and Americanness qua "proper" use of English on the other, the cosmoderns propose that both the standards and the linguistic and national identities are ceaselessly formulated and reformulated in language outside the strictures of this equivalence. More to the point: what it means to speak like—and thus be identified as—an American is not preordained by certain apperceptions of linguistic nativity. It is rather the other way around: laid down in linguistic performance, Americanness fluctuates, can mean as many things as the performance itself. In the final analysis, it is the latter that fashions and invents America and the Americans. The nation and the natives speaking in its behalf are no longer the only measure of linguistic nationality and fluency but, to the contrary, join in the performative decoupling of "nation" and "language," "American" and "(American) English," "native" and "correct."

"We only ever speak one language" is one of the two "propositions" on language Derrida puts forward in *Monolingualism of the Other*. Completing another aporia of his linguistic philosophy, the other is: "We never speak only one language."[11] The second statement is less problematic, so I begin with it: it does not mean that we all speak several distinct languages, even though many of us do, but that our own one language is neither our own proper nor one. It is not because it is hardly "pure," an ahistorical monolith into which we are born and which we in turn reproduce. Therefore, our affiliation by birth with the ethnic group or the country speaking it does not or should not represent a monopoly. Language is not our property, nor are we its standard-bearers, guardians of speech propriety and gatekeepers of linguistic nationality.[12] Granted, we speak "our" language as Americans, but to do so we (*a*) articulate a heteronomy of discourse and cultural history, bear with-ness to the "other" speaker who makes "our" speech possible, and (*b*) further enlarge that heteronomy ourselves in an ever-diversifying and evolving vernacular. If, as Baudrillard fears, the New Order's "hegemonic fantasy of a global and perpetual communication" involves "ultrasimplifying" the world by "reduc[ing] the same to the same" through inscription into a reductive language of automatic equivalences and denotative exchanges, we can still hark back to language itself, more specifically, to its "vernacularizing" force. "The strongest resistance" to the pseudoidentification of the world's "singularity [and] irreducibility" as selfsameness is, the philosopher argues, the "radical alterity" language both flows from and begets. This alterity or "ontological absence" renders it less identical to itself, hence an unreliable instrument of "total identification." A singularity itself, falling short of the presumed standards and so ever "inadequate," language's constitutive "vernacularity" runs counter to the world's egological "adequation" to our words.[13]

Uncommonly keen on language as vernacularizing practice that flouts the nation-state's repertoire of codifications, cosmodernism transcribes the cornucopia of accents, connotations, styles, and idiomatic vacillations issuing forth in what otherwise we may hear (and utter) as one, as the monoglossic touchstone of identity building and expression. The cosmodern analytic of language turns up languages inside language, the "Englishes" inside our shared English but also those into which the English "norm" is being further "creolized" as more and more "nontraditional" and nonnative speakers adopt it. We cannot ignore, of course, that our language and country are not in the world as other languages and countries are. English pulls this world together as well as *around* the words and significations of English-speaking nations, the United States first and foremost. In and through English, the United States enunciates itself into a privileged position of self-styled global norm linguistically and otherwise. But again, to the cosmoderns, this norm is not one, nor would it be at all if it was not for the miscellany of noises and meanings of the world over which it now presumes to speak yet by which it continues to be modulated visibly and invisibly. Enlightenment cosmopolites thought the answer to the modern world's disorienting Babelization was a rational and universal idiom, and many believe English fits the bill better than any other natural language. A step ahead of both recent generic incitements to "vernacular cosmopolitanism" and postmodernism's still U.S.-based "neo-vernacular" stylistic, today's cosmoderns suspect that English-derived tech lingos and English as late-global-era equivalent to Medieval Latin or Hellenistic Greek are doing to regional idioms what McDonald's has done to local cuisines.[14] The hope for self-expression and communication, they posit, does not lie in a one-language but in our ability to speak each other's language and give it the intonations and connotations likely to reinscribe it into the multivocality it comes from. As the cosmoderns insist, the self *articulates* itself in the strongest sense of the word, that is, it enunciates itself as it ascertains its link, its articulation unto an other. Even in our monologues we con-verse, turn to others' strange idioms and the strangeness whispering in it. We speak, and thus speak in tongues and versions, mutter the other's vulgate. As such, we dramatize *a* possibility, try out *a* sound, don *a* face or facet of the said. Yes, our language is not ours, because it is not one either. In this cosmodern awareness, we give up the master's "jealousy," thus giving ourselves and our native entitlements over to language.[15] Vice versa, nonnatives take up—act out—an honorary nativity of sorts, claim their place in "our" language, in what used to be and ever so often still is the "language of the master." This is how self and other ultimately face each other in language, converse: *through* the versions of being and language they be/speak rather than "in spite" of them. "We" address "them" as others, in our language, a tongue that happens not to be theirs by birth. But only in part does speech, our interpellation, originate in us. Inherently a medley of voices, it places us fundamentally in relation to "other" linguistic versants and faces of language.

Norm, Mastery, and the Vernacular

> The first true Germany was that of Luther's vernacular.
> —GEORGE STEINER, *After Babel*

As we speak, our words speak to this relation. By the same token, we enter into an ethical contract. The contract, however, is breached daily by perceptions and arrangements tilted to a normative mythology of native mastery. Derrida is apprehensive of this seldom-examined prerogative, but its dismissal in *Monolingualism of the Other* is both theoretical and inconsistent. True, we are reassured that language's self-appointed "master"—an ethnic, racial, or religious group, a political class or a whole nation-state—"is nothing," does not possess anything "naturally," "giv[ing]," instead, "substance to and articulat[ing]" an "appropriation only in the course of an unnatural process of politico-phantasmatical constructions" such as "cultural usurpation," colonization, exclusion, and other "impositions" by means of a particular idiom defined "as 'his own'" (23). Derrida does not entirely practice what he preaches, though, and this becomes apparent as soon as we start asking, Who is this native master? Who are the native speakers here? More broadly, to whom does the whole argument apply? As the discussion so far has made clear, the natives are those who traditionally stand in the circle of "we": not the dispossessed of the former colonies who are entitled to retake possession of the histories and languages they have been long cut off from, but the natives of old and new metropolitan centers—the French in Derrida and Federman, the Americans in Lee—who raise linguistically proprietorial, exclusionary-regulatory claims to language. The distinction is capital. As Doris Sommer notes in her critique of *Monolingualism of the Other*, speakers of different backgrounds are positioned differently with respect to language and the polity built on it. It makes a big difference, she says, if you are, or are viewed as, a native/originary speaker, and thus a normative participant in the national conversation, or if you are or are perceived to be a newcomer, an immigrant, an alien whom, at most, an ESL class might assimilate into the country's legitimate body of speakers. Abdelkebir Khatibi, Arab French author of *Amour bilingue*, from which Derrida draws in *Monolingualism*, and Derrida relate, by virtue of their both congruous and incongruous inscriptions into French and the colonial/postcolonial histories of Frenchness, asymmetrically to language in general and authority over language and the nonnatives learning it, in particular. Magisterial delusions of "appropriation" play out differently here. Derrida and Khatibi may share Maghrebian "fellowship," but it is not at all certain that it grants them the same "posture" with respect to French and Frenchness. Khatibi's French-Arabic bilingualism rubs up against French (and Derrida's own French "monolingualism") in ways Derrida's nonexistent Arabic or Hebrew does not. Compared to Derrida's, Khatibi's French is "supplemented," additionally—and decisively—*versi*fied, "intonated" by versions, alternatives, and alternate "norms," creolized, destabilized, and destabilizing, a challenge to the monism of monolingualism from a bilingual position of enhanced polyphony. In exchange, the French language, *le bon français*, aggressively reinforced by L'Académie Française since 1635, homologates Khatibi and Derrida in unlike ways. The latter's "versifications" and plays on language are better accommodated, assigned a comfortable *marge de jeu* in French, whereas Khatibi's or Federman's raise suspicion. Derrida's point on the "heteronomous" (39) makeup of French is well taken, but, while calling for a new, heteronomy-informed "politics of language," he still deems certain versions of French "incompatible" with the "intellectual dignity of public speech" (46); he is both skeptical of "pure" language and "admits" to its "purity" (47). Accordingly, in "surrendering" to the idiom, he buys into a soft "normativity" or "purism" that, explicitly abhorred at places (47), comes back to rescind the linguistic hospitality elsewhere offered to the other. Sommer is thus right to ask if what ultimately carries the day in the guise of an ideal, untainted, and unaccented French is not a "residual universalism" that "den[ies] linguistic/cultural differences," thereby making language's sine qua non otherness and "impurity" a hypothesis of little consequence.[16]

Is Derrida still useful, then? I think so, provided we do not take his first "proposition" above—"We only ever speak one language"—to endorse the "one-norm" view of language that otherwise he himself refutes at times. If he is indeed serious about his adage "There is nothing but plurilingualism" (21), then are we not better off, I wonder, if we dispense with the "one-language" notion altogether? What strikes me as critically fertile is the juncture where Sommer's multilingualism, which she uncovers in typically bilingual situations, and Derrida's monolingualism, which he opens up as polylogue, overlap. The Babelic hustle and bustle Sommer hears in several languages spoken together Derrida makes out in one, and, his normative lapses notwithstanding, these "anomalous" noises and faces crowd in on the linguistic *nomos,* dispute vociferously the putative master's authority. They use language and other it as they go along. "[C]ulture [may] institut[e] itself" as "monolingual obstinacy" (57) in moments and through institutions of linguistic-political exclusion, but locutional praxis pluralizes. A space of otherness originally—other become discourse—language lends itself to this diversification of grammar, dictionary, and pronunciation, and thus carries the speaking self beyond "monolingual solipsism" (22) farther afield into the uncharted and unsaid. We discourse, the cosmoderns assert, from scripts not of our making only to arrive in others' wordings and meanings.

It is this *langue d'arrivée,* this "language of arrival," that the linguistic fables I survey here listen to. Vocally inventive if not iconoclastic; anomalous or, more accurately, polynomous; paradigmatically fluid, rarely "at one with itself" (65); neither "corrupt" nor "degenerate" but, Dante would say, "natural," the "noblest" of dictions: this language is fundamentally vernacular.[17] In it, speakers accede to a "*uniqueness without unity*" (68) that "permits" them to recognize and address an "other" (69). For, a vernacular composite, the national idiom is not only a priori vernacularized but also actively vernacularizing. It continuously yields further configurations of language and citizenry, of association with the body linguistic and politic. The idiom springs from a condition of relatedness and sets up, against prescriptive statutes of correctness, accuracy, and legitimate enunciation, new ways of relating the speaker to others.

Authors from Eva Hoffman (*Lost in Translation: A Life in a New Lan-*

guage, 1989), Julia Alvarez (*How the García Girls Lost Their Accents*, 1991), Marie G. Lee (*Finding My Voice*, 1992), Demetria Martínez (*Mother Tongue*, 1994), and R. Zamora Linmark (*Rolling the R's*, 1995) to Sigrid Nunez (*A Feather on the Breath of God*, 1995) are among those who, against the normative-ordering sway of the post–Cold War "linguistic order," have pondered this condition inside and outside the nation. Missing from this ostensibly incomplete list are novels like DeLillo's *The Names* (1982), one of the first American fictions to get a grip on the global-age spread of English, as well as classical examples from other traditions, such as Coetzee's *Foe* (1986), David Malouf's *Remembering Babylon* (1993), Assia Djebar's *L'amour, la fantasia* (1985), *Oran, langue morte* (1997), *Ces voix qui m'assiègent . . . en marge de ma francophonie* (1999), and *La Disparition de la langue française* (2003), Jean-Christophe Rufin's *Globalia* (2004), and Zahia Rahmani's *"Musulman" roman* (2006). If I do not cover books like DeLillo's here, that is because, as mentioned earlier, what I want to throw light on is the nation as a site of national language performance. Needless to say, the local and the global, the national and the international collide, intersect, and combine in this arena to the point that the nation's inside and outside get almost impossible to pick apart. But this *is* the point: in the late-globalization nation's loquacious bazaar the internal-external divide is eroded by "outside," "nontraditional" speakers—immigrants, migrant workers, travelers, alien residents, ethnoracial groups—while normative-nativist codifications of language set out to reinscribe it. Designed to check national tongue's vocalizations by voices presumably exterior to the nation, these restrictive interpellations clash against locutional performances in which those voices act out and further enrich the polyvocality of language. It is interesting to observe not only how this agon plays out in the space of the nation but also how it evokes this space anew along the lines of a more comprehensive cultural cartography. It is, to be sure, an evocation in the sense described earlier, but also an invocation. The former tests the national ear's "tolerance" for vernacular "malapropisms" of pitch, word choice, and grammar still to be featured in the nation's code of "proper" use; the latter is a culturally symbolic strategy of inclusion and legitimation. The outsider's vocalization of the nation's voice is looked upon with suspicion. We shall see momentarily, this speaker is treated as intruder, "spy" (in Lee), or "traitor" (in Federman); his speech is "deviant," "aberrant," and abnormal, a "vocal" violation (it is "strident" and "cacophonic"). In response, the speaker—Lee and Federman as authors speaking for themselves and on, another level, their heroes—turn to tactics of homologation that invoke intertextually linguistic-aesthetic standards of excellence such as Walt Whitman and Samuel Beckett, respectively. Once more in colloquy—with these classics as precursors who wrestled with the same dilemmas of language, identity, and recognition—Lee and Federman fine-tune their cosmodern message of inclusiveness. One deals with English, Korean, and the United States as a forum of cross-ethnic logomachy. The other goes back and forth between French and English and France and America. Both writers vent, however, the same anxieties, put up the same drama of language, and convoke a similarly exigent proximity of voices, speakers, and citizens.

2. Glossolalia: Chang-rae Lee's *Native Speaker* and Cosmodern Nativity

Legends, Spies, and "Ethnic Coverage"

Lee's 1995 novel *Native Speaker* has been called a spy thriller and rightly so.[18] Its Glimmer & Company uses "ethnics" like Korean-American Henry Park, Lee's narrating protagonist, to gather information on immigrants and the recently "hyphenated." "Each of us," Henry confesses, "engaged our own kind, more or less. Foreign workers, immigrants, first-generationals, neo-Americans. I worked with Koreans, Pete with Japanese. We split up the rest, the Chinese, Laotians, Singaporans, Filipinos, the whole transplanted Pacific Rim. Grace handled Eastern Europe; Jack, the Mediterranean and Middle East; the two Jimmys, Baptiste and Perez, Central America and Africa. . . . Dennis Hoagland had established the firm in the mid seventies, when another influx of newcomers was arriving . . . and there were no other firms with ethnic coverage to speak of. . . . He was the cultural dispatcher" (17–18).

Before dispatching him on a new "assignment," Korean-American businessman and community leader John Kwang, Hoagland urges his employee to "work carefully through" the "legend" (story or cover) under which Henry would get close to Kwang. The legend calls for an unassuming act, a *soft* identity performance. "Just stay in the background," Hoagland says. "Be unapparent and flat. Speak enough so they can hear your voice and come to trust it, but no more" (181). Eventually, Henry puts together a plausible legend. But so does his author, in his own way and for his own purpose. To Hoagland, the term equates fiction and disguising ploy, but *legend* also designates something we need to read first so we can read further. After all, *legenda* are "things to be read." To consult a map, for instance, we must begin with its list of cartographic symbols and their explanations ("keys"). It is through them that we read the chart or text to which they are appended. In this view, *Native Speaker* is a legend twice: because it furnishes the "legible" appearance, the story in which Lee comes before his readers, but also because this story itself appears and lends itself to reading (is made *legible*) via a legend in the etymological sense of the word. Embedded in the novel, this key is Whitmanesque and thus central to Lee's engagement with America.[19] Whitman, the "legendary" native forerunner, helps Lee lay his own claim to Americanness, specifically to American writer status. Korean-born Lee becomes a "natural," naturalizes himself into America, its language, and letters via the emblematically American, Whitman intertext lodged inside his novel. Lee wants his story of tongues and voices to be heard across Whitman's voice and so sets up his novel as a ventriloquial narrative that at once emulates and reworks the precursor's symbolically capacious idiom. Thus, *Native Speaker* presents us with a novelistic glossolalia, speaks to us in tongues: in Whitman's emblematically "native" and multitudinous tongue, as well as in others whose inclusion in the national conversation, Lee implies, is as legitimate as his bid to be part of the American canon. Not only does he stage his Koreanness in relation with the American classic; he also recycles the Whitmanesque vistas of U.S. linguistic-cultural identity into a script for *Native Speaker*'s spectacle of selfhood.

This spectacle and its lead actor are cosmodern, or become so, rather, for they start out in a problematically cosmopolitan mode. Dispatched according to background, Hoagland's ethnic spies cook up their stories so they can write the true stories of "others" (18). This is how Henry comes to see himself as a "mundane" chronicler of their "cultural manner" and mannerisms (19). His debriefings feed off the resilient idiolect of strangeness. For this, Hoagland opines, white Americans possess too parochial an ear, unable as they now are to turn to the world their "*other* ear"[20] and listen for otherness. Moreover, they betray themselves before getting to betray (inform on) others. They give themselves away—blow their cover—easily, out of some "charge or vanity of the culture, à la James Bond and Maxwell Smart" (172–73). This "cultural excess" makes them the "worst spies" because it prevents them from approaching the target as a cosmopolitan, "world-political creature" (19) whose private worries and mysteries may matter and therefore may be worth nosing into from a perspective larger than the immediate community, nation, state, or culture of the spy. So what Hoagland needs is an analogously cosmopolitan type of spy. This "secret agent" must possess, first, cosmopolitan *propensity*, in other words, a balanced, "natural" albeit carefully understated interest in others like him, be those his kin or not, then a level-headed openness toward them, an inherent if tactically deployed neighborliness outside the native neighborhood, country, or religion; second, cosmopolitan *ability*, consisting primarily in multiple linguistic-cultural competencies; third, cosmopolitan *compatibility*, a like-mindedness of the spy and the "assignment," a shared feel for the "big picture" beyond the self and its enclave. Common to these skills is the capacity to operate in more than one world and go back and forth between them, to screen people and lives perceptively, sift through their often culturally unfathomable texts, sort out the relevant and the trivial and write it all out by translating and formatting it into a "story" the firm can read. This means that the cosmopolitan spy must also be a *translator*, and both are actually implied in the figure of the cultural go-between. As Van der Veer writes of Dutch "Orientalist" and "scholar-spy" of Muslim law Christiaan Snouck Hurgronje, "The cosmopolitan person is not only a translator, but also a spy who commands more languages than the people he spies upon, as well as the ability to translate their languages into the languages of rulers. It is the ultimate cosmopolitan fantasy, well expressed in Kipling's writings, that the colonial hero has a perfect grasp of the language and the customs of the 'natives', the 'locals', but still in his crossing over remains true to himself and returns to his own world where he uses his acquired knowledge for the improvement of colonial rule."[21]

Lee's is more than a cosmopolitan fantasy. It is, in fact, a counterfantasy that goes against the voyeuristic, "intelligence-gathering" sort of cosmopolitanism in which his hero is engaged on behalf of other, "vastly wealthy voyeur[s]," hypothetical "xenophobe[s]," and chauvinistic America-firsters, overt and covert devotees of "national vigilance."[22] Undoubtedly, not all cosmopolitans are spies and informers on empire's payroll, even though Henry does spy and inform. Nor are his world and moment colonial any more, and, as we shall see, location and nativity no longer play out the way they did back in imperial and immediately postimperial settings. Van der Veer's analysis of spying applies to late Victorian empire, its Kiplings, and Conrads, a moment defined by the external, extrametropolitan, exotic foreignness the British, French, and other empires were stumbling upon in their expansion, by the unsettling cultural enigmas imperial secret agents were called on to solve.[23] Colonization and espionage did go hand in hand at the time, with the cosmopolitan the ideally positioned operative. In Lee, however, the settings and thrust of cosmopolitan contacts have changed. The latter are unprecedented, indeed "world-political." Foreigners no longer fascinate from afar but as a worldly presence concurrently "over there," in the homeland never quite left behind in the age of "networks" and "border-crossing," as well as "over here." Capable of rendering alien, complex, and incoherent the idioms and texts of their new home, they stand poised to interpolate American cultural-historical narrative, to "adulterate" the land's language.

In this new global context of surging encounters, cosmopolitan aptitudes and knowledge can be put to a more ethical, cosmodern work beyond the intelligence sought by "agencies" and empires old and new. A whole new dynamic of self and other obtains in *Native Speaker,* a postdivisional distribution of linguistic and cultural markers across ethnic and other categories, which complicates and partly redeems the practice and trope of cosmopolitanism as spying. For, in a sense, Van der Veer is right: cosmopolitan dealings do entail predispositions and talents also required of spies, undercover agents, and reconnoiterers of unknown lands. Conversely, a good spy is an effective scout of another's culture, a proficient reader of that culture's map. He or she must be able to detect traces of life, significant gestures, "mannerisms," and events, to unravel that which for another might remain insignificant, illegible, irrational. In this respect, Hoagland's own "reading" of Henry is warranted: spying comes to the latter "naturally" as a matter of calling ("nature") rather than training ("nurture") because it inheres in his cross-cultural mobility, in the gift of being at ease, "himself," in the demanding proximity of the "ethnic subject." Henry admits, in fact, that Hoagland "had conveniently appeared at the right time, offering the perfect vocation for the person I was, someone who could reside in his one place and take half-steps out whenever he wished" (*Native Speaker,* 127). But Hoagland and Henry relate to this subject differently. Hoagland seizes it as distinct from himself and white America. Instead, Henry senses a kinship, a connection not only with Kwang, but also with other "neo-Americans" who have undergone acculturating experiences comparable to his own. Hoagland polices the gap. He fetishizes the ethnic-cultural rift but uses people like Henry to bridge it lucratively. Henry is much closer to Kwang by background, "appearance," and cross-cultural adeptness. It is this closeness that almost makes Kwang Henry's "classical psychological double"[24] and helps him step over the gap; it is this sameness, this linguistic and cultural code-sharing, that facilitates Henry's approach, and it is this too that determines his spying as betrayal, which in turn, Lee hints, reenacts Kwang's "originary" act of community "disloyalty."

Such betrayal or self-betrayal, rather, is part and parcel of immigration and acculturation to the extent that they entail the loss of a "mother tongue," "ancestral graves," mores, and reflexes (279), as well as self-forgetting and self-remaking. And as far as this ur-betrayal of sorts goes, Kwang and Henry are alike. Yet Henry is as Korean as he is American. He does take "half-steps" (127) out of his home and into the other's—Kwang's—much like Kwang himself, who learned early in life how to "exis[t] outside the intimate community of his family and church and the street where he conducted his business" (182). Henry and Kwang are "cosmopolitely compatible"; they show off the same cultural mobility and worldly adroitness, feel at home in and out of their homes. Nonetheless, Henry is always a half step ahead of the unsuspecting, targeted other, not just because the other has no idea what Henry's job and real identity are but also because America, Henry's home, has transformed Henry, a first-generation U.S. national, more than Kwang, for whom Korea remains the home to go back to. On the other hand, Hoagland's assumptions notwithstanding, Henry's Korean-Americanness is as akin to his wife Lelia's "white" Americanness as it is to Kwang's Koreanness. Therefore, the sameness on which Henry trades to draw near Kwang—and draw him out—is also something he works hard at, if gently, without overdoing it. It rewards his conscientious efforts to cross a preexistent bridge no less than to overcome a whole set of demarcations and inscriptions of otherness. Where the colonial and postcolonial cosmopolitan spy went native to become native-like, like the other, and thus fluent in the colony's idiom, Henry is the native or the quasi native scrambling to get beyond this nativeness, beyond his American, "assimilated" persona so as to reconstitute a sort of "pre-native," pre-Americanized profile presumably conducive to a bond, to a window into Kwang's native Korean self. Linguistic as much as cultural, this struggle also makes Kwang into an other to Henry, a challenge both inside and outside the horizon of the familiar. This comes as no surprise since Kwang remade himself into this amphibological identity whose foreignness claims a chunk of America, while making his new country, through an "identity leap," a part of himself (211). Similar and dissimilar to Lelia *and* Kwang though not in the same way, as non-American to the former as non-Korean to the latter, Henry wields the complex languages of both worlds, benefits from the insider's insights, and so is able to turn his educated gaze to either one.

Yet while he can spy on Kwang and betray him without Kwang's knowledge, Lelia feels that something is amiss. In fact, she does not hesitate to call him a "spy." Lelia is family, after a while Henry's only family member. So her charges count, on two levels: ethical and cultural. Here is the indictment-love poem she hands him before leaving for a soul-searching trip to Italy: "You are surreptitious / B+ student of life / first thing hummer of Wagner and Strauss / illegal alien / emotional alien / genre bug / Yellow peril: neo-American / great in bed / overrated / poppa's boy / sentimentalist / anti-romantic / ———analyst (you fill in) / stranger / follower / traitor / spy" (5). An illuminating coda to the poem is provided on a paper scrap Henry later finds under their bed: *"False speaker of language"* (6). The innuendos, the ethnic clichés regurgitated half tongue-in-cheek, half in earnest, and the overall double-entendre of the farewell note blend earnest incriminations and not-so-earnest flattery, ultimately conveying Lelia's "despair" (5) over Henry's true meaning. She has been trying to "read" him and failed. Or she has partially failed because she has at least learned the reason of her failure: Henry's resistance to her attempts to get through to him and figure him out. What Henry has put together for her daily perusal, she realizes, is a decoy text, another legend. No more than a cover, this legend is unethical; it is designed to lead people on and away from him. Instead, Lee's Whitmanesque legend is ethical, for it invites the reader in, decodes.

The Whitman Code

The rare, cosmical, artist-mind, lit with the Infinite . . .
    —WALT WHITMAN, *Democratic Vistas*

I make a pact with you, Walt Whitman . . .
We have one sap and one root—
Let there be commerce between us.
    —EZRA POUND, "A Pact"

In intertextuality, ethnic literature renews itself as a project capable
of exceeding—indeed, risking—its own bounds and its willingness
to view difference not separately but crosswise.
    —YUNG-HSING WU, "Native Sons and Native Speakers: On the
    Eth(n)ics of Comparison"

Encapsulated by the famed "lists of peoples, occupations, and possibilities," the "Great Enumerator"'s "cosmopolitanism" and "ethos of representational inclusiveness" have drawn writer after writer.[25] Mukherjee's

The Holder of the World (1993), Paul Auster's *The New York Trilogy* novels (1985–86), Maxine Hong Kingston's *Tripmaster Monkey* (1989) and *The Fifth Book of Peace* (2003), Michael Cunningham's *Specimen Days* (2005), and Vijay Seshadri's shorter piece "Whitman's Triumph" (2005) are some of the recent prose "invocations" of Whitman as a modern founder of American cosmopolitan philosophy. In *Native Speaker* and then again in the later books I take up in *Cosmodernism*'s next part,[26] Lee suggests that both this philosophy and the American cosmopolis built on it must be re-founded, for, on the one hand, late-twentieth-century America comes short of Whitman's inclusive vision, but, on the other, this vision too seems insufficiently equipped to embrace the linguistically and culturally multifarious post–Cold War world. Similarly ambivalent is Whitman's treatment as a literary forerunner. Like Mukherjee or Kingston, the Korean-American writer pays homage to Whitman as an epitome of an "accommodating," "native" tradition that has opened up the American pantheon to immigrant voices like Lee. At this level, the Whitman legend offers a literary prophecy and a critical endorsement; Whitman is an ally, the cosmopolitan forebear authorizing *Native Speaker*'s cosmodernism. Notably, he also is the host who issues an invitation, calls out to his Korean-American guest. Lee answers, and in so doing positions himself at the same time inside and outside Whitman's America. He both relies on the poet's outlook and revises it to take it into the "postethnic" and "postnative" age. He rehearses and updates Whitman's representation of the national self, redrawing the boundaries of the nation and its nativeness domain. A container of multitudes, the postnative and postnational self is, or ought to be, Lee thinks, the terrain on which others do not merely feel at home but also play host for other Americans, "native" or not.

Central to the American self, the immigrant experience as narrated in *Native Speaker* and the novel as that experience's narration by an immigrant writer stake out their joint claim to Americanness by reclaiming Whitman.[27] This claim is also a *clamatio* calling back to the cosmopolitan precursor. It is the voice, Lee's, in which *Native Speaker* revisits Whitman's own "visitation" of the book, responds to the intertextual call the *Leaves of Grass* author makes on Lee's work beginning with its opening epigraph.[28] Excerpted from Whitman's poem "The Sleepers," the motto places Lee's whole project under the patronage of the American bard: "I turn but do not extricate myself, / Confused, a past-reading, another, / but with darkness yet."[29]

As Henry would say, Lee is here "cracking the lid" of the novel (90). The character does so occasionally and only to throw dust in the eyes of Kwang's entourage, whereas the writer means (and does) what the Whitman legend says (or implies). Through it, Liam Corley explains, Lee shows himself as attempting a social and political "turn," a shift in his position and place in American history and society as an Asian-American. Yet he cannot—nor can his character for that matter—wholly "extricate" himself from a certain status quo of public misrecognition, from how he and others like him have been "read." Confusing and obsolete (a "past-reading"), the American map's Asian-American legend is nonetheless resilient. It still "gets wrong" the "others" as it latches onto their "darkness" and thus further others them racially and nationally, marking them as non-American, as "outsiders" to the national body.[30] Read in turn this way, the Whitman "counter-legend" helps Lee recenter himself as an insider, as an Asian-American man and writer already inside America and its tradition.

Opening up with the poem fragment, the reverential-revisionary "commerce" with Whitman goes on with the telltale scene featuring Lelia and Lee among the "sleepers" in an El Paso park (12), then continues with the image of the "slumber[-]bound," sinking swimmer in the "Peanut Butter Shelley" lines reproduced later in the novel (233), and otherwise runs through the entire text at several levels simultaneously.[31] Plotwise, it is indeed noteworthy that "[t]he spectacle from which Whitman turns [in his poem] is a shipwreck."[32] The poet turns away from his vision of solitary albeit grandiose fall only to zoom in on the collective tragedy off the shore. Helpless, he looks on while a boat's passengers reenact the death of a "beautiful gigantic swimmer." Lee incorporates this particular event into his book explicitly and allusively. Toward the novel's end, he references the 1993 wreck of *Golden Venture*, a freighter that sank in the New York harbor (246–47, 327). The ship was smuggling hundreds of Chinese, some of whom drowned, while the rest were rescued but only to be imprisoned and deported. Corley, whose discussion of the incident I follow here, is also right to highlight the cultural impact of this catastrophe, which the news networks spun as an assault on America by Asian illegals.[33] This is the legend/construction government agencies and the press put on the episode, and this is precisely the reading of the *Golden Venture* affair *and* the reading of the Asian-American venture into full-fledged American-ness that Lee sets out to displace with help from the Whitman intertext. In this light—the light Whitman casts on *Native Speaker*—it is highly relevant that "The Sleepers" does not simply mourn the drowned. The poem is also an obituary that, albeit posthumously, finds a place for the dead in the house of which they failed to make a home. The "sleepers that lived and died," the "Asiatic and African," "the European and American" sleepers the poet watches while they "lie unclothed, / flowing hand in hand over the whole earth from east to west," on the one hand, and, on the other, the drowned—those asleep in their beds and the dead the poet helps "lay . . . in rows in a barn"—rest side by side in the poem, limbs of the same cosmopolitical body. A most astute, *ethical* voyeur of American culture, Whitman sees through others' legends and covers naturally and morally. His gaze does not expose to "set up" and exclude but to embrace. It is his gaze, his "art of looking" that identifies—"IDs" and legitimates—the observer as one of the observed, "boss" and "pet" at once. He is so much one of them, capable of understanding what it is to be "the emigrant and the exile," "the homeward bound and the outward bound," that "they [can] hide nothing." Nor need they disguise their distinctive selves anymore. In Whitman's America "the diverse shall be no less diverse, but they shall flow and unite" so they can forsake their deceptive legends, "lift their cunning covers."[34]

The poem's present tense accelerates time, sucks the future, utopias' usual abode, into a visionary *hic et nunc* where the cosmopolis can take place without having arrived at its place yet. More realistic, *Native Speaker* offers that the late-twentieth-century United States shortchanges the Whitmanesque ideal, for the country is still reading Asian-Americans as unreliable, "treacherous" intruders infiltrating the nation to observe "us" from within; we continue to misread "colored" and "foreign" bodies generally, to take them as what they are not and so threaten what they actually are; we view their identity performance as a coverup and menace. This social anxiety feeds into the vicious circle of misperception and deception. Within this circle, on one side we construe the other as what he or she is not; on the other side, this other puts on a calculated, defense-mechanism-type show of identity that plays up to our misconstructions. Lee's America is a site for this contest of cross-cultural representations, a field of interaction no less than confusion, of successively unsuccessful misunderstandings where people do not feel encouraged to "lift" their covers. It makes little difference if the other actually wears a mask or I only believe he or she does, nor does it matter if his or her mask, when real, just responds defensively to my suspicious gaze or feigns "bearing out" my presuppositions. Practically speaking, what counts is how I see him or her, *how I read his or her face*, as natural physiognomy or as cultural stratagem.

This is Lelia's conundrum: she does not know what to make of Henry's face, whether to read it as "truth" or "show." But it is the very impossibility of reading Henry's legend unequivocally that ultimately tilts the balance and adjudicates (while further complicating) the amphibology by "seeing" the face's other, "true" face—the face as "ploy" and "mask." Consequently, Lelia's text closes with a charge. As she ends her "anti-Whitmanesque" poem, her husband must be a traitor, a spy. The "falsehood" of his cover or persona, she concludes in her "signature," gathers itself up and is forefronted in language, in his very "front" or mask where legend and language are one and where Henry appears to her as a "false speaker of language" (6). Henry's legend, how he wants to be viewed, is indeed constructed by his speech, by his use of language, and ultimately *is* language. Etymology proves here once again helpful. *Legend* does not only foregound an obligation/expectation concerning reading, that which is to be read. *Legenda* also result from speech acts. Evolved from the same linguistic stem, *lego, legere* and *loquor, loqui, locutus sum* (Latin for "to speak") convey their common origin. In other words, Henry "speaks" his legend. He produces a tactical "locution," *speaks himself into a certain way of being heard or "read."* His speech, what Lelia calls "Henryspeak" (6), coaxes others into a particular reading (*lectura*) or perception of himself and thus lends him a convenient appearance or "face."

The Face, the Voice, and the Voice-over

Truth is in a face.
—ZADIE SMITH, *On Beauty*

My passport says one thing, my face another; my accent
contradicts my eyes.
—PICO IYER, "The Nowhere Man"

A human face consists of other faces—the faces you inherited
or picked up along the way, or the ones you simply made up—laid
on top of each other in a messy superimposition.
—ALEKSANDAR HEMON, *The Lazarus Project*

In the other's face, Levinas writes in *Totality and Infinity,* the other's truth presents itself: the other as "naked truth." This nudity comes forth in the locutional "face-to-face," in language as con-versation, when self and other "turn" to one another and, "no less diverse," communicate. This is how they become part of a "human community instituted by language" where the "interlocutors" can "remain absolutely separated"—*distinct yet bearing with-ness,* in a relation that presupposes and safeguards distinctiveness.[35] As far as this cosmopolitan desideratum goes, Henry's face both helps and hurts him. This "double-bind" of the face largely accounts for the overall "double-bind experienced" by Henry, Kwang, and millions of "neo-Americans" stereotypically "bound" to the "other America" and thus kept apart.[36] For two things happen here. On the one hand, Henry puts on a linguistically native face despite the occasional struggle with the idiom and his good ear for dialect. He sounds like a "real" American, "speaks" himself a successful face so that what others hear is an American. He "Henryspeaks" himself into Americanness, into belonging to a community of speakers-listeners. Unlike Djebar's adopted French, his English is not a "vivisector's scalpel," does not "unveil" to expose and violate but to authenticate and thus recognize a right to belong.[37] Gadamer's translators are right to remind us apropos of the conversational theory developed in *Truth and Method* that *gehören,* German for "to belong," contains *hören,* "listen to."[38] "Belonging together," Gadamer himself emphasizes, "always also means being able to listen to one another," grounded as it is in the mutual "openness" of the speaker and the listener.[39] In Henry's case, though, there is nothing "genuine" or "natural" about this openness. He works hard at his "locutions" so that his interlocutors hear what they expect: an orally flawless national performance through which he cuts himself a serviceable profile, a rhetorically American figure. But again, this figure is the result of acculturation, of hard work, and what his former classmates call "practicin'." He puts himself together as a native speaker. He produces—in a thespian sense—his "nativity" linguistically while inside still hearing and feeling the plural rustle of idioms, multiple and shaky pronunciations, phonetic dilemmas and phonation challenges. His "standard" English, his linguistically performed nativity, is only apparently monological, flat, pure. In reality, it is a dissimulating sound for a wealth of noises and tones, for the compound "static" of otherness that any standard carries within and implies and any lingua franca bespeaks while trying to scour out and speak over. His English voice-over gives him an acoustically American facade, but like his Americanness, this shields other sounds and varieties of America. This "master" English can and does screen these variations out but cannot discard them; it muffles them yet keeps them inside. The one he makes himself into publicly through his speech fronts for multitudes, for others and their languages. Unheard albeit throbbing in his speech, this otherness comes to the fore in his complexion, which shows what his listeners cannot hear.

Thus, on the other hand, his face takes back what his voice gives him. Like Julia Alvarez's Yoyo in *How the García Girls Lost Their Accents,* he "takes root" in English.[40] But his countenance disfigures his American figure, renders it alien, unreliable, possibly a "fifth columnist."[41] His Asian face—"Charlie Chan, face as flat as a pan," his little son Mitt called him once "innocently" (103)—"defaces" his identity or complicates what the voice strives to simplify, wedges heterogeneities and discontinuities into the continuum of Henry's identity and between Henry and the "natives" listening and looking at him. To them, his being seems out of sync; they recognize the "native" voice, but his face "says" otherwise, for it does not strike them as a signifier of nativeness. Unable to square what they hear and what they see, they are at a loss. The whole point, Henry learns from Hoagland, is to play the face's double-bind right by showing/saying no more and no less than his audience is comfortable with. It all comes down to a balancing act of vocal and visual appearance. Looking like an Asian and speaking like a Euro-American, Henry has in principle an insider's access to both worlds but not in the same way. Nor do his voice and face unlock the same doors or mean the same things to different people. His "amenable Asian face" (89) "seem[s] to assure" (85) Asian-Americans and other "others." Instinctively, Kwang and his staff intuit in Henry's complexion a familiar presence, a bridge into sameness; his American accent, however, inevitably marks him as distinct and distant to the same audience. With the "natives," it is the other way around. The idea then is either to show himself and speak tactfully to stress commonalities and compatibilities without overplaying them and thus drawing too much attention, or, to the contrary, to deemphasize them, to "overmark" himself as different and thus cash in on the misconceptions built into his presumed otherness. Again, Henry uses the former tactic in "neo-American" situations and the latter in more "mainstream" American encounters. One counts on the benefits of a guarded intimacy with his "kind"; the other deploys the careful reserve of an alterity playing deliberately into the "natives'" representation of his visage to the point that that representation and related presumptions displace him as a real human being. In this context, his face does not make him present and familiar but erases him, cancels his visibility out. Among Asians and other immigrants, his studied invisibility is of a different type, trading as it does on his ability to fit, be like, and appear like them. Among "Americans," what makes him stand out and inconspicuous at once is his Korean complexion. People notice him but only to file his presence under what they think they know about him—under what his face "tells" them.

One more time, his face supplies the dissimulating legend under which he can remain alert and observant. And, to weave Henry's plausible cover or story, Lee turns to a multi-significant American story, perhaps *the* American story of invisibility, observance, and "critical voyeurism," Ralph Ellison's *Invisible Man*. If Whitman's is the omnipresent and overexposed voyeur, taking in the multitudes while stepping into the spotlight of American visibility, Ellison's remains outside, below, unnoticed. He watches the American show from the "darkness" into which he has been "chased" by people who "refuse to see [him]" (13, 3). This culturally induced blindness has consequences on both sides of the racial divide. The black man may not be a "spook," a "phantom" (3, 4), but he is treated like one. In turn, this spectral quality bestowed on him by those incapable of seeing him for what he is gives them the appearance of people asleep, entranced in a ghostly world of fuzzy shapes. Like Whitman, Ellison surveys a sleeping world, "walks softly so as not to awaken the sleeping ones" (5). Unlike Whitman, Ellison is pointing up the noctambulism of the whole culture, of a people risking to become a nation of sleepwalkers if they continue to see through others and ignore their presence.

A victim of his invisibility, Ellison's hero observes rather defensively, from the outside. Henry has learned instead how to turn the others' blindness into an advantage, into a profitable cover by smartly juggling his linguistic and "complexional" faces. To spy on "natives," for example, he puts on a show of Koreanness, effaces his American face by "grunting his best Korean" (in which he is approximately fluent) and thus antagonizing his father, who thinks that a display of linguistic nativity might get more people into his store. "I saw," Henry observes, "that if I just kept speaking the language of our work the customers didn't seem to see me. I wasn't there. They didn't look at me. I was a comely shadow who didn't threaten them" (53). But then the self-effacing shadow, the face that despite its Asian features does not stand out, "in the face" of the native one, blends into the background, gets itself the perfect cover—the cover of America—no less than an ideal "observation post." This is how the espionage novel and the American narrative become one. Or this is how Lee uses the same language to spin both his spy story and the story of American becoming, with Henry the Asian/spy assimilating into / "infiltrating" the nation, an aspiring citizen and "mole" at the same time, devising his Americanization and his "instant live burial" (202)—his American posture and his "imposture."

The former puts other Americans at ease because it tells an American story of self-reliance and reliability, of honesty and "obedien[ce]" (202)—the story of an "invisible underling" (202). Henry is supposed to efface himself into the broader American narrative through hard work and an unflappably "Asian" devotion to the "dream." And this is also what Hoagland hopes to get from his report: "clean" writing, a product of "the most reasonable eye" "present[ing] the subject in question like some sentient machine of transcription" (203). "Undo[ing] the cipherlike faces" under the cover of a verisimilar legend and "writ[ing] out" those "face[s]" (170–71) are both a matter of psychological sangfroid and stylistic phlegm. Henry should be no more than a "scribe," a storyteller who "keep[s] his face in the shadows" (204). Luzan is the only one who manages to get close enough to "look into [Henry's] face" and "read" it, that is, formulate for his pretend patient the "insistent question" Henry has been unconsciously asking of himself all along: "Who, my young friend, have you been all your life?" (205) Responding to the face looking into his own, Henry does not fess up, though, to the ethical responsibility of the face-to-face, does not name his legend, nor does he confirm Luzan's reading—or he does not do so explicitly, by making his identity entirely visible. Instead, he tells his doctor "of [his] invisible brother with no name" (205).[42] That is, he tells, speaks of himself while keeping himself unspoken, unrevealed. He "cracks" his legend's lid but only to test out the cover, not to blow it. During the (pseudo)conversation with Janice he puts on the "confidence grin" (89) that tricks others into reading him the way he wants to be read. This is the decoy type of mask, the deliberately "over-the-top," overwritten legend. In another sense, cracking the lid, partial/pseudo-self-exposure, may mean just pointing to his "regular" mask but not to what it hides. His "Asian poker face" is all here: impassible, understated and underwritten, un-remarkable in its seemingly zero-degree of emotional writing. It is this face that he shows—without showing himself—in the scene where he "show[s] Lelia how this [i]s done, sometimes brutally, my face the peerless mask, the bluntest instrument" (96). From behind it, he can "see your face, hear your voice, make certain that you live how you say" (280)—that what you show is no mask. This is the face he turns to Kwang in a face-off of sorts, a competition between the prying and the protecting faces, with the former keeping the latter in its "sights" (140) until the other's face "cracks" its own door open and lets out even more than Henry has hoped. "My job," he says, "was never to spy out those moments of his self-regard, it was not to peer through the crack of the door and watch as he bore off each successive visage. My appointed plan was just to give a good scratch to the surface, come away with some spice or flavor under my nails. As Hoagland would half-joke, whatever grit of an ethnicity. But then all that is a sham" (140–41).

Facing others as unethical positioning, as posturing and "sham": but so is ethnicity itself, "on the face of it" at least. It is deceptive, Lee seems to imply, not only insofar as it assumes that Henry and Kwang are the same and so they must "get" each other "naturally," as Koreans, but also to the extent that ethnicity is an "invention," in this case one of Kwang's many inventions along the road of American self-invention. Ethnic identity, though, is embedded in Kwang's deepest mask or face, which is what he wears to step into the open when he is assaulted by an angry mob. It is this face too, "his wide immigrant face," that he "shield[s]" from Henry's gaze (343), precisely because in it being and image come together, making the mask a "mirror" in which Henry "beheld" at last the man Kwang was (140). Henry does get a glimpse of Kwang's most intimate disguise, but that is still a level of being to peel off, to read through. At that level, however, the other's face-as-mirror reflects the spying gaze back to the gaze itself so that understanding (an other) becomes ultimately a self-understanding vehicle. As David Cowart points out, "[I]n Kwang's final mask . . . Henry Park discovers his own face."[43] What Henry discerns in the other's figure, I would further argue, is himself as a text to figure out. No longer a self-effacing observer, a transparent-eye-cum-spying-scribe, the self now centers on himself, finally able to reflect not only objects, information, but also *on* himself, make himself into an object of his own gaze, hence institute and dignify himself as a subject.

Vocation and Calling: From Gaze to Language

> . . . the locally honed, cosmocentric idiom of New York . . .
> —DELILLO, *Falling Man*

Unfolding under the aegis of "The Sleepers'" compassionate voyeurism, Henry's subject-becoming is on a collision course with Hoagland's surveillance philosophy. "To be a true spy of identity," the boss tells him, "you must be a spy of the culture" (206). Since the role requires cosmopolitan

flair, Glimmer & Company, Henry thinks, "offer[ed him] the perfect vocation for the person [he] was, someone who could reside in his one place
and take half-steps out whenever he wished. . . . [He] thought [he] had
finally found [his] truest place in the culture" (127).

A professional and moral notion, vocation determines aptitude as
"calling." But Henry's actual work renders this aptitude unethical, for his
job involves duplicity, a two-faced "act" at odds with cosmopolitan ethics.
Accordingly, his "truest place in the culture" circumscribes in reality a theatrical space of untruth. Henry occupies a zone of "double-dealing" identity performance where, for all this show's fluidity, he remains vulnerable
both to manipulatory pressures such as Hoagland's and to "native" apprehensions. Either way, he comes off as a spy capable of betraying others like
him, so the firm takes advantage of his aptitude, while white Americans
just fear it and, on this ground, resent his "infiltration." It is with a deliberately Whitmanesque voice that Henry talks about his own exploitation
and his exploitation of others (319), as well as about the anxieties raised by
an alien "penetration" of the national body: "I and my kind . . . will learn
every lesson of accent and idiom, we will dismantle every last pretense and
practice you hold, notable as well as ruinous. You can keep nothing safe
from our eyes and years. This is your own history. We are your most per-
ilous and dutiful brethren, the song of our hearts at once furious and sad.
For only you could grant me these lyrical modes. I call them back to you.
Here is the sole talent I ever dared nurture. Here is all my American education" (320).

The passage is key. It marks out Henry's place in *Native Speaker* while
it pinpoints Lee's own self-positioning in the history of American culture
by means of a modulating dialogue with Whitman, with a visionary *other*
and his vision of otherness. Henry's—no less than Lee's—cosmopolitan
"vocation" and "voice," his ability to hear and respond to an other's call,
enables him to pick up on the language of America and the symbols and
legends of Americana. His education, his cultural and conversational apprenticeship are complete only when the novice/newcomer makes full use
of the language by evoking, by "calling back" all these voices and lyrical
modulations. This is Kwang's, Henry's, and Lee's ultimate performance as
speakers and writers. Admittedly, they are all speaking and writing
"against a xenophobic nativism,"[44] and one way to displace its claims is to
reperform linguistic nativeness itself as a plausible show (233–34), thereby
redefining it as cultural achievement whose true place may well be *outside*
birthplace and kin. Both Kwang and Henry speak American English "per-

fectly" (12, 179). Their voices flesh out a plausible Americanness, for voice itself is the "flesh of language," as Hélène Cixous says.[45] In fact, they speak English too well, with unusual "care," "outspeaking" the natives themselves. Neo-Americans like Kwang, Henry, and Eduardo "call back" the standard's melody and tones so deftly that they modulate and almost "versify" it into another "version" of the standard as they seemingly act it out without a difference. But the linguistic surplus is right there, in the flawless repetition itself. The other leaves his mark in this apparently unremarkable, unalloyed return of the same voice—another sign that he has been there all along, despite the native myth of homogeneity. Answering the normative call of the same, the other calls back, yet, as critics like Derrida are eager to point out, he or she cannot call "except in multiple voices."[46] Whatever he or she says, it is either more or less, other. In turn, his or her "cacophonic" response only reveals retroactively the voices, assonances, and uncoordinated inflexions in the native's own, supposedly standard and inflexible idiom, alters it by inscribing an *alter* native language, a vernacular alternative of sorts, into American Englishness. The other's voice voices multitudes, but so does the native voice whose "polyglossia" Lee retrieves and sets up, with Whitman's help, as a more welcoming and capacious "standard."[47]

Reflecting "the stratification of any national language," this nonnormative norm rests at the core of Lee's cosmodern project.[48] Where modern cosmopolites were looking for a common language to set straight "those misguided centuries that had witnessed the scattering of nations and the bedlam of tongues," Lee pins his hopes on the linguistic jumble itself.[49] Set against monoglossic cosmopolitanism, his polyglossic cosmodernism does not ride on the ecumenic compass of one voice but values the many voices' concert, people's rights not just to idioms not theirs by birth but also to idiomatic uses of these idioms.[50] This cosmodernism welcomes a whole spectrum of "Englishes," from Lelia's own "standard"—a speech therapist, she calls herself, self-ironically, the "standard-bearer" (12)—to Kwang's and Henry's quasi-unremarkable "versions" thereof to the more markedly dialectal. Under Whitman's tutelage, the novel gradually drifts away from an exclusive paradigm of homogeneity and correctness to a more flexible model. This sanctions as "acceptable" American performance not only the impeccable, self-effacing reproduction of the deceivingly monolithic "standard," but also Asian and, more broadly, immigrant variations. Like people's faces, the English facets these faces express demand a place in the American house of language in spite of—better still, due—to their accents, for these too speak America. Significantly, the shift away from the absolute locutory mimesis of the "assimilist" immigrant (160) to verbal allotropy parallels the switch out of the mode of invisibility and facelessness into a position of assumed visibility and social presence. The point, made by Whitman's texts and remade by Lee intertextually or "intervocally," by an in-vocation of Whitman, is no longer to be *like* an "American," to play an other's part as though you too were the "real deal," but to rewrite this part so as to make it more hospitable to other representations and sounds of Americanness. The former, masquerading posture is geared toward deception and, sooner or later, self-deceptiȯn. It is certainly a questionable stance (45), involving as it does spying, betrayal, and self-betrayal (314). Implied in the performance, the face is here still a mask, an "unassailable body of cover" (161). Opposed to this unethical posturing of the face is the face-to-face in which what self and other practice is not identity mimicry, "blending in" and into each other's representations. They do not turn toward one another a cover but their being's text itself, the actual voice and face where the distinctions appearance-reality, surface-depth, act-existence, impersonal norm–dialectal variation, native-nonnative collapse. Notably, it is not performance per se that authentic, community-fostering conversation goes up against but the dissimulating act in which the actor or actress rubs out his or her individualizing marks so that he or she can appear and be heard like "us." A linguistic-cultural tactic, this act sets out to preempt the anxiety of difference, the panic "we" may experience before an alter-nation of the national body by alien bodies and noises.

Recalled by Lee, Whitman's vision counters this difference-expunging, putatively "appeasing" assimilation show. The poet does not urge others to melt into an undifferentiated America but to write their distinctiveness into an already plural body politic. It is not the other's fictive alterity that he welcomes into an also fictitiously homogenous house of the nation, but an actual entity into a real space. Whitman's Americans and America are not generic, normative notions but palpable and concrete *because* multitudinous, ever differentiating, idiomatic yet able to converse. No supracultural standard of Americanness is needed for this intercultural, multipronged dialogue to take place on the national stage. Nor do "others" need to enact—put on the show of assimilating into—this standard by leaving behind, in the offstage of their particular communities, their true voices and complexions. Listening to Kwang, but also to himself talking to strangers, Henry "couldn't help but think there was a mysterious dubbing going on" (179), a conscientious attempt to "stylize" his speech and render it "Anglo" (180), a sonorous badge of Americanness; as Whitman and, after him, Lee propose, Americanization should take neither a radical makeover to hide the other's face nor a radical voice-over to muffle this voice, its tone, and its accented English.

Speaking in the voice-over mode is a veiling—pseudo-revealing— show that shows a *prima facie* face, so to speak, and thus gives a first-glance or "first-face" impression. Derived from a superficial—"surface"—reading of the other's identity, it differs from what a deeper insight into the other's being could turn up *ultima facie*. In the pseudodialogue between the already assimilated and the assimilating others, the surface face and the deep face, on one side, then, on the other side, the onlooker's *prima* and *ultima facie* readings of the other stay distinct. In ethical tête-à-tête, they overlap or make the overlap a goal to work toward. False dialogue relies on the linguistic parameters and ideal of becoming-similar, of sounding if not looking like the same by eliminating the accented, the dialectal, the "storefront patois" (336). Instead, refraining from rubbing out people's physiognomic and phonetic faces, authentic exchange values this whole vernacular phenomenology because it is in it that being truly "appears." The point is not that Kwang and Henry—and, on another level, Lee—do something wrong as they speak "like" Americans or write "like" an American writer (Whitman), but that in the process of looking/sounding/writing like an other they suppress that which otherwise Whitman himself posits as a vital feature of America's geocultural "aspect." This is precisely the point Lee makes via his Whitmanesque legend, the face he ultimately shows his readers. Not a or *the* face actually, but faces and facets of Americanness and American English; not the over-voice of the cut-to-size voice-over but voices; not America's definitive, uncorrupted text, but its versions, ever apocryphal: at the end of the day, this is what *Native Speaker* speaks of. "There are as many versions of India as Indians," Rushdie writes in *Midnight's Children*.[51] "There are as many versions of America as Americans, and there are as many Americans as their voices," Lee replies. We hear them all in an unorchestrated crescendo from the opening episode with Lelia and Lee in the park—"Everywhere you heard versions" (12), Henry reports—to the end, where the recent versions and voices have transformed New York into a polyloquial Babel of globalization. After Rome and before L.A., New York is indeed the "second Babel" (237), a "city of words," its citizenry the "strangest chorale," with Henry-as-Lee-as-Whitman passionate New Yorker and *flâneur* walking around and taking in all "shades of skin I know, all the mouths of bad teeth" speaking "too loud" in good English but also in whatever they can utter "to get by" (344). Kwang is here, too, the American neither the natives nor the newly arrived have ever "imagined" (304). Not a polyglot per se, he is a ventriloquist of the national tongue, "speak[ing] the language like a Puritan and like a Chinaman and like every boat person in between" (304).

Both the "earnest" Asian face and flawless English are publicly "reassuring" performances.[52] The face may be different from an "Anglo" complexion but does not threaten. Nor does Henry's English. Both are sameness devices, portals into a new kind of invisibility: the invisibility of the "assimilated." Unlike in Ellison, this invisibility is not otherness- but sameness-derived. It does not result from how different others see you (and therefore do not see you at all) but from how "like them" you "appear" to them on the stage of your physiognomic and linguistic appearance. Ellison's facelessness was imposed; Henry's is self-imposed. An intricate corporeal act balancing voice and complexion, it involves "playing the face" artfully so as to efface/show himself to his advantage by toning down the physicality of his face. Playing up his English voice—a mark of Americanness—Henry plays down the Asianness of his complexion to the point that his look conveys "reliability" rather than "foreignness." In other words—American—he speaks himself another face. Whitman helps Henry/Lee face up to the theatrically acquired invisibility of the face and inaudibility of the voice, with the un-remarkable voice helping erase the "different" face and both fading into mainstream faces' and voices' supposed uniformity. Henry's initial face/legend dubs in his "other" face and thus consolidates the de-differentiating paradigm of the faceless voiceover. The Whitmanesque legend shaping and elucidating *Native Speaker* faces out this model of voiceless anonymity, turns a critical face to it, so to say, by working the plurality of voices and complexions into the cultural sketch of America. Through Whitman, Lee's novel gradually becomes a cosmodern project, not against but, let me reiterate, across the welter of American lilts and countenances.

Whitman's American cosmopolis is, Lee contends, a dream deferred. In its ecology of language and culture, speakers are under egological pressure to pledge allegiance to the nation in linguistic performances—"flat," "unapparent," Hoagland would say—that reprise the native norm and otherwise bear out expectations of "native" assimilation. It is then quite telling that in the end Lelia, the "speech therapist," does not embody the norm any more and that the immigrant no longer is a signifier of abnormality. Back together, Lelia and Henry work as a team. Her "speech work" (349) aims now less at "curing" the nonnative speakers, at "regularizing" the other's English, than at welcoming it as it is into American English and America. Henry is at her side playing "the Speech Monster" (348). He helps her "show and tell," de-monstrate the inflections of the language but also naturalize, prove "legible"—rather than pathologize, quarantine, and "sanitize"—the English varieties he hears. He bodies forth one version of English/America himself, is a "monstrous" deformation of what America "should" look like. And yet the monster speaks English with native ease, reassuring the kids that visual *and* vocal disfigurations are "normal" figures of the native. The face and the voice used to be props in a "two-face" tactic disruptive of the "equation" (12) of look and speech, "dead-ringer" mien and the words "just spoken" (220). In the "aberration" of their grimaces and sounds, in that which draws attention yet *cannot* serve as camouflage, the face and the voice get now on the same page/face. No longer pretending, they position themselves ethically, alongside others.

It is this monstrosity of the voice-look unit, this saliently differential and "idiosyncratic" incorporation, that welcomes the students' Babel of Englishes into America. The monster does not scare them off. On the contrary, it weaves them into this linguistic-political Americanness from a position marked, much like theirs, by conspicuous difference—difference to be encouraged and strengthened, brought out in bold relief rather than "remedied" through speech therapy. Thus, the monster encourages them to play with the language rather than play up to an abstract benchmark. And so does Lelia herself, who "wants to offer up a pale white woman horsing with the language to show them it's fine to mess it all up" (349). They do so, and the "standard-bearer" recognizes them as speakers and citizens of a community in which membership can be acquired through linguistically differentiating rather than homogenizing routines: "Everybody, she says, has been a good citizen." But then the former "healer" of otherness can be no exception. She too must apply for citizenship, must reveal her own "speakerly" face as one of the standard's faces and facets. Submitting her application—producing her own English—she tries to speak the speakers' names, "call[ing] out each one as best as she can, taking care of every last pitch and accent." Listening to her "messing it all up," Henry "hear[s] her speaking a dozen lovely and native languages."

In Lelia, the native at last speaks in tongues. Le(e)lia finally earns her nickname, "Lee" (128). Thus, it is she, rather than Henry, who becomes Lee's "alter alter-ego"—the American becomes the *gook* ("American") she has been all along without knowing it—by speaking in the language of the other, a language of languages that in retrospect sanctions the native language's "thick," heterogenous yet unacknowledged fabric (242). The native, her idiom, and national identity are so redefined under the aegis—are reread *with* the legend—of a Whitmanesque "chorale" that arises "*within* the moment of articulation," a moment both native and nonnative speakers alike must go through and whose pluralizingly "monstrous" effects they must face.[53] Lelia too must submit to this process, cannot but give herself to language. In so doing, she relinquishes her presumptive mastery over it. This is how whiteness as a signifier of Americanness and white America as a signifier of nativeness, on one side, and "ownership of the language," on the other, are no longer "equated."[54] At once similar to Henry and different from him, Lelia is the native master who forfeits her mastery, aware of all the idiom's hypostases that she does not command and in which others can make themselves at home.

In its last pages, *Native Speaker* takes us into the language house of the nation via Whitman's vision and, through it, beyond whatever residue of norm, universal practice, or center surviving in his garrulous America or in Derrida's monolingualism. What Lee implies is that if today's United States still fails to fulfill Whitman's dream, Whitman himself bears some responsibility for it insofar as he assigned his national utopia a racially, ethnically, and otherwise culturally-historically "stable" core. Not unlike Derrida, who overcomes his "purist" aversions in order to appoint himself guardian of *le bon français,* Whitman subsumes his panorama of American diversity to a unifying self, to an advantageous poetic vantage point and culturally organized authority under which "others" fall in line ("unite") while remaining "different." No one, Lee retorts, can assume the politically "centering" role the poetic self purports to play in Whitman.

In Whitman's voice, through a vocalization critical of the celebrated "score," Lee posits that as new speakers bring about new versions of the national language, they set themselves up in dialogue with others and their Englishes, acquire a linguistically cosmodern citizenship. Lee's neo-Americans sing—versify and diversify—America. They put forth linguistic, cultural, and political alternatives, question historically solidified meanings and representations. What Sommer writes of bilingualism applies to Lee's "Babelized" English. "Troubl[ing] the expectation of easy communication," this English "upsets the desired coherence of romantic nationalism and ethnic essentialism, . . . interrupts the dangerous drama

of single-minded loyalty."[55] Awareness of grammar, structures, vocabularies, and the like in many cases leads to broader critical vigilance toward
words and things alike. Allegiance to more than one language and culture—allegiance to language and culture as idiomatic-cultural alloys—
bears on actual or self-described monolingual and monocultural environments, gives more depth to both language and culture, looks for
exceptions, substitutes, and new solutions, queries the status quo. The
"broken Englishes" into which "they" break up "our" national standard
yield "new possibilities and fresh contradictions."[56] "Messing up" reigning
arrangements of language and culture, multilingualism reshuffles lexicons
as well as mores and mythologies.

3. Cacophony: Federman the Lingovert

> Only returning to the native land after a long absence can reveal
> the substantial strangeness of the world and existence.
> —MILAN KUNDERA, *Testaments Betrayed*

> What of this being-at-home [*être-chez-soi*] in language toward
> which we never cease returning?
> —JACQUES DERRIDA, *Monolingualism of the Other*

> Perhaps my French and English play in me in order to abolish my
> own origin. In the totally bilingual book I would like to write, there
> would be no original language, n[o] original source, no original
> text—only two languages that would exist, or rather co-exist
> outside of their origin, in the space of their own playfulness.
> —RAYMOND FEDERMAN, *Critifiction*

The Grammar of Betrayal

If Henry is a "spy," Federman—the character and the author—is a "traitor." *Un traître à la cause:* this was the actual charge brought against him.
As we learn from a 2005 autobiographical fragment, on the account that "a
Frenchman who writes in a language other than French is a traitor to the
cause, . . . one of France's big-time publishers" refused to publish a French
translation of Federman's first book, *Double or Nothing*. So be it, but
which "cause" are we talking about, the writer wonders. The cause of
French "tradition," "culture," or "history"? As it turned out, the bone of
contention was "la cause de la langue française." This was what *Double or*

Nothing had actually betrayed, and it made for the ultimate infidelity because all the other "causes" were tied into it. The French language *is* French "tradition," history and culture both in one and carefully managed as faces of this oneness. Further, in using the word *patrimoine* ("patrimony") for "tradition," Federman hints that French identity and linguistic expression were, as they undoubtedly still are, regarded as monist, exclusionary (of others), and codependent (of each other), and that this codependence defines the speaker's membership in the French "family." And vice versa: one risks "falling" from Frenchness—one is out of the nation's linguistic and cultural fold—if one gives French up, if one adds more tongues to one's native repertoire, or if one "defamiliarizes" *le bon français* through language use that ends up rendering the idiom "strange" by speaking and writing it outside the family and its notorious language codifications and policies.

But *Double or Nothing*'s author makes no bones about his "treason." He recognizes that "My French had become foreign [*étrangère*]. It had become a foreign language. And in France, foreigners are not always well liked and welcome. This is common knowledge. I know this. My father was a foreigner who spoke seven languages, including French. That is why I too speak French today. The language was France's gift to me. And now," he goes on, "I want to give France back what she gave me: my French language. That is, the language that I took with me to America and which, over there, in my books, has transformed. Thus, like François Villon, I leave all my books to France. This is a free gift. All I am asking from France is one day to put up somewhere a plaque that reads: 'Here lived Federman, a traitor to the cause.'"[57] This is no admission of guilt but an ironical rebuttal. Federman too speaks in several tongues at once (one of them certainly in cheek). Beyond the refutation itself, I find particularly illuminating how the linguistic and the patrimonial intersect and shore each other up in a cosmodern "testament" that rejects a univocal take on Frenchness. Univocality is what Federman deflates here—the expected and obsessively reinforced "one voice" and way of sounding and being French, of speaking, and speaking for, the national patrimony. Federman does to "Francophone" and "French" what Lee does to "Anglophone" and "American" and, more broadly, to "national idiom" and "nation": he pulls them apart. "Spies" and "intruders," they wedge themselves into the ethnolinguistic complex and "dislodge" the "national predicate" that has historically bestowed "ownership" of language X on ethnicity Y.[58] But the "mushiness" of what it means to be American or French after the umbilical cord to the national tongue has been cut follows from the writers' (and their characters') "messing" with language. On this account, it is worth pointing out that Federman's filial patrimony, the French—and with it the Frenchness—his father passed on to him, strikes a discrepant note. It also speaks in tongues. The idiom is just one of Szmul (Simon) Federman's languages, an ingredient of paternal polyglotism. Its speaker was himself a foreigner/stranger. In his mouth, French had to adapt to other idioms and accents, and also to those of the "Russians, Poles, Hungarians, Romanians," and other "foreigners" in the father's entourage.[59] Accurate and "authentic," even colorfully idiomatic, as we shall see presently, Federman's French is thus concomitantly "strange." Spoken by his Jewish family—"strangers" not exactly "bien vus et bienvenus" in France—the language is already on its way of becoming "une langue étrangère." Its speakers, the French they speak, and the whole public "patrimoine" their speech is assumed to carry are greatly complicated by this other linguistic, ethnic, and cultural inheritance, so much so that retrieving the patrimony, going back to it in writing, has a critically antinostalgic thrust. In effect, driven throughout by an autobiographical circling back to its French "roots," Federman's oeuvre is a counternostalgic project, one of the most consistently pursued in recent American letters. Over and over again, this work enacts a return, but this is no homecoming. What Federman repeatedly goes back to stands jarringly at odds with the myth of the French patrimony: all of a piece, homogenous linguistically and ethnically, sounding the same and basking in the fiction of ahistorical sameness. Instead, he recovers a wholly different French, France, and Frenchness, a place and time of the many and their voices, a plurivocal and "fallen" world tragically entangled in history. The writer may set out to recuperate the "one," *illo tempore* France of childhood, the once-upon-a-time familial and familiar place, but he ends up in the strange and unsettling place the native country has been all along. What he revisits is then an essentially alien geography of divergent representations, coordinates, and rumors.

It is this multivociferous hubbub of tonalities and modes of being that Federman's return captures, with French, English, and the rest of the Babel in between, linguistic and cultural signals "intersecting" and "threaten[ing] to displace one another" despite the author's own attempt to "translate" or "transact"[60] them into each other till they "complement" reciprocally, make one another "whole" again.[61] No wonder Beckett is Federman's "figure tutélaire." Modernism's great bilingual, whom Federman has frequently taught and written about, helps him get a handle on his own bilingualism or, as I suggest above, patrimonial multilingualism. It is Beckett who, in *Critifiction,* makes it easier for Federman to listen to himself only to hear the self's many "voices."[62] It is the "voice[s] within the voice," the "voice[s] in the closet"[63] and out of it, consistently fine-tuning the "twofold vibration" of being across an astoundingly encyclopedic and "recyclopedic"[64] register of textual, intertextual, and typographic arrangements ever in congress, echoing each other's sonorities, playing and pla(y)giarizing one another. Remembering things past, Federman revoices this discordant concerto as he recalls people, places, or things for that matter. As Nietzsche says in an epigraph to Federman's *Take It or Leave It,* things too speak, of themselves and ourselves in their midst, and when we reminisce about them, we set in train a total recall of sorts. What they speak to us as they bespeak us is "many more languages than one imagines"[65] and more than just language. They speak language as much as culture; it is in this sense that, as Federman stresses in *Critifiction,* "bilingualism and multilingualism [are] related . . . to the current concern for multiculturalism."[66]

Who should cut through the nation's contractual fantasy of homogeneity and retrieve this abundance of feeling and expression if not somebody steeped in the with-ness of language, a "lingovert"? As the narrating hero discloses in *Aunt Rachel's Fur,* "[I]t's in the French language that I suffered the most in my life, perhaps that's why I write mostly in English, to escape my suffering, and now I'm part of that notable exception of multi-linguists, those *lingoverts,* as my buddy Peter Wortsman calls us, what a smart guy Wortsman, he has a gift for inventing new words, *lingoverts,* great word to define all the uprooted writers who bring chaos into borrowed languages, yes I belong to . . . that literary foreign legion made of runaway aristocrats, political deportees, indigent adventurers, travelers without luggage, soldiers of fortune, roving intellectuals, refugees of all sorts, survivors, who leap-frog the linguistic and geopolitical boundaries to create an alternative tradition, a literature of the elsewhere."[67]

No "luggage"? Hardly. A "multi-linguist" travels with a lot of language—and that is a lot of luggage, a whole "patrimoine." This is more than the ethnos engrained in one idiom (French). It also comprises a linguistically and culturally pluralizing ethos. Both native and "borrowed," French remains for father and son an alien('s) language, and the writer repeatedly underscores his "native" fluency no less than the alterations, the playful Franco-phony of his French. Following his father, living up to the family's "patrimoine," Federman defamiliarizes French, renders it "strange." French becomes strange and France estranged in his work, forever displaced onto a space always to come and time impossible to come back to, to talk about in any clarifying way. For one thing, the native land to which Federman attempts a number of "returns" in his career proves unrepresentable, or hard to represent in conventional, unproblematic fashion. For another, indispensable to such representation, as the author himself recognizes, the native language opens a window into the *most* problematic: the unspeakable itself. The French and France Federman resuscitates in his books are scenes of unspeakable pain and loss, which further explains why the "patrimoine" cannot be evoked, at least not in the grand, extolling style demanded by the patrimonial rhetoric of the nation. In fact, whenever he does go back, his aborted homecoming reminds him not only of his "disloyalty" to French language and *traditio*. He also feels out of place in the country that had betrayed him and his family during the French Holocaust before the "traitor" himself carried out his own "treacherous" acts.

The Repetitive, the Patrimonial, and the Ethical:
Return to Manure

Repetition, Gilles Deleuze argues, is not exactly repetitive because it opposes re-presentation of that which has been.[68] It does not "repeat" the past nor anything reassuringly familiar or familial ("patrimonial"). What comes back to us and what we go back to more often than not perplexes and unsettles, even frightens us, Freud says, because it is not the same but the uncanny other, not the homely coherent topography of childhood but the elsewhere, the otherwise, the manifold. Accordingly, the mother tongue may end up "scaring" us later in life, and it certainly does scare Federman, "foreign and restrictive" as it sounds to him.[69] His return returns him not to *heimliche* sounds and images but to unexplored grounds, unheard noises, new understandings and facets of life—in brief, to what Deleuze identifies as "singularities." This is anything but comforting homecoming that sanctions the *déjà-vu*, things taken for granted. A repetition in the antireiterative sense of Kierkegaard's *Repetition*, Federman's return makes precisely the move the Danish philosopher's Constantin Constantius recommends, that is, away from the traditionally "ethnical [*ethniske*] view of life" and toward an "ethical view."[70]

Taking us beyond the ethnical and its patrimonial codifications, this project cuts in the 2006 "nostalgic tale" *Return to Manure* through French linguistic norm and culture of "normality" to unearth life forms and sounds the ethnolinguistic *nomoi* have quelled. "In th[e] tribal or traditionalist view," Edward J. Mooney comments on *Repetition,* "self-identity is secured by successful assimilation into prevailing cultural currents. In contrast, repetition requires for identity that we step back from these common currents to a stance ready for *individual* evaluations and individual self-choice. This flows naturally from the idea that 'repetition is a task for freedom.'"[71] Supposing that, like *Aunt Rachel's Fur* and Federman's other counternostalgic narratives, *Return to Manure* ultimately seeks if not to restore a lost presence then at least to recuperate a fuller "identity," it sets itself this "task" over and against an identitarian nomality that, in language as much as in other areas of life, strives to regularize the singular, the idiosyncratic, the foreign, and the strange, to integrate their voices into the national choir. To this "tribal" pressure Federman responds à la Kierkegaard, who speaks to us through Constantin Constantius, who in turn addresses the reader through the German of Johann Georg Hamann, who, at last, admits to "express[ing] myself in various tongues and speak[ing] in the language of sophists, of puns, of Cretans and Arabians, of whites and Moors and Creoles, and babbl[ing] a confusion of criticism, mythology, *rebus,* and axioms, and argue now in a human way and now in an extraordinary way."[72] Anything but a "lie" meant to throw the reader off, the confession clues us in instead, helps break the code of Kierkegaard's obscure text itself and, albeit indirectly, casts revealing light on Federman's own "repetition."

An "other-initiated grant,"[73] Federman's return wreaks havoc in the French Arcadia of selfsameness. As *Return to Manure* shows, what definitively blocks a "recovery" of French and Frenchness in line with the censorious routines of the nation is the fact that, as suggested earlier, the native idiom and place were, and during the "return" become once more, unspeakable. To be sure, Federman is still fluent, and in *My Body in Nine Parts* and again in *Return to Manure,* he legitimately boasts of his "genuine proletarian Parisian accent."[74] Granted, he "messes" with French as his father did before him, wants to "corrupt" it. There is something else that we need to consider, though: in speaking and further "estranging" and creolizing the strange French he inherited from his parents, he simultaneously voices the unspeakable, the horror, the family tragedy.[75] The quintessential French "patrimoine" gives him the voice with which to articulate the irretrievable family patrimony, the silenced voices and shadows of those whom the Nazis and their Vichy buddies wanted to expunge from French collective identity. So going to France and speaking French again is a journey in time and language, yet this voyage does not carry Federman's reader to the bucolic French countryside but "au bout de la nuit." It is an infernal enterprise and also a trip to the inferno complete with an eschatology, or scatology, rather, because it gives us a glimpse into that which, according to Federman, people can be made (or unmade) into when they are treated worse than animals and things: shit. The book is jam-packed with it as much as it is filled to the brim with words. Fecal matters and matters of speech: they both matter, and they do so together. Intriguingly—sacrilegiously—the outhouse provides the language to talk about the lofty "patrimoine" freely. Neither the ludicrous "Toubon Law" nor broader French "linguistic chauvinism" can do anything about it.[76]

Being, Speaking, and the Unspeakable

Following his family's 1942 Nazi roundup and murder at Auschwitz, thirteen-year-old Federman shoveled manure ("fumier") on a French farm for three years. Three more years thereafter, he left "ce fumier de pays" ("[that] crappy country") for the United States. On his way to Cannes sixty years *après*, he is searching for the place of his wartime ordeal. As we have noticed, the homecoming is bound to fail for several reasons, all of which pertain to language, to its lure and loss, to what it repeatedly promises—and fails—to retrieve. In *My Body in Nine Parts*, Federman declares:

> What one hears in a work of art . . . is a voice—always a voice—and this voice that speaks our origin [the nothingness whence we came before we uttered our first word], speaks at the same time our end [the nothingness towards which we are crawling] . . . my voice, in this sense, is my human adventure. . . . When I speak, . . . I am telling myself. . . . That's about all I can say about my voice. Except that when I speak English I have a pronounced French accent. An accent, I confess, carefully cultivated for social and sentimental reasons. I have domesticated my French accent. . . . The somewhat incoherent cadence of my voice certainly corresponds to the cadence of my life. And to make things worse, I often speak myself in two languages at the same time without making any distinctions between the two. . . . I speak therefore I am. . . . After all without my voice I'd be nothing. I would have no story.[77]

If presence is shorthand for co-presence and if the measure of co-presence is colloquiality, then presence, being ultimately, is *being heard.* Being is speaking and being listened to. If we are at all, we are in and through language. When we are written out of it, left out, silenced, devocalized, our being is deeply threatened. Federman's narrative ontology forms around voice, which is both tenor and vehicle of life. Yet, for one thing, this voice is not one, as he makes plain and as we shall see in more detail subsequently. For another, it always borders on voicelessness, on silence, arises from it and risks ending up back in it, to things unspoken or unspeakable. "The voice at the center of the circle," he muses in *Critifiction,* "can no longer express what lies outside it. It can only repeat its own void, its own emptiness, its own absence of fullness." Therefore, voice ultimately voices, on the one hand, "excessive" vocality, confusing cacophonies, on the other hand, "speechlessness," that is, "nothingness."[78] Returning to the manure emporium and its hardships is a vocal and existential challenge because it takes Federman back to a linguistic and existential nothingness made more terrifying and traumatizing by its literal meaning: this is were his "origins" had been "erased," where familiar and familial voices had been rendered speechless, reduced to nothing. All his voice can and must make heard, no matter how loud and colorful it may seem to us, is the unspeakable, the patrimonial silences and absences. This is the impossible yet necessary, emphatically ethical task Federman's revisiting of the French village takes on. Speaking what cannot be spoken, about "self and others," his "repetition" acts out a profound "responsibility."[79]

The French camp(agne) and the Nazi camp are hardly the same thing. *Toutes proportions gardées,* as the French say, what happens in the former on a lower scale of pain and humiliation does smack of the latter and its full-blown carnage. They both are places of forced labor where Federman and, hundreds of miles away, his family toiled at the same time. The only difference is that while Auschwitz embodied the unspeakable horror—the unspeakable pure and simple—the French farm bordered on it, implied it, signified on it as its oblique metonymy. This is why the story of those three years, not unlike most Holocaust stories, while demanding to be told, ultimately cannot be, at least not in the expected, representational-teleological form of traditional realism. This is why telling and untelling—deferring, "complicating," interpolating, glossing, and otherwise "subverting"—the story are one and the same thing, odd as it may sound. If that story can be captured, if revealing and responsible mimesis can be somehow carried out, it cannot happen other than in this textually baroque, self-interrogating form where linguistic and narrative "experiments" are not a luxury but a necessity.

It is the unspeakable that forces you to go on when you cannot. So does Federman, zipping along the "autoroute" toward the unspeakable itself, his destination all along. An assumed dead end? An impasse that might account for the storytelling about-faces and delays, for the neo-picaresque incidents, or for the splitting (doubling?) of the narrating protagonist? Possibly, because we are presented here with the Beckettian conundrum that Federman's work has restaged repeatedly. Yet, once again, restaging is not reiteration but genuine "production," lexical performance. A brisk linguistic dance, the story is woven around the untellable and the unnamable. This is the charged silence of the silenced, of absented presences and otherwise maimed, obliterated life, not the peaceful quiet of pastoral scenery, and Federman brings it all back to life with stupendously chromatic sonority. The accusing intonations just cannot sound—cannot be—other than what they are: a voluminous signifier of life, the index of a thorough, autobiographical recall. It is the voice or the voices rather that speak, as much as they can, the "gamin" Federman back into life.

Retrieving the unspeakable past is then an overly vociferous proposition. The present in which "Federman" and "Erica" are traveling is thus kilometer after kilometer and one "péage" after another sucked into a past of complications, complexities, and perplexities. This past, Federman's, is also not one. It too speaks in tongues, bears witness to a richness of being the brutal farm treatment threatened to pare down to an "abrutie" machine. The journey does not lead back to an idyllic "dolce far niente" in postcard-perfect French countryside but to the absolute opposite: hard labor dehumanizing the young boy and pushing him closer and closer to the other "brutes" (animals) and into their scatological world. *Return to Manure*'s Lauzy farm lies literally sunk in its excreta and noises, drowned in ca-ca-phonies. Its story is (what else?) "une histoire de merde," a "shitty story" in more senses than one.[80] Rejected by the outside world, harshly "refused" by it, the Jewish boy is here further assaulted by refuse, its stench, and the racket of the creatures that make it. The beasts, the cows in particular, overproduce it. Nature mimics them when "[il] pleut comme une vache qui pisse" ("it rains like a pissing cow") as the farm owner waxes lyrical (173). The field looks like one big latrine, and the politics of the time is full of it too. "The Pétain fascist propaganda was founded on this sordid condition that stank of cow shit," Federman informs us (24). The farmer even cogitates that "[m]anure is the essence of life, . . . and each time he would hurl a pitchfork of manure in my face" (85). The philosophy of refuse and the literal refusal-cum-humiliation of the other converge in this gesture, a moment as political as any on the farm, where "Everything made [the boy] angry. Everything that was free, or that had the freedom to do nothing but eat and shit all day" (175).

Remembrance thus mounts a serious olfactory challenge, for this abject Proustianism brings back a whole phenomenology of excretion, as well as a "dejective" politics complete with the stink of decay, decrepitude, and servitude. But remembrance must also happen in writing, and, with another paradox, if this writing is effective, it must modulate that which it is about, even if it combines fiction and recollection, or perhaps especially if it does that. After all, good writing emulates its subject matter formally, and the manure story is no exception because "the journey in search of the farm" and the "journey in search of the book" turn out to be one. Past travail and its present writing are analogous if not equivalent. The former is excretal by condition, which the latter must willy-nilly assume. Both are hard work; both require getting your hands dirty, messing with dirt and soil and soiling yourself in the process. And both can wind up a mess. As far as writing goes, this mess may consist in a different sort of waste—of time, for the story's audience. "You know Federman," one of the voices interpellates our storyteller, "you could discourage a good listener with your digressive bullshit" (89). But digression—the kind of textual residues in turn refused by the impatient reader—is not necessarily the flatulent staple of a b(ogu)s aesthetics. It may not seem "economic," to the point, but there is no point but points, no meaning but meanings, no story but stories, no storyteller but storytellers and their multiple voices while the space of their contest and quarrels, the text itself, is limited. So meaning-making (of the past) involves choices and making a choice, deliberation with oneself and other selves, playing with narrative possibilities, trying them out and often abandoning them, in brief, "digressing"—narratively speaking—"all over the place" (89).

A number of Federmans participate in this cacophonic storytelling, some of them speaking, some of them writing, and the rest kibitzing. As they do so, they bring before us another cacophony: the foul dissonances of the Vichy years (see Gk. *kakos*, "bad," "wretched"), but also, and more importantly, the Federmans' sonorities, tongues, and voices, all muffled by history yet wrapped up and still pulsing in Raymond's own voice. History, French history more exactly, during and after the war, has tried repeatedly to tone them down, to limit them to a certain monovocalism, or deauthorize them as atypical forms and sounds of Frenchness. But Federman's "excremental souvenirs" (13) tell of all the sounds abuzz amid the farm's sonic hell, of that which, in French, *wants to be heard* outside the French ethnos and hearth. If the nostalgic return is, much like the kind of fiction usually chronicling it, just that—a fiction, a doctored impossibility, "b.s."—in this case homecoming makes no sense first and foremost because the French country(side) was hardly an Arcadian home. Thus, quite befittingly, Federman returns to manure, to a stall and a barnyard, not to a house or home. The returning outcast ends up in the privy of Frenchness one way or the other, on the outside of the official language and of the French nation as a Jewish man living in the United States and writing in both French and English. He had been there already, and painfully so, following "la Grande Rafle" of 1942, doubly displaced, and all he can do now is project that place, put it together through the one thing nobody can take away from him despite his own displacements and rejections: language or, better still, languages, the voices of his past and present, talking to one another above and against the exclusive constructions of French nationhood, nativity, and "fluency." On his way to the farm and at long last at the destination, the world talks to Federman, is an open dictionary of terms and phrases through which he "remembers"—and because he does so through language, he also reinvents. This linguistic realism is the flip side of what earlier I identified as abject Proustianism. Through French, through the words associated with objects and events tied to his farm years, Federman takes us and himself back there, even though language hurts and the whole experience is painful, "emmerdante."

The Voice and the Name

Federman's real "buddy" and "être de papier" in *Aunt Rachel's Fur*, Peter Wortsman is a "man of [his] word" and "man of words" at once.[81] Both real and fictitious, the friend is a "multilinguist" and by the same token Federman's "ethical double." For, in keeping his word, Wortsman/Federman hardly keeps *to* words and wordings of accredited repertoires and styles. A "man of honor" honors the plurality of the logos. A "man of his word" is not a man of one word but of many. He steps over linguistic-textual boundaries to shake up oral and written language, to mix it up and into aggregates, patterns, and solecisms friendlier to new ideas and speakers, thus rendering the national standards and canons more accommodating to alternatives, to the nation's native and nonnative others. These proce-dures are a matter of linguistics as well as ethics because they lay bare a certain "vocation" of trading in words, and this matter is explicitly named in the name itself, in "Wort(s)-man" no less than in "Feder-man." Both are German-Jewish surnames, with the latter renaming—translating, con-verting, or "lingo-verting"—the former. Notably, as the narrator of *Return to Manure* reveals, his own artistic calling is "inscribed in our [family] name."[82] *Feder* means "feather" and by extension "pen" in German. A painter whose craft was also written into his name, Federman's f(e)ather thus "transmitted his dream and artistic vocation into my body, into my skin, my flesh, my bones. Into my head."[83] "Federman," *der Mann der Feder*[84] or "*l'homme de plume*,"[85] "penman," "anticipated," Raymond him-self acknowledges elsewhere, his "vocation,"[86] designating penmanship as part and parcel of the name bearer's "patrimonial" calling.

A "polylingual pun,"[87] *Federman* is also more than an onomastic joke or nom de plume—the author's name has a *plume* in it, but the Feder/feather is his father('s), names him (it). Thus, *Federman* is not a pseudonym but a patronym. However, the name is not just an etymologi-cal gloss on the *pater*/patron. True, the name and with it the "calling" (vo-cation) of the son name the father's name and skills, and so the names and the named blotted out by history come to us. Yet they are recalled in keep-ing with the lingovert's calling itself, that is, across other names, words, and voices. For spelled out in the father's name is a lineage, a line of blood and culture running deep into the past, but also the essence of Federman's "penmanship": "polylingual" techniques, "double-" and multi-talk, rau-cously subversive plurivocality, crisscrossing texts and traditions. Feder-man's patrimony as an artist and as his father's son connects then back to patronymy while linking up patronymy itself—the family name and things familiar—horizontally to the names, labels, rubrics, and categories of life outside it.

In Federman, Lee, and other cosmoderns, vocalizations of voice (*phōnē*) bring out a linguistically and culturally stratified phonology, an echo-logy. Hospitable con-vocation of other voices in the echo chamber of voice, this echo-logy is also an ecology. Structurally and ethically au-thentic in the cosmodern sense, voice convokes, bears with-ness. And so does the name. Just as voice is simultaneously unique and a *portavoce*, a mouthpiece of others' voices, a name names the self and his or her her-itage as it names others, in fact—and this is typical of cosmodernism—employs those others' names to call the self and tell his or her story. As with voice and the linguistic imaginary recording its chromatic riffs in cosmodernism, others and their names are not "in the way" to authentic expression and self-identification; they *are* the way. Quite telling ("vocal") in this regard, "Wortsman"/"Federman," the friend's/father's name, is an onomastic knot of sorts into which other names and stories are tied and via which Raymond reaches out to a whole catalog of things, people, places, and their names—Jewish, French, German, English, Southeast European, and more. The father made Raymond a Federman and a federman. In the family name, he passed on to the son a Babel of names and voices, the talent to listen for them, and with it the ability to develop his "own voice." Raymond comes into his own, completes his individuation as a person and writer, and becomes famous ("makes a name for himself") in the other's name, as it were. This name comes from the other not only because it belonged to the father, as Lacanians would stress, but also because it comes from others in a vaster, cultural sense.[88] Cosmodernism's onomastic imaginary, to which I move on now, pivots precisely on this mutual "nomination"—designation and identification—of self and other in the act of naming.

PART 2 ⊕ ONOMASTICS

Our names contain our fates.
— SALMAN RUSHDIE, *Midnight's Children*

[Responsibility] is always exercised in my name *as* the name of the other.
— JACQUES DERRIDA, *On the Name*

1. The Names of the World

Heritage, Contingence, Cosmonomastics

There are then, roughly, two ways of thinking about patronymy, patrimony, and more broadly about the names, denominations, and values that make up tradition—two ways, you might say, to conceptualize America and its identity. In the introduction, I labeled them the root and the route models and argued that the latter gets a boost in the post–Cold War years. This is, in essence, what Amin Maalouf points out in his discussion of heritage. "Each of us," he writes, "has two heritages, a 'vertical' one that comes to us from our ancestors, our religious community and our popular traditions, and a 'horizontal' one transmitted to us by our contemporaries and by the age we live in." The "horizontal" heritage of the present world is, the Lebanese novelist goes on, "more influential" and "becomes more so every day." But, he adds, "this fact is not reflected in our perception of ourselves, and the inheritance we invoke most frequently is the vertical one."[1]

Cosmodernism is changing all this. Consider Alda's "Americanist" revelations in China or, parallel to Lee's Whitmanesque apprenticeship, Lelia's relearning English from her students: these are testimonies to an adjustment of identity perception to the "thickening" of the cloth from which "being" is worldwide "woven . . . as a result of cultural globalization."[2] I have called these scenes relational, but I might as well have called them "horizontal," for they are mise-en-scènes of the *lateral ancestry* that is playing an ever more decisive part in who we are and in how we see ourselves nowadays. Factoring this component into the formula of being, cosmodern self-awareness is thus closing "the gulf" not only "between what we are and what we think we are"[3] but also that between the two kinds of heritage. Precisely because cultural "threads" that have not touched or crossed each other before now do so in places, under circumstances, and at angles unexpected, the cosmoderns do not see the two heritages as separate or divergent, which is why they need not uproot themselves in order to take up "exogenous," "lateral" affiliations. As I also underscored in the introduction, some roots can grow sideways. Vice versa, horizontal routes of culture can run aslant, downward or upward, and so intersect other cultural horizons, lines, and alignments and fertilize them, set themselves up as their *Urphänomena* of sorts while being in turn cross-pollinated by them. To restate one of *Cosmodernism*'s central contentions: those "other" tracks, flows, and ways do not stand in our way; they provide the way. The route *is* the root; the longer way home is the safest.

Cultural identity comes about via this detour. Its anthropological uniqueness—that which makes it "ours"—*supervenes* in the strong sense of the word, the cosmoderns insist. It "comes after," characteristically ensuing from a "wayward" narrative of oblique addition, filtering, and refracting. What makes it authentic is a transcultural chain of deviations, divagations, and interpolations. A *dérive* in space and meaning bearing out late globalization's emblematic relationality, this route is a routine of derivation that splices together diachronic ("vertical") filiation and synchronic affiliation or rather maps the former onto the latter, a displacement somewhat analogous to Jakobson's definition of the poetic function as a "project[ion of] the principle of equivalence from the axis of selection into the axis of combination. Equivalence," the critic specifies, is "promoted to the constitutive device of the sequence."[4] In our terms, the self's historical transcendence, his or her ties with a past and its patrimonial paradigm, vertically, this self now projects horizontally onto the planetary sequence of cultures to the point that worldly contingence—self and other's juxtaposition in the world—assumes some of the grounding roles hitherto performed within presumably discrete paradigms primarily by the patrimonial metaphors of root and depth. Contingence becomes heritage as en-routeness takes on the attributes of enrootedness. Still, the self is no less authentic for that. It is just that the coordinates of authenticity are changing. Patrimony remains key, but its geometry is altered by the cosmodern self's ability to retrofit affiliation with others as filiation, to assign horizontal appositions the traditionally rooting function of verticality, and conversely, to bring those others' filiations and histories into the present and root itself in that multidimensional temporality.

Patrimony, Patronymy, Heteronomy

> A bricolage kind of identity: this is what plays out in a name.
> —RADU TURCANU, "L'identité selon le 'id,'" *La Revue de psychanalyse du Champ lacanien*

Reflecting the shift in how we understand patrimony and the "vertical" attributes it bestows on identity—"historical," "rooted," hence "authentic"—cosmodern patronymy and cosmodern proper names generally delink, as Alain Finkielkraut would say, ancestral territory—the places where we are identified by our ancestors' names as we receive or adopt these names—and patronymy. It is not so much that "evil comes to the world through fatherlands and patronyms" and "the dead" are "taking hold of the living" by proclaiming "the dictatorship of family names over first names";[5] the point is not that traditional names are not markers of agency, that they rarely express our choices onomastically and otherwise, but that names' birthplaces and our own need not coincide, and yet names can still be authentic, "ground" our being. Simply put, cosmodern names—names of "others," from other places, cultures, and onomastic repertoires—identify us as any name would, but, more than other names, they identify us *as* an other. Better put: they do not equate us with those others whose names we bear; they only reveal us to the world by revealing our ties to others. Cosmodern names thus denote not only an expansion of the patronymic but also of the patrimonial across the boundary of our community, making it possible to think of those others (the name givers) in terms comparable if not synonymous to kin and inheritance and of ourselves (the named) as authentic, legitimately identified by "other" names. "Historically," Julia Watson observes in her discussion of "heteroglossic naming," critics have "read the name not as a sign of process or migration but as a guarantor of authenticity, of irreducible singleness and authority."[6] Cosmodern onomastics, or cosmonomastics, extends the realm of authentic naming along the lines of cosmodern authenticity into *heteronomy*, the "names of others," culled on the go, in motion, from "alternative" inventories and texts, from unwonted or faraway stories and histories quite irreducible to the authority to which the named and their lives may be otherwise subject.

A point worth making—but surely not overstating—in this context is that traditional patronyms attest to culture's "dream of autarchy."[7] Arguably, they seal a place's or a heritage's sway over us. Not only do they assign us a serial identity, but they are usually also "passed on" to us within a tradition and thus tend to lock us in it to the extent that, as we are given those names, we are also given over to a lineage, to an ancestry, to a community and its memory, and all we can be must be and is presumed to take place inside that place, in the *patria's* patronymic territory. In the following, names refute this autarchy. The stories they tell are parables of cross-cultural engagement. In them, the name, the proper name more exactly, is not just an identity denominator coming after this identity solely in order to tag it. The name is part and parcel of identity formation. Furthermore, naming frames that identity itself—and by extension the culture it "belongs" to—in terms of formative connection with an other not from here-and-now or not like "us" and "our" people. The lead character in these stories, the cosmodern name has singularly de-finitional force; it de-fines the name bearer most profoundly, that is, links him or her to "others" across the confines of the culture so as to bring into the open the signification of his or her being. If the name is, to recall DeLillo's *Ratner's Star,* not just a "badge" I happen to carry, a free-floating signifier, but over time becomes one with whom it names, then it also designates the instituting relatedness undergirding the named self. For, Brecht writes in *Mann ist Mann,* "When you name yourself, you always name another."[8] If our names are "substitutes," associations awaiting interpretation, as Freud famously said, then, the cosmoderns posit, what names associate is self and other into denominative, cultural, and existential configurations spilling over the confines of the serial, the repetitive, and the selfsame.[9]

However, we seldom name ourselves. Whether we like it or not, naming does constitute one of those ties "imposed on us," and as such it references communitarian and familial authority, cognominal and otherwise, the whole cultural and jurisdictional "topology" Finkielkraut's globetrotting hero is poised to leave behind by severing those ties and "choosing" his "relationships freely."[10] The philosopher's irony is well aimed; this freedom is theoretical: we are usually born into a system of "ties" within our culture linguistically, onomastically, and so on. The "system" predates us, and there is little we can do about its vocabulary, classification principles, rubrics, or denominations. As names are bestowed on us, as they provide condensed descriptions of identity, they tend to limit what we are or are perceived as. But not all names ascribe strict descriptive limits to our being—not all onomastics need be "topological" or "toponymic," reminding us and the world that we are "from" place X and "belong" there. The cosmoderns would in fact acknowledge, as they do in what follows, that names bequeathed on us "within" can also inscribe us into the wider world. In the cultural other's name, in the name of somebody from a different topology, we overflow our initial toponymy. We do not necessarily "break out" of it nor write it off. But we link the realm of birthplace with new places on earth, where the earth is no longer only the ground from which the dead keep an eye on us, but a vaster ecumene. We will see immediately, this relation and celebration of identity itself can obtain onomastically, in a particular culture and tradition yet against cloistral or sectarian constraints as "people . . . give their child a name from any place on earth."[11] As I am given an other's surname or forename, my self is set up and advertised socially, within and without "my" culture, in the other's name, and so a new relation forms outside and across kind, blood, and place, with this other my new relative, for it is in relation to him or her that I am being "identified" and called up in the world's interlocutory arena.

As Charles Taylor stresses in *Sources of the Self,* "the close connection between identity and interlocution also emerges in the place of *names* in human life. My name is what I am 'called.' A human being *has* to have a name, because he or she has to be *called,* i.e., addressed. Being called into conversation is a precondition of developing a human identity, and so my name is (usually) given me by my earliest interlocutors."[12] This is the general case. Below, we notice something more intriguing: the twofold interlocution of naming where appellation entails interpellation as a linguistic and cultural or, more accurately, intercultural act. As the narratives of names examined here suggest, I am not only addressed and thereby acknowledged as a "human being," but nested in the calling itself lies another one, a broader conversation with or calling out to an other whose name those calling on me must use. My humanness is projected through this dialogue with an other, with whom those talking to me talk and whom they name as they speak to me. And there is no other way, for I bear his or her name; I am *named-with.* So this other, my not-here "namesake," indirectly participates in this dialogue, and, notably, it is through the larger, cultural dialogism associated with this presence that my own persona is socially recognized, here and now. In a very fundamental way, then, the name of the other, as Levinas propounds in *Proper Names,* helps us speak to one another no matter where we are, including within the topological horizon of this here and now, insofar as the most trivial chitchat turns on our ability to identify, to name our interlocutor.[13] A decisive mediation of the dialogue must and does arise as a sine qua non of the dialogue itself, and in this view we would do well to remember that the Greek *dialogos* (from *dialego*, "to converse") does not refer to "two" (cf. Gk. *duo*) but to *dia*, "across" or "through," and *legein*, "to speak." Which is to say, I manage to get across, to speak to you, via an other—again, in his or her name. Originally his or hers, my name, much like my overall language, testifies to this very locutory indebtedness, to the fact that I am— for I am "identified"—in and through his or her name. Beauvoir talks about "alienation" in our *own* names, about how all names are ultimately *allonyms* and as such hurt the named; on the contrary, the cosmoderns figure "alien" names as onomastic sites where we "catch up" with ourselves, with who we are or dream of being.[14]

We often establish ourselves, step on the social stage in an act of deceptive autonomy. We "make a name" for ourselves, and that self-making, that personality poiesis, points toward us, the putative source of the name, of the well-known noun. Yet "when a name" truly "comes," Derrida meditates in *On the Name*, "it immediately says more than the name: the other of the name and quite simply the other, whose irruption the name announces."[15] The other arrives in his or her name first, in "my" name, that is. A dispatcher of otherness, my name is a sign for something or somebody not yet fully present, a deferral of presence and a cultural *approximation* thereof simultaneously, for while standing in for the other, his or her name—now mine—also draws me closer, into the heat of a proximity that is numinous, profusely enriching, not just nominal. He or she is not here, but his or her name already teaches me about that presence not present. The name tells a story that makes up for an absence while in its turn that story calls forth and restores other presences by retelling, re-storying their stories and re-naming their names.

This onomastic intertextuality operates within particular traditions[16] and still more forcefully these days across them, thus making up for an important vehicle of cosmodernism. The other's name is not solely a repository of otherness. In saying or listening to it, in "reading" and "bearing" it, I learn not just things about others, their traditions, and communities. "In the other's name" I also learn things about myself and those surrounding me. This is how the cosmoderns learn more and more that the other's name, like his or her language, story, and culture generally, concerns them deeply, names them, summons them up. The other's name calls up his or her own being, and in that it does remain a signifier of otherness, of what continues to be different from me. At the same time, I feel that it is this very difference that carves me out, takes part in the construction of my own presence and endorses my bonds with others of my kind. The "moorings" of my being, the "roots" of my self no less than my self's ties into other selves this side of the cultural divide are not "original," *ab quo* phenomena but, as I contend throughout, offshoots of an affinity with others across the divide, with that which I am not but which is nonetheless woven into what I am.

In the cosmodern imaginary, the name is a marker of this affinity. Names concurrently enact and signify this constituting closeness over natural or native gaps and frontiers, a shared liminal space where other and self still preserve their distinct profiles while drawing nigh and "bordering on" each other, revealing each other's compatibilities, swapping representations and codes, talking to each other and borrowing each other's talk. This is a distinctive affinity in that it does not jeopardize the distinctiveness of self and other. The name builds a bridge to the other('s) side, which the other crosses not to assimilate me but to help me get a purchase on myself. The name brings the other so close, and he or she gets so intimately involved in the algorithms of my being that he or she becomes my namesake. Thus, I bear his or her name, yet we are not the same. *Our* name designates a homology, not an identity, and so we do not get identical. My name names others while it whispers my own name and my own kind's, and therefore my nominal bond with the other, what we share "in our name," does not sap my local ties and allegiances. Quite the opposite, it enables and strengthens them. My namesake lends me a language in which such issues can be best couched and thought through.

2. Namesakes

Global Gogol: Jhumpa Lahiri's *The Namesake*

> ... a sense of himself reconstituted in another ...
> —JHUMPA LAHIRI, *Unaccustomed Earth*

Following in a cosmodern line that runs through recent works by Rushdie, Mukherjee, Lee, Coetzee, Peter Carey, Hanif Kureishi, and Arundhati Roy among many others, Lahiri's 2003 novel *The Namesake* is a case in point.[17] A Bengali-American saga chronicling the Ganguli family's resettlement in

North America, shuttling back and forth between worlds, cultures, and people simultaneously wounded and nurtured by dislocation and relocation, the book revolves around the foundational name of the other and thus recalls Willa Cather's 1907 story "The Namesake," another fable of Americanization, cultural-onomastic kinship, and reading.[18] Also as in Cather, the other's name provides a fertile if not completely stable ground for family bonding and continuity during unsettling times. It would be inexact, though, to view this name and, along with it, the other's nominal presence, as an adulteration of an original, unalloyed makeup. This presence is there from day one, not to disrupt the collective presence, the sustaining co-presence the Gangulis extend to each other, but to bolster it, to give it meaning; not to interrupt family rites, to break up traditions of intimacy but to break ground for them and help them survive the tests of displacement, diasporic readjustment, and acculturation.

What Dostoyevsky said about Gogol—"We all came out of Gogol's overcoat"—also applies to the Gangulis (*The Namesake*, 78). Ashoke, the father, quotes Dostoyevsky to his son to comment not on what Russian writers owe to Nikolai Gogol but on what the Gangulis do. He is not implying that his family has Russian origins either. Or, if you will, the implication is that origin, tradition, and ancestry more largely should be reframed, reoriented away from the localist-nativist paradigm of blood, place, and sedentary roots, and tied more closely into a culturalist, indeed cross-culturalist one, which grants others unprecedented, *originating* centrality. Thus it can be argued that the Gangulis "came out of"—were "fathered" by—Gogol. Concomitantly, Gogol is not an "original" tradition but a *tradition adopted,* and *adopted father.* For Gogol, too, had been "taken in" by the Bengalis a long time ago. A devotee of classical Russian literature, Ashoke's grandfather had urged his nephew to "read all the Russians, and then reread them." "They will never fail you," he assured him (12), and Gogol proved him right one October day in 1961 when "The Overcoat" saved his life: Ashoke was reading Akaky Akakyevich's story when the train he was riding derailed, and it was a page of the Gogol text he was clutching in his hand that caught the eye of the rescuing crew who pulled him from the wreckage. Gogol authored then, one might say, his text as well as its reader or readers, rather, an entire line of fathers and grandfathers related to each other not just by blood but also by their passion for Gogol's work. They passed this passion on from grandfather to nephew and from nephew to his son, forming a Gogolian chain of readerly devotion that comes to define the Gangulis, "explain" them to each other, and bring them together under the auspices of an other's word and name. They bond as they introduce and read Gogol to each other, and the numerous Gogolian scenes strewn throughout the novel cobble together a whole patrilineal tradition inching steadily along, generation after generation and reading after reading, "in the margins" of another's stories. No doubt, the Ganguli family is certainly more that a gloss to Gogol, just as tradition, theirs included, goes beyond reading, let alone reading only the Russian realist. But Gogol becomes something of a rite of passage no less than a way of passing the torch, so much so that his presence in the family cannot be separated from the family history. In fact, he shapes the latter, makes it by making himself part of it, part of the Ganguli heritage. Gogol writes himself into the family story, into their patrimony, while they insert themselves into his world, "immers[e] in the sartorial plight of Akaky Akakyevich" (17), see themselves in a Gogolian, strange yet "oddly inspiring" (14) light.

This cosmodern interface of the patrilineal, the patrimonial, and the patronymic is truly arresting. On the one hand, as I have proposed and as Ashoke himself implies, Gogol authors, "makes" his Bengali fans, a readership lineage inside the Ganguli family, and by the same token molds the family narrative. On the other hand, the Bengalis appropriate him, include the unfamiliar and unfamilial other in the family patrimony as somebody whom they make theirs and then make over to those coming after them. Thus they establish and transfer a legacy as much as they pass Gogol's name along as, and in, their own. Grandfathers, then fathers, hand the other's text down, and sons and nephews come of age as they come into this inheritance of otherness, once they are finally able to read—and read themselves into, see themselves through—the Russian's work. So Gogol comes both before and in the aftermath of this genealogy of passionate readers, concomitantly from the outside and inside, makes, and is made by, his Bengali aficionados. In a way, he is already there, awaiting only to be "introduced" to the young; in another, he cannot but come after the young have "assumed" him and, in so doing, have crossed into adulthood while awakening into a new sense of duty and belonging. The Gangulis' sense of identity springs from their relation to the only one among them who is *not* one of them, from a relation of a different kind because not grounded in kind, in a commonality of ethnicity and blood, but in commerce with Gogol. Some of most defining in-group protocols—individual self-identification, other selves' recognition in the family, or the preservation of family customs across generations and continents—play out under the other's name, through and in "Gogol," with such an intensity that that other so crucial to these psycho-cultural rites cannot *not* be Gogol, cannot bear another name. And neither can the Gangulis.

The novel conveys this inevitability from the outset. To be sure, this is a symbolic beginning—and the "right call." As with *Native Speaker,* the beginning lies elsewhere, in an other's voice. To get started, Lahiri calls out to the unlikely ancestor, Gogol. And, like Lee's Whitman, Gogol answers with an excerpt from his work, a sentence from "The Overcoat," which Lahiri uses as an epigraph where she sets off her book's tenor. "The reader," Gogol says in this fragment, "should realize himself that it could not have happened otherwise, and that to give him any other name was quite out of the question." The passage alludes to "The Overcoat"'s protagonist but also to *The Namesake*'s, Ashoke's son, Gogol. Ashoke gives his first American-born child the name of his favorite author, and this is how the Russian writer becomes the namesake of Ashoke's son. Naturally, this occurs after Ashoke takes up Gogol and decides to name his son after him. But we also know that Gogol has been part of the family already, and family members have been close to each other "in his name" before this presence manifests itself in the name given to Ashoke's first born. Moreover, this patrilineal passion for the other's text that brings him into the family and institutes him as patrimony has a patronymic flip-side suggesting that Gogol has been a Ganguli, already there in *their* name, before they "adopted" him. In Calcutta, Ashoke's son is amazed to discover whole pages of Gangulis in the local phone book and remembers that his father had told him that "Ganguli is a legacy of the British," an "anglicized way of pronouncing his real surname, Gangopadhyay" (67).

Paronomasia; or, Embracing the World

Ganguli is a colonial anagram, a British disfiguration of the original name and injustice done to the name and its bearer. Resulting from this egological abuse of the name is, however, a revealing paronomasia. The Greek *paronomazein* means to name, call, or designate someone or something by using a slightly altered name. What happens to the initial Bengali patronym is an onomastic metonymy for the larger process of colonial cooptation, metamorphosis, and survival, through which the entire Bengali culture went under the British. Mangled and rendered "official" in the "anglicized" form, Ganguli still recalls its origin—notably enough, the name calls up origin itself, Ganga, the river goddess, and with it the land (Bengali, or Bangla) it gave life to. But the name's colonial disfiguration figures, *projects* (throws forward, shoots up) *another* root, another origin altogether. Like *Akaky* and *Ashoke, Ganguli* and *Gogol* are so close euphonically (if not culturally) that the Russian name can be said to figure into the Bengali already as a symbolic if not actual etymon. Misappropriated by the British as *Ganguli,* the Gangulis reappropriate themselves as they take possession of that which their name intimates that they have a right to: Gogol. Giving his American-born son the latter's name, Ashoke sanctions this heteronomous narrative of naming, misnaming, and renaming, acknowledging the apocryphal etymology of the patronym, reinscribing the Russian name "officially" into the Ganguli so as to hint that the writer's name has been there along.

In Gogol's name, tradition and innovation, inside and outside, self and other, bloodlines and text lines feed into and off each other. By custom, Gogol's grandparents were charged with picking a first name for him, but the Calcutta letter carrying their name choice never made it to Boston, so Ashoke gave his son the provisional "pet name" of Gogol himself. An unofficial appellative and signifier of intimacy, privacy, and care simultaneously, this *daknam* (25) is used by family and close friends and only later "paired" with a "good name," a *bhalonam* fit for official bureaucracy (26). A reminder of an earlier, less formal world of childhood, pet names are often "meaningless, deliberately silly, ironic, even onomatopoetic" (26). Not so Gogol's: the pet name already *means* something. "Temporary" as it may be, it has long been marking, textually and onomastically, that other's presence in the heart of the Bengali family, for Gogol is the name of what they have been reading, the name of the other and concurrently theirs— what they could read into their own. Gogol is the nickname, the cognominal surrogate, the "other name" and the other's name all in one. But it also designates a long-standing, defining, hence identifying knot of traditions in the family: the Ganga/Bangla/Ganguli onomastic complex, which Gogol recalls, on one side; on the other side, the preoccupation encapsulated in the other's proper name. For this reason, Gogol is the name proper, a true name, and indeed, in the Russian writer's words, "to give [Gogol] any other name was quite out of the question." Which is to say, to identify him other than by a cultural recall of the other's stories and names was impossible.

Nor does onomastic identification stop here. The pet name is soon followed, possibly superseded by the "good name." Yet in Gogol's case, the pet name's "other" is not another name but the other's "other name" and possibly an even more appropriate name since what is at issue here is not the family name, the *Ganguli* in which the Russian author's lives on, but the first name. And the new first name is even closer to Gogol than Gogol itself not only because it is the Bengali version of Nikolai Gogol's given name but because it is simultaneously Russian and Bengali. The name, "Nikhil, is artfully connected to the old. Not only is it a perfectly respectable Bengali good name, meaning 'he who is entire encompassing all,' but it also bears a satisfying resemblance to Nikolai, the first name of the Russian Gogol. Ashoke had thought of it recently, staring mindlessly at the Gogol spines in the library, and he had rushed back to the house to ask Ashima her opinion. He pointed out that it was relatively easy to pronounce, though there was the danger that Americans, obsessed with abbreviation, would truncate it to Nick" (56).

Uncovering the name's age and cultural texture, the double-barreled etymology of the new name is quite striking. But the name does not signify just the Russian-Bengali co-presence and survival in that which, on American soil, might become "Nick." At play in Nikhil is a whole cosmodernism of appellation, for the name names, *in Bengali,* Nikhil's native language—the language of family and heritage—a "horizontal" transcendence that embraces all and derives a sense of wholeness from its propinquity of "en-compassing" everything and everybody. The name takes Bengali tradition with it as it takes the whole (world) in, because, once again, *in the other's name,* on which his father decided while staring at Gogol's books in a Boston library, Nikhil connects back to his Bengali parents, to who they are and what they mean to him—what they name— *in their own names: Ashoke,* we find out, signifies "he who transcends grief," and *Ashima,* his mother's name, "she who is limitless, without borders" (26), and so here, on the *other* onomastic ground, the patrilineal and the matrilineal finally meet to correct an older imbalance, and all family roots are acknowledged, nourished, and push deeper. They will continue to do so for Nikhil's sister, Sonia, another cosmodern name. "Though Sonali is," Lahiri writes, "the name on her birth certificate, the name she will carry officially through life, at home they begin to call her Sonu, then Sona, and finally Sonia. Sonia makes her a citizen of the world. It's a Russian link to her brother, it's European, South American. Eventually it will be the name of the Indian prime minister's Italian wife" (62). *Sonali,* "she who is golden," according to her Bengali "good name," implies perfection, roundness, all-encircling and all-embracing propensity. Thus the name re-relates her, so to speak, to her family's first names and to her family more broadly, in particular to her brother as the good name spins off the pet name and, further, as the more culturally idiomatic pet name evolves into something that it has harbored all along, Sonia.

What the name stands for in the small and wide world; the name as a cultural allegory of the name bearer's standing in both; the name as a matter of destiny and individual agency; the name's pre-scription in Gogol's writings and names but also in the grandmother's letter, with which the initial good name got lost; and, at last, the name as choice, as voluntary and individualistic inscription—all these reveal themselves fully later in life as Ashoke's children come to understand and honor their names. At first, Gogol is unhappy with *Nikhil*. Although he will have *Gogol* changed to *Nikhil* legally later, he doubts *Nikhil* means anything "in Indian," and finds it "ludicrous, lacking dignity or gravity" (76). He does not understand Ashoke when his father says that he "feel[s] a special kinship with" the writer (77). The "kinship" with the other, one more time redefined culturally outside the blood line, does not mean much to Gogol when Ashoke gives him a book by the Russian as a birthday present. Like Ashima, who becomes "true to the meaning of her name, . . . without borders, a resident everywhere and nowhere" (276) only after her husband's untimely passing, Gogol/Nikhil overcomes his onomastic "burden" in his father's absence, realizing that the Gogolian text is not an embarrassment but a vital opportunity. For many years, he refused to read Gogol and never bothered to open *The Short Stories of Nikolai Gogol* received years back. Now, at *The Namesake*'s end, he is ready to immerse himself into the other's word.

Commenting on Gogol, Levinas points out that, extraordinary as the event described in "The Nose" may be, it does not "upset" the course of things. "Posit[ing] itself in itself," the "uncanny" occurrence does not wreak havoc in a world that goes on without learning much from Major Kovaleff's ordeal. "Great poet of the surreal," Gogol surveys a landscape of "solid-being," self-sustaining objects. [19] In it, a "scandal" is ontologically unlikely because these objects—people, things, habits, culture largely speaking—appear to need nothing else except themselves to account for what they are. In fact, to provide this account, they exclude other people, things, and accounts, other views and explanations of life. But precisely because such foolproof ontology rules authoritatively, its very dominion becomes an ethical problem, and if Gogol's universe does not scandalize ("stumble") ontologically, it does so ethically. The distinct, the atypical, the singular, the sui generis have survened, yet Russian society has managed to suck them into its routine. This is one of "The Nose"'s implications, and the word is apt, for, Levinas notes, this remains no more than an undeveloped suggestion. It seems to me, though, that in taking up Gogol, Lahiri builds on this suggestion, extending it to Gogol's entire oeuvre and ultimately to the writer himself. In her work, Gogol becomes what "The Nose" never quite did for its initial audience: an occasion for the self to look at itself in the mirror of the other.

3. "Through a filter of associations and links": The Name of Homeyness

A Gesture Life and the Onomastic Contest

In Lee, this cultural autoscopy is coextensive with the work itself. It starts off, as we saw earlier, with *Native Speaker* and continues with *A Gesture Life*.[20] Tracing the discourse of "accommodating" Americanness past Whitman to Benjamin Franklin, the 1999 novel reinforces intertextual affiliation in Franklin's name, onomastically but also ideologically, that is, in the name and life story of Franklin Hata, *A Gesture Life's* narrating protagonist. If the first book's genealogy of nativism dwells on the Whitmanesque euphoria of the multitudinous self, the second cuts deeper, to this self's liberal-individualist, self-reliant premise to ask how instrumental this Franklinesque concept is to a narrative of Americanization that spans the better half of the twentieth century and must come to grips with its traumatic memory.

It is this assumption that Franklin Hata mulls over early in the novel. "Being alone," he ruminates, "is the last thing I would wish for now . . . I've known myself best as a solitary person, and although I've been able to enjoy the company of others, I've seen myself most clearly when I'm off on my own, without others in the mix" (68). "This may seem," he goes on, "an obvious mode for most, but I think a surprising number of people prefer to imagine themselves through a filter of associations and links. . . . There is nothing inherently wrong with this. Indeed, there was a time when I held my own associations quite close to who I was, in the years leading up to and during the Pacific war, when in the course of events one naturally accepted the wartime culture of shared sacrifice and military codes of conduct. But then I eventually relinquished those ties for the relative freedom of everyday, civilian life, and then finally decided to leave Japan altogether, for the relative—though very different—liberties of America." In the United States, Franklin completes his confession, "You sadly find that the most available freedom is to live alone. There is an alarming surplus of the right" (68).

Living alone, picturing oneself as a "discrete" entity of the polity, is, Franklin realizes, a principle, if not *the* principle of American *communality*, of nationhood and communities "in my town and every town" (68). This is a custom whose contradictions his immigrant life has been struggling to work out, the double-bind of his self-refounding project. This is a project he "gestures" at, or names, in his own name by giving himself Benjamin Franklin's name—the name of a Founding Father, a founder of the nation as well as of a dominant if admittedly contradictory modality of the national self, coagulated around the cardinal "gestures" and discourses of autonomy, independence, initiative, self-proving isolation and trials, thrift, and discipline. From Franklin's own *Autobiography* to Lee's Franklin, passing through the defining moments marked by transcendentalism, Whitman, Horatio Alger's *Ragged Dick,* Jack London, Mary Antin, Carl Sandburg, Hemingway, F. Scott Fitzgerald, all the way to postmoderns like Robert Coover and Eva Hoffman, these social calisthenics and discourses have spun a "Grand American Narrative" of sorts.[21] While earlier authors tended to contribute new chapters to the Franklinesque tale of national selfhood and thus further legitimate it, more recent writers query it. Especially after *The Great Gatsby,* which at once buys into the self-reliant paradigm and disputes it, artists and thinkers respond more and more ambivalently to this narrative. Playing into Franklin Hata's musings, the ambivalence is behind the ironic fate, the "gesture" his life has come to embody following his emigration to the land of reputedly unfettered remaking. This irony is enacted in the hero's name itself, more precisely, in what, it turns out, Benjamin Franklin's name did *not* harbinger in his namesake's: a triumphantly autonomous self-invention story woven in an American present unencumbered by either personal or collective histories.[22]

This overhaul of the self fails or meets with limited success for reasons that have to do with the affiliated status of identity and, derived from this status, with the intertextual, cross-narrative makeup of such histories. Undoubtedly, like the new story it sets out to write for itself in America, the self does not form in a vacuum. Neither starts with a clean slate, for neither can be its own origin. To the contrary: both obtain by brushing up against others and their own selves and stories, past or present. Reinvention is not transcendent but contingent, much though it fancies itself free-floating, self-origination, independent of those others no less than of the self's own prehistory, in this case, Hata's "pre-Franklin" life as Jiro Kurohata—worth mentioning here is that his former first name, Jiro, means "second son" in Japanese (in a way, this is what he is to his Japanese foster parents), while, we shall note later, *Kurohata* anticipates Franklin Hata's business.[23] Nevertheless, under an other's name and in the name of the creed that name is popular for—the American philosophy of *un*affiliated, individualistic self-fashioning—Jiro strives to become an other. His dream is not to be an other like Franklin or other Americans literally; he wants to be an other with respect to whom he was in the stories he scrambles to forget as he is spinning his American story.

Yet as soon as he associates himself symbolically with an other—as soon as he gives himself Franklin's name—he plunges into a world of political and textual associations; he *affiliates* himself. He cannot write his new life script, and thus rewrite himself into a novel self other than in an other's name, and this rewriting is culturally binding, ties him into another world, history, and narratives. No matter how he pictures Benjamin Franklin and Benjamin Franklin's America—no matter how Franklin Hata reads the namesake's name—a relation has been set up, and it undercuts the other, unrelated relation or story the self means to produce for himself. "Others" cannot but be "in the mix" (68), and they make this personal epic and the narrative-cultural re- and self-invention it tells of "relative" in a number of ways. Hata both "relates" his story and acknowledges its "relativity." He narrates his relation and implicitly relates its narrator, the "self-begotten" Hata, to others. It does not matter these are not blood relatives, for they can be, and Benjamin Franklin surely is, a source of empowering language about what we are or about how free we could be. By the same token, the American saga Hata composes and lives out is constructed narratively and existentially (is made "relative" to) by the Franklinesque relation (discourse) of "freedom," the "individual," "community," and "duty," and their imprint on American history. Far from inhering in "being alone," in the self-sustaining solitude where the self-writing self gives itself a "second chance," self-revamping does presuppose a "filter of associations and links." It is a necessarily communal project. It trades on Hata's relation to what he has been no less than to those with whom he is now without being like them culturally, ethnically, and racially. This undertaking turns, in brief, on relatedness, which enhances rather than "relinquishes" the self's "ties" and "links" (68), past or present, with those "close" or "remote" to him. Unlike Benjamin Franklin's America Jiro Kurohata had dreamed of, true America is not a connection-free, narratively "untainted" Eden, but a *relative*, narratively and ideologically charged structure. Therefore, in this America, he attempts the existentially, culturally, and narratologically impossible.

His failure is no less instructive for that. Franklin Hata may have failed, but the author manages to uncover the underpinnings of his character's defeat, of the onomastically symbolic contest in which "Jiro" ultimately wins over "Franklin." That is why this victory is not absolute and a cosmodern message emerges, tactfully formulated by Lee. This lesson, this ethical gesticulation points to a kind of complexly "relative," binding, cultural-ideological, and narrative contract that Jiro enters as soon as he calls himself Franklin. This compact is not visible, or it is not visible to Jiro-as-Franklin right away. But Lee makes it legible to us, reads it between the lines of his hero's story. This is how the story, a monologue in more than one way, becomes dialogical, engages with itself critically by revealing its cultural, political, and textual ramifications.

The layered ambivalence of relatedness, to begin with, is part of this unwritten agreement. In all fairness, the lengthy passage reproduced previously suggests that Franklin Hata is not totally unaware of this stipulation. He senses that America's liberties, first and foremost the freedom of self-making and remaking, are relative. There is only so much one can do, or redo, remake, rather, for one never starts from scratch. The fabled clean slate bears the scratches and marks of otherness. The self's "autonomous" reconstruction, advertised in Franklinesque terms as it may be, is actually a cosmodern enterprise, occurs via "associations quite close to [who]" and where Franklin Hata no longer is. Autonomy is hardly the rule of the self-making game: the "alarming surplus of the right" renders the right suspect, hence deficient, unreliable, and ultimately, if paradoxically, in short supply.

The mythology of stand-alone selfhood notwithstanding, Franklin Hata associates and relates "routinely" by routes and routines not of his own making across narratives, symbols, and voices that speak for him in the cultural silence in which he has not been heard yet. Voiceless and faceless, he too is "figured out" before his face pops up in the national "mix." If his cosmodern self is a work in progress unfolding in "alternative," nonnative settings, the native actors and actresses of this drama both help and hurt. In ways that remain, as Lee's hero notices, noncommittal, ambiguous, they provide the overall set for the reinvention script. However, they have already cast him in a part at odds with the one he seeks to play on the American stage. As soon as he walks onto this stage, he is stepping into an a priori egological scenario and, inside it, into the status of an "Other to the (European) American self," an Asian-American extra in the national show. As in *Native Speaker*, undermining self-remaking in *A Gesture Life* is the "Orientalizing" construction the natives put on the "visible difference" of his face and voice.[24] Alone Franklin Hata certainly is. His solitude, though, is neither philosophical (Franklinesque) nor sociological, but ethical. He lives amid the people of Bedley Run, where he moved after the war, but is hardly "with" them. Neither are they. They see him daily but only to enmesh him into a cobweb of visible and invisible "relations" (anecdotes, gossip, etc.) that tie him down and jam the narrative and social mobility he thought America would afford him.

A panoptical isolation of sorts under native eyes and imaginings, Franklin Hata's loneliness is fraught with and cancelled out by ideology. This is, also as in *Native Speaker*, an ideology of Americanness[25] that operates on two, intersecting levels. On one level, it takes up the generous form of Franklin's American Dream, that grand, generic, and transcendent narrative of which we all can be part regardless of individual circumstances if we commit ourselves to the ethic of hard work, self-improvement, and frugality. On another level—the level of Franklin Hata's everyday dealings with the townsfolk—this narrative proves rhetorically geared toward particular sociopolitical differentiations hinging on race, ethnicity, religion, sexual orientation, and so forth. On this level, Franklin Hata is made into that which jeopardizes his own remaking project. That is to say, in and precisely due to the complications of Benjamin Franklin's America, *Jiro* remains, in a sense, Franklin Hata's "truer" name. Unnamed yet firmly nestled in the Japanese name a past of multiple trauma lives on.

Relations, Relatives, Realty: Belonging and the Ethics of Naming

> Everything is real estate.
> —DON DELILLO, *Underworld*

In another sense, though, Jiro "gets over." Yet this does not happen, as he hoped, in Benjamin Franklin's name or, more accurately, it does not happen as he imagined it would. His reinvented life is another success story only in part, on the surface, as a sum of perfunctory "gestures." It does bear out the namesake's self-making theory but chiefly economically as Franklin Hata becomes a successful owner of the local Sunny Medical Supply and well-respected member of the community. The respect, too, is rather formal and distant, another social "gesture" without consequences. Nor is his relation with white Americans like Mary Burns more consequential. For most people, he is a reassuringly unthreatening presence, a reliable citizen living in a vintage "two-story Tudor revival" house Liv Crawford of Town Realty has set her eyes on.

Beautifully maintained as it may be, Franklin Hata's house is not so much a home as real estate, counts as property value for itself and surrounding properties. Its owner is not a neighbor to those properties' owners either, but a financial reassurance. The Bedley Run people do not relate to him, and what he is, as neighbors but rather through him to what they own: in "Doc Hata," they relate to realty, to an "impressive" listing. For this matter, neither the neighborhood nor the town feels like a home, much as "people t[ake] an odd interest in telling [him] that [he] wasn't *un*welcome" (3). A "feeling," a "happy blend of familiarity and homeyness and what must be belonging," does form over time, but it eventually "begin[s] to disturb [him]" (21) once he realizes that he has become "a quantity known, somebody long ago counted" (21). "Discomfiting" in "all this rapport" is what Levinas would identify as the unethical—"unneighborly"—structure of the knowledge embedded in this "known," "counted," and "categorized" human quantity. Like Henry and, before him, Ellison's hero, Franklin Hata rightly suspects that he has "develop[ed] an unexpected condition of transparence here, a walking case of others' certitude" (21). Henry, we may recall, encourages such "certitudes." To the extent that Franklin Hata does the same—and, to a lesser degree, he does—he bears some responsibility for his treatment. A long time ago he took it upon himself to become a "business and civic elder and leader" (136), a "citizen and colleague and partner" (135). Making his "job to be the number-one citizen" (95), he built, however, his "whole life out of gestures and politeness" (95)—one big "polite" gesture toward the place and its citizenry.

To Bedley Run, Franklin Hata submits "freely," but the town is at once "welcoming and not," a home and a "burden" (135). The place both takes him in and keeps him out, on the "outside looking in" (356). This curiously epidermal positioning in the civic body of its "number-one citizen" marks a twin ethical quandary. The first is collective. Because, as Lee reemphasizes in *Aloft*, homeyness rests on with-ness, Franklin Hata's home makes him oddly uneasy. He is not with others, hence he cannot possibly "feel" at home. Civility alone does not build a civitas, does not guarantee a sense of community. In fact, courteous proximity is here a venue of asociality, the scene of a polite pantomime in which the "civic leader" himself excels.

But home is not only unhomely; it is also *unheimlich*. Present asociality—the polite displacement of the other as socius, and thus of the polity itself—restages Franklin Hata's earlier disengagements from other lives. Bedley Run is the place where this uncanny past returns to haunt its most honorable resident. His house and town cannot be a true home, a hearth, a center and place where the self can finally center itself, and the house and the town alike remain a site of exteriority as long as he himself remains intellectually and morally exterior to the memories he has carried with him across continents. The present time is an encumbrance for the same reason and to the extent that the past is burdensome, a receptacle of "external" gestures and neutralities whose significance, years thereafter, still nag at him but he is unable to assume. In fact, the burden has less to do with the present, with the civic responsibilities of which he has otherwise acquitted itself, than with the obligations whose test he had failed to pass decades ago; it pertains to who Jiro had been and what he set out to overcome *as* Franklin to finally "come home" to Bedley Run (376) and make himself at home in Benjamin Franklin's name.

Remarkably, nobody in town wants to call him Franklin but Doc Hata, another way of Lee's underscoring *Jiro*'s symbolic resilience. *Doc Hata* is the onomastic version of the distant and distancing, vaguely patronizing gaze. Others name and thus (mis)identify him by giving him a name "other" to the one he has chosen. But Lee also implies that the onomastic badge of change, self-renaming and self-reinventing under Benjamin Franklin's name, must be equally earned, must occur ethically. True, Benjamin Franklin himself would encourage onomastic initiative, the bestowing of a changed name—and of the name of change—on oneself as a volition act and agency token. Yet again, Lee tells us that one cannot give oneself new names and lives other than in the others' midst, that these things and the freedom we associate with them are obtained in cultural-existential "associations." Differently put, *Franklin* must be *given* to Jiro; Hata must be named, and thus changed, made into a new man, by an other. Franklin is by no means an inappropriate name, yet it has not been earned. Others' refusal to use it has not rendered it useless, but naming—self-naming—has not gone through the ethical channels and territories of alterity, and so *Franklin* has been a self-conferred rather than other-bequeathed gift.

But who is this other who finally gives Franklin the name in which Jiro can—at last—unburden himself? Or, what kind of "other" are we talking about? The neighbors cannot call Franklin by his self-given name because that would imply a rapport, understanding and genuine welcoming, and those have been forfeited by their "not *un*welcoming" gestures. An authentic gesture presupposes a true relation, which is exactly what the "realty" approach to place and sodality has displaced. Nor can a true welcome to a new place, life, and name come from Franklin Hata's sole "relative," Sunny. For one thing, Sunny is not a blood relative, which is also relevant, as we shall see immediately. For another, his dealings with Sunny, Mary Burns, and women generally are tainted by the past and past self he thought the United States would help get away from. But it becomes obvious that this "getaway" life is unethical, another reason his American name is not socially recognized and cannot do much for him. As long as he leads this kind of life, as long as he does not.assume his biography's entirety and not just its American chapter, his new life cannot get under way. Arguably, he tried to "jump-start" this process by adopting Sunny, but he does not manage to set up a true relation with her because the African American–Korean girl reminds him of the "lowly quarters of my kin," that is, of his own Korean background.

It turns out, indeed, that Jiro Kurohata is actually a Korean Japanese whom his "real parents . . . wished as much as I," he tells Kkutaeh, would "become wholly and thoroughly Japanese" (235). So they gave him to the Kurohatas, a Japanese couple who raised him as a Japanese, and it was as such that he served in the Imperial Army during World War II. Kkutaeh, whose name too was forced upon her (a name Jiro shortens to K), was also Korean and among the sex slaves on a Burma Japanese military base where Lieutenant Jiro was posted as a medical assistant. Jiro's "associations" with women had always had an uncomfortable edge to them and got forever complicated, guilt-ridden, on a certain level even blocked by his relationship with K. Before Sunny, yet arguably setting up Franklin Hata's relation with his adoptive daughter, K charged him with "gestural" behavior. Infatuated with her while she and her companions were being sexually tortured by the Japanese, he was incapable of doing anything for her and did not refrain from having sex with her regardless of the circumstances. Adding insult to injury, he invited her to play, despite the horror she had to go through, a pseudocosmopolitan, "pretend game" of sorts, which made up phantasmatically—"superficially," immorally, on the skin of things and in the shadow of actual gestures and stances—for what he was unable or unwilling to do for her in reality. For a while, it looked as though a bond, albeit feeble, was not impossible. A certain cosmopolitan premise seemed to be there and help K and Jiro reach some common ground. The premise lay not just in shared "legacy" and "background," and in the Korean "ethos" (233) inhering in what they shared by birth, an ethos to which Captain Ono kept referring disparagingly, but also in a transnative, cooperative ethos undergirding Korean and Japanese cultures alike. On both sides, though, this ethos was tentative, never a full-fledged notion. K's father, for instance, believed that "whether Chinese or Japanese or Korean we were rooted of a common culture and mind and we should put aside our differences and work together" (249). Yet he equally resented non-Asian "influences," denied K a basic education, and ultimately did not hesitate to sacrifice her to save her brother. In turn, Jiro backed up the "pan-Asian" vision of K's father. "This is," he told K, "our Emperor's mandate, . . . to develop an Asian prosperity, and an Asian way of life" (249), and, ironically, only a few pages thereafter, Ono would lecture Jiro on the "Pan-Asian prosperity as captained by our people" (268).

The rhetoric of this "regional" cosmopolitanism was delusional at best. And so was the cosmopolitan fantasy that, also temporarily, appeared to provide a respite from contingent horror. Drawing from those Western novels K's father loathed, Jiro conjured forth a surrogate world in which K and he could fancy a common future. K was not totally unresponsive. "I wish," she confessed, "that we could read one of those novels. . . . A story set in another land and time in history, with completely different sorts of people. Since I was a little girl, I always wanted to live a completely different life, even if it might be a hard one. I was sure I wasn't meant to belong to mine. Maybe you can describe the stories to me, and we could pretend we were in their lives" (249). So Jiro carried on with his pipe dream story and its vain hope in some kind of "nearness," "correspondence between us, an affinity of being" by "pretending to be other people, like figures in a Western novel, imagining how we could somehow exist outside of this place and time" (263). K played along yet declined to pretend it was not a pretend game, a "gesture" that substituted itself for ethical action, just as the "Asian way of life" was, she also pointed out, no more than "Japanese life" (249) and female "volunteering" sex slavery.

K is, then, the name of an aborted association, an associative model that undercuts Jiro Kurohata's—later, Franklin Hata's—attempts to "associate" himself with others. With another irony, Jiro fulfills K's prophecy by expatriating himself into the world of Western fiction, yet his new name fails to sanction the desired new life. His past is still with him, pulling him back, preempting the fresh start under the self-given name and in the name of the hopefully redeeming relationships with Sunny, Mary Burns, the Hickeys, Liv, Ronney, and others. "With" them (and not quite), his worst nightmare comes true as novel situations reenact his wartime inaction and superficial response to others and their ordeals (a theme resurfacing in Lee's 2010 novel *The Surrendered*). The symmetrically pro forma acknowledgment by his Bedley Run neighbors is thus the mirror image of his past treatment of others, and so is his rejection by his own "daughter." From her, a "relative," he cannot get what he himself denied to his K(in); his redemption cannot come from or be of this kin(d), from or in this type of relationship. Yet it is not far from the latter either. Otherwise put: it does come from Sunny, from a Sunny whose life Franklin Hata endeavors to change and does change to a notable degree but without sublating it into the kind of "association" he denied himself, if on another level, in his brief encounter with K. The more we learn about his past, the more Sunny's unqualified yet staunch rebuke qualifies this past, constructs itself as a censure of his past and present existential "gesticulation." She senses the symbolically proxy, vaguely redemptive role she is assigned in Franklin Hata's life, in his self-refurbishing/self-vindicating drama, and turns the part down. This is why Jiro cannot rename and remake himself in relation to "Sunny-as-another-K." His new name and lease on life cannot come from her because she is at once biographically too close to him, as a Korean and "daughter," adopted like him into another family and culture, and phantasmatically too remote, separated by her "father"'s youth insofar as she is K's stand-in.

Concurrently too loaded and too tenuous to work, this relation is nevertheless the template for another one, more indirect but more fruitful, with Thomas, Sunny's black Korean son. More African American than his mother and more American than his "grandfather," Thomas is twice removed from the Jiro of the Burma years. A generational, ethnoracial, and cultural gulf pulls them apart but also toward each other. The boy is at last Franklin Hata's relative, moreover, his "twin" of sorts (*Thomas* means "twin" in Aramaic). Yet Thomas is no less Jiro's other for that, and it is from this position of heightened yet sympathetic otherness that he gives Jiro another opportunity to take stock of himself and his misconceptions (the racial ones included), to touch somebody's life for the sake of that person.[26] Thomas no longer is the symbolic substitute for an other not here and not present. In his dealings with his "nephew" and multiple other, Franklin Hata does not suspend this other's presence to reconnect himself with this other's other (K), with whom he did not have the courage to be fully, ethically. The boy "allows" Franklin Hata to share in his life (and actually save it), which Jiro, and then Franklin, did for neither K nor, later on, Sunny. More importantly, Thomas is the one who, at last, calls him Franklin (276), releasing him from Jiro Kurohata's clasp—from the spell of his name, that is. For, we find out earlier in the novel, "Hata is, literally, 'flag,' and a 'black flag,' or *kurohata*, is the banner a village would raise by its gate in olden time to warn of a contagion within. It is the signal of spreading death. My adoptive family . . . had an ancient lineage of apothecaries, who had ventured into stricken villages and had for unknown reasons determined to keep the name, however inauspicious it was" (224–25). Ono alluded to Jiro's name to "belittle" the name bearer (225), while K "crie[d]" it out to unburden herself and cry herself to sleep, if "fitfully," "saying over and over very quickly what sounded most peculiarly like *hata-hata, hata- hata*" (261), but also to appeal to Kurohata and thus burden him with the responsibility for her life and death.

K, Ono, and "other specters of history" (353) keep Franklin Hata hostage in Jiro Kurohata's name and world. He cannot journey into another name and life without a nod from an other, without a relation, an "association" into which otherness is effectively embedded. Thomas is just that kind of relation. He is perfectly positioned between past and present, the former's spectrality and the latter's blood-and-flesh immediacy, between Kurohata-the-apothecary or World War II medical assistant and the Bedley Run medical supply store owner, in brief, between what the protagonist was and cannot deny or disown, on the one hand, and, on the other, that which he might still become, in Benjamin Franklin's name and in the vicinity of those close and not so close to him. In this challenging nearness, in this relation in which Thomas is both a signifier of otherness and a relative in and through whom the other reveals himself in all his kindness as Franklin Hata's truest kin, Lee's protagonist can finally write his Franklinesque story. Only, it goes without saying, this story is nothing he imagined. In it, he does not "get away" from, or "over," Jiro. Nor should he, given that identity reconstruction must revisit and incorporate the past. Thus the relation with Thomas enables another one, another relation and story, as K "finally come[s] back for [him] (286)." But she does not return to castigate. She no longer allegorizes a doomed "life of gestures"

(299), of botched responses to others, for which both K and Sunny reprimand him and Bedley Run pays him "in kind." Another kind of repayment or reward and another kind of story become possible only after Thomas enters his world: a story where the past world and the world in general are not sanitarily roped off or narratively excised in order for the story's hero to make himself at home in a better world and home, but a story in which Koreans, Japanese, Americans, and everybody else can be at home because they are with each other. To this home and this cosmodern realization Franklin Hata can come—in his namesake and his own name, this time around—by assuming his entire life, by constructing his story ethically. And, as he comes full circle and recollection seeps into ongoing narrative and ruminations, "Franklin" impacts on "Jiro" and opens up for him the possibility of a future, in Bedley Run and anywhere else in the world.

4. The "Infamous Other": Onomachy

Aloft's Embattled Names

The same ethical circularity and, within it, recognizable themes shape Lee's third book, *Aloft*. Reviewers have called the 2004 novel's author "a writer . . . who feels expansive enough in his spirit and ambitions to encompass not just his close kinsmen but the infamous Other."[27] As we saw in *Native Speaker*, this expansiveness is Whitmanesque. It remains so in *Aloft* but not without qualifications. It is, in fact, Whitman's "encompassing" logic itself that Lee queries at the same time that he falls back on it to make room for the "infamous Other" in the house of the American self. Similarly to *A Gesture Life*, this "expansion," this cultural "home improvement," plays on the relation/realty trope, which in turn retrieves Whitman's symbolic "Mall of America" figure. In *Aloft*, people flock to the Walt Whitman Mall to bask in the discount emporium's simulacrum of conviviality. Here, they blend into the "like-mindedness" of shoppers or at least attempt to do so, like the aging father of Jerry Battle, the storytelling hero. Foreshadowing Battle Sr.'s mall exploits, Jerry's early retirement features frequent trips "to the nearby Walt Whitman Mall (the poet was born in a modest house right across the street . . .) for what I would always hope was the easeful company of like-minded people but would end up instead, depending on the selling season, to be frantic clawing hordes or else a ghost town of seniors sitting by the islands of potted ficus, depressing and diminishing instances both" (3–4).

Opposite to "expansive" and "encompassing," "depressing" and "diminishing" are counterintuitive attributes for a place named after Whitman. An onomastic antiphrasis—the name means the contrary to what it stands for culturally and historically—"Whitman" is marketed as marketplace itself. Under Whitman's name, a rather un-Whitmanesque space unfolds, for the mall perpetuates *A Gesture Life*'s logic of realty where, fracturing and ultimately dislocating "real" community and neighborhood, suburbanite real estate weakens relations among people, unravels fellowships, devalues mutual responsibilities, and pushes self and other apart. The disintegration of collective, communal, as well as familial selfhood is arguably even more advanced in *Aloft* than in the previous novel, and to account for this decline one must turn to the stronger role real estate and the adjacent themes of property maintenance, landscaping, gardening, home improvement, and interior design play in the story.

Lee ties these topics and naming together from the outset in Jerry's succinct presentation of Battle Brothers Brick & Mortar, a masonry and landscaping company started by Jerry's grandfather in the 1930s and now run by Jerry's son, Jack. The company and family name, we discover, "was originally Battaglia, but my father and uncles decided early on to change their name to Battle for the usual reasons immigrants and others like them will do, for the sake of familiarity and ease of use and to herald a new and optimistic beginning, which is anyone's God given right, whether warranted or not" (24). Battle, Jerry goes on, "is a nice name for a business, because it's simple and memorable, ethnically indistinct, and then squarely patriotic, though in a subtle sort of way. Customers . . . have the sense we're fighters, that we have an inner resolve, that we'll soldier through all obstacles to get the job done, and done right. . . . My father insists that the idea for the name originated with him, and for just the connotations I've mentioned, which I don't doubt, as he was always the savviest businessman of his brothers, and talked incessantly through my youth about the awesome power of the words" (25). *Battle* is to *Battaglia* what *Franklin* is to *Jiro*: a complex appellation that conjures up more than it designates. For, while others call the Battles by their new name, in this very calling, in calling as interpellation and profession, the Battles advertise themselves as Americans, call on their American callers ("clients") to include them, treat them as "kin," "for the sake of familiarity." The Americanization/translation of the Italian name betokens of course Americanization itself, understood reductively as Anglo-becoming, which is seized on, erroneously yet typically, as a washing out of ethnicity, in this case Italianness. What the name appears to lose, to "unname" ethnically, is compensated economically and culturally: Americans call the Battles on their American(ized) name to ply their old-country trade, and, as the name proves good for business, the named drift farther away from their ethnic and social origins. A self-bestowed mark of Americanness, *Battle* demarcates a truly fresh chapter ("beginning") in the family's history only when they "make it." In making it, they finally remake themselves. The future "heralded"—announced and called on—by the American name at last arrives and Americanization is complete when their "horizontal" move into the ethnic "indistinctness" of the American body politic is followed by a move up the social ladder as Battle Brothers thrives.

Yet the company ultimately fails, and the failure suggests that the ethic of hard work is not enough. What the Battles lack, Lee offers, is the deeper ethic of relatedness. Missing here is the realization that whatever we attempt or even achieve plays out in a space that is more than just setting for frantic individualism and its solitary battles against difficulties where others count as either something to control and get the better of (competition, hard-to-please customers, suppliers) or, if closer to us (neighbors, coworkers, relatives), as entities to acknowledge superficially and in whose lives we get minimally involved. This unethical, adversarial self-positioning of the Battles in general and Jerry in particular in the social field implicitly and explicitly sets others up as enemies or nuisances. Ideally, the field itself should be "others-free"; if that was not possible, "they" should take up strictly defined spaces that would not hinder the self's relentless march through life. Here, the self is egologically self-centered, and this is what *Battle* signifies in the final analysis: a self-centeredness "obstructed" by others, whose "battling" (overpowering, ignoring, etc.) parallels the Battles' own struggle to efface themselves as others to America by renaming themselves into ethnic in-distinction. Cleared of "them" as objects of preoccupation, attention, intimacy, or care, the social is reduced, not unlike the Whitman Mall, to a zone of mercantile transactions, to landscape and impersonal suburban topography. In short, this is realty really—realty that dislodges social reality if not "the Real" itself, as Jerry himself comes to admits.

"Declining the Real," as Jerry puts it (243), has been the family business privately and publicly. When the business goes under, a crisis breaks out financially as well as ethically. In turning down the Real, he suspects, we forego that part of the world which sets the stage for our self-centering. As Alda learns from Yuan Long Ping and Franklin Hata from Thomas, we are not born on this stage. We spend our lives striving to come on it, and thus into our own, from offstage. Following the Freudian theory of the ego's "radical heteronomy," Lacan asserts "the self's radical ex-centricity to itself," and it is this deeply seated decenteredness that renders autonomous self-making and remaking an uphill battle.[28] The "real" constitution of the self necessarily runs through other selves, occurs in conjunction, collision, and cultural friction with people who cannot be ignored or brushed aside, just as we cannot discard our own background, memories, and habits. As Hans Bertens comments on Lacan's view of the self, since "we need the response and recognition of *others* and of *the Other* to arrive at what we experience as our identity," the latter is ineluctably "*relational*."[29] The Real cannot be imagined in the absence of languages, codes, and representations. It cannot lie outside culture and what culture presupposes—those others whose presence in it marks off our own place. Their recognition (of us) is a prerequisite of our own cognition of ourselves, a stepping stone to self-knowledge. For that, turning our back to the Real means undercutting self-knowledge itself, failing to know ourselves because we have failed to know others, to take an interest in their lives, in short, to care. Unknowable as it may be according to Lacan, the Real nevertheless calls on us to know it, to take a stab at it over and over again not because it will reveal itself to us eventually but because as others interpellate us and respond to our interpellations, we are revealed to ourselves.

Benjamin Franklin to Roland Barthes

Inserting us into the culture, philosophers like Charles Taylor insist, this conversation is predicated on names. To be talked to and thus be socially sanctioned, we must be called on. Our recognition is, then, always first and foremost onomastic, takes place in our names, *in the name's name.* And vice versa: we take notice of others in their own names. But *Battle* does not bring into play this ethical reciprocity, evoking instead an allergic ideal of self-contained, autonomously organized identity in a world where other identities are perceived as hindrances or distractions. This worldview goes bankrupt along with Battle Brothers. The latter's decline no longer sustains the declining of the Real, and what starts out as managerial troubles develops into an ontological, ethical, and phantasmatic crisis, drilling in the self's solipsistic armor a hole through which the Real rushes in. Nor is Jerry unaware of what is going on. Rejecting the Real, he surmises, actually does the "contrary," "inviting it in" (243). This intuition marks a breakthrough, an incipient form of self-knowledge, for, as in *A Gesture Life*, retrospection starts playing an analytic, self-scrutinizing role: "invited" in by Jerry and encapsulated by his life story, the Real carries with it a heteronomous content, those others whom he has ignored (has not "known") or has disconsidered throughout his "soldiering." This invitation, we will note momentarily, is more than a Lacanian metaphor, although it is extended, half in earnest, half jokingly, in Lacan's very name. Jerry has most certainly not read *Écrits*, but his daughter, Theresa, a college professor, has, and peppers her sentences with references to Lacan, Roland Barthes, "the Real," and "the Other." Jerry is not an intellectual, although he looks up things mentioned in his presence and does not hesitate to educate himself, read up on this or that topic, even plow through the experimental fiction published by Paul, his son-in-law. While unquestionably out of his league, Lacanian stuff somehow appeals to him. He picks it up from Theresa, Paul, and their friends' "language whose multi-horned relativistic meanings I feel," he admits, "I should but don't much understand" (212). In a rudimentary sort of way, though, he somehow "gets" it and, quite ironically, drops its lingo here and there in his monologue yet not without effects themselves Lacanian. For what purports to convey an irony "and nothing else" spills over into seriousness, yields surprising clarifications. This paradoxically illuminating overflow of meaning is set up early on in a passage that brings together all of *Aloft*'s major issues, not least the Lacanian problematic of otherness. The fragment begins by describing a family photo taken at the house of Jack and his wife, Eunice, a picture that "might appear in a fashion magazine spread titled something like 'The Spoils of Battle.'" "We," Jerry reflects,

> [woul]d probably be just right, too, for such a shoot, not only because we have a nice generational mix going (white-haired patriarch, sportive young parents, peach-cheeked toddlers) but also because we're an ethnically jumbled bunch, a grab bag miscegenation of Korean (Daisy) and Italian (us Battles) and English-German (Eunice) expressing itself in my and Jack's offspring with particularly handsome and even stunning results. As a group you can't really tell what the hell we are, though more and more these days the very question is apparently dubious, if not downright crass, at least to folks like Theresa and Paul, whose race-consciousness is clearly quite different from mine. I

suppose what's critical to them is who's asking the question, for if it's an average guy like me there's only awkwardness and embarrassment ahead, the assumption being I'm going to blindly buy into a whole raft of historical "typologies" and "antecedents" and turn around and plonk somebody with the label of Other. (72–73)

If Jack, who has "always *passed*," seems "totally unconcerned about such matters" (73), Paul "writes about the terribly conflicted and complicated state of being Asian and American and thoughtful and male" (78). These are *Aloft*'s two conflicting models. Initially, Jerry identifies with Jack's, that is, with unexamined, or seemingly unexamined, life and identity. These remain delusive, unlived to the fullest because people like Jack, Jerry, and Jerry's father ignore what makes them what they are, namely, the other within and around them. Such subjects—themes and people—are either avoided or skirted. Thus, the typical Battle stands alone, aloof and aloft, aside from and above others and the Real, like Jerry, self-proclaimed "Numero Uno" or "Solo Flyer" (298) moving "high" and "fast" in his Cessna (288). Such people, Paul tells Jerry, "think they can go anywhere and do anything, as if none of their actions has any bearings except on themselves, like they are in their own mini-biosphere, all needs self-providing, everything self-contained, setting it up like God would do himself. It doesn't matter that there are people on the outside tapping at the glass, saying, 'Hey, hey, I'm here. Look out here'" (298). And Jerry is right: his son-in-law is "striking closer to home than [Jerry']d prefer" (298), for the "Chairman Me" or the "Client Zero" type Paul is talking about is no one else than Jerry himself. An authorial alter-ego, Paul indirectly charges Jerry with the egotism his father-in-law no longer disputes in the wake of his recent family crisis—or crises, rather, because even more worrisome than the financial situation of Battle Brothers is Theresa's health. Jerry admits that "shirking almost all civic duties save paying the property taxes and sorting the recycling" (260) made for the kind of conduct that got him in trouble in the first place. And, in hindsight, his successful battles do turn out as so many personal defeats in disguise, with those once close to him committing suicide (Daisy), leaving him (Rita, Kelly), keeping their distance (Theresa), or threatening to perpetuate his own alienating behavior (Jack). For what Jerry has spent his life doing is precisely wielding his life, in its intimate and public aspects alike, as a buffer zone, an emotionally aseptic hinterland across which others are perfunctorily acknowledged.

Neither a racist nor a xenophobe, he is not incapable of seeing through labels, buzzwords, and clichés. But this capacity did not translate into authentic responses to other lives after Daisy's death, and Theresa does complain about Jerry's "supernatural ability to short-circuit dealing with the needs of others," about how he "could never bear doing anything purely for someone else" (300).

The wake-up call comes later, with the different sort of battles he must fight alongside Jack, Theresa, his father, and others rather than solitarily and for the purpose of retaining his "solo flying" station. The new predicaments "are new instructions from above (or below or beyond), telling me in no uncertain terms that I cannot stay at altitude much longer, even though I have fuel to burn, that I cannot keep marking this middle distance" (288). An unethical space, this distance pertains to the neutral logic of what Jerry himself identifies as "realty responsibility" (288), which does imply the notion that "existence" is "shared." But this sharing has been minimal, a pseudoinvestment affectively. Allegorized by his airborne "aloftness," his private and public aloofness has blocked his self's growth. Jerry has prospered economically by pulling away from others, through a self-involvement predicated on the other's affective erasure. Daisy's and Theresa's deaths sanction the empathic deficit of a self who, locked into his self-absorbed life, cannot respond to others ethically.

In this regard, Jerry is Jiro's avatar, as the quasi homophony of their names suggests. Also like Jiro, Jerry changes his ways by trading "realty responsibilities" for real, emotional ones. He quits living in denial of others, pushing them out, across spaces nicely maintained. Instead, he invites them in. But, if Jiro/Franklin gives up his home in hopes of coming home in a more profound way, Jerry keeps it, yet only to take the others in. For a long while, and especially after Daisy's death, Jerry's dealing with the Real and those "out there" in it has taken place in between spaces of intimacy, in between homes, in the realm of realty, of gardening and landscaping. Now, it is staged inside, in his own house, which has become a home at last, for its owner and others alike. After Theresa's death, Paul sticks around, caring for their son, while Jerry's father has also moved in, and so have Jack and his family, who had to sell their mansion following Battle Brothers' bankruptcy. They "all had to come around in the last few weeks, dealing with one another's daily (and especially nightly) functions and manners and habits and quirks," which are, Jerry confesses, "one hopes not half as telling of our characters as are our capacities for tolerance and change" (352). To signal this change, Jerry does not change his name. He does not rename himself Franklin to "herald" onomastically "a new and optimistic beginning" (24). This shift, the self's ethical reorientation and reconsideration of others, comes along symbolically in an other's name, under the auspices of the name of Theresa's son, Barthes Tae-jon Battle, named after Roland Barthes.

The name choice threw Jerry off at first. He vaguely knew that Lacan and Barthes were among the "theory" gurus worshipped by Theresa and her friends, yet to him the names stood for "multihorned" and "relativistic" lingo. A shibboleth of academic fatuity, *Barthes*, he thought, was part of a discourse shield of sorts underneath which others lived their no less aloof lives. Yet that changes after the crisis. Like Jiro/Franklin's relationship with Thomas, the French-Korean-Italian-American name of Jerry's grandson signals ethical adjustments inside the Battles' world and house, which become a family and a home. Neither is a configuration of sameness, though, of inherited commonalities and duties. The Battles come to a sense of kinship, togetherness, and reciprocal obligations, discover the strengthening ritual of family life as they, and Jerry in the first place, recognize the others in their midst, the ethnoculturally heteroclite texture of their individual and collective being. Similarly to Jerry and Jiro, Gogol and Ganguli and Nikhil and Nikolai in Lahiri, Brick and Brill in Auster's 2008 novel *Man in the Dark, Barthes* and *Battle* are not homonyms but paronyms, nor do they denote the same things, but they sound alike and thus imply a possible bridge between the distinct entities they stand for. And "Barthes" is just the theoretical rationale for this bridge; in his name, more to the point, in the spirit of his famed text theory, "Life" and "Text" merge in the self's very life. "Barthes" is originally "other" to Jerry, an epitome of otherness, of the impenetrable stuff others say and, in saying it, exclude him as audience, as a presence in *their* midst. Toward the end of the novel, though, the critic's name points to Jerry's realization of what life and its responsibilities entail. This understanding is not "theorized," nor need it be. Jerry simply hints at it. He names it in a name that remains both "other" to him and a mark of his newly acquired suspicion that there are no autarkic battles, that the self is already enmeshed in the text of otherness much as that text already interpolates our lives and stories, which calls on us to acknowledge those others' right to dwell and be taken care of in our home. For there is no other way "we" and "our" families can become a "decent lot" (352).

Onomastic Transference

Following Freud's and Antonin Artaud's works on drama, René Major approaches this onomastic dynamic as "transference." By-products of theatrical production, the complex transfers or position exchanges among characters or between characters and their audience allow a character or spectator to trade unconsciously his or her place with another character and thus assume the latter's inner life, take up its fantasies, and even act on its desires and repressions. According to Major, proper names can operate as transaction vehicle or currency. Through them, people develop an "imaginary relationship" with others, shift into a position of otherness where they live out subliminally those others' dreams and terrors.[30] In other names, they "nominate" themselves for tasks and postures not theirs originally. In identifying a namesake, in naming myself after him or her, I forge an onomastic association; I throw a bridge into another existence and identity, and I also cross it to experience them as I lend myself that other person's identity. This is how in the play-in-the-play episode of "The Murder of Gonzago," Hamlet "renames" himself after Lucianus, who poisoned Gonzago, much like, in the frame-tragedy, Claudius murdered Hamlet's father. Therefore, Hamlet "swaps roles" with Lucianus, and hence also with Claudius, with whom he arguably shares "regicidal desire." But because Lucianus is also Gonzago's nephew, Hamlet also identifies with his father. In so doing, he bolsters unconsciously the homonymy of their name(s), which shores up their equivocal alliance and fashions an identity that makes it possible for the son to take action on his father's behalf and name and so exact his—his own and his father's—revenge on Claudius.[31]

Since Major's take on homonymy is psychoanalytic, the "elective identity" derived from onomastic transference is not exactly a matter of choice. Neither the public nor the dramatis personae choose to rename themselves after others and thus share in their longings or anxieties. But Jiro does make this choice. A complete swap would imply an equivalence of self and other, transference as incorporation and assimilation of an other whose place and private life the self takes over and carries on by proxy, *as* an other. This would go against the relational ethics that gets so much play in cosmodernism, for this homonymy would be de facto a synonymy, not only an identity of the name but also an identity of the named. What onomastic homonyms render possible in the narratives examined above, however, is not unconscious transference that evens up performatively but a relation that evolves into a more complex kind of homology, into a togetherness wherein Franklin (Hata) does not become (Benjamin) Franklin. In the other's name, Franklin's, Hata embarks on a life-changing narrative, but even though his first name and Benjamin's last name coincide, his story does not collapse into Benjamin's; in actuality, Hata adopts an other's name to take charge of his personal story. Likewise, Alice Randall's Push[kin], we will learn in part 4, does not reincarnate Alexander Pushkin. Nor does Lee Siegel's Indian-American Lalita become Lolita, although his 1999 novel *Love in a Dead Language* alludes "paronymically" to Vladimir Nabokov's *Lolita* to work out a whole theory of cosmodernism as "transmigration."[32] Nabokov's book and heroine do supply *Love in a Dead Language* and Lalita with a narrative and cultural "score" to perform, but Lalita hardly rehearses Lo's fate. Reenacting the nymphet's subaltern position in late-global settings, Lalita faces quandaries similar to Lolita's, yet her solutions reinforce this difference. Notorious for her intertextual nomadism, Nabokov's heroine catches her breath in Lalita; in exchange, in Lolita's name, Lalita gains an insight into other worlds and, across them, back into her own.

Andrei Codrescu's 2004 novel *Wakefield* plays on this nomadism even more pointedly. Writer, traveling lecturer, and man of the world, Codrescu's protagonist is a self-professed "nomad" in more than one way.[33] Both hero and plot wink at Hawthorne's "Wakefield." As in the *New York Trilogy* and elsewhere in Auster, Hawthorne's character rises from the dead to "transmigrate" in a late twentieth-century namesake. But, also as in Auster, Codrescu's Wakefield is more than another body for the illustrious predecessor. Onetime resident of a hotel across from his home, he is a philosopher of nomad life and ever on the go himself. For one thing, "Wakefield"'s and *Wakefield*'s central figures share a name, are alike onomastically. For another, through the Hawthornian plot and name, Codrescu rounds off his Wakefield by tapping into a resistant social philosophy advocating withdrawal from forms of lucrative public involvement that level things out, co-opt, and typify—much like the software corporation headquartered in the Midwestern town of Typical. Under Hawthorne's tutelage, the writer subjects the cultural-corporate ideology of the typical and typifying to an itinerant critique across America as *Wakefield*'s expert-at-large "lecture[s] in places he's already written about, giving the natives a quaint 'outsider' perspective on their familiar world" (11). Prompted by the illuminating vicinity of the namesake and the "outsider" position he takes up in "Wakefield," Codrescu's hero removes himself from his home and habits to live out the "perspective" from which he "defamiliarizes" the "familiar world" of his audiences. His speeches argue for the imaginary, the oddball, and the unfamiliar, and against worldwide mass reproduction of the selfsame. But again, and following from this very argument, Hawthorne's and Codrescu's heroes are not interchangeable; the former only reauthorizes the latter's quirky dissent at a time nonconformism has become another lucrative "gesture."

Naming, Translating

Onomastic yet not identitarian, homonymy and similar onomastic plays call out the name's origin, name the other in the self's name and, *as such*, afford individuation rites without which the self would not come into its own. In short, homonymy is and further fosters a heteronomy. Hata's first name is the name of an other, but he does not morph into him. Instead, he leads a new life under his alias as he relates to others around him, "gets" them and through to them in *A Gesture Life*'s conclusion. Late in their lives as it comes, Jiro's and Jerry's ability to connect with others who remain so—other—this emotional and cultural capacity to be with those unlike them, pertains to empathy rather than transference and therefore cannot be sorted out by psychoanalysis alone but by a broader, cultural and cross-cultural psychology. For pivotal here are a propensity of putting oneself in the other's place ethically, a proclivity grounded in shared feelings, which in turn hinges on the self's knack for seeing itself in that very place, shouldering the other's burden, "feeling" alongside and "for" him or her.

In this sense, cosmodernism's imaginary, its onomastic imaginary in particular, is distinctively empathic. In a large number of American authors who become better known after the 1980s, culturally "transferable" proper names are anthropological vehicles of compassion through which the self empathizes with others, slides imaginatively into predispositions and perspectives from which those others' positions can be intuited, "infelt." Mapping being-with onto the language of affect, in-feeling is feeling-with. Fellow feeling, feeling with somebody or in his or her place, boils down in cosmodernism to having those feelings or, more accurately, to imagining what it would "be like" to feel them in that person's situation— but *not* in his or her stead—for his or her benefit rather than for vicarious purposes. If naming is "meaning-making" that sets off "a process of self-engagement transacted and performed both socially and textually" through actions that may end up refashioning the selfhood under my name, assuming an other's name projects this cultural-semiotic "engagement" outward, ethically.[34] I am still "re-creating" myself by "heteroglossic plays," but I am making the most of them now as I "wield" a Janus-faced name, mine and an other's, one and two at once, *my* window into a vibrant not-me.[35]

Cosmonomastics is a vestibule to with-ness, an ecological terrain of naming. Here the proper name does not appropriate but approaches, draws near, and teaches. I take your name, or you take mine, yet neither of us takes anything away from one another. Nor do we give anything up. Or, if we do, it is a cultural complacency of sorts that the stranger's name estranges us from. We bring him or her nominally into the family, and by the same movement we bring everything into question, into the epistemological estrangement that awakens us to the atypical, the unfamiliar, and the aserial in the typical, familiar, and the series. The cosmoderns reshuffle these polarities into an eponymous correlation where "our" names repeat "theirs" (and vice versa) so as to write new cultural narratives rather than submit to old ones. Cosmodern cognominal mimesis is not the colonization Brian Friel's 1980 play *Translations* famously castigates. At the same time, a translation is in play, and this is, I might add, both translation and self-translation. For not only do we translate ourselves into others' names; not only do we disclose ourselves in those names and in the stories behind them. But, in us and in the stories we also write under those names, we rename those names' meanings, translate the names as we ascribe them the meanings of our own time, place, and language. The next part explores this Janus-faced, cosmodern logic of translation in greater detail.

PART 3 ⊕ TRANSLATIONS

It seems that she needed to love one culture to be able to love the other one.

—SUKI KIM, *The Interpreter*

1. The Translational, the Relational, and the Cosmodern

No Joking Matter: The Chasm and the Chiasma

Nothing is more serious than a translation.

—JACQUES DERRIDA, "Des Tours de Babel"

In Zadie Smith's 2002 novel *The Autograph Man*, Adam, an American-born black Jew living in London, tells Alex, who is half-Jewish and half-Chinese, a joke. The little story features a "debate" between the pope and Rabbi Moishe. Neither speaks the other's language, so the contest is "silent." Its stakes, however, are high. Should the pope win, the Jews will be expelled from Italy. "On the day of the great debate," we learn,

> the Pope and Rabbi Moishe sat opposite each other for a full minute before the Pope raised his hand and showed three fingers. Rabbi Moishe looked back and raised one finger.
>
> Next, the Pope waved his finger around his head. Rabbi Moishe pointed to the ground where he sat. The Pope then brought out a communion wafer and a chalice of wine. Rabbi Moishe pulled out an apple. With that, the Pope stood up and said, "I concede the debate. This man has bested me. The Jews can stay."
>
> Later, the cardinals gathered around the Pope, asking him what happened. The Pope said, "First I held up three fingers to represent the Trinity. He responded by holding up one finger to remind me that there was still one God common to both our religions. Then I waved my finger around me to show him that God was all around us. He responded by pointing to the ground to show that God was also right here with us. I pulled out the wine and the wafer to show that God ab-

157

solves us of our sins. He pulled out an apple to remind me of original sin. He had an answer for everything. What could I do?"

Meanwhile, the Jewish community crowded around Rabbi Moishe, asking what happened. "Well," said Moishe, "first he said to me, 'You Jews have three days to get out of here.' So I said to him, 'Not one of us is going to leave.' Then he tells me the whole city would be cleared of Jews. So I said to him, 'Listen here, Mr. Pope, the Jews . . . we stay right here!' "

"And then?" asked a woman.

"Who knows?" said Rabbi Moishe. "We broke for lunch."[1]

Adam calls this "the founding joke of all the others" yet does not elaborate.[2] But *The Autograph Man* and Smith's other two novels, *White Teeth* and *On Beauty,* teem with clues as to what the anecdote might found. Noteworthy is, in this light, that Adam has taken an interest in Hebrew symbolic numerology, a hermeneutics of subtextual connections among seemingly unrelated text units, while Alex, a "philograph"—collector and trader of autographs, of "others'" quintessential writings, as it were—is a kind of writer himself, at work on a "book" listing in two contrasting columns all things "typically Jewish" and "goyish."

The point, in Smith and in cosmodernism broadly, is contrast itself, more exactly the unwonted with-ness it bears, its relational undertow; the gap dissimilarity opens, but also the bridge; the chasm between identities no less than the chiasma, the "crossing over" and the crisscrossing of these identities and their expressions, linguistic and otherwise; in short, cross-cultural and cross-linguistic communication, as it turns out, both possible and impossible, arduous yet necessary. A cultural-identitarian parable, the founding narrative founds—and, Adam glosses, "enlightens" us on—the very foundation of culture and identity: the self-other relation. Specifically, the joke sets up translation as a modality of relatedness and by the same token the culturally-existentially foundational role translation plays despite its fated shortcomings.[3] Since relationality is the keystone of the cosmodern and translation is a relational form, translation scenes and, with them, an entire translational way of seeing the world take up a central position in the cultural projections of cosmodernism. Charting the translational imaginary of turn-of-the-millennium American narrative, part 3 looks closely at Nicole Mones's and Suki Kim's fictions of translations. To frame the discussion, I attend first to the interface of the translational and the cosmodern. As I do so, I ask: Are all translations cosmodern? Or is there a cosmodern shift in the history of translation? If there is one, when does it occur and what does it entail in view of my book's overall argument?

One of the most inherently transcultural and metalinguistic—in Jakobson, "phatic"—genres, the joke almost invariably pivots on cultural discrepancies and tensions as much as it does on its teller's ability to tell it "right," without "ruining" it, which in turn hangs on his or her talent in both drawing on the asymmetries and conflicts involved and shuttling back and forth between them so as to help the audience "get it." Therefore, the joke-teller must be a translator, a "chiasmic" artist or go-between yo-yoing from one side to another while the "parties" remain "discrete," unassimilated into a controlling totality (unlike in racist jokes) and yet brought into colloquy.

This is as much as saying that all jokes are translational, are about, and simply are, translation; and that they problematize translation itself, what it does and does not do, and, in revealing its own limits, what it also reveals about its scene, cast, and historical ambiance. In flaunting and, successfully or less so, performing translation, jokes show how culture works; how much it is about translation, about crossings back and forth between tongues, styles, and mannerisms; and how much language, culture, and community rest on plurilinguism and pluriculturalism, on the many underneath the veneer of oneness. Jokes' dead serious transgressive thrust inheres precisely in this translational mobility. "[R]oughening conventional material in unconventional ways," they "defamiliarize," Doris Sommer observes. We notice here what we also did with respect to names and language broadly in cosmodernism: jokes shed new light on the familiar and the familial, on mother tongue, motherland, and "us" generally. A technical or aesthetic matter in formalist poetics, this Brechtian *Verfremdung* has deep cultural-ideological consequences, for it "exposes" the "strangeness" of one's culture, enables this culture's critical anatomy.[4] If, according to Sommer, aesthetics is a joke, so is culture. Better yet, jokes are cultural, are culturally revealing content-wise, as cultural "documents," but they are also metacultural in that they uncover culture's nuts and bolts, its "rules."

Adam's story is a case in point. It makes, in fact, for a particularly germane case given the conspicuousness of its translational theme. Here, everybody is a translator, lives or barely gets by in translation, good or bad: the pope and the rabbi, who engage or attempt to engage in cross-cultural or "interlinguistic" translation during the contest, but also their people, to whom they retranslate afterward what they think the opponent said and for whom such (mis)translational exercises are part and parcel of the daily grist. The retranslation is, or fancies itself, interlinguistic but (still in Jakobson's terminology) also "intersemiotic" since the debaters render body language into another semiotic system (words); lastly, this retranslation is "intralinguistic" as the pope and the rabbi interpret for their linguistic, ethnic, and religious communities what they suppose the rival meant.[5] Of course, they are—in their different ways—wrong, more precisely, at once right and wrong. They are wrong insofar as they assume there is just one, literal meaning of the other's gestures, and go for it, thereby rehearsing the either/or, "right-or-wrong" translation model that reinforces the "categorical" divorce between Jews and gentiles in Alex's book. And they are right in that, even though they "get" each other neither during nor after the debate, the coming together of self and other in the agonal face-to-face is "supplemental" or, translation theorists would say, "added value."[6] "Translation-cum-supplement," as Rey Chow calls it, "adds" to the "conversation," especially in the rabbi's case, further conversational, interrogative, and self-interrogative implications to the self and its group.[7]

These implications are local, story- and history-bound to the extent they account for the narrative *dénouement,* an unlikely solution to an otherwise all-too-real problem that may or may not refer specifically to Italian Jewry's sixteenth-century persecutions under Pius V. But the joke has broader bearings. To clarify, let me point out that it unearths a culturally, religiously, and linguistically composite setup where gentiles and Jews, Italian, Judeo-Italian (La'az), and possibly Ladino speakers, not counting more scholarly and theologically oriented users of Latin and Hebrew, live virtually side by side. While this sharing of space and power is uneven and the parties appear divided by any number of things including limited insight into one another's language and culture, deals are not out of the question. In reality, they are vitally important and do happen. The two peoples and religions are both apart and "stuck together" and so have no choice but to work out arrangements and relationships. This means, symbolically as well as practically, con-versing, turning to each other, testing—if also contesting—the other in and through language exchange and quotidian give-and-take. Indeed, this existential conversationalism tests how self and other feel and what they know about one another, but it also tests their feelings and knowledge about themselves. The joke's debate foregrounds pointedly the shortcomings of mutual knowledge, and with them the failure of translation, whereas the postdebate briefings are where the contest's loss-loss, in which both debaters gave "wrong" answers, if it does not become a win-win (certainly not from the pope's viewpoint), at least warrants the status quo of co-presence as modus vivendi.

A generic and primordial condition of *communality* as *cross-cultural commonality*, the status quo, this compound makeup of language, culture, and identity, pertains not only to the Italian Jews but to any community. None is ever pure, and so all attempts to purify or "cleanse" it are bound to fail since, as cosmoderns emphasize, self and other share an *ab ovo* proximity culturally as well as linguistically. This would be one way to interpret the final part of the encounter, where the pope hints that God would absolve him of the sin he is about to commit by running the Jews out of the city, to which the rabbi "retorts" (so the pontiff says, at least), that that sin is original or, originary rather. This means that the sin was not, and will not be, remitted, for it is part of what we are as humans. More notably still, it also means that whatever we are in well-defined configurations of culture, history, religion, and idiom, we are so because we are with others, profoundly bound up with them. Thus the conversation the contestants do not manage to carry, and which their translations could not possibly capture, is made up for in another plane and place. The "misunderstanding" and its mistranslation translate into profit in kind, into understanding and self-understanding.

On this score, the Jewish perspective is more instructive. For one thing, the debate's outcome buttresses a certain notion of heterogeneous, jointly although unequally occupied territory. It is in this space that, for now, the Jews' survival is ensured in translation, in the negotiation of the everyday across tongues and mores. For another thing, if the rabbi does not know how to translate the pope's signs, in his attempted rendition he finds, first, that all translation is interpretation and, second, that, if the goal is "truthful" transposition of an other's words, this interpretation may be off base and yet somehow spot-on. What gets translated, then, is not so much or solely the other's meanings and the other in general as *the translator himself to himself and his kin*. In the debate's aftermath, the rabbi's "Who knows?" and the urgency of knowledge it conveys are refocused on himself and his people as conversation and contestation across community boundaries now move within and translation initiates a self-translating, self-clarifying effort. The other as translation quandary, as question mark, sets up doubt as a cosmodern stepping stone to the rendering self's self-questioning. In their strange names, words, and gestures, others prompt us to revisit our own body language and language overall, and with them the linguistic, semiotic, epistemological, and ethical paradigms fashioning selfhood. While Adam's joke does not flesh out this autoanalytic process, it nevertheless "founds" it, finds its premise—and promise of paradoxical "gain"—in translational loss, in that which resists translation and may well be untranslatable.

The Un/translatable; or, Founded in Translation

An Impossible Necessity . . .
—MARTHA J. CUTTER, *Lost and Found in Translation*

[I]n the very tongue of the original narrative there is a translation.
—JACQUES DERRIDA, "Des Tours de Babel"

World literature is writing that gains in translation.
—DAVID DAMROSCH, *What Is World Literature?*

What makes language untranslatable, though? Why is translation both impossible and indispensable? Further, why is linguistic translation insufficient? Do linguistic translations fall short because they are not also cultural? The questions have elicited a range of responses. One of the most frequently rehearsed, Walter Benjamin's 1923 essay "The Task of the Translator," may help us see more clearly why the rabbi and the pope's "problem" is not only lack of bi- or multilingual skills, why this may not even be a translation problem per se but a larger one, language itself, and why the "problem with language" may not be just a linguistic matter either. We learned in part 1 that my language is neither wholly mine nor a single whole, one, inscribing as it does an other into discourse and thus divulging a heteronomy, a relation with a being not me nor my kind, regardless of what else I may be communicating. Whatever I say, I tell of a presence already worded into my language, of room set aside for meanings "other" (than mine). What my saying carries across, what it translates into the realm of the said, is an other. Thus, my speech is always-already translated, a translation, and by the same token unfinished. It bespeaks—without fully speaking or spelling out—the unspoken, and so remains incomplete.

It is translation's effect, if not job proper, to round off my speech, to translate this translation into the completeness, the totality, or identicalness to itself original speech, originals, and origins do not enjoy, as Derrida comments on "The Task of the Translator."[8] My linguistic and cultural other, the translator comes along to carry through my project, to render my inchoate language into a more accommodating albeit never absolutely accurate expression of whatever I may have meant. It is in this sense that "[i]n translation the original rises into a higher and purer linguistic air," as Benjamin writes.[9] But again, translation does not simply "come after," and on this account it is as original as the "original" itself. Moreover: not only is translation not a "secondary and derived event in relation to an original language or text";[10] translation also comes first because it has already come in the "original," which may explain why so many writers have let out that they do not write but translate, make accessible. Unfortunately, this translation—the source text as translation—fails or, as Benjamin says, history dulls it, wears it out. This is where "actual" translation comes in to either speak what the text has left unspoken or to check the ebb into meaninglessness of that which the text did speak. The translator, then, is no longer a cultural Cinderella (nor is his or her work derivative) but an author's equal-footing partner, for, inexorably sketchy, *imperfecta* (Lat. for "unfinished"), writing calls for somebody capable not just of rendering it "equivalent" in another language but of finishing it up. Carrying over as carrying through; translation as (co-)authorship, as crucial to the authored writing as the "original" authoring itself: translation constitutes, Derrida stresses, both a debt and a moral necessity. I am indebted to the "original" as much as this is indebted to the other originals it incorporates, and thus translates, in hopes of carrying forth into expression a certain meaning. But the "original" is also indebted to the still unknown translator to come. This person will attempt to fully bring that meaning out and, because he or she *will necessarily fail to do so*, others will have to take up the same task much though they themselves will come up short, over and over again. For successful translation would entail respeaking the text into the One Language that would make us all one, the same, and haul us into the world of selfsameness. This was the "negative" universality God warded off by mixing up the Tower of Babel builders' tongues, thus "founding" the "necessary and impossible task of translation, its necessity *as* impossibility."[11] Consequently, the Tower (*tour* in French) was left unfinished. But this incompleteness too turned out to be *foundational*, for across ages it has afforded the more "productive" and indispensable incompleteness of ever-partial, hence ever-reattempted translation, and with it human fellowship over the gulfs of language and culture. Because there is no universal language, because a national idiom or an utterance can only say so much, one depends on an other and his or her language, on a de*tour* through the geography of otherness to carry out the discourse. Authorship and, bound up with it, the "originality" of what I say or write are then authorized by an other's presence. This presence founds, gives me a toehold before *and* after I speak or write. It permeates my speech or writing originally—authenticates it, as I argued in the introduction—and comes to its assistance thereafter. The other's idiom marks my words' incompleteness *as* the translation they already are, but also their chance for completion *in* the translations to come.

Philology, History, Critique

> They did not know the delights of the historical sense; what was past and alien was an embarrassment to them; and being Romans, they saw it as an incentive for a Roman conquest. Indeed, translation was a form of conquest. Not only did they omit what was historical; one also added allusions to the present and, above all, struck out the name of the poet and replaced it with one's own—not with any sense of theft but with the very conscience of the *imperium Romanum*.
> —FRIEDRICH NIETZSCHE, *The Gay Science*

Analogous to the shift in reading theory described in part 4, the cultural turn in translation studies put a slightly different spin on the issues raised by Benjamin. The turn "meant," in Susan Bassnett's view, that the "questions asked were more descriptive than evaluative and concerned how translations circulate in the world, how they contribute to the formation of literary canons, and what the role of the readers of translations might be." This change "has altered the way in which translation and the translator are perceived. In addition to the difficulties posed by linguistic constraints, by norms of literary acceptability, and by different horizons of expectations, contemporary research in translation studies has added a whole additional layer of difficulties posed by questions of unequal power relations across cultures."[12] The "difficulties"—the questions the "cultural answers" themselves begged—sprang up in the transition from a translation model centered on the "source" text to another revolving around translation's own author, text, and context. A venerable philosophy and practice of translation has assumed that, "unfathomable" as it may be, this text's meaning can be tackled methodically and "correctly," like a textual-stylistic cipher, and that the challenge it mounts concerns principally the translator's learning and command of language. This translator would use his or her competencies to cut through whatever stands between him or her and the text's "message," which would have to be retrieved and represented accurately, with no omissions or additions. Not unlike the traditional critic, this translator supposedly circumvents contingency. A variety of the antiexpressive (and anti-self-expressive) mimesis doctrine, such a translation dismisses or plays down translational historicity. Translation may be interpretation, but interpretation is, primarily if not solely, linguistic. The only context it takes into account is the text and its idiom. This is how the pope interprets the rabbi's hand signs and also why he misinterprets them. Not only does he assume that the gesticulatory language they argue in is unbounded, "catholic." He also takes for granted the contest's frame of reference by presuming that the argument cannot be but about what he knows and cares for. That explains why in his decoding of his opponent's motions, he disregards the rabbi, his community, and concerns. "Interlinguistic" the pope's translation may be, but it is not intercultural. In consequence, it misses the mark.

Critics from Umberto Eco to Bassnett have drawn from the "Sapir-Whorf hypothesis" to show that one translates from a language as much as from its culture.[13] They have insisted that not even the words for "staple elements" like *bread* or *coffee* are "culturally equivalent" across tongues and countries given that the mores and values such "trivial" lexicon designates vary from one idiom and place to another, "produc[ing] stories" that make sense in one idiom and place more than in others. In Eco's example, the sentence "'Ordinai un caffé, lo buttai giù in un secondo ed uscii dal bar' (literally, 'I ordered a coffee, swilled it down in a second and went out of the bar'),"[14] conveys one thing to an audience of espresso drinkers and another to those who "sip" their brew from large mugs and for whom downing a coffee in a single gulp would be quite a feat. Eco's coffee drinking is similar to the pope's gestural semiotics: one must assume, as the protagonist of Philippe Vasset's 2003 dystopia *ScriptGenerator©®™* does, that neither "travels" well, does not signify abroad what it does at home, and therefore requires a translation as linguistic (or "literal," in Eco) as cultural.[15] This way, one establishes a relation to the other culture, turns to it and "targets" it as much as one does the "target language." This is not what the pope does, though. His translation concurrently *deculturates,* that is, deals with the other's idiom in vitro culturally speaking, ignores the rabbi's "situation," and *acculturates,* maps Christian cultural and religious references onto what the rabbi "expresses," and so ultimately "rewrites" him into a version of the translator. Thus, *The Autograph Man* forefronts "c(o)lonial" translation, more broadly, representation of an other as "cloning" of the same. Testimony to globalization's "darker side,"[16] the "hegemonic"-"exploitative" thrust of this egological sort of translation has been pinned down in a plethora of works from Carlos Fuentes's short story "Las dos orillas" (The Two Shores) to Cormac McCarthy's *Blood Meridian*, Barbara Kingsolver's *The Poisonwood Bible*, and T. C. Boyle's *The Tortilla Curtain*.[17]

A century before, Nietzsche's *The Gay Science* also pictured translation as "conquest" and appropriation of an other's idiom and culture, with specific reference to "dehistoricizing" Latin renditions of Greek authors and the ensuing "forced" assimilation of those authors into Roman styles and concepts. But the translations in question also attest, and demonstrably led, to a "Hellenization" of the Roman mind, after Cato the Elder a hot-button issue in Rome.[18] German classicist and biblical scholar Friedrich Schleiermacher's 1813 essay "On the Different Methods of Translating" is the locus classicus for this age-old dilemma that either "moves" the translated writer toward, and eventually "transforms" him or her into, his or her audience or, conversely, carries the target public backward into the writer's world.[19] The former kind of Latin translation would "Romanize"; the latter would "Grecize." True, Schleiermacher and his followers seek a more "dialectic" alternative to the "domesticating"/"foreignizing" dichotomy, but overall they tend to favor the dyad's second member and understandably so given that the opposite category has had the upper hand historically. Either way, what we risk "losing in translation," Nietzsche writes in *The Gay Science* and then again in *Beyond Good and Evil*, is a certain "tempo," pacing, or "style" of culture. Like Goethe before and poststructuralist thinkers after him, he deems some of this "untranslatable," for not only does language in general always say, in the source texts and in their renditions alike, either "too much" or "too little,"[20] but, he reflects later in *The Will to Power*, words also "make the uncommon common," serialize the unique.[21]

The pope certainly purports to make the uncommon common. First, he takes for granted a deeper commonality of language, where language is not a particular tongue but a cultural idiom more broadly articulating a "view of things," a repertoire of values and issues. Yet, second, he is the one who gets to define this commonality or "universality," and so, as in

Native Speaker, the joke's philosophical-ideological lingua franca disenfranchises because it is encoded egologically, that is, no matter what the other signals, the signs are bound to reference the code-holder and his agenda. The rabbi does not step out of this pseudoconversation entirely either, but its linguistic, cultural, and political lopsidedness betrays arrangements of language, representation, and polity for which the pope, rather than his "adversary," bears responsibility. In fact, it is these institutions, formations, and images that construct the rabbi and his community as an adversarial entity with whom one sorts things out in win-or-lose contests and more broadly in either-or, disjunctively confrontational engagements. The pontiff thinks he can win out by "catholicizing" the other, by rendering him "common," in-different. His is a translation and, more largely, a *cultural politics of in-difference* that sets out to boil the other down—as I say, egologically—to the same, to render similar to, and ultimately co-opt into, the rendering ego. He believes this kind of transposition of uncommonality and difference can be done. To put it otherwise, he knows in advance, or thinks he does, what the rabbi means (signifies and is). The rabbi, however, is not so sure, hence he does know, if not everything about the pope, then at least that he, the rabbi, has to question what he knows about him. For the pope, translation is unquestionably doable and unproblematically so because it works "vertically" as the translator reaches "across" the other's discourse "down" to the unrevealed "meaning" at the expense of any substantial dealings with discursive contingencies and those "others" in them. For the rabbi, translation takes the longer road, "horizontally" or "laterally."[22] It still strikes out for a "depth," for what the other means, but not i(m)-mediately, without "mediation." Thus, to quote Appiah's adaptation of the "thick description" formula, what is in play here comes close to "thick translation," for it transcends neither the context of communication nor those participating in it.[23] In translating, "doubling" the other in another language, both the pope and the rabbi ultimately "translate," double back onto themselves. But where vertical (transcendent) translation is narcissistic and runs in a vicious circle that "bears out" the already-known, horizontal translation effectuates a spiral-like movement. It does not put the translator back where he was prior to the encounter with the other's language but into a place where the possibility of translation, and with it of all knowledge, becomes, indeed, something to wonder about.

Culturalism, "Relational Semantics," Cosmodernism: Translation and Difference

From textuality to contextuality, from translation as relating *about* an "original" to translation as relating *to* its own milieu: traceable to Renaissance polemics "call[ing] into question more naïve or literalist notions of translation equivalence," the cultural studies turn in translation scholarship, especially the theorized scrutiny of translation's "effects" on the social imaginary, is a late twentieth-century development.[24] But, in the shift from a semantics to a pragmatics of translation, critics have not abandoned semantic concerns altogether. Instead, they have pointed to another "semantic shift," from "referential" to "relational semantics," that is, from preoccupations with what translation says about the translated text to what translation imparts about its own author, time, and place.[25] This way, culturalist relationality eventually expands to bring into focus the translator himself or herself, thus completing the veer from the referential-objectualist paradigm centered around translation's "object" with a self-reflective move across the object, that object's author and world, back toward the translating subject. Like old-school realism's, traditional translators' is an ideology of objectuality and, derived from it, objectivity. They claim to bring out for one "side" (theirs) what "the other side" meant while making sure not to "take sides." What I said above about the historical-material context of translation applies to the translated text as it does to the translating text and its author. The pope hardly serves as example in this respect, but overall, as far as the translator's "empirical" person goes, the idea (and the ideal no less) is self-transcendence. He or she must disappear, "lose" himself or herself in translation. This is the price for translation's complete transparency and unequivocalness, for a success defined in a terminology and within an aesthetic-philosophical framework translation studies has long shared with the classical theory of representation. Clashing against conventional notions of representation and rendition according to which the commitment to self-transcendence ensures translation's fidelity, objectivity, and straightforwardness, cosmodern translation makes no bones about a translational *politics* that acknowledges the translator's "involvement."

Carrying on and refining the culturalist project, cosmodern critics and fiction writers alike suggest not only that the translator cannot rub him- or herself off the translation scene where he or she holds a leading part, but that that part appertains to the broader script of knowledge and self-knowledge. Of course, translation is still about something foreign to itself linguistically and otherwise. In being about it, though, it is also about itself and its author. To clarify, along the lines of the economy of relatedness sketched out in this book's introduction: translation cannot be about the translator unless it is first and foremost about the translated. Translation is not simply self-translation, nor are the other and his or her idiom just pretexts for the translating self to take another look at himself or herself. It is, to be sure, not the codex of selfhood that this self sets out to translate from but the chronicles of otherness, and yet as it applies itself to the latter—and *because* it does so—it also elucidates the former. To reiterate a core tenet of cosmodernism, self-knowledge does not come about egologically, as I self-center and shut others out, but translationally—ecologically—as I take them in and reword their words into mine. To put it differently: dedication to an other, to understanding his or her word and world, is rewarded with the gift of self-understanding; both arrive through the same effort, stake the same space, and are couched in the same text.

It is in this sense that something like another—let us call it cosmodern—turn in how we think about translation seems to be under way now. This is a turn from translation as relation between texts rendered and texts that render to translation as relation of the rendered text and self to the rendering self and finally of this self to itself—in Michael Cronin's formulation, from "dwelling" on "*translations and texts*" to a "greater focus on *translations and translators*,"[26] or from translation as reflection, ideally and idealistically *reflective* of the "original"'s truth,[27] to self-*reflexive* translation that holds up for scrutiny the translator, his or her presuppositions, standards, and life philosophy.[28] Prefigured in *The Autograph Man* and vividly dramatized in the translation episodes reviewed later in this part, this shift pulls us further away from issues of textuality, philology, aesthetics, hermeneutics, and their largely rational-formalist take on linguistic meaning, and toward questions of identity, cultural politics, hegemony, and a relational and self-relational approach to the translator as meaning-maker.[29] The semantics of profundity and corresponding transcendent hermeneutics looked deep into the text for its "truth." Relational semantics and the contingent critique it capacitates have not given up on this sort of search, but they also look "laterally," around the translator's world and into him- or herself. Reference-relation-self-relation: the search for meaning elsewhere sets in motion an epistemological quest inside, for what the translator's self means, whereas the rational, "vertical" model of translation-as-transcendence retroactively "corroborates" the translator's "intuitions," so that culturally and ideologically the target text proves to have been its own source all along. Spurred by fantasies of sameness, translations of this stripe are unethical. Lawrence Venuti got it right: "Institutions, whether academic or religious, commercial or political show a preference for a translation ethics of sameness, translating that enables and ratifies existing discourses and canons, interpretations and pedagogies, advertising campaigns and liturgies—if only to ensure the continued and unruffled reproduction of the institution." At the same time, translation can ruffle culture's feathers, is institutionally "scandalous," for "it can create different values and practices, whatever the domestic setting." "This is not to say," the critic cautions, "that translation can ever rid itself of its fundamental domestication, its basic task of rewriting the foreign text in domestic cultural terms. The point is rather that a translator can choose to redirect the ethnocentric movement of translation so as to decenter the domestic terms that a translation project must inescapably utilize. This is an ethics of difference that can change the domestic culture."[30]

Lost and Found: Translation, Self-Translation, and the Production of the Human

> But nothing's lost. Or else: all is translation
> And every bit of us is lost in it
> (Or found . . .)
> —JAMES MERRILL, "Lost in Translation"

> Where is the lost-and-found, we ask, if we have left something
> somewhere? Where, indeed, but in translation? Translation as
> trope finally constellates a lost-and-found—a locale that holds
> items/languages until such time as they can be reclaimed,
> exchanged, or claimed by another user/speaker. The lost-and-
> found of translation represents a site of simultaneous linguistic
> loss and gain, of reduction and reimplication of codes, of both
> the destruction and resurrection of language.
> —MARTHA J. CUTTER, *Lost and Found in Translation*

Rational, decontingent translation, translation that thinks of itself as dispassionate language exercise, ends up "domesticating" or "overdomesticating." It aspires to seize the "naked truth" of an other's word, to transcribe it into another language "as is," by short-shrifting that word's cultural embeddedness. But, we have noticed, this deculturing tack actually accultures. It "Romanizes," "Westernizes," and so forth. It is only an apparent paradox that the more this translation type scrambles to lay hold of the "truth itself" beyond and above any contingencies and interests, the more that truth, once delivered, looks like what the translator, his or her public, and the institutions putting out the translation have expected. Brought into sync with available inscriptions of sameness, the truth of an other's word and world scarcely touches off cultural self-interrogation. On this account, Bassnett is spot on: "Perhaps the principal contribution of contemporary translation theorists to the longstanding debates about faithfulness in translation and definitions of equivalence is the assertion that equivalence as sameness is an impossibility."[31] The larger point, though, is perhaps not what we cannot do but what we should not attempt in the first place, in other words, not the inescapable limitations of our semantic-hermeneutical toolkit but a procedural ethics committed to curbing the other's "domestication."

If with the rational, transcendent model "the traffic goes" in "one direction only,"[32] toward the text at first, across it after that, and, at last, into the semantic beyond, relational translation becomes a two-way and even a three-way street, a triangulating process linking up the rendered text, the rendition, and the renderer. Looping back onto itself and its author, translation is here a reflection of and on identity—the identity of translation and translation as identity, the translator's identity and identity largely, both grasped as translational "aftershocks": on the move, fluid, unsettled and unsettling; tentative, in-progress versions of "originals" of otherwise impure origins and hence analogously ever-imperfect, "defective"; "neither here nor there," "mixed bags," pidgin renderings into creolized lingoes of stuff that may have never been the "real thing." Incurred in translation and so making up for what we might "lose" in it, this instability of process—this process of instability of being and understanding—unhinges hardened ontological, epistemological, and cultural categories, thus clearing the decks for seeing ourselves and our world anew. As Martha J. Cutter observes, much though "[p]ostmodern theorists have argued that we are all alienated from language, that we are all 'lost in translation,'" translation and translators do "offer," even when they seem "at a loss," "productive ways of acknowledging this loss but also of finding ourselves in and through translation—ways of locating a mode of cultural voice that renovates the racial and linguistic politics," overall the cultural politics of the "textual and actual worlds we inhabit."[33]

Counterintuitive as it may strike some, this *productivity of loss*—the loss converted, translated into gain—is what I wish to underscore here.

For we do find ourselves in translation as soon as we bring an other's language into our surroundings. We translate an other, carry him or her over into the landscape of our feelings and references, but that translation repositions us too, transports us into a self-exploratory position within that space. The topological and the epistemological, *where* the new location takes us and *what* it does for us there, are two faces of the same coin. Philosophically speaking, this new place "surprises" us: we may lose some of the other's nuances and even ourselves as we search for them, but we are also, emotionally and cognitively, "surprised in translation."[34] "Impenetrable," resistant to our *metaphrasis*, the other's phrases and thoughts may nonetheless jolt us into rephrasing and rethinking our own formulas and cogitations and thus into wonder, curiosity, and reflection—into the rabbi's groundbreaking "Who knows?" The fact that it may not be entirely possible to know and verbalize what the rabbi himself knows and is—a broader provision about otherness *Cosmodernism* has made from the outset—should not deter us from taking upon ourselves to know, and thus translate, him.

A number of critics have put us on guard against giving up prematurely our engagement with the idiomatic, "untranslatable" other. It is in this context that Zhang Longxi worries that the "relativist emphasis on difference" may "serve to legitimize a position of cultural supremacy."[35] In the same vein, Apter warns that "[i]f translation failure is acceded to too readily, it becomes an all-purpose expedient for staying narrowly within one's monolingual universe. A parochialism results, sanctioned by false pieties about not wanting to 'mistranslate' the other. This parochialism is the flip side of a globalism that theorizes place and translates everything without ever traveling anywhere."[36] To sidestep the twin dilemmas of translatability/untranslatability and globalism/parochialism, Apter too turns away from translation as "adequate" rendition/recovery of the original and toward a global-era Benjaminian "model" that deems everything "translatable and in a perpetual state of in-translation,"[37] subject, that is, to in-translatability and as such at once resisting and calling for translation. Drawing from Badiou's *Petit manuel d'inesthétique,* she acknowledges the "incommensurability" of the original, in-translatability as *un*translatability; but she also recognizes the flip side: the untranslatable *as* in-translation, provisional stage inviting the "completing" labor of translation. The world, its languages, and discourses, in Apter's rehearsal of Benjamin, move back and forth between these two poles: the untranslatable and that which we nevertheless must and do translate; the translation that falters or fails and the translation that *for this very reason* must be undertaken. "Cognition," therefore, cannot but reckon with a "worldly dialectics" that calls on us to wrestle with the "interlocking singularities" and "incommensurabilities" nested in the seemingly monolingual.[38] "The implications of planetary criticism" for the humanities, Apter says, lay "emphasis on a unidimensional formalism—univocity, singularity, irreducibility, holism, quantum cosmology, the Event" while retaining the commitment to "an earthly politics of translation and nontranslatability."[39]

To be in today's world more than in any other before, the cosmoderns intimate, is to be in the "Zone"—in the "translation zone" of in-translation singularities; it is, to recall Apter's Russell Banks metaphor, "drifting" from place to place and version to version;[40] it is being at once inside and outside your circle of relatives and cultural alphabet, in transit and "relative," making sense of yourself in relation to others while recognizing that such sense-making may get neither those others nor yourself exactly right; it is, as Judith Butler insists, experiencing culture as intersection of various "cultural horizons" and by the same token as translational domain.[41] More basically then, *being in the cosmodern world is being in translation,* to wit, in translation understood "laterally." And equally, being in the world is *translation itself as being,* as inching toward that which you end up being, transiting to your humanity and eventually becoming human as your words and deeds are weighed and recast by an other and as you do the same unto him or her. "We are translated men," Rushdie said of himself and fellow English-language Indian authors in his 1982 essay "Imaginary Homelands."[42] If Rushdie revised the statement today, he would probably make sure nobody felt left out, not only Indian-born women. For, a quarter century *après,* is this not the portrait of the writer as a human being? How many of us are not "translated," translational if not necessarily transnational even though more and more of us are "borne across the world"? How many of us are not, as Rushdie also observes, "at once plural and partial," on the go, growing in transit from place to place a quintessentially translational selfhood by adopting and adapting others' languages, styles, and worldviews?[43] To be sure, fewer and fewer—if any of us ever—can make an earnest claim to the contrary. A matter of codependence and mutuality, our humanity arises and blossoms in translation. Moreover, as Augustine offers in a famous passage from Book XIX of *The City of God,* "[I]f two men, each ignorant of the other's language, meet, and are compelled by some necessity not to pass on but to remain with one another, it is easier for dumb animals, even of different kinds, to associate together than these men, even though both are human beings."[44] Thus not only is humanity translational, born in translation insofar as it is the latter that distinguishes us from beasts, but, as a communication tool, translation also makes us human by enabling, indeed, requiring the pope, the rabbi, and us all to overcome silence, solitude, and monolingualism and step into our full humanness by being with one another. In sum, translation provides for human fellowship, for relatedness as a foundation of being human. "It is normally supposed that something always gets lost in translation," Rushdie remarks in the same essay, but he adds: "I cling, obstinately, to the notion that something can also be gained."[45] This is what we gain, what we find in translation, and what translation ultimately founds: being *as* translation, the very meaning of being. By the same token, translation ontologizes a new analytic of identity, institutes a post-Heideggerian ontological hermeneutics. That is, my being takes shape, and so I become what I am, in translation of an other. Yet, as I translate an other, I also translate myself; I ask what he or she means but also what I mean to him or her, to myself, and the world.

Given that my being obtains, is exercised and warranted in translation, translation must lie "at the centre of any attempt to think about questions of identity in human society"[46] now more than ever. Now more than at any point in history, "life is translation, and we are all lost in it," as Geertz paraphrases James Merrill.[47] An existential process leading up to what I am, care about, and stand for, translation both settles me into an onto-cultural structure of mind and soul, beliefs and passions, *and* unsettles, prods me to query them all. This query, the ontological analytic or the hermeneutics of being, is growing more relational day by day in that it yields a certain knowledge about myself and my culture as I wrestle with questions about an other, his or her idiom, and culture. "In the kind of translation that interest me most," James Clifford confesses in his essay "Traveling Cultures," "you learn a lot about peoples, cultures, and histories different from your own, enough to begin to know what you're missing."[48] What we "find" in the translation of such histories and stories—rather than "lose"—is the chance to "recognize aspects, dimensions, and elements of ourselves that we did not even know existed."[49] This is, as we will learn in more detail in this part's final section, re-cognition that does not solidify what our cognition already possesses (or thinks it does). In Geertz's words again, this is not "epistemological complacency" but self-discovery as, and through, the discovery, be it fragmentary, of an other.

The anthropologist is right: we can never "apprehend another people's or another period's imagination neatly, as though it were our own."[50] But we can apprehend, or reapprehend rather, our own world of images and ideas as we look into the worlds of others.

2. Geopolitics of Desire

Remade in China: Nicole Mones, *Lost in Translation*

> Where does a dialogue begin if not in the space of desire, in the space of the interrogative that allows one to cross over into the word of the other?
> —JAMES RISSER, "The Voice of the Other in Gadamer's Hermeneutics"

> Translation is the performative nature of cultural communication.
> —HOMI BHABHA, *The Location of Culture*

Mones's 1998 bestseller *Lost in Translation* may not bring to mind Marguerite Duras's *L'Amant* (*The Lover*) as promptly as it does Merrill's poem, Eva Hoffman's 1989 memoir *Lost in Translation: A Life in a New Language*, Sofia Coppola's 2003 movie *Lost in Translation*, or Frost's definition of poetry as that which "gets lost in translation."[51] However, Duras's celebrated 1984 "Oriental romance" resembles Mones's book closely. Both are set in the Far East, *The Lover* in Indochina, *Lost in Translation* in China, and they feature the same type of erotic plot. Duras's "lover" is Chinese, and so is Mones's, but neither story centerstages him. Unlike colonial love stories such as Mircea Eliade's 1933 *Maitreyi*—to which the prototype of Eliade's heroine responded with her own version four decades thereafter—both *The Lover* and *Lost in Translation* revolve around a Western woman, French in Duras, American in Mones.[52]

The two romances bear witness to distinct moments, however. *The Lover* is an imperial romance, whereas *Lost in Translation* has already outgrown John McClure's "late imperial romance" to step into a new era. Mones's China has gone global.[53] In the throes of fast-forward globalization, middle and late 1990s China, in which Mones's later novels *A Cup of Light* (2002) and *The Last Chinese Chef* (2007) also take place, flaunts an odd blend of Communist and corporate politics both tolerant and apprehensive of the new pouring in as capital, Big Macs, Madonna, communication technologies, and American expatriates like Alice Mannegan,

Mones's main heroine. A freelance translator, Alice is hired by one Dr. Adam Spencer, an American paleoanthropologist on his way to the Chinese northwest. In hopes of boosting his flagging academic career, he sets out to recover the famous Peking Man (*Sinanthropus pekinensis*), the remains of which were discovered by the French Jesuit, paleontologist, and philosopher Pierre Teilhard de Chardin in 1928 but vanished mysteriously in 1941. The search is important both to the American and the Chinese, who suspect Spencer might try to sneak the Peking Man out of the country. Therefore, scientists Lin and Kong are assigned to help him but also to make sure the precious bones stay in China.

The cosmodernism of Mones's book stems not so much from setting as from the kind of translator Alice is. Conversant with local idioms, dialects, and culture, she also proves painfully aware of the self-stock-taking in play in their translation. She realizes that she is crossing over into the territory of others, their tongue, and world as soon as she attempts to translate them. She understands too that her translations are seldom flawless, ever less (or more) than the original. An exacting task, interpretation is, she feels, hardly exact. In practice, it is usually just that: an interpretation, an approximation. She is therefore deliberately wrestling with that which may well remain a cipher, impossible to read and transmit to a third party. What matters most is this very struggle with Chinese, the translation process itself rather than rendition accuracy, in short, translation as a cultural "act," as a performance allowing her to step over to the other's side. This move carries more weight than the exactness of her "interpretations" because even if she fails to understand others' utterances completely, her failure opens the door to self-understanding. Here and elsewhere, the cosmodern scene of translation does not obligatorily enact episodes of successful linguistic conversion but rather, and characteristically, larger dramas of cross-cultural encounters that *translate the translator* himself or herself, deliver the interpreter's self to itself. Once more, in this relational sense, translation may be of and "about" others, but it also is about the translating subject, about the intellectual translation this subject makes toward itself and its own quandaries under the spell of an other's words.

A translator in the rich meaning of the term, Alice is a go-between with a keen sense of her fluctuant, "conjunctural" identity, which in James Clifford's view holds out the promise of successful "crosscultural translation."[54] That is, she does not simply play the linguistic and cultural broker, nor does she merely translate *for* others like herself *from* others unlike herself. She is also translating herself, remaking herself into something or somebody she has not been prior to the linguistic act of translation, "losing," but only to "find," herself into a new cultural "positionality," as Bhabha might put it, which warrants a fresh purchase on herself and her America. For, through Alice, Mones also manipulates translation as a master trope and cultural operator concurrently complicit with and resistant to modernity's expanding narrative. Variously tied into the motility and exchanges of globalization, translation does the latter's bidding to a certain degree; as a global vehicle, it acts out modernity's unifying drive.[55] On closer inspection, this act turns out to be a more elaborate performance, though. In it, translation, transgression, and identity transaction dovetail to "unwrite" or at least provide critical footnotes to this grand story as Alice becomes less and less complacent about her work. More than a cogwheel in the egological economy of globally manufactured equivalence via conversion of languages, selves, and cultures into one another, she gradually learns that the untranslated "remainder," whatever is left unparaphrased, uninterpreted, unequaled, "other," can help her make a life-changing leap, translate herself to the other side of complacency, commonplace, and routine.

La planétisation: A grand récit?

Mones deploys the translation theme in an intertextually conspicuous fashion by revisiting—"translating"—texts that have taken up similar "transgressions": contact with others, longing for what we are not, nor can become unless we look beyond ourselves. Of course, it comes as no surprise that the most important intertexts are Teilhard de Chardin's works, primarily his 1955 essay Le Phénomène humain (The Human Phenomenon) and the Letters of Teilhard de Chardin and Lucile Swan. Both are acknowledged in the "Author's Note" and again in the "Historical Note." Teilhard's biography and bibliography tell Mones a captivating story. She is intrigued by his scientific-theosophical writings but also by the letters, which portray Lucile Swan and Teilhard's unconsummated relationship in China, right after Teilhard had dug up the Peking Man and gone on to participate in the famed paleontological American Central Asian Expedition. Notably, Spencer's own fieldwork reenacts this expedition much as Lost in Translation on the whole recapitulates Teilhard's life and work: Alice and Lin's affair parallels Lucile and Teilhard's; diffidence toward foreigners and Communist taboos stand in for Catholic strictures; translation—linguistic, cultural, even sexual—builds an analogy to Teilhard's "system" of metamorphoses and continuities between the organic and the anorganic, spirit and matter, religion and science.

"[Teilhard] was," Mones writes, "an explorer, a scientist—a real man of the world" who "fascinated" women (28). In fact, love—love of a certain sort—is the cornerstone of Teilhard's worldview, as a passage from *Le Phénomène humain,* reread by Alice late at night, reveals. And yet, while Alice does not question Teilhard's "total commitment," she realizes that he "could love Lucile, could care about her and be close to her—as long as he never became her lover." By contrast, Alice is aware that she herself "entered the sexual heart of China all the time—but only the sexual heart" (40). That will change before long, but at this point it bears observing that her Chinese exploits repeat Teilhard's own explorations with a sexual difference since for him love is a desexualized, theosophical-pantheistic concept, namely a Christian, scientific-humanist instead of purely theological one. In Teilhard's philosophy—a mix of Neoplatonism, Thomism, Hegelian *Phänomenologie des Geistes,* and a natural sciences-shaped view of genetics and biological evolution—a cosmic eros, or logos rather, draws everything together, with planetary "communion" both step toward and proof of a universal unity in the making. In his system, the cultural and physical cosmos—the cosmopolitan and the cosmological—go hand in hand: as Mones hints, Teilhardian paleontology is a generous albeit, we shall discover, not unproblematic metaphor of connectedness across all ages and spaces of cosmo-human development, a Christian "romance of totality" from which Mones's own global romance draws critically. In effect, her translational imaginary and more broadly her cosmodernism take shape in dialogue with Teilhard's modernist cosmopolitanism, particularly with the ecumenical philosophy of globalization from *Le Phénomène humain*'s part 4, "La Survie" ("Superlife" or "Super-Consciousness").[56] A thumbnail sketch of this philosophy should therefore help.

Teilhard's thought is modernist on several accounts. First, it presents a typical, early to middle twentieth-century synthesis of philosophical modernity and aesthetic modernism: on one side, humanism, anthropocentrism, rationalism, and positivism, with Darwin's *The Origin of Species* as a prime source; on the other, challenges to all of these in a criticist spirit redolent of Kierkegaard, Nietzsche, and Marx.[57] Second, Teilhard was also a physicist, a geologist, and a paleontologist. These "modernist" preoccupations worried the church, and for good reason. During the first years of the last century, a host of Catholic thinkers sought to "modernize" the Roman Catholic Church. Matei Calinescu points out that "the Modernists," as Pope Pius X derogatorily called them in 1907, "were involved in an effort to make Church doctrine more compatible with the tenets of modern scientific knowledge (for instance the theory of evolution) or of modern historical criticism."[58] Granted, Teilhard did not consider himself a theologian proper. Nor did he join in this "loose theological movement of 'modernization'" led by theologians such as Alfred Loisy, Friedrich von Hügel, and George Tyrell (Teilhard was ordained a priest in 1911 and received his doctorate in geology about a decade thereafter).[59] But the church would not allow him to publish or even return from Asia, which speaks to the same dogmatic, "antimodernist" (antiscientific) position. It is also worth mentioning that Teilhard's works start coming out only a few years before the Vatican begins to "vindicate" the "modernists."[60]

Third, more notable still is the modernist philosophical form Teilhard adopts: phenomenology. As N. M. Wildiers writes, in Teilhard, Husserl, and later in Merleau-Ponty, whose *Phénoménologie de la perception* will appear a few years after *Le Phénomène humain* had been completed, phenomenology is "an endeavor . . . to give as completely as possible expression to the world in its totality and inner orientation."[61] An "archescience" of sorts, Teilhard's is neither philosophy nor metaphysics but a sort of "biography" of the cosmos, a hybrid "science of totality" attempting a holistic description by tapping into a range of sciences and working toward a synthesis of the religious and scientific spirit. A recurring term in Teilhard and his critics,[62] *totality* is a multifaceted phenomenological concept, a method of inquiry stressing the focus on its object as a whole and, in that, also a fundamental insight into this object's makeup insofar as the cosmos represents, *Le Phénomène humain* assures us, a "unity, a *Totum*" (39). Conveying Teilhard's modernism in a fourth sense, this *Totum* designates a modernist construct, a totality or totalizing projection of the cosmological and biological "grand narrative" *Le Phénomène humain* uncoils chapter by chapter with teleological confidence.

It is in conjunction with "totality" and the "totalist" paradigm hammered out in *Le Phénomène humain* that the philosopher theorizes the "global." He actually uses the term, if in a rather general sense.[63] The spread of life on our planet, he tells us, already bears out the hypothesis of a "global [*globale*] unity" (118). But to refer to modern, worldwide social and spiritual developments, he speaks of *planétisation* (234). Roughly, this is a synonym of *mondialisation,* which in French criticism designates both an equivalent and, we saw earlier, an alternative to *globalization.* In Teilhard, *planetization* covers the last stage of a universal, coherent, and convergent progress that has gone through three moments, to which on our planet correspond a first, anorganic period (*la prévie*), when matter (the "geosphere") was created, then a biological phase (*la vie*), when life and the "biosphere" arrive, and third, but also flowing from the preceding step, an intellectual-rational stage, *la pensée.* As its name suggests, the latter witnesses the advent, in "hominized" life form, of thought, which brings about the "noosphere." Coined from the Greek *noos* (or *nous*), "intelligence," "intellect," and "mind," this covers all of them plus their sociocultural manifestations—simply put, human civilization.

Throughout history, Teilhard writes in the third chapter ("The Modern Earth") of part 3, "Man thought he was facing a 'historical turn'" (237). But what we are dealing with in the late 1930s, when Teilhard was completing his book, and all the more so at the dawn of the twenty-first century, is a deep-running crisis. According to the evolutionary logic of Teilhard's cosmo-noological narrative, this is a planetary crisis set off by the "Neolithic metamorphosis," that is, by unprecedented social and "socializing" processes (227). In their wake, the "noosphere has already started to close in on itself by embracing the whole Earth" (229). More than just turning nature into culture, noological expansion presupposes an exponential increase in the "socialization" that will end up "unifying" the planet into a cultural "megasynthesis" (270). Ominous at it may sound, this is, according to Teilhard, "the natural culmination of a process of cosmic organization, which has been following its course invariably since the childhood of our planet" (270). Crowning this evolution will be, he believes, "a harmonious collectivity of consciousnesses, equivalent to a sort of superconsciousness; not an Earth overlaid with myriads of isolated grains of thought, but one wrapped in one continuous thinking cover so completely that it makes up a single, vast grain of thought on a cosmic scale; a plurality of individual reflections coming together in one unit and growing stronger in the act of a single, unanimous reflection" (279). If we have not reached this point yet, that is because we have not been able to handle the growing "hyperorganicity," the abundance of global connections (*liens sociaux*), in short, because we have mismanaged modernity (280). This is how the crisis that broke out in the Neolithic reaches its climax in modern times to define modernity as a time of crisis.

The crisis is twofold. First, it results from a "[p]rise *en masse* de l'Humanité," from the fact that humankind has been integrated as or into a *global mass* (280). Another Teilhardian formula, this *prise en masse* is synonymous with *planetization* (280). Following Teilhard's evolutionary dialectic, planetization sums up our present global condition as well as the condition—in the sense, this time, of prerequisite or stepping stone—for future growth as "peoples and civilizations have attained such a degree of peripheral contact or economic interdependence that the only way they can grow any further is by interpenetration" (280). Second, the crisis of globalization originates in our inability to use our strengths effectively. We face a "*chaotic outbreak of untapped energies,*" but we react to this confusing world by adjusting national frontiers as we scramble to expand physically, in space. Yet, Teilhard warns, unless we readjust ourselves spiritually, we will end up "crushed against one another" on an ever-smaller planet. What we lack, then, is "a new domain of psychic expansion" rather than new borders and imperial expansion; a "totalization" of an inner kind of the world itself (281), capable of carrying on and translating into spiritual terms geopolitical planetization. This will take place in the "point Omega," or the *Parousia,* Christ's advent at the end of time, which coincides with the final intensification of noospheric "unanimity" (321) as all centers of thought and spiritual energy coalesce into one "super-personal" and simultaneously superhuman center (303).

Granted, the "super-personal" or "hyper-personal" (283) obtains beyond the collective (*au délà du collectif*). But it comes along quasi mystically, by a quantum leap happening as we heighten our "love energy" (*l'amour-énergie*) (293). This is, again, universal love. We have it in us as much as the rest of the universe does because it is this love that has created us all in the first place. The unity of life forms evidences love's universality and also goes to show that the same kind of creative-spiritual energy stands behind the birth of life, the evolution of species, the development of the human race and thought, and the noospherical rise up to, and into, the Omega point. We need to recognize, we are told, in the latter our inevitable "ultimate destination" as intelligent creatures. If we do, the Omega point becomes a "noble enterprise" that we must take upon ourselves conscientiously. It is our job to "brin[g] the cosmos to its completion,"[64] that is, into Christ, which would be "wholly consonant with St. Paul's teaching" (134). Thus cosmology and Christology name the same "science." Jointly, they provide a rationale for a *cosmopolitan Christianity,* for a Pauline global brotherhood in Christ.[65]

It has taken us ages to get here, but in Teilhard's narrative the Alpha is an Omega in the making; earlier chapters foreshadow the denouement. To quote other Teilhardian titles, "the vision of the past" (*La Vision du passé*) projects "the future of man" (*Le Futur de l'homme*). It is on this basis that paleontology can divulge what awaits us, and it actually does so, in Teilhard's account, by lending support to the Christological hypothesis. To be more accurate, "hypothesis" is a misnomer here. Teilhard contends that if we turn to the evolutionary argument to account for anthropogenesis, then we must accept its full consequences, which are "noogenetic" on a planetary scale and ultimately eschatological. To put it otherwise, studying human phylogeny opens a window into our common future: the earth qua cosmopolis. As Teilhard concludes, "[T]he Pithecanthropus and the Sinanthropus are more than just two interesting anthropological types. Through them, we gain an insight into the great panorama of humanity" (*Le Phénomène humain*, 215). Accordingly, the rise—and therefore the crisis—of planetary community becomes *legible* for the phenomenologist in the remains of the Peking Man; it is these paleoanthropological intimations of globality that draw Mones to Teilhard.

Paleontology, Totality, Diversity

As Wildiers reflects on Teilhard's comparative anatomy, one can view paleoanthropology as a philosophy of linkages between humans and other species, between humankind and the cosmos, and among people themselves.[66] The connections are indicative of both continuity and discontinuity, unity and difference, and, truth be told, Teilhard does not lose sight of "diversity." Moreover, he deplores "massification" as "bad globalization," pointing to its de-differentiating and "depersonalizing" pull. "Real community," Wildiers comments on *Le Phénomène humain*, "far from making men undifferentiated, creates diversity; and the larger and more complex the community, the more opportunity it affords each individual to develop his peculiar gifts and express his personality." Thus, diversity ought to be the ultimate goal of the "community of nations"; in any event, the "global solidarity" the "planetization of mankind" brings about should not arise at the expense of individual and regional values.[67]

At the same time, the medley of biocultural varieties provokes in Teilhard a fair amount of uneasiness about multiple life types, nuclei, and their interaction. This becomes increasingly apparent in the review of the planetization phase, which his "new Christian humanism" keeps in check by pulling it all together around a Christian-Pauline hub.[68] We noticed earlier, love leads naturally and supernaturally to the Incarnation. But the "supernatural unification of mankind"[69] into the *Parousia* implies a cultural-spiritual unification, and this makes Teilhard's cosmopolitan *Summa* quite ethnocentric, for it privileges a certain confessional and cultural space. In "The Neolithic Extensions and the Rise of the West" chapter, the philosopher hints at the "centering" of his cosmological narrative not only around a "super-human" axis in the sense specified above but also on a geocultural pivot. Planetization and Westernization seem here closely bound up with one another if not interchangeable. Teilhard promises to uncover later the role "other fragments of humanity" have played in our collective reaching of "planetary plenitude" (*la plénitude de la Terre*). Until then, he contends, one can hardly dispute that "throughout history, the principal axis of anthropogenesis has passed through the West. . . . [E]ven those elements that had been known elsewhere for a long time could take up a definitive human value only by getting integrated into the system of European ideas and actions. . . . [A]cross the world, to preserve or enhance their humanity, all peoples have inevitably had to formulate the hopes and concerns of the modern world precisely in the terms in which the West has couched them."[70] Ontological, life-spawning energy is thus channeled along a single track in Teilhard's "romance of totality." Questioning this modernist *metarécit* of teleological, integrative progress of all material forms, Mones queries the undifferentiated, culturally lopsided construction of "globalization" as subcategory and stage of "totality." This is where translation comes in.

No longer in touch with her "expat friends," who are too hung up on their "Westernness" (25), Alice has "drifted away" into a territory where the ruling idiom, faith, rationality, or cultural center is hard to pin down. Teilhard's "planetization" was modernist and totalist. Its rationality had ontologically "holistic" implications. To be was to be part of, and give oneself over to, a *totality*, to a sui generis Catholic-Wallersteinian world-system, while in Mones being is being in relation and comes about in language negotiation—quite literally, in translation. In it, being is found, and founded, no matter how much meaning otherwise might get lost.

Now, it goes without saying, Wallerstein's world-system has been spreading out a great deal since *Le Phénomène humain*. This expansion accounts for a major paradox in Mones's critical update of Teilhard's worldview: although globalization in his pre–World War II China was hardly what it is today, Teilhard's planetization chimes in with the "noospheric," all-embracing, equalizing developments of the 1990s, whereas Mones's romance, set in a country deeply reshaped by planetary forces sixty years later, looks to translation as a cultural-existential means to cope with the changes. Contrary to Teilhard's "convergent" cosmological narrative, coping involves an attempt at de-equalizing and untranslating the forcibly evened up, at preserving the unique and the off-kilter, the still untranslated and possibly untranslatable other, and, indirectly, the similarly singular, "askew" self. This effort results in two translational, or countertranslational, procedures. More of a "philosophical" kind, the first inheres in a translation that takes aim directly at Teilhard's *totalist* philosophy. Rather forthright, conspicuously political, the second shows Alice handling explicitly *totalitarian* and hegemonic ideologies and situations. The two types naturally intertwine since Teilhardian intertexts inform both. For example, Alice rejects Horace, her politician father with a prosegregation past, who would want only "Anglo-Saxon grandchildren" (156). Nor do the Chinese officials think very differently. They simply place the genetic (racial, ethnic) and cultural center, the *fons et origo* of human civilization, on the Asian side of the East/West divide. This explains their approval of Spencer's project, whose "worldwide importance" (18) they sense. Han, vice director of a Beijing paleontology institute, is skeptical about Spencer's chances, but should the American find the Peking Man, he is confident that "[t]he entire world would be reminded that China was not only, of course, the oldest continuous culture on earth but also—quite possibly—man's point of origin" (18). Besides, the "American hypothesis" has "potential for ruling out the distasteful possibility that the Chinese race might be descended from Africans" (19–20). *Homo erectus* has evolved, Han and Lin think, "separately in China" (115). In point of fact, Chinese paleontology officially deems Asian *Homo erectus* not only a distinct species, a different race, but also the source of all races. Betraying science's subordination to politics and hence the totalitarian nature of the regime, this totalist theory is one of the many Stalinist/Maoist anachronisms of "modernized" China. Han and Lin's argument is separatist; its disjunctive logic underlies a loose system of competing anthropological and cultural paradigms, with the Chinese one as center and "origin" of later varieties. As Alice quotes from *Le Phénomène humain*, Teilhard believes that, seen "*from* within," "the true natural history of the world . . . would appear no longer as an interlocking succession of structural types replacing one another, but as an ascension of inner sap spreading out in a forest of consolidated instincts" (84). It would seem, then, that his universalism is at odds with "differentialism," Han and Lin's anthropological party line, but the conflict is superficial. Underwritten by fetishized difference, Sinocentrism is only the flip side of Teilhard's Eurocentrism, for they both posit a common, original essence to all beings, and they both are universalist ontologies postulating a global "synthesis" that comes at a price. As Alice recalls Teilhard again, "Every final synthesis costs something. . . . Something is finally burned in the course of every synthesis in order to pay for that synthesis" (156–57).

So where does Mones stand? To answer the question, we need to figure out the position of her protagonist and, apparently, surrogate. For one thing, Alice is drawn to Teilhard's thought; as a translator, she cannot ignore the promise of cross-cultural communication and understanding it holds out. For another, she is enthralled by his love for Lucile, which her own relationship with Lin restages. Lucile was the same age as Alice, "just like [her]" (54–55). Nor is Alice impervious to Teilhard's shortcomings as a philosopher of humanness and human being himself. Lin's theories do not win her over either, yet she enjoys in his presence the intimacy Teilhard denied Lucile. Her "Chinese lover" steps over to the "outside woman," breaks the rules accepted by the Frenchman. In a way, Teilhard and Lucile reenacted the "calamitous" love story of Abélard and Héloïse. As Thomas M. King notes, there were other women beside Lucile in Teilhard's life. With one of them, Léontine Zanta, the philosopher also exchanged affectionate letters.[71] But it is the correspondence between Teilhard and Lucile that fleshes out the French Jesuit's outlook on love and sexuality. According to him, the two are, or should be, separate. As Teilhard wrote in a 1934 essay on "The Evolution of Chastity," sex "burns up" and "deadens" the soul, rendering it no longer "whole" and thereby jeopardizing its integration into a larger aggregate.[72] Mary Wood Gilbert observes in the prologue to Teilhard's and Lucile's letters that this may be the crux of the problem: "For Lucile, physical consummation was fundamental to the love between a man and a woman, a seal of what they felt for each other. Teilhard's consistent and continual response was a rejection of this point of view, offering in its place a redirection of the energy of sexual union towards God."[73] Remarkably, in a 1933 letter from Beijing, where he refers to himself in the third person, Teilhard owns that "because your friend, Lucile, belongs to Something Else, he cannot be yours."[74] A 1934 epistle brings additional clarity to the argument. "My line of answer," Teilhard specifies, "does not exclude the 'physical' element. . . . All the question is to decide whether, amongst the natural 'effects' which you alluded to, some have not to be avoided (in certain cases) precisely because they have, in themselves, something of an end, or of an achievement, or of an internal completion, which makes them rather a *terminal* stage than a *step* towards the only complete spiritual union."[75] In his epilogue, King concludes that Teilhard sees "the Feminine . . . as the force that calls man out of himself and into Life," but the critic goes on to say that, idealized as Virgin Mary by Catholic faith, woman in Teilhard rather "inspires the spirit to rise beyond the world and unite with God."[76] This is precisely the role of Teilhard's "Eternal Feminine," as an early essay with this title suggests. Hypostatized as Virgin Mary or Dante's Beatrice, the feminine is essentially a transcendent symbol. One wonders, then, into what kind of "Life" Teilhard's feminine pulls him. An artist herself, interested in spiritual matters Western and Eastern, Lucile seems to have found eventually peace of mind by returning to Christian faith.[77] But a more pugnacious stance comes through one of Lucile's 1935 diary entries, pulling the rug out from under Teilhard's spiritualistic totalism.[78] Here, she turns Teilhard's argument on its head. The repression of sexuality, she notes, ties into a broader denial of the physicality without which one cannot be whole nor partake of a higher wholeness. Built around restraint, Teilhard's cosmos remains fraught with prohibitions, divisions, and barriers across which "mystical" translation—transcendental rather than transgressive—dematerializes, leaving passions, bodies, and ultimately the body of culture itself behind.

"The natural mutation of things"

> Translation, whether we practice it or not, is a key metaphor for
> the age in which we live.
> —SUSAN BASSNETT, "Translation Theory"

Lucile's point on human "materiality" concerns chiefly gender and sex, but, in focusing on Alice and Lin's relationship, Mones extends the observation to culture to show that translation is neither "evasive" nor immaterial.[79] Quite the contrary, it works through contact and dialogue that set in motion becoming rites in which physicality holds a principal role. Granted, in linguistic communication generally, meaning and means, what we mean to say and the phonetic-corporeal apparatus saying it, in brief, mind and body, all become one. But Mones brings this solidarity into sharp relief. Furthermore, not only do mind and body become one. They also become something else, effect a translation, move or morph into a "position"—linguistic, cultural, existential—in and from which the translating self, now itself translated, can "find" or rediscover itself. In translation, Alice feels, we can translate ourselves into, *perform like* an other if we do not actually become, and thus substitute, for it. The performative of language and identity translation has nothing to do with genetics and genetic identicalness, with Teilhard's "inner sap" or anthropological "*Ur*-type" that would presumably allow Alice to body forth the historically documented subtypes ("Euro-American," "Asian," etc.). But it has a lot to do with cultural makeover through language and translation. If identity has a "source," performance is its name, as a whole Foucauldian tradition tells us. We "perform" our race and gender, even our sexuality. True, our culture imagines them for us, yet we respond through "acts" reimagining them outside, across, and often contra given representations and rubrics.

It is imperative, cosmodern writers and critics propose, that we take another look at language transactions in today's worldwide "chameleonic" protocols of being. Enabling mimetic reproduction of native cultural models, such protocols are a hallmark of our globalizing world—for better or worse, I should add. It seems to me, though, that *Lost in Translation* dwells on the progressive facet of these protocols, because struggle with and for language and linguistic authority here ties into resistance to political authoritarianism. Echoing an "acute demand" for translation in general and "cultural translation" in particular, "chameleonism" of this sort challenges language and culture monopoly, reinforcing the Derridean doubt that language can be "owned," while allowing the translator to put up on "authentic" speech acts.[80] What the latter denote—and this is remarkable given the resilient belief in the all-sufficiency of English as lingua franca—is that "other" idioms can indeed be "learned," appropriated, reproduced, and circulated worldwide. As we also saw in part 1, "desacraliz[ing] the transparent assumptions of cultural supremacy,"[81] this understanding and practice of language refute the notion that an identity, idea, value, or standard is the exclusive attribute of an immutable place, context, version, or representation of that identity, idea, value, or standard, be it English (American), Chinese, or anything else.

A multivalent, phonetic-bodily performance, translation encroaches in Mones upon the political, upon alignments of power, place, and subjectivity. This explains why Alice's skills make the Chinese officials uneasy. Spencer's interpreter during his first meeting with Han, Alice undergoes a transformation that startles the others. Speaking with Han, "Unconsciously she, too, was now rolling and drawing out her *r*-sounds, unable as always to check this chameleon quality of her Chinese-speaking" (20). "Chinese-speaking" is a way to performing "Chineseness." "This woman actually wanted to be Chinese!" Han discovers. He feels "compassion for her dislocation" (21), but he also feels threatened. Yet the "enemy" does not come from the outside, for there is no reassuring, outside-influence-free inside in *Lost in Translation*. In fact, Alice finds in Chinese itself the very prompt and matrix of her linguistic-existential morphing. The mobility of being, the capacity for self-fashioning and reinvention on the model of the other, does inhere in a deep-reaching, originary heterogeneity and in-tertextuality of being, which have always been "down there." But these fea-tures are first "spelled out," *spoken* in (and by a) Chinese. As her Chinese language teacher told her, in Chinese "'each phrase'" could be "'inter-preted in different ways—especially in spoken Chinese. Never one mean-ing, always many. Not like English. And our idioms—the best ones are not literal . . . instead they are oblique, they make reference to legends, stories, famous dramas, and books. They do not offer specific information. . . . They produce a state of mind! Ah, so few of you outside people grasp the pleasure of speaking a truly civilized language—never base, never obvious and therefore clunky and painful, as English is.'" But "Alice had under-stood. Chinese was a huge maze-world: stable yet evasive. Nothing was permanently what it seemed. *Yes* meant maybe and *no* meant maybe and so did everything in between—other Westerners saw this as Chinese pre-varication," but to Alice "it was simply the natural mutation of things. Natural *and* welcome—because here in China the self could always be reinvented. She, too, could become someone else" (247–48).

Being on the "inside" is being on the side of language and thus an "in-sider" or sorts, not postulating an outside, a cultural dualism. It is just the other way around. This interiority voids all dualisms, not only those of linguistic nature ("yes"/"no"). It replaces a world of disjunctions and seg-regations with one of relations, laying the groundwork for a critique of the dichotomies that block the self's "reinvention" in the inspiring proximity of an other's body and whispers. Alice does think this Chinese-becoming may never be complete. On the phone with her father, she cannot repress a "rush of belonging" (126), and this is a telling moment because in striv-ing to remake herself she is to a certain degree unmaking herself by getting away from what her father is and stands for (317), much though Lin re-minds her of her Americanness and whiteness (316). There is some sub-stance to her "acultural" creed—"The truth is, I don't really think of myself as having a culture" (316)—but only insofar as this claim opens up the possibility of multiple *acculturations*, of successive becoming cycles. Introduced to the "insideness" of language, to the idiomatic zone where monotonous ideology gives way to the dialogics of tongues and voices, Alice gains an insight into the intimate, cultural relationality of selfhood, into our plural makeup and the imprints of others on it. And so, as anticipated above, translation starts out linguistically but ends culturally and ontologically as it binds together language and body, then different bodies, and finally the geopolitical worlds around those bodies. Desire for communication and contact, desire for the other—desire pure and simple—is in Mones at play underneath the translator's apparent desire for *equivalence*, linguistic and otherwise. Therefore, words are and remain, even "in translation," as eroticized as the body, while sex affords bodies an eloquence that makes up for what, in the same translation, falls through the cracks.

In this sense, sex with Chinese men is, as Alice confesses, "sex with China" (155), an intercourse of a higher order. In this sense too, Mones's is a "global romance," for in *Lost in Translation* sex acquires a symbolic, vitalist value while preserving the human materiality missing from Teilhard's spiritualism. "We are fucking now in the center of the anvil," Lin whispers to Alice in Chinese (314), and, as they make love, they tell one another Western and Chinese legends of creation, translate each other's bodies and stories in caresses and phrases that continue to be what they are while "making sense" in other idioms and codes. Through language and sex, homonymous incarnations of the same translating desire, the translator accedes if not to a "condition" of otherness" then to a place where she proves able to enact this condition's parameters and codes. What Alice does "eventually" bears on what she is in that it alters how she views herself. "You can never be Chinese" (42), she is often told, and she does understand that she may never carry through her morphing. Yet that is only because any identity is scarcely whole unto itself, self-contained, complete, but provisional, partial, and dependent on others for its various parts and embodiments. Since, like Lin himself, we are permanently in flux and incomplete, those trying to be (like) us cannot but play catch-up with our always-already outdated versions. For this reason, there can be no endgame to Alice's identity games. At the same time, her ability to pick up on the rules and play the game gets her a new grip on what it means to have a self, particularly on what her American self means. In that, translation is, once more, about the translator as much as it is about the translated.

3. Translation, Mistranslation, Countertranslation

Cognation, Cognition, Re-cognition

> [T]he measure of an idea is often taken, first and last, "abroad," in "foreign" countries.
> —JACQUES DERRIDA, *On Touching—Jean-Luc Nancy*

"The tourist's supreme wish," Franco Moretti assures us, is "re-cognition." Tourists travel not to "see the world, but in order to see once more— *through* the world—[their] own encyclopaedia." Somewhere between the "American Monkey King" of Gerald Vizenor's 1990 *Griever* and the sexually impetuous American teacher of Anchee Min's 2003 *Katherine,* both of whom are also "displaced" in China, Alice is not exactly a tourist. But if tourism "reveals the difficulties of appreciating otherness except through signifying structures that mark and reduce it," then she probes just the cultural, epistemological, and ethical problem pinpointed by the Italian critic.[82] I say "probe" rather than "solve" because Alice does not find a solution per se. She does not come up with a "dictionary equivalence" to Chinese words—nor should she, for, as Bassnett posits, if we "assume" such an equivalence without factoring in "differences that are more cultural than linguistic, the resulting loss of meaning could render the translation useless."[83] And so Alice is right not to rationalize these differences into an "absolute" rendition, which in reality would reproduce the "signifying structures" of the English language and American culture. We have seen, her interpretation is not an exclusively rational "thing of the mind," nor does she treat Chinese as if it lent itself to such a reductive, re-cognitive, self-referring approach, characteristic of modern translators, tourists, and modernity broadly. What they all "desired" as they were making contact with others was themselves. More bluntly, the object of modern cultural romance is egological. Cognition is therefore narcissistic, repetitive re-cognition, or pseudocognition. In view of the discussion so far, I find it quite remarkable that Mones's interpretive cosmodernism retools critically the modernist problematic of "touristy" re-cognition by discarding the repetitive while retaining the self-examining component. In other words, not only is Alice "cognizant" of the linguistic difficulties and cultural traps hindering her attempt to capture the intricacies of Chinese in English for her American client, but she turns this predicament into a self-re-cognition opportunity. Zeroing in on an emblematic reaction of the modern mind to the alien, the uncharted, and the exotic far-off, Moretti takes issue with that which in cognition only re-cognizes, re-learns what it has learned at home. To him, re-cognition rehashes the same, retrofits available knowledge. In Mones and other cosmoderns, interpretive acts give rise instead to self-assessment moments. To them, there is nothing wrong—repetitive or redundant—with this self-evaluating desire. For a different kind of self-centering seems to be in play in it as Chinese words lead Alice to reexamine her own dictionary and encyclopedia, to relearn the American cultural lexicon, as it were, and test not just how well she knows it but also the knowledge stored in it.

To summarize: the cosmodern scene of translation showcases linguistic interpretation as part and parcel of both ampler and more intimate translations, of a cross-cultural erotics, with language exchange a vehicle of intimate semiotics, of private transactions and reciprocal initiations in the idiomatic semantics of otherness. At the same time—and this speaks to the cultural turn in translation studies as it does to cosmodernism's transactional proclivity—this scene brings into view the translator as much as what/whom is translated or the party the translation is done for. However much gets lost in it, translation proves, at the end of the day, not only a scene of loss but also one of finding, of self-finding more exactly, insofar as the translator becomes at last able to "triangulate" to himself or herself (to recall Eva Hoffman) under the guidance of others. Let me reemphasize: re-cognition works as critical self-study that does more than just reprise stuff already learned, and that is because cognition and cognation are no longer bound up in this place of displacement. Transposed into this space, the translator submits to a cosmodern pedagogy of otherness and unfamiliarity. If traditionally societies learn (or assume they do) from themselves, if their members look largely to those to whom they are related—*cognati*, in Latin—for relations (cultural narratives) laying down the norms and ways of operating in their communities, the cosmodern translator become generally cognizant and particularly self-cognizant in cognitively heteronomous setups. Simply speaking, he or she learns about the world and himself or herself inside other cultures while attempting to carry them and their lexicons outside themselves. One more time, it is the presumed translator who is translated back to himself or herself, into an idiom in which the self can get a better grip on itself.

The problem our "other" teachers pose is not that the grammar of their languages and cultures is utterly "impenetrable" to "outsiders" like Alice, but that these outsiders have been living on the outside of their own idioms and cultural vocabularies. The relationship that Alice and Lin have brings them together across a linguistic and cultural gap, which makes individual romance into a symbolic one, of cultures and geopolitical "systems." But her relationship to an other is also the building block of a relation to herself; transposing itself, translating itself in the position where conversing with an other becomes possible, the self ends up interpellating itself, discovers itself as complicated, problematic, and ambiguous, hence *in need* of translation. Translation of others culminates in self-translation; the latter rounds off the former, is its cosmodern corollary. This is what a flurry of recent translational narratives tell us, from post-Borgesian, Argentine novelistic allegories such as Pablo De Santis's *La traducción* (The Translation), Néstor Ponce's *El intérprete* (The Interpreter), and Salvador Benesdra's *El traductor* (The Translator), all published in 1998, to Lahiri's "Interpreter of Maladies," Lee Siegel's *Love in a Dead Language*, Demetria Martínez's 1994 *Mother Tongue*, Leila Aboulela's 1999 "halal novel" *The Translator*, Ward Just's 1999 thriller *The Translator*, John Crowley's 2002 popular *The Translator*, Paul Auster's 2002 novel *The Book of Illusions*, Jonathan Safran Foer's 2002 debut *Everything Is Illuminated*, and the 2005 movie *The Interpreter*.[84]

Fudging the Answers: Suki Kim's *The Interpreter;* or, Translation as Hubris

> [T]ranslation is always a shift, not between two languages, but between two cultures.
> —UMBERTO ECO, *Experiences in Translation*

Korean-American Suki Kim's 2003 murder mystery *The Interpreter* shows poignantly not only how conducive to self-scrutiny translation can be but also how political this analysis is. What we noticed of Lee's Henry apropos of *Invisible Man*'s echoes in *Native Speaker* applies to Kim's Suzy Park too. She is supposed to be a transparent and transitive medium, to self-efface in the act of visualizing others and their meanings as a Korean language translator of witnesses' depositions in trials and official inquiries. In actuality, she does get in on the act(ion), which helps Kim hammer home her cosmodern notion of translation and, linked into it, that of identity. For the author herself defines linguistic "interpretation" as a multifold metaphor of cultural transformation and identity (re)making.[85] To her, this is a richly existential trope, a figure of human life *as* life refiguration, cutting to the heart of, if not specifically *what* we are, then *how* we are: ever in changeover mode, in transit from one place, idiom, and being hypostasis to another, in brief, relational, translational. And because this is how we are, always transitioning from one side to another while carrying our own sides on our backs, in our words and worldviews, the metaphor and the practice flowing from it in *The Interpreter* dispute the translator's "impartiality." Aware of the parts, parties, and sides in play, Suzy has no qualms about playing parts and taking sides that legally she should neither play nor take. The contract her agency had her sign "included a clause never to engage in small talk with witnesses. The interpreter is always hired by the law firm on the side opposing the witnesses. It is they who need the testimony translated. The witness, summoned to testify without any knowledge of English, inevitably views the interpreter as his savior. But the interpreter, as much as her heart might commiserate with her fellow native speaker, is always working for the other side. It is this idiosyncrasy Suzy likes. Both sides need her desperately, but she, in fact, belongs to neither. One of the job requirements was no involvement: Shut up and get the work done. That's fine with her." Except, Kim adds, "Suzy often finds herself cheating. Sometimes the witness falters and reveals devastating, self-incriminating information. The opposing counsel might ask how much he makes a week, and the witness turns to Suzy and asks what he should say. Should he tell him five hundred dollars, although he usually makes more money on the side? Suzy knows that the immigrant life follows different rules—no taxes, no benefits, sometimes not even Social Security or green cards. And she also knows that he should never tell lawyers that." "So [Suzy] might fudge the answer. She might turn to the lawyer innocently and translate, 'My income is private information; approximately five hundred dollars, I would say, but I cannot be exact.' Or the opposing side might try to make a case out of the fact that the plaintiff, when struck by a car, told the police that he was feeling fine and refused an ambulance. 'Surely,' the lawyer insists, 'the injury must not have been severe if you even refused medical attention!' But Suzy knows that it is a cultural misunderstanding. It is the Korean way always to underplay the situation, to declare one is fine even when suffering from pain or ravenous hunger. This might stem from their Confucian or even Buddhist tradition, but the lawyers don't care about that." Suzy knows "it is wrong to embellish truth according to how she sees fit," but truth, "she has learned, comes in different shades, different languages at times, and lawyers with a propensity for Suzy Wong movies may not always see that. The job comes naturally to her. Neither of her parents had spoken much English. Interpreting is almost a habit."[86]

Kim's entire novel and translational identity allegory are here in a nut-shell—the deontological, contractually reinforced premise, but also the breach, of nonpartisan translation. More than an interpreter, Suzy is a cultural critic, an interpreter in a broader sense. Capable not only of hauling truth across tongues and cultures "as is" but also of weighing the epistemological deflections ("misunderstandings") of linguistic and cultural difference, Suzy gets "involved" and eventually self-involved. As in Mones, self-involvement has little to do with egological self-servience and everything to do with a connective notion of truth that relates to us and regards us, turns its face to us as we do the same unto others, care, help, and otherwise treat them ethically much as this treatment may not jibe with the classical ethic of objectivity. We already get a sense that this truth "concerns" Suzy personally at the end of the last fragment quoted above. The implication there is that she can protect the truth of others because her immigrant family, if not she herself, has been in that tough place once. As it turns out, this would be ironic if it was not tragic in more ways than one: Grace, her older sister, translated for their parents at meetings with U.S. Immigration officers to whom the Parks apparently reported undocumented Koreans. With Grace, then, the older, transitive model of interpretation sets up translation as hubris, as overstepping of moral bounds twice. First, and once more reminiscent of *Native Speaker*, Grace respeaks for the government the unspeakable uttered in Korean by her parents and in so doing becomes responsible for—"party" to—the ultimate "immoral act" somebody in their position can commit (240); oddly enough, "veracious" translation makes here the *traduttore* a *traditore*, a "traitor." Second, the Parks were murdered in reprisal for their "betrayal," for a "revealing," "truth"-laden translation that, while it got the whole family American citizenship, in truth—one deeper than "legal status" and identity papers—neither made them more American nor earned them a place in the Korean-American community. To the contrary, it cut them off from everybody including their daughters. Resenting her having been forced to participate in her parents' transgression of the immigrant ethos and more broadly reenacting the translational asymmetries between generations so abundantly illustrated in works from Kingston's *The Woman Warrior* (1976) to Amy Tan's "Mother Tongue" (1990), Gish Jen's *Typical American* (1991), *Mona in the Promised Land* (1998), and *Who's Irish* (1999), Lan Cao's *Monkey Bridge* (1997), Chang-rae Lee's "Mute in an English-Only World" (1996), and Jean Kwok's *Girl in Translation* (2010), Grace pulls away from her mother and father, then from Suzy as well, to protect her from the family's "truth." Instinctively, Suzy does nothing else: if Grace disapproves of her parents' haste to be legally recognized as Americans by sacrificing others like them *in* translation, her sister is dismayed at how steeped in the "old-country" culture, how *lost* in the translation and transition from Korean and Koreanness to English and Americanness their ways were. Because, as she felt at the time, "She could not become American as long as she remained their daughter," she *"betrayed them, so she might live"* (212). Having a life and being a translator are one and the same and together convey, both for Grace and Suzy albeit for different reasons and with different implications, a sense of betrayal.

Making up, in a way, for this betrayal, translation is for Suzy profoundly personal, a side-taking or "participatory" act. What she "finds" in translation as she purposefully mistranslates on behalf of others in need is that they bear witness not so much to their own troubles as to Suzy's and her family's tragedy. During one of the testimonies, she learns that the person on the stand has information about her parents' killing, and instead of translating into Korean the questions posed by the "opposing side," she starts asking her own questions. Step by step, still a "shadow," "invisible" (12) to lawyers, she gets between the "sides" and carves out her own, triangulating the conversation as she seeks her own answers. Thus the translator translates herself into a detective pursuing the family's dark secret and more largely the mysteries of linguistic, cultural, and legal relations and transactions behind identity fashioning in 1990s America.

Lolita in the Bronx

Grace has been doing the same and is always a step ahead of her sister. With Suzy, though, the whodunit develops into a quest narrative not so much geared to revealing the culprit as to revealing Suzy to herself. And what she *is* comes out in what she *does,* in her work: like Alice, she is a translational being. She is in translation, on the move between places and "sides" as she translates them to one another, mindful of how impartial, "verbatim" in her rendition of an other's words the legal system wants her to be yet no less aware of how lacking "language[-]as[-]equation," this aseptic philosophy of "exactness" (90–91), is, of how superficially it retrieves the truth of one's life and culture. "What she possesses," Kim writes, "is an ability to be at two places at once. She can hear a word and separate its literal meaning from its connotation. This is necessary, since the verbatim translation often leads to confusion. Languages are not logical. Thus an interpreter must translate word for word and yet somehow manipulate the breadth of language to bridge the gap. While one part of her brain does automatic conversion, the other part examines the linguistic void that results from such transference. It is an art that requires a precise and yet creative mind" (91). "You must never forget your language; once you do, you no longer have a home," their father told the sisters (45). Suzy has not forgotten Korean, and, having arrived in the United States when she was five, her English is virtually native. Therefore, to quote her father again, her "home" is "ensured" (46)—or her homes, rather. For she is "polytopic," makes her home in between homes, languages, races, ethnicities, and family rites when she does not make it against them as her relations, relationships, and affairs run counter to "family values." Not the "nonplace" or "nowhere" person described by critics and globe-trotters like Marc Augé, Pico Iyer, and Aleksandar Hemon, Kim's character maps out a sort of flowing "somewhere," a location from which she brings places and people together, makes them relate to one another as she relates (relays) each other's meanings to them and, at last, to herself.

This is no smooth sailing. "Being bilingual, being multicultural," Kim writes, "should have brought two worlds into one heart, and yet for Suzy it meant a persistent hollowness. It seems that she needed to love one culture to be able to love the other. Piling up the cultural references led to no further identification. What Damian," a former lover, "had called a 'blessing'"—that is, being raised in what he deemed the "cultural vacuum" of the Parks household—"pushed her out of context, always. She was stuck in a vacuum where neither culture moved nor owned her. Deep inside she felt no connection" (166). The passage can be read in a several ways. Not so much multicultural as "postmulticultural," one of them becomes more tenable in light of Bruce Robbins's reaction to Étienne Balibar's indictment of "the cosmopolitan's supposed absence of feelings."[87] Even more notable in cosmoderns like Kim than in Robbins's cosmopolitans is the extent to which the lack of a central, "exclusive," or "separate" emotional connection or allegiance to one culture and the "hollowness" following from this apathic, decentered experience of a number of cultures set the stage for Suzy's cultural-linguistic brokerage, "contextualize" her translational-relational knack for the host of connections and identifications she makes possible for herself and others across cultural boundaries. In Kim and cosmodernism at large, love, emotion, "feeling" for and understanding of one's own culture rest on the capacity, if not to feel exactly the same about another culture, then at least to "connect" with it on a level sufficiently deep psychologically, linguistically, morally, and so on. Self-identification, defining oneself and one's obligations are not premised on identity as *identitas* ("immutability"), as fixity of an ever-the-same (*idem*) being inside unchanged frontiers of idiom, mores, and loyalties. Yes, this is the paradox of cosmodern cultural feeling: to love one's culture one must love the other's. To love, one must possess the "context," the outside "connection," perspective, and element of comparison accounting for the logic of affect, for the "why" of its privileging fervor. It is this "external" connection that is originary and thus founds our innermost feelings, those by which we reconnect with kin and kind.

If *Lost in Translation* charts this oblique trajectory of passion and knowledge also obliquely by a detour through Teilhard, *The Interpreter* takes a similarly road across Nabokov. The intertextual scope is not as extensive as in Mones, nor does Kim dwell specifically on *Lolita* as much as Siegel in *Love in a Dead Language* or, as we will see in part 4, Nafisi in *Reading Lolita in Tehran*. But Suzy assumes the role of a "smooth-talking" "Bronx Lolita" early in the novel (85), and, frivolous as this "part" may look at that point, it will later help clarify her overall participation in the life of culture, her "involvements" with others and herself. Where Grace "declar[es] herself separate, apart" (169) and in the end runs off, Suzy seems keen on becoming a part of other lives, "Lolita-style." Reminding one of *Native Speaker*'s colloquy with Whitman this time, Kim's conversation with Nabokov is centered around themes such as earning one's place in the nation's imaginary museum, the cultural politics of location, identity, inclusion, and affiliation, and, most relevant to Suzy's translational view of people and idioms, the critique of "neutrality." The conversation's venue is also dialogical: a chat between Suzy and her friend Jen, a literary magazine editor but also "the image of what Suzy was not, what Suzy could never be—the ultimate emblem of the American dream" (160). Jen tells her about the article a famous writer, Harrison, Nabokov's former student at Cornell, has recently submitted on his teacher's alleged "hatred" of English and America. The friend's story is briefly interrupted by Suzy's third-person question to herself—*Whose side is she on?* (159)—and the italics are warranted both narratively and thematically, for the next pages will indeed be about Nabokov and the sides he did or did not take as much as about the side Suzy herself takes, if not in the Nabokov controversy triggered by Harrison, then in life and culture generally. In Jen's account, Harrison is wrong. Nabokov did not hate America and its language; his "citizenship" was not a cover for his "anti-Americanism," nor was *Lolita* a "metaphor for how Nabokov felt toward the English language" (163). She also thinks it is significant that Nabokov retired to Switzerland ("talk about neutral ground!") and, like Suzy, suspects that he did not love Russia that much either. "I don't believe," Jen goes on, "he was capable of that kind of love or hate for a country. He was too selfish. You can see that in his writing. He picked each word as though his entire life was at stake. He was notorious for jotting down every thought on three-by-five index cards. His life was a string of exile, from England to Germany to France to America to Switzerland. It was right after renouncing Russian that he threw this verbal masturbation of a novel called *Lolita* at the American public. Here's this Russian guy who's only been in the U.S. for a decade or so, tripping on English prose like Faulkner on acid!" (166). Jen is right: whatever haunted Nabokov drove him from one place to another, yet that was neither the Russia nor the Russian he abandoned; this hypothesis is "too simple" (166). But so is the other, with its emphasis on the writer's pedantry and "masturbatory" stylistics of selfishness.

This portrait of the artist as a roving, unaffiliated modernist attracts and repels concurrently. The canvas is surely a palimpsest. At an angle—at a critical angle—one can make out, also as in *Native Speaker*, a self-portrait: the author's and the character's alike, for writing and translation parallel each other and trace the same identity genealogy. Nabokov's "problem" is conspicuously Suzy's; his exile prompts her to reflect on her family's (167). But toward the end of Jen's Harrison rebuttal Suzy all but stops listening. A solidarity of sorts seems to take shape at that juncture between the Russian-American writer who cannot defend himself anymore and the Korean-American eager to put her own "selfishness" on trial. This trial or critique builds on the critical portrait of *Lolita*'s author. On the one hand, Nabokov and Suzy treat language in general and English in particular with the same respect, which is all the more remarkable as their English is not native. In court, Suzy too "pick[s] each word" but, also similarly to Nabokov, "trips" on language, makes up words, invents. Her translations mix in mistranslations and, for all practical purposes, countertranslations, made-up "renditions." Further, one might ask, is Nabokov's fictional logomachy "selfish," wrapped up around itself? Critics like Harrison claim that he was an American citizen pro forma, that his heart was elsewhere. But Nabokov does stake his claims to citizenship linguistically and culturally, on *Lolita, Pnin, Pale Fire,* and their uncanny stylistic mastery and cultural insight, on the massive investments in *other* words and the worlds behind them. Yielding a still unparalleled x-ray of America, these investments laid the foundation of postmodern fiction this side of the Atlantic and thus taught "us" a new way of looking at ourselves. On their account, the case for his "self-absorption," "perversity" (167), and phobia of commitment becomes harder to make.

On the other hand, though, in a move again redolent of Siegel and Nafisi, and partly of Pia Pera's 1995 *Lo's Diary*, Kim bestows on her Lolita attributes the 1955 prototype lacks. Not only is Suzy conspicuously more "philosophical" about relationships; she is also aware of the "impossibility of desire" (160) drawing Humbert Humbert to his nymphet and, on another level, Michael and Damian to herself. Further, both her lovers are white and married. The latter is in his late forties, and so is his wife and research partner, Japanese-American Yuki Tamiko, who also teaches East Asian literatures and cultures at Columbia. What "ruins" their marriage is not nineteen-year-old Suzy but the equally impossible desire behind it. Better put (by Tamiko herself), it was not this desire per se but what fueled it. Damian "could never love an Asian woman," Tamiko enlightens her, because what had gotten him in the relationship in the first place was not love for an other but self-hatred. His "searching [for] the other," where the distinction between "search" and "love" makes his "desire" rather academic, was no more than a reflection of his "running from his whiteness" and from himself in general (288).

History and politics arguably foreordain Tamiko and Suzy's rivalry, but their views of relations among people and cultures are not as far apart as they may look at first. A supervisor of Suzy's senior thesis on *King Lear* and Akira Kurosawa's 1985 movie *Ran*, Tamiko does not seem very excited about her student's "central argument [on] the impossibility of harmony between the East and the West" (80); at the same time, her critique of the project retains the antinomies of ethnicity, race, and gender, and overall the "us and "them" vocabulary (82) Suzy's father—another Lear—used (81). No wonder neither the thesis nor the affair with Damian goes anywhere; they are both on the wrong track. Suzy is unprepared to tease out the meanings of Kurosawa's sophisticatedly cross-textual and cross-cultural masterpiece, to notice how much *Ran* is "neither here nor there" but turns on an eerie aptitude of tying together the "East" and the "West." Not impervious to such implications, Tamiko is nevertheless prisoner of a language that cannot lay them out for Suzy either. Nor could they be presented to her from the outside, translated to her into a language she could understand. This translation has to be personal; in and with it, Suzy has first to stop running away from herself, her family, and background, has to get "involved" more profoundly and ethically than before; its revelations, the translator's investment—not unlike Nabokov's own, in his style and work broadly—have to be total, and they become so as she discovers the self-translating dimension of translation, how the other's words speak to her deepest secrets. This is how the translator turns detective, and detection, self-detection. What Suzy at last "finds" is not as clear as the hardcore fans of murder mysteries might hope. *Where* she finds herself, however, in what place her quest leaves her, does become apparent as she stops withdrawing, "exiling" herself from others like her à la Nabokov in the affective Switzerland of pseudorelationships, and starts working (quite literally) to initiate relations between "sides" that otherwise would not relate. So where Kim's cultural and linguistic go-between ends up is, as I say, a postmulticultural zone, a site of feelings, languages, and values beyond the "us"/"them" multicultural divisiveness and stand-aloneness of her parents, of Tamiko and Damian, and even of the Korean-American "1.5 generation" (126): a place defined not as placelessness but as a site of contacts, passages, and transitions among places, a knot of words, discourses, and contentions about Americans, America, and the world.

Translatability and Readability

As Sanford Budick comments on Karlheinz Stierle's discussion of Renaissance translation terminology, the word itself, *translation,* "harbors a crisis of translation, specifically a crisis in attempting to translate the other," insofar as "translation necessarily marks the border crossing where, if anywhere, one culture passes over to the other, whether to inform it, to further its development, to capture or enslave it, or merely to open up a space between the other and itself."[88] Here and throughout Budick and Iser's *Translatability of Cultures,* translation designates any number of things. Across the board, though, translation as word-for-word transposition meets with little enthusiasm. Instead, it is theorized as a form of interpretation, a practice coming under hermeneutics and reading as much as it does, some argue, under writing itself, conceived as it is by many as "mosaic technique" or intertextuality—ever quotational, transtextualizing, in transit from a precursor text to its sequel, pastiche, or rewrite.[89] Now, to be sure, to the extent that translation crosses into another culture—to the extent the other makes up its object—translation is interpretation, and vice versa;[90] the translated cannot be conveyed, "carried over" without semiotic modification. A "case" of cosmodern selfhood, Suzy repeatedly runs into this problem: how to translate by interpreting and how to interpret or read without misreading others; how to render them without further othering them (a risk, we saw earlier, Budick also keys on); last but not least, how to make sense of those others and thereby of herself—how to make "legible" the "other side"'s "testimonies," its way of seeing and bearing witness to America without missing that which available American codifications of legibility and legality may deem illegible, culturally "impenetrable" and forever "mysterious," or worse, illegal. Either way, for Suzy and pretty much for all of us these days, the question is otherness as mysterious text, more and more ubiquitous and unavoidable, demanding our reply. And one more time, it is of utmost importance that we do not lose sight of what or whom this mystery of meaning and being ultimately refers to. It is easy to get confused since, as Sacvan Bercovitch reminds us, the public perception of self and other has been traditionally underwritten by a "hermeneutic of transcendence" stipulating that, first, "to interpret is not to make sense of a mystery out there. It is to discover otherness as mystery (something 'overwhelming,' 'incomprehensible'), and then to explain the mystery as the wonders of an invisible world, a realm of meaningful 'silence,' resonant with universals. Second, to investigate those wonders is not to come to terms with the new or unexpected. It is to domesticate the unknown by transferring the agency of meaning from the mystery out there to realities we recognize, and so to invest the familiar—ourselves, or our kind—with the powers of a higher reality. . . . Third, to establish the laws and rules of that higher reality is not to break through the limitations we experience. It is to deny our conditions of dependency by translating those limitations into metastructures of culture, history, and of the mind."[91] This philosophy of translation-as-interpretation, then, "transcends" and thus "controls and incorporates" the new and the mysterious it bumps into.[92] It does not actually know them nor aim at their effective "cognition." Instead, it "re-cognizes" them in the repetitive sense discussed before, reduces them to realities already known or so deemed. This is the path to mistranslation as misreading.

There is another itinerary, however, which I have charted in response to Moretti's critique of the epistemology of recognition, and to which Bercovitch's transcendent hermeneutics brings us back. This alternative trajectory of knowledge does not dismiss the recentering of cognition on the close, on the familiar, and ultimately on ourselves, provided two conditions are met. First, this refocusing of interpretation on the interpreting self, interpretation's doubling as self-interpretation, comes at the end as an upshot of the original encounter and epistemological attempt at an other's cognition. And second, as we bring self, family, community, or nation into focus, we do not re-"invest" them with the transcognitive, "domesticating" prerogatives they have never earned. This encounter encourages us to do quite the opposite: divest this intimate and proximal world of its convenient, oftentimes blindfolding and pseudoexplanatory powers. If successful, translating an other translates into a translation of one's own hitherto untackled mysteries or, at the very least, translates, brings the translator into a position from which these mysteries present themselves as something in urgent need of tackling. In sum, translation as interpretation and deciphering—as reading test—prompts self-reading. This is what the cosmodern scene of translation teaches. This lesson is nuanced on the cosmodern scene of reading, to which I turn now.

PART 4 ⊕ READINGS

1. Cosmodern Interpretive Communities

> [T]he ethnographer of Bali, like the critic of Austen, is among
> other things absorbed in probing what Professor Trilling . . . called
> one of the significant mysteries of man's life in culture: how is it that
> other people's creations can be so utterly their own and so deeply
> part of us.
>
> —CLIFFORD GEERTZ, *The Interpretation of Cultures*

Other-Reading

> [C]ulture proves to be a kind of network that interlinks levels,
> positions, attitudes, and last but not least, otherness in order to
> gain its individuality.
>
> —WOLFGANG ISER, "Coda to the Discussion,"
> *The Translatability of Cultures*

A drop of human blood, Mukherjee muses in her 2004 book *The Tree Bride,* is "a hemo-synecdoche of the world"; "like the novel, it contains the world."[1] This Whitmanesque definition of the genre—and of the human genus no less—fits especially cosmodern novels, including Mukherjee's, in particular those published after *Jasmine.* More emphatically than her previous narratives, the 1989 title puts up the identity makeover drama on the stage of global travel, transience, and migrancy. Besides the protagonist herself, the other lead actors are language, textuality, and certain texts, the old and new "patrimonies" Jyoti/Jasmine/Jase/Jane appropriates to own herself fully and thus carry through her "metempsychosis."

In *Jasmine, The Holder of the World, Leave It to Me, Desirable Daughters, The Tree Bride,* and elsewhere in Mukherjee, metempsychosis is a rich cultural trope. To take ownership of herself and become the self she wants to be, the heroine "wants" that which has articulated other selves into being: language, more exactly, *their* language. Specifically, it is the relation with English that underpins her self's constitutive relation with itself. At the same time, she senses that "to want English is to want the world."[2] As in Mones, to desire the "foreign" idiom means—Lacanians would tell us—desire *tout court,* for "erotology" inheres in heterology;[3] the desire for the world entails longing for those "others out there," who make the world what it is, so desirable and colorful, as "multitudinous" as a novel. The author implies that, far from denying us places, dreams, and forms of being in the world, other cultures and others generally open up the world to us. This world awaits us, yet we never take possession of it directly, without assistance or mediation. In effect, we are ushered into it by others and their words, images, and books, and if we are not—as in *Native Speaker* and repeatedly in Mukherjee's fiction itself—we ought to be. For it is as we watch, listen to, and read these others, as we plunge into their novels, that we put together our own stories and in fact become the voluminous narratives capable of embracing the world. Cosmoderns like Mones, Kim, Mukherjee, and Lee suggest that we must make a detour through other lands, real and imaginary, pass through other novels and novel situations in order to come home, into our own. So do Jasmine/ Jane as she "crosses" *Jane Eyre* and Tara Bhattacharjee in *Desirable Daughters,* where she revisits Daphne du Maurier's 1938 novel *Rebecca* (and the movie made after it), to "explor[e] the making of [her own] consciousness" (5). Charlotte Brontë's and du Maurier's works are of course as fictional as the Mukherjee episodes featuring them. Nonetheless, what Mukherjee's readers—characters inside her works and actual audiences alike—pick up from the reading scenes enacted by these dialogues across centuries, continents, and cultures helps them get a better sense of the world they live in. It is something *Cosmodernism* acknowledges consistently and this part dwells on in detail: the stories the characters pore over, but also the stories in which they do so, are relations (narrative accounts) that set up new relations (bonds) with the stories' authors and strengthen old ones. Not only does Jasmine/Jane "learn" about other places and people as she reads about them. She also connects with them, *is* with them. And because she is with them, she is at last able to be with—and simply be—herself.

A with-ness subset, reading an other pertains to "information" ("reading about"), to literacy and knowledge acquisition, as much as to ontology and, Levinas would say, to ethics before anything else.[4] As information relays itself to the reader, the relay, or the relation, shapes his or her identity in a profound sense, and thus he or she consents to a debt, to an obligation, and to an ethics. Other-reading reaches beyond the informative; it is formative. We shall see later, the reader's identity and identity overall arise in cosmodernism characteristically as a result of intensifying textual-cultural commerce with others around the world. It is this reading scenario that draws writers like Mukherjee as they try to figure out what it means to evolve a self in the new millennium's global context. What these authors suspect is, first, that reading acts of this sort have never been more identity-shaping no matter how "rooted" this identity chooses to remain or is coerced into remaining; and second, that such an identity need not form at the expense of local ties and commitments. On the contrary—and this sets off a key distinction between cosmopolitanism and cosmodernism once more—reading the remote other creates or takes part in the creation of the self by establishing a relation that enhances extant affiliations or spawns new ones within the reader's community. It is in this admittedly counterintuitive sense that Yi-Fu Tuan views the "external other" as a prerequisite to communal bonding and, in an effort to get a handle on herself *as* an heir of Tata Lata, the Bengali Tree-Bride to whom Mukherjee devotes her novel, Tara turns to *Rebecca* and thus in another direction, seeks out an other's voice.[5]

As I underscore throughout, this double movement where the relation to an other serves as a prologue to self-relation is growing quickly into a subjectivity procedure in the United States and elsewhere. The phenomenon itself is not unprecedented, but its magnitude is, as people worldwide are constituting themselves "by reference to each other" more intensely than ever, as they become self-reflective—more fundamentally, "just" become, acquire a selfhood—by "relocating" themselves "imaginatively . . . in the narratives and fables of other cultures."[6]

The predilection for placing oneself in an other's relations (stories) and thus culturally, ontologically, and epistemologically in relation— "self-discovery" in and across an other's narrative accounts—plays out conspicuously in what critics from Yunte Huang to Appiah have characterized as "intertextual travel"[7] and "traveling in books"[8] or in what I call other-reading, part 4's focus. Discovery and understanding of the self via discovery and understanding of an other, story-made self are a matter of, if not synonyms to, reading, reading as answering the call of an other's text and with it, with and in this text, the call of otherness: to comprehend yourself as you comprehend an other is to approach his or her story as a site and occasion of a decisive "encounter," of a halfway meeting of "I" and "you."[9] For the twofold movement of "relocating" in an other's stories so as to locate, to "find" one's own narrative and ultimately oneself corresponds—reenacts and responds—to a move made first by what one reads. Poetry and writing overall, Auster reflects in *The Art of Hunger,* are (or should be) "a moving toward the Other."[10] The story I tell or write carries me toward somebody else at the other end of telling and writing; as I narrate and speak, my story bespeaks my "craving" for an other and so defines itself as "hungry art." Auster's critics have traced the intertwined themes of hunger and otherness—of hunger *for* otherness—to Knut Hamsun's 1890 novel *Hunger* and Kafka's short story "The Hunger Artist," but Levinas and Judaic tradition are also there. Glossing on the Spinozian "struggle to be," Levinas propounds that "here, in the *conatus essendi,* hunger is astonishingly sensitive to the hunger of the other man. The hunger of another awakens men from their well-fed slumber and their self-sufficiency." This is how we come to "liste[n] to the other," "ste[p] out" of ourselves "toward the other."[11] Auster and Levinas have in mind specific social categories such as the "downtrodden" and the outcast, largely those in "need," but also more general and more radical aspects of otherness toward which our innermost yearnings nudge us. A deeper hunger, this is, to go back to Spinoza, a "craving" for that which we lack in order to wholly be, in this case whatever cultural-existential need the other's tale responds to and, in responding to it, addresses us and so calls for our own response.

Call, Response, Transaction

Increasingly consequential as an artistic practice and theoretical awareness over the past century, the call-and-response protocol has expanded through modernism to become a cosmodern staple of late. "Konstanz School" phenomenology-derived *Rezeptionsästhetik* from Hans Robert Jauss to Rainer Warning and reader-response criticism in the Wolfgang Iser–Stanley Fish–Norman Holland–David Bleich line, then what Jane Tompkins deems the "historicizing" of reading theory by identity and cultural studies, with Elizabeth Flynn and Patrocinio Schweickart breaking new ground in the late 1980s have all worked through a number of receiver-oriented, "transactional" reading models for which the nation-state or group of adjoining nation-states, usually Western, has proved a less and less accommodating framework.[12]

Initially set out in a 1976 article, Fish's "interpretive community," followed by further, primarily race- and gender-oriented qualifications of the communal, complicates this framework indirectly. Notably, Fish does not talk about *a* community but communities sharing distinct expectations about "interpretive strategies not for reading" but "for writing texts, for constituting their properties and assigning their intentions. In other words," he clarifies, "these strategies exist prior to the act of reading and therefore determine the shape of what is read rather than, as is usually assumed, the other way around."[13] The critic designates no group or association as his communal model. Therefore, the community invoked in "Interpreting the *Variorum*" could in principle surface both inside "classical," political, cultural, and linguistic units such as the nation and astride national or geographical borders. While Fish does not elaborate on either possibility, what one comes away with is the notion of a rather limited, geoculturally bound readers' community and competency. Not only does he suggest that members of a group apply conventions considered legitimate *within* that group, but he also appears to posit a fairly tightly knit, homogenous and potentially if not effectively "homogenizing," "coherence-building" interpretive community. In it, people interact through face-to-face dealings on the basis of reading "strategies" that, "prior" as they are to the actual readerly encounters, risk "produc[ing] sameness out of [the] difference" they come upon.[14] "The only 'proof' of membership" in such circle, he notes, "is fellowship, the nod of recognition from someone in the same community."[15]

What about a nod from others and their communities? Deliberate or implied, this nod or interpellation is both a condition of life and a challenge at a time when those others' stories get to us faster and faster and, culturally "thick" and hard to unpack as they may be, furnish us with self-fashioning opportunities. On this account, Fish is not particularly helpful. By and large, his focus is "intra-communal." In his view, people produce meaning inside communities rather than *across* them; meaning making (response) fluctuates from community to community; reading reinforces community as a "discrete," unrelated, largely "local" and unchanging entity; resting on a presumably "unitary, coherent reading consciousness" and thus dedicated to coherence-building, reading—more accurately, the theory framing it—tends to reduce lives and texts to a central "ego" and so activates an "egology."[16] The interpretive community notion and reader-response theory overall, then, must be, I propose, "rehistoricized," adjusted to the ongoing realignments of communities in general and communities of readers in particular, in the United States and abroad. The cropping up of at-distance, transnational sodalities of discussion and interpretation, remarkably active in digital venues such as Internet blogs and chat rooms, is certainly another symptom of highly networked globality. In this area, we surely have our work cut out for us. We still know little about how people of different backgrounds navigate and transact together, as a group, the same texts. So inquisitive in other regards, global studies has left the question of global-era literacy and reading largely unasked. Of course, some have contended that our "visual" or "postliterate" age renders the issue less relevant—people, we hear all the time, read less and poorly; when they still do it at all, they "consume," rather, stuff such as supermarket paperbacks, comics, tabloids, or cereal boxes, like DeLillo's "full professors" in *White Noise*. Others, with Baudrillard, Paul Virilio, and Ben Agger among them, think that, customarily a slow-motion, repetitive ceremony, reading cannot be possibly accommodated by our speed culture, whose unsettling vitality rests, we are told, on its virality, on its self-distribution as fast-circulating data. I am not persuaded by either argument. As far as I am concerned, reading remains a basic rite of perception and intellection, *the* modality of taking in the world and its representations and so part and parcel of self-representation and self-becoming. If anything, reading must be rethought alongside the other, individual and collective routines and sites of learning and interpretation shaken up by the "network society."

Online, "virtual" reading communities may not supplant the "real" ones but are here to stay. If, in the following, I attend to "classical" reading and the groups and bonds coalescing around it, that is because this structure too evolves as others and their discourses make up its self-perception horizon more and more. Amounting to a "cosmodernization" of this community, the evolution reflects the nature of the texts read and debated and in whose margins, as it were, readers' identity construction is undertaken. As I show in this part, these are works ("nods") by distant and distinct others; not exclusively but growingly, in the post–Cold War environment *reading means reading of the cultural other.* "Classical" as it may be, homogeneous or perceiving itself so, largely stable or just caught in a moment of historical stability, "in-situ" when not roped off by isolationist regimes, this community has been opening up in order to come together *as such,* as an actual community springing from, and honoring, a place and time. Authors like Nafisi, Iyer, and Randall show how members of such groups or partnerships acknowledge and call on one another by answering the call of an other not with them, an other whose call itself calls for sustained reading, first and foremost for an ability to hear this call over the chasms of geography, politics, and mores. Reading may sometimes take place in isolation, but as it unfolds, as the other's texts are shared, a relation with other worlds and worldviews begins to obtain, and through it, a relation of the reading self to itself. The "here," "now," and "ours"—the cultural grammar of this community—does not drop away. In fact, it forms fully, and helps formulate self-understanding, once the "out there," "then," and "theirs," encrypted in the other's story, are taken in and localized by the perusing selves.

Cultural Studies without Cultures? Cosmopolitan Reading

But how is decryption possible across such distances and cultural-stylistic asymmetries? Can we hear the other's call at all? Suppose we can, can we also "get" it, and thus, ourselves? At last, what makes—assuming it does—this understanding ecological rather than egological? From among the answers given over the past decades to these questions, I want to pick up on a few relevant to our discussion. Objectivist, or "anti-perspectivist," the first, E. D. Hirsch's, disputes Fish's. The same year "Interpreting the *Variorum*" came out as an article, Hirsch asked in *The Aims of Interpretation:* "If all interpretation is constituted by the interpreter's cultural categories, how can he possibly understand meanings that are constituted by different cultural categories?" On this issue, Dilthey "was straightforward and perfectly within the sponsoring Kantian tradition. We can understand culturally alien meanings because we are able to adopt culturally alien categories," which means that "Cultural subjectivity is not innate, but acquired; it derives from a potential, present in every man, that is capable of sponsoring an indefinite number of culturally conditioned categorical systems. It is within the capacity of every individual to imagine himself other than he is, to realize in himself another human or cultural possibility."[17]

This is the transcendental premise on which cross-cultural communication rests in post-Enlightenment thought. Accordingly, cultural subjectivity may be acquired, but one's ability to acquire it and thus picture oneself "as" an other, is inborn, built into our common humanity. An assumption of modern cosmopolitanism, this humanistic-universalist a priori also overhangs Appiah's "cosmopolitan reading," his endeavors to leave "past universalisms" behind notwithstanding.[18] Reacting to anthropology's "professional bias toward difference," the philosopher sets out to "defend a kind of cosmopolitanism—but not as the name for a dialogue among static, closed cultures, each of which is internally homogenous and different from all the others." "If we are going to do cultural studies," he continues, "let us at least do it without cultures"[19]—an odd undertaking, to say the least. What it comes down to becomes clear when Appiah specifies that old humanism was not mistaken to assume that we must "share" something in order to understand one another; it only got wrong what exactly we shared: not atemporal categories of experience, axiologies, grand narratives, and generally grandiose things such as "human nature," "reason," and other "universals," but, as Appiah calls them, "particulars." What we run across in a novel, in that "message in a bottle from some other position, even if it was written and published last week in your hometown," he expounds,

> derives not from a theoretical understanding of us as having a commonly understood common nature—not, then, from an understanding that we (readers and writers) all share—but from an invitation to respond in imagination to narratively constructed situations. In short, what makes the cosmopolitan experience possible—in reading as elsewhere—is not that we share beliefs and values because of our common capacity for reason: in the novel, at least, it is not "reason" but a different human capacity that grounds our sharing: namely, the grasp of a narrative logic that allows us to construct the world to which our imaginations respond. That capacity is to be found up the Amazon, the Mississippi, the Congo, the Indus, the Yellow River, just as it is found on the banks of the Avon and the Dordogne.[20]

As Appiah would have it, not only is this capacity one for all; the world in which we exert it is one too. In this world, novels go places and are read differently because "people are different." At the same time, "common conversations" about these "shared objects" are possible, and with them "cosmopolitan reading," yet what makes them so is not necessarily "shared culture" or "understanding" but the "capacity to follow a narrative and conjure a world." This "little" universal and a number of other little things of such sort is what brings us all together, not what eighteenth-century philosophers thought we had in common. On this account as on others, they were, according to Appiah, "dismally unimaginative" rather than exceedingly presumptuous.[21]

What we get above is an account of a cosmopolitan reading cautious—but not cautious enough—to tiptoe around the pitfalls of Enlightenment universalism. As I see it, and as the writers examined in this part see it, cosmodern reading takes the next step, which Appiah's model seems ready for but stops short of. Vector of the greater move from cosmopolitanism to cosmodernism, the leap or turn pertains to a significant degree to the business of "sharing." In both old-school and "revised" humanists like Hirsch and Appiah, respectively, the emphasis falls on what we must share so as to read each other, which poses problems Appiah's insistence on a commonality of "particulars" does not solve. The novel's genre structure, storytelling technique, Bremondian *logique du récit,* and so on, are not exactly universals.[22] They do hold a cultural-symbolic function largely varying from community to community. This function lies behind narrative and, more broadly, meaning making. Whatever the story, when presented with it we may recognize, or assume, rather, that its whole point ("logic") is to make a point, to "conjure" a world—but what about the literature of the illogical, the nonsense, and the absurd, what about the post-Dada "poetics of pointlessness," I am tempted to ask. In any event, understanding *how* the point is made and thereby what the point ultimately *is* takes cultural competence. Generally speaking, all stories feature narrative and character, but neither is everywhere the same. Their formal makeup is a cultural variable. Narrative structures too are "constructed," enmeshed with local systems of representation and power. Not only does the typical Chinese detective novel differ formally from a Raymond Chandler thriller, but the difference, in novels and literature overall, is also cultural, and thus a deterrent against reading a Chinese thriller as we would an American one. Of course, we can learn the appropriate decoding principles, but before learning them, we must recognize the limits of our own logic, narrative or otherwise.

There are places in "Cosmopolitan Reading," *The Ethics of Identity* (which rehashes the 2001 essay), *Cosmopolitanism,* and elsewhere in Appiah where such limitations get little play. His cosmopolitan banner may be "universalism plus difference," but because in practice he seems determined primarily to keep at bay the "skeptical antiuniversalism" of the Lyotard and Rorty kind, his "dialogical universalism" ends up more universal than dialogical. It is thus noteworthy that, to Appiah's mind, that "other position" an African novel speaks from embodies, presumably to a Western reader, the same otherness and by the same token poses the same "decryption" problems as a novel "written and published last week in [his or her] hometown."[23] In the universalism-cum-difference formula, then, it is not cultural difference, the universalism *of* difference—or, rather, differences—but the propensity to bridge gaps and distinctions, to communicate above and against them, that drives Appiah's case for cosmopolitanism and accounts for his whole rhetoric of "sharing" and "agreeing."

What the cosmoderns agree on, instead, is that transparent in all agreements is a privileged location; that "sharing" ultimately speaks to formulated or unformulated assent and so bodies forth a concession; and that the latter pulls toward a center that has not conceded much in exchange. Ever lopsided like universalism itself (claims to the contrary notwithstanding), "sharing" in something or with somebody ordinarily takes some "identifying" with that other person, group, and their values. Or, as I often stress in these pages, the real challenge in a world bent on becoming everywhere the same is to talk to one another and to read each other on the assumption that we do *not* share much nor do we operate with similar (let alone identical) narrative/reading logics prior to opening each other's books and that, after we have closed them, we may still stick to our dissimilarities. For the whole point of cosmodernism as cultural ecology is to work out relations in which self and other do not become interchangeable, and this is not possible unless these relations arise while self and other keep intact—and thus communicate by—their differences, disagreements, and discrepant logics of writing and reading. That is why Fish's theory would not make much sense to cosmopolitans like Appiah, as it does not to cosmopolitans like Hirsch. According to Fish, narrative logic is not an attribute of the story but, like all textual elements, a readerly construction, something assigned to the text by the interpretive community. This community may or may not take the trouble to acquaint itself with the logic of the writing community in which the story was authored. But there is nothing in Fish preventing a reading "we" from acquainting itself with "their" writing conventions.

Appiah does not ignore this issue—the very question of difference—completely, but treats it inconsistently. While completely consistent, Hirsch acknowledges the problem but only to throw it out. Since a story's meaning, as he would put it, exists "objectively," only from the author's perspective, a "valid" take on the story must reflect that perspective. As a consequence, cultural difference and the potentially divergent interpretations stemming from this difference are not to be factored into a culture-("perspective"-)sensitive reading model but, one more time, are to be overcome. As a good reader, I would be expected to take up the author's position, to *be(come)* the author, which, I might point out, is not the same as "relocating" myself *in* that author's story. Anything short of this "identification" with the author's position would not be interpretation but "authorship."[24]

This perspectival adjustment comes close to Georges Poulet's *critique d'identification*.[25] With Hirsch, the reader goes over to the "other side," where he or she sees things as it does. With Poulet, it is the other way around. It is the "consciousness of another" that my "innermost self" hosts, so much so that what "I" end up thinking is somebody else's thoughts. The Swiss critic's conclusion is extreme: "Reading, then, is the act in which the subjective principle which I call *I*" gets "modified in such a way that I no longer have the right, strictly speaking, to consider it as my *I*." "I am," he insists, "on loan to another, and this other thinks, feels, suffers, and acts within me." For that, we can safely infer, this "identification" goes, pace Iser, beyond "the establishment of" balanced "affinities between oneself and someone outside oneself—a familiar ground on which we are able to experience the unfamiliar."[26] Thus, no matter what side one finds oneself, the reader's or the author's, one winds up harboring the other's brainwork, forfeiting his or hers—"receding" (if "temporarily") into the background"[27]—in order to emulate an other's. I am not sure that, in a world that has extensively experimented with giving up the rights to an "I," this sounds like an attractive proposition. Nor does Gadamer's "fusion of perspectives" (*Horizontverschmelzung*), and by implication Jauss's "horizon of expectations" (*Erwartungshorizont*), provide the remedy just because Hirsch rejects it. He does so, I would submit, for the wrong reason. The right reason would be, I think, the equivalence of "fusion" and "sharing." If the "subject-object division" gets "removed," as is the case with both Poulet's and Iser's reading models, who is "fusing" with whom?[28] What is the privileged element here? On what cultural terrain, on whose terms is the fusion taking place?

Cultural Studies *with* Cultures: Cosmodern Reading

As we have observed, Hirsch is "objectivist," "authorial." To him, the literal meaning maker, the author, runs the show, foreordaining the readerly encounter. In Poulet, things change only superficially. In Gadamer and Jauss, we move slightly to the center along an axis running from authorial objectivism to Fish's "communal" subjectivism to "individual" subjectivism à la Bleich and Holland. Somewhere toward the more formalist middle lies Iser's Roman Ingarden–based notion of reading as "filling in" the gaps. A blueprint or set of instructions for its own completion (*Vollendung*) through reading rather than a finished product, the "formulated text" "shade[s] off through allusions and suggestions" another text "that is unformulated though nonetheless intended." "Only in this way," the German critic observes, "can the reader's imagination be given the scope it needs; the written text furnishes it with indications which enable it to conjure up what the text does not reveal."[29]

In a famous exchange with Iser, Fish has challenged the distinction between the formulated and unformulated text, or between textual determinacy and indeterminacy.[30] Did the American critic come out on top, as some have concluded?[31] I think he did to the extent Iser's *implizite Leser*, theorized in *The Implied Reader* and further qualified in *The Act of Reading*, is identified as "those predispositions necessary for a literary work to exercise its effect—predispositions laid down, not by an empirical outside reality, but by the text itself." Its "roots firmly planted in the structure of the text," this reader is a "textual structure anticipating the presence of a recipient" yet "without necessarily defining him: this concept prestructures the role to be assumed by each recipient, and this holds true even when texts deliberately appear to ignore their possible recipient or actively exclude him." "Thus," Iser asserts, "the concept of the implied reader designates a network of response-inviting structures, which impel the reader to grasp the text."[32] Iser lost out, and for that his usefulness here diminishes, insofar as *The Act of Reading* accentuates the textual pre-figuration of reading: if the "particular role" I am to play as a reader is (pre)scripted, if I am "impelled" by the text to "grasp" it in a certain way, then its "appeal structure" (*Appelstruktur*) calls to a preexisting (textual) *order* of form and meaning and so is hardly a call proper. For the latter, if authentic, implies a response that has not been given nor pre-figured yet.[33] But this pre-figuration is not consistently strict, let alone that, according to Fish, it is just another interpretation effect anyway, something figured *into* the text *post scriptum*, so to speak, by the actual reader, rather than a preexistent, built-in guideline—this reader formulates *both* the "unformulated text" and the directions (the "user's manual") for this formulation. At any rate, there is, above and elsewhere, a fair deal of "indeterminacy" in Iser's own language. This leaves room both for a genuine call and, accordingly, for a culturally more substantial, "original" and un-(pre)figured reader's role where textual formulas seem to allow for the reader's more thorough self-"formulation" and self-"discovery" during reading.[34] We are thus told that the "implied" reader does not necessarily "define" the actual audience, nor is it enough for the reading to take place. As in Appiah, the reader's "imagination," his or her own figurative capacity, is a vital ingredient; the implied reader sets it off in the actual or external reader. Channeled by the text with varying degrees of firmness, the receiver's imagination remains in Iser equally "defining" and, thus, self-defining, since "the role he [the reader] is to play in uncovering the hidden reality of the text will lead ultimately to his uncovering and correcting the hidden reality of himself."[35]

This sounds encouraging. Only, in order for self-uncovering to occur, this role cannot be pre-figured as mechanically as it seems to occur in Iser at times. For what does it mean to pre-figure it? It means to read reading before its advent and thereby block its "event," as Iser and others call it. It means to fake, in writing, that movement toward an other's figure or face and then control or even obstruct the actual reading of that writing; it boils down to muffling the writing's call to its audience, the self's ecological address to an other *as* other. Iser's user's manual "excludes" to the extent that it "includes." It encodes/programs a user. That user—that other—and *the meaning of the text with it* are, accordingly, foregone conclusions, "known" in advance by the text (and/or its author—the distinction is not terribly important here), and this knowledge precludes or at the very least restricts reading as self-knowledge, textual "uncovering" as the reader's autodiscovery. In this vein, Derrida ventures in *La carte postale* that textual experience is more exciting when the other at the other end of the writing process, the "addressee," is unknown or only slightly "implied." After all, we largely write—and, I should say, publish—for others these days, for those who have or will have soon historically unparalleled access to what we put out, much as we do to their own output. Who exactly we address is of course seldom spelled out, and even if it were, even if our writings were one big cultural in-joke, their "nominal" addressee would still make for a small fraction of their readership. So it may not be too self-aggrandizing to assume that the unknown out there and the alien, the foreign, and the strange are or are becoming our writings' broadest destination in a world where more and more texts, images, and tunes reach ever-widening audiences outside our "hometowns." Thus our writings imply "strangers" even when these writings "imply" or self-professedly "cater" to a familiar reader—even when they fall back on an *ethnos-grounded ethos of writing*. In this sense, they are indeed "written as a defense of the dignity of the strange."[36]

If truly ethical, all defense and care start out with or as recognition. To be con-cerned, one must first look at the object of one's concern—the Latin *cernere* means to "perceive" and "discern"—with ethical "discernment" and so acknowledge this object as subject. This is another way of saying that to defend the strange, one must first recognize it as such, namely, re-cognize what this word too teaches us about recognition as "knowing af-ter" opposed to the a priori egology of precognition, pre-figuration, and other Iserian "implications" of this kind. If genuine, the defense of the other, I maintain, presupposes as much as it further opens up the wiggle room of self-figuration, allows for that other "to figure it all out" for him-self or herself in the context of his or her culture. It is only in this context, where the other's/reader's face emerges whole and new, "un-pre-faced" and unscripted by any readerly prescriptions, that it will have received, in the read text, full, ethical con-sideration. This is why, pivoting on such context as it does, cultural studies has not rushed to take up reception the-ory of the phenomenological brand so far covered; this is why cultural studies cannot be done if that means doing it "without" culture; and this is also why, by contrast, one can define cosmodern reading theory and practice—cosmodern cultural studies, if you will—as cultural studies *with* culture. This model approaches, we learn in the following sections, both writing and reading as a "call" to others across geopolitical and cul-tural disjunctions yet without the "implications" and predeterminations that directly or indirectly narrow down the response and by the same movement curtail the reader's—the other's—ability to con-figure himself or herself. What this model provides for is an *Appelstruktur* lax enough to "appeal" to an other without calling him or her to order (be it textual), an *answerability structure* of the loosely Bakhtinian sort that posits that the text itself would not be—*will not have been*—whole, "complete" had it not called, in its own textuality, for a response as unfettered, un-pre-figured, and "whole" as possible. This consummate reaction is the only one that would allow the unknown reader to respond and thus read himself or her-self into an authentic figure and identity.

Of course, it is primarily the text (the novel) rather than its reading that Bakhtin deems an answer to previous texts and "utterances."[37] Con-temporary with Bakhtin's early thoughts on authorship but otherwise coming from a direction (Hasidism) distinct from Bakhtin's Hegelianism, Buber's reflections on reading might help us carry this answerability over into the cosmodern space of cross-cultural reception where, in answering a text, the reader launches a relational project as much hermeneutic as ex-istential because, and in the first place, that text calls out to him or her with an ethical "consideration" that does not "imply" much beyond the obligation of a response in kind. Throughout *I and Thou,* Buber remains adamant about the mutuality of such an obligation. As Walter Kaufmann comments on Buber's reading philosophy, "We must learn to feel addressed by a book, by the human being behind it, as if a person spoke directly to us. A good book or essay or poem is not primarily an object to be put to use or an object of experience: it is the voice of You speaking to me, requiring a response."[38] Readers, Buber thinks, all too often reify texts, treat them as objects or utensils; what they hear and respond to in a text is an "It," not a "You." Therefore, their response, whatever they "say" to the work they read, is not "whole," and because "being I and saying I are the same," the readers are not whole either.[39] Nor can this saying (reading), which is I-saying as much as You-saying, say itself verily if the reader has been already objectified, partially scripted ("implied") as an "It" and thus handed the "script" of the about-to-be-said. For this is what an "actual relation" does: in it, the aesthetic "form" I am presented with, and the "You" in it, "acts on me as I act on it."[40] This condition of "true" relatedness—the reciprocity of action and reaction—is in Buber key to the "wholeness" of reading and writing alike. "This is," he avers, "the eternal origin of art[:] that a human being confronts a form" that "wants to become a work through him." Notably, this is "not a figment of his soul but something that appears to the soul and demands the soul's creative power. What is required is a deed that a man does with his whole being: if he ... speaks with his being the basic word to the form that appears, then the creative power is released and the work comes into being."[41] So reading can be—and, insofar as it follows out a relational, "nonscripted" situation, should be—a form of freedom as well as of creativity.[42] In it, the reader's "creative power" reigns supreme. This is an imagination that does not "invent" the work yet still "conjures" a world "creatively," which, we noticed earlier, both Appiah and Iser determine as a core attribute of reading.[43] The reader, though, must effectuate this "projection" with his or her "whole being," and for that, his or her being cannot be pro-jected (pre-figured) beforehand. All the reading self and the authoring other (or the authoring self and the reading other) "share" is this "conjuring" faculty. Otherwise, when my whole being is engaged in projecting a world in relation with what I am reading, the projection works through the text at hand in the concrete circumstances of my culture. As *studium*—etymologically preoccupation, concern *for* the text—reading is cultural studies or reception-oriented cultural studies, cultural studies *with* culture, informed by communally "embedded" preoccupations.

The cosmodern reader thus fully "creates," and this creation honors the other, the "You," and thus the higher "Thou," as reading arises in relation.

At the same time—and the writers discussed subsequently also illuminate this fundamental feature of reading as being-in-relation—this text/other-derived, readerly relation both comes about within, and in turn bolsters, community. *The other's story is the "You" around which ("Our") community comes together, the "original phenomenon" of community.* Artistically and sociologically, we are dealing with the same apparent paradox: like art, community emerges, as Buber tells us, in response to an other. Art production is a reception effect—the effect (reception) "causes" (produces) it—for in the last analysis it is this "experiencing" (cf. Gk. *aisthesis*) of the other's discourse, this perceptive or aesthetic act, that gives birth to community. Routinely thought of in ethnic terms, *the communal has the aesthetic at its heart, and even deeper than that, the ethical,* "the central presence of the You."[44] In a profound way, this presence brings community into presence as the community's readers project "worlds" in conjunction with their other-readings yet for the benefit of their peers. "True community," Buber explicates, "does not come into being because people have feelings for each other (though that is required, too), but rather on two accounts: all of them have to stand in a living, reciprocal relationship to a single living center, and they have to stand in a living, reciprocal relationship to one another."[45] The You—your poem, your story, coming from strange worlds in strange wordings—lies in this pulsing center; if it does not, my (our) readings draw it there. Through them, I and others in my community relate to "You," and through "You" we relate to each other, and bond. Again, we read "locally," and our readings are positional, "contingent." We read others culturally in that we read them "with" our culture. Reading-as-answering is then a relation/response to an other and, through it, a relation/response to local circumstances within equally local communities of reading. It is under such circumstances that cosmodern readers hear the other's call, experience the other's text and thus themselves authentically. Once we have read it, that text becomes communal glue, a crucially constitutive nexus for readers as they configure themselves individually and collectively through and around a relation with an other's "storied" relations. Consequently, "we" incur a personal and public debt to what and whom we read. To anticipate a suggestion made by the authors investigated in this part's remainder, the ethical-aesthetic "bonds" forged in cosmodern reading's "contact zone"[46] can rival the binding force (*Verbindungskraft*) of the collective consciousness "rooted" in the presumably unmediated "*ethnos* of nationals (*Volksgenossen*)."[47] "With reading," Iser echoes Erving Goffman, "there is no *face-to-face situation*."[48] This is not an absolute rule—I can read your poem while you are here with me—but even if it was, the reading of that other whose face is not among those coming together around his or her story pulls these figures and minds together with wondrous "binding force." Nowhere is this force more salient than in Nafisi.

2. Against Solipsism

> I would like to think of my own status as what you called "citizen of the world."
> —AZAR NAFISI, interview by Robert Birnbaum

Meteorology of Reading: *Lolita* in Tehran

Reading Lolita in Tehran: A Memoir in Books made such a splash when it was released in 2003 that Random House reissued Nafisi's book in paperback only months thereafter.[49] Translations into over a dozen languages were under way a year later. The author was born and educated in Shah Pahlavi's Iran (which she treats in *Things I've Been Silent About* [2009]), continued her studies at Oxford and in the United States, then went back home in 1979, a few months after the breakout of the Islamic Revolution and the return of Ayatollah Khomeini from exile and less than a year before the takeover of the American Embassy by militants. In Tehran, she did her best to carry on as a woman and academic passionate about introducing her students to Austen, James, Fitzgerald, and Nabokov. She navigated the rough waters of religious totalitarianism and censorship, surviving the purges, the mock trials, the scapegoating of the Iraq war years, the "morality squads'" raids, the implosion of the curriculum, the burning of public libraries' books, and more. She taught on and off, was expelled for refusing to wear the veil, but after Khomeini's death in 1989 was persuaded by friends to resume teaching. By 1995 the Iranian perestroika had fizzled out, however, and she quit her job to run a clandestine reading group from her living room until 1997, when she left the country for good.

The impact of Islamic theocracy on Iranian life and women's lives in particular has been documented in a number of extraordinary autobiographies by Azadeh Moaveni (*Lipstick Jihad*), Marjane Satrapi (*Embroideries* and the *Persepolis* series), Roya Hakakian (*Journey from the Land of No*), Firoozeh Dumas (*Funny in Farsi*), Haleh Esfandiari (*My Prison, My*

Home), and Shirin Ebadi (*Iran Awakening*), to list just a few. To this archive of plight, Nafisi contributes the testimony of a reader who meets in secret with other readers—her former students—to lead them through *Pride and Prejudice, Daisy Miller, The Great Gatsby,* and *Lolita.* The risks they take are considerable. Some of them, all women at this point, end up in jail, where they are tortured or murdered.

Clandestine or vaguely tolerated, group reading and discussion were venues of political dissent in "Cultural Revolution" China, as Dai Sijie's 2000 international bestseller *Balzac and the Little Chinese Seamstress* testifies so touchingly, and in the former Communist countries, from the USSR's "Bakhtin circle" to the Romanian "Păltiniş Group."[50] Little known outside the country, the group (or "school"), its leader, philosopher Constantin Noica, and some of its members became household names in Romania after the 1983 release of *Jurnalul de la Păltiniş* (The Păltiniş Diary) by Noica's closest disciple, Gabriel Liiceanu.[51] Playing Plato to his master's Socrates, Liiceanu gave Noica to an audience hungry for something different from the official cultural model and the "formative" ideology behind it. Indeed, what Noica offered, principally via Liiceanu's diary (subtitled, in translation, A Paideic Model in Humanist Culture), was a "pedagogical" countermodel, where the qualifier *paideic* references directly the title of *Paideia,* a three-volume work published between 1933 and 1947 by German classicist Werner Jaeger, and indirectly *Paideia*'s subtitle, *Die Formung des Griechischen Menschen* (The Fashioning of the Greek Man). Founder of "the third humanism" in Nazi Germany—*Paideia*'s second volume came out in 1944—Jaeger is an ambiguous figure, but Liiceanu wrestles the pedagogical concept from national socialism's clutches and uses it subversively during the twilight years of Nicolae Ceauşescu's socialist nationalism.

Largely inspired by Heidegger's work and lifestyle and named after the southern Transylvanian mountain resort where Noica moved late in life and where cohorts of disciples-to-be went to see him, the group remains controversial to this day, as does its founder, for reasons not unlike those for which Heidegger himself became the subject of heated dispute: a past of far right-wing politics coupled with a nationalist language philosophy. Disproportionately influential in post-Communist Romanian politics, the group started out small in the late 1970s, with an older Noica and a few others in their twenties interested in matters of readerly and cultural-philosophical nature: what and how to read, where to begin, and so forth. In hindsight, their reading choices and approaches seem conservative, yet back then they struck many as a breath of fresh air. What Noica and his circle were striving to retrieve by returning to the sources and issues the master had debated before the war with friends like playwright Eugène Ionesco, historian of religions Mircea Eliade, and philosopher E. M. Cioran was a cosmopolitan canon at odds with the regime's literacy policies and politics, with what Romanians studied in schools, where, especially in philosophy and the social sciences, curricula were vetted by official Marxism. Via Liiceanu, Noica recommended starting from culture's square one, a "literacy from scratch" or radical "paideic model"—radical in that it sought to go back to "roots," more precisely, to the European roots. Derived from *pais*, "child," *paideia* is Greek for "cultural formation," "education." This formation, *Formung* or *Bildung*, entails first and foremost *unlearning* what the regime has forced people to read, and then reading anew, and new works. Accordingly, one would start with the Greeks, move on to the Romans, later to classics in several European traditions, whenever possible in the original. And one would be well advised to ignore things Romanian at least for a while—a remarkable advice given Noica's personal investment in such things. In this alternate reading, philology and politics were one. Reading began, too, with a canon war of sorts, with what the reader needed to pick out or set aside, with a preliminary value judgment that was aesthetic as it was political. And for many years, kilometers away and above Bucharest, in a famously cold room and under relentless surveillance, Noica and his followers would get together to make such judgments, read, and comment on their readings.

Some of the "school" members, the master himself included, had spent long years in the Romanian gulag for reading and circulating banned texts—a charge all too familiar in the Stalinist 1950s. Bursting at the seams with students, teachers, academics, writers, and other intellectual categories, the prisons of the time were places of deprivation, torture, and extermination, yet they also offered opportunities to discuss blacklisted authors in fairly expert circles and in response to what Noica called euphemistically "politically" inclement "weather." Released from incarceration and house arrest, he noticed that the climate had not changed. As historians of totalitarianism have only of late acknowledged, Stalinism did not end with Stalin's death in 1957 but continued well into the following decades for intervals varying from country to country and with later relapses such as the Romanian middle and late 1980s. Noica, Liiceanu, and others would meet to translate and talk about Plato and Augustine as a way of overcoming the elements, not to weather history but to carve out a space inside it where another history could be imagined. To do so, these "resisting readers," as Judith Fetterly might say, clustered around the milestones of what they saw as "high performance" culture, and around those texts from other places and times they forged a nurturing community. Turning to one another as they turned to others' words, they built a new and complex togetherness against the strictures of place, time, and times, against adverse "meteorology."

Up to a point, *Reading Lolita in Tehran* is an Iranian *Păltiniş Diary*. The similarities are striking, hence the little East European detour just taken. But so are the differences.[52] Both are antitotalitarian, cultural-political projects. Elitist, exclusive, and exclusively male despite the large number of people to whom otherwise Noica's doors stayed open, the *Diary* follows in the tradition of European cosmopolitanism. Its modernism, however, is as questionable as Heidegger's (*Sein und Zeit* was the group's philosophical guide). The alternative it supplies to official cultural politics is classical if not classicist, ostensibly Eurocentric, and conservatively canonic. The *Diary*'s "high culture" pathos did have political reverberations, but they were barely fleshed out in its first edition, which was butchered by censorship. Composed after the author left "the gaze of the blind censor" behind her, *Reading Lolita in Tehran* is conspicuously political in spite of the group leader's claims and efforts to "prevent the political from intruding on our individual lives" (273). Noica had something similar in mind when he likened the regime to climate: since you, the individual, cannot control the weather and since the weather has admittedly little influence on your work, you might as well ignore the political blizzard and keep on reading and writing. Noica's Hegelian mystique of culture as absolute and sufficient life form and value cut off from other values and forms of social expression, his assessment, in effect, of such values and forms as "distractions" had, as one might expect, depoliticizing effects, which explains why his legacy is a bone of contention to this day.

So is Nafisi's insistence that the personal and reading as a private, quasi-exclusive aesthetic experience, on the one hand, and the political, on the other, be kept separate.[53] Nor is her formalist, self-professedly nonfeminist if not antifeminist (and anti-"postmodern") reading method innovative or "subversive." It has been denounced, actually, as "(neo)conservative" and has been upbraided for "actively participat[ing] in the agenda of an overtly 'depoliticized' cultural study that is in fact profoundly *political*." "Compelling" as "extrinsic evidence" may be—critics have adduced "her position as director of the Dialogue project at [Johns Hopkins's Paul

H. Nitze School for Advanced International Studies] (SAIS), her support from the Smith Richardson Foundation, and her participation in the public relations' campaigns of SAIS to promote the United States as the 'protector' of the Free World"[54]—and no matter how odd her overall New Critical pronouncements in early 1990s Iran may sound to us here and now, Steven Mailloux's and Susan Friedman's arguments on the "positional" meaning of Nafisi's approach to Austen and Nabokov ultimately carry the day.[55] To be sure, Tehran and its fundamentalist-repressive regime make up the context that defines—gives meaning, aesthetically as well as politically, to—*Reading Lolita in Tehran*'s sense-making protocols. No question about it: it surely matters whether one reads *Lolita* in ("with") Tehran or in (again, "with") the Idaho where John Carlos Rowe "read[s] *Reading Lolita in Tehran*." In the Idahoan context, Rowe's critique of Nafisi's sense-making model makes sense, but so does Nafisi's take on Nabokov *in* Tehran. Only the American West and the "totalitarian" "dangers" its "liberal individualism" poses (according to Rowe) are *not* Nafisi's original "historical" context no matter where she wrote about that context.[56] Under those circumstances, what she and her students did with the likes of *Lolita* was—could not *not* be—political regardless of her apolitical claims and later, U.S. associations. On this account, Rowe is right, or half right, rather, because her politics—a politics of reading—is genuinely antititotalitarian. Self-confessedly "ignorant" of what oppression meant in Nafisi's Islamic Republic, Rowe cannot appreciate her subversiveness, once more, in *that* context, the one that counts most.[57] Therefore, Rowe's article "Reading *Reading Lolita in Tehran* in Idaho" judges Nafisi unfit for the treatment Nafisi gave Nabokov in Iran. That is, Rowe does not set up her work as a mirror in which "we," Americans, Idaho ranchers included, might take another look at ourselves. The mirror and the mirrored, he implies, are too much alike for that.

I want to argue, instead, for a substantial difference between the two and with it, for a reading politics in turn warranted, according to critics like Mailloux and Friedman, by a politics of location. What I mean by this is "situational" reading, interpretation where the position of the interpreter bears on the interpreted. Nafisi's reading of *Lolita* may be "traditional." But this traditionalism, formalist, "elite," or otherwise, must be historicized by the cautious reader, that is, reinscribed and weighed carefully within the historical context from which it sprang. Once we take the trouble to historicize this "aestheticism," it no longer comes across as conservative or politically crippling but as profoundly destabilizing and even politically explosive. Striking in Nafisi's account of Iran is an element that also marked Noica's Romania and, in it, the political play of the same formalist-individualist values at issue here. More to the point: given the all-out, distinctively totalitarian assault on the individual, the private, and the subjective in former socialist Romania as well as in Nafisi's Islamic Republic, the focus on the personal and the personal, aesthetically oriented approach to texts could not have been more political. Defining the entire society as a political space, on the one hand, and taking up that space entirely, on the other, the totalitarian apparatus rendered political—more precisely, oppositional—any attempt to secure within the social domain a privacy zone of reflection and expression, be they "merely" aesthetic. Islamic, Communist, or otherwise, autocracy *hyperpoliticizes* the world, makes everything political while denying political agency to the individuals in this world. By the same token, events and stances that may not seem politically remarkable, including those self-avowedly "apolitical," become or are judged political, hence subversive in *this* type of milieu—no wonder, as Pico Iyer writes in *Video Night in Kathmandu,* "the ruling mullahs in Iran were fretting that their capital's newly formed clandestine Michael Jackson clubs could easily turn into revolutionary cells."[58] "I gave," Nafisi herself tells her interviewer Robert Birnbaum, "a talk once on *Madame Bovary,* on Flaubert—there was almost a riot." This could hardly happen in the United States, Birnbaum retorts, and he is probably right.[59] No matter how akin to Nafisi's may seem reading and female bonding protocols in book groups such as those portrayed by Mary McCarthy's *The Group* (1991), Mary Alice Monroe's *The Book Club* (1999), Lorna Landvik's *Angry Wives Eating Bon Bons,* (2003), or Karen Joy Fowler's *The Jane Austen Club* (2004), the "riotous" politics of perusal and commentary remains alien to these novels' heroines, as it largely did to the actual reading groups that have picked Nafisi's memoir.[60]

Traveling in Books

In *Reading Lolita in Tehran,* this politics is cosmodern. Unlike Noica's, it embraces a world vaster than Europe and articulates itself in an emotional relation with that world. Nafisi and her group set up a new type of community in a particular time and place, not necessarily or programmatically against that time and place but valiantly across their "climatic" limitations. This is not escapist politics either, which calls into question one more time the line the author draws between the "personal" and the "political." *Lolita* is no safe haven, no Baudelairean *paradis artificiel.* Its covers are not the shelter under which Nabokov's devotees read *Lolita,* sip tea, and sit out Iranian history any more than *Lolita* itself is about the Tehran of the 1990s. Nor is Nabokov your typical "political" writer. Among the twentieth century's greatest cosmopolites, he could have declared, as Nafisi herself does: "I would like to think of my own status as what you called 'citizen of the world' or a 'citizen of the portable world,' if not of the world. . . . My life has been the life of a vagabond."[61] In a society under cultural lockdown, however, the aesthetic cosmopolitanism of foreign authors like Nabokov is twice undermining, if not thrice. For in play here is not just tasting the forbidden fruit, reading the other's cosmopolitan work on the sly. A cosmodern reading is applied to Nabokov, and a certain community emerges as a result. Nabokov may not be political, and he is not big on "community" either, as Suki Kim's characters suspect. It is this reading that politicizes him, making him, to recall Buber, into the "living center" of a whole communal politics of gender.

How does this happen? To answer, let me note first that the politics of a text is most often thought of thematically ("topically," Nabokov would say), as a way of foregrounding a certain subject (in this respect too, Rowe's considerations are edifying). "In" the text, a novel's politics is "content." Accordingly, some authors are political, and others are not. For argument's sake, suppose the latter is Nabokov's case. The Russian-American author *is* political or, better still, the reading he calls for is political in the cosmodern sense that a certain politics obtains or stems not from a politically marked content or theme *inside* the text but transactionally, *in between* this text and its readers. Separated from the writer by geography, history, language, ethnicity, and other boundaries, the readers nonetheless engage with him intimately. They feel the Habermasian "binding force" of his words and connect with them affectively as they read them and thus reach across such boundaries into a place where self and other can converse, weather through, and sustain each other against the bad weather of history. Fostered here, in the generous interstice of cosmodern reading, is a *local* alliance of Iranian readers that sets itself up *supralocally,* courtesy of an other elsewhere. This is all the more remarkable in a regime like Iran, which made into law its citizens' isolation from the outside and especially women's sociopolitical isolation, deploying as it did a whole repressive apparatus to reinforce both national borders and gender boundaries. A typical counterreaction in politically denied spaces around the world, the cosmodern politics of collective perusal and discussion seeks to "sublate" the state-policed territories and distances. A distinctive spatial politics, it plays out in and through the space of reading, which unfolds between text and reader as an invisible bridge spanning the physical expanse and narrowing the epistemological gap between the Russian-American writer and his Iranian audience. In this sense, across such bridges, travel is possible and, as Appiah meditates, we do travel in books; still in this sense, there is nothing "intrinsically wrong with the safari."[62] But we need to make sure that we travel ethically, as good cosmoderns.

To understand what this means—and why Nafisi and her students' journey to Nabokov, and back to themselves, is ethical—I would suggest that embedded in the Nabokovian novels and ahead of their time is what I would term cosmodern *appeal*. I define the concept as a configuration of plot, character, style, and critical-ironic ethical stances that call out to, and pull in, fellow human beings living, as they may be, on the other side of ethnocultural, linguistic, or geopolitical divides but subject to comparable or compatible cultural-political codifications, sanctions, and injunctions. Built into Nabokov's text is, I submit, a dialogical constellation of problems, situations, and narrative forms that issue forth a resounding call to the world. This thematic-formal matrix features a rare ability to draw out and to elicit responses from the disenfranchised, from people trapped by history in ethical-political conundrums and predicaments resembling those faced by Nabokov's characters. Thus, undergirding the appeal structure of his oeuvre is a textually constructed yet no less deeply seated empathy, so much so that the heart of his oeuvre goes out a priori to people caught in real struggles analogous to the fictitious ones staged by *Lolita, Pnin,* and *Pale Fire.* At the end of the day, Nabokov may prove a cosmopolite typical of Europe's "belated modernism,"[63] yet his work's empathic instigation is cosmodern or, more correctly, has cosmodern *effects* insofar as it is answered by an other in so many ways different from the self behind the text and the selves in the text and this answer raises a bridge of analogies and symmetries across a host of rifts. True, in texts like *Ada,* Nabokov himself builds that bridge as he carves out a cross-cultural utopia where East and West can meet. But what attracts the Iranian readers to his work is this work's call for a reading that it itself would be the bridge. While Nabokov does not encroach upon their territory, the way they approach him allows them to touch his world by opening up theirs, by looking out over their horizon and then back into it enriched, with a better grip on themselves. As Nabokov's readers step into his world, they "conjure" another. In so doing, they unbolt the doors to theirs, challenging those who took over it.

Nabokov's texts welcome their beleaguered, persecuted, and excluded readers. Nafisi and her students find in his work what is missing from their lives. His novels inaugurate a political venue where judgment and self-judgment can take place by taking up the vacant place of "actual" political participation denied to his Iranian fans, and I find it intriguing that the masculinist, elitist, and "classist" exclusions habitually enacted by Western cosmopolitanism, and from which Nabokov's work is far from free, are in Nafisi's group reconstructed into their opposite. Unlike traditional cosmopolitanism, the cosmodernism at work in *Reading Lolita in Tehran* is not male, metropolitan, and upper-crust. Rowe is right that Nafisi's "reading group" cannot be "substitut[ed . . .] for 'Iranian women' or even Iranians opposed to the policies of the Iranian state."[64] What the memoir brings before us, though, is hardly a socially exclusive "class of cosmopolitans," but a kind of "exoteric" "cosmopolitanization," or cosmodernization rather, of "classes,"[65] another sign that our time's cosmodernism does not want to be "the prerogative of an elite."[66] Both the former Oxonian and her otherwise modestly educated followers can assume this prerogative. Class—social, intellectual—is in play but no longer stands in the way to this sodality of reading. The cosmodernism founded in Nafisi's home does not brush aside the idiomatic, the local, the ethnic, the religious, cultural traditions generally, does not replace the place of reading with some aesthetic utopia, and does not abolish time. Nor does it ignore context, and so our reading of *Reading Lolita in Tehran* should not either. Nafisi spells it out for us: this is *our Lolita. We* have made it ours, against all the odds and in Tehran of all places. Nafisi and her female students read *Lolita;* then, Lolita's plight, much like Daisy Miller's, becomes a lens through which they reread their daily lives. As Holland would say, the Nafisi group make themselves part of *Lolita* so they can make it part of their own "psychic economy" and thus "re-create" *themselves* (and so set themselves free) around the Nabokovian text.[67] Reading is, like individuality itself—in this case like that individuality the regime seeks to control—a "variation on the [reader] identity theme."[68] This identity occurs within the threefold "horizon" of Nabokov's novel, of the self, and of the self's "experience of life." The latter shapes reading while spreading out an "ethical realm" where the experience of reading sets going a "radicalizing" reflection that "anticipates unrealized possibility, broadens the limited space of social behavior for new desires, claims, and goals, and thereby opens paths of future experience" outside "religiously or officially sanctioned morals."[69]

To reemphasize: Nabokov is not a pipe dream. Through him, his readers plug themselves back into history, theirs, painful as it may be. His fiction is an invitation to rethink what Nafisi herself calls "social experience,"[70] an unexpected mode of understanding and challenging, via a silenced Lolita, Muslim women's coerced voicelessness and invisibility. We register the same reaction to Nabokov's *Invitation to a Beheading,* where the Russian-American writer "capture[s]," Nafisi notices, "the texture of life in a totalitarian society, where you are completely alone in an illusory world full of false promises, where you can no longer differentiate between your savior and your executioner."[71] If *Lolita* can be read as "the confiscation of one individual life by another"—and Nafisi's group does read it along these lines—then, she concludes, "Nabokov had taken revenge on the Ayatollah Khomeini" and all the "solipsists who take over other people's lives."[72]

Solipsism, Egology, Autocracy

> I require a You to become [I]; becoming I, I say You.
> All actual life is encounter.
> —MARTIN BUBER, *I and Thou*

> There are[, the solipsist says,] other beings outside me, but I am the only self.
> —BERNADETTE DELAMARRE, *Autrui*

Euphemistically as it may have been made, the reference to abusive "solipsizers" and solipsism points up what is ultimately at stake in cosmoderns like Nafisi: the self, unthinkable outside "individual life," outside culture as individuation practice and repertoire of alternatives.[73] For it is the alternative itself, that *other* to what one has been or is presumed to become by education, religion, birthplace, ethnicity, gender, or sexuality, that sets in train the narrative of selfhood. Since the authentic self, the self as "individual life" symptom, is essentially "impure" by origin, brought into being by the play of alterity, it is "in its nature" to seek out opportunities to further alter, "edit," and creolize itself. The cosmodern cultural modality rests on this realization.

Individualist *absolutely*—the only individual there is and ought to be, or so he or she thinks—the solipsist is an egological subset and therefore abhors the individual's heterogeneous matrix, that other which founds the self as an *other* presence in, and hence a threat to, the solipsist's world. As political solipsism, autocracy turns against the individual for similar reasons. The autocrat tolerates no individuality except his or her own, which feeds off all others' and so sets itself up as their hecatomb. An antinomy of cosmodern with-ness, the tyrant is fundamentally alone, *solus ipse.* Yet his of her solitude is not just political but also cultural, and deliberately so given the other's role in the birth of the individual self. This explains why autocracy is usually autarchic culturally, aggressively "allergic," programmatically anticosmopolitan, and decidedly nationalistic or ethnocentric underneath the occasional internationalist veneer. So were Stalin, Mao, Enver Hoxha, and Ceauşescu, proponents not only of a one-leader society but also of a "one-culture" world, a monolith produced and reproduced ceaselessly under strictly formalized and monitored conditions. The threat of otherness was such an important catalyst in this reproductive cycle that if the impure other was not there to play the straw man, it had to be produced. The egological manufacturing of cultural self-sameness was in fact predicated on this *other* invention, on the fabrication of the subversive *heteros.*

This means that the autocratic solipsist does not necessarily deny the existence of others outside and even inside his cloistered, aseptic world—the world of the putatively self-begotten self, in whose official biography homogenesis replaces heterogenesis. Instead, the solipsist denounces the "pathogenic" effects of the other, of an other constructed as "virus" in a way analogical to the selfsameness virus discussed in part 5. Epidemic by nature, we are told, the other infects and ends up altering the self. This alteration is unwarranted and must be thwarted because it runs counter to the homogenetic myth, "corrupting" the self's purity matrix and by the same token spreading the contagion of individuation. To contain the disease of selfhood, the solipsist stages the high drama of purity and impurity and its discordant we/they, here/there, inside/outside rhetoric where the boundaries, apocryphal as they may be, are nonetheless painstakingly policed. Ever under siege, the self's taintlessness must be protected by keeping the contaminating agents at bay. If already *intra muros,* either as historical residues from the culture's past or as intruders from the outside, they must be exposed and eradicated. Again, the solipsist may acknowledge the other. What he or she cannot accept is its participation in cultural and social life alongside the self precisely because this participation's upshots would be "viral," at once *pluralizing and endemic,* unlocking the self's world and allowing for the spread of the alternative truths, "pockets" of otherness, dissenting formations, "deviations," "perversions," and blends within which individual life thrives. If the psychological solipsist believes that, while there may be other "true beings" besides himself or herself, no true self—and no self in possession of truth—exists except himself or herself among those worthless "others," the cultural solipsist admits that there may be other cultures besides his or her own but only his or her culture preserves the one-truth. Repository of this religious or political truth, "true culture" is a culture of selfsameness, whereas solipsistic regimes reinforce one-truths (*solae veritates*) through cultural policies of sameness. Suspecting that "others" interrupt the phantasmatic consistency of selfhood by opening up the gaps of individuation, the wrinkles and cracks of being wherein the self sows its seeds, the solipsists do all they can to exorcise otherness.

As they read Nabokov, Nafisi and her students set up a nurturing, readerly-interpretive community, a binding "collegiality" that hinges on another, invisible yet no less real community. For the bonds among the Iranian Nabokovians, how they read and are with one another, depend on how they relate to Nabokov, on how they respond to the other's call. Appiah maintains, as we saw, that such call-and-response stands on a certain "cross-cultural sameness." For one thing, this sameness argument falls back on "universals," "human nature," and other similarly hazy notions. For another, a quick look at Nabokov's and Nafisi's books suffices to drive home the striking differences between the worlds they describe. To be with the other's book and thus be with one another, that is, to be "colleagues," "reading partners" of one another and, together, of the one not there, Nabokov's readers must deal with these contrasts; to shore up their threatened, familiar world, they have to delve into the unfamiliar. Ensuing cosmodern togetherness does not predate cultural practice, interaction, and exchange, is not a notion, an idea, a taste, a value, or trait that somehow they share with Nabokov prior to sharing his work and impressions thereof. *This togetherness arises through reading.* There is no foundation of sameness on which they can build their bridge but just an "appeal" they can make out and respond to. As Nafisi shows, if a foundation exists, it awaits its founding in the call-and-response. In this light, reading the other—reading the cultural other—fulfills a foundational function. But reading does not equalize, does not found a community of the same or based on sameness, and this is where classical reading theory hits a bump on its road to coming to grips with *Reading Lolita in Tehran*. After all,

Nafisi's young women are so different from each other. They do not become "like" Lolita or "like" Nabokov. They scarcely convert to his "values."
Quite the opposite. As Nafisi writes, while "*Lolita* gave a different color to
Tehran, . . . Tehran helped redefine Nabokov's novel, turning it into this
Lolita, our *Lolita.*"[74] Making Nabokov's book *theirs:* this is a readerly re-
creation act in which the audience is "wholly" involved. The Iranian readers may be "removed" from *Lolita* culturally and otherwise, yet they feel
they can play a "role in its creation," a role that is, Bleich stresses, of ultimate import.[75]

Reading-engendered togetherness is both representation and "binding" event, produces representations that set up connections. As "I" read, I
visualize "you," the other on the other side; I picture you and your world.
That world's pull can be tremendous, but it does not make me "like" you.
I can still remain this side of the looking glass, but looking, looking and
seeing, the educated eye—in short, reading—are paramount here. As
Nafisi teaches her students to read, they go through motions taking them
to the *other* side of the mirror. They do not give up what they have or
are—Nabokov and James do not "Westernize" them—but as they relate to
Lolita's and Daisy's outlandish exploits, they do just that, launch a relationship, a tie into another world, and so manage the ultimate feat as they
cross over: look at themselves from outside, imagine themselves from a
position of otherness, against the "tyranny" of time and meteorology:
"[T]o steal the words from Humbert, the poet/criminal of *Lolita,*" Nafisi
writes, "I need you, the reader, to imagine us, for we won't really exist if
you don't. Against the tyranny of time and politics, imagine us the way we
sometimes didn't dare to imagine ourselves: in our most private and secret
moments, in the most extraordinarily ordinary instances of life, listening
to music, falling in love, walking down the shady streets or reading *Lolita*
in Tehran. And then imagine us again with all this confiscated, driven underground, taken away from us."[76] So can "we," in the here and now of
Idaho or Brooklyn, imagine Nafisi as much as Nafisi and her followers
imagined Nabokov in Iran? How can we make *Reading Lolita in Tehran*
"our" *Reading Lolita in Tehran?* How can *we* step over to Nafisi and *her*
world and thus carry on the work? In sum, how should we read *Reading
Lolita in Tehran?* Given that the memoir invites a reading ethically attuned
to the reading applied, inside the text, to Nabokov and other Western writers, a befitting take on her book would be, it seems to me, cosmodern too.
This reading was, in Iran, and it would have to be again a reading "against

the odds," if not for the same "meteorological" reasons, then because it would have to factor in a wide range of entrenched asymmetries and complacencies. The dissimilarities, disjunctions, and other geocultural and political apples and oranges are certainly scandalous in the ancient sense evoked earlier. Reading *Reading Lolita in Tehran* in the United States is indeed a scandal. Critics like Rowe have been scandalized, and we have seen why. My reaction is identical but for somewhat different reasons. Needless to say, to read and chat about Nafisi, Americans need not go underground. Her work is available to us, as are broadly speaking information, culture, their expression and sharing, and so forth. Is Boise (like) Tehran? Methinks not. Idaho's "frontiersmen" may sport beards, but they have yet to do unto Californian "tree-huggers" what Khomeini's "Basij" have done to women and dissidents. To reiterate, our "context," our hurdles, urgencies, and immediate objectives could not differ more from those of *Lolita*'s Iranian readers. Still, if "we" read Nafisi "over here" along the lines of Nafisi and her followers' reading of Nabokov "over there," if we make the cultural-epistemological effort to reach across to her the way she and her students did to answer *Lolita*'s call in Tehran's particular place and time, then we may reach another conclusion as to what Nafisi's book might mean politically in Idaho or California. She is, let us not forget this, an Iranian-American author. No matter what side of the hyphen one might privilege, the questions that her work and cosmodernism in general pose is, What happens to the imagined other as I imagine him or her? How does he or she come alive in my reading?

Interpretations that disregard *Reading Lolita in Tehran*'s historically determining frame of reference cannot possibly do justice to the book's own subversive politics of interpretation and on this ground cannot be appreciative of how "scandalous" the text might be to Idahoans and Californians either. What we are ultimately talking about is a deficiency of the critical imagination, a failure, "ours," as hermeneutical as ethical, to imagine Nafisi's otherworld from its position of otherness. It goes without saying, this imagining is easier from "our" position, hence the neoconservative charges. Reading *Reading Lolita in Tehran* on its own terms, on the other hand, is a more laborious proposition. Would it pay off? I believe so. Not only would it be fairer to Nafisi's work, to how she imagines herself, her group, and her Iran. It would also be more culturally salubrious to "us," for it would involve an other-reading that prompts another look in the mirror, a critical imagination whose aftereffects are self-imaginative and self-critical.

3. "Each was the hidden key to the other": Reading the Sufis in California

I've brought you a mirror. Look at yourself,
and remember me.
  —RUMI, *The Essential Rumi*

[A] true cosmopolitan, after all, is not someone who's traveled
a lot so much as someone who can appreciate what it feels like
to be the Other.
  —PICO IYER, *The Global Soul*

Bright Ardor

The stranger whose voice we recognize as our own.
  —PICO IYER, *Abandon*

"I recognise in Nabokov," Iyer writes in his 1997 essay "The Nowhere Man," "a European's love for the US rooted in the US's very youthfulness and heedlessness; I recognise in him the sense that the newcomer's viewpoint may be the one most conducive to bright ardour. Unfamiliarity in any form breeds content."[77] "Ardour": a bow to Nabokov's 1969 novel *Ada or Ardor*? Possibly. Let us note too, the outsider's inquisitive passion is "bright." It brightens. It bathes things in the raw light that in turn "enlightens" those who have been living in their shadow. Nabokov's relative unfamiliarity with the natives' world, a world ingrown, become too familiar perhaps, defamiliarizes, is both relative (approximate) and relational in its upshots. The exile's passionate scrutiny catches on, fanning the insiders' self-reflexive ardor and adding a glowing intensity to how they feel about themselves. This is how *Lolita* "bred" new "content," giving new meaning to our 1950s and, on another level, to Nafisi's Iran. Unlike V. S. Naipaul's, Nabokov's "way," as Iyer labels it, lies in an epistemological exposure if not in an exposé altogether, in an in vivo cultural-political dissection. Naipaul's "congenital displacement" provides a unique insight into the modern state. Modernity, the Indian-Trinidadian-British Nobel Prize laureate intimates, spawns rootlessness and estrangement from, or loss of, the nation-state's culture. A "citizen of the world," he lives out world citizenship as exile and alienation in the modern sense that renders geopolitical separation anthropological inadequacy.[78] Less so Nabokov; much less so Nafisi. Crossing, albeit inconsistently, into postmodernity, the Russian-American writer embodies a different cosmopolitan variety. I have called Nabokov an exile, and I agree with Michael Seidel's assessment that "Of all novelists who have lived in exile and written its traumas and its imaginative opportunities into the texture of their fictions, Vladimir Nabokov reigns, in his way, supreme."[79] But *Ada*'s author also illustrates the displaced type that rises, in Seidel's Joycean formulation, to "postexilic eminence."[80] A reality of late modernity and postmodernity already, this becomes, with notable exceptions, a post–Cold War "condition."

What this means is that in the post-exile age of global access and media coverage, spaces out of or into which we may be forced, limiting spaces or spaces off-limit, unknown and strange, are shrinking. A cosmodern harbinger in this respect, Nabokov is one of the first twentieth-century writers to feel "stranger nowhere in the world"[81] and therefore "partially adjusted everywhere."[82] The point is not simply that exile, exteriority, and "alienation" now make up "our natural state,"[83] but that the outlander and the "alienated" are no more—and no less—than an *alienus*, an "other" complete with an analytically "othering" gaze, a probing eye whose semiotic "plight," Iyer glosses in *Sun after Dark*, is to see through the "games" of culture, otherwise.[84] In Iyer's nomadic epistemology, the wanderer retains the "non-parochial" capacity for "wonder"[85] that gathers us all around culture as a site of "perplexity."[86] To him or her, culture, native or adopted, is neither lost cipher nor inscrutable enigma but object to fresh distinctions that may prove epistemologically and morally contagious. As the writer quotes Adorno in *The Global Soul*, "It is part of morality not to be at home in one's home,"[87] and we do get more intellectually restless, more observant, hence more "moral," in the clarifying proximity of the "connoisseur"-"outsider at the feast," because, Iyer insists, "[he] does not have to sit in the corner alone, taking notes" any more; "he can [now] plunge into the pleasures of his new home with abandon."[88]

"Abandon," either the guest's or the host's, has less to do with giving up or relinquishing and more with their antinomies, with taking up and giving oneself over passionately, almost mystically, without the usual calculations and disclaimers, to a certain preoccupation, in this case to cultural experience, reading, and self-reading. This is what abandon signifies here, as it does, more alluringly still, in the 2003 novel Iyer published under this title.[89] Like Mones's *Lost in Translation*, *Abandon* is a romance of culture flaunting a similarly many-layered erotics of cross-cultural, textual, and human intimacy. In Iyer, as in Mones, Lahiri, Lee, Nafisi, Randall, and their cosmodern peers, intimacy trades on relatedness. To be "intimate" is to be with an other, with an other here with you or with an other's consummate proxy, with his or her book, to wit, with America and its stories in Nabokov's *Lolita*, with Nabokov's *Lolita* in the Middle East, with *Reading Lolita in Tehran* in Rowe's Far West or, as in *Abandon*, with Iran's Sufi tradition in Santa Barbara. *Jouissance* in action, "ardent" competency that picks up where scholarly rationality leaves off helpless, "intimate knowledge" is philology etymologically understood, empathic expertise that reaches across playfully and jubilantly once it has mastered the exacting art of self-abandon. What is forsaken is not the self altogether—we noticed that Nafisi and her students never renounce it—but its egological mold. The consummate readers of an other's work push themselves conscientiously to banish whatever presumptions warp an ethical relation with that which they are reading and indirectly with themselves. "Banish," *Webster's* informs us, is an old meaning of *abandon*, and a "ban" on our cultural egotism must be imposed, or self-imposed, if abandonment is to complete its hermeneutical-ethical cycle and set up a connection, if not, indeed, a "bond" between self and other. After all, *ban* is morphologically part of *band*, which is related, and implicitly ties *abandon* itself, to *bond* (cf. the German *Band, binden,* and *Bund*), thus forming a relation that gestures to separation and difference and, *through them*, to the deeper semantics of relationality.

Ruminations: Pico Iyer's *Abandon*

> I, being self-confined,
> Self did not merit,
> Till, leaving self behind,
> Did Self inherit.
> —RUMI, *The Wisdom of the Sufis,* ed. Kenneth Cragg

> Texts read us as much as we read them.
> —PICO IYER, *Video Night in Kathmandu*

This semantics and its ethical corollary are less apparent in the travel literature for which Iyer is better known. Britain-born, California-raised, and current resident of "the world's great Significant Other," as he dubs Japan,[90] Iyer has established himself as a *Time* magazine contributor and author of *Video Night in Kathmandu and Other Reports from the Not-So-Far-East* (1988), *The Global Soul: Jet Lag, Shopping Malls, and the Search for Home* (2000), *Sun after Dark: Flight into the Foreign* (2004), and a few other "books about the romance between cultures."[91] Now, this sort of romance does not shy away from the cultural-political contextualizations without which any ethics of relationality sounds hollow. Neither fictions like *Lost in Translation,* which follow the erotic genre closely, nor more experimental travel stories mixing up the fictional and the nonfictional from Tété-Michel Kpomassie's *An African in Greenland* (1981) to Yoko Tawada's German-Japanese *Where Europe Begins* (1991) to William T. Vollmann's *Europe Central* (2005) slight the "conditions of coercion, radical inequality, and intractable conflict [that] usually" shape the production of "relations" in "contact zones."[92] Besides, what with the whole world becoming a with-ness zone of adjacent living and testimonials, cultural romance— Mary Louise Pratt's "transculturation"—is evolving quickly into a staple narrative formation of late globalization. Still, unlike travelogues such as Amitava Kumar's more scholarly *Bombay-London-New York* (2002), Iyer's "romances" have been faulted for overromancing the "new order of man."[93] Nonplused by Iyer's globetrotting euphorias, commentators have balked at his sometimes unqualified celebrations of "homelessness" and "mobility."[94] Particularly vexing have been the "unaccountability" and "duty-free" elations smacking, to some, of modern cosmopolitanism's debonair "detachment."[95] Redolent of this ambiguous legacy, Iyer's jet-lagged Emersonianism—the "Over-Soul" retrofitted as "unaffiliated" "Global Soul"[96]—has been reprimanded for a noncommittal approach that, it has been objected, ends up aestheticizing indiscriminately and subsequently universalizing the self-other relations while the "radically asymmetrical relations of power" underlying the "contact zones'" overall relationality are largely left out.[97] To the extent this is true—and, in part, it is—Iyer's own "contacts" remain perfunctory. Outside the jealous "reach of the nation-states," a "fellow in-betweener"[98] frolicking in the world's "playpen," the reporter dons the self du jour from his vast identitarian "wardrobe"[99] to sample the idiosyncratic, the off the beaten path, and the all but extinct before moving on to the next place on his list. A just-in-time obituary of the exotic, the scarce, and the endangered, his frequent-flyer reportage publicizes their imminent demise. The freelancing "global soul" goes through customs after customs only to get to places about to turn into the nondescript "nonplaces" the world's other places have already become and about which he wrote during the previous stopover.[100] "Everywhere could be home if everywhere was homogeneous," Iyer cogitates in *Video Night in Kathmandu.*[101] Obviously, everywhere is not everywhere the same, or not yet. On this account, neither is home, the reporter's included. It is not everywhere the same, nor can it be built on a foundation of sameness. One comes away, though, with the impression that, like the hero of Aleksandar Hemon's 2002 novel *Nowhere Man,* Iyer makes himself at home amid spreading, unaffiliated, and "disaffiliating" place-lessness and homelessness, that, notwithstanding the people he meets on his trips, he cultivates a tactical loneliness, a lucrative self-centeredness, and that his ethnographic eulogies—as many egologies—not only "re-port" but also somehow thrive on, and wind up compounding, the world's withdrawal inside the hardened hull of sameness.

Abandon charts a different course. Neither eulogistic nor egological, the story does not take us to an elsewhere on the wane, to a nowhere in 'the making and thus to an impossible home, but to an "otherworldliness" (164) that holds out the possibility of home. We saw with the Montaignean *ailleurs*—thought's abode—something we see, or rather hear, throughout the philosophical tradition of dwelling as thinking and, again, in Iyer's tit-ular metaphor: the cosmodern exhortation to abandon a certain place or home cognitively if not literally, to leave behind not necessarily the place we inhabit but the place as commonplace, as unexamined habit and "sec-ond nature," so we can rediscover the place's meaning and, within it, ours. This is where this "transport" gets us—to unfamiliar places that defamil-iarize the familial to render it familiar anew, places and postures where we go so that what we know or think we do by origin, location, or usage, al-most as a birthright, as a gnoseological entitlement, in turn "comes to us" and meets us halfway as new "content." To get there, we must first admit, with the thirteenth-century Sufis whom Iyer's hero, John Macmillan, stud-ies at UC Santa Barbara, that we "are mysterious to ourselves" (28). Mys-tery is where what we know or presume to know ends, but also the tran-scendent, tautological topology where dwelling and knowing overlap, where true knowledge dwells; we belong there too even though we pitch our tent in this world. Accordingly, the latter is home that triggers "home-sickness," "longing to get back to the place that is our rightful home" (28). Running through the poems of Attar, Hafiz, and the other Sufis on whom John is completing his doctoral dissertation, the notion of world as "exile" (28) from truth, true selfhood, and their home is quintessentially mystical. Rumi's ghazals in particular, which cast an overwhelming spell on John, couch this metaphysical nostalgia in an exquisite stylistics of loss, separa-tion, and the abnegation—self-denial or abandonment—any retrieval or return calls for.

Hermeneutically, this raises serious problems, the very problem of reading, in fact. For the poem's textual space, and then the space or interpretive discourse in which a textually and culturally "receptive" interpreter might set out to accommodate the poem participate in the same economy of lack, absence, and displacement, and as a result can be only an imperfect home to the poet's meaning no less than to the critic's attempt to make sense of that meaning. Not a mystic himself, John is nevertheless committed to "empathic" reading and writing about the Persian mystics. Thus, he emulates them analytically by acknowledging their "negative" semiotics and, ensuing from it, their poetic "strangeness" and opaqueness, their limited readability. His failure to read the Sufis is limited too, though, not only because he does "get" them to a degree apparently acceptable to Sefadhi, his Iranian supervisor, but also because whatever John learns in the process helps him reacquaint with himself. The Sufis do "resist" analysis no matter how thorough his research; they remain unyielding, mysterious. But the other's "mystery"—surviving in Shiite *taqiyya*, which John translates as "sacred dissimulation" (72)—more precisely, the reflections the obscure other occasions throw light on the reader. Other-reading sets off self-reading, is rechanneled inward. John's brooding over how hard Rumi is to figure out, his scholarly ruminations, we might say, refract back onto himself. *Taqiyya* "tells us," he writes in his diary, "that we're all other—better—than we seem" (72). In other words—words forever other, "hiding" as they word the elusive truth *taqiyya*-style (72)—betterment and the good we might reach as we work to improve ourselves are inexorably altruistic. We become better, and are good, once we have done so unto others; we owe them our good life.

"Falling into a new relation": The World of Symbols

"There is a way to be good again," an older friend reassures Amir, the protagonist of Khaled Hosseini's 2003 Afghan-American odyssey *The Kite Runner*.[102] In Hosseini, Iyer, and other cosmoderns, this way is an "alternate route," running as it does through that which or who we are not, yet with which or whom we must be. "Your real country," John quotes Rumi, "is the place where you're going, not the place where you are" (73). Rumi's work itself shows the way there, though not as a life philosophy to follow *ad litteram*—Abandon is no *Imitatio Rumi*—not even as a body of work to retrieve and define critically, but mainly as a self-defining experience. This is the experience of reading, Appiah's "reading as elsewhere" with a cosmodern twist where, analogous to the translation dialectic worked out in part 3, the shortfall of reading concurrently marks the reader's "fall" into a "new relation" (180) with an other and eventually, courtesy of what sets self and other apart, into "something else" (191): a new relation of the reading self with himself. Kim's Suzy does not translate perfectly. At times, her renditions are barely accurate. She translates or transposes herself, rather, into another position, epistemologically speaking. In Iyer, this transposition is the very protocol of reading as abandonment, as ecological "transport" or leap, across an other's strange stanzas, "outside [our]sel[ves]" and our quirks, notions, and apperceptions (191). "We wall ourselves in," reads another note in John's diary, "with what we think we know, and then what we don't know, which is what can save us, is left knocking on the door" (114). But what he does not know and will not find a key to, try as he might, does provide a window into himself (230). Before long, the reflection on the stranger's voice and the reflecting voice merge (28), "round one another out" (129) into a togetherness of which Islam's crescent moon is an aptly relational allegory. Accordingly, the self is just partly visible—intelligible, "readable"—and more generally "is," to itself alone, in and of itself, inside its "solipsistic" walls. To the whole that it truly albeit unapparently represents, the self is what the crescent is to full moon: an ethical-ontological synecdoche, a prompt to think about ourselves and those close, visible, and similar to us in relation to those less so yet with whom we make up something bigger than our immediate turf and worries.

This vaster juxtaposition of selves and passions is the "symbolic," steadily growing ("crescent") world of with-ness. "The English word 'symbol,'" John "remember[s], comes from the Greek *symbolon*, referring to one half of the knucklebone carried as a token of identity to someone who has the other half. Only when the two halves, the two people, are brought together does the whole have a meaning" (280–81). The noun and, more markedly still, the verb (*symballein*, "throw" and "bring together") forefront worldly relationality. Their etymology teaches us that to be in the world, "thrown" in it, as the existentialists would say, is to be "thrown together" with others. Cast out in the world, "we" cast our lot with "them." Being human, though, cosmoderns like Iyer hint, is sharing in our "symbolic" condition without also falling back on our "common humanity," for that condition, and with it the chance of "encountering" and "joining" the "other half" (cf. Gk. *symbolē*), turns on the two halves' "disjointedness," on split and difference. Conversely, Rumi's poems "symbolize" not, or not in the first place, because they shelter "esoteric" meaning but because they play on the umbilical coarticulation of here and there, now and then, visible and invisible, "me" and "you" in world architectonics. Insofar as John "gets" this symbolism, and he ultimately does, he also "gets" the Sufis' "dark" poetics (141) and implicitly the empathic imperative to read their poems and the greater "world in terms of darkness" (129). This darkness, he gathers, is revealing, a locus of *correlative* meaning. This is not merely the hideaway where others and what they mean keep out of sight but an epistemologically refractive medium that, as it deflects exploration, tests the explorer's self-knowledge. The "dark" in which the Sufis "believe" (141) and with whose ink they write tells us, then, more about ourselves than about them. Himself hiding out in California's "Pynchonland" (122), Talmacz, the famed translator whom John consults, is an authority, *the* Sufi translator, actually—his Hungarian name means "translator"—not only because his translations are exquisite but also because they are premised on the notion that "Farsi epistemology" (126) translates, carries over cross-culturally, and thus, in and through its own obscurity, has something to convey to, and about, Persian poetry's American readers and their America.

An art of abandon in more than one way, this epistemology is, also as in Mones, an erotology and, with that, a heterology. Its truth hands itself in as and across an other, is and barely seems to be at the same time. It gives itself and withdraws in the chiaroscuro of meaning, steps into darkness so as to appear, and absents itself on the brink of presence. No stable configuration of self and other, surface and depth, form and content, symbol and symbolized but only the certainty of symbolization, of being thrown together over distances and discrepancies that decline to shrink; no certainties, no firm ground or *Grund,* no rationality or mode of rationalizing what exactly pulls together self and other, the nearby and the faraway, the semilune and the moon's other half, but only relationality, the aching certitude of togetherness—John's relationship with Camilla Jensen, who is Danish-Iranian-American and whose name, an "anagram" of his, "hid[es] out inside 'Macmillan'" (94), makes for a not-so-veiled metaphor of this elusive yet no less actual nexus. The relationship seems to be fading away in the end, and yet, in a Rumi pastiche written in Farsi, translated by John into English, and, in translation, reproducing John's first name in vertical acrostic, Camilla reassures him that their "hands" remain forever "connected" over Rumi's hand(writing). "No division in / Our hearts," the poem closes (353), not to decree that there are no divisions at all but that over an other's words, protected by the words' strangeness and translation alike, self and other may come together. "If two beings throw themselves fully together," John comments on the mystic Attar, "they can so lose themselves in something higher that the result is what looks like nothing" (135). But neither Talmacz, who refuses to teach "mysticism" (126), nor John, as we saw, is a mystic or, more exactly, a dogmatic. The whole "point of Sufism" may be "emptying" yourself, "d[ying] to every notion of yourself" (135), receding into the nothingness and "nowhere" where you can become anything and thus everything, "universal" (287), almost God-like and therefore similarly "unknowable" (333). Bordering on nihilism, this point may lead to a dead end. Or, as John also suspects, it may well be that what the Sufis recommend that we lose or "burn" is that which keeps us from seeing farther than ourselves. To actually see ourselves as we are so we can get to a "better" place and into a better self, as Camilla says (291), we must in actuality start with ourselves. We must look for and bracket off whatever inside us prevents us from seeing more than ourselves in the world and *thus from seeing ourselves completely, authentically.* This is what second-century AD Arab Gnostic Monoimus meant, in John's interpretation, by "taking [o]ursel[ves] as the starting point" (135). We should do so but, in Camilla's words again, only to eventually "ste[p] out of [our]sel[ves]" autocritically, that is, into an "alternative" (290) or awareness of other places and thoughts apt to get us to rethink our own place.

In this view, the "Sufi problem" is a U.S. problem. The problem "with" reading Sufi poetry, more broadly with the tradition the Sufis come from and also with the more recent Iranian tradition of managing Persian inheritance, is indeed the very problem of with-ness and, as such, poignantly problematizes America's meaning and position in the world. "The problems of Iran," a German scholar, another character in *Abandon*, asserts at a conference in Seville, "are now the problems of everyone. Globalism has made of Tehran an international syndicate" (83).

I will come back to the notion of a world "syndication" of culture in this part's conclusion. Here, what bears underscoring in the critic's argument, then in the paper on Rumi and San Juan de la Cruz ("Abandon: East and West") John delivers at the same gathering, and overall in Iyer's book, is the impulse to think through the global problematics ethically, as a subset of the problem of with-ness, of that which being-with entails and requires. If, according to other conferees, the post–Cold War "new postmodern order" indeed enmeshes America in the disjunctive syntax of *Jihad vs. McWorld* (85), then *Abandon* points to a logic, and an ethics, of necessarily co-participatory, overlapping, and deeply reciprocal arrangements and definitions. As I explain in *Cosmodernism*'s introduction, these obtain in, and further extend, worldly legibility as a geography of reading-with. For this reading- and being-with, for this collegiality that is a utopia yet to fail, Iyer's readerly imaginary proposes a plausible model. Why? Because the reader and the read signify, produce meanings, and reproduce themselves into new significations within an *apriorily* relational textual-cultural setup where, without converging or rescinding their institutive differentiations, the parties always-already traverse and reflect each other prismatically, trade on these mutual modulations, mediations, and reflections to reflect the world. What "we" mean and are is of necessity a joint venture, a "symbolic" enterprise. "We" read "them" so that we can break our own codes. This implies, Iyer notes in *Video Night in Kathmandu,* that "their" books read us too[103] and have done so all along. It all comes down, then, to "learn[ing] to feel addressed"[104] by others not only when we read their books, as Kaufmann proposes in his Buber commentary, but also when we read our own; when we work our way through Rumi's ghazals and Omar Khayyam's rubaiyyats but also when we run into Thoreau's meditations on the social hygiene of "abandonment" and into Emerson's Persian translations;[105] when we read or listen to Iranians in Tehran but also, as Iyer writes in "The Nowhere Man," when, walking down Santa Monica Boulevard, we hear Beverly Hills's "second tongue," Farsi.[106]

4. Friendships across Death: Alice Randall's Pushkin

> . . . looking at one's self through the eyes of others. . . .
> —W. E. B. DU BOIS, *The Souls of Black Folk*

The Russian Shakespeare

What Gogol does for Russian literature (according to Dostoyevsky) and for the Bengali family (according to Ashoke) in *The Namesake* Alexander Pushkin does for African American Vanderbilt professor Windsor Armstrong and her son, pro football player Pushkin X, in Randall's 2004 novel, *Pushkin and the Queen of Spades.*[107] Randall's work strengthens the feminist component of the post-"New Black Aesthetic," hip-hop metafiction that after the late 1980s builds on the experiments of Clarence Major, Ishmael Reed, and Charles Johnson to gain momentum with writers such as Trey Ellis and Percival L. Everett. Like Ellis's *Platitudes* (1988, reissued in

2003 together with the "New Black Aesthetic" essay first published by Ellis in 1989) and Everett's *Erasure* (2001), *Pushkin and the Queen of Spades* indulges in provocative rereading and rewriting of the literary past. The book consolidates, in fact, the reputation of a brazen "literary meddler"[108] its author earned in 2001 with *The Wind Done Gone,* a retelling of *Gone with the Wind.* No less meddlesome, the second novel features, among other things, a spunky update of Pushkin's unfinished story "The Negro of Peter the Great" to drive home a different point. For what Randall "meddles" with this time around is a work and a tradition she and her own tradition have been "mixed up with" from the word go. Etymology is here once again revelatory: "meddling" implies being "mixed in"; the "meddler," the novelist hints, is already in the "mix," one of its original ingredients and so akin to it.

Randall is not the first African American writer to dwell on this kinship. In a 1900 series of articles titled "The Future American," Charles W. Chesnutt adduced Pushkin's African background as evidence for worldwide "race-amalgamation" or "admixture."[109] Much as in Randall, "the Russian Shakespeare"[110] attests in Chesnutt to a racial future anterior: this future of race, of all races, has already arrived because races, the Indo-European included, have never been "pure" to begin with;[111] Pushkin is just a more salient instance of age-old, worldwide racial intermingling. While shifting the focus away from genetics onto cultural genealogy, Randall does not abandon the former either. In effect, she uses it to ground her "meddling" ethically. This is the crux of her novel's entire cosmodern argument and also that which "vindicates" her Pushkin "remix":[112] since Pushkin's great-grandfather was African, the writer, *Pushkin and the Queen of Spades* tells us, is "Afro-Russian" (4), so Randall's borrowings from and plays on Pushkin are legitimate. Moreover, they are part of a whole African and African American tradition in its own right, without which black literary and cultural history would be inconceivable—the tradition of Signifyin(g). Windsor, her fictional alter ego, actually mentions Signifyin(g) as well as its most prominent critic, Henry Louis Gates, Jr., and those moments lay bare her Signifyin(g) novel's "poetics," how her text operates and comes to be what it is, as well as the novel's "thematics," what the text talks about, more precisely, Randall's dilemmas and politics of identity. This is how *Pushkin and the Queen of Spades* legitimates itself twice, as form and content. As form, it represents, beginning with the title, a dialogue with the Russian classic. Further—and here we see how form and content prove inseparable—the intertextual conversation and appropriation are not inappropriate because Pushkin's life and work embody multiple identities, unfold both this side and the *other* side of the self/other divide. Pushkin's African Russianness, the "Africanness" of his "Russianness," makes him compatible—albeit not identical—to Pushkin X, a befitting namesake, a verisimilar "relation." Randall exploits this plausibility ingeniously by mining the Russian writer's biography and oeuvre for episodes and texts that, smartly maneuvered, illuminate the conflicts in Windsor's and her son's lives. Coming full circle, the latter cast light on Pushkin, the not-so-strange other, and in so doing span the gap between sameness and otherness by reenacting situations from Pushkinian biography and bibliography. As with Lahiri's recourse to Gogol, this does not render Randall's characters mere footnotes to Pushkin's. Also as in *The Namesake*, the other is the magnifying glass through which the novelist qua reader of the Russian's life and work puts up a psychologically and culturally authentic identity drama that plays itself out as it speaks through the other writer's actual or fictional torments. For not only did Pushkin have African ancestry; he also had, Randall submits, identity anxieties many African Americans did and do. Couching these concerns and quandaries in memorable language, his life and fiction thus have a lesson to teach, a commonality of plight to share, the same uncertainties and tough choices to go through—as many reasons Randall's "meddling" in Pushkin's texts is not unwarranted.

Like Lee, Nafisi, Iyer, Lahiri, and other cosmoderns, Randall extends postmodern intertextuality cross-culturally by thinking and writing "in the margins" of the other's thoughts and texts. But, one more time, her own thinking and writing come both after and before her "source," for they are at once derivative and original. She may be following Pushkin but, like Windsor, a "scholar of Afro-Russianness" and Pushkin specialist, only to "shelter" in the "shadow of W.E.B. Du Bois" (7). She then goes back to Pushkin and reads him through Du Bois's racial-cultural theory from *The Souls of Black Folk,* which forefronts a cosmopolitan mind-set that in hindsight has proved even more ahead-looking than that embedded overtly in *Color and Democracy* forty-odd years later.[113] Thus she finds in Pushkin, first, what Du Bois reveals to her about the complexity of African American psyche, that is, remarkable insights into "double-consciousness." Then, tied into this complexity, she detects an uncanny, cross-racial and cross-cultural ability to leap across the self/other rift and provide the other with a unique perspective on his own otherness "from the inside"—from the very "insides" or "bowels" of the other's culture, from what Du Bois calls the "entrails" of this otherness. Pushkin, Randall intimates, has a lesson to teach others elsewhere, in this case his African American readers. His work is deeply "instructive," an act of what Du Bois identifies as anthropological "clairvoyance" to describe his own purchase on the "other" American psyche in his 1920 essay, "The Souls of White Folk." "Of them" [white Americans], Du Bois confesses, "I am singularly clairvoyant. I see in and through them. I view them from unusual points of vantage. Not as a foreigner do I come, for I am native, not foreign, bone of their thought and flesh of their language. Mine is not the knowledge of the traveler or the colonial composite of dear memories. . . . Nor yet is my knowledge that which servants have of masters, or mass of class, or capitalist of artisan. Rather I see these souls undressed and from the back and side. I see the working of their entrails."[114] Searching into others' soul from a positioned of otherness, Du Bois makes out capital truths about the other as well as about the self, about "the strange meaning of being black here in the dawning of the Twentieth Century."[115] Pushkin has similar insights and, looking into his tormented soul, so does the Pushkin scholar, who feels that he has something to say—at once obliquely and straightforwardly, from the "points of vantage" of his foreignness—about herself and her son, about being black and white over centuries and continents, life and death, Russianness and Americanness, blackness and whiteness. Du Bois and Pushkin reassure Windsor that the hybrid structure of the Afro-Russian or African American psyche itself is ground for alliances, friendship, and community across all kinds of "Veils" rather than an impediment, that racial identity's inner "split" and the "double consciousness" presumably anchored in it can heal splits and close gaps between cultures, races, and people.

Politics of Friendship

Owing to the name, friendship begins prior to friendship.
—JACQUES DERRIDA, *Politics of Friendship*

[A]ll dramas begin with human connection.
—MATTHEW ROBERSON, *1998.6*

Windsor does not quote Du Bois's later work on "The Riddle of Russia," a chapter of *Color and Democracy*,[116] presumably the more explicitly "cosmopolite" Du Bois,[117] but *The Souls of Black Folk*'s chapter "Of the Training of Black Men," where "he concludes, . . . 'I sit with Shakespeare and he winces not. Across the color line I move arm in arm with Balzac and Du-

mas, where smiling men and welcoming women glide in gilded halls'"
(*Pushkin*, 7). Windsor's quotation ends here, but in the original Du Bois
goes on to round off his cosmopolitan vision: "From out the caves of
evening that swing between the strong-limbed earth and the tracery of the
stars, I summon Aristotle and Aurelius and what soul I will, and they come
all graciously with no scorn nor condescension. So, wed with Truth, I
dwell above the Veil."[118] The vision is founded on "Truth," hence the reference to Aristotle. In turn, this truth, the self-evidence of basic human
rights, reveals itself transcendentally, from a nonsectarian perspective
possible only outside Plato's cave as people rise up and "soar" above the
twice enslaving ground of oppression and ignorance. But Du Bois is not
advocating free-floating, metaphysical rootlessness. His cosmopolitanism
censures, rather, the rootedness that chained blacks down to Georgia's
"dull red hideousness"[119] by spawning the "counter-bond" of bondage
outside the self, between enslaved self and master and at the same time a
pseudorelation of the self to itself, a false relation that, steeped in ignorance as it was, closed self-knowledge out. Endorsing this cosmopolitan
project of overcoming a confining locality without leaving behind the
physical place and its people is the author of *Meditations,* a seminal text in
the history of cosmopolitan thought. Like Aristotle, if more eager to listen
to "the reason that embraces all things"[120] and look over the *polis's* walls,
Marcus Aurelius heeds Du Bois's invitation. "Observe," Windsor comments on Du Bois's "summoning" of his friends, "one of the little-recog-
nized habits of the oft-unrecognized African American intellectual—the
making of friendships across the chasms of death, particularly the friendship of authors, especially white authors." "Somehow," she adds, "friendships with dead white poets and novelists and theologians feel less disloyal
than friendships with living ones. I shared with Pushkin [her son] my passion for Emily Dickinson. Have I disclosed that once upon a time I considered Emily to be one of my best friends? Did my love for Emily somehow prepare Pushkin to love Tanya?" (*Pushkin*, 7)

"[T]his subject is deranging" Windsor (7), for she cannot ignore the historical ambiguity of interracial bonds and, derived from it, the potential for
pain and disappointment in friendships across Du Bois's "Veil." In other
words—Derrida's—a whole "politics of friendship" is in play here and
"nags" her. In *Politics of Friendship,* the philosopher turns to the famous section "On Friendship" from Montaigne's *Essays* to propose that we can reach
out to others and their places, especially to other writers, above the chasms
of life and death, and thus "make friends" in the friend's very absence.[121]

Still, the subject is "irritating," "political" in another sense: if Du Bois's wedding to the "Truth" imparted by the company of Aristotle, Marcus Aurelius, and Balzac warrants Windsor's love for *Eugene Onegin*'s author and Dickinson, as well as the relationship with her Russian lover—his first name is, like Pushkin's, Alexander—Windsor's infatuation with these "others" may have triggered her own son's love for Tanya, a Russian stripper.

In Tanya, old worries beleaguer Windsor alongside new ones, and she cannot but feel ambivalent about her son's matrimonial designs. Detailing her misgivings about the impending wedding, the novel has been read as "one long apologia from Windsor to her son."[122] Yet nested inside the apologetic rhetoric lies her struggle to deal with a conflictual situation outside the context of classical miscegenation anxieties, and here the Russian writer proves helpful again. His life and work, Windsor realizes, also speak to this struggle. He was where she is now, in the hot seat of historically justified apprehensions and hard choices. He is or becomes her ancestor not only because his name is also an homage to her father but also because, in her reading, Pushkin's trials and challenges foreshadow hers, thus bestowing on them a strange familiarity.

Ruslan and Ludmila, Boris Godunov, and *Tales of Belkin,* which includes "The Queen of Spades," had been published before Gogol's first volume, *Evenings on a Farm near Dikanka* (1831), and critics have pointed out that if realism, Dostoyevsky's included, came out of Gogol's "Overcoat," Russian literature as a whole had sprung out of Pushkin. He "fathered" them all, in turn finding inspiration in Byron (which made him the "Byron of Russia") and in "our father Shakespeare,"[123] hence his other nickname, "the black Shakespeare" (*Pushkin,* 203). But Pushkin "invent[ed]," as Windsor suspects, not only modern Russia's language and literature:

> No one outside Russia read Russian before Alexander Pushkin. European nobles learned Russian to read Pushkin. . . . Hemingway wrote, "First there are the Russians." . . . Can you imagine the dimensions of [Pushkin's] mind's geography? . . . Father Pushkin. . . .
>
> Push [Windsor's son], does the vastness of you, the immensity of the territory covered by your speed and strength, have anything to do with the vastness of Pushkin's brain, the vastness of the Siberian plain, the vastness of my body undisciplined?
>
> Why is Pushkin not enough? Pushkin has fed us and clothed us and housed us for many more years than football and far better than most fathers.

> Do you remember that his mother's father's father was a slave given
> as a present to Czar Peter the Great? Do you remember that the czar,
> impressed by the intelligence of the slave, raised him to the nobility
> and gave him a noble wife? And that wife bore him a son, . . . and that
> son's daughter spawned Pushkin? And Pushkin invented the modern
> Russian language and fell in love and married. But he feared that his
> wife did not love him. Feared that she could not love his kinky hair,
> inky skin, and broad nose. He believed that she was unfaithful. He
> challenged the man he thought was her lover to a duel. Pushkin was
> shot in the duel and took days to die. (22, 55–56)

Windsor talks to her son about his "namesake" (222), sliding into the
writer's biography, then out of it and into her son's. She draws parallels between the two, fearing that actual similarities might bring about more
ominous if less obvious commonalities, in other words, that the black
American's life might rehearse the torments in the black Russian's. This is
the troublesome amphibology of the writer's "invention": he invented not
just a whole tradition, Russian no less than American, as Hemingway implies; he also reinvented, both in his life and work, Othello's plight for the
modern era (276–77), picking up where "father Shakespeare" left off and,
Windsor worries, passing Othello's anguish on to her son. With Pushkin,
a whole literary culture originates but also a culture of suffering. Bound
up in Windsor's and Push's background, they are simultaneously enriching and portentous. Pushkin bodes well and ill at the same time, makes up
for an inheritance to honor yet hardly for a prophecy to fulfill. Revisiting
Pushkin, Randall aims to "correct" his life and fictions of gloom and
doom, to recast the Russian genius and his "heir," Tanya—who comes
from his village (6)—in a story of hope countering Pushkin's.

There is, first, the story *in* the story, Randall's own version of "The Negro of Peter the Great." Letting out his racial apprehensions in this
unfinished novella, the writer "doubts his own humanity" (107) and worries that his protagonist Ibrahim's interracial marriage might be hurt, as
his "confidant" Korsakov presumes, by Ibrahim's "passionate . . . nature,"
"flat nose, thick lips, and coarse wool."[124] Given racial prejudice, chances
are the matrimonial future may only confirm Ibrahim's station of "a man
alone in the world, without birth and kindred, a stranger to everybody."[125]
Thus, Randall/Windsor does not hesitate to rewrite the story "preemp-
tively." As she tells Push, "I would rewrite God if it would make you feel
better" (*Pushkin,* 223). Her "audacious" (223) rewrite (228–64), which
works into its verse rendition of the story Pushkin's own biography, "fixes"

the original (222), completing and ending it on a far more encouraging note. Instead of hoping to "die before the consummation of the odious marriage," Natasha "taste[s] eternity" beside her husband Abraham (the name of Pushkin's African ancestor).[126]

Likewise, the broader story, the novel as a whole, revisits "The Queen of Spades" to "prevent" Tanya from doing to "Push" what the game card did to Pushkin's unfortunate Hermann. The novella "signifies" (187) to her glaringly. As she reads the text, the text reads her life back to her. In Windsor's interpretation, the story "announce[s] the deal life had dealt me," telling of Pushkin's romantic hero no less than of Windsor and her family—"Lena was my Queen of Spades; the Queen of Spades was my mother" (187), who did not hesitate to hurt people. At first, Windsor's reading does not give much hope: "It is the story of a woman who is apparently giving assistance but is in fact sealing doom. A woman who makes relationships to effect damage. Suddenly I knew why I was born. The Queen of Spades signifies secret ill-will. Lena had me to have someone hurt. If my daddy didn't understand this, Pushkin did" (190). But as the novel progresses, she discovers that neither history nor story, neither Pushkin's life nor Hermann's, need repeat itself. Therefore, Randall's story does not "restore" Pushkin's. In other words, Tanya, fictional "mother" and, before long, actual daughter-in-law, is not a queen of spades. She does not mark the meaning of blackness at the dawn of the new millennium and so does not bring Push misfortune. Pushkin's fate—Abraham's, Ibrahim's, Othello's—does not repeat itself in Push's because Tanya proves able to carry on ("repeat") Pushkin's cross-cultural legacy, emulating not the plot of his stories but the generous spirit behind them.

It is this kindred spirit that Windsor eventually discovers in Tanya. The rap lover is not a gold digger. Nor is she a dooming queen of spades but a "spade" of sorts. And, since "spades are black people, people like Spady and me" (187), Tanya is also a woman not unlike her, equally "audacious" (268) because, Windsor admits, "no longer white" (271). "Pour[ing] blackness in [Tanya's] ear" (277), Randall's/Windsor's manuscript—the "modified" Pushkin—"blackens" Tanya's mind (271) so that the Russian's bride decision to read a Countee Cullen poem to her groom during the wedding ceremony no longer seems contrived. Tanya can appreciate, from "inside," the beauty of the poem as much as she can see Push's own beauty (269). Windsor is certain that her text "changed" Tanya culturally and even racially, but Randall reminds us that the text of race has never been "pure" in the first place. Pushkin's "heir" and invention in more than one way, Tanya's identity has always been more complicated than Windsor has assumed. Windsor's "rewriting" of Tanya into "understanding," "sympathetic" blackness, no less than the multiple Pushkinian readings and rewrites throughout the novel, only builds up the subtextual and intertextual complications already in play in the "original" and ends up rewriting the rewriter herself. This is possible because Pushkin's text, like Nabokov's in Nafisi, already has a cosmodern texture of sorts and, inscribed into it, the promise of a "profound communion." Pushkin reading has already transformed the reader, and the transformation is parallel to Tanya's. As such, it will not happen because it already has: written into the text of identity, as in Pushkin's own identity and texts, then reinforced by Windsor's reading, is already the possibility of crossing over to the other side and embodying it fully:

> And I will be Russian. I am Russian. It seems to me so clear now how it has come that my own son chose a Russian woman. I fed my soul bites of Pushkin's poetry and prose. When I supped on syllables of Pushkin, it was a profound communion. When I sipped the syllables of Pushkin, I drank the blood of Mother Russia. In the water and the wine Christ appears. In the water and the wine Christ is present. In the poetry and the prose, in the syllables of the sound, Russia arises from the past, vast and languorous, snow-covered and thawing. When I was small and the world grew too complicated, when I, the daughter of a refugee from Montgomery, Alabama, discovered myself to be exiled from Motown, from Detroit City, discovered myself shipwrecked on the Potomac, when I stopped longing for a home that was lost, destroyed, exploded, when Martha Rachel died and I did not attend her funeral, when I stopped hearing my own heartbeat, I heard Pushkin. I had Pushkin. It was almost all I had. (272–73)

"Perhaps I am more Russian than you," she confesses to Tanya (273) at the end of this hymnal, recapitulative self-reading of sorts, with Pushkin's work a magnifying glass through which Windsor's life unveils a new cohesion and meaning. Coming about under the auspices of the other, this significant coherence is not "derived" but authentic. It does not weaken the self's clarifying relation to herself but, to the contrary, lays its foundation, grounding it in the self's originating, live-giving relation to other selves and the greater world beyond them.

"There is such shelter in each other,"[127] Carlene tells her friend Kiki in Zadie Smith's 2005 novel *On Beauty*, a line critics have traced to *Howards*

End's famous epigraph and chapter 22: "Only connect! . . . Only connect the prose and the passion, and both will be exalted, and human love will be seen at its highest. Live in fragments no longer. Only connect, and the beast and the monk, robbed of the isolation that is life to either, will die."[128] Smith in her reading of E. M. Forster; Derrida in *Politics of Friendship*'s *Essays* glosses; Nafisi and her students in their enthusiasm for *Lolita;* John Macmillan in his study of Rumi; Windsor in her passion for Pushkin: they all "take shelter" in the other's work to overcome fragmented life and understanding, to achieve the wholeness born from with-ness. Other-reading is a homecoming of the mind, an elsewhere where the reader "connects" in order to self-connect and belong. As Camilla tells John, "Montaigne felt as if he were leaving everything he knew for some better, truer place which was the place where he belonged (*Abandon,* 187).

With Iyer, Smith, and other cosmoderns, things are changing. As John says, "community" is now "global" (261). More than Montaigne, Forster, or Du Bois, today's "people of the world" (85) find themselves hard-pressed to gauge the extent to which global community leads to Randall's "communion." Is late globalization a time of coming together? Or is it, as another hero of *Abandon* wonders, an "age of global scattering" (172), of exacerbated "fragmentation" of selves and cultures? One can look at this "scattering," the same character offers more encouragingly, as mobility and dissemination of cultural material entering planetary circulation, now that "texts have shed their authors, as much as they've lost their [original] readers[, . . .] float[ing] without names, without addresses, like refugees with only transit papers moving from airport to airport" (172). On the other hand, one might point out that, "uprooted" violently by politics and history, others' writings, with Sufi manuscripts the perfect example, can be "uploaded in an instant," "translated into languages that have no word for 'fire' of the Sufi kind," "paraded before the ignorant as once women from Egypt, or Chinese men were paraded before the laughing crowds of Europe," and otherwise presented and represented, multiplied and manipulated until they "shrink" into meaninglessness. We have access to them but seldom the "eyes with which to read them," and so we risk reducing them to hackneyed "love songs," "cries to drunkenness and dissipation" (173), and cultural déjà vu. We take the roving texts in, only to recast them into our fantasies. And vice versa, we reproduce ourselve in artifacts and discourses that travel farther and make an impact deeper than at any other time in the world's memory. It is to the imaginary of this reproduction that I attend in *Cosmodernism*'s last part.

PART 5 ⊕ METABOLICS

There is more reason in your body than in your best wisdom.
　—FRIEDRICH NIETZSCHE, *Thus Spoke Zarathustra*

Who were they, these psychic shapes each to be defined by the invasion of the other? With different skins came different glands, different smells, different hair, different self-images, different histories.
　—JOHN UPDIKE, *Brazil*

1. The Metastatic

All around him the American self was reconceiving itself in mechanical terms, but was everywhere running out of control. The self talked constantly about itself, barely touching on any other topic.
　—SALMAN RUSHDIE, *Fury*

Cosmodernism, Inc.: The Body, the World, and the Haptical

Of the flesh but not the world? How peculiar. How can that be?
　—THOMAS PYNCHON, *Against the Day*

. . . the body cosmos . . .
　—DON DELILLO, *The Body Artist*

Le Corps cosmos . . .
　—MICHEL COLLOT

Here comes the world of bodies.
　—JEAN-LUC NANCY, *Corpus*

"To exist is to be a body," the Stoics taught.[1] To be a body, they also suggested, does not mean simply to be *in* a body, within a carnal shell. What puts us in a body by the same token places us in the world of bodies. Being in a body, then, is being in the world, with others. As third-century BC philosopher Cleanthes argued, corporeality represents the keystone of universal interaction (*sympatheia*) both inside individual bodies, where soul and flesh touch on one another by virtue of their shared materiality, and among separate somatic entities.[2] Of course, *separate* may not be the best word choice since the Stoic cosmos makes up a "sympathetic" ensemble held together by a "relation [of] mutual intermingling"[3] and, again, bodies "intermingle" owing to their physicality. Nor does this intermingling stop where political bodies traditionally do, at the national borders, for example. It is intrinsically transnational and transcultural, making us "all . . . members of one body."[4] Since, according to the Stoics, "one and the same nature has fashioned [us] all from the same elements for the same destiny,"[5] we all participate in the "*logos* that draws everything together across time and space."[6] This is true cosmically—we are one with the natural cosmos—as it is politically—"all men are brethren," proclaims Epictetus.[7]

Stoic universalism is not without its pitfalls. What I want to highlight for now in its *logos*, however, is not universal rationality but an essentially bodily relationality, which, across and beyond Stoicism, underwrites our dealings with one another. Roughly speaking, we make and have contacts, "keep in touch" insofar as we are bodies. Conversely, our bodies supply us with encounter venues and communication tools. We have bodies, live, and develop a self as long as we "make contact," live up to what the body structurally is. Thus, growth, successful metabolism—the narrative of individuation—boils down to an incorporation of exchanges, negotiations, and relations, so much so that *our* bodies, which, by force of habit, we deem as fundamentally belonging to us and ending with us, representing and being us most intimately and exclusively, cohere around and reference those not us. It is the dialogue with those presences that our bodies body forth. The conversation would be unthinkable, and so would be thinking itself, if it were not for the *pathos* of physical contact. As the Stoics assure us, there is no depth without surface, no "principle" without substance, no spirit without a body fashioning it, hence no territory without limit and no access without its threshold and the trials of crossing. This is what Derrida repeats throughout his career and once more at its end in *On Touching—Jean-Luc Nancy*, where truth, being, and selfhood are closely tied into the "haptical" (from Gk. *haptomai*, "to touch") and its themes: corporeality, finitude, and liminality. It is by contact with other bodies that we reach, he emphasizes, "a limit *at the limit*," that we "go the limit" and so, in "extreme," geoculturally and epistemologically "liminal" situations, we learn about the world and ourselves.[8] These bodies open windows into unexplored versions of the world and ultimately into the world itself as a whole, a *mundus* above and beyond whatever "ties us down" to our "finite" bodies, as Nancy says, or to the collective (ethnic, religious, etc.) bodies to which we are supposed to belong and be confined.

"The greatest thinker about touching of all time," as Derrida calls him, Nancy builds originally, in *Corpus, The Sense of the World,* and elsewhere, on corporeality and corporeal interchanges in Aristotle and Stoicism.[9] Noteworthy here is Nancy's case for thinking the complex, bio- and cultural-political thematics of the body over and against that into which the world's body, the *mundus,* once globalized, threatens to turn. As noted in the introduction, Nancy rejects globalization, not "mondialization." Published during the perestroika, *La communauté désoeuvrée* (1986) is an earlier effort to envision a body politics for the aftermath of a Communist totalitarianism approached as ethnosomatic management—a set of policies, disciplinary representations, and practices regulating particular bodies and their inscription into the nation's body. In fact, Nancy prefers *immanentism* over *totalitarianism,* and this is more than terminological nitpicking. As he explains, in the ex-Eastern bloc countries "private" bodies were pressured to "fus[e] into a *body* or under a *leader*" and thereby "expose [and] realize," "necessarily in themselves," the "essence" of humanness laid down by national ideology.[10] Posited as strict instantiations of the communal body, they were presumed to arise "immanently" instead of by exposure to other finite beings, to appear rather than "co-appear" by rubbing up against other bodies in the world's "shared space"; they were not forming in relation, were not relationalities, and for this reason they were not "singularities" either.[11]

The events of 1989, Nancy will point out later, did not bring large-scale immanentist constructions of the body and body politics to an end. In fact, stepped-up globalization seems set on a "literalist" mise-en-scène of the Stoic "one body" as a oneness unmatched in world history. Not only is the world conglomerate of interlocking singularities, the world body as *bodies,* demonstrably more homogenous today than twenty years ago because of the expanded range and force of leveling phenomena. It also is, in effect, on the brink of becoming a dedifferentiated system, a "nonworld." Bent on indistinctiveness, the world, Nancy alerts us,[12] is less and less of a world, an unworlding world falling into "immundity," or abjection.[13] In his account, globalization parades before us an indiscriminately self-centered, egological totality where touching equalizes those in touch and bodily configurations and boundaries are disfigured, violently redrawn, or abolished.

This is one haptical model and, derived from it, one corporeal or meta-bolic modality to which I attend in part 5. As the first section shows, the global "one body"—the world as globe—comes about by contagious contacts, via a logic whose recursive rationality the cosmoderns limn as pathogenic haptics, that is, as contamination, viral outspread, cloning, metastasis, and the like. Especially in DeLillo, this is a logic not so much of physical bodies as of certain cultural bodies; in actuality, we will also note apropos of the post-*Underworld* novels, the blood-and-flesh body resists this rationality. Otherwise, the distinction body-culture is notori-ously tenuous. Much like in fiction writers and critics from Pynchon, Up-dike, Joseph McElroy, Philip Roth, Kathy Acker, Yamashita, Leslie Mar-mon Silko, Mark Leyner, David Foster Wallace, William Gibson, Bret Easton Ellis, Powers, and Vollmann, to Lacan, Foucault (and Fou-cauldians like Judith Butler), Deleuze and Guattari, Kristeva (and nearly entire French feminism), N. Katherine Hayles, Donna Haraway, and Su-san Bordo, in DeLillo culture and the body are multiple and significantly isomorphic. Similarly to the onomastic or the translational, the somatic "images" how culture comes along, how it works and molds us, how it goes around, passes, and renews itself. Keen, in DeLillo's words, on the "writer's market" and on culture broadly as a "living organism" that "changes," "palpitates," "grows," "excretes," "sucks things," and "spews them up," this imaginary charts, in sum, cultural metabolism.[14] Given its bodily-biological implications, "metabolism" provides a befittingly dy-namic allegory of cultural output, distribution, and exchanges. The cos-moderns picture culture as a complex, loosely systemic, and corporeal as-semblage governed by ever-amplifying rhythms and transformations, and vice versa, identify bodies as symbolic sites of cultural action, re-ac-tion, and interaction less and less effectively served by modernity's pace and geo-intellectual maps. What cosmodernism canvasses, then, is, on one side, the body of culture, culture as one body of texts, images, and sounds with their lives, deaths, and itineraries; on the other side, the cul-ture of and in bodies, the cultural-aesthetical constitution and cycles of human bodies. On the former, the culture into which bodies are born; on the latter, the culture a posteriori inscribed into them, made into, and re-made, in and across them: as I have said, the two sides are practically im-possible to pry apart. But, for the sake of presentation, I will take them one by one. We will discover, accordingly, that DeLillo's metabolic narra-tives of cultural making, remaking, and circulation, principally *Under-world* (1997), document with rare acumen the egological workings of the haptic model mentioned earlier, whereas the episodes of performative embodiment and bodily transactions in Updike, Yamashita, later DeLillo, and other authors examined in this part's closing section give center stage to a different paradigm.

Totalizing, egologically self-repetitive, recycling the cultural-political codes and locations out of which it spins, the first paradigm speaks to the world as globe; the second, to the world as *mundus*. One is a symptom of globalization; the other, of mondialization. A "mondializing" world is still a world, more precisely, a *mundus*, because its "haptical" makeup—its self-touching, its overall connectivity—does not result in the kind of "self-relation" that only bolsters one self, thought, or worldview.[15] The *mundus*-like world is a nontotalistic *totum*, a whole where, while touching, mingling, and turning into one another, bodies nevertheless preserve their differential identities, as Nancy insists in *The Sense of the World*.[16] A plural, variegated *corpus, le monde* is a body-with; it is a body of, and as, difference. Within it, bodies converge, interact, intersect, and thus participate in the world's *totum*.

The globe's haptics is metastatic, immanentist—metastasis is "immanent," Baudrillard specifies—autoreferential, self-reproductive, and self-assuredly "rational." The haptical modality of the *mundus* is metamorphic, cross-referential and in that more "transcendental,"[17] humbly relational, and therefore productive—productive of knowledge, of new understandings. For the other's body is, as Barry Smart comments on the Levinasian "face-to-face," a face itself.[18] In turning to, and at times even into, others' bodies and corporeal structures, we face the face, the "aspect" of somebody or something of crucial import to who we are or aspire to be. This "turning" or "morphing," this *metabolē*, is symbolic. It is about physical and individual bodies as much as about cultural and political bodies, about national bodies and about the world's larger *corpus*. It latches, as we will discover in this segment's second half, onto biological bodies and their reembodiments as metaphors of reaffiliations and transgressions that pull the "ekstatic" subject out of immanentist "self-containment" and into the broader world.[19] If indeed "the boundary of the self as well as the distinction between the internal and external is established through the ejection and transvaluation" of an "otherness"[20] originally constitutive of the self, the cosmodern imaginary dwells so copiously on how bodies touch one another, on how they change into other bodies and swap shapes and meanings, not just because corporeality is "contingent," but also because it is profoundly contingent on otherness.

The Perfect Crime

> As integration increases, we are becoming like primitive societies once again, with all their vulnerability to the slightest germ. . . . In place of conviviality, convirality.
> —JEAN BAUDRILLARD, *Cool Memories II*

> A virus reproduces itself outside history.
> —DON DELILLO, *Falling Man*

Thriving at the expense of others, the virus is the quintessentially allergic body. It cannot and will not be "with." It will only be: "immanently," insatiably, ever the same. It will not change but adapt to change others so as to replicate itself in their bodies, again and again. Viral haptics is by and large one-directional. While viruses touch others (they are "con-tagious"), little if anything touches them. They mutate strategically to sidestep real transformation. Reasserting each and every time the egological fiction of a body unto itself, absolute and absolutely self-begotten, their mutation is a repetitive ploy and thus, for thinkers like Baudrillard, a critical hyperbole that cuts to the quick of the networked society's cultural pathology.

Released one year after *La communauté désoeuvrée*, the first volume of *Cool Memories* muses about global-age "viral revolution" apropos of wire transfer, a banking method no longer "revolutionary" at the time.[21] Money remains, however, a typical instantiation of the overall de-objectualization and corresponding "viralization" of objects in modernity and of modernity itself. To move around the globe unhampered by locations and their borders—to go viral, hence global—money had to go through simulacral transformation and so became virtual. The simulacral, then, marks the prehistory of the viral. To spread virally, objects first deobjectify, lose their materiality and moorings in material contexts. As they do so, they turn into their own, self-displacing specter, the real's "self-reflexively" imaginal or hyperreal other. Hyperreality is "static" infancy of virality, even though, via a reference to Virilio's germane theories of worldly dematerialization and "disappearance" from *Pure War*, the initial installment of *Cool Memories* also remarks on the "virus of virtualization" and on the "ecstasy of indifference" the world's simulacral becoming and virtualization bring on.[22] *Simulations* details this transformation's substages, but more relevant here is that, once completed, this involutionary process sets off pandemic multiplication. From object to its "deterritorialization" and deobjectifying representation; from there to the nonreferential image, to the digital version that has little to do with the object;[23] and from the object's data-becoming, from its virtuality, to its virality, to its ever-speed-ier global distribution: this is a fair synopsis of Baudrillard's viral chronicles. I single out their last chapter because in it objects get "transparent" and eventually "disappear" as objects to reappear, spectral and omnipresent, as pixels and computing code.

"Information virus" par excellence, the virus is, as Baudrillard elaborates in the third volume of *Cool Memories*, "a communicable idea, thought, ideology, image, notion or concept, that is created by someone, for no one in particular but everyone in general, which purpose is to infect, seduce, subvert, and ultimately transmute the host society, culture, metropolis centre, nation-state or any other system or cultural circuitry, seemingly on a self-propelling redundancy overload that is rushing toward its own collapse, destruction or annihilation, armageddon and/or demise."[24] This is another way of saying that viruses "communicate" *themselves*, the *same* information all the time. Vehicle of sameness, they do not carry information proper. They are not reflective of something or somebody else but self-reflective; they are redundant and redundancy itself at work. The "repetition" they enact is "senseless," will never make sense because it always makes the same sense.[25] To Baudrillard, "objectual" modernity prized originality and worshipped difference, the iconoclastic, the idiosyncratic, and the idiomatic. Instead, viruses haul us headlong into a "radical modernity" that, we read in *America*, "is founded on the absence of difference."[26] In the vortex of metastatic dedifferentiation, cultures bleed to death—death as deculturation and indistinction. As with bodies, so with cultures: "absolute death," the philosopher writes in *The Vital Illusion*, "is not the end of the individual," but "a regression toward a state of minimal differentiation among" entities, "a pure repetition of identical beings."[27] "In evolutionary terms," he goes on, "the victory goes to beings that are mortal and distinct from one another," yet "the reversion is always possible." The relapse can occur in the "viral revolt of our cells," when they "forge[t] *how* to die" and "g[o] on again and again, making thousands of identical copies of [themselves], thus forming a tumor." Or it can happen in "[our] enterprise" of "reconstruct[ing] a homogenous and uniformly consistent universe—an artificial continuum this time—that unfolds within a technological and mechanical medium, extending over our vast information network, where we are in the process of building a perfect clone, an identical copy of our world, a virtual artifact that opens up the prospect of endless reproduction." The "revenge taken on mortal and sexed beings by immortal and undifferentiated life forms" from viruses and clones to

Facebook avatars, this "immortality" is "pathological" biologically, cultur-ally, and otherwise, for it "actively work[s] at the 'dis-information' of our species through the nullification of differences." Equally viral on their mi-cro- and macro-levels, genetic cloning and globalization's cultural cloning "may well be," Baudrillard ventures, a "deliberate project to put an end" to the "game of difference, to stop the divagations of the living," and ulti-mately to "eradicat[e] . . . the human" by setting up a techno-mediatic and mass educational system geared to making "singular beings" into "identical copies of one another."[28] In brief, "we all have fallen victim to" a "virus de-structive of otherness." A "site of the perfect crime against otherness," our "world [has been] given over entirely to the selfsame [*le Même*]." With global culture restaging privileged bodies of culture, a wholesale "liquida-tion of the Other"[29] is under way, which menaces with-ness in its relational essence by substituting "convirality" for "conviviality."[30]

We saw in the introduction, the other is our "convive." As such, he or she is key to the world, and thus to our welfare. But as American cosmoderns of the Baudrillardian stripe like DeLillo warn us, in the holocaust of vi-rally displaced otherness the world itself is receding, and with it the self's chance to come into its own. In Nancy's terms, the world's "ebbing" fol-lows from the degrading of the *mundus* to globe on the heels of what in the introduction I called, with a nod to Giddens, runaway egology. This egology, DeLillo observes, is disproportionately self-indexing—"The world has become self-referring," he writes in *The Names* in 1982[31]—and "overhaptical"—the planet is a "near-circular system of rings intersecting across the globe," he tells Anthony DeCurtis in 1990.[32] As *Underworld* shows extensively, the two attributes are intertwined. More to the point, self-referentiality, or self-connectivity, stems from *hyper*connectivity, is an upshot of excessive contacts. This excess is just that: "too much," happen-ing in less and less time, to the point that eventually nothing but the same things occur, over and over, faster and faster. Not only does network over-load—the webs' "immoderate" haptics—result in glut, in *wasteful* pro-duction. Waste is what the cultural network (over)produces by definition, for it is the surplus, the "redundancy," that piles up as the network reflects, repeats, and keeps multiplying some of its nodes on an ever-larger scale. And, since making is remaking, making is not making it new but already old, used and used up, ready to be disposed of. It is "in [this] sense," Bau-drillard observes in *The System of Objects*, that "*consumption precedes . . . production.*"[33] In the novel, Nick and his wife "se[e]" new products "as garbage even when they sat gleaming on store shelves, . . . unbought" yet somehow ready to be discarded.[34] This is among countless other places in *Ratner's Star, White Noise, Mao II,* and *Underworld* indicating that, more than a signature theme, waste is DeLillo's cultural archeconcept. It is so not only because this is how cultures, old and new, reach us, as the bits and pieces we rummage through and sometimes salvage from archives and digging sites, as in *The Names,* or as "brand-new" rubbish, but also because household or public, cultural or industrial, nuclear or toxic, biodegradable or less so, waste is both testimony to the environmental gamble we take to produce and consume and—exactly because waste bears witness to our productive-consumptive habits—a cultural text worthy of perusal. Production may be disposal, reproductive and thus counterproductive, but what we dispose of is highly instructive of the cultural body we are and its sociopolitical, aesthetic, and ethical metabolism.

Underworld's Dietrology; or, Know Thy Garbage

> Everything is connected.
> —DON DELILLO, *Underworld*

As William G. Little contends in his study of waste from naturalism through postmodernism, DeLillo underscores the "creative aspect" of garbage, refuse, and junk.[35] If, the critic reminds us, in *The Sacred and the Profane* Mircea Eliade makes out a "cosmogony" of waste across a number of creation myths, *Underworld* sketches out, in Nick's own words, the "cosmology of waste" (88). Oddly enough, in this intertextual ontology of ever-tainted, "spoiled" origins—of rot as root—waste signals a beginning rather than an end. Hardly a by-product devoid of purpose and meaning, it is ur-product, *the* product and condition of possibility of all production and origination. According to Detwiler, the "waste theorist" hired by Nick's company, "garbage comes first, then we build a system to deal with it" (288). I would take, therefore, Little's point on "the creative aspect of waste" a step further: if there is a demonic-apocalyptic dimension to consumption and its residues in DeLillo's work—"What we excrete comes back to consume us," Nick fears (791)—there is a "creative" one too in that, like "risk analysis" in *The Names,* waste analysis in *Underworld* is cultural analysis, with all its ideological, political, and moral ramifications. Differently put, to "get" waste in American and world culture—and both are one in DeLillo after *Underworld*—is to understand what "creates" ("originates") that culture, where and how it starts, its metabolism, not just how it ends up. For not only are a culture's leftovers and debris semiotically revelatory; they are its prime hermeneutic sites because they cut to the heart of what culture "is made of," where it comes from and how, what it was and is. As in a Heideggerian ontological hermeneutics or sorts, waste equally covers up and shows off the meaning of culture. If there is a philosophy of life, a global outlook to a community or place, it comes through as a "Weltanschauung" of waste, as Nick calls it (282). Detwiler is right: rather than neglect, bury, and otherwise put out our trash "uncritically," we should "bring [it] into the open" and listen to what it says about us (286). "Get to know your garbage" (286) so you can know yourself, urges the landfill sage.

This is what DeLillo sets out to accomplish by accentuating the profusely epistemological import of waste. Ultimate signifier and narrative "knot" in *Underworld,* waste is "the best-kept secret in the world" (281) because it is a secrecy site per se, locus and product of *secretus* and secretions, of refuse and bodily by-products that we use, excrete, and then secrete, separate out and off, and finally hide away from where we live, produce, and consume (cf. Lat. *secerno,* "separate off," "treat as distinct"). Once more, waste menaces *and* brings forth a world in a sense that is both productive and explanatory. It "makes" our material universe rather than simply consecrating its use, abuse, and depletion. It unearths something not here or not now, or neither, the signification of things past and their present traces as memorabilia. Like in *The Names,* this revelation obtains "archaeologically." More than a theorist, Detwiler is a "garbage archaeologist" (281), an expert in what lies underneath America's landfills, with a unique purchase on its stratified meanings. His "landfill meditation," to recall Gerald Vizenor's 1991 Native American allegory of refuse, is a cultural critic's.[36] He works from the present's outer layer of visible, "disposed-of" signifiers backward toward the invisible depth, the beyond and the before, whereas, as we will remark subsequently, painter Klara Sax tackles the same problem from the other end, of the past, and applies another layer of meaning on top of history-laden salvage. One reads through culture's extant writing, traces the remnants back to previous life, production, and consumption; so does the other by overwriting the inherited symbology, thus bringing out its semantic underworld—its "underwords," *Underworld*'s commentators quip.[37] The archaeologist and the painter are both drawn to the country's wastelands, to America *as expressive* wasteland, a land whose dreams and drives are both encoded and spelled out by its waste.[38] More than a public nuisance, our detritus and leftovers are vehicles for a cultural tenor lying "underneath," "behind," "out back," in the Western outback, and elsewhere, as waste goes West and awaits its discerning critics "out there."

The critic is, in fact, the dis-cerning mind per se; this is what makes him or her a *secrecy* expert: in Greek, Latin, and several modern Indo-European languages, the words for *discriminate, discern,* and *critique* share the same ancient root, *c[e]r.* The redundant phrase and the cultural expertise it designates are sanctioned by what we already know about secrets: not only are they associated with, if not necessarily identical to, waste, to private and public, individual and socioeconomic "secretions." "Secreting" equally implies that secrets and garbage are "taken out" to Staten Island (whose "unique cultural deposit" Nick's colleague Brian visits), or to the collective psyche's unconscious landfill (whose effigies visit us). Either way, they are "classified" and thus deemed typical, hence meaningful, out of sight, which implicitly calls for archaeological scrutiny, for critical sifting through. Indeed, as the words' structure suggests, the secret (the meaning)—the signifying object's castoff, hidden "residue"—lends itself to the critic's discerning gaze. After all, the Latin verbs *discerno* and *secerno* both denote separation, literally (physically) or metaphorically (epistemologically), sorting things out before disposing of them as the recycling-minded characters of *White Noise* and *Underworld* do, or going through discards and leftovers in hopes of retrieving something they both contain and cloak. Corroborating the revealing synonymy is the formal-etymological kinship, which also bears out the "discrete" (*discreta*) nature of all *secreti:* "the biggest secrets [may be] the ones spread open before us," as Brian recalls Marvin Lundy's Lacanian piece of wisdom while looking out over the Fresh Kills "mountain of wrack" (185), but these secrets still call for some digging up and sifting out. For the "mass metabolism" (184), the cultural history they preserve, is fundamentally "prehistory" (184), behind us temporally, or "underhistory," beneath our feet. As Nick's Russian partner Victor reflects, "[W]aste is the secret history, the underhistory, the way archeologists dig out the history of early cultures" (791).

"Underneath" and "behind," in the shadowy "back," away from "our" Apollonian, intellectually safe geography of here and now—this is the ever-ambiguous, shifty, and dusky *Unterwelt* of the apocryphal, Eisenstein movie, and pretty much of all DeLillo cult films and footages from *Running Dog* to *Falling Man.* It is also the under- , outer-, and back-world of waste and secrets, of waste *as* secret. If Detwiler's approach to waste is archaeological, Nick's is "dietrological." Dietrology or, the original Italian word, *dietrologia*, is, he explains to Sims, "the science of what is behind something, . . . [t]he science of what is behind an event" (280). As in *Running Dog, The Names, White Noise*, and particularly *Libra*, the writer retains dietrology's analytic appeal. What draws DeLillo to this "parascience" of "dark forces" are not the "forces" themselves but the possibility—rather than the Pynchonian necessity—of connectedness left open by the critical imagination built into the "science." In this respect, *Underworld* is a dietrological enterprise purporting to tell the understory of post–World War II America, to throw light, that is, on what took place in the shadow of the official narrative, "behind" and "beneath" the immediately discernible and generally in the "back," *dietro,* where meaningful waste lies. The treatment of garbage as cultural signifier—the novel's scavenging semiology—is a branch of dietrology because *dietro* is the locus of waste and secrecy alike but also because in the stuff we dispose of, in the household refuse we cast around our cities no less than in the nuclear waste Viktor's company allegedly "destroys" in the earth's invisible bowels, surface and depth, "out here" and "out (back, down) there," visible and invisible, what we can see and touch and what we can only infer connect and, at the same time, hold up connection as an interpretive tool.

Heterology: The Decalogue of Waste

> [T]he question turns from a question of disposing of this "trash" to a question of appreciating its qualities.
> —DONALD BARTHELME, *Snow White*

> It is necessary to respect what we discard.
> —DON DELLLO, *Underworld*

In DeLillo's cosmodern imaginary, wastelands deploy a latticework of vertical and horizontal links that organize the world into a *suggestive* structure, putting it together while hinting at what, how, and where it means. Waste disposal, then, is meaning retrieval. Compost composition is "telling." Rubbish bares our culture's defining if not all-too-apparent, converging tenets and protocols. Following are the most relevant to our discussion:

(1) The very meaning of our culture "over here" may well lie in what we throw away and dis-place "out there," a correlative metabolics *Underworld* sets up transparently against Cold War polarization.[39]

(2) Uncovering this meaning is inherently a matter of relatedness and depends on our ability to spot relations.

(3) Such relations are elusive, and so they must be reconstructed "archaeologically" by stepping into "dietral" obscurity.

(4) Elusiveness does not foreclose actual connectedness, continuity across boundaries. In reality, because waste is "everywhere," as Sims notices (283), because it has become a salient global presence, it "unifies" the planet by determining globalization as a waste world-system and testimony that "everything is connected" (289). Waste's global ubiquity refashions our perception of the world, gives us a sense of globality. As Nick says, "[P]eople look at their garbage differently now, seeing every bottle and crushed carton in a planetary context" (88).

(5) The "best-kept secret" is waste itself as *the* global secret. At home and abroad, waste "discloses" America as much as it does a dark side of the global, of the late-global, to be more precise: the global as totality driven by late twentieth-century, technological-managerial hyperintegration, a geopolitical-economic script writing itself over "vestigial" times and "spaces of otherness"[40] harboring "atypical" communities, individuals, and styles. If, according to Sims, "everything [we] see is garbage" (283), garbage also helps us see everything, "see it all," the world as world, the imperiled *mundus*.

(6) These intimations of totality occur dietrologically, in the "back" or "behind." Wastelands are the hinterland of critical revelation, the underworld of concealed and repressed truths. But this underworld shelters an otherworld, the realm of alternatives, of *others*, and is therefore key to DeLillo's critical ecology. Once more etymology clues us in: the heterological purview of dietrology's exploits is set forth in the word's prefix, *dietro*. This particle has evolved from the combination of the preposition *di* (cf. Lat. *de*, "of," "from") and the adverb *retro* ("back" or "behind" in Latin), which in turn contains the Indo-European, Greek, and Latin *t[e]r* root of *heteros, alter, other*, and so on.[41] Dietrologists, then, deal with what lies outside, behind, or before mainstream cultural production and consumption, with the by-products and the bygone, the "retro" and the "arche" to dis-cern things not right away obvious, to retrieve an "other" to official histories and generally to tell stories about others. Again, what they salvage is unmetabolized meaning—meaningful alternations, the untold, the hard-to-stomach versions.

(7) Rubbish in general and nuclear waste in particular—"the dark multiplying product" (791)—builds up exponentially. Ironically, Viktor's company adds to the radioactive waste it blows up in the Kazakh *Untergrund*. Proliferation thus masquerades as lucrative destruction, with waste

disposal disposing of (ruling over) the world itself by globalizing certain "arrangements" of power, commerce, and culture.

(8) Better marked in *disposer* and *disposition,* the French etymons of *dispose, disposal,* and *disposition,* such arrangements and their ordering politics are not missing in English either. Political and waste disposal illuminate one another. Further, if what goes on at U.S. waste sites defines America and the world, then the "multiplying" of the "dark product" ad infinitum, the multiplication of the *same* product as production formula *urbi et orbi* foreground a process affecting the world in its worldly essence, making it "dirty" and thus less a *monde*—in French, *immonde* means "impure," "dirty," and *les immondices* are "residues," "trash." There is a politico-ethical aspect to this littering of the world: the "product" begetting more of the same points more generally to self(same)-begetting as a reigning ("disposing") form of cultural production, of production as *re*-production or self-production in locales and moments from which others and their histories have been removed.

(9) Waste discloses the world and disposes of it. Our throwaways recover lost meanings and open up new perspectives. At the same time, consumption residues consume the world's expanse as inbreeding waste reproduces itself virally and thus institutes reproduction and repetition as the late twentieth century's distinctively egological cultural routines. So waste in DeLillo is not only an epitome of the global but also, similar to the global itself, an amphibology. A semiotic topos, a place for significant positionings, dispositions, and decisions, it is fraught with inconsistencies and flirts with the undecidable, with the "open-ended," a term DeLillo himself uses to describe his prose.[42] Waste draws attention to secrets and mysteries but hardly spells them out. A system in and of itself, with the smudged, timeworn ball a piece of salvage at its heart—much like its symbolic double, the baseball-size plutonium core of an A-bomb—it remains semantically unstable because, mimicking its center, it never stands still. It shifts and never settles, circling—and so "integrates," makes "one"—the globe like pollution, the MAD-era B-52s later salvaged by Klara, or the rumored toxic-waste Flying Dutchman. Continuously shuttling back and forth between various times, places, and owners real or hypothetical, the ball is ultimately untraceable to the "original" one hit by Bobby Thompson. *Underworld*'s "center" is, then, decentering. On the face of it, it makes for a "textual nexus, linking virtually all of the novel's themes and motifs—including the theme of connectedness itself."[43] But the novel's thematic hub or core link is faulty. As Marvin admits, that which links it to its

first owner cannot be verified. There nests, then, here as in *Amazons, Running Dog*, or *Falling Man*, a collective mystery hidden deep inside our collections and recollections, in trash collection and personal memories, in junkyards and memorabilia like the fabled baseball, for everything intersects in them.[44] A microcosm of the production, consumption, and control apparatuses in turn undergirded, crossed, paralleled, and allegorized by the multilayered waste structures locally and globally, Nick's treasure supplies what the larger ensembles also do on another level: a way of connecting the dots, of tying together top and bottom, "here" and "there," "front" and "rear," *davanti* and *dietro*, which gives us a sense of the "big picture" without spoon-feeding us its meaning. That is why waste remains in DeLillo a multifaceted enigma defying solution. It poses a still "undisposable" problem—it does not stop being a global eyesore and threat— while presenting us with a range of other issues and conundrums. It both litters our roads and shows the way. It is an environmental hazard and a heuristic opportunity even though it is only partially recyclable into environmentally safe and epistemologically stable stuff.

(10) *Underworld* is vague on the "what" and "who" but tackles the "how," the forms and workings of the discourses behind the imaginal construction of Cold War and post–Cold War private and public spheres. While the trash "master system" instantiates, subsumes, and supplants other systems, it stops short of decoding them. It does not show what lies underneath them but how the seen and the unseen fold into one another to stake their claims to history.

The Aura of Reproduction

> Waste has a solemn aura now.
> —DON DELILLO, *Underworld*

Roughly, these claims fall into two categories. The first is totalistic and, in places, totalitarian, of the "hard" version during the Cold War and of the "soft" sort thereafter. In the post-1989 era, socially marginal and aesthetically subversive *unterweltliche* sodalities and groupings raise a second kind of claims or counterclaims. The division is by no means clear-cut. Nor are the author's leanings. Overall, though, he seems to fault the former type for its exceedingly systemic, "ordering" thrust. Indeed, cultural contentions of this sort call to order. They systematize and regularize. In them, American culture "appears" to itself as one, homogeneously ordered inside and hegemonically ordering outside, quick to dispose of anything that does not follow its prescriptive dispositions. Within such a setup, production is de facto *re*production of a stock catalog of shared fantasies masquerading as novel effigies, styles, and rhetorics, which renders space a space of sameness and, analogously, flattens time into a temporality where the same resurfaces under different masks. These disguises cover up their own formulaic structure. In this respect, we are living in a culture that dissimulates its repetitive and scavenging nature, the pressure on us to *repeat,* to rehash extant repertoires and, with them, culture's "stable" oneness. Culture itself as "one thing," as a "whole"—its perception as such if not its actuality—is culture's utmost claim. The louder this contention, the stronger normative pressures on the particular community, and this is why in her book on the "claims of culture" under globalization Benhabib advocates bringing culture back under the scrutiny it tries to dodge if not inherently, in and through what it truly is, then in how it "wants" to be seen, in the kind of cultural epistemology it projects.[45]

In the 1997 essay "The Power of History," DeLillo makes an identical recommendation.[46] He is concerned here with the receiving end of cultural production as reprise of preset topoi and schemes. Most damaging is, in his view, that this production algorithm and its outcomes reembody themselves in the consumer. If our visual culture's "epidemic of seeing," as *Underworld*'s Sister Edgar calls it, has not spread into the Bronx's otherwise disease-stricken Wall, that is because the place has been "unlinked to the usual services" (812). Out there, popular culture has not exacted its "revenge" (323)—not yet, because Ismael is "planning to go on-line real soon, . . . go, like, global" (812). Should that happen, the "pathogenic element" (812) of glances, the optic contagiousness of what he and his friends would view might rub off on them. Like the woman who "showed" the "modern stigmata"—the symptoms of "the illnesses and diseases of the celebrities" (378) she had been watching on TV—we all risk becoming if not what we watch, read, and listen to, then similar to it. Our serialized commodities and interests clone themselves in us: we become like what we buy or read but also like one another as we build our selves in response to the same things. So we ourselves turn into sequels, repetitive subjectivity configurations rehashing their egological makeup within a closed circuit of feelings, values, and representations. In a culture that "repeats itself, again and again," self-replication is the dominant self-making recipe, putting out as it does, "sub, sub, sub, sub, sub, [s]ubjects" (418), "lesser"—because iterative—subjects who stutter themselves into being. The self makes itself in the present while making this precarious present the only time of identity making. This is the "official time" of what DeLillo indicts as "the culture of the instantaneous."[47]

Is there a way out of this self-contained playback horizon? Is there any chance to step out of the egological prison-house into the ecological house of being? DeLillo thinks so. We can seize this chance, he propounds, if we reclaim language—largely, representation—as a form of "counter-history" opposed to the dehistoricizing ("disremembering"), temporally flattening drive of dominant culture, and, pace Jameson and his post-modern pastiche argument, he adduces Doctorow's *Ragtime* as an example of novelistic idiom that withstands the thrust of what it otherwise describes. For this is what Doctorow and DeLillo himself do, the strategy of their metalinguistic no less than metacultural critique: respeak a cultural and political system's language to speak it otherwise, to play it back to the system itself with a critical twist. The essay theorizes this dissenting kind of recycling, while *Underworld* narrativizes it in detail. As DeLillo proposes in the 1997 *New York Times Magazine* piece, certain archival instances, flashes of history, and echoes of things past such as Russ Hodges's radio voice calling the famous 1951 Giants-Dodgers ballgame and newsreel footage featuring Thomson's home run—both of which went into *Underworld*'s prologue—somehow escape "the debasing process of frantic repetition that exhausts a contemporary event before it has rounded into coherence."[48] Unlike most movie stars, "iconic products of the moment" who "disappear into the very context of their emergence,"[49] "Thomson and Hodges are unconsumed. And the work a novelist may do in examining the recent or distant past may strike him as similarly blessed, at least in theory, at the outset, before the book becomes recalcitrant in his hands or, later, before the hypermarket squeezes it off the shelves." A novelistic form that staves off co-optation into the repetitive and the selfsame rituals of "monotonous" states, "corporate entit[ies], and "assembly line[s]," "counterhistorical" dialect that rearticulates history as actual time and memory and reinstitutes distinct pastness, presentness, and futurity, this is language that regains, on *our* behalf, the cultural murmur of "otherness"; it is language as "life-giving" force, "shap[ing] the world" as it "break[s] the faith of conventional re-creation" and so ultimately creates us *because* it opens up a time and space for others. For "language," DeLillo avers, "lives in everything it touches and can be an agent of redemption, the thing that delivers us, paradoxically, from history's flat, tight and relentless designs, its arrangements of stark pages, and that allows us to find an unconstraining otherness, a free veer from time and place and fate."[50] Or, as Nick stresses, "The Thomson homer continues to live because it happened decades ago when things were not replayed and worn out and run down and used up before midnight of the first day. . . . Because it's something that's preserved and unique" (98).

The point on language and resistance to depersonalizing repetition brings to mind Benjamin. "Even the most perfect reproduction of a work of art," he famously wrote, "is lacking in one element: its presence in time and space, its unique existence at the place where it happens to be."[51] However, "reproduction can bring out those aspects of the original" that we might otherwise miss or can "put the copy of the original into situations which would be out of reach for the original itself." For example, enlarged photos may show more, and more clearly, than their "original"; the camera lens may help us make out things the naked eye would not; and all pictures "take us" at least "halfway" to places where we may not be able to go.[52] Furthermore, the "authority" of the aesthetic object, its inscription into a specific "fabric of tradition," its inaccessibility, and its related "pure art" status and ritual-related, "cult value" are all challenged, with positive outcomes, by modern reproduction mechanisms. Triggered by the latter, the "depreciation" of the "actual" artwork's "presence" is substantially offset by replication and distribution that bring the work before wider audiences.

Mechanical reproduction thus has an upside in Benjamin. Nor does it mean the same thing in the two authors. For the most part, "The Work of Art in the Age of Mechanical Reproduction" refers to the multiplication and circulation of a single art object; *Underworld*, chiefly to the dissemination of a stylistic and cultural pattern, code, or form under the guise of "new" objects. The philosopher acknowledges the "auratic" dwindling of the original but deems it a reasonable trade-off in a democracy of consumption. For the novelist, the main problem is no longer access but excess, not the public absence of originals but the overabundance of representations that, in setting forth the same things time and again, deploy a chronology of sameness where less repetitive formulas and designs are either brought into line or crowded out.

Hegemonic as this metastatic chronotopia may be, it is not airtight, which leaves room for another cultural metabolics. The possibility does not lie outside the system of reproduction but is built into it, and *Underworld*'s network of potentially meaningful links allegorized by the global structure of waste at once conceals and divulges this alternative. If this system and generally the world we live in are overall shaped by a reproductive logic whereby clichés and stereotypes recycle themselves endlessly, there is, or there can be imagined, according to DeLillo, a less totalistic, more creative system, or countersystem, of recycling. This works with, and works over, what the "macrosystem" of production, reproduction, and consumption disposes of, and also works against that system's material and political "dispositions." This subsystem sets in motion a reproductive apparatus that scavenges "with a difference," foraging through discards to recuperate lost meanings or lay out new ones. Where "epidemic" production is in actuality reproduction, this reproduction is productive, originating, for so is or can be waste itself. This second-order production can manufacture its own aura: there is an authenticity of the original in the sense of Benjamin's modernist aesthetics, and then there is another one, cosmodern, according to which creation is not so much clean-slate invention as it is refurbishing, salvaging, working over—painting over, in Klara's case, or writing over, in DeLillo's.

Redolent of the postmodern double-bind that leaves artists no choice but to work with the material of that which they work counter to, *Underworld* dramatizes the one-becoming of the post–Cold War world body at the same time that it disrupts this mimetic-repetitive process through aesthetic repetitions of a rather different kind. What interests me is primarily the latter because they set forth the second, cosmodern type of cultural claims within the taxonomy laid out earlier, but also because the novel itself stages them. Indeed, *Underworld* enacts such repetitions as it reenacts post–World War II history. DeLillo zeroes in on both the macrohistorical and the microhistorical, on the grand canvas of the national and international events with McCarthyite witch hunts and J. Edgar Hoover's tantrums on one side and the minutia of the everyday, the private, the neighborly, and the genial ethnic tableaux on the other, mining them both for embodiments of "unconstraining otherness." This is how inside the text's historical or, rather, counterhistorical framework plot-level counterhistories begin to unfurl; what DeLillo does with the novel as a whole artists like Klara perform in it. The novelist goes through the individual and global memories and memorabilia of the last fifty years to dig up specific yet unconsumed moments, and so does the character. She recycles aesthetically—if quite literally—Cold War history by painting the B-52s decommissioned in the Arizona desert while "salvaging" (her own word) what was humanly unique, ethical about them: not the weapons but the life-loaded trivia such as the name of a woman drawn on a plane's nose.

Montage and "Ethical Strength"

> Power works best when it makes no distinctions.
> —DON DELILLO, *Cosmopolis*

> [T]here is no singularity on the [I]nternet. . . . In this virtual
> secluded world, there is no alterity.
> —JEAN BAUDRILLARD, "Between Difference and Singularity"

Painting the painted plane: this is Klara's counterpainting of the historical canvas, much as *Underworld* paints its own, with Klara in it as if in a campy *Las Meninas*. The planes, Klara tells Nick, were part of power arrangements that "held the world together" for decades (76). Stretching across a "split" and the "curtain" marking it variously multiplied around the world, this togetherness was certainly spurious. A balance of sorts was maintained, though. A geo- and chrono-political standstill was achieved, where self and other clustered together around a semblance of difference but also around an array of effective distinctions enforced all over the world despite this admittedly oversimplifying polarization. Back in Hoover's day, the world was "held together," as it were, by division. The "connection between Us and Them," the FBI director felt, lay in the polarity itself (51). Conjunction inhered in disjunction, actual or tactically played up as in *Unterwelt*, according to Klara, a "film about Us and Them" (444) that staged the "contradictions of being, . . . the inner divisions of people and systems" (444). If Eisenstein "remade" Brueghel to put a human face on Cold War Manichaeanism, Klara uses graffiti techniques on Cold War weaponry to "unrepeat" and thus "find an element of felt life" (77). The bombers and, she insists, the "systems" the big planes came out of, "repeated endlessly" (77), standing as they did on a self-metabolic, apprehensive logic on either side of the divide, with "Us" and "Them" "spooked by [each other's] otherness" (395). The face-off recycled into a panoply of ambiguously overlapping, private and public haptical "disorders" from Hoover's sanitary phobias of trash, grime, germs, "infections," influenzas, and "outside" influences to policies of segregation, quarantine, containment, and deterrence.

After 1989, the *horror coniunctionis* flips over into its symmetrically excessive antinomy: the haptical frenzy encapsulated by the "fasten, fit closely, bind together" (827) globalist mantra. What Sister Edgar observes of the cyberworld holds truer and truer of the world as a whole: [O]ut here, or in there, or wherever she is[,] [t]here are only connections. Everything is connected. All human knowledge gathered and linked, hyperlinked, this site leading to that, this fact referenced to that, a keystroke, a mouse-click, a password—world without word, amen." Logged-in, DeLillo's heroine "feels the grip of the systems" of knowledge production and storage, the "paranoia of the web, the net," and the "perennial threat of virus" embedded in them all as they lead her, one after another, to the H-bomb site. There, "she begins to understand. Everything in your computer, the plastic, the silicon and mylar, every logical operation and processing function, the memory, the hardware, the software, the ones and zeroes, the triads inside the pixels that form the on-screen image—it all culminates here" (825). The bomb is an apotheosis of virality, but so are the bomb webpage and the entire World Wide Web. In them, rationality unveils its deep teleology or, Nancy would say, its "immanentism." "Culmination" obtains as self-fulfilling prophecy. The apex is already in the first link and, before it and its html inscription, in the "primeval" digital input, in the initial "binary black-white yes-no zero-one hero-goat" (465–66), which repeats itself ad infinitum like radiation and AIDS and repeats the world in its own self-repetition, writing the world's unconsumed moments, monuments, and sites into Baudrillardian "indifference" much as the thermonuclear tests blotted out "the foreignness, the otherness of remote populations implied in the place names, Mururoa, Kazakhstan, Siberia" (825). As the readers of *The Names* and *Ratner's Star* will recall, this toponymy is a marker of the stand-alone and unrepeatable, of an otherness threatened by extinction decades ago and again today, when "intersecting systems" are "pull[ing] us apart" by "fusing us" with one another. So did the "atoms forcibly combined" by the 1950s bomb-heads, and so do cyberspace links, for their "coupling" is nothing but "a way of seeing the other side and a settling of differences that have to do" with "difference itself, all argument, all conflict programmed out" (826–27).

A fully integrated and serialized system whose cut-to-size pieces spend their lifecycle quoting one another, DeLillo's cyberspace is a postdifferential world that paints a symmetrically totalistic picture of the late-global world. By contrast, Klara's project—and DeLillo's with it—is transrepetitive. It recycles the humanness couched in the wrecks but employs the desert to block the recycling of the system in which the flying machines participated: "This is a landscape painting in which we use the landscape itself" (70) as a "framing device" (70) "unconducive . . . to industry[,] progress" (71), and the other venues and narratives in which systems and networks of power perpetuate themselves. The repainted planes may not be original in Benjamin's sense, yet they are no less auratic for that because, objets trouvés of sorts, they are not "readymade" but ready to use: they are "found" and then remade into something at odds with their initial meaning.

No different is Nick's "language therapy." Under Jesuit supervision, he circles back to the underworld of "everyday things" to bring it out and thus "build up" the "fullness of [his own] identity" (538). This can be accomplished, Father Paulus tells him, through calisthenics that are no "mere repetition" (539), through the "rote" that "helps build the man" (541). What the potentially artistic language of military discards is to Klara the "found language" of "quotidian things" and the "commonplace" (542) is to Nick: a treasure chest of "overlooked knowledge" about others and himself, and more notably still, about others as guides to the "fullness" of the self. Tactfully Pauline, Father Paulus is quite adamant on the cosmodern benefits of what he calls "the physics of language" (542): to "produce serious men," one needs to "develop" inside them an *ethical space*, a "spacious quality" of body and mind that translates into "respect for other ways of thinking and believing." According to DeLillo, this plenitude of being derives from a paradoxical heteronomy or studied incompleteness, which in turn results from an "openness" toward others, from the room we save "them" inside "us" so that *our* "ethical strength" (538) can have a place to grow. In the egological self, this topology of otherness is permanently under siege. Instead, DeLillo's ecology both presupposes and boosts it through "de-ego[ing]" exercises that take us to the "spatial ethics" beneath the "spatial esthetics" of surfaces and its self-centered "autoworld of pain and loss" (457).

The exercises build moral stamina, for they "repeat with a difference," reusing used-up language. "This is," Nick says, how you "escape the things that made you" (543). Klara, the "bag lady," poaches the thick-layered, American and world waste system to "unstratify the culture" (571) and fashion an other to it; Nick raids language to make himself over and thus break out of the "hypnotic repetition" (443) in play in copycat killings and copycat culture at large, in the "human presence"-free (63) assembly line where his rental Lexus was put together, and in the "infinite regression" of the "endless fitted links" in the warheads' "alpha particles" (251) awaiting mass-destructive self-replication underneath the equally repetitious "alfalfa fields" (458).[53] He re-cites the already-said, calls it forth and out of the selfsame cycle. His drills help him "veer" from "the dumb sad sameness of the days" in which superficially distinct objects "collaps[e] in on themselves" (512) to reinforce "the sameshit thing you'd said a thousand times before" (711) under the pressure of "same[-]thing" entities such as "the state, the nation, the corporation, the power structure, the system, the establishment" (575). This pressure "compresses" time and space into "interval[s]" inside which things and people can be reproduced immediately— "serial murder," DeLillo points out, finds its ideal medium in instant "taping-and-playing" (159). This serialized reproduction is what *Underworld*'s artists fight, whether it is Eisenstein's "montage," the "scrounging" (492) style of Sabato Rodia's Watts Towers decorations, Lenny Bruce's standup, Ismael's "mural tagging," Wolfman's "bandit" broadcasts, or Klara's neocamp: like Bruce's brows, "set at a cosmopolitan arch that seemed to function as an open challenge to his hustler aspect" (505), they all stage repetitions that take exception to what they repeat.[54]

2. The Metamorphic

Not mere repetition.
　　—DON DELILLO, *Underworld*

Performance

. . . always in the process of becoming another . . .
　　—DON DELILLO, *The Body Artist*

We are embodied agents.
　　—CHARLES TAYLOR, *The Ethics of Authenticity*

From *Unterwelt*'s monstrous bodies tragically reembodied in the Kazakh victims of Soviet nuclear tests to the angelic holograms of New York freeway billboards to Klara's palimpsestic commemoration of "Long Tall Sally" on aircraft bodies to Rodia's acrobatics to Bruce's impersonations, and from the 1997 novel back and forth to the rock stars, movie directors, stunt men, photographers, and writers of DeLillo's previous and later books, art involves, as often as not, incorporation or, better still, reincorporation. Regardless of medium, in DeLillo the artist is a body virtuoso and to make art is to metabolize: a body of work takes bodies at work but also bodies working on, with, or by other bodies, biological as much as cultural, which renders art making remaking, and incorporation, *re*incorporation—commemoration, intertextuality, recycling. This somatopoetics runs the full gamut of the metabolic: from Baudrillard's "senseless" repetition of cultural materials and the socio-aesthetical contracts under-lying them to repetition as production; from quantitative reproductions that rehearse the very "culture of reproduction of late capitalism" and in the process incorporate the artist himself or herself into the "sociosym-bolic order" to qualitative reenactments that "avoid incorporation";[55] from the iterative to the transiterative or transformative; in short, from metabolics as metastasis to metabolics as *metabolē* in the Greek sense of "change."

DeLillo's bodies and bodily practices illustrate these extremes and everything in between. In his oeuvre, some bodies metabolize superfi-cially, merely "regurgitate." Organically repetitive, they repeat themselves into indistinction and symbolic extinction. Bill Gray in *Mao II* (1991), Rey Robles in *The Body Artist* (2001), and Eric Packer in *Cosmopolis* (2003) are just three of DeLillo's characters who corroborate this repetitive model and its egology. Gray and Robles are artists who struggle to avoid repeat-ing themselves into commodifying ("digestible") discourse, while Packer is a currency trader, hence arguably on the other side, and "part of the problem." They all end up, however, in the same place, the very place of absolute sameness—death—and their deaths all are more or less suicides because their lives act out, with varying degrees of deliberateness, what earlier I identified as recursive rationality. This rationality is egological and thus assimilative; what recurs in its repeated self-reproductions is ex-ponentially more of the same. Packer exemplifies this metastatic self-in-stantiation in mind and body alike. His digital models purport to "pre-dict" digitality itself, repetitiveness, more specifically, repetitive phenomena in foreign markets, and he runs his body through the same routine day after day. He works out regularly, monitors his vital indicators continuously, and is so obsessed with his prostate's slight asymmetry (an echo of Gladney's troubles in *White Noise*) that he has daily proctological examinations in his limo. But here, in the car on whose screens he follows the digital pulse of the yen and of his own heart, and inside his extended automotive body, in his actual body, is where physicality reveals itself as the very rhetoric of consciousness, showing us, as an *Underworld* charac-ters explains, how the mind "looks," "what's happening" to it (511). Ac-cordingly, it is in the body that the logic of the selfsame jams, and this is exactly the point Packer's killer, Benno Levin, makes during their final chat: "The importance of the lopsided, the thing that's skewed a little. You were looking for balance, beautiful balance, equal parts, equal sides. . . . But you should have been tracking the yen and its tics and quirks. The little quirk, the misshape. . . . That's where the answer was, in your body, in your prostate."[56]

Levin is spot-on. The body has answers. As in *Cosmopolis,* it alerts us first to itself, but to itself as *l'Étranger,* as other:[57] to the misshaped, lop-sided, and "twisted," to what does not confirm and conform, to the other-than-usual, and thus to the world's otherness, to that which makes the world tick. "Suddenly it becomes possible," Ricoeur wrote half a century ago, "that there are just *others,*"[58] and, still in Benno's words, our organs and limbs tell us too that "there is nothing in the world but other people,"[59] other fellow human beings and others generally: the bodyguard from the former Yugoslavia, the Romanian "pastry assassin," the Sikh cab-bie, the little chapel Packer thought he could buy, the Siberian taiga's white tiger, the lonely shark in its tank, indeed, the world. *Others* are the world. And we must be with them—"an 'other' among others," Ricoeur also says in *Histoire et vérité*—so we can be.[60]

Latter-day Stoics, DeLillo and other cosmoderns endorse this prescrip-tion by shifting emphasis away from the metastatic, the disjunctive, and the confrontational, in which one element reproduces itself in, and thus suspends, an other, to the metamorphic and the relational, where one term performs, or morphs into, another and thus gestures to overlaps, compatibilities, and affiliations that either can be reconstructed—they have always been there, are "organic"—or can be constructed for the first time. Either way, the cosmodern body can turn into an other, and thus latches onto otherness. For in cosmodernism the somatic matrix is intrin-sically transcorporeal, a heterogeneous collage of body parts put together as in Peter Carey's 2003 novel *My Life as a Fake* or in Kingston's *Tripmas-ter Monkey,* body of texts leaning on other textual bodies for ampler rhetorical and cultural sustenance as Carey's story does on Mary Shelley's "modern Prometheus" and Kingston's on Whitman and Chinese folklore in her version of the Monkey King roaming California as Wittman Ah Sing and using his "seventy-two transformations" to "integrate" people into the larger "fraternité" of the "World"'s "Humanity."[61] With typical frequency, bodies are in the cosmodern imaginary worldly connectors. They embody culture, or cultures rather, and on this score Kingston's Wittman is once more paradigmatic. Her *Tripmaster Monkey* hero does not turn away from kin to embrace others. Instead, as he portrays his fam-ily, "we are connected to one another in time and blood," but, he adds, "Each of us is so related, we're practically the same person living infinite versions of the great human adventure, . . . all the multitudinous ways of being human."[62] It is, in fact, Chinese mythology's bodily metamorphic repertoire that allows him to see himself under another angle. "I think," he confesses, "that history being trapped in people means that history is embodied in physical characteristics, such as skin colors."[63]

In Kingston, culture and history are incorporated as skin pigment and "slanted" eyes; in Zadie Smith, quite famously after her 2000 international bestseller, in teeth, tooth roots, and racially and ethnically marked bodies. Not unlike in Kingston, deep as the roots may be, they are intertwined in Smith's *White Teeth* with other roots and thus make selfhood impossible to "isolate" as "pure" ontological and cultural unit. The harder you dig— the deeper Smith's "root canals"—the more the vertical cut through the individual's biography proves to be a cross-section through other biographies, individual and collective, and the political and ethical bearings of this cosmodern revelation cannot be underestimated. *White Teeth* explicitly cautions that, considering the heteroclite architecture of who we are, literal self-repetition—"autogamy," Smith calls it—is philosophically dubious, a repression of or "political" cover for a process the author deems "cross-pollinating."[64] So is, of course, Smith's novel itself, what with all its Rushdie and Kureishi textual "implants," to name just a few.[65] The "Rushdie affair" is certainly referenced in *White Teeth* and before it in Kureishi's *The Black Album,* leading in both to heated arguments over cultural and religious identity.[66] It is not impossible, although it is not highly likely either, that Smith has worked the debates into her book via Kureishi's own working through of the widely publicized incident. Regardless of the volume of borrowings, ultimately defining in all three authors is the struggle to chart a middle course between a worldview of disconnected, a-haptical monads and another, overly haptical yet everywhere the same. As in Smith and Rushdie, in Kureishi the cosmodern balance is reached in the characters' bodies themselves, especially in Shahid's. The corporeal self proves to Shahid that the meaning of belonging, allegiance, and membership is not carved in stone but in the body, in bodily inscriptions of gender, sexuality, race, and ethnicity. These are, however, subject to performative reinscription, and Shahid is a performer—a performer and a bricoleur—many times over. Torn apart by his "warring selves" in "a room of broken mirrors," he scrambles to put the pieces back together as pictures of bigger worlds.[67] To do so, he employs his own body in acts of travesty and masquerade that reenact the transgender performances of Prince, who had released his own *Black Album* the year before Kureishi's came out. A Pakistani fan of the African American pop star, Shahib reperforms his idol's "Funk Bible" opus by reproducing himself, no less shockingly, into a white woman like Deedee, his teacher and lover.

"Engineered Transpositions"; or, Updike's Tropical Romance

> We are not Brazilians only—we are citizens of the planet!
> —JOHN UPDIKE, *Brazil*

Physical-intertextual metamorphosis has been a hallmark of the last decades in American and other literatures. A range of postcolonial, magical realist, late modern, and postmodern authors from Coetzee, Julio Cortázar, Pynchon, and Cynthia Ozick to Mircea Cărtărescu (*Nostalgia*), Marie Darrieusecq (*Pig Tales*), and Yoko Tawada (the "Tongue Dance" chapter of *Where Europe Begins*) set to "out-Kafka" their famous precursor, as Philip Roth writes in *The Breast*, his own version of "The Metamorphosis." In Kafka as in Roth, metamorphosis does not "scrap" the original self but repositions it, allowing it to "turn" and thus see itself and the world in a brutally new light. As a *Kreatur*, first more amusingly as a female breast, then on the more somber side as a "human stain" or "dying animal" (to quote the titles of two recent novels by Roth), the self steps into a strange zone of being, into being itself as strangeness, as alienation in the sense discussed in part 4. In a way, cosmodernism's ethnoracial, transgender, and cross-cultural impersonations, morphings, and swaps up the ante, for they "historicize" the somatic transformation and thus render it more drastic, more material, and more prominent. By the same movement, though, they take the metamorphic self farther afield beyond modernist alienation and its postmodern aftershocks, into a different strangeness of being—into a world of strangers; after all, they are marked as such by their skin, hair, and eyes. A strange world, a geo-somatic allegory of difference, this is no longer the world of existential solitude and alienation, however. It is the world where I am—with the stranger.

Published in 1999 and included in *Licks of Love* (2000), Updike's "Metamorphosis" does not centerstage this discovery, or does not do so as explicitly as he had done five years before in *Brazil*, a novel premised on an identical somato-cultural transmutation. In "Metamorphosis," Anderson undergoes plastic surgery initially to have a skin cancer removed yet ultimately to get himself the look of the surgeon, a Korean-American woman. Updike's "idler" winds up wanting to be like Dr. Kim, even *be* her.[68] Wearing the other's face, though, looking like her, does not necessarily mean facing her in any profoundly Levinasian sense. Prevailing in the short story is indeed the "epidermal" turn into an other, the kind of "skin-deep" tropism that identifies one with, and further reinforces, a complexional-cultural stereotype, in this case the "Oriental in its impassive expression."[69] Here as in *Native Speaker,* it is this other that is "excised" in the cliché. Unlike the shorter piece, the novel deploys a whole cluster of cosmodern tropisms whose physical shifts and refigurations turn the characters toward each other's figures ethically.

In "Metamorphosis," tropisms are cosmetic. In *Brazil,* they are textual and contextual, literary and cultural, cosmodern. The 1994 novel opens, also as in Lee, with a Whitmanesque motto, an excerpt from "A Christmas Greeting" welcoming the "Brazilian brother" into the world's "ample place." More significantly still, the story reworks other works to narrate the rich tropicality of bodies and the ways of being they embody. A tropical romance, not only is the book set at the tropics, but it also unfolds as bodies, striking in their original, socio-physiognomic contrasts, move toward and into one another and thus step into other worlds of values and feelings. Its elaborate tropical apparatus lays out an equally transtextual and transcultural space of "fraternal" ties and "liaisons" across bodies of race, ethnicity, class, history, and geography. A cultural romance comparable to *Lost in Translation* and *Abandon,* Updike's book would not have been possible without the literary "affair" inside it, namely, without its textual romance with another romance, *The Romance of Tristan and Iseult* in Joseph Bédier's 1900 version.

Updike acknowledges Bédier in the afterword for the "tone and basic situation," but a side-by-side reading of the two texts turns up borrowings that are both substantial and selective. Tristan's intense "ownership" of his body, Iseult the Fair's dazzlingly golden hair, the changes in Tristan's facial skin color and voice, then the plot itself down to such minutia as the lovers' separation and Tristan's ring are all recast in *Brazil.*[70] In Updike, Tristan becomes Tristão and Iseult, Isabel. Star-struck lovers—he is a poor mulatto from Rio's favelas; she is rich and white—they too elope, to the Mato Grosso's woodlands. With a nod to Lévi-Strauss's comment that journeying across Brazil is like treading through the country's social structure and history from one class and century to another, the characters trek over hundreds of miles and years and thus retrace Brazilian identity-building from the Portuguese colonization to the post-Kubitschek era to the globalizing late 1980s.[71] Decades ago, Mário de Andrade's Macunaíma took a similar trip and underwent the same racial-ethnic, fantastic transformations Updike's characters go through the farther inland they press on. It is, we learn in *Brazil*'s "Mato Grosso" chapter, as if Tristão and Isabel are "moving back in time" (159). Away from what has kept them apart, they are now free to fully "define" (151) each other. Set in train the day they met, when Tristão "stamped himself" on Isabel's body, on "her eyes, on her soft young fibres," the "de-finition" that reveals us to ourselves by opening us up to the world of others is only carried through when they swap their bodies magically—"as one chang[es] into the other and back again in the endlessly repeating distances of the Mato Grosso" (150). The extraordinary *metabolē* is not complete—Isabel does not become a "masculinized" black woman, nor does Tristão "soften up" as an educated, well-off white man—until Isabel, accompanied by her onetime lover Ianopamoko, an aborigine woman, meets a shaman who helps her effectively "chang[e] her self" (186). The holy man describes the miraculous change in pointedly "structuralist" language. "As far as [Isabel] could understand" it, the sacrificial logic stipulates that "[m]agic can merely transpose and substitute, as with the counters of a game. When something here is placed *there*, something there must be placed *here*" (186), that is, in relation and in line with the cosmic rule of equitable distributions. And since Isabel wants it all—she wants Tristão's love and welfare, in brief, wants him—she must surrender something of equal weight in return. Of course, the absolute equivalent is Tristão himself, whom she will give up for good at the end as he reenacts Tristan's fate on the very beach they met. Until then, she would have to trade her next most prized possession, "her [own] self," for him, that is, for that other self most closely resembling, if not in reality being, Tristão and for its people, race, and memory. On one side, "something in the smoke" in the medicine man's hut "eat[s] away at the boundary between" Isabel's "minds" (185). On the other, the more these boundaries volatilize and the shaman gets a better look at Isabel's masculine "heart," the more her "white," "feminine" core shrinks so that "what is eventually left is somebody else" (187).

This somebody else is body and mind, yet the two are not separate. They make up one body, are both in the body and, together, are it. The shaman and Isabel's Uncle Donaciano, a cosmopolite "who knew so many languages that his mind was always translating" and whose "tongue had no home" (72), could not come from more discrepant worlds, yet they both suspect, in the Brazilian aristocrat's words, that "we *are* our bodies" and because of that, our lovers' bodies can "create" and re-create us as

bodies of flesh, emotions, and thoughts (73). So, as much as Tristão remade Isabel's into what she is away from the comfort of her Rio apart-
ment, she is remaking him once her own physical metamorphosis gets under way. They trade bodies across the subtropical expanse while they are
apart and retain their swapped bodies after they reunite. Vaguely reminiscent of Alejo Carpentier's treatment of Pauline Bonaparte, who becomes
a "mulatta" in his 1949 novel *The Kingdom of This World*, Isabel is a "black"
woman now. Thus, "a different inheritance" "descend[s]" on her, "a
strength not merely passive," while his newly acquired whiteness "glim-
mered in the shadows of the hut" (*Brazil*, 203). Racial, ethnic, social, and
so forth, the switch also has a sexual component as Isabel takes the lead
and opens herself a window into the "underside of the real world" (204)—
the world she has so far deemed real, familiar, hers. The same goes for
Tristão. Now that Isabel's body is "no longer the color of clouds and crystal but that of earth," it reveals her to him, for the first time, as a complete
person, with a physicality of her own (206). The other in her self, then, is
not an extraneous element but that which rounds the self off, makes it
whole, and "de-fines" it as such.

The "transpositions" Isabel "engineered" (208) with the shaman's help,
Tristão gathers, do not simply reposition us so we can see, "from within,"
others and what they themselves see and feel. What the bodily exchanges
and alterations achieve is not temporary. They neither come "later," re-
warding us for keeping an "open mind," nor unearth an ontological acces-
sory, an addition to or extension of what we "deep down" are. Instead, they
retrieve something we have always been in order to be what has been so far
visible, under a certain skin and sexual, economic, and cultural identity.
They bear witness to our "true self"—if not to the other as this self, at the
very least to the other as a sine qua non selfhood ingredient. Tristão makes
precisely this point when he tells Isabel that, as a black woman, she has
"become [her] true self" (207). Become what they have been—invisibly—
all along, the lovers are at last giving each other the "gift . . . of a drowsing
oneness with the universe" (210).

" . . . fresh as if just finished / and taken off the frame": this is how Elizabeth Bishop sees Brazil's luxuriously vegetative world in her poem "Brazil,
January 1, 1502." Updike's canvas is darker. The novel ends on a somber
tone not entirely derived from *Tristan et Iseut*'s tragic dénouement. Nor is
this ending completely shaped by Bishop's poetic frames, which render ex-
otically lush Brazil a pictorial artifice, a matter of craft. At its most exu-

berant, the country is, in Bishop, a painting, a representation, a "technical" problem. Some of this vision has passed into the novel, and Updike does credit Bishop's "Brazil" too in the afterword. More important than the acknowledgment itself, though, is what happens in his own *Brazil*'s last pages, where, "on a globe dominated by Japanese and German methodology," the lead characters and the whole country rush to endorse the "new arrangements of mutual dependency and satisfaction" (234). Technology, overdevelopment, tourism—Tristão and Isabel now travel the world— seem poised to "ea[t] up the planet" (235). Here and elsewhere, Updike proves a keen observer of what in *Bech at Bay* he indicts as globalization's "deep-fried homogeneity."[72]

This homogenization is at odds with the "oneness" achieved by Tristão and Isabel. Arising in and across bodies, oneness with an other and the world sheds fresh light on people, things, and places alike, on the bodies of the two characters as much as on Brazil's body of land. A caveat on what can beset both nature and history, the Brazilian forest's body reproduced in Bishop becomes, in Updike, Brazil as manufactured and no less manufacturing, industrial body. In adopting world-unifying, "standard" ("Japanese and German") reproduction methods—in "going global"—this body risks reproducing itself in their ossifying likeness, whereas what Tristão's and Isabel's change-prone bodies "produce" across landscape, contending histories, and social stations is the unremitting play of biocultural difference, the very drama of culture.

Tropics, Tropisms, Allotropes

In Updike and, we will see shortly, in Yamashita, Brazil epitomizes the generic condition of culture: tropicality, culture as tropological apparatus. Brazil is a tropical culture not just because it lies at the tropics but also because the ebb and flow of its cultural metabolics performs the country's geographical coordinates. This tropical performance, in which the Bakhtinian carnivalesque is flamboyantly at play, is hardly a Brazilian monopoly but, both Updike and Yamashita imply, is more noticeable here than in other traditions. Accounting for this is, as one might expect, Brazil's colonial past. A former Portuguese colony, the country has a long history of metropolitan expansion, adaptation, local configuration, and refiguration, and the ensuing "tropicalization"[73] of culture, to borrow Srinivas Aravamudan's "tropicopolitan" riff on Pratt's "transculturation," seems to be better marked somatically in Brazil than elsewhere.

Yamashita's reference to Brazil as a "tropical Transylvania" is, along these lines, strikingly apt, offering an insight into the "othering"-antinomian rationality of the metropolis.[74] For the better part of modernity, the Brazilian tropics served as a subliminal dumping ground where the metropolis cast off an otherwise constitutive part of itself. An exorcizing topography in which Europeans have externalized their "other" self only to run across it later in unwonted and unwanted cultural tropisms, the tropics became the West's haunting antipodes. The Euro–North American colonial imaginary reified the geocultural and biological tropical bodies into culturally inferior, grotesquely sexual, and violent-demonic incorporations putatively "antipodal" to Western bodies. Actual and imagined, fascinating and feared, controlled and out of control, rationalized and irrational, the tropical body, Aravamudan comments, "exists both as a fictive construct of colonial tropology *and* actual resident of tropical space, object of representation *and* agent of resistance."[75] Repressed and represented according to this polar logic, it remains inescapably "opposed," "out there," "external."

Marking colonialism, postcolonialism, and the global studies influenced by the postcolonial paradigm, this logic has undergone some adjustments of late. The changes fall short of a complete shift. They do point, however, to new mechanics and meanings of somatic tropisms in the literature, theory, and philosophy after 1989. If the antipodal model of subject and culture spoke to the modern and modernist world of compartmentalized, hierarchically structured *worlds* and bodies, the cosmodern perception of self and other "at the antipodes" is no longer predominantly divisional. The colonial, indeed, the recolonizing thrust of globalization, and with it modernity's surviving, discrete-discrepant logic, has been abundantly documented. Less attended to, yet diagnostic of the post–Cold War era, is a biocultural tropology that switches emphasis from the dichotomic and antagonistic to the analogical and codependent, from *separate* and unambiguously adversarial bodies and cultures to co-, cross-, and trans-corporeality. To restate a key part of *Cosmodernism's* argument, the problem of our world is not how different we are or how defining for who we are our differences will likely remain, but how to deal with one another ethically, that is, how to be with one another via our dissimilitudes.

The cosmoderns respond to this problem by reimagining the body as a contact point, or continuum rather, a haptical locus where bodies meet and acknowledge one another, where they touch, switch places and shapes, and even turn into each other: the body as a morphic and meta-morphic site, the body itself as *tropos*. The tropics provide cosmodernism's metabolic imaginary with a germane space where the body and its reincorporations as "other"—its *allotropes*—can stand side by side, distinct *and* juxtaposed instead of divided and isolated, not necessarily similar and yet woven into the same world syntax. This is where bodies turn to and into one another, toward others and their "customs," "modes of life," and cultural "characters" (*tropoi*). Structurally theatrical, this corporeal tropicality is, we have noticed in Updike and we will notice again, an identitarian *show*—and tell. Obliquely, by various figurations, it tells of an identity notion according to which a body, along with that somebody inside it, becomes like, or simply becomes, some other body and thus somebody else so as to hint not only that it can relate to others and thus enter new configurations of humanness but that relating, interacting, and joining in such aggregates is what the body does qua body.

Cultural amalgams and venues of further amalgamations, tropisms, permutations, and combinations that allegorize emerging cross-cultural alliances and mélanges, bodies are intercorporeal as much as they are intertextual. One might say that at the tropics they are in their element, for the tropics make for a saliently rhetorical-intertextual environment. As Yamashita also shows, the "turning" to and into other bodies works through other bodies of work, as montage or bricolage that turns to, morphs, and refigures others' works, images, and figures. Conversely, not only do bodies "from the tropics" embody tropisms, that is, not only are they allomorphic linguistically, culturally, racially, and otherwise, but they also incarnate tropicality itself, the very metabolic possibility of morphing, change, and transgression, the limit and its crossing into other bodies and modalities of being. Whether incorporated as geographical coordinates, cultural dominant, or human bodies, the tropics contour a space of change, of cosmic and cultural revolutions. In this regard, they are the globe's motile zone per se. As spatial markers and marked spatiality simultaneously, they cannot be an exception to this global mobility either, and so they too are on the move, shifty, boundaries changing location and the locations, lives, and stories they cross into. The tropics are no fixed barriers. Signposts and operators of an essentially metabolic cosmodernism, they corporealize, much like the actual bodies inhabiting them, a perpetually evolving, amphibological liminality; they set up the limit and its unlimitation, the boundary and its breaking protocols; they distinguish among places, cultures, and people and knit them together.

Tropical Tilt: Karen Tei Yamashita's *Tropic of Orange*

> When I visit Los Angeles or San Francisco, I am at the same time in
> Latin America and Asia. . . . I oppose the sinister cartography of the
> New World Order with the conceptual map of the New World
> Border—a great trans-, and inter-continental border zone, a place
> where no centers remain. It's all margins, meaning there are no
> "others," or better said, the only true "others" are those who resist
> fusion, *mestizaje*, and cross-cultural dialogue.
> —GUILLERMO GÓMEZ-PEÑA, *The New World Border*

This deterritorializing-reterritorializing motion across bodies of territory, style, and flesh is Yamashita's constant theme and stylistic protocol in *Through the Arc of the Rain Forest* (1990), *Brazil-Maru* (1992), *Circle K Cycles* (2001), and especially *Tropic of Orange* (1997). Traveler, anthropologist, cultural critic, and author of multimedia performances, plays, poems, short stories, and novels, Yamashita has explored variously what Ursula Heise calls, apropos of the 1990 novel, the "infinite mutability of the physical world." As the critic glosses, "this transformability [is] foreground[ed]" in the novel's opening epigraph:[76] "I have heard Brazilian children say that whatever passes through the arc of the rainbow becomes its opposite. But what is the opposite of a bird? Or, for that matter, a human being? And what then, in the great rain forest, where, in its season, the rain never ceases and the rainbows are myriad?" Another motto of sorts, the "Author's Note," placed right before the book's first part, mentions *Tristes Tropiques'* "reading" of South American tropicality as a *novela brasileiro* setting. *Through the Arc of the Rain Forest*, we infer, renovelizes—retextualizes and renews—the tropical soap opera and its dramatic mix of joy and pain by employing the technique of "tropical tilting," to quote the title of the novel's closing fragment. What Yamashita "tilts"— what she reworks and puts a personal twist on—is not only Lévi-Strauss but also the magical realism tradition of García Márquez and Andrade before him, a tradition that has dwelt on the tropics as a stage of racial-cultural and somatic metamorphoses and reembodiments.[77]

The "tilting" is inherently tropical twice. Another name for bricolage as textual refiguration and transformation, it is also the locus where natural and cultural bodies change and exchange shapes magically, where objects like Kazumasa Ishimaru's ball tell stories, people grow additional breasts and arms, pass into one another and as each other so as to substantiate Yamashita's notion that the local, the idiomatic, the archaic, and the seemingly cloistered are not "opposite" to locations and values usually deemed "universal." She is, no doubt, skeptical of the "Plastics Age," but worldly "plasticity," the morphic capability that leads to "jungle plastic," is the same that jump-starts the metabolism of the "old forest's" body "once again, secreting its digestive juices, slowly breaking everything into edible absorbent components, pursuing the lost perfection of an organism in which digestion and excretion were once one and the same." Nor is this the return of the same—"But it will never be the same again," announces the ball, and this seems to be the whole point.[78] A full comeback would mean aligning tropical metabolics to the system of opposites and contrasts already in place. The novel looks, instead, to displace the system, to destabilize what appears stable, defined and confined in terms of location and formula and thus unrecognized outside available descriptions, taxonomies, and axiologies.

Even more emphatically than Yamashita's first book, *Tropic of Orange* suggests that this stability is, at the tropics and around the world they circle, a convention, a trope—a tropic. At a time millions are still tied down to places of want, persecution, and toil, the suggestion has something visionary to it. The author looks ahead to a world organized not by top-down agreements like NAFTA but by a popular, "multitudinal" politics of mobility. The world as managerial totality, as *corporate corpus,* on the one hand; on the other, and quite literally, as an *alternative,* the world as a body in motion and bodies on the move turning into and to one another to locate and relocate themselves and thus build new sodalities and coalitions—this is what *Tropic of Orange* envisions. In it, ever on the move, bodies produce movement and movements, culturally, politically, and otherwise. In the bodies' nature and flowing from them, motility is innately corporeal, "natural," but also political. Source of the change affecting bodies of people and countries, it opposes stasis and that which curbs movement itself—the atropical limit, the frontier—while resisting "deregulations" and de-limitations that tend to assimilate tropical geographies and economies into supranationally exploitative totalities.

Both vectors play lead roles. The former makes its first appearance on the book cover, where the Berlin Wall, now restored as the United States–Mexico border fence, à la Boyle's *The Tortilla Curtain,* repositions the Cold War's West-East divide along a North-South axis. If NAFTA calls for frontiers' elimination on behalf of TNCs—corporate entities that work tautologically to reproduce themselves across borders—Yamashita's migrant laborers and refugees do not abolish borders but break through them to link up hitherto unconnected bodies and thus fashion a world body in which cultures, lands, and people appear as what they have always been no matter where they have been: hybrid "organisms," *mixta composita* undergirded by a network of links and interdependences. These are, according to the author herself, the defining features of the bodies populating *Tropic of Orange*'s kinetic landscape beginning with Arcangel, the protagonist.

Emblematic incorporation of the book's intricate tropology, Arcangel crosses into the United States and "tak[es his] culture and landscape with [him]." Setting in motion the "landscape itself," he "distort[s] the geo-political grid that defines the region."[79] Eminent "representative of a place and a body where the borders are being redrawn," he is the cosmodern messiah of the disenfranchised, reincarnation of the Aztec prophet Chilam Quetzal.[80] The arc(h)wetback/Arc(h)angel greatly complicates our representations of nativity and belonging. Born elsewhere, he is nevertheless the quintessential Angeleno, and so is Japanese-American Manzanar, a fellow body artist who "knows the arteries of the body" as a one-time surgeon and whose former profession prepares him "for his role as a transient who comes to know the transportation arteries and the sewage system of a city existing as a corpus" reminiscent of Mike Davis's *City of Quartz: Excavating the Future in Los Angeles*.[81]

Arcangel does a bit of "reverse" excavation of his own. He reconstructs L.A.'s multifarious history while holding up this past as the city's future to come—one more time, not a return of the same but of the other and the many, of the city as perennial urban bricolage. It is of course only befitting that Arcangel is a bricoleur himself. On one side, he is an intertextual body; as the writer discloses, he constitutes both a "Pablo Neruda-figure"[82] and a "literary interpretation" of Guillermo Gómez-Peña," the Mexican-American writer-provocateur and performer. Author of the mock-NAFTA performances collected in *The New World Border, Dangerous Border Crossers*, and elsewhere, Gómez-Peña is a central presence in Yamashita's own *borderismo*. Her trickster/superhero reembodies transparently Gómez-Peña's "Supermojado," described by his creator as "Border hero, conceptual carnal of Superbarrio, champion of undocumented workers' rights, and archenemy of Migrasferatu and Pito Wilson."[83] As in Gómez-Peña, in Yamashita the "border is both political and semiotic."[84] "Sinister political cartography," according to the Mexico City–born artist, it evokes "outdated fragmentation," "static identities," "fixed nationalities," and "pure languages."[85] Once rendered fluid—shifty limit of a "fluctuating cartography," as Gómez-Peña calls it[86]—the border becomes a signifying and resignifying place, a culturally metamorphic zone.

Tropic of Orange bodies forth the zone and its motility in Arcangel's roving and hyperelastic body, a body always ready to be somewhere else and in other shape. In fact, in his body, Yamashita both incorporates and "metaphorizes" geography. For one thing, she employs his body figuratively to personify the landscape and its markers, including the tropic itself; for another, *Tropic of Orange* "literalizes this tropic."[87] The literalization plays out on several levels but primarily in and through Arcangel's crossover bodily performance. A master of impersonation and metamorphosis, he takes it upon himself to do what others would not or could not with or to their bodies. Like Gómez-Peña's, his feats break with inherited customs and expectations of somatic and cultural-aesthetic behavior, step over its visible and invisible lines to expose its historical "constructedness." As both Gómez-Peña's intertextual reincarnation and "El Gran Mojado," Arcangel gets, at last, to L.A., dragging the Tropic of Cancer with him across the border and into the "Pacific Rim Auditorium," where he performs before an audience of "legal" and "illegal" workers from both sides of the border. The show is billed as "The Ultimate Wrestling Chammmpppionnnnshhhipppp! El Contrato Con América. Sponsored from a generous grant from the Ministry of Multicultures. Brought to you by the CIA, the PRI, the DEA, and the INS."[88] El Gran Mojado is the champion, Supernafta his comic-book challenger, and their fight is announced by *Rocky*'s theme song. If Supernafta gives a speech about progress and "money go[ing] around," Arcangel / El Gran Mojado tells the audience, in a Gómez-Peña-pastiched poem, that there is neither past nor future, archaic and modern, First World and Other Worlds, but only never-ending change of one into another. "We are not the world" echoes the battle cry of antiglobalization demonstrators, yet, he implies, we are changing the world so we can make it ours against and above whatever freezes it into exploitative antagonisms, rubrics, and maps.

After each contender morphs into various martial heroes and weapons successively, the superchamps end up destroying one another, however. So it bears asking, is North-South a correlation or a disjunction? What makes it more than a relapse into Cold War schizophrenia? Are we still hostages of those land-, culture-, and policy-locked bodies Gómez-Peña wants us to morph out of? The discouraging showdown notwithstanding, the grand finale also prefaces a new beginning, with the Chinese-American immigrant Bobby stepping in to pick up the torch. He is skinny and yet somehow also an "Atlas." He holds the body of the world and is one with it as the nomadic orange's "lines"—the globe's tropics—"ri[p] through his palms" and become bodily and cosmic "connections" at once. This may well be what Yamashita wants us to come away with by reincarnating Arcangel as Bobby in the last pages of *Tropic of Orange:* the image of a many-faceted world body and of our bodies in it, with the "invisible bungy cords" pulling us all, friend and foe, kin and "alien," toward one another.[89]

DeLillo's Body Art: Cosmetics and Cosmoderns

It is about who we are when we are not rehearsing who we are.
—DON DELILLO, *The Body Artist*

Bobby, Arcangel, Manzanar, and Gómez-Peña before them; *Brazil*'s Tristão and Isabel; *Underworld*'s Lenny Bruce, André Petrescu, the pie-throwing, urban ambusher of *Cosmopolis,* and, in DeLillo's 2007 novel *Falling Man,* the "Falling Man" himself, re-posing all over New York in the tragic pose of the 9/11 victim immortalized by the Richard Drew photograph: these are bodies that morph into other bodies of flesh and culture concurrently reproducing and, DeLillo writes of *The Body Artist*'s Lauren Hartke, taunting "rueful reproduction."[90]

Lauren, the "body artist," is Klara's successor and, like her, "unrepeatingly" repetitive.[91] Earlier, I offered Spanish filmmaker Robles, Lauren's dead husband, as an example of containment of artistic discontent. Robles's first movies, reviewers claimed, paint "landscapes of estrangement" and other "alien places" where "characters are forced toward life-defining moments" (29). But since life in a mass-reproduction and mass-consumption society is substantially "defined" by a repetitive temporality at loggerheads with such a-serial instances, "his subsequent movies failed commercially and were largely dismissed by critics" (29). "The answer to life" may be, as Robles declared, "the movies" (28), but, one might be tempted to add, not *his* movies; it may supervene in a cinematic flash of "estrangement" and "alienation" but, as I have suggested, not if the notions mean what they do in modernism. If they do, and this appears to be the case here, the films drawing on them are sooner or later isolated, commodified as "oddities," metabolized commercially into socially "palatable" representations, used up by circulation, and finally discarded. Sanctioned by the death of the artist himself, the death-bound, public recycling of artistic insurgency is, *The Body Artist* hints, largely built into the avant-garde's "estranged" aesthetics. In it, estrangement and alienation boil down to unmitigated separation from those strangers with whom, cosmoderns like DeLillo think, the self must connect in order to make a difference politically, aesthetically, and otherwise.

Arguably, Robles's art is self-defeating. Not so Lauren's. Still a performance of estrangement, it works, however, through and with strangers, through and with their bodies rather than apart from them. It is the stranger's body—Mr. Tuttle's—that plugs Lauren back into a world from which, after Robles's suicide, she stood disconnected, her body literally his body's "echo" (9), "ruefully" retracing its down-spiraling trajectory. Itself recursive despite its experimentalism, this course carried over into Lauren's own life and art as mechanical embodiment of the quotidian at its most repetitive and formulaic. "She tended lately," we learn, "to place herself, to insert herself into certain stories in the newspaper." "Daydream variation[s]" (14) scarcely at variance with what they purported to be "version[s]" of (20), her imaginary conversations with these stories' characters (23–24) or her desktop trips to the "dead-time" "[o]ther world" of the Finnish town of Kotka (38) were forays into the ever-returning identical and thus into the atemporal: "You separate the Sunday sections and there are endless identical lines of print with people living somewhere in the words and the strange contained reality of paper and ink seeps through the house for a week and when you look at a page and distinguish one line from another it begins to gather you into it and there are people being tortured halfway around the world, who speak another language, and you have conversations with them more or less uncontrollably until you become aware you are doing it and when you stop, seeing whatever is in front of you at the time, like half a glass of juice in your husband's hand" (19). Lauren inserted herself "between the lines" and into them, even "bec[a]me someone else, one of the people in the story" (20), but, as with Robles and other DeLillo artists before him, this becoming and the "conversations" it enables were ultimately inconsequential. They failed to establish a relation—the strangers in the papers remained strangers—and for this reason Lauren was assimilated into the media narrative, disappeared in her self-inscriptive performances instead of appearing in new, enabling postures.

Things change, however, courtesy of "Mr. Tuttle," who shows up one day unexpectedly. More than any other character in DeLillo, he is sheer embodiment and by the same token strangeness itself. Possibly autistic, the boy seems minimally communicative, and his rudimentary intellectual behavior proves highly repetitive. Seemingly "just body," he is, however, an antithesis to Nancy's corporeal immanentism, for "he exists only in relation to other references."[92] He "is not himself" in the common, psycho-rationalist sense of the phrase, and as such he stands for an "other" to our notions of "normal," "functional," and "coherent" self. As a perpetual other to himself, he steadily backs away from whatever structure of self-hood is gelling inside him, so much so that his interiority "exists" only as a place where other selves make their appearance. He effaces himself so that they show their face; he is solely in relation to them, his body a raucous "library" for words and voices "not his" (86) but theirs, not a link in a Lacanian chain of references but the very possibility of linking and referencing.[93] Purely relational, he does not engender discourse but mimics others' to the point that in and to him being is mimicry, repeating—not himself, despite what his name might connote, but others. To Lauren's consternation, he even mimics Robles's sentences and demeanor in an act of startlingly accurate if unwitting ventriloquism.

In the stranger's performance, Robles is at once himself and somebody else, but more important than the fidelity with which Mr. Tuttle "reappears" Robles is the lesson in somatic mimesis the boy teaches Lauren. This is a lesson in the humbleness of being as ethical "appearance" that does not do away with disappearance per se but, quite the contrary, is predicated on it. Disappearing does not signify melting away, though. It is a self-cleaning or self-erasure of sorts, which "scours" off the part of us that, in "resembling" too closely the images, stories, and conventions surrounding us, blocks out others' appearance on the stage of our self. Not only does this partial yet critical disembodiment clear the decks for Lauren's reembodiment performances; it is, in and of itself, serious body work: "This was her work, to disappear from all her former venues of aspect and bearing and to become a blankness, a body slate erased of every past resemblance." She cuts and bleaches her hair, exfoliates, applies rubs and "fade" creams to "depigment herself," uses "astringents" to remove all possible "residues," "dirt," and "impurities." More than "secretions" and "glandular events" of the "body cosmos" (84), these are cultural footprints. By embodying a wide spectrum of norms, expectations, and exigencies, Lauren's body has grown into a Foucauldian "microcosm of [her] culture."[94] If this growth has indeed stabilized and "rigidified" Lauren into lesser morphic ability by inscribing her body into the restrictedly performative symbolic order, what she attempts in emulating Mr. Tuttle is an artful regression past the symbolic back into the semiotic and its unbridled performativity.[95] Cutting through the crust of cultural reflexes, Lauren steps beyond the body as cosmetic, superficial, and self-referring microcosm into the body as cosmos, the body as cosmic stage where others can appear. "Closing off" the repetitive order's "outlets to [her] self," the body artist retools her self into an outlet to other selves (97).

Now hers is "body art in extremis" (103). As Mariella, another character, comments on one of Lauren's performances, "Hartke is a body artist who tries to shake off the body—hers anyway. . . . Hartke's work is not self-strutting or self-lacerating. She is acting, always in the process of becoming another or exploring some root identity. . . . Hartke's piece begins" with a woman "gesturing in the stylized manner of Noh drama, and it ends seventy-five minutes later with a naked man, emaciated and aphasic, trying desperately to tell us something." "Alter[ing] her body and voice," Lauren makes her "body jum[p] into another level," the level or the world of alterity itself. "Stripped of recognizable language and culture," her body "flies" her various subjects "out of one reality into another" no less real, "live" rather than "taped," across cultures and their boundaries of idiom, ethnos, and gender: a Japanese woman, adolescents, Pentecostal preachers, "a one-hundred-and-twenty-year-old woman sustained by yoghurt," Mr. Tuttle himself and, in his voice, Robles's Spanish intonations and masculinity, which Lauren's body impersonates so well that Mariella "can almost believe [Lauren] is equipped with male genitalia . . . [o]r she has trained her upper body to deflate and her lower body to sprout" (104–9). The "agonic" theatricality of Lauren's female body works out connections with others—men, women, and a "number of nameless states" in between—who would otherwise remain alone and unseen, "in solitary otherness" (109). The connections are not of the all-encompassing, impersonal, and impersonalizing kind, for their "agony" is "never the grand agony of stately images and sets" restaging themselves all over the world. Intimate and evocative, Lauren's "mysterious" body renders otherness "familiar and even personal" without serializing it, makes it less "solitary" by embodying it publicly and at the same time shields its mystery (109–10).

The piece Mariella refers to is called *Body Time* for a reason. "In [Mr. Tuttle]," DeLillo's critics contend, "time has slowed to a full stop."[96] In Mariella's judgment, Lauren too "clearly wanted her audience to feel time go by, viscerally, even painfully" (104). In Mr. Tuttle's and her "viscera," then in those watching her and in bodies generally, time slows down. It surely does not stop nor end. Our being "is" still in it—"You are made out of time. This is the force that tells you who you are," Lauren reflects (91–92). But in and as body, time starts measuring another temporality and, in it, other possibilities of being. In closing, I take up DeLillo's recent work once more to expand on this temporality and subsequently on cosmodernism as a cultural paradigm in late-globalization America.

EPILOGUE ⊕ POSTMODERNISM
INTO COSMODERNISM?

Time . . . is a carrier of significance, a form through which we define the
content of relations between the Self and the Other.
> —JOHANNES FABIAN, *Time and the Other:*
> *How Anthropology Makes Its Object*

Time, Achrony, and "Furtive Sameness"

Time is the only narrative that matters.
> —DON DELILLO, *The Body Artist*

. . . timeless time . . . the dominant temporality of our society . . .
> —MANUEL CASTELLS, *The Information Age,* vol. 1,
> *The Rise of the Network Society*

Manuel Castells concurs: "We are embodied time."[1] Time makes and
defines us. We tell it, but it tells us too. It measures us individually and collectively, biologically and historically. Can we ask, then, what time is it
now in U.S. culture, twenty years after the Wall went down? And can we
tell this time in and of America solely, in and of "us" alone? I will qualify
my answer to the latter question—a "no," as one might surmise—by pos-
ing the former first because it raises the issue of "now," of the present and
its cultural logic, in friction with which cosmodernism asserts itself. It is
this logic that troubles DeLillo in "The Power of History":

> You're watching a video-tape of hooded men emerging from a bank
> and they move with a certain choreographed flair, firing virtuoso
> bursts from automatic weapons, and you wonder if they are repeating
> a scene from a recent movie, the one that disappeared overnight when
> the weekend gross was flat, and the tape is played and replayed, ex-
> hausting all reality stored in its magnetic pores, and then another tape
> replaces it, a car chase through a startled suburb, and the culture con-
> tinues its drive to imitate itself endlessly—the rerun, the sequel, the

theme park, the designer outlet—because this is the means it has devised to disremember the past.

Or you're staring at the inside of a convenience store on a humdrum night in July. This is a surveillance video with a digital display that marks off the tenths of seconds. Then you see a shuffling man with a handgun enter the frame. The commonplace homicide that ensues is transformed in the image-act of your own witness. It is bare, it is real, it is live, it is taped. It is compelling, it is numbing, it is digitally micro-timed and therefore filled with incessant information. And if you view the tape often enough, it tends to transform you, to make you a passive variation of the armed robber in his warped act of consumption. It is another set of images for you to want and need and get sick of and need nonetheless, and it separates you from the reality that beats ever more softly in the diminishing world outside the tape.

Against these flashes, these lonely fleeting images, against the ritual arrangements of these serial replays, events and documents of the past have a clarity and intactness that amount to a moral burnish. A Matthew Brady photograph, a framed front page—"Men Walk on the Moon." These things represent moments of binding power. They draw people together in ways that only the most disastrous contemporary events can match.[2]

Inside its shorter and shorter cycle, repetitive culture dreams its dream of unsullied synchrony. A "fall into amnesia," culture no longer evokes but revokes.[3] It "disremembers" and disowns the past in the ever-shrinking encore present of the playback, the spin-off, and the remake, and the briefer this present, the more achronic its synchrony—the more atemporal the temporality in which mainstream American culture reruns itself. In its attempt to presentify itself, cultural egology becomes chronology, projects itself onto the time axis as a temporality, or atemporality rather, of sameness. No less egological, this chronology of sorts, one that has lost its historical sense of becoming, transformation, and differentiation, plays out as an eternal and eternally self-canceling present—Lenny Bruce's culture of "instant and quick."[4] Perpetually *in statu nascendi* and "disposed of" before its time, so to speak, this present is sheer provisionality. It never begins—is ahistorical—because, in its *fuite en avant*, it begins over and over, and for the same reason it never ends either, in time or space.

Its culture's liquid diffusion across "every wall, home, life, and mind" mimics and is spurred by liquidity itself, by cash.[5] "Money has no limits," Klara tells an interviewer in *Underworld* (76). Moreover, the World Trade Center's "twin towers," "a model of behemoth mass production, units that roll identically off the line" (377), hint not only that money reproduces itself worldwide as credit and venture finance ever more freely after 1989 but also that it reproduces, on the same scale, metastatic reproduction as *the* form of cultural production. Echoing Klara, Nick makes a similar point in "Das Kapital," the book's "Epilogue," during a chat in a bar with "old buddy Brian" while "repetitive" rock pounds in the background:

> Capital burns off the nuance in a culture. Foreign investment, global markets, corporate acquisitions, the flow of information through transnational media, the attenuating influence of money that's electronic and sex that's cyberspaced, untouched money and computer-safe sex, the convergence of consumer desire—not that people want the same things, necessarily, but that they want the same range of choices. . . .
>
> Some things fade and vane, states disintegrate, assembly lines shorten their runs and interact with lines in other countries. This is what desire seems to demand. A method of production that will custom-cater to cultural and personal needs, not to cold war ideology of massive uniformity. And the system pretends to go along, to become more supple and resourceful, less dependent on rigid categories. But even as desire tends to specialize, going silky and intimate, the force of converging markets produces an instantaneous capital that shoots across horizons at the speed of light, making for a certain furtive sameness, a planning away of particulars that affects everything from architecture to leisure time to the way people eat and sleep and dream. (785–86)

The Cold War and its strategically repetitious planning, Fordist or socialist, may lie behind us, but market-driven instantaneousness culture is "planning away" the world's "particulars" with escalating fury. This culture feeds "nuance" into an historically unrivaled dedifferentiation machine, a "system of connections in which," *Underworld* specifies, "you can't tell the difference between one thing and another, between one soup can and a car bomb, because they are made by the same people in the same way and ultimately refer to the same thing" (446). Bronzini, Nick's former teacher, understands full well that this time's hysterical present cannot be a stage of self-other co-presence, that time's "presentist" foundering into achrony and the same-becoming of particulars go hand in hand to enhance the world's self-referring egological structure. This is why he would like to "stop everything for half a second, atomic clocks, body clocks, the microworld in which physicists search for time" (234). Against the ambivalent "heroism" of the momentousness so intimately tied into the American cult of the serializing "do-it-now," "fuck-the-past" (377), Bronzini wants, like Klara, to "rewind life, give us all a chance to do it over" (234). In the same vein, DeLillo notes in his 2001 essay "In the Ruins of the Future," the antiglobalization protesters of Genoa, Prague, Seattle, and, in *Cosmopolis,* New York City hope "to decelerate the global momentum" so as to write another narrative of the contemporary, in which instants and instances of "particular" styles, codes, and rituals can be rescued and with them our cultural ecology. This "unhurried" historical narrative or, as DeLillo puts it, "counter-narrative"[6] sets out to preserve the uniqueness of life past and present in a planetary "landscape of consumer-robots and social instability, with the chance of self-determination probably diminishing for most people in most countries."[7]

This is not nostalgia. The novelist does not retreat into a prior authenticity where the contemporary can be disavowed. In fact, *Underworld* dismisses this "pornography of nostalgia" (320) openly as much as "In the Ruins of the Future" condemns the murderous "narrative" whereby, in DeLillo's view, the 9/11 terrorists sought to rescind the present and thus push us "back in time."[8] This narrative essentially defies technology-propelled "modernity," purporting not only to "slow things down, even things out, hold off the white-hot future" (34) but to "bring back the past"[9] by walking the fine line between two philosophies of time. Underlain by what on first blush seem incompatible values, they are similarly globalistic in their agendas, and, although in different ways, they both trade on the past. On one side, the hijackers', the past is the ideal antimodern bulwark of the "global theocratic state, unbounded and floating and so obsolete it must depend on suicidal fervor to gain its aims." On the other, analogously "totalistic" if not outright totalitarian, lie the temporal outlook and practices of increasingly digitalized "capital markets" that "ha[ve] dominated and shaped global consciousness" in the Cold War's aftermath. One is a throwback to pastness. Its present is a gaunt memorial to the bygone; its fantasy, that time's total recall. The other, what with the 1990s' "dramatic climb of the Dow and the speed of the Internet," calls on "us all to live permanently in the future, in the utopian glow of cyber-capital, because there is no memory there and this is where markets are uncontrolled and investment potential has no limit." Encrypted, stored, and moved digitally, capital "summons" us into a particular modality of time and culture or, better still, of time *as* culture. This is the post–Cold War culture of, and in, "accelerated time," as DeLillo describes it in an interview right after the release of *Cosmopolis*,[10] a culture that produces the future by reproducing the present into this present's instantly passé effigies.[11]

Future and Futures: The Digital Imperative

> Basically, we've bet the farm on the digital imperative.
> —BRUCE STERLING, *Unstable Networks*

In culture and finance alike, we noticed apropos of *Cosmopolis*, the digital is the repetitive itself, thus at the center of an endogenous chronoculture where production is reproduction, the present self-re-presenting, and the future a futures chart, that is, another if more distant self-re-presentation of this present. To Packer, the future, in the stock exchange sense of chartable commodity, and time itself ultimately open up an interval where the increasingly formalized, "purer" (77) model, scheme, or theory that has worked out before needs must pan out again later. "Destroy the past, make the future," his "chief of theory" Vija Kinski goads him (93), and Packer obliges. Noteworthy too, though, is that the future into which fast-forward culture and financial transactions drag us is presumed to bear out the present about to pass, restaging it and thus consecrating both past and future as selfsameness domains, "disremembering" history's living complexity in its very reenactment while leaving little room in the future's computer-generated picture for things that do not reprise what has been. Working from equivalences and homologies, the concept, the cogito, the mathematical projection recover themselves in the symmetry of the past and the future, with the present a flickering interlude of consumption. If Lauren "want[s] to create her future, not to enter a state already shaped to her outline,"[12] Packer seeks to work out an outline the future will fit into. To him, a true future sanctions the truth of its past. This future is predictable or, as Bertrand de Jouvenel would say, a "conjectural" affair, even though in it time as temporal scene of becoming and difference cancels itself out and so does not happen because it already has. In a reference to Jouvenel's "futuribles," "futures that can be *made* to happen," Toulmin rightly objects in his own *Cosmopolis* that "[a] well formulated approach to the future—a realistic range of available futuribles, within reasonable horizons of expectations—does not depend on finding ways to quantify and extrapolate current trends[.] "[T]hat," he adds, "we may leave to enthusiastic weather forecasters, stock exchange chartists, or econometrists. Rather, the questions are, 'What intellectual *posture* should we adopt in confronting the future? What eye can we develop for significant aspects of the years ahead? And what capacity do we have to change our ideas about the available futures?'"[13]

This is, I submit, the crux of the problem in DeLillo's cosmopolis as much as in ours: How should we think about the future, about time broadly? More specifically: *How willing are "we" to entertain a nonteleological notion of a time that does not merely verify our notions and self-perceptions?* DeLillo stresses that not even a hardcore "chartist" like Packer, who has amassed a fortune by pleonastically (pre-)telling ("predicting") the future of currency markets as their retold past, is to be trusted with such extrapolations. In fact, DeLillo lets on, the problem is extrapolation itself, the chart, the model made obsolete by stocks' unchartable, futural hysteria. The diagram, the computerized venture, and the venturesome rationality behind them are, he implies, not just financial procedures and instruments. They are themselves "postures," ideologies of time and culture in which a certain temporality is made "available" to us. But do we really want to avail ourselves of it?

"A high point of that highly problematic intersection of money, time, and space as interlocking elements of social power," virtually unrepresentable market "volatility"[14]—the turn-of-the-millennium pecuniary sublime—mounts a challenge indeed capital to Packer's spreadsheets, forcing them to play catch-up with a market always ahead of the curve, fluid, and hard to stabilize into a representation. Superficially influenced by our will to represent, to bring them into being by tracing them into the future's present-to-be and thus presentifying them in the future, currencies and the jittery yen in particular dodge prognosis. Granted, they appear to be representable, subject to theories and forecasts, yet they do so only in the deceptively "extrapolating," future anterior modality as developments that *will have taken place,* will have "charted" because we have already drawn up their charts and projections. Worsening the postmodern time-space "condition" David Harvey talks about, late globalization's "interaction between technology and capital" in *Cosmopolis* (23) speeds up the "superannuation" of money, values, and images and more broadly "hurries" the world into a representational cycle that short-circuits time altogether. Intriguingly enough, on his stretch limo's monitors Packer sees himself doing things he is only about to carry out and later previews his own death on his digital watch, which does not show time anymore but his owner's dead body. Coterminous and coterminal, Packer's death and the death of time reinforce one another as a "conflation of all worlds," where "all possible states become present at once" only to toll the death knell of the present and presence, of the time in which being can present itself (204–5). The collapse of the past-present-future sequence into the one-dimensional future; the copycat futurality of all time and times, parallel to the concentration of all places and moments in one point of fallacious immutability; the barely moving Lincoln: this is the premise and promise, the means and the end, in all senses, of Packer's self-converging, "conjectural" logic of temporality.

Critics from Baudrillard and Ben Agger to George Marcus and Meric Gertler have focused primarily on the tempo-spatial "construction of capital" through high-speed, supralocal, and, as Caitlin Zaloom calls it, post-"face-to-face" electronic futures trading.[15] Lately, artists and philosophers have attended to the opposite, namely, the temporal and "spatial implications of money," as Giddens writes in a gloss to Simmel's *The Philosophy of Money*.[16] Under the disembodying and "disembedding"[17] pressure of Kinski's "free market system" (79), time, they have noticed, is made and remade by cash. It used to be the other way around: time was money because it made money. In earlier modernity, well-defined physical location and time were prerequisites of labor as process, hence also of profit. In the new millennium, Kinski "theorizes," "money makes time" (79), or unmakes it, rather. A "corporate asset now" (79), *time's time is up*. Time as we know it has come to an end, for the ouroboric rite of reproduction, investment, profit-taking, and digital trading has flattened time's cultural-historical multidimensionality into a vacuous coevalness without remainder. The past, Kinski briefs Packer, "is disappearing" because, if "all doubt rises from past experience," computer networking and charting software dispose not only of "doubt" but also of human memory. We do not know the past any more (86). All we know, or think we do, is the future, the *future anterior* our computers retrieve for us. Nor is the present better off. "Harder to find" (79), it "leaks," implodes, goes to waste in the "cultural drama" of "instant obsolescence,"[18] and is otherwise "being sucked out of the world to make way for the future of uncontrolled markets and huge investment potential" (79). This is, after all, what the presentified past and the already passed present are: spectral potentialities still to "express" themselves (74), "latent" (63) "pattern[s] that wan[t] to be seen" (86), and which we do see, later, when the potential is actualized and the present becomes, for a fraction of a second, present in its digitally conjured-up representation.

"Let us make this potentiality an actuality! Let this future come!" If not in so many words, this is Kinski's "digital imperative" (24). Its postethical "zero-oneness" now "define[s]," in her account, "every planet's living billions, . . . the heave of the biosphere. Our bodies and oceans, . . . knowable and whole" (24). This fantasy of "knowability" and wholeness, of knowledge as wholeness—as epistemological globalization—betrays the same totalist gambit, the drive to oneness recognizable in the recalibration of all time and times to market time. According to Packer's "theorist," nothing takes place outside this temporality because "there is no outside anymore"—"The market culture is total"—and so what occurs in actuality recurs, is a recurrence. Whatever is is "traded" (90) on this market and so instantly traded *for* pre-dictions, redundancies, and other forms under which the same returns. In the sole futural dimension possible in this chronototality, time is "always a wholeness, a sameness. We are all tall and happy there" (91). Resulting from time's "unification" on a "world scale," "world market" time is, as Guy Debord observed, "time-as-commodity" because, first, it is a time itself commodified, "devalued," and dehistoricized into the pseudoduration of "echangeability" in which all segments are quantitatively and qualitatively equivalent,[19] and second, because what is produced in this temporality perforce extends the realm of sameness by reproducing the world—past or present, nearby or remote, familiar or alien—into preexistent stylistic and thematic repertoires.

This time standardizes the many into one while this standardization atemporalizes, reduces all temporalities to one, the time of oneness and of the one's arrogant solitude. In *Underworld* already, the microsystems (825) that integrate us all into circuits of representation and desire crisscrossing within the same macrosystem of cultural reproduction bypass time and space, first in cyberspace, then in "real" space to the point that "[t]here is no space or time" in either. "Hyperlinking" (825) and the digital generally cut up and contract time ("microtime" it) to replicate it more easily. As we saw earlier, intrinsically viral, digitalization is geared to self-reduplication and self-distribution, "mix[ing] in whole cultures and geographies and cross-references" (545) and rerunning them "to the ends of the earth" "until everyone on the planet ha[s] seen [them]," and then all over again until they "pres[s] time flat" (232–33). The pixels, the zeroes and the ones, the germs, viruses, and alpha particles make up an infinitesimal code that rewrites discrepantly timed world cultures into a cybernetic coextensiveness where identity in time translates into identity of essence. By the same token, this identity of essence threatens historical time in its essence. The temporal flattening of ontology—of what "is"—in turn streamlines time into an interval where, under the crust of novelty, only identicalness can be.

Time and Its Others, History before Time:
The Cosmodern Imperative

> Solitude is an absence of time.
> —EMMANUEL LEVINAS, *Time and the Other*

The cookie-cutter culture of repetitiveness is *chronophagic*. It abridges and ultimately "consumes" time, as "The Power of History" concludes.[20] Vice versa, the time of repetition is *culturophagic*. It eats, *Underworld* discloses, into "particular" cultural formations to make time for the "benign totalitarianism" in which you "becom[e] indistinguishable from your neighbor" and "everybody's the same" (368). The digital imperative issues a stern call to selfsameness, but, as *Underworld*, *The Body Artist*, *Cosmopolis*, and other texts discussed in *Cosmodernism* evince, the self-identical is just the antinomy of the neighborly. Counterintuitive as it may sound—certainly not to thinkers like Levinas—neighborhood rests on distinctiveness. Any neighborhood and any community's building block, with-ness presupposes an other, the distinguishable and the distinct. DeLillo puts it plainly in the paragraphs reproduced in this epilogue's opening: the a-serial, the unrepeated, and the dissimilar "draw people together." Historically asynchronous and culturally asymmetric, discrepancies possess "binding power." They bind us together during and by their inconsonant times, in short—and fundamentally—give us time. As Scott Lash comments on Derrida's *Given Time*, difference "gives being and gives time."[21] It is in the generous horizon of "differential" time that we *can be*, in the "thick," fruitfully "out-of-synch" temporality whose unscripted and uneven effulgence we share with others. And we *are* as long as we do the "neighborly thing to do," the sharing. Packer does not, so he is not. Nor are the other individualists, solipsists, and egotists we have met in *Cosmodernism*. Quite literally, they do not have time for it. Frantically recurrent and autoreferencing, their time is one and the same, a time of sameness and thus of solitude, spent in forty-eight-room apartments or in cork-lined ("prousted") limos. In their "solitarist"[22] time, even when they are around others—relatives, lovers, business partners—they are still entrenched "self-totalities" (191) honing into perfection the pitiful art of "how to be alone together" (185).

Over against late-global world's Packers and their "compact"-autarchic maneuverings of time and culture, cosmodernism urges us to be together together, as it were. It holds out the ethical imperative of togetherness.

This imperative is ethical twice. First, it recognizes in the temporal continuum not only the self but also what *The Body Artist* views as "other reaches of being, other time-lives" (92). The cosmoderns acknowledge, in fact, that the relation between self and other predates any time making, any communal saga or foundational story, any cultural narrative, and any narrative for that matter. To clarify, it may help to remember that in the 1947 essay *Le temps et l'autre* Levinas contends that the two elements in his title are interdependent. They are so because death, as a "future of the event," is "not yet time. In order for this future, which is nobody's and which a human being cannot assume, to become an element of time," he explains, "it must also enter into relationship with the present." "What is," the philosopher wonders, "the tie between two instants that have between them the whole interval, the whole abyss, that separates the present and death, this margin at once both insignificant and infinite, where there is always room enough for hope?" It is, he answers, "certainly not a relationship of pure contiguity, which would transform time into space, but neither is it the élan of dynamism and duration, since for the present this power to be beyond itself and to encroach upon the future seems to me precisely excluded by the very mystery of death. Relationship with the future, the presence of the future in the present, seems all the same accomplished in the face-to-face with the Other. The situation of the face-to-face would be the very accomplishment of time; the encroachment of the present on the future is not the feat of the subject alone, but the intersubjective relationship." Therefore, "the condition of time" rests on "the relationship between humans, or in history."[23] What makes time possible is history—history as a stage on which self and other enact their ethical relatedness.

Could we say, then, that history comes before time? I suspect we could, in the sense that the face-to-face, the ethical itself, antedates *and* sets off temporality, and so we "have got time"—for ourselves, for those close to us, and for the world —because time has been given us during this confrontation, in an "intersubjective" transaction prior to any egology and ontology of being. Consequently, as we learn from DeLillo and as Levinas corroborates in *Totality and Infinity,* "[S]olitude is the absence of time," a "tragedy" that may not follow immediately or conspicuously from not being with an other but that surely is an upshot of the other's absence.[24] Going back, at last, to the first question I posed at the outset of these closing considerations, the invitation the cosmoderns extend us is to think of American culture overall and post-1989 U.S. culture in particular as a *gift of an other* in the full, ethically engaging amphibology of the genitive: this time is the gift to "us" from an other while presenting us with this other as a gift. In the irreducibility of the giver, the temporal gift of cosmodern authenticity—the time in which the American arts and culture develop *their own* individuality relationally—is both initiated and preserved. "[D]eclin[ing], as Levinas specifies across his work, "the concept and withstand[ing] totalization," the giver "has its own time" that is "not absorbed into the universal time."[25] It is not that others such as Alda's Chinese friend bestow on us *their* time; they do not "chrono-colonize" us. They only make time our own. More exactly, they make it available to us during and through our dealings with them. With the cosmoderns, we can then safely assume, today more than ever in American and world history, that the only time there is, hence the only time when we can be, where we can figure out who we are and build a culture in the process, is the time of self-other interaction. A temporalization of mutuality, this time *determines culture as a deeply transactional, ethical project.*

Second, let us not lose sight, however, of what "project" means, more to the point, of why this determination is not an unequivocal ascertainment but rather a morally driven ascription of meaning—not a strict assessment of where American culture stands now but a suggestion that this is where it may and *should* go. *The cosmoderns project a world and charge us with their projection.* As we have seen repeatedly and as DeLillo helps us see again, cosmodernism is not necessarily the cultural model late globalization is fostering in the United States and elsewhere, or not the reigning one by a long shot. And yet many cosmodern writers and critics "bet the farm" on it. Ethically speaking, they do not have much of a choice once they feel, as they consistently and characteristically do, the "moral burnish" of other times and traces of style, form, and worldliness. Stemming from this feeling, from this recognition of worldly otherness in the biography of America and the makeup of Americana, is a cosmodern concept of discourse fundamentally, self-consciously, and overtly indebted to other temporalities and practices of culture. If time is indeed distributed to our dreams, projections, and stories in the self-other give-and-take—if we are, as Bronzini assures us, "way stations for the distribution of time"[26]—then, cosmodernism stipulates, our narratives and fantasies must afford temporal and cultural redistributions, representations, codifications, and inscriptions recognizant of this recognition itself. Kinski makes no bones about it: Packer's egological time has no future because future—that is, Packer's approach to it—"always fails."[27] Therefore, we need, she concedes, a "new theory of time."[28]

We need, our cosmoderns add, not just a theory, and certainly not one in Kinski and Packer's "conjectural," digital sense. What we also need is a new practice of time, a whole other way of imagining and doing culture capable of owning up to the kind of indebtedness that inside and outside post-1989 America becomes deeper and better marked. As Soja contends in a commentary on Buber's 1957 essay "Distance and Relation," this capacity derives from "a will to relate, a necessary impulsion to overcome detachment," for this is "the only means whereby we can confirm our existence in the world," thus "overcom[ing] meaningless and establish[ing] identity." "Human consciousness" may begin with separation from others, in space as well as in time.[29] But, for one thing, the critic himself points out that consciousness achieves full humanness by overcoming that distance. For another, provided we buy into this originary demarcation from others in the first place—a hypothesis historians start querying well before Martin Bernal's *Black Athena* (1987–2006)—separation is separation from. As such, it already postulates others, is a *protorelational form of with-ness.*

Often celebratory of what it surveys, Soja's 1980s "postmodern geography" proves on closer inspection unevenly receptive to what writers like DeLillo were intimating around that time, namely, to the hardening of relatedness old and new, original and recently forged, into an achronic, dehistoricizing, and fast globalizing temporal-cultural dimension in which those others were being expunged. One might ask, then, How well prepared is—should I say with Brian McHale, *was?*—postmodernism to handle a globalizing crisis that has meanwhile become the very crisis of globalization? I have raised the question, rather tangentially, in my 2001 book *Rewriting* and more straightforwardly four years later in its sequel, *Memorious Discourse,* particularly in the closing chapter on postmodern intertextuality and the network society.[30] What was insufficiently clear to me then and what I think I see better now can be formulated in a series of eight concluding propositions, attending reasonings, and outright provocations as follows:

The Cosmodern Turn

> You are contemporary if you turn your eye not to your time's
> clarity but to its obscure side.
> —GIORGIO AGAMBEN, *What Is the Contemporary?*

> Certainly, I know less about postmodernism today than I did thirty
> years ago, when I began to write about it. This may be because
> postmodernism has changed, I have changed, the world has
> changed.
> —IHAB HASSAN, "From Postmodernism to Postmodernity:
> The Local/Global Context"

> We have to conceive of the postmodern era in global terms.
> —ULRICH BECK, *What Is Globalization?*

(1) *Because, on the one hand, the postmodern does not make a clean break
with the modern and, on the other, the postmodern in "postmodernism,"
"postmodernization," and "postmodernity" is basically the same, postmodernism cannot offer a solution to this crisis.* With Linda Hutcheon, Cornis-
Pope, Paul Maltby, and others, I have argued for a critical, "dissenting,"
and "resistant" postmodernism. There are indeed postmodern authors,
works, and styles capable of talking back to "late capitalist" ideology, not
to mention that capitalism does not now seem what it was back in Ernest
Mandel's and Fredric Jameson's 1970s and early 1980s, nor are all societies
in which postmodernism has flourished market economies. But even a
comprehensive survey of postmodern literatures and cultures like Bertens
and Fokkema's *International Postmodernism*, otherwise so careful to account for regional and national "postmodernisms," deals with non-Western phenomena under the heading "The Reception and Processing of
Postmodernism."[31] The title says it all: much as certain varieties of postmodernism do enable a "critique" of late globalization, this critique is un-
dercut by postmodernism's historical "hubris"—by postmodernism's
globalizing thrust. What the title implies, and what I want to reinforce
here, is that Tokyo's postmodern architecture or Bulgarian theory of the
"post-paranoid condition"[32] represents, to a degree that after resounding
interventions by Jameson, Stuart Hall, and others, no scholar can dismiss
offhand, the outcome of the global "reception" and "processing" of a cultural model largely Western, and especially American, in its origin and expansionist in its history.[33] It is noteworthy that both aesthetically oriented,
traditional liberals like Ihab Hassan and committed leftists such as Spivak

and Ziauddin Sardar highlight the paradox that the fragment-, difference-, and indeterminacy-celebrating postmodern distrust of grand narratives and systems has been behind a postmodern*ism* that has spread worldwide not only as an epistemological-literary school of self-inquiring, antitotal-ist, and delegitimating suspicion but also as the all-embracing, cultural-economic and hypertechnological postmodern*ity* termed, by some, glob-alization.[34] "[T]he discourse of postmodernism," Spivak states perhaps too bluntly, can "suggest that the *cultural* (not merely) the economic logic of microelectronic capitalism is universal, that the *cultural* logic that holds for London and Paris and Liverpool and Nevada City also holds for Hong Kong or Bankura or Beirut."[35] I doubt postmodernity is globalization's more befitting name, and I think lumping the two together Jameson-style is overly reductive.[36] Nor do I believe that globalization and universaliza-tion—of the West, that is—are synonymous, much as I hesitate to seize on postmodernism as "the new imperialism of Western culture."[37] Nonethe-less, despite recurrent references to otherness, marginality, and the like as axial categories of postmodern poetics, politics, and ethics,[38] there is something to be said about the "generalization" of postmodernism—the postmodernization of the non-Western world—not only as textual termi-nology and methodology but also as "manipulation of geopolitical or-der."[39] Postcolonial critics in particular have pinpointed the "classic irony"—a subset of the foregoing paradox—that has postmodernism ul-timately *universalize* a certain stress on or approach to alterity and thus a whole philosophy of being, meaning, and culture, no matter how antiuni-versalist and emancipating this philosophy deems itself. That is, the critics insist, a "positional" politics of postmodern interpretation is here in play: recentering this culturally-historically circumscribed philosophy on the "other" means one thing in Paris and another in Beirut. In effect, "when generalized from one context to another, hybridity," "otherness," and "the subaltern" may not only "los[e] their political significance,"[40] but may also be put through ratiocinations liable to render the postmodern "attemp[t] to preserve the infinity or unapproachability of the other" a continuation of the "modernist work [of] reduc[ing] the other to a theme."[41]

Declarations of intent notwithstanding, the postmoderns have often failed to heed this distinction. This is why their realization that "we need to cultivate a keener, livelier, more dialogical sense of ourselves in relation to diverse cultures, diverse natures, the whole universe itself"[42] has not yielded commensurate cultural work. The result has been that what Hutcheon describes as the "internationalizing [of] postmodernism" has come to stand not so much for a "challenge [to] the dominance" of the West and the "U.S. in the domains of both theory and practice"[43] and thus possibly for "postwesternization"[44] as for the internationalization of "white" and North Atlantic postmodernism. Fair or not, the prevailing perception of postmodernism's globalization lays emphasis on the latter term, making postmodernism preponderantly a globalization issue, an aspect of the global crisis rather than its solution culturally, philosophically, or otherwise.

(2) *Postmodernism is not an egology structurally, in its core principles. Its "original guilt" is not so much paradigmatic as it is historical.* Unlike cosmopolitanism, postmodern universalism is not intrinsic but acquired. Yet, this time *not* unlike cosmopolitanism, postmodernism risks becoming, and some believe it has become, egological in its geopolitical unfolding insofar as this dissemination perpetuates the colonizing impetus of cultural-aesthetic metropolitan modernism and of modernity broadly. There are two "conflicting and interdependent modernities," as Calinescu has observed. One is "rationalist, competitive, technological"; the other, "culturally critical and self-critical, bent on demystifying the basic values of the first."[45] Modernity number one lives on in the kind of standardizing globalization with which neither postmodernism as an aesthetics nor postmodernity as epoch or zeitgeist seeks to be linked with, and yet, as we have seen, both have been. Modernity number two bleeds into a range of postmodern discourses of "otherness" from "heterological" epistemology to self-reflective metafiction to performance- and hybridity-grounded theories of subjectivity to sexual politics, all vehemently opposed to globalist projects of totalization and homogenization and yet viewed, once again, with a great deal of skepticism by those whose communities bear the brunt of globalizing developments.[46] So, if globalization signifies, as it does in some quarters, the "globalising of modernity" and, further, if we understand, as Habermas, Giddens, Wallerstein, Charles Taylor, and others do, modernity itself as a "Western project,"[47] then, as the famous argument goes, neither aesthetic-epistemic postmodernism nor historical postmodernity has thus far made a persuasive case that their "post" and *post*-colonialism's are the same.[48] Put differently: at loggerheads with its own philosophical and political agenda—and, unquestionably, in some situations more than in others—postmodernism carries on modernity's utmost egological project, Western colonialism. As one of postmodernism's most vituperative detractors contends, "While postmodernism is a legitimate

protest against the excesses of suffocating modernity, instrumental rationality and authoritarian traditionalism, it has itself become a universal ideology that kills everything that gives meaning and depth to the lives of nonwestern individuals and societies."[49] Thus, postmodernism only opens another chapter in the narrative it sought to "deconstruct." Or, worse, it designates, alongside postcolonialism, an "*effec[t] that reflec[s] or trace[s]* the expansion of the world market and the passage of the form of sovereignty," hence "point[ing]," as Hardt and Negri claim, "toward Empire."[50] Either way, "postmodernization" is "modernization" by other means—hypermodern à la Gilles Lipovetsky perhaps, and thus hypertroubling, what with "hyper-dedifferentiation" kicking into high gear.[51]

Once more, this may not be and, for the record, I do not think this is what the postmodern "is" *ab ovo* or purports to be. But if this is something it nevertheless ends up being, then, its proclamations to the contrary aside, the relational or, as Hassan says with a wink at Bakhtin, the "dialogical" refounding of identity and culture cannot be the postmodern's "*spiritual project*."[52] Alternatively, this can be postmodernism's and, in a vaster perspective, postmodernity's "project" in the sense that they may take it on, but it is not certain at all that either can complete it. The more reasonable thing to do at this juncture in American and world cultural history would be to give the postmoderns credit for laying the groundwork, setting the basic agenda, and developing, in the interval between the late 1960s and the late 1980s, the terminologies and methodologies for a project whose completion by and large lies beyond the postmodern's purview.

(3). *If modernity, principally in its Euro-American form and, inside this form, in the leading aesthetic-philosophical embodiments, is and views itself as an expanding, abstract, and atemporal rationality, postmodernity and, within it, postmodern culture and "theory" indicate an* inchoate, *historicizing move toward relationality.* Granted, modernity and modernism are far from monolithic; this shift goes back to works and incidents too well known to be rehearsed here. But what I want to punctuate is, first, modernity's "hegemonic" logos and the "cultural dominant" reflecting it and, second, the postmodern as a challenge to this reigning modern strain. In U.S. prose, it is late moderns like Nabokov and his immediate successors, the early metafictionists of John Barth's generation, who flung down the gauntlet initially. Similarly defying positions are taken up in theory and the humanities with poststructuralism, to gain momentum with "identity studies" a bit later. This is a time of profound and wide-ranging transformations that promise to cure modernity of its genetic "allergy." It is also a time of indecision and half-steps. Modern America opens up and falls back on itself and on an insular perception of the American self, simultaneously discovering "the world of others" and pulling back from it. Comparable to the mutations affecting the scholarly imaginary around the same time, the relational shift under way in the U.S. literary-theoretical postmodernism of the 1970s and early 1980s is partial and conflicted, held in check by the postmoderns' ongoing cultural-epistemological allegiance to the nation-state model and to its ethnolinguistic and geopolitical "supracategory," Western tradition. Postmodernism's is a burgeoning with-world, but, generally speaking, this world is still culturocentric. I have repeatedly rebutted the resilient orthodoxy regarding postmodernism's "ahistoricity," so I will not do it again here.[53] I will only say that the postmodern rehistoricizing of representation through recycling of past stories and histories usually obtains intranationally and intraculturally. The scope of the thematic and intertextual "redistribution" of time as times and site for the recovery of history as histories and of those in them—"us" but also others unlike "us"—is mainly if not exclusively the nation and its immediate environs. Thus, echoing the Cold War's disjunctive and antagonist externalization of others in a "not-us, not-here" alter-geography, postmodernism bears limited with-ness.

Following Johannes Fabian, critics like Rey Chow fault explicitly the poststructuralists and implicitly the postmoderns for an approach to differential temporalities ("allochronies") that de facto suspends the "coevalness" in which "others" can coexist with "us."[54] Ultimately, I may subscribe to this conclusion, but, in fairness to the postmodern arts, at least, I would like to give first credit where credit is due. That is, where modernism's ideal is, and often unfolds in, absolute synchronicity—the sole time in which the world can be timed and integrated as globe—postmodernism marks the allusive and jocular return to the diachronic as relation with other times and their others. A cross-section through the nation's cultural memory, this relation is vertical, connecting as it does with other moments, feelings, and representations mostly *inside* the same tradition and its tradition of sameness. If, as Charles Jencks has argued, postmodernism "fuses" the heterogeneous temporalities its self-advertised pluralistic eclecticism calls forth, one should perhaps ask about which fuses with what and where the center of the ensuing "time fusion" might lie.[55] To the extent the postmoderns have not confronted such questions adequately, they still operate within the framework of modern egology.

(4) *Beginning with the late 1980s, the relational shift picks up speed, expands, and combines with cognate developments in multiculturalism, ethnic and new immigrant literatures, and other sectors and discourses of American culture to set in train a more radical, cosmodern turn. Roughly, this turn is to U.S. and, in some cases, world culture what the Wall's fall is to post–World War II history.* I should add, the analogy goes only so far. As I have underscored, the paradigm to which this turn gives birth, cosmodernism, proves both reflective and critical of late globalization's highly networked environment—this is, I have also said, cosmodernism's "double-bind." In keeping with post-1989, worldwide amplifying and densification of human relations, cosmodernism projects postmodernism's newly found historical relationality horizontally across national and regional traditions and their unsynchronized temporalities. Thus, cosmodernism starts replacing postmodernism's conceptual unit, the nation-state, with an ever more worlded world.

Postmodern intertextuality drove home a point made previously by Kenneth Burke, yet it did so with a force Burke did not anticipate. " 'Reality,' " Burke says,

> could not exist for us, were it not for our profound and inveterate involvement in symbol systems. Our presence in a room is immediate, but the room's relation to our country as a nation, and beyond that, to international relations and cosmic relations, dissolves into a web of ideas and images that reach through our senses only insofar as the symbol systems that report on them are heard or seen. To mistake this vast tangle of ideas for immediate experience is much more fallacious than to accept a dream as an immediate experience. For a dream really is an immediate experience, but the information that we receive about today's events throughout the world most decidedly is *not*.[56]

Despite exceptions such as the "Oriental" forays of Barth's "Dunyazadiad" or, in poetry, the Beats, American postmodern intertexts generally roam the room of the nation or of the Western family of nations. In essence, this room and the systems postmodernism plugs us into are coextensive; diachronically and synchronically, this is the postmodern space of Burkean immediacy. With cosmodernism, however, this horizon enlarges dramatically to incorporate the formerly less immediate and less contingent ("out there") worldly "web of ideas and images." This is a transnational rather than postnational process. It leaves the nation behind altogether neither physically nor analytically but works it into broader, "international" and "cosmic" assemblages. Along these lines—the lines of the cosmodern imaginary itself—cosmodernism articulates and in turn can be represented critically as a vision of cross-traditional and polycentric intertextuality and interculturality that builds on the typically yet largely theoretical, fantastical, or mystical-Kabbalistic idea of "world" ("Babel") library or "arena."[57]

(5) *The cosmodern vision declines to be another egological extrapolation of U.S./Western nuclei of values, ideologies, and intertextual repertoires. Mindful of the culturocentric risks historically involved in such macro-systemic undertakings, cosmodernism is an imaginary of worlded aesthetic relations as much as it is one of ethical relatedness.* Not only is the cosmodern problematic of otherness more authentically—heterologically—"other," vaster, more capacious ethnically, racially, or religiously, and not only is it more extensively explored than in postmodernism; not only are "others" becoming the master theme of the American literature of the past twenty years, but this "theme" is also ethically explored. This actually means that the other's presence in cosmodern discourse is no longer just a matter of "theme," and hence of thematization, of rational reduction. The other's presence founds, organizes, and orients cosmodern representation rather than merely supplying it with the subject *du jour.*

"Relational"[58] writing and reading in postmodernism are writing "about" and reading "for" the otherness theme textualized or, better still, intertextualized through a range of formal devices from ironic allusiveness, bookishness, and bricolage to "ludic" self-referentiality and Chinese-boxes-style metalanguage. These "forms" are not exclusively postmodern but become mainstream and emblematic in postmodernism. A subset of postmodern relationality, intertextuality is the postmodern writing technique or form of thematizing other works and others generally, as well as a method of interpreting this kind of writing. Cosmodernism does follow in postmodernism's footsteps thematically and formally, as we have noticed throughout. Yet the cosmodern authors grow increasingly uncomfortable with an approach that, on an important level, continues to do the bidding of an older worldview that conceptualizes and thus further "others" and externalizes alterity qua "theme" and "form." As we have learned, cosmodernism seeks to engage with otherness beyond the thematic and the formal, ethically. Now, if this is *the* cosmodern benchmark, then not all works billed as cosmodern may make the cut while works that usually come under other rubrics may, depending on how one reads them. As with the epistemic reshufflings of the 1980s, so with the with-ness-revolving structure grabbing hold of the American literary-cultural imaginary more and more markedly after 1989: this structure arises, as my prologue warned, across a series of authors not all of them, and certainly not all of them at the same time, cosmodern.

(6) *Cosmodernism is a cross-canonical and "soft" epochality.* In other words, the critics of the future may conclude that cosmodernism lacks some of the features of earlier, better demarcated "epochs" such as Romanticism, modernism, and even postmodernism. Let me clarify by reasserting, first, that there has been, in the United States and beyond, a cosmodern turn, a sweeping cultural change that can be described as cosmodern or, if the term sounds tired now after hundreds of pages of use, as "something" fitting that which I have been presenting as cosmodern. This turn marks the onset of a new paradigm and epoch in American literature, theory, and culture. However, because what we are talking about is a highly complex and deep-reaching reordering of the world as we know it, it is going to take a while. It did begin in the late 1980s, but, for all intents and purposes, the 1989 late-global milestone marks decisively the turning point within, as I have said, an otherwise lengthier, contradictory, and multipronged turn. Nor has this shift been taking place within a single, cosmodern series of authors or within a sole, cosmodern cultural model but, again, across and through works also known as late modern, postmodern, postcolonial, and so forth, on both sides of the eventful 1989.

(7) *A cutoff year in the post–World War II history of globalization, 1989 is putting growing pressure not only on political scientists and historians but also on literary and cultural critics to think their timelines over.* Central to the debates around the periodization of the "contemporary" and, in particular, of postmodernism has been the modernist-postmodern sequence. Its main historical signposts have been placed around World War I—or a bit earlier, "about the year 1910," as Virginia Woolf famously if "arbitrarily" offers in her 1924 essay "Mr. Bennett and Mrs. Brown"[59]—and then in the late 1950s—or, according to Jencks, ten odd years thereafter.[60] While modernity is surely centuries older, the first decade of the twentieth century witnessed the dawn of modernism in postimpressionist and avant-garde form or forms (the "isms") succeeded by the high modernism of the 1920s and 1930s; the interval between the last part of the 1950s and the early 1970s, with the demise of "official" Stalinism and its McCarthyite

version at one end and 1968 and the civil rights movements at the other, heralds modernism's twilight.

Is this unduly "evolutionary"?[61] Maybe. Does this "sequentialism," or Jencks's own "stagism" for that matter, give some people pause? It has, actually. But McHale is right: this is too serious a game not to play it. And many critics have, expressing either joy or "discontent" at the thought of a "past tense," "passed," passé, or (post)-postmodernism. Attending the postmodern's wake—asking "what . . . postmodernism [was]" or what comes after the "after" ("post-post")[62]—two decades since the resoundingly publicized "postmodern turn" has been a bit awkward.[63] But then, weary as we should be of "dichotomist" ploys in historical and aesthetic accounts,[64] how helpful is the suggestion offered by Lyotard and Lyotardians like Bill Readings and Bennet Schaber, who maintain that, because, on the one hand, "it is the other that the modern forecloses" and, on the other hand, "the work of the postmodern is rather to produce an other to modernism," postmodernism "comes before modernism?"[65] Not very helpful, I must say, if the idea is to take stock of postmodernism by inscribing it into a cultural-material context that could not have arisen in pre-postmodern times. Nor does the suggestion further my own discussion, which, similarly, makes a point to historicize cosmodernism by placing it in a cultural-material and geopolitical context that came *after* postmodernism's *années folles* and could *not* have possibly come *before* a certain moment in U.S. *and* world history. This moment is 1989, cosmodernism's not-so-"arbitrary" birth year. With 1989, we start measuring another time in American culture. To quote Woolf again, no only do "human relations" change about that year;[66] they are radically and irrevocably refounded on large-scale relatedness, on what more and more American thinkers and artists deem a historical reality, a practical necessity, and an ethical ideal. It is in this sense that, with historically unmatched vigor and self-awareness, post–Cold War American culture takes steps toward becoming a culture of relatedness.

What happened "about the year 1989" will probably force future critics to move the two aforementioned signposts so as to revise the modern-postmodern sequence—along with all the divides, periodizations, and controversies derived from it—as a *modern-cosmodern narrative*, with World War I and the late 1980s (rather than, say, the 1960s) as the main turning moments in recent cultural history. In the long run, the Wall's crumbling may turn out to be more consequential geopolitically *and* culturally than the "collapses" of modernist buildings that between the 1960s and the early 1970s, Jencks argues, allegorized the general collapse of modernism. We would have, then, a "long modernism" followed by a "cosmodernism" that at present is too young to afford a satisfactory description. Let me also repeat another observation from the prologue: cosmodernism is not postmodernism's only successor and in that is not unlike the postmodern, which has been sharing modernism's "post" with any number of trends and directions.[67] Nor is postmodernism "over." The postmodern project too is "incomplete." There have been, in fact, some attempts to retool the postmodern paradigm for our global era by setting up a "postcolonialized," "diversified," Third World, even "worldist" postmodernism as this era's "cultural logic" or, on a more combative note, "counter-logic."[68] These endeavors have not been without merit. I agree, however, with critics who point instead to the overall superannuation of the postmodern paradigm in the age of networks, hence the need to move "beyond postmodernity."[69] Contradictory, both recapitulative and critical of postmodernism, this movement is part and parcel of the complicated cosmodern dynamic. The post-1989 period—the contemporary in a strong sense, as I call it—is the scene of this movement. Cosmodernism's initial stage, our immediate present is a transitional act in an unfolding drama that will end in a sea change eventually.

(8) *The cosmodern turn may also bring about a revolution in style. However, while over the last decades the United States has been transitioning out of a cultural dominant and critical awareness thereof, our culture as a whole has not settled into another, formally configured constellation of emotions, representations, and discourses yet. Still relying copiously on postmodern techniques, at present cosmodernism is insufficiently "paradigmatic" stylistically. But its devotion to the concept that "the subject can no longer be conceived of as closed up in itself"*[70] goes beyond the stylistic and the conceptual, and thus beyond the postmodern, into the ethical. For this reason, and for now, cosmodernism is best understood as an ethical rather than "technical" project. This project has considerable bearings on how we think not just about the subject but also about discourse, history, culture, community, patrimony, and tradition. The cosmoderns complicate all these issues by rewriting them as paragraphs in a worldly phenomenology of self-other mutuality. I welcome this complication. I predict, too, that it will expand and America will be better off for it.

NOTES

PROLOGUE

1. Jean-Paul Sartre, *No Exit,* in No Exit *and Three Other Plays* (New York: Random House, 1973), 47.

2. "Mais 'l'enfer, c'est les autres' a toujours été mal compris. On a cru que je voulais dire par là que nos rapports avec les autres étaient toujours empoisonnés, que c'étaient toujours des rapports infernaux. Or, c'est autre chose que je veux dire. Je veux dire que si les rapports avec autrui sont tordus, viciés, alors l'autre ne peut être que l'enfer. Pourquoi? Parce que les autres sont au fond ce qu'il y a de plus important en nous-même pour notre propre connaissance de nous-même. Quand nous pensons sur nous, quand nous essayons de nous connaître, au fond nous usons ces connaissances que les autres ont déja sur nous. Nous nous jugeons aves les moyens que les autres ont, nous ont donné de nous juger. Quoique je dise sur moi, toujours le jugement d'autrui entre dedans. Ce qui veut dire que, si mes rapports sont mauvais, je me mets dans la totale dépendance d'autrui. Et alors en effet je suis en enfer" (Sartre, "*Huis clos* de Jean-Paul Sartre," http://www.alaletre.com/sartre-huisclos.htm [accessed May 20, 2006]).

3. On Thomas Nagel's 1974 essay "What Is It Like to Be a Bat?" and Coetzee's response to Nagel, see the South-African writer's novel *Elizabeth Costello* (New York: Penguin, 2003), 75–82.

4. David Hollinger, *Cosmopolitanism and Solidarity: Studies in Ethnoracial, Religious, and Professional Affiliation in the United States* (Madison: University of Wisconsin Press, 2006), xxii.

5. Rey Chow, *The Age of World Target: Self-Referentiality in War, Theory, and Comparative Work* (Durham, NC: Duke University Press, 2006), 31, 41.

6. Friedrich Nietzsche, *Beyond Good and Evil,* in *Basic Writings of Nietzsche,* trans. and ed., with commentaries, by Walter Kaufmann (New York: Modern Library, 1992), 218. On the "stand-alone" American Adam, see R. W. B. Lewis's classical 1955 account, *The American Adam: Innocence, Tragedy, and Tradition in the Nineteenth Century* (Chicago: University of Chicago Press, 1984), 5.

7. Hollinger, *Cosmopolitanism and Solidarity,* xxii, 57–58.

8. Homi Bhabha, "The World and the Home," in *Dangerous Liaisons: Gender, Nation, and Postcolonial Perspectives,* ed. Anne McClintock, Aamir Mufti, and Ella Shohat (Minneapolis: University of Minnesota Press, 1997), 454.

9. Hollinger, *Cosmopolitanism and Solidarity,* 73, 36.

10. Samuel P. Huntington, *The Clash of Civilizations and the Remaking of World Order* (New York: Simon & Schuster, 2003), 129. Also see Benjamin Barber's *Jihad vs. McWorld: How Globalism and Tribalism Are Reshaping the World* (New York: Ballantine Books, 1996). In *La Peur des barbares: Au-delà du choc des civi-*

lizations (Paris: Robert Laffont, 2008), Tzvetan Todorov deflates the antinomies and anxieties underlying "clashist" theories.

11. Trinh T. Minh-ha, "Not You/Like You: Postcolonial Women and the Inter-locking Questions of Identity and Difference," in McClintock, Mufti, and Shohat, *Dangerous Liaisons,* 416.

12. Minh-ha, "Not You/Like You," 418.

13. Karl Marx and Friedrich Engels, *The Manifesto of the Communist Party,* in *The Communist Manifesto: New Interpretations,* ed. Mark Cowling, including, in full, *The Manifesto of the Communist Party,* trans. Terrell Carver (New York: New York University Press, 1998), 16–17.

14. Giorgio Agamben, *The Coming Community,* trans. Michael Hardt (Min-neapolis: University of Minnesota Press, 1993), 5, 10.

15. Hélène Cixous, "Sorties," in *Modern Criticism and Theory: A Reader,* 3rd ed., ed. David Lodge, with Nigel Wood (Harlow, UK: Longman, 2008), 364.

INTRODUCTION

1. Alan Alda, *Things I Overheard while Talking to Myself* (New York: Random House, 2007), 72–73.

2. On Lacan and the "ex-centricity" of the self, see, among other places, "The Insistence of the Letter in the Unconscious," in *Modern Criticism and Theory: A Reader,* ed. David Lodge, revised and expanded by Nigel Wood (Harlow, UK: Longman, 2000), 83. On Lacan, identity, and "L'Autre," see the whole issue "L'i-dentité en question dans la psychanalyse" of *La Revue de psychanalyse du Champ lacanien* 6 (March 2008), especially Jean-Jacques Gorog, "L'identité est 'de l'Autre,'" 59–65.

3. Milan Kundera, *La vie est ailleurs,* trans. François Kérel (Paris: Gallimard, 1976).

4. Drawing from Levinas, Adam Zachary Newton discusses the remote, the strange, the "not-here," and their "liberating" role in *The Elsewhere: On Belonging at a Near Distance; Reading Literary Memoir from Europe and the Levant* (Madi-son: University of Wisconsin Press, 2005), 116. On Levinas's *sortie de soi* and how this "exit," *ex-cedence* (in Newton), or ex-cessive repositioning of the self outside of itself in the "proximity of the other" empowers the self's life and mind, see "La proximité de l'autre," in *Altérité et transcendence,* preface by Pierre Hayat (Paris: Fata Morgana, 1995), 108.

5. Mark C. Taylor, in a commentary on Richard Rorty in "Paralectics." See Robert P. Scharlemann, ed., *On the Other: Dialogue and/or Dialectics; Mark Tay-lor's "Paralectics,"* with Roy Wagner, Michael Brint, and Richard Rorty (Lanham, MD: University Press of America, 1991), 18.

6. Nicole Lapierre glosses on Montaigne's dictum "Nous pensons tousjours ailleurs" ("Our thinking always takes place elsewhere") in *Pensons ailleurs* (Paris: Gallimard, 2006), 11–20.

7. Following Freud, Lacan also elaborates on the heteronomy of the self in "The Insistence of the Letter in the Unconscious" (83) and elsewhere.

8. Giles Gunn is one of the critics who have formulated such questions in

terms of cultural translation. See his book *Beyond Solidarity: Pragmatism and Difference in a Globalized World* (Chicago: University of Chicago Press, 2001), 23.

9. Camilla Fojas, *Cosmopolitanism in the Americas* (West Lafayette, IN: Purdue University Press, 2005), 132.

10. Basarab Nicolescu, *La transdisciplinarité: manifeste* (Paris: Rocher, 1996). The American reader can consult *Manifesto of Transdisciplinarity*, trans. from the French by Karen-Claire Voss (Albany: SUNY Press, 2002). Also see Nicolescu, *Théorèmes poétiques*, preface by Michel Camus (Paris: Rocher, 1994); Nicolescu, "The Challenge of Transdisciplinarity: From Postmodernity to Cosmodernity," paper abstract, Centre of Transdisciplinarity: Cognitive and State-System Sciences—Indexicals, http://indexicals.ac.at/abstractvienna05bnicolescu.html (accessed December 31, 2006); Basarab Nicolescu, Corin Braga, Ruxandra Cesereanu, Sanda Cordos, Anca Hatiegan, Marius Jucan, Doru Pop, Vlad Roman, Nicolae Turcan, and Mihaela Ursa, "Ce este cosmodernitatea?" [What Is Cosmodernity?], Center for the Research of the Imaginary, Cluj, Romania, http://phantasma.ro/dezbateri/masa-/masa14.html (accessed September 23, 2007). On the "new vision of the world," the reader can turn to the *Manifesto*'s seventh chapter, 39–47.

11. Nicolescu, *Théorèmes poétiques*, 78.

12. Immanuel Wallerstein, *The Modern World-System*, vol. 1 (New York: Academic Press, 1974), 7–8.

13. Immanuel Wallerstein, *Geopolitics and Geoculture: Essays on the Changing World-System* (Cambridge: Cambridge University Press / Paris: Maison des Sciences de l'Homme, 1991), 198–99. See too Wallerstein's *Utopistics, or Historical Choices of the Twenty-first Century* (New York: New Press, 1998).

14. Yi-Fu Tuan, *Cosmos and Hearth: A Cosmopolite's Viewpoint* (Minneapolis: University of Minnesota Press, 1996), 187–88.

15. Gérard Raulet, *Critical Cosmology: On Nations and Globalization—A Philosophical Essay* (Lanham, MD: Lexington Books, 2005), especially 65–80.

16. Félix Guattari, *Chaosmose* (Paris: Galilée, 1992).

17. Anne Phillips, *Multiculturalism without Culture* (Princeton, NJ: Princeton University Press, 2007), 42–72.

18. Nicolescu, *L'homme et le sens de l'univers: Essay sur Jakob Boehme, suivi d'un choix de texts,* preface by Antoine Faivre and Joscelyn Godwin (Paris: Lebeau, 1995). The original edition of the book came out in 1988. On *Naturphilsophie,* see the *Manifesto,* "The Death and the Resurrection of Nature" chapter, especially 57–59.

19. Novalis, *Journal intime suivi des* Hymnes à la nuit *et des* Fragments inédits, trans. from the German by G. Clarette and S. Joachim-Chaigneau, introduction by Germaine Clarette (Paris: Stock, 1927), 102–3.

20. Novalis, *Journal intime,* 102.

21. Nicolescu, *Théorèmes poétiques,* 211.

22. Nicolescu, *Théorèmes poétiques,* 119.

23. Nicolescu, *Manifesto of Transdisciplinarity,* 131.

24. Nicolescu, *Théorèmes poétiques,* 149–50.

25. Nicolescu, *Manifesto of Transdisciplinarity,* 151.

26. Among recent works on nontraditional "proximity" and "neighborhood," I refer the reader only to Slavoj Žižek, "Love Thy Neighbor? No, Thanks!" in *The*

Psychoanalysis of Race, ed. Christopher Lane (New York: Columbia University Press, 1998), 154–75 ; Slavoj Žižek, Eric Satner, and Kenneth Reinhard, *The Neighbor: Three Inquiries in Political Theology* (Chicago: University of Chicago Press, 2005); Nenad Miscevic, "Close Strangers: Nationalism, Proximity, and Cosmopolitanism," *Studies in East European Thought* 51 (1999): 109–25; and the whole "Ethics and the Politics of Proximity" section *Postmodern Culture* published in 2005 (vol. 15, no. 2), which featured essays by Robert Meister, Laura O'Connor, and Dana Cuff, with a preface ("Approaching Proximity") by Rei Terada.

27. Tuan, *Cosmos and Hearth,* 146.

28. Jean Baudrillard, "Global Debt and Parallel Universe," in *Digital Delirium,* ed. and introduced by Arthur Kroker and Marilouise Kroker (New York: St. Martin's, 1997), 38–40.

29. Bhabha, "The World and the Home," 454.

30. Tuan, *Cosmos and Hearth,* 146.

31. Gunn, *Beyond Solidarity,* xx.

32. Dominique Wolton, *L'Autre mondialisation* (Paris: Flammarion, 2003), 9, 15.

33. Clifford Geertz, "The Uses of Diversity," *Michigan Quarterly Review* 25, no. 1 (1986): 112.

34. On "connection" to others *"despite* differences" in Appiah's cosmopolitan ethics, see his *Cosmopolitanism: Ethics in a World of Strangers* (New York: W. W. Norton, 2006), 135; on Habermas, his book *The Inclusion of the Other: Studies in Political Theory,* ed. Ciaran Cronin and Pablo De Greiff (Cambridge, MA: MIT Press, 1999), xxxvi; on the "space of difference" as "groundless ground," Scott Lash, *Another Modernity: A Different Rationality* (Oxford: Blackwell, 1999), 11.

35. Maurice Blanchot, *The Unavowable Community,* trans. Pierre Joris (Barrytown, NY: Station Hill Press, 1988), 12. Jean-Luc Nancy follows Blanchot in *The Inoperative Community,* ed. Peter Conor, trans. Peter Conor, Lisa Garbus, Michael Holland, and Simona Sawhney, foreword by Christopher Fynsk (Minneapolis: University of Minnesota Press, 1991).

36. I allude here to Charles Taylor's "The Politics of Recognition," for which see Charles Taylor, *Multiculturalism: Examining the Politics of Recognition,* with commentary by K. Anthony Appiah, Jürgen Habermas, Steven C. Rockefeller, Michael Walzer, and Susan Wolf, ed. and introduction by Amy Gutmann (Princeton, NJ: Princeton University Press, 1994), 28. Also see a class-oriented revisiting of Taylor's basic concept in Nancy Fraser's article "Rethinking Recognition," *New Left Review* 3 (2000): 107–20.

37. Timothy J. Reiss, *Against Autonomy: Global Dialectics of Cultural Exchange* (Stanford, CA: Stanford University Press, 2002), 67, 73.

38. Charles Taylor, *The Ethics of Authenticity* (Cambridge, MA: Harvard University Press, 1992), 91; James Clifford, *The Predicament of Culture: Twentieth-Century Ethnography, Literature, and Art* (Cambridge, MA: Harvard University Press, 1988), 12.

39. Paul Gilroy, *Against Race: Imagining Political Culture beyond the Color Line* (Cambridge, MA: Belknap Press of Harvard University Press, 2000), 275.

40. Emmanuel Levinas, *Proper Names,* trans. Michael B. Smith (Stanford, CA: Stanford University Press, 1996), 5.

41. Pico Iyer, *Sun after Dark: Flights into the Foreign* (New York: Random House, 2004), 10–11. For Habermas, see *The Inclusion of the Other,* xxxvi.

42. On the other as "primordial," see Wolfgang Iser, "Coda to the Discussion," in *The Translatability of Cultures: Figurations of the Space Between,* ed. Sanford Budick and Wolfgang Iser (Stanford, CA: Stanford University Press, 1996), 298.

43. Michel de Certeau, *Culture in the Plural,* ed. and with an introduction by Luce Giard, trans. and with an afterword by Tom Conley (Minneapolis: University of Minnesota Press, 1997).

44. Walter Benn Michaels, *Our America: Nativism, Modernism, and Pluralism* (Durham, NC: Duke University Press, 1995).

45. Agamben, *The Coming Community,* 68.

46. Lou Freitas Caton, *Reading American Novels and Multicultural Aesthetics: Romancing the Postmodern Novel* (New York: Palgrave Macmillan, 2008), 39. Mark Taylor discusses the "self-transforming" impact of the relation with an other in "Paralectics," 17.

47. Sacvan Bercovitch, "Discovering America: A Cross-Cultural Perspective," in Budick and Iser, *The Translatability of Cultures,* 150. "*What is proper to a culture is not to be identical to itself,*" writes Derrida in *The Other Heading: Reflections on Today's Europe,* trans. Pascale-Anne Brault and Michael B. Naas, introduction by Michael B. Naas (Bloomington: Indiana University Press, 1992), 9. See also Julia Kristeva's *Strangers to Ourselves,* trans. Leon S. Roudiez (New York: Columbia University Press, 1991).

48. Bhabha, "The World and the Home," 454.

49. On Bakhtin and the "world of others," see Richard Bauman's *A World of Others' Words: Cross-Cultural Perspectives on Intertextuality* (Oxford: Blackwell, 2004), 1.

50. Montesquieu, *Persian Letters,* trans. with an introduction and notes by C. J. Betts (New York: Penguin, 1993), 83.

51. Paul Valéry, "Préface aux *Lettres persanes,*" in *Variété II* (Paris: Gallimard, 1930), 66.

52. On Montesquieu, Valéry, and Cioran, see Matei Calinescu's chapter 10 in Matei Calinescu and Ion Vianu, *Amintiri în dialog* (Bucharest: Litera, 1994), 224.

53. Mark C. Taylor, "Introduction: System . . . Structure . . . Difference . . . Other," in *Deconstruction in Context: Literature and Philosophy,* ed. Mark C. Taylor (Chicago: University of Chicago Press, 1986), 4.

54. Simone de Beauvoir, *The Second Sex,* trans. and ed. H. M. Parshley, introduction to the Vintage edition by Deirdre Bair (New York: Vintage, 1989), xxii, xxv. On the Heideggerian *Miteinandersein,* see Martin Heidegger, *Being and Time, A Translation of Sein und Zeit,* trans. Joan Stambaugh (Albany: SUNY Press, 1996), 111–12.

55. For the Cartesian cogito and the "annihilation" of the world, see Georges Poulet, *Entre moi and moi: Essais critiques sur la conscience de soi* (Paris: José Corti, 1977), 100.

56. G. W. F. Hegel, *Phenomenology of Spirit,* trans. A. V. Miller with analysis of the text and foreword by J. N. Findlay (Oxford: Oxford University Press, 1977), 342.

57. Beauvoir, *The Second Sex,* 248, 139, xxii–xxiii.

58. Hegel, *Phenomenology of Spirit,* 21.

59. James Risser, "The Voice of the Other in Gadamer's Hermeneutics," in *The Philosophy of Hans-Georg Gadamer,* ed. Lewis Edwin Hahn (Chicago: Open Court, 1997), 396.

60. Roland Barthes, *Mythologies,* selected and trans. from the French by Annette Lavers (New York: Noonday, 1993), 151.

61. On Barthes and cultural anthropomorphism, also see *The Eiffel Tower and Other Mythologies,* trans. Richard Howard (Berkeley: University of California Press, 1997), 29.

62. Barthes, *Mythologies,* 151.

63. See Arthur Anthony Macdonell's *Practical Sanskrit Dictionary* for Sanskrit *barbara* (London: Oxford University Press, 1924), 192. The *Unabridged Webster's* too mentions the Sanskrit and "inhumane" as a meaning of the Greek "barbarian." "Babbling" is also listed as a meaning for "barbarous." The Liddell-Scott *Greek-English Lexicon* lists *barbarizo,* "speak broken Greek, speak gibberish," "violate the laws of speech," whence the modern term, "barbarism." The *barbaroi* were, we learn, originally "all non-Greek-speaking people" (Oxford: Clarendon Press, 1940), 1:306.

64. Gianni Vattimo, *The Transparent Society* (Baltimore: Johns Hopkins University Press, 1992), 70.

65. Fred Poché, *Penser avec Arendt et Lévinas: Du mal politique au respect de l'autre* (Lyon, France: Chronique Sociale, 1998), 82.

66. For Levinas and the "eternal return of the self," see Derrida's commentary on Levinas's *Nine Talmudic Readings* in Jacques Derrida, *Adieu to Emmanuel Levinas,* trans. Pascale-Anne Brault and Michael Naas (Stanford, CA: Stanford University Press, 1999), 2.

67. On "other" and "similar" ("fellow"), see *L'Autre et le semblable: Regards sur l'ethnologie des sociétés contemporaines,* compiled and introduced by Martine Segalen (Paris: CNRS, 1989). On Descartes and "autrui comme autre moi," see Bernadette Delamarre, *Autrui* (Paris: Ellipses, 1996), 7.

68. Emmanuel Levinas, *Humanism of the Other,* trans. from the French by Nidra Poller, introduction by Richard Cohen (Urbana: University of Illinois Press, 2003), 65–69.

69. Emmanuel Levinas, *Totality and Infinity: An Essay on Interiority,* trans. Alphonso Lingis (Pittsburgh: Duquesne University Press, 1961), 213–14.

70. Žižek, "Love Thy Neighbor? No, Thanks!" 167. On the "contingent" nature of the other, see Richard Rorty, "Comments on Taylor's 'Paralectics,'" in Scharlemann, *On the Other,* 78.

71. Sylviane Agacinski, *Critique de l'égocentrisme: L'événement de l'autre* (Paris: Galilée, 1996), 13.

72. Levinas, in Emmanuel Levinas and Richard Kearney, "Dialogue with Emmanuel Levinas," in *Face to Face with Levinas,* ed. Richard A. Cohen (Albany: SUNY Press, 1986), 21. On objectivity and objectification in Levinas, see his *Proper Names,* 19–20.

73. Beauvoir, *The Second Sex,* 140–41.

74. Hegel, *Phenomenology of Spirit,* 20.

75. Derrida, *Adieu to Emmanuel Levinas,* 91.

76. On "inter-culturation," see Jacques Demorgon's *L'interculturation du monde* (Paris: Anthropos, 2000) and *Critique de l'interculturel: L'horizon de la so-*

ciologie (Paris: Anthropos, 2005). For the relational definition of cultures, see Gabriel Motzkin, "Memory and Cultural Translation," in Budick and Iser, *The Translatability of Cultures*, 265. On "intersectional" cultural identity and culture as "heterogeneity," also see David Theo Goldberg, "Introduction: Multicultural Conditions," in *A Critical Reader*, ed. David Theo Goldberg (Oxford: Blackwell, 1994), 28. On world literature—or, in my account, on all literture and its production—qua circulation, also see David Damrosch, *What Is World Literature?* (Princeton, NJ: Princeton University Press, 2003), 5, 283.

77. Heidegger, *Being and Time*, 35.

78. Levinas, "Dialogue with Emmanuel Levinas," 24.

79. Martin Buber, *I and Thou: A New Translation with a Prologue "I and You" and Notes by Walter Kaufmann* (New York: Simon & Schuster, 1996), 67.

80. Buber, *I and Thou*, 78.

81. Levinas, "Dialogue with Emmanuel Levinas," 25.

82. Derrida, in Stanislas Breton and Francis Guibal, *Altérités: Jacques Derrida and Pierre-Jean Labarrière*, with essays by Francis Guibal and Stanislas Breton (Paris: Osiris, 1986), 70.

83. Jean-Luc Nancy, *Vérité de la démocratie* (Paris: Galilée, 2008), 25, 62.

84. David Held puts forth the "strong globalization thesis" in the afterword to his anthology *A Globalizing World? Culture, Economics, Politics* (London: Routledge in association with The Open University, 2000), 171. Christopher J. Kollmeyer takes up Held's weak/strong globalization distinction in "Globalization, Class Compromise, and American Exceptionalism: Political Change in 16 Advanced Capitalist Countries," *Critical Sociology* 29, no. 3 (October 2003): 369–91.

85. See, among others, Martin Albrow, *The Global Age: State and Society beyond Modernity* (Stanford, CA: Stanford University Press), 1997.

86. John Tomlinson, "Globalization and Cultural Analysis," in *Globalization Theory: Approaches and Controversies*, ed. David Held and Anthony McGrew (Cambridge: Polity, 2007), 150.

87. On "context," see Jonathan Culler, *Literary Theory: A Very Short Introduction* (Oxford: Oxford University Press, 2000), 67.

88. Tomlinson, "Globalization and Cultural Analysis," 150.

89. Manuel Castells, *The Information Age: Economy, Society, and Culture*, 2nd ed., vol. 1, *The Rise of the Network Society* (Oxford: Blackwell, 2000), 500, 508.

90. Thomas L. Friedman, *Longitudes and Latitudes: Exploring the World after September 11* (New York: Farrar, Strauss and Giroux, 2002), 3; *The World Is Flat: A Brief History of the Twenty-first Century*, further updated and expanded (New York: Farrar, Strauss and Giroux, 2006), 10.

91. Jean-Pierre Warnier, *La mondialisation de la culture*, 3rd ed. (Paris: La Découverte, 2004), 32.

92. Albrow, *The Global Age*, 77; Arif Dirlik, "Globalization as the End and the Beginning of History," http://www.scribd.com/doc/2546826/Globalization-as-the-End-and-the-Beginning-of-History (accessed July 27, 2008); Francis Fukuyama, *The End of History and the Last Man* (New York: Free Press, 1992).

93. On Pierre Chaunu's *univers cloisonné*, see his book, *Histoire, science sociale: La durée, l'espace, et l'homme à l'époque moderne* (Paris: Société d'édition d'enseignement supérieur, 1974).

94. Roland Robertson, "Mapping the Global Condition: Globalization as the Central Concept," in *Global Culture: Nationalism, Globalization, and Modernity. A Theory, Culture, and Society Special Issue*, ed. Mike Featherstone (London: Sage, 1990): 27.

95. Friedman, *The World Is Flat*, 53, 63.

96. Ken Jowitt, *New World Disorder: The Leninist Extinction* (Berkeley: University of California Press, 1992). Bauman refers to Jowitt's book in *Globalization: The Human Consequences* (New York: Columbia University Press, 1998), 59. For Todorov, see *Le Nouveau Désordre mondial: Réflexions d'un Européen*, preface by Stanley Hoffmann (Paris: Robert Laffont, 2003). On the "chaos" of contemporary world, also see Amin Maalouf's recent book *Le dérèglement du monde* (Paris: Grasset & Fasquelle, 2009) and Immanuel Wallerstein's article "Revolts against the System," *New Left Review*, 2nd ser., 18 (November–December 2002): 37.

97. Valéry, "Préface aux *Lettres persanes*," 53–60.

98. Gilbert Durand, *Les structures anthropologiques de l'imaginaire: Introduction à l'archétypologie générale* (Paris: PUF, 1963), 11.

99. Durand, *Les structures anthropologiques de l'imaginaire*, 51–52.

100. On another way of distinguishing between the "fictive" and the "imaginary," see Wolfgang Iser's book *The Fictive and the Imaginary: Charting Literary Anthropology* (Baltimore: Johns Hopkins University Press, 1996), especially the first chapter, "Fictionalizing Acts," 1–21.

101. Thomas Peyser, "Globalization in America: The Case of Don DeLillo's *White Noise*," *CLIO* 25, no. 3 (Spring 1996): 256.

102. Daniel Cohen, *La mondialisation et ses ennemies* (Paris: Grasset, 2004), 85.

103. Arjun Appadurai, *Modernity at Large: Cultural Dimensions of Globalization* (Minneapolis: University of Minnesota Press, 1999), 3, 5, 7, 15, 33.

104. Martin Heidegger, "What Are Poets For?" in *Poetry, Language, Thought*, trans. and introduction by Albert Hofstadter (New York: HarperTrade, 1981), 102–4.

105. Heidegger, "What Are Poets For?" in *Poetry, Language, Thought*, 92.

106. Heidegger, "What Are Poets For?" in *Poetry, Language, Thought*, 101.

107. Saul Bellow, *Herzog* (New York: Penguin, 1996), 49–50.

108. Bellow, *Herzog*, 323.

109. Anthony Giddens, *The Consequences of Modernity* (Stanford, CA: Stanford University Press, 1990), 146.

110. Deborah Lupton, *Risk* (London: Routledge, 1999), 8.

111. Niklas Luhmann, *Risk: A Sociological Theory*, trans. Rhodes Barrett (New York: Aldine de Gruyter, 1993), 219. For Barry Smart, see his book *Facing Modernity: Ambivalence, Reflexivity, and Modernity* (London: Sage, 1999), especially 47–49; for Lash, *Another Modernity*.

112. Ulrich Beck, *Risk Society: Towards a New Modernity*, trans. Mark Ritter (London: Sage, 1992), 10.

113. Jacques Derrida, *Of Grammatology*, corrected ed., trans. Gayatri Chakravorty Spivak (Baltimore: Johns Hopkins University Press, 1998), 44–65, 157–58.

114. Anthony Giddens, *Modernity and Self-Identity: Self and Society in the Late Modern Age* (Stanford, CA: Stanford University Press, 1991), 3.

115. Giddens, *The Consequences of Modernity*, 125–26. Giddens elaborates on

the claim Beck makes in *Risk Society* regarding "the end of 'others'" (*The Consequences of Modernity*, 125).

116. Beck, *Risk Society*, 19.

117. Michel Foucault, *Technologies of the Self: A Seminar with Michel Foucault*, ed. Luther H. Martin, Huck Gutman, and Patrick H. Hutton (Amherst: University of Massachusetts Press, 1988), 146.

118. See Lupton, *Risk*, 7.

119. R. Castel, quoted in Lupton's *Risk*, 7.

120. Levinas, *Totality and Infinity*, 44.

121. "[W]hat happens with the shift to the global information culture?" asks Lash in *Another Modernity*. And he answers: "What happens in a multimediatized cultural space of not difference or perplexity or ambivalence, but instead of *indifference*" (11).

122. John Tomlinson, *Globalization and Culture* (Chicago: University of Chicago Press, 1999), 2.

123. Erick Schonfeld, "Analysis: Yahoo's China Problem," *Business 2.0*, http://money. cnn.com/2006/02/08/technology/yahoo_china_b2o/ (accessed January 19, 2008).

124. See Alain Finkielkraut and Paul Soriano, *Internet, l'inquiétante extase* (Paris: Fayard, 2001); Alexander Bard and Jan Soderqvist, *Netocracy: The Power Elite and Life after Capitalism* (London: Reuters, 2002). For a net-skeptic rebuttal of Bard and Soderqvist, see Slavoj Žižek, "The Ideology of the Empire and Its Traps," in *Empire's New Clothes: Reading Negri and Hardt*, ed. Paul A. Passavant and Jodi Dean (New York: Routledge, 2004), 258–61. Baudrillard calls the network "public enemy number one" in *Cool Memories IV: 1995–2000* (trans. Chris Turner [London: Verso, 2003], 24).

125. On Hardt, Negri, and the political ambiguity of global networks, see their *Empire* (Cambridge, MA: Harvard University Press, 2000), xv, and *Multitude: War and Democracy in the Age of Empire* (New York: Penguin, 2004), 79–91. See too Jodi Dean, "The Networked Empire: Communicative Capitalism and the Hope for Politics," in Passavant and Dean, *Empire's New Clothes*, 265–88. In Peter Day and Douglas Schuler's collection, *Common Practice in the Network Society* (London: Routledge, 2004), see especially the editors' introductory essay, "Community Practice: An Alternative Vision of the Network," 1–20. For "glocalization," Roland Robertson's *Globalization: Social Theory and Global Culture* (London: Sage, 1992) is still the *locus classicus*. On "glocalization" and "heterogenization," helpful is Robertson, "Glocalization: Time-Space and Homogeneity-Heterogeneity," in *Global Modernities*, ed. Mike Featherstone, Scott Lash, and Roland Robertson (London: Sage, 1995), 40. Relevant to the notion and the debate around it is, in the same collection, Timothy W. Luke's essay "New World Order or Neo-world Orders: Power, Politics, and Ideology in Informationalizing Glocalities," 91–107.

126. On globalization as "homo-hegemonization," see Derrida, *Negotiations: Interventions and Interviews, 1971–2001*, ed., trans., and with an introduction by Elizabeth Rottenberg (Stanford, CA: Stanford University Press, 2002), 373.

127. Friedman, *The World Is Flat*, 92–93.

128. Friedman, *Longitudes and Latitudes*, 3.

129. Bellow, *Herzog*, 165.

130. Giddens, *The Consequences of Modernity*, 49.

131. Ulrich Beck, "Risk Society Revisited: Theory, Politics, and Research Programmes," in *The Risk Society and Beyond: Critical Issues for Social Theory*, ed. Barbara Adam, Ulrich Beck, and Joost Van Loon (London: Sage, 2000), 226.

132. Finkielkraut and Soriano urge a "critique of connective reason" in *Internet, l'inquiétante extase*, 72.

133. Levinas, *Totality and Infinity*, 47. On recent applications of the Levinasian egological versus ecological distinction, see Adam Potkay's article, "Wordsworth and the Ethics of Things," *PMLA* 123, no. 2 (March 2008): 391. Potkay refers to Silvia Benso's book *The Face of Things: A Different Side of Ethics* (Albany: SUNY Press, 2000).

134. Leslie Head, "Cultural Ecology: The Problematic Human and the Terms of Engagement," *Progress in Human Geography* 31, no. 6 (2007): 840. Important interventions in cultural ecology along postmodern lines rather distinct from the present discussion have been made of late by Paul Maltby, Laura Barrett, John W. Coletta, and Jim Tarter. On "cultural ecosystems," see Armand Mattelart's *Diversité culturelle et mondialisation* (Paris: La Découverte, 2005), 92–100. Mattelart calls for an "info-ethics" (100), that is, for an ethics of biocultural diversity in the "new world order of networks" (99).

135. P. B. Bridgewater, "Biosphere Reserves: Special Places for People and Nature," *Environmental Science & Policy* 5 (2002): 9.

136. Hubert Zapf, *Literatur als kulturelle Ökologie: Zur Kulturellen Funktion imaginativer Texte an Beispielen des amerikanischen Romans* (Tübingen: Max Niemeyer, 2002), and the anthology *Kulturökologie und Literatur: Beiträge zu einem transdisziplinären Paradigma der Literaturwissenschaft* (Heidelberg: Universitätsverlag Winter, 2008); Ursula Heise, *Sense of Place and Sense of Planet: The Environmental Imagination of the Global* (Oxford: Oxford University Press, 2008); Michael Wutz, *Enduring Words: Literary Narrative in a Changing Media Ecology* (Tuscaloosa: University of Alabama Press, 2009). Worth mentioning here is too the anthology published by Wutz and Joseph Tabbi, *Reading Matters: Narrative in the New Media Ecology* (Ithaca, NY: Cornell University Press, 1997). Also, in the preface to *Idylls of the Wanderer: Outside in Literature and Theory* (New York: Fordham University Press, 2007), Henry Sussman touches on the "ecology of writing" (xv).

137. See Head, "Cultural Ecology," especially the section "From Other to Self," 840.

138. Peter Singer, *One World: The Ethics of Globalization* (New Haven: Yale University Press, 2002), 1–2.

139. Jacques Derrida, "Autoimmunity: Real and Symbolic Suicides. A Dialogue with Jacques Derrida," in Giovanna Borradori, *Philosophy in a Time of Terror: Dialogues with Jürgen Habermas and Jacques Derrida* (Chicago: University of Chicago Press, 2003), 121.

140. Jean-Luc Nancy, *The Creation of the World or Globalization*, trans. and with an introduction by François Raffoul and David Pettigrew (Albany: SUNY Press, 2007), 27–28. On "globalization" as "transparent"-rendering of the world through unproblematic translation, also see Raffoul and Pettigrew's introduction to their translation, 2.

141. Jean-Luc Nancy, *Being Singular Plural*, trans. Robert D. Richardson and Anne E. O'Byrne (Stanford, CA: Stanford University Press, 2000), 189.

142. Nancy, *The Creation of the World or Globalization*, 28.

143. Nancy, *Being Singular Plural*, 185.

144. Nancy, *Being Singular Plural*, 186–87.

145. Jean-Luc Nancy, *La création du monde* ou *la mondialisation* (Paris: Galilée, 2002), 58, 72.

146. Jean-Luc Nancy, *The Sense of the World*, trans. and with a foreword by Jeffrey S. Librett (Minneapolis: University of Minnesota Press, 1997), 8.

147. For a rebuttal of Alain Badiou's "rejection of difference" and of the ethics rooted in the concept, see Shu-Mei Shih's essay "Global Literature and the Technologies of Recognition," *PMLA* 119, no. 1 (January 2004): 27–29. On Masao Miyoshi and "the problem with the logic of difference," see his article "Turn to the Planet: Literature, Diversity, Totality," *Comparative Literature* 55, no. 4 (Fall 2001): 294–96.

148. Emmanuel Levinas, "Ideology and Idealism," *The Levinas Reader*, ed. Seán Hand (Oxford: Oxford University Press, 1989), 244.

149. Nancy, *The Sense of the World*, 9.

150. Derrida, in Breton and Guibal, *Altérités*, 82.

151. Nancy, *The Sense of the World*, 9.

152. Jacques Derrida, *On Touching—Jean-Luc Nancy*, trans. Christine Irizarry (Stanford, CA: Stanford University Press, 2005), 54.

153. Stephen R. Yarbrough, *Inventive Intercourse: From Rhetorical Conflict to the Ethical Creation of Novel Truth* (Carbondale: Southern Illinois University Press, 2006), 167.

154. On Charles Taylor, selfhood, and authenticity, see once more his book *The Ethics of Authenticity*. Regarding today's "webs of interlocution," also see Charles Taylor, *Sources of the Self: The Making of Modern Identity* (Cambridge, MA: Harvard University Press, 1989), 36. For Bakhtin's "world of words," see M. M. Bakhtin, *Speech Genres and Other Late Essays*, ed. Caryl Emerson and Michael Holquist, trans. Vern McGee (Austin: University of Texas Press, 1986), 89, and Richard Bauman's *A World of Others' Words*, 1.

155. Michael Holquist, "Introduction: The Architectonics of Answerability," in M. M. Bakhtin, *Art and Answerability: Early Philosophical Essays*, ed. Michael Holquist and Vadim Liapunov, trans. and notes by Vadim Liapunov, supplement trans. Kenneth Brostrom (Austin: University of Texas Press, 1990), xxx–xxxi.

156. Jacques Derrida, *Monolingualism of the Other; or, The Prosthesis of Origin*, trans. Patrick Mensah (Stanford, CA: Stanford University Press, 1998), 19.

157. This is a reference to Werner Sollors's work, primarily to *Beyond Ethnicity: Consent and Descent in American Culture* (Oxford: Oxford University Press, 1986) and "The Invention of Ethnicity," for which see his anthology *The Invention of Ethnicity* (New York: Oxford University Press, 1991), ix–xx.

158. In *Postethnic America: Beyond Multiculturalism* (New York: Basic Books/HarperCollins, 1995), David Hollinger makes the valid point that his "postethnic" approach is in reality "more respectful" of ethnic identity (5). Also see Frederick Luis Aldama's *Postethnic Narrative Criticism: Magicorealism in Oscar "Zeta" Acosta, Anna Castillo, Julie Dash, Hanif Kureishi, and Salman Rushdie* (Austin: University of Texas Press, 2003). For the study of the "interethnic imagination," see Caroline Rody's *The Interethnic Imagination: Roots and Passages in Contemporary*

American Fiction (New York: Oxford University Press, 2009). On the indigenous as "globally disseminated material," see Frederick Buell, *National Culture and the New Global System* (Baltimore: Johns Hopkins University Press, 1994), 243.

159. Georg Simmel, "Bridge and Door," in *Simmel on Culture: Selected Writings,* ed. David Frisby and Mike Featherstone (London: Sage, 1997), 174.

160. Reiss, *Against Autonomy,* 68.

161. Hans Bertens, *Literary Theory: The Basics* (New York: Routledge, 2001), 161. On cultural heritage as debt to others—which may involve fair or "inequitable indebtedness"—see also Joseph Roach's essay "World Bank Drama," in *Shades of the Planet: American Literature as World Literature,* ed. Wai Chee Dimock and Lawrence Buell (Princeton: NJ: Princeton University Press, 2007), 172.

162. Reiss, *Against Autonomy,* 67.

163. Clifford Geertz, *Local Knowledge: Further Essays in Interpretive Anthropology* (New York: Basic Books, 1983), 48.

164. Ulrich Beck, *The Reinvention of Politics: Rethinking Modernity in the Global Social Order,* trans. Mark Ritter (Cambridge: Polity, 1997), 2.

165. Taylor, *The Ethics of Authenticity,* 59.

166. Don DeLillo, *Falling Man* (New York: Scribner, 2007), 176.

167. Milan Kundera, *The Art of the Novel,* trans. Linda Asher (New York: Grove Press, 1988), 17.

168. Lupton discusses at some length the risk "posed" by otherness and the various groups deemed to embody it, in the "Risk and Otherness" chapter of her *Risk,* 123–47.

169. On "tak[ing] the risk of the other," see Derrida's *Of Hospitality: Anne Dufourmantelle Invites Jacques Derrida to Respond,* trans. Rachel Bowlby (Stanford, CA: Stanford University Press, 2000), 34–36.

170. Of late, efforts to rethink "collegiality" across a range of cultural-institutional environments have been made by contributors to the special-topic issues of *symploke* 13, no. 1–2 (2005): 7–218, and *Profession* (2006): 48–176.

171. Ethically and otherwise, my scholarly (epistemological) imaginary concept involves a with-ness structure far more consequential than Appadurai's "research imagination." For the latter, see Appadurai's introductory essay "Grassroots Globalization and the Research Imagination" in his anthology *Globalization* (Durham, NC: Duke University Press, 2001), especially 14–15.

172. Thomas Peyser, *Utopia and Cosmopolis: Globalization in the Era of American Literary Realism* (Durham, NC: Duke University Press, 1998), 9. On the world as "hermeneutic" (approach) see Buell, *National Culture and the New Global System,* 6–7. In his discussion, Buell takes his cue from an earlier article by Roland Robertson.

173. Stephen Greenblatt, "Racial Memory and Literary History," *PMLA* 116, no. 1 (January 2001): 59.

174. Greenblatt, "Racial Memory and Literary History," 60.

175. Friedrich Nietzsche, *Human, All Too Human: A Book for Free Spirits,* trans. Marion Faber with Stephen Lehmann, introduction and notes by Marion Faber (Lincoln: University of Nebraska Press, 1984), 29. Albrow also mentions Nietzsche's "age of compariso[n]" in *The Global Age,* 115.

176. "Thick description" is a phrase Clifford Geertz borrowed from philosopher Gilbert Ryle. See Geertz's essay "Thick Description: Toward an Interpretive

Theory of Culture," in *The Interpretation of Cultures: Selected Essays* (New York: Basic Books, 1973), 6–9.

177. Taylor, "The Politics of Recognition," in Taylor, *Multiculturalism*, 73.

178. Just a few examples from an endless list: Christopher Schedler's *Border Modernism* (New York: Routledge, 2002); Stephen Clingman's *The Grammar of Identity: Transnational Fiction and the Nature of the Boundary* (Oxford: Oxford University Press, 2009); Paul Gilroy's *The Black Atlantic* (1993), but also the recent tradition of transatlantic cosmopolitanism reconstituted by Susan Manning and Andrew Taylor in their *Transatlantic Literary Studies: A Reader* (Baltimore: Johns Hopkins University Press, 2007); Ralph Bauer's "Hemispheric Studies," *PMLA* 124, no. 1 (January 2009): 234–50, as well as the contributions to *Hemispheric American Studies*, ed. Caroline Field Levander and Robert S. Levine (Rutgers, NJ: Rutgers University Press, 2008); Caren Kaplan's *Questions of Travel: Postmodern Discourses of Displacement* (Durham, NC: Duke University Press, 1996); Yunte Huang's *Transpacific Displacement: Ethnography, Translation, and Intertextual Travel in Twentieth-Century American Literature* (Berkeley: University of California Press, 2002); Emily Apter's *Continental Drift: From National Characters to Virtual Subjects* (Chicago: University of Chicago Press, 1999) and *The Translation Zone: A New Comparative Literature* (Princeton, NJ: Princeton University Press, 2006); Julio Ortega's "Transatlantic Translations," *PMLA* 118, no. 1 (January 2003): 25–40; Mary Louise Pratt's *Imperial Eyes* (London: Routledge, 1992); John Carlos Rowe's collection *Post-Nationalist American Studies* (Berkeley: University of California Press, 2000); Paul Giles's "Transnationalism and Classic American Literature," *PMLA* 118, no. 1 (January 2003): 78–89; the Spring 2003 *Modern Fiction Studies* special-topic issue "Fictions of the Trans-American Imaginary" guest-edited by Paula M. L. Moya and Ramón Saldivar; Carlton Smith's *Coyote Kills John Wayne: Postmodernism and Contemporary Fictions of the Transnational Frontier* (Hanover, NH: University Press of New England, 2000); James Clifford's *Routes: Travel and Translation in the Late Twentieth Century* (Cambridge, MA: Harvard University Press, 1996); and Steven G. Kellman's *The Translingual Imagination* (Lincoln: University of Nebraska Press, 2000). On "geomodernisms," see Laura Doyle and Laura Winkiel's anthology *Geomodernisms: Race, Modernism, Modernity* (Bloomington: Indiana University Press, 2005), including the editors' introduction, "The Global Horizons of Modernism," 1–16. On Jameson, aesthetics, and the "geopolitical," see his *The Geopolitical Aesthetic: Cinema and Space in the World System* (Bloomington: Indiana University Press, 1995); Gearóid Ó Tuathail, Simon Dalby, and Paul Routledge's *The Geopolitics Reader* (London: Routledge, 1998); Dominique Moïsi, *La Géopolitique de l'émotion* (Paris: Flammarion, 2009). For "geocriticism," see especially Bertrand Westphal's *La Géocritique: Réel, Fiction, Espace* (Paris: Minuit, 2007). Regarding the "transnational" and "global imaginary," see, among many other titles, the earlier book by Wilson Harris, *The Womb of Space: The Cross-Cultural Imagination* (Westport, CT: Greenwood, 1983); Rob Wilson and Wimal Dissanayake, "Introduction: Tracing the Global/Local," in Rob Wilson and Wimal Dissanayake, eds., *Global/Local: Cultural Production and the Transnational Imaginary* (Durham, NC: Duke University Press, 1996), 6; Ulf Hannerz, *Transnational Connections: Culture, People, Places* (London: Routledge, 1996); and Manfred B. Steger, *The Rise of the Global Imaginary: Political Ideologies from the French Revolution to the Global War on Terror* (Oxford: Oxford University Press, 2008).

179. Charles Bernheimer, "The Bernheimer Report, 1993: Comparative Literature at the Turn of the Century," in *Comparative Literature in the Age of Multiculturalism,* ed. Charles Bernheimer (Baltimore: Johns Hopkins University Press, 1995), 39–48.

180. Mary Louise Pratt, "Comparative Literature and Global Citizenship," in Bernheimer, *Comparative Literature in the Age of Multiculturalism,* 58.

181. Haun Saussy, ed., *Comparative Literature in an Age of Globalization* (Baltimore: Johns Hopkins University Press, 2006). In the same volume, also see Roland Greene's essay "Not Works but Networks: Colonial Worlds in Comparative Literature," 212–23.

182. See Reingard Nethersole's "text-without-context" notion of networks in her essay "Models of Globalization," *PMLA* 116, no. 3 (May 2001): 640.

183. The examples are not as plentiful as one would expect, and most of them are articles and essays in collections. A more systematic analysis of literature and culture under late globalization is still unavailable, and discussions of *particular* works *sub specie globalitatis* are few and far between. An earlier and rather partial exception is Michael Valdez Moses's *The Novel and the Globalization of Culture* (New York: Oxford University Press, 1995), especially its brief epilogue (193–202). Also see, along these lines, Marietta Messmer, "Reading National American Literary Historiography Internationally," *Comparative Literature* 52, no. 3 (Summer 2000): 193–212, and A. E. B. Coldiron's sketchy considerations on "world lyric"— or "political lyric in global contexts"—in "Toward a Comparative New Historicism: Land Tenures and Some Fifteenth-Century Poems," *Comparative Literature* 53, no. 2 (Spring 2001): 97–116. Focusing on early modern literature, Coldiron is not unaware of his reliance on twenty-first century concerns and methodologies. Also, *PMLA, Comparative Literature, symploke, Public Culture, Modern Language Notes,* and *Modern Fiction Studies* have been among the North-American journals that have devoted whole issues to "cultural globalization," the "globalization of literary studies," the "globalization of English," and so forth. On globalization as the "absolute horizon" of the "future," see Jameson's article "New Literary History after the End of the New," *New Literary History* 39, no. 3 (Summer 2008): 375.

184. John Pizer, "Goethe's 'World Literature' Paradigm and Contemporary Cultural Globalization," *Comparative Literature* 52, no. 3 (Summer 2000): 213. Pizer also points up the "Eurocentric" limits of Goethe's *Weltliteratur.* On the latter's misuses—as influential in the history of comparatism as *Weltliteratur*'s legitimate employment—see Hans-Joachim Schulz and Phillip H. Rhein, eds., *Comparative Literature: The Early Years* (Chapel Hill: University of North Carolina Press, 1973), 3. On the *Weltliterarische* revival in the new (post)postcolonial, global-transnational context, see, among others, Homi Bhabha's *The Location of Culture* (New York: Routledge, 1994), 11–12, and "The World and the Home" essay; Pascale Casanova, *The World Republic of Letters,* trans. M. B. DeBevoise (Cambridge, MA: Harvard University Press, 2004), whose original French edition came out in 1999; David Damrosch, *What Is World Literature?;* Franco Moretti, *Modern Epic: The World-System from Goethe to García Márquez,* trans. Quintin Hoare (London: Verso, 1996); and Kate McInturff, "The Uses and Abuses of World Literature," *Journal of American Culture* 26, no. 2 (June 2003): 224–36.

185. "Literary History in the Global Age" is the title of a recent special-topic issue of *New Literary History* (39, no. 3 [Summer 2008]) featuring contributions by

Jameson, Brian Stock, Walter F. Veit, Anders Pettersson, Damrosch, David Bleich, Hans Ulrich Gumbrecht, Karyn Ball, Chow, Apter, Nirvana Tanoukhi, Dimock, Jerome McGann, Frances Fergusson, Mark Poster, Amy J. Elias, Hayden White, and Jonathan Arac. *American Literary History* has also published, in 2006, a special issue devoted to the transnational reframing of national literary history (18, no. 2).

186. See Robert A. Gross, "The Transnational Turn: Rediscovering American Studies in a Wider World," *Journal of American Studies* 34, no. 3 (2000): 373–93; Ursula Heise, *Sense of Place and Sense of Planet: The Environmental Imagination of the Global* (Oxford: Oxford University Press, 2008); Wai Chee Dimock, *Through Other Continents: American Literature across Deep Time* (Princeton, NJ: Princeton University Press, 2008).

187. Wai Chee Dimock and Lawrence Buell, eds., *Shades of the Planet: American Literature as World Literature* (Princeton, NJ: Princeton University Press, 2007), especially the introduction and the contributions by Arac, Paul Giles, Joseph Roach, Bhabha, Buell, and Dimock.

188. On DeLillo and Houellebecq, see my article "The Genomic Imperative: Michel Houellebecq's *The Possibility of an Island*," *Utopian Studies* 19, no. 2 (2008): 265–67.

189. Peter Coulmas, *Les citoyens du monde: Histoire du cosmopolitisme*, trans. from the German by Jeanne Étoré (Paris: Albin Michel, 1995), 21.

190. Derek Heater, *World Citizenship: Cosmopolitan Thinking and Its Opponents* (New York: Continuum, 2002), 30.

191. Jacques Derrida, *On Cosmopolitanism and Forgiveness*, trans. Mark Dooley and Michael Hughes, preface by Simon Critchley and Richard Kearney (London: Routledge, 2001), 19–20; Giorgio Agamben, *The Time That Remains: A Commentary on The Letter to the Romans*, trans. Patricia Dailey (Stanford, CA: Stanford University Press, 2005); Alain Badiou, *Saint Paul: La fondation de l'universalisme* (Paris: PUF, 2004); Wolfgang Feneberg, *Paulus, der Weltbürger* (Munich: Kösel, 1992); Pope Benedict XVI, "Paul, the Apostle: Teacher for Today," http://www.ewtn.com/library/PAPALDOC/b16stpaul1.htm (accessed February 14, 2009).

192. See Kant's 1784 essay "Idea for a Universal History with a Cosmopolitan Purpose," in Immanuel Kant, *Political Writings*, 2nd ed., enlarged, ed. with an introduction and notes by Hans Reiss, trans. H. B. Nisbett (Cambridge: Cambridge University Press, 1991), 48–51. On Kant and Enlightenment cosmopolitanism, Thomas J. Schlereth's *The Cosmopolitan Ideal in Enlightenment Thought: Its Form and Function in the Ideas of Franklin, Hume, and Voltaire, 1694–1790* (Notre Dame: University of Notre Dame Press, 1977) remains very useful. Also see Andrea Albrecht, *Kosmopolitismus* (Berlin: Gruyter, 2005), and the essays by Nussbaum, Karl-Otto Apel, Habermas, and Held in James Bohman and Matthias Lutz-Bachmann's collection *Perpetual Peace: Essays on Kant's Cosmopolitan Ideal* (Cambridge, MA: MIT Press, 1997).

193. On the "global turn," see too my articles "Cosmopolitics, Paroxism, Global Talk: Emerging Issues and Approaches," *symploke* 7, nos. 1–2 (1999): 197–202, and "The Global Turn in Critical Theory," *symploke* 9, nos. 1–2 (2001): 80–92.

194. Simon During, "Postcolonialism and Globalization: Towards a Historicization of Their Inter-relation," *Cultural Studies* 14, nos. 3–4 (2000): 402.

195. Gayatri Chakravorty Spivak, *A Critique of Postcolonial Reason: Toward a History of the Vanishing Present* (Cambridge, MA: Harvard University Press, 1999), especially the appendix ("The Setting to Work of Deconstruction"), 423–31; *Death of a Discipline* (New York: Columbia University Press, 2003).

196. On the postnational, see Jürgen Habermas, *The Postnational Constellation: Political Essays*, trans., ed., and with an introduction by Max Pensky (Cambridge, MA: MIT Press, 2001); Ulf Hedetoft and Mette Hjort, eds., *The Postnational Self: Belonging and Identity* (Minneapolis: University of Minnesota Press, 2002); Azade Seyhan's *Writing outside the Nation* (Princeton, NJ: Princeton University Press, 2001); Anne Holding Rønning and Lene Johannessen's anthology *Readings of the Particular: The Postcolonial and the Postnational* (Amsterdam: Rodopi, 2007). On the tensions between the postcolonial and the global, see During's "Postcolonialism and Globalization"; Revathi Krishnaswamy and John C. Hawley, eds., *The Postcolonial and the Global* (Minneapolis: University of Minnesota Press, 2007); Clara A. B. Joseph and Janet Wilson, eds., *Global Fissures: Postcolonial Fusions* (Amsterdam: Rodopi, 2006); Joel Kuorti and Jopi Nyman, eds., *Reconstructing Hybridity: Post-Colonial Studies in Transition* (Amsterdam: Rodopi, 2007).

197. During, "Postcolonialism and Globalization," 387.

198. Masao Miyoshi, "'Globalization,' Culture, and the University," in *The Cultures of Globalization*, ed. Fredric Jameson and Masao Miyoshi (Durham: Duke University Press, 1998), 248–61.

199. Warnier, *La mondialisation de la culture*, 107.

200. Fredric Jameson, "Notes on Globalization as a Philosophical Issue," in Jameson and Miyoshi, *The Cultures of Globalization*, 57.

201. For a critique of the simplifications involved in equating "transnational mobility" with "Americanization," see Bruce Robbins, *Feeling Global: Internationalism in Distress* (New York: New York University Press, 1999), 43.

202. In literary-cultural studies, Americanists of "global" persuasion include, among others, Frederick Buell, Lawrence Buell, Arac, Giles, Dimock, Peyser, Heise, Carolyn A. Durham—see her *Literary Globalism: Anglo-American Fiction Set in France* (Lewisburg, PA: Bucknell University Press, 2005)—and James Annesley, whose *Fictions of Globalization: Consumption, the Market, and the Contemporary American Novel* (New York: Continuum) came out in 2006. For a broader international perspective, I will mention only older works such as Jameson and Miyoshi's *The Cultures of Globalization*, Michael Valdez Moses's *The Novel and the Globalization of Culture*, and Tomlinson's *Globalization and Culture* and more recent contributions like Amitava Kumar's anthology *World Bank Literature*, with foreword by John Berger and afterword by Bruce Robbins (Minneapolis: University of Minnesota Press, 2003), an application of Kumar's cultural model by Roach, in "World Bank Drama," Paul Hopper's *Understanding Cultural Globalization* (London: Polity, 2007), and Suman Gupta's *Globalization and Literature* (London: Polity, 2009). A number of literature anthologies of declaredly "global" scope would also have to be listed here, even though, to give just two earlier examples, the titles of Arthur W. Biddle and Gloria Bien's *Global Voices: Contemporary Literature from the Non-Western World* (Upper Saddle River, NJ: Prentice Hall, 1994) and Elisabeth Young-Bruehl's *Global Cultures: A Transnational Short Fiction Reader* (Middletown, CT: Wesleyan University Press, 1994) suggest that critics and editors are still trying to figure out what "global" means. As a curiosity,

also see the "new encyclopedism" of projects like *The Dictionary of Global Culture: What Every American Needs to Know as We Enter the Next Century—from Diderot to Bo Diddley,* ed. Kwame Anthony Appiah, Henry Louis Gates, Jr., associate editor, Michael Colin Vazquez (New York: Knopf, 1997).

203. Here are only a few of the more significant monographs and anthologies in the swelling new cosmopolitan studies bibliography: Guy Scarpetta, *Éloge du cosmopolitisme* (Paris: Bernard Grasset, 1981); Stephen Toulmin, *Cosmopolis: The Hidden Agenda of Modernity* (Chicago: University of Chicago Press, 1990); Derek Heater, *World Citizenship and Government: Cosmopolitan Ideas in the History of Western Political Thought* (New York: St. Martin's Press, 1996) and *World Citizenship;* Timothy Brennan, *At Home in the World: Cosmopolitanism Now* (Cambridge, MA: Harvard University Press, 1997) and *Wars of Position: The Cultural Politics of Left and Right* (New York: Columbia University Press, 2006); Pheng Cheah and Bruce Robbins, eds., *Cosmopolitics: Thinking and Feeling beyond the Nation* (Minneapolis: University of Minnesota Press, 1998); Vinay Dharwadker, ed., *Cosmopolitan Geographies: New Locations in Literature and Culture* (New York: Routledge, 2001); Derrida, *On Cosmopolitanism and Forgiveness;* Amanda Anderson, *The Powers of Distance: Cosmopolitanism and the Cultivation of Detachment* (Princeton, NJ: Princeton University Press, 2001); Jessica Berman, *Modernist Fiction, Cosmopolitanism, and the Politics of Community* (Cambridge: Cambridge University Press, 2001); Steven Vertovec and Robin Cohen, eds., *Conceiving Cosmopolitanism: Theory, Context, and Practice* (New York: Oxford University Press, 2002); Carol A. Breckenridge, Sheldon Pollock, Homi K. Bhabha, and Dipesh Chakrabarty, eds., *Cosmopolitanism* (Durham, NC: Duke University Press, 2002); Ulrich Beck, *Der Kosmopolitische Blick oder: Krieg ist Frieden* (Frankfurt am Main: Suhrkamp, 2004); Hollinger, *Cosmopolitanism and Solidarity;* Margaret C. Jacob, *Strangers Nowhere in the World: The Rise of Cosmopolitanism in Early Modern Europe* (Philadelphia: University of Pennsylvania Press, 2006); Anthony K. Appiah, *Cosmopolitanism: Ethics in a World of Strangers;* Seyla Benhabib, *Another Cosmopolitanism,* with commentaries by Jeremy Waldron, Bonnie Honig, and Will Kymlicka, ed. and introduced by Robert Post (Oxford: Oxford University Press, 2006); Rebecca Walkowitz, *Cosmopolitan Style: Modernism beyond the Nation* (New York: Columbia University Press, 2006); Nicolas Di Méo, *Le cosmopolitisme dans la littérature française: De Paul Bourget à Marguerite Yourcenar* (Geneva, Switzerland: Droz, 2010). I supply overviews of emerging neocosmopolitan scholarship and its tensions with postmodernism and cosmodernism in "Cosmopolitics, Paroxism, Global Talk" and "Postmodernism, Cosmopolitanism, Cosmodernism," *American Book Review* 28, no. 3 (March–April 2007): 3–4.

204. Henry Lefebvre, *The Production of Space,* trans. Donald Nicholson-Smith (Oxford: Blackwell, 1991), 365.

205. Coulmas, *Les citoyens du monde,* 66, 301–4, 59.

206. Marcus Aurelius, *Meditations,* a new trans., with an introduction, by Gregor Hays (New York: Random House, 2002), 136.

207. Julien Benda, *The Treason of the Intellectuals,* with a new introduction by Roger Kimball, trans. Richard Aldington (New Brunswick, NJ: Transaction, 2007), 85, 98–100.

208. Brennan, *Wars of Position,* 136–37. Brennan ranks twentieth-century cos-

mopolitan proponents with other "champions" of globalization. For Rowe, see his article "Post-Nationalism, Globalism, and the New American Studies," in Rowe, *Post-Nationalist American Studies*, 31.

209. Peter Van der Veer, "Colonial Cosmopolitanism," in Vertovec and Cohen, *Conceiving Cosmopolitanism*, 169.

210. Coulmas, *Les citoyens du monde*, 205.

211. Coulmas, *Les citoyens du monde*, 169.

212. Heater, *World Citizenship and Government*, 7.

213. For a brief discussion of the Buddhist tradition of cosmopolitanism reaching back to 500 BC, see Dharwadker's essay "Cosmopolitanism in Its Time and Place," an introduction to his anthology, *Cosmopolitan Geographies*, 6–7.

214. Carol A. Breckenridge, Sheldon Pollock, Homi K. Bhabha, and Dipesh Chakrabarty, "Cosmopolitanisms," in Breckenridge, Pollock, Bhabha, and Chakrabarty, *Cosmopolitanism*, 1.

215. Hollinger, "The New Cosmopolitanism," in Vertovec and Cohen, *Conceiving Cosmopolitanism*, 228.

216. Breckenridge, Pollock, Bhabha, and Chakrabarty, "Cosmopolitanisms," 1. On "micro-cosmopolitanism," see Cronin's *Translation and Identity* (New York: Routledge, 2006), 15.

217. Robbins, *Feeling Global*, 100.

218. For Appadurai's "postnational imaginary," see his *Modernity at Large*, 177. On Beck's distinction between "the national perspective" that "excludes" "monologically" "the otherness of the other" and "the cosmopolitan perspective" and its "alternative imagination," see his article "The Cosmopolitan Society and Its Enemies," *Theory, Culture, and Society* 19, no. 1–2 (2002): 18.

219. Walter Mignolo, "The Many Faces of Cosmo-polis: Border Thinking and Critical Cosmopolitanism," *Public Culture* 12, no. 3 (2000): 721–48.

220. Emmanuel Levinas, "Peace and Proximity," in Emmanuel Levinas, *Basic Philosophical Writings*, ed. Adriaan T. Peperzak, Simon Critchley, and Robert Bernasconi (Bloomington: Indiana University Press, 1996), 168.

221. See, for example, Patrick Brantlinger, *Crusoe's Footprints: Cultural Studies in Britain and America* (New York: Routledge, 1990), 16.

222. Robert Eaglestone, *Ethical Criticism: Reading after Levinas* (Edinburgh: Edinburgh University Press, 1997).

223. I will refer only to Mark C. Taylor's *Altarity* (Chicago: University of Chicago Press, 1987); Adam Zachary Newton's *Narrative Ethics* (Cambridge, MA: Harvard University Press, 1995) and *The Elsewhere;* Paul Ricoeur's *Oneself as Another*, trans. Kathleen Blamey (Chicago: University of Chicago Press, 1992); Thomas Docherty's *Alterities: Criticism, History, Representation* (Oxford: Clarendon, 1996); T. M. Scanlon's *What We Owe to Each Other* (Cambridge, MA: Harvard University Press, 1998); Crystal Parikh's *An Ethics of Betrayal: The Politics of Otherness in Emergent U.S. Literatures and Culture* (New York: Fordham University Press, 2009); Singer's *One World;* Charles Taylor's *The Ethics of Authenticity;* Habermas's *The Inclusion of the Other;* and Butler's *Giving an Account of Oneself* (New York: Fordham University Press, 2005).

224. See, for instance, Eaglestone's *Ethical Criticism;* J. Hillis Miller's *Others* (Princeton, NJ: Princeton University Press, 2001); Jill Robbins's *Altered Reading: Levinas and Literature* (Chicago: University of Chicago Press, 1999); Todorov's *La*

conquête de l'Amérique: La question de l'autre (Paris: Seuil, 1991), *Nous et les autres: La réflexion française sur la diversité humaine* (Paris: Seuil, 1992), and *La Vie commune: Essai d'anthropologie générale* (Paris: Seuil, 2003); Patrick McGee's *Telling the Other: The Question of Value in Modern and Postcolonial Writing* (Ithaca, NY: Cornell University Press, 1992); Linda Bolton's *Facing the Other: Ethical Disruption and the American Mind* (Baton Rouge: Louisiana State University Press, 2004); W. Lawrence Hogue's *Postmodern American Literature and Its Other* (Champaign: University of Illinois Press, 2008); François de Singly's *Les uns avec les autres: Quand l'individualisme crée du lien* (Paris: Armand Colin, 2003); Bertrand Badie and Marc Sadoun's excellent collection *L'autre* (Paris: Presses de la Fondation Nationale des Sciences Politiques, 1996); Gisela Brinker-Gabler's anthology *Encountering the Others: Studies in Literature, History, and Culture* (Albany: SUNY Press, 1995); Derrida's *Of Hospitality* and the first part of his book *On Cosmopolitanism and Forgiveness;* the 1997 issue of the French journal *Communications* dedicated to "the question of hospitality today"; Žižek, "Love Thy Neighbor? No, Thanks!" and the anthology edited by Žižek, Eric Satner, and Kenneth Reinhard, *The Neighbor.*

225. Levinas, "Ideology and Idealism," 244.

PART 1

1. Roland Barthes, "The Death of the Author," Lodge and Wood, *Modern Criticism and Theory,* 2000 ed., 146.

2. Joshua A. Fishman, "The New Linguistic Order," in *Globalization and the Challenges of a New Century: A Reader,* ed. Patrick O'Meara, Howard D. Mehlinger, and Matthew Crain (Bloomington: Indiana University Press, 2000), 436.

3. Emily Apter, *The Translation Zone: A New Comparative Literature* (Princeton, NJ: Princeton University Press, 2006), 246.

4. Domna Stanton, "On Linguistic Human Rights and the United States 'Foreign' Language Crisis," *Profession 2005,* 66.

5. Dante, *Literature in the Vernacular,* trans. with an introduction by Sally Purcell (Manchester, UK: Carcanet New Press, 1981), 20.

6. Julia Kristeva, *Nations without Nationalism,* trans. Leon S. Roudiez (New York: Columbia University Press, 1993), 41.

7. Derrida, *Monolingualism of the Other,* 24; *Of Hospitality,* 135.

8. Apter glosses on Derrida's "aporetic" deconstruction of monolingualism in *The Translation Zone,* 246–47.

9. Derrida, *Monolingualism of the Other,* 24.

10. Jacques Derrida, "Structure, Sign, and Play in the Discourse of the Human Sciences" in Lodge and Wood, *Modern Criticism and Theory,* 2000 ed., 95–96.

11. Derrida, *Monolingualism of the Other,* 7.

12. "Once the national predicate is dislodged," Apter comments in *The Translation Zone,* "no speaker maintains exclusive ownership of language properties; the right to language is distributed more freely as language is classed as the property of X-many lease-holders" (247).

13. Jean Baudrillard, *The Vital Illusion,* ed. Julia Witwer (New York: Columbia University Press, 2000), 69–71.

14. Hall issues the call to "vernacular cosmopolitanism" in his "Political Belonging in a World of Multiple Identities" contribution to Vertovec and Cohen's *Conceiving Cosmopolitanism* anthology, 30. On postmodernism and vernacularism, see Jim Collins, *Uncommon Cultures: Popular Culture and Post-Modernism* (New York: Routledge, 1989), 128–36.

15. Derrida, *Monolingualism of the Other,* 24.

16. Doris Sommer, *Bilingual Aesthetics: A New Sentimental Education* (Durham, NC: Duke University Press, 2004), 45, 8.

17. Dante, *Literature in the Vernacular,* 15.

18. Chang-rae Lee, *Native Speaker* (New York: Riverhead, 1995).

19. Critics who have underscored the role Whitman plays in *Native Speaker* include, among others, Liam Corley, David Cowart, Tim Engles, and Daniel Y. Kim.

20. Jacques Derrida, *The Ear of the Other: Texts and Discussions with Jacques Derrida; Otobiography. Transference. Translation,* English ed. by Christie McDonald, trans. by Peggy Kamuf of the French edition ed. by Claude Lévesque and Christie McDonald ("Otobiographies" trans. by Avital Ronell) (Lincoln: University of Nebraska Press, 1988), 4. For an analysis of white America and whiteness in general in *Native Speaker,* see Tim Engles, "'Visions of me in the whitest raw light': Assimilation and Doxic Whiteness in Chang-rae Lee's *Native Speaker,*" *Hitting Critical Mass: A Journal of Asian American Cultural Studies* 4, no. 2 (Summer 1997): 27–48, http://www.ux1.eiu.edu/~cftde/-hcmns.html (accessed October 10, 2005).

21. Van der Veer, "Colonial Cosmopolitanism," 168.

22. Lee, *Native Speaker,* 295.

23. See James Der Derian's discussion of espionage and the spy thriller genre, with references to Terry Eagleton's essay on Conrad's *Secret Agent,* in "Spy versus Spy: The Intertextual Power of International Intrigue," an essay from *International/Intertextual Relations: Postmodern Readings of World Politics,* ed. James Der Derian and Michael J. Shapiro.(Lexington, TN: Lexington Books, 1989), 162–87.

24. David Cowart, "Korean Connection: Chang-rae Lee and Company," chap. 5 of *Trailing Clouds: Immigrant Fiction in Contemporary America* (Ithaca, NY: Cornell University Press, 2006), 174.

25. Tom Lutz, *Cosmopolitan Vistas: American Regionalism and Literary Values* (Ithaca, NY: Cornell University Press, 2004), 3, 37.

26. Chang-rae Lee, *A Gesture Life* (New York: Riverhead, 1999) and *Aloft* (New York: Riverhead, 2005).

27. "Through his narrative," Liam Corley remarks in "'Just Another Ethnic Pol': Literary Citizenship in Chang-rae Lee's Native Speaker" (*Studies in the Literary Imagination* 37, no. 1 [Spring 2004]: 74), "Lee revises Whitman's heritage of representative Americanness to include the immigrant experience as central."

28. Also see Corley, "'Just Another Ethnic Pol,'" 73–74.

29. Lee, *Native Speaker,* xi.

30. Corley, "'Just Another Ethnic Pol,'" 73.

31. See Cowart's *Trailing Clouds* for a cogent discussion of Shelley's "moral vision" in Lee's novel (177–78).

32. Corley, "'Just Another Ethnic Pol,'" 74.

33. Corley, "'Just Another Ethnic Pol,'" 62–63. On the *Golden Venture* shipwreck, also see Rachel C. Lee, "Reading Contests and Contesting Reading: Chang-

rae Lee's *Native Speaker* and Ethnic New York," *MELUS* 29, no. 3–4 (Fall–Winter 2004): 341–52.

34. Walt Whitman, *Complete Poetry and Selected Prose,* ed. with an introduction and glossary by James E. Miller (Boston: Houghton Mifflin, 1959), 298–302.

35. Levinas, *Totality and Infinity,* 74, 213–14.

36. Corley underscores "the double-bind experienced by both Kwang and Lee—of being fluent and acculturated yet also constructed as foreign and other" ("'Just Another Ethnic Pol,'" 75).

37. Assia Djebar, *Fantasia: An Algerian Cavalcade,* trans. Dorothy S. Blair (Portsmouth, NH: Heinemann, 1993), 157.

38. Translators' preface to Hans-Georg Gadamer, *Truth and Method,* 2nd revised ed., translation revised by Joel Weinsheimer and Donald G. Marshall (London: Continuum, 2004), xv.

39. Gadamer, *Truth and Method,* 355.

40. Julia Alvarez, *How the García Girls Lost Their Accents* (New York: Penguin, 1992), 141.

41. See Tina Chen's article "Impersonation and Other Disappearing Acts in *Native Speaker* by Chang-rae Lee" (*Modern Fiction Studies* 48, no. 3 [2002]: 637–57) for a discussion of the role *Invisible Man* plays in *Native Speaker*'s encoding as a spy thriller. On Lee and other African American writers including Ellison and Richard Wright, I also refer the reader to Yung-Hsing Wu's article "Native Sons and Native Speakers: On the Eth(n)ics of Comparison," *PMLA* 121, no. 5 (October 2006): 1460–64.

42. In Henry's "invisible brother," Cowart writes, "readers may recognize a variant of Fa Mu Lan, the narrator's heroic alter ego in Kingston's *Woman Warrior*" (*Trailing Clouds,* 171).

43. Cowart, *Trailing Clouds,* 175.

44. "Lee's novel" overall, Daniel Y. Kim maintains, is written "explicitly . . . against a xenophobic nativism." See Kim's article "Do I, Too, Sing America? Vernacular Representations and Chang-rae Lee's *Native Speaker,*" *Journal of Asian American Studies* 6, no. 3 (October 2003): 245.

45. Hélène Cixous, "Le sexe ou la tête," quoted in Stephen Heath's essay "Difference" featured in *Literary Theories: A Reader and Guide,* ed. Julian Wolfreys (New York: NYU Press, 1999), 225.

46. This is one way of translating the Derrida epigraph to J. Hillis Miller's *Others:* "l'autre appelle à venir et cela n'arrive qu'à plusieurs voix" (1). The motto is from Derrida's *Psyché: Inventions de l'autre* (Paris: Galilée, 1987), 61. J. Hillis Miller renders the passage as "the other calls [something] to come and that does not happen except in multiple voices" (*Others,* 1).

47. M. M. Bakhtin, *The Dialogic Imagination: Four Essays,* ed. Michael Holquist, trans. Caryl Emerson and Michael Holquist (Austin: University of Texas Press, 1981), 67.

48. Bakhtin, *The Dialogic Imagination,* 67.

49. In a 1784 essay on the topic of the "universality of the French language," Franz Thomas Chastel deplores "ces siècles d'erreurs qui avaient vu la dispersion des nations et la confusion de langues." For Chastel's text, see Stefano Gensini, "La varietà delle lingue da Babele a Cosmopoli," in *L'idea di cosmopolitismo: Circolazione e metamorfosi,* ed. Lorenzo Bianchi (Napoli, Italy: Liguori Editore, 2002), 134.

50. On "linguistic imperialism" in *Native Speaker* and other works by John Okada, Chin Frank, and Donald Duk, see Eugene Eoyang's article "English as a Postcolonial Tool," *English Today* 19, no. 4 (October 2003): 23–29.

51. Salman Rushdie, *Midnight's Children* (New York: Penguin, 1991), 308.

52. See Corley, "'Just Another Ethnic Pol,'" for a nuanced treatment of the novel's "claim that American identities are performative through language" (79).

53. Crystal Parikh, "Ethnic America Undercover: The Intellectual and Minority Discourse," *Contemporary Literature* 43, no. 2 (Summer 2002): 281.

54. Corley, "'Just Another Ethnic Pol,'" 78.

55. Sommer, *Bilingual Aesthetics*, 19.

56. Colin MacCabe, "Broken English," in *Futures for English*, ed. Colin Mac-Cabe (Manchester, UK: Manchester University Press, 1988), 12.

57. "Ma langue française était devenue étrangère. Elle était devenue une langue étrangère. Et en France les étrangers ne sont pas toujours bien vus et bienvenus. C'est connu. Je sais. Mon père était un étranger qui parlait sept langues. Même le français. C'est pour ça que moi aussi je parle le français. C'était un don de la France. Et maintenant je veux rendre à la France ce que la France m'a donné. Ma langue française. Celle que j'ai emmenée avec moi en Amérique et qui là-bas s'est transformée en mes livres. Je lègue donc à la France, comme a fait François Villon, tous mes livres. Je les donne gratuitement. Tout ce que je demande à la France, c'est de mettre un jour une petite plaque quelque part qui dira: *Ici a résidé Federman. Un traître à la cause.*" See Raymond Federman, "Le traître à la cause," http://www.montbouge. info/spip.php?article412 (accessed April 5, 2007). Slightly altered, the text is reproduced, in original or translated form, in *My Body in Nine Parts* and in the *Manure/Fumier* books.

58. Apter, *The Translation Zone*, 246–47. Also see Sommer, *Bilingual Aesthetics*, 191.

59. Raymond Federman, *Return to Manure* (Tuscaloosa: University of Alabama Press/Fiction Collective Two, 2006), 128–29.

60. As Federman declares, "I do not translate myself. I transact myself. Or better yet I plagiarize the original version when I rewrite it in the other language" (letter to the author).

61. See Marcel Cornis-Pope, *Narrative Innovation and Cultural Rewriting in the Cold War Era and After* (New York: Palgrave, 2001), 203–4.

62. Raymond Federman, *Critifiction: Postmodern Essays* (Albany: SUNY Press, 1993), 76–84.

63. Federman, *Critifiction*, 77.

64. See Larry McCaffery, Thomas Hartl, and Doug Rice, eds., *Federman A to X: A Recyclopedic Narrative* (San Diego: San Diego State University Press, 1998).

65. Raymond Federman, *Take It or Leave It: An Exaggerated Second-Hand Tale to Be Read Aloud Either Standing or Sitting* (New York: Fiction Collective, 1976).

66. Federman, *Critifiction*, 77.

67. Raymond Federman, *Aunt Rachel's Fur: A Novel Improvised in Sad Laughter; Transacted from the French by Federman and Patricia Privat-Standley* (Tallahassee: FC2, 2001), 248.

68. Gilles Deleuze, *Difference and Repetition*, trans. Paul Patton (New York: Columbia University Press, 1994), 57.

69. Federman, *Critifiction*, 82.

70. Søren Kierkegaard, *Fear and Trembling; Repetition*, ed. and trans. with introduction and notes by Howard V. Hong and Edna V. Hong (Princeton, NJ: Princeton University Press, 1983), 149.

71. Edward J. Mooney, "*Repetition:* Getting the World Back," in *The Cambridge Companion to Kierkegaard*, ed. Alastair Hannay and Gordon D. Marino (Cambridge: Cambridge University Press, 1998), 282–307.

72. Kierkegaard, *Fear and Trembling; Repetition*, 149.

73. Mooney, "*Repetition:* Getting the World Back," 300.

74. Raymond Federman, *My Body in Nine Parts: With Three Supplements and Illustrations*, photographs by Steve Murez (Buffalo: Starcherone Press, 2005), 70; *Return to Manure*, 26.

75. Federman, *Critifiction*, 83.

76. Federman, *Return to Manure*, 10.

77. Federman, *My Body in Nine Parts*, 68–69.

78. Federman, *Critifiction*, 59–60.

79. Mooney, "*Repetition:* Getting the World Back," 297.

80. Raymond Federman, *Retour au fumier: Récit nostalgique pour mon vieux chien Bigleux*, translation from the English (U.S.) by Éric Giraud (Romainville, France: Éditions Al Dante, 2005), 10.

81. McCaffery, Hartl, and Rice, *Federman A to X*, 396.

82. Federman, *Return to Manure*, 134.

83. Federman, *Return to Manure*, 134.

84. McCaffery, Hartl, and Rice, *Federman A to X*, 123.

85. Federman, *Critifiction*, 58.

86. McCaffery, Hartl, and Rice, *Federman A to X*, 123.

87. McCaffery, Hartl, and Rice, *Federman A to X*, 123.

88. Collete Soler, "Les noms de l'identité," *La Revue de psychanalyse du Champ lacanien* 6 (March 2008): 11.

PART 2

1. Amin Maalouf, *In the Name of Identity: Violence and the Need to Belong*, trans. Barbara Bray (New York: Penguin, 2000), 102.

2. Maalouf, *In the Name of Identity*, 103.

3. Maalouf, *In the Name of Identity*, 103.

4. Roman Jakobson, "Linguistics and Poetics," in Lodge and Wood, *Modern Criticism and Theory*, 2000 ed., 38.

5. Alain Finkielkraut, *In the Name of Humanity: Reflections on the Twentieth Century*, trans. Judith Friedlander (New York: Columbia University Press, 2000), 107.

6. Julia Watson, "What's in a Name? Heteroglossic Naming as Multicultural Practice in American Autobiography," *Prose Studies* 17, no. 1 (April 1994): 96.

7. Finkielkraut, *In the Name of Humanity*, 106.

8. On the *Mann ist Mann* passage and its discussion by Toril Moi, see her book *Sexual/Textual Politics* (London: Routledge, 2001), 160.

9. Sigmund Freud, "Lecture 6" of *Introductory Lectures on Psychoanalysis*, in Lodge and Wood, *Modern Criticism and Theory*, 2008 ed., 58–60.

10. Finkielkraut, *In the Name of Humanity,* 105–6.

11. Finkielkraut, *In the Name of Humanity,* 106.

12. Taylor, *Sources of the Self,* 525.

13. Levinas, *Proper Names,* 4.

14. Beauvoir, *The Second Sex,* 47.

15. Jacques Derrida, *On the Name,* trans. and ed. Thomas Dutoit (Stanford, CA: Stanford University Press, 1995), 89.

16. See Mark C. Taylor's *Altarity.*

17. Jhumpa Lahiri, *The Namesake* (Boston: Houghton Mifflin, 2004).

18. For a discussion of cross-cultural kinship, intertextual onomastics, and the theme of reading in Cather's "The Namesake," see Walter Benn Michaels's *Our America,* 33–38.

19. Levinas, *Proper Names,* 10. For a reading of the Gogol passage in the context of Levinas's essay on Schmeul Josef Agnon, see Robbins, *Altered Reading,* 143.

20. Lee, *A Gesture Life.*

21. On Coover and the "Grand American Narrative," see Paul Maltby, *Dissident Postmodernists: Barthelme, Coover, Pynchon* (Philadelphia: University of Pennsylvania Press, 1991), especially 51 and 121.

22. See Young-Oak Lee's article, "Gender, Race, and the Nation in *A Gesture Life,*" *Critique* 46, no. 2 (Winter 2005): 153. The critic acknowledges his debt to Sau-Ling Wong for "associating the name 'Franklin' to Benjamin [Franklin]" (158, n. 1). In chapter 6 of his book, *Trailing Clouds,* Cowart also glosses the name of Chang-rae Lee's hero.

23. Mike Campbell, "Jiro," in *Behind the Name: The Etymology and History of First Names,* http://www.behindthename.com/php/view.php?name=jiro (accessed March 8, 2007).

24. Lee, "Gender, Race, and the Nation in *A Gesture Life,*" 153. In his discussion of Asian Americans as "others" to American self-projected national identity, Lee quotes David Leiwei Li's *Imagining the Nation: Asian American Literature and Cultural Consent* (Stanford, CA: Stanford University Press, 1998).

25. Lee, "Gender, Race, and the Nation in *A Gesture Life,*" passim.

26. Mike Campbell, "Thomas," in *Behind the Name: The Etymology and History of First Names,* http://www.behindthename.com/php/view.php?name=thomas (accessed March 8, 2007).

27. This *Washington Post* book review fragment opens *Aloft*'s "Extraordinary Praise" section.

28. Lacan, "The Insistence of the Letter in the Unconscious," 83.

29. Hans Bertens, *Literary Theory: The Basics* (New York: Routledge, 2001), 161.

30. René Major, "Names: Proper and Improper," trans. John Forrester, in *Postmodernism: ICA Documents,* ed. Lisa Appignanesi (London: Free Association Books, 1986), 186.

31. Major, "Names," 187, 189–91.

32. Lee Siegel, *Love in a Dead Language: A Romance by Lee Siegel Being the Kamasutra of Guru Vatsyayana Mallanaga as Translated and Interpreted by Professor Leopold Roth with a Foreword and Annotation by Anang Saighal following the Commentary of Pandit Pralayananga Lilaraja* (Chicago: University of Chicago Press, 1999).

33. Andrei Codrescu, *Wakefield* (Chapel Hill: Algonquin Books, 2004), 241.

34. Watson, "What's in a Name?" 98.

35. Watson, "What's in a Name?" 99.

PART 3

1. Zadie Smith, *The Autograph Man* (New York: Random House, 2002), 120.

2. Smith, *The Autograph Man*, 119.

3. Smith, *The Autograph Man*, 119.

4. Sommer, *Bilingual Aesthetics*, 29.

5. Roman Jakobson distinguishes between "intralinguistic," "interlinguistic," and "intersemiotic" translation in his classical essay "On Linguistic Aspects of Translation" included first in Reuben A. Brower's 1959 anthology *On Translation* and more recently in Lawrence Venuti's *The Translation Studies Reader*, 2nd ed. (New York: Routledge, 2004), 138–43.

6. Michael Cronin quotes C. Y. Lee's 2001 essay "Small Can Be Even More Beautiful," which in turn cites Gunther Höser's reference to the assumption that "translation doesn't represent any added value." See Cronin's *Translation and Globalization* (New York: Routledge, 2003), 61.

7. See Rey Chow's "Translation and the Problem of Origins" chapter in *Primitive Passions: Visuality, Sexuality, Ethnography, and Contemporary Chinese Cinema* (New York: Columbia University Press, 1995), 186.

8. Jacques Derrida, "Des Tours de Babel," in *Difference in Translation*, ed. with an introduction by Joseph F. Graham (Ithaca, NY: Cornell University Press, 1985), 188.

9. Walter Benjamin, "The Task of the Translator," in *Illuminations: Essays and Reflections*, ed. and with an introduction by Hannah Arendt, trans. Harry Zohn (New York: Schocken Books, 1968), 75.

10. Jacques Derrida, "Letter to a Japanese Friend," in Wolfreys, *Literary Theories*, 282.

11. Derrida, "Des Tours de Babel," 171.

12. Susan Bassnett, "Translation Theory," in *The Johns Hopkins Guide to Literary Theory and Criticism*, 2nd ed., ed. Michael Groden, Martin Kreiswirth, and Imre Szeman (Baltimore: Johns Hopkins University Press, 2005), 911–12.

13. Bassnett, "Translation Theory," 910.

14. Umberto Eco, *Experiences in Translation*, trans. Alastair McEwen (Toronto: University of Toronto Press, 2001), 18.

15. Philippe Vasset, *ScriptGenerator*, trans. Jane Metter (London: Serpents's Tail, 2004), 84.

16. On global-era "c(o)lonial" translation that makes the translated into a clone/duplicate of the translator's cultural identity and thus speaks to globalization's "darker side," see Cronin's *Translation and Globalization*, 128–30.

17. "Although the history of colonialism varies significantly according to place and period, it does reveal a consistent, no, an inevitable reliance on translation," Lawrence Venuti observes in *The Scandals of Translation: Toward an Ethics of Difference* (New York: Routledge, 1998), 165. On "colonizing"/"Orientalizing" translation, also see Tejaswini Niranjana's book *Siting Translation: History, Post-*

Structuralism, and the Colonial Context (Berkeley: University of California Press, 1992), especially the first two chapters (1–86), and the "Politics of Translation" chapter in Gayatri Chakravorty Spivak's *Outside in the Teaching Machine* (New York: Routledge, 1993), 179–200. Chow's *Primitive Passions* too features a nuanced discussion of the issue (189–92). Both *Primitive Passions* and Cronin's *Translation and Globalization* (90, 139–40) query some of Niranjana's contentions. On Mc-Carthy's *Blood Meridian,* Kingsolver's *The Poisonwood Bible,* Boyle's *The Tortilla Curtain,* and translation as "hegemonic discourse over disenfranchised people and marginalized dialects," see Martha J. Cutter's *Lost and Found in Translation,* 12–13. Fuentes's "Las dos orillas" has been included in his 1994 short story collection *El naranjo* [The Orange Tree]. For a discussion of the story, see Ian Barnett's article "The Translator as Hero" at http://www.biblit.it/translator_hero.pdf (accessed December 2, 2007).

18. Nietzsche, *Beyond Good and Evil,* 230.

19. Friedrich Schleiermacher, "On the Different Methods of Translating," in Venuti, *The Translation Studies Reader,* 43–63.

20. George Steiner quotes from Nietzsche's *The Will to Power* in his considerations on language's power to "conceal" meaning and resist translation. See Steiner's *After Babel: Aspects of Language and Translation,* 3rd ed. (Oxford: Oxford University Press, 1998), 237.

21. Friedrich Nietzsche, *The Will to Power,* a new translation by Walter Kaufmann and R. J. Hollingdale, ed., with commentary, by Walter Kaufmann (New York: Random House, 1968), 428.

22. For a completely different meaning of "vertical" and "horizontal" translation, see Karlheinz Stierle, "Translatio Studii and Renaissance: From Vertical to Horizontal Translation," in Budick and Iser, *The Translatability of Cultures,* 55–67.

23. See K. Anthony Appiah's "Thick Translation," in Venuti, *The Translation Studies Reader,* 389–401.

24. Cronin, *Translation and Identity,* 104.

25. Cronin, *Translation and Identity,* 104.

26. Cronin, *Translation and Globalization,* 9–10; *Translation and Identity,* 105.

27. Chow, *Primitive Passions,* 182–95. In the same chapter, the critic takes issue with the "*rationalist* understanding of translation" (191) based on a facile distinction between correct and incorrect renderings.

28. Cronin distinguishes between "*translation as reflection*" and "*translation as reflexion.*" The opposition resembles mine only in part. As he specifies in *Translation and Globalization,* "The first term we define as the unconscious imbibing of a dominant language that produces the numerous calques that inform languages from Japanese to German to Irish. The second term refers to second-degree reflection or meta-reflection which should properly be the business of translation scholars and practitioners, namely, the critical consideration of what a language absorbs and what allows it to expand and what causes it to retract, to lose the synchronic and diachronic range of its expressive resources" (141).

29. "The easiest way to see what has happened in translation theory" since the late 1980s "is to think of a movement from the hermeneutical to the hegemonic," Bassnett proposes in "Translation Theory" (912).

30. Venuti, *The Scandals of Translation,* 62.

31. Bassnett, "Translation Theory," 910–11.

32. Chow, "Translation and the Problem of Origins," 183.

33. Cutter, *Lost and Found in Translation*, 30.

34. Mary Ann Caws, *Surprised in Translation* (Chicago: University of Chicago Press, 2006).

35. Zhang Longxi, *Allegoresis: Reading Canonical Literature East and West* (Ithaca, NY: Cornell University Press, 2005), 17.

36. Apter, *The Translation Zone*, 91.

37. Apter, *The Translation Zone*, 7.

38. Apter, *The Translation Zone*, 243–46.

39. Apter, *The Translation Zone*, 93. The critic returns to Benjamin's essay in her recent article "Taskography: Translation as Genre of Literary Labor," *PMLA* 122, no. 5 (October 2007): 1403–15.

40. Emily Apter, *Continental Drift: From National Characters to Virtual Subjects* (Chicago: University of Chicago Press, 1999), xiii.

41. Judith Butler, *Gender Trouble: Feminism and the Subversion of Identity* (New York: Routledge, 1999), ix.

42. Salman Rushdie, "Imaginary Homelands," in *Imaginary Homelands: Essays and Criticism 1981–1991* (London: Granta, 1991), 17. Pascale Casanova talks about the "tragedy of translated men" in *The World Republic of Letters*, 254–59.

43. Rushdie, *Imaginary Homelands*, 17, 15.

44. Augustine, *The City of God against the Pagans*, ed. and trans. R.W. Dyson (Cambridge: Cambridge University Press, 1998), 928. In the introduction to *Translation and Identity*, Cronin also comments on Augustine's *The City of God* fragment on translation.

45. Rushdie, *Imaginary Homelands*, 17.

46. Cronin, *Translation and Identity*, 1.

47. Geertz, *Local Knowledge*, 44.

48. James Clifford, "Traveling Cultures," in *Cultural Studies*, ed. and with an introduction by Lawrence Grossberg, Cary Nelson, and Paula A. Treichler, with Linda Baughman and assistance from John Macgregor Wise (New York: Routledge, 1992), 110.

49. Gunn, *Beyond Solidarity*, 23.

50. Geertz, *Local Knowledge*, 44.

51. Nicole Mones, *Lost in Translation* (New York: Random House, 1999).

52. Mircea Eliade published *Maitreyi* in Romanian in 1933. The novel has been translated into a number of languages, including French (*La nuit bengali*, 1950) and English (*Bengal Nights*, 1993). Maitreyi Devi came out with her counterstory, the romance *Na Hanyate* (It Does Not Die), in 1974. The University of Chicago Press released both books together in 1994.

53. In *Late Imperial Romance* (London: Verso, 1994), John McClure contends that romance "*requires* the very condition threatened by the successful establishment of the global order. It requires a world at war—starkly divided, partially wild and mysterious, dramatically dangerous" (2).

54. Clifford, *The Predicament of Culture*, 11, 4.

55. On Mones and modernism/modernity, also see Theo D'haen's essay "Post/Modernist East," in *Re-Imagining Language and Literature for the 21st Century*, ed. Suthira Duangsamosorn (Amsterdam: Rodopi, 2005), 319–30.

56. "Super-consciousness" is how N. M. Wildiers renders Teilhard's *la survie*

in *An Introduction to Teilhard de Chardin*, trans. Hubert Hoskins, preface by Christopher F. Mooney (New York: Harper & Row, 1968), 101. Sarah Appleton-Weber, the author of the new translation of *Le Phénomène humain*, prefers to play it safe ("superlife"). See Pierre Teilhard de Chardin, *The Human Phenomenon*, a new edition and translation of *Le phénomène humain* by Sarah Appleton-Weber, with a foreword by Brian Swimme (Brighton, UK: Sussex Academic Press, 1999), 165.

57. See Wildiers's *Introduction* for a discussion of Teilhard's relations to Kierkegaard (166), Nietzsche (101, 107, 166), and Marxism (101–2, 105–6).

58. Matei Calinescu, "Modernity, Modernism, Modernization: Variations on Modern Themes," in *The Turn of the Century: Modernism and Modernity in Literature and the Arts*, ed. Christian Berg, Frank Durieux, and Geert Lernout (Berlin: Walter de Gruyter, 1995), 43.

59. Calinescu, "Modernity, Modernism, Modernization," 42.

60. Calinescu, "Modernity, Modernism, Modernization," 45.

61. Wildiers, *Introduction*, 50.

62. In the "Avant-propos" to the 1955 edition of *Le Phénomène humain*, N. M. Wildiers observes that the essay's reader is "struck especially . . . by *the profound sense of totality* that the author shows constantly." See Pierre Teilhard de Chardin, *Le Phénomène humain* (Paris: Seuil, 1955), 12.

63. On Teilhard's "globalist" terminology, the reader may rely on Bernard Sesé's essay "Pierre Teilhard de Chardin: Prophète de la mondialisation?" *Etudes*, no. 3964 (April 2002): 483–94.

64. Wildiers, *Introduction*, 103.

65. As Wildiers observes, "In the Christian idea of things the whole of history is directed toward the building up and unifying of the entire human race into a supranatural community of which Christ is the head and all of us the members" (*Introduction*, 135).

66. Wildiers, *Introduction*, 69–71.

67. Wildiers, *Introduction*, 97–100.

68. Wildiers, *Introduction*, 150.

69. Wildiers, *Introduction*, 136.

70. Teilhard, *Le Phénomène humain*, 235.

71. See Pierre Teilhard de Chardin's *Lettres à Léontine Zanta*, introduction by Robert Garric and Henri de Lubac (Paris: Desclée De Brouwer, 1965). Most letters were written during his 1923–34 Chinese travels. In an epistle dated December 14, 1929, the philosopher-paleontologist mentions the discovery of a Peking Man skull (109).

72. Quoted in *The Letters of Teilhard de Chardin and Lucile Swan*, foreword by Pierre Leroy, ed. Thomas M. King and Mary Wood Gilbert (Scranton, PA: University of Scranton Press, 2001), 296.

73. *The Letters of Teilhard de Chardin and Lucile Swan*, xvii.

74. *The Letters of Teilhard de Chardin and Lucile Swan*, 7.

75. *The Letters of Teilhard de Chardin and Lucile Swan*, 19.

76. *The Letters of Teilhard de Chardin and Lucile Swan*, 295–96.

77. Mary Wood Gilbert, in *The Letters of Teilhard de Chardin and Lucile Swan*, xvii.

78. *The Letters of Teilhard de Chardin and Lucile Swan*, 34.

79. "Matter he loved: people, landscape, stones," Annie Dillard, another con-

temporary American author interested in Teilhard, writes about him in *For the Time Being* (New York: Knopf, 1999), 43. Judging from her examples, though, it becomes clear that "landscapes" and "stones" fare better than "people"; "matter" actually designates the "materials" of Teilhard's research.

80. Butler, *Gender Trouble*, ix.

81. Bhabha, *The Location of Culture*, 228.

82. Moretti, *Modern Epic*, 161. Moretti quotes from the "The Semiotics of Tourism" chapter of Jonathan Culler's 1988 book *Framing the Sign: Criticism and Its Institutions* (Norman: University of Oklahoma Press).

83. Bassnett, "Translation Theory," 910.

84. Lahiri's story "Interpreter of Maladies" has been included in her 1999 Pulitzer Prize–winning collection bearing the story's title (Boston: Houghton Mifflin), 43–69. Cronin discusses the De Santis thriller in *Translation and Globalization*, 6–7. In "The Translator as Hero," Barnett surveys briefly the works of De Santis, Benesdra, and Ponce alongside Fuentes's "Las dos orillas," concluding that "the three novels are crying out for translation into as many languages as possible as soon as possible."

85. See "Interview with Suki Kim, author of *The Interpreter*" by Cindy Yoon, *AsiaSource,* March 24, 2003, http://www.asiasource.org/arts/sukikim.cfm (accessed July 12, 2006).

86. Suki Kim, *The Interpreter* (New York: Farrar, Strauss and Giroux, 2003), 14–16. Further references to the novel are keyed to this edition.

87. Robbins, *Feeling Global,* 70.

88. Sanford Budick, "Crises of Alterity: Cultural Untranslatability and the Experience of Secondary Otherness," in Budick and Iser, *The Translatability of Cultures,* 11. For Stierle, see Karlheinz Stierle, "Translatio Studii and Renaissance."

89. Wolfgang Iser, *The Range of Interpretation* (New York: Columbia University Press, 2000), 5–12.

90. Klaus Reichert, "The Buber-Rosenzweig Bible Translation," in Budick and Iser, *The Translatability of Cultures,* 175.

91. Bercovitch, "Discovering America,"149.

92. Bercovitch, "Discovering America," 149.

PART 4

1. Bharati Mukherjee, *The Tree Bride* (New York: Hyperion, 2004), 10, 236.

2. Bharati Mukherjee, *Jasmine* (New York: Grove, 1989), 68.

3. Julia Kristeva, *Polylogue* (Paris: Seuil, 1977), 49.

4. Levinas, *Totality and Infinity,* 44–47.

5. Tuan, *Cosmos and Hearth,* 146.

6. Gunn, *Beyond Solidarity,* 23.

7. Yunte Huang, *Transpacific Displacement: Ethnography, Translation, and Intertextual Travel in Twentieth-Century American Literature* (Berkeley: University of California Press, 2002).

8. K. Anthony Appiah, "Cosmopolitan Reading," in Dharwadker, *Cosmopolitan Geographies,* 207.

9. Andrew Gibson talks about reading as "encounter" in a commentary on

Gadamer in *Postmodernity, Ethics, and the Novel: From Leavis to Levinas* (London: Routledge, 1999), 51.

10. Paul Auster, *The Art of Hunger: Essays, Prefaces, Interviews, and* The Red Notebook (New York: Penguin, 1993), 22.

11. Emmanuel Levinas, *God, Death, and Time,* trans. Bettina Bergo (Stanford, CA: Stanford University Press, 2000), 171.

12. See *Gender and Reading: Essays on Readers, Texts, and Contexts,* ed. Elizabeth A. Flynn and Patrocinio P. Schweickart (Baltimore: Johns Hopkins University Press, 1986), and, also edited by Schweickart and Flynn, *Reading Sites: Social Difference and Reader Response* (New York: Modern Language Association of America, 2004).

13. Stanley Fish, *Is There a Text in This Class? The Authority of Interpretive Communities* (Cambridge, MA: Harvard University Press, 1980), 171.

14. Gibson, *Postmodernity, Ethics, and the Novel,* 187, 196.

15. Fish, *Is There a Text in This Class?* 173.

16. Gibson, *Postmodernity, Ethics, and the Novel,* 187.

17. E. D. Hirsch, "Faulty Perspectives," in Lodge and Wood, *Modern Criticism and Theory,* 2000 ed., 238.

18. Appiah, "Cosmopolitan Reading," 217.

19. Appiah, "Cosmopolitan Reading," 222–23.

20. Appiah, "Cosmopolitan Reading," 223.

21. Appiah, "Cosmopolitan Reading," 222–23.

22. See Claude Bremond's *Logique du recit* (Paris: Seuil, 2001).

23. Appiah, "Cosmopolitan Reading," 202, 216, 208.

24. Hirsch, "Faulty Perspectives," 239.

25. On Georges Poulet's "critique of identification," see his essay "Criticism and the Experience of Interiority," in *Reader-Response Criticism: From Formalism to Post-Structuralism,* ed. Jane Tompkins (Baltimore: Johns Hopkins University Press, 1980), 41–49.

26. Poulet, "Criticism and the Experience of Interiority," 45. On Iser and Poulet's "identification," see Iser's *The Implied Reader: Patterns of Communication in Prose Fiction from Bunyan to Beckett* (Baltimore: Johns Hopkins University Press, 1978), 291.

27. Iser, *The Implied Reader,* 293.

28. Iser, *The Implied Reader,* 293.

29. Iser, *The Implied Reader,* 31.

30. See Fish's polemical review of Iser's *The Act of Reading* in "Why No One's Afraid of Wolfgang Iser," *Diacritics* 11, no. 1 (1981): 2–13. Iser replies in "Talk Like Whales," *Diacritics* 11, no. 3 (1981): 82–87.

31. Robert Holub, *Reception Theory: A Critical Introduction* (London: Methuen, 1984), 104.

32. Wolfgang Iser, *The Act of Reading: A Theory of Aesthetic Response* (Baltimore: Johns Hopkins University Press, 1978), 34.

33. On Iser's *Appelstruktur* and its relation to the determinacy-indeterminacy distinction, see his essay "Die Appelstruktur der Texte" in *Rezeptionsästhetik,* ed. Rainer Warning (Munich: Wilhelm Fink, 1988), 228–52, originally published in 1970 as *Die Appelstruktur der Texte: Überstimmtheit als Wirkungsbedingung literarischer Prosa.* The English version of the text came out in 1971 and then again, two

years after the German edition of *Der implizite Leser* (1972), as chapter 5 of *The Implied Reader* (1st ed., 1974). *The Act of Reading* also develops ideas from the 1970 essay.

34. Iser, *The Implied Reader,* 294.

35. Iser, *The Implied Reader,* 36.

36. Kristeva, *Nations without Nationalism,* 51.

37. In "Author and Hero in Aesthetic Activity," Bakhtin explains at length why I obtain my complete picture, experience, "constitute," and understand myself wholly only through others. See Bakhtin, *Art and Answerability,* 24–25, 38.

38. Walter Kaufmann, "I and You: A Prologue," in Buber, *I and Thou,* 39.

39. Buber, *I and Thou,* 54, 61–63.

40. Buber, *I and Thou,* 61.

41. Buber, *I and Thou,* 60.

42. Buber, *I and Thou,* 103.

43. Appiah, "Cosmopolitan Reading," 222–223; Iser, *The Implied Reader,* 31. Reading can be "a creative process," Iser also writes in *The Implied Reader,* 271.

44. Buber, *I and Thou,* 95.

45. Buber, *I and Thou,* 94.

46. On reading the "multicultural text"—rather than reading of texts in general—see Laurie Grobman's use of Mary Louise Pratt's "contact zone" theory in "Rhetorizing the Contact Zone: Multicultural Texts in Writing Classrooms," in Schweickart and Flynn, *Reading Sites,* 256–85.

47. Habermas, *The Inclusion of the Other,* 132.

48. Iser, *The Act of Reading,* 166.

49. Azar Nafisi, *Reading Lolita in Tehran: A Memoir in Books* (New York: Random House, 2003).

50. For Dai Sijie, besides his *Balzac and the Little Chinese Seamstress* (trans. Ina Rilke; London: Chatto & Windus, 2001), see also *Mr. Muo's Travelling Couch* (trans. from the French by Ina Rilke; New York: Knopf, 2005), and *Once on a Moonless Night* (trans. from the French by Adriana Hunter; New York: Knopf, 2009).

51. Gabriel Liiceanu's *Jurnalul de la Păltiniș* came out in 1983, was revised and reissued in 1991, and then was translated into English as *The Păltiniș Diary: A Paideic Model in Humanist Culture,* trans. James Christian Brown, with a preface by Sorin Antohi (Budapest: Central European University Press, 2000). *Epistolar* (Collected Letters), edited by Liiceanu (see 2nd ed., revised and expanded, Bucharest: Humanitas, 1996), and Liiceanu's *Ușa interzisă* (The Forbidden Door) (Bucharest: Humanitas, 2002) are also of interest. See Katherine Verdery's "The 'School' of Philosopher Constantin Noica," in her book *National Ideology under Socialism: Identity and Cultural Politics in Ceaușescu's Romania* (Berkeley: University of California Press, 1995), 256–301.

52. I compare Liiceanu's diary and Nafisi's memoir in my article "Jurnalul de la Teheran" (The Tehran Diary), trans. Laura Savu, *Observator cultural* 257 (January 25–31, 2005): 15–16.

53. John Carlos Rowe, "Reading *Reading Lolita in Tehran* in Idaho," *American Quarterly* 59, no. 2 (June 2007): 259.

54. Rowe, "Reading *Reading Lolita in Tehran* in Idaho," 271.

55. Quoted in Rowe, "Reading *Reading Lolita in Tehran* in Idaho," 258.

56. Rowe, "Reading *Reading Lolita in Tehran* in Idaho," 272.

57. Rowe, "Reading *Reading Lolita in Tehran* in Idaho," 263.

58. Iyer, *Video Night in Kathmandu and Other Reports from the Not-So-Far-East* (New York: Knopf, 1988), 6.

59. Azar Nafisi, "Azar Nafisi: Author of *Reading Lolita in Tehran* converses with Robert Birnbaum," interview by Robert Birnbaum, identitytheory.com: a literary website, sort of, February 5, 2004, http://www.identitytheory.com/inter views/birnbaum139.php (accessed January 14, 2005).

60. In the same interview, while pointing to "all these [American] subversive book groups where people are reading on their own," Nafisi insists that "Unfortunately you have to be deprived of something in order to understand its worth. I keep telling people, it's like your arm, if you have it, you are not thinking about it—being thankful everyday it exists—but if it is chopped off . . ."

61. Nafisi, the Birnbaum interview.

62. Appiah, "Cosmopolitan Reading," 207.

63. On Nabokov's cosmopolitanism and late modernism in the context of the transition to postmodernism, see my book *Memorious Discourse: Reprise and Representation in Postmodernism* (Madison, NJ: Fairleigh Dickinson University Press, 2005), 40–53.

64. Rowe, "Reading *Reading Lolita in Tehran* in Idaho," 258.

65. Ulrich Beck, "The Cosmopolitan Perspective: Sociology in the Second Age of Modernity," in Vertovec and Cohen, *Conceiving Cosmopolitanism*, 74.

66. If indeed, as Daniele Archibugi argues, "cosmopolitanism remains the prerogative of an elite," cosmodernism no longer preserves nor claims this privilege. See Archibugi's essay "Demos and Cosmopolis" in his anthology *Debating Cosmopolitics* (London: Verso, 2003), 258.

67. Norman Holland, "UNITY IDENTITY TEXT SELF," in Tompkins, *Reader-Response Criticism*, 124.

68. Holland, "UNITY IDENTITY TEXT SELF," 120.

69. Hans Robert Jauss, *Toward an Aesthetic of Reception,* trans. Timothy Bakhti, introduction by Paul de Man (Minneapolis: University of Minnesota Press, 2005), 24, 41–45.

70. Nafisi, *Reading Lolita in Tehran,* 18.

71. Nafisi, *Reading Lolita in Tehran,* 23.

72. Nafisi, *Reading Lolita in Tehran,* 33.

73. Nafisi, *Reading Lolita in Tehran,* 33.

74. Nafisi, *Reading Lolita in Tehran,* 6.

75. David Bleich, "What Literature Is 'Ours'?" in Schweickart and Flynn, *Reading Sites,* 311.

76. Nafisi, *Reading Lolita in Tehran,* 6.

77. Pico Iyer, "The Nowhere Man," *Prospect* 30, no. 3 (February 1997): 32.

78. Iyer, "The Nowhere Man," 32.

79. Michael Seidel, *Exile and the Narrative Imagination* (New Haven, CT: Yale University Press, 1986), 164.

80. Seidel, *Exile and the Narrative Imagination,* 4.

81. See Jacob's *Strangers Nowhere in the World.*

82. Iyer, "The Nowhere Man," 32.

83. Iyer, "The Nowhere Man," 32.

84. Iyer, *Sun after Dark,* 194–96.

85. Iyer, *Sun after Dark,* 24.

86. Pico Iyer, *The Global Soul: Jet Lag, Shopping Malls, and the Search for Home* (New York: Random House, 2000), 24.

87. Iyer, *The Global Soul,* 258.

88. Iyer, "The Nowhere Man," 32.

89. Pico Iyer, *Abandon: A Romance* (New York: Random House, 2003). All references are to this edition.

90. Iyer, *Video Night in Kathmandu,* 331.

91. Iyer, *Abandon,* biographical note.

92. Pratt, *Imperial Eyes: Travel Writing and Transculturation,* 6.

93. Iyer, *The Global Soul,* 258.

94. Iyer, *The Global Soul,* 24.

95. Iyer, *The Global Soul,* 19, 24.

96. Iyer, *The Global Soul,* 125.

97. Pratt, *Imperial Eyes,* 7.

98. Iyer, *The Global Soul,* 17, 19.

99. Iyer, "The Nowhere Man," 32.

100. Iyer, *The Global Soul,* 41.

101. Iyer, *Video Night in Kathmandu,* 228.

102. Khaled Hosseini, *The Kite Runner* (New York: Penguin, 2005), 226.

103. Iyer, *Video Night in Kathmandu,* 8.

104. Kaufmann, "I and You: A Prologue," 39.

105. Iyer, *Abandon,* 85, 134.

106. Iyer, "The Nowhere Man," 32.

107. Alice Randall, *Pushkin and the Queen of Spades* (Boston: Houghton Mifflin, 2004).

108. Lizzie Skurnick, "Menace II Russian Society," *New York Times Book Review,* May 23, 2004, 8.

109. Charles W. Chesnutt, "The Future American: A Complete Race-Amalgamation Likely to Occur," in *Essays and Speeches,* ed. Joseph R. McElrath, Jr., Robert C. Leitz III, and Jesse S. Crisler (Stanford, CA: Stanford University Press, 1999), 131, 133.

110. Chesnutt, "The Future American," 128.

111. Chesnutt, "The Future American," 122.

112. Skurnick, "Menace II Russian Society," 8.

113. Brennan places Du Bois's later work in the context of post–World War II cosmopolitanism in *At Home in the World,* 28–31.

114. W. E. B. Du Bois, *Writings* (New York: Library of America, 1986), 923.

115. Du Bois, *Writings,* 359.

116. W. E. B. Du Bois, *Color and Democracy: Colonies and Peace* (New York: Harcourt Brace, 1945), 114–22.

117. See Brennan's comments on the "Riddle of Russia" chapter of *Color and Democracy* in *At Home in the World,* 30–31.

118. W. E. B. Du Bois, *The Souls of Black Folk,* in *Writings,* 438.

119. Du Bois, *The Souls of Black Folk,* 438.

120. Marcus Aurelius, *Meditations,* new trans., with an introduction, by Gregor Hays (New York: Random House, 2002), 112.

121. Jacques Derrida, *Politics of Friendship*, trans. George Collins (London: Verso, 1997), 251.

122. Skurnick, "Menace II Russian Society," 8.

123. Lillian Herlands Hornstein, ed., and G. D. Percy, coed., *The Reader's Companion to World Literature*, 2nd ed. (New York: Penguin, 1984), 436–37.

124. Alexander Pushkin, *The Poems, Prose, and Plays of Alexander Pushkin*, selected and ed., with an introduction, by Avrahm Yarmolinsky (New York: Random House, 1964), 782.

125. Pushkin, *The Poems, Prose, and Plays of Alexander Pushkin*, 778.

126. Pushkin, *The Poems, Prose, and Plays of Alexander Pushkin*, 786.

127. Zadie Smith, *On Beauty* (New York: Penguin, 2005), 93.

128. E. M. Forster, *Howards End: Complete, Authoritative Text with Biographical and Historical Contexts, Critical History, and Essays from Five Contemporary Critical Perspectives*, ed. Alistair M. Duckworth (Boston: Bedford/St. Martin's, 1997), 168.

PART 5

1. A. A. Long and D. N. Sedley, *The Hellenistic Philosophers*, vol. 1, *Translations of the Principal Sources, with Philosophical Commentary* (Cambridge: Cambridge University Press, 1987), 7.

2. Cleanthes quoted by Nemesius, in Long and Sedley, *The Hellenistic Philosophers*, 1:272.

3. Eduard Zeller, *The Stoics, Epicureans, and Sceptics*, trans. from the German by Oswald J. Reichel, new and revised ed. (New York: Russell & Russell, 1962), 136.

4. Zeller, *The Stoics, Epicureans, and Sceptics*, 328.

5. Zeller, *The Stoics, Epicureans, and Sceptics*, 328.

6. Michel Spanneut, *Permanence du stoïcisme: De Zénon à Malraux* (Gembloux, Belgium: Duculot, 1973), 14.

7. Zeller, *The Stoics, Epicureans, and Sceptics*, 328.

8. Derrida, *On Touching—Jean-Luc Nancy*, 297.

9. Derrida, *On Touching—Jean-Luc Nancy*, 4.

10. Nancy, *The Inoperative Community*, 3.

11. Nancy, *The Inoperative Community*, 28. Also see Fred Dallmayr's commentary on this and related places in Nancy's work in "An 'Inoperative' Global Community? Reflections on Nancy," in *On Jean-Luc Nancy: The Sense of Philosophy*, ed. Darren Sheppard, Simon Sparks, and Colin Thomas (London: Routledge, 1997), 181.

12. Nancy, *The Sense of the World*, 9.

13. Derrida, *On Touching—Jean-Luc Nancy*, 54.

14. Don DeLillo, *Great Jones Street* (Boston: Houghton Mifflin, 1973), 27.

15. Derrida, *On Touching—Jean-Luc Nancy*, 53.

16. Nancy, *The Sense of the World*, 35, 62–63, and passim.

17. Jean Baudrillard, *L'autre par lui-même: Habilitation* (Paris: Galilée, 1987), 49.

18. Smart, *Facing Modernity*, 124–30.

19. Dallmayr comments on Nancy's "'ekstatic' self-transgression" in "An 'Inoperative' Global Community?" 178.

20. Butler, *Gender Trouble*, 170.

21. Jean Baudrillard, *Cool Memories*, trans. Chris Turner (London: Verso, 1990), 173.

22. Baudrillard, *Cool Memories*, 30.

23. Baudrillard, *Cool Memories*, 110.

24. Jean Baudrillard, *Fragments: Cool Memories III, 1991–1995*, trans. Emily Agar (London: Verso, 1997), 39.

25. Baudrillard, *America*, trans. Chris Turner (Verso: London, 1996), 1.

26. Baudrillard, *America*, 97.

27. Baudrillard, *The Vital Illusion*, 6.

28. Baudrillard, *The Vital Illusion*, 5–16, 25–26.

29. Jean Baudrillard, *The Perfect Crime*, trans. Chris Turner (London: Verso, 1996), 107, 111–12, 115.

30. Jean Baudrillard, *Cool Memories II: 1987–1990*, trans. Chris Turner (Durham, NC: Duke University Press, 1996), 51.

31. Don DeLillo, *The Names* (New York: Random House, 1989), 51.

32. See "'An Outsider in This Society': Interview with Don DeLillo," by Anthony DeCurtis, *South Atlantic Quarterly* 89, no. 2 (1990): 299.

33. Jean Baudrillard, *The System of Objects*, trans. James Benedict (London: Verso, 2005), 172.

34. Don DeLillo, *Underworld* (New York: Scribner, 1997), 121. All references are to this edition.

35. William B. Little, *The Waste Fix: Seizures of the Sacred from Upton Sinclair to* The Sopranos (New York: Routledge, 2002), 7. Other critics who have sifted through *Underworld*'s meaningful waste include David Cowart in *Don DeLillo: The Physics of Language*, rev. ed. (Athens: University of Georgia Press, 2003), especially 181–210, and Paul Gleason in "Don DeLillo, T. S. Eliot, and the Redemption of America's Atomic Waste Land," included in *UnderWords: Perspectives on Don DeLillo's* Underworld, ed. Joseph Dewey, Steven G. Kellman, and Irving Malin (Newark: University of Delaware Press, 2002), 130–43. John N. Duvall has also written an article on the topic, "Excavating the Underworld of Race and Waste in Cold War History: Baseball, Aesthetics, and Ideology," which can be found among the contributions to *Critical Essays on Don DeLillo*, ed. Hugh Ruppersburg and Tim Engles (New York: C. K. Hall, 2000), 258–81. Duvall follows up with a reader's guide, *DeLillo's* Underworld (New York: Continuum, 2002), where waste is subject to further scrutiny.

36. Gerald Vizenor, *Landfill Meditation: Crossblood Stories* (Middleton, CT: Wesleyan University Press, 1991).

37. See the *UnderWords* collection edited by Dewey, Kellman, and Malin.

38. For a survey of *Underworld*'s "semiotics of waste" and, in particular, for a comparative analysis of the novel and Eliot's *Waste Land*, see Gleason's essay "Don DeLillo, T. S. Eliot, and the Redemption of America's Atomic Waste Land."

39. Peter Knight calls *Underworld* "both a product and a creative response to the new World Order of connectedness" in "Everything Is Connected: *Underworld*'s Secret History of Paranoia," *Modern Fiction Studies* 45, no. 3 (Fall 1999): 832. See Cornis-Pope's *Narrative Innovation and Cultural Rewriting in the Cold*

War Era and After for a substantial discussion of the "polarized ideologies" of the Cold War self-other antagonisms in recent fiction.

40. Julian Murphet, "Postmodernism and Space," in *The Cambridge Companion to Postmodernism*, ed. Steven Connor (Cambridge: Cambridge University Press, 2004), 126.

41. See A. Ernout and A. Meillet's *Dictionnaire étymologique de la langue latine: Histoire des mots* (Paris: Klincksieck, 1959) on the related "histories" of *alter, in* and *inter,* and *re-* and *retro,* 22–23, 311–14, and 565–66.

42. DeLillo insists on the "open-ended" structure of his book in the interview with DeCurtis, "'An Outsider in This Society,'" 293.

43. Cowart, *Don DeLillo,* 192. In his article "Awful Symmetries in Don DeLillo's *Underworld*," Arthur Salzman also analyzes the "totalizing" trope of parallels, homologies, and connectivity and its bearings on the mysteries of life in DeLillo's novel, with references to previous works. See Salzman's text in Ruppersburg and Engles, *Critical Essays on Don DeLillo,* 302–16.

44. See Little, "Trash Recollection" subchapter, which focuses on *White Noise,* in *The Waste Fix,* 113–16.

45. Seyla Benhabib, *The Claims of Culture: Equality and Diversity in the Global Era* (Princeton, NJ: Princeton University Press, 2002), especially 3–11.

46. Don DeLillo, "The Power of History," *New York Times Magazine,* September 7, 1997, http://www.nytimes.com/library/books/090797article3.html (accessed May 23, 2007). Cowart makes a good case for reading DeLillo's essays "The Power of History" and "In the Ruins of the Future" (2001) alongside *Underworld* and *Cosmopolis* to tackle the themes of language, repetition, recycling, and obsolescence. See his *Don DeLillo,* 181–96 and 210–26. The latter chapter, on *Cosmopolis,* appeared first as "Anxieties of Obsolescence: DeLillo's *Cosmopolis*" in *Science, Technology, and the Humanities in Recent American Fiction,* ed. Peter Freese and Charles B. Harris (Essen, Germany: Die blaue Eule, 2004), 159–79. All future interpretations of DeLillo's recent work will have to take into account Cowart's sagacious analyses. I might add here that DeLillo's 2001 *Harper's* article also throws revealing light on his 2007 novel *Falling Man.*

47. In a French interview published under the title "Don DeLillo: Retour vers le futur" (*Magazine littéraire* no. 425, November 2003, 81), the author refers to "la culture de l'instantané" and its "destructive" effects on people.

48. DeLillo, "The Power of History."

49. DeLillo, "That Day in Rome: Movies and Memories," *New Yorker,* October 20, 2003, 76.

50. DeLillo, "The Power of History."

51. Walter Benjamin, "The Work of Art in the Age of Mechanical Reproduction," in *Illuminations,* 220.

52. Benjamin, "The Work of Art in the Age of Mechanical Reproduction," 220.

53. Steven Kellman talks about the "logogenetic" thrust of *Underworld* in an essay that opens with an analogy between Nick's Lexus and the "lexis" DeLillo "driv[es] through the windy expanses of preverbal thought." See Kellman's essay "DeLillo's Logogenetic *Underworld*" in *UnderWords,* ed. Dewey, Kellman, and Malin, 68.

54. On "montage" and DeLillo's own style as both "replication" and critique of the "power structure it wants to oppose," see Philip Nel, *The Avant-Garde and*

American Postmodernity: Small Incisive Shots (Jackson: University of Mississippi Press, 2002), particularly the chapter "'Amid the Undeniable Power of Montage'": Modern Forms, Postmodern Politics, and the Role of the Avant-Garde in Don DeLillo's *Underworld*," 97–107. Catherine Morley specifically addresses the influence of Eisensteinean montage on *Underworld* in her article "Don DeLillo's Transatlantic Dialogue with Sergei Eisenstein" published in *Journal of American Studies* 40, no. 1 (2006): 17–34. Despite the rather ill-informed treatment of Proletkult aesthetics and politics, Morley's account of the role played by Eisenstein's techniques in DeLillo's book is useful.

55. See Anne Longmuir's clarifying discussion of DeLillo's "two artistic paradigms" in "Performing the Body in Don DeLillo's *The Body Artist*," *Modern Fiction Studies* 53, no. 3 (Fall 2007): especially 529–33.

56. Don DeLillo, *Cosmopolis* (New York: Scribner, 2003), 200.

57. Jean-Luc Nancy, *Corpus* (Paris: Métailié, 2000), 11.

58. Giddens uses this Ricoeur fragment as an epigraph to *The Consequences of Modernity.*

59. DeLillo, *Cosmopolis,* 195.

60. See note 58 to this part.

61. Maxine Hong Kingston, *Tripmaster Monkey* (New York: Random House, 1990), 17, 65.

62. Kingston, *Tripmaster Monkey,* 102–3.

63. Kingston, *Tripmaster Monkey,* 312.

64. Zadie Smith, *White Teeth* (New York: Random House, 2000), 257.

65. Critics have agued that Zadie Smith has used specific thematic and narrative elements from Rushdie's *Midnight Children* and Kureishi's *The Black Album.* See Claire Squires, *Zadie Smith's* White Teeth: *A Reader's Guide* (New York: Continuum, 2002), 16–18.

66. For references to the "Rushdie affair" in Smith's book, see *White Teeth,* 193–94. For similar places in Kureishi, see his *The Black Album* (New York: Simon & Schuster, 1996), 179, 182, 193.

67. Kureishi, *The Black Album,* 157.

68. Martha Stoddard Holmes, "John Updike: 'Metamorphosis,'" *Literature, Arts and Medicine Database,* http://litmed.med.nyu.edu/Annnotation?action=view&annid=12403 (accessed September 24, 2007).

69. John Updike, "Metamorphosis," in *Licks of Love: Short Stories and a Sequel* (New York: Knopf, 2000), 176.

70. Joseph Bédier, *The Romance of Tristan and Iseult,* trans. Hilaire Belloc and Paul Rosenfeld (New York: Pantheon Books, 1945), 20, 31, 225–27.

71. Claude Lévi-Strauss, *Tristes Tropiques,* trans. from the French by John Weightman and Doreen Weightman (New York: Atheneum, 1974), 85–86.

72. John Updike, *Bech at Bay* (New York: Knopf, 1998), 238–39.

73. Srinivas Aravamudan, *Tropicopolitans: Colonialism and Agency, 1688–1804* (Durham, NC: Duke University Press, 1999), 6. To name only a few recent critics, "tropicalizations" of culture have been tackled by the contributors to Frances R. Aparicio and Susana Chávez-Silverman's collection *Tropicalizations: Transcultural Representations of Latinidad* (Hanover, NH: University Press of New England, 1997), by Robert Stam in *Tropical Multiculturalism: A Comparative History of Race in Brazilian Cinema and Culture* (Durham, NC: Duke University Press, 1997), and

José Quiroga in *Tropics of Desire: Interventions from Queer Latino America* (New York: NYU Press, 2000), respectively.

74. Karen Tei Yamashita, *Through the Arc of the Rain Forest* (Minneapolis: Coffee House Press, 1990), 160.

75. Aravamudan, *Tropicopolitans*, 4.

76. Ursula Heise shows how Yamashita's *Through the Arc of the Rain Forest* "link[s] issues of global ecology with those of transnational culture." See Heise's article "Local Rock and Global Plastic: World Ecology and the Experience of Place," *Comparative Literary Studies* 41, no. 1 (2004): 126–52. On "transformability" in the novel, see Heise's "Local Rock and Global Plastic," 144. Approaching the novel within the framework of the modern-postmodern distinction, Molly Wallace tackles the same problems in her essay "'A Bizarre Ecology': The Nature of Denatured Nature," *Interdisciplinary Studies in Literature and Environment* 7, no. 2 (Summer 2000): 137–53.

77. On Yamashita's "reworking" of *One Hundred Years of Solitude*, Andrade's *Macunaíma*, and their metamorphic imaginary, I refer the reader to Heise's "Local Rock and Global Plastic," 139–44.

78. Yamashita, *Through the Arc of the Rain Forest*, 212.

79. "An Interview with Karen Tei Yamashita" by Jean Vengua Gier and Carla Alicia Tejeda, *Jouvert* 2, no. 2 (September 2001), http://social.chass.ncsu.edu/jouvert/v2i2/yamashi.htm (accessed June 10, 2004).

80. Yamashita, "An Interview with Karen Tei Yamashita."

81. Claudia Sadowski-Smith, "The U.S.-Mexico Borderlands Write Back: Cross-Cultural Transnationalism in Contemporary U.S. Women of Color Fiction," *Arizona Quarterly* 57, no. 1 (Spring 2001): 105.

82. Yamashita, "Interview with Karen Tei Yamashita."

83. Guillermo Gómez-Peña, *The New World Border: Prophecies, Poems, and Loqueras for the End of the Century* (San Francisco: City Lights, 1996), and *Dangerous Border-Crossers: The Artist Talks Back* (New York: Routledge, 2000). For Supermojado and other "borderismos," see the glossary of *The New World Border*, 240–44. Somewhat dismissively, Molly Rauch has called Yamashita "the hybridized godchild of Gloria Anzaldua and Guillermo Gomez-Peña" in "Fruit Salad," *Nation*, March 2, 1998, 28. In her article "Tropics of Globalization: Reading the New North America," published in *symploke* 9, nos. 1–2 (2001): 145–60, Molly Wallace also names Anzaldúa's *Borderlands/La Frontera* and Leslie Marmon Silko's *Almanac of the Dead* (148), as well as Gómez-Peña, Octavia Butler, Mike Davis, and García Márquez, as main intertextual ingredients in a "blend of magical realism, political satire, and postmodern metafiction" geared toward a "metaphorical representation of NAFTA" (148). Part and parcel of globalization, Yamashita's NAFTA is, Wallace proposes following Paul de Man's *Resistance to Theory* and Hayden White's *Tropics of Discourse*, both an economic (material, "referential," "literal") and a figural ("tropic," or "literary") phenomenon while declining to be (n)either exclusively (151–58). In other words, the treaty is "real," but its reality has been continuously debated, produced discursively, and Wallace credits Yamashita with forefronting this discursive-"literary" (158) production. In an astute critique of Appadurai's "free trade zone" metaphor from *Modernity at Large*, Wallace adduces the novel as an example of how the "gap" and asymmetries

of power and profit between economic-cultural exchanges enacted in and across the zone can be laid bare.

84. Smith, *Coyote Kills John Wayne*, 153.

85. Gómez-Peña, *The New World Border*, 7.

86. Gómez-Peña, *The New World Border*, 7.

87. Wallace, "Tropics of Globalization," 153.

88. Karen Tei Yamashita, *Tropic of Orange* (Minneapolis: Coffee House Press, 1997), 258.

89. Yamashita, *Tropic of Orange*, 269–70.

90. Don DeLillo, *The Body Artist* (New York: Scribner, 2001), 112.

91. On *Underworld* and *The Body Artist* and Klara Sax and Lauren Hartke, see Longmuir, "Performing the Body in Don DeLillo's *The Body Artist*," especially 531.

92. Tim Adams, "The Library in the Body," http://www.guardian.co.uk/books/2001/feb/11/fiction.-dondelillo (accessed January 22, 2009).

93. Adams, "The Library in the Body."

94. Longmuir, "Performing the Body in Don DeLillo's *The Body Artist*," 539–40.

95. Longmuir, "Performing the Body in Don DeLillo's *The Body Artist*," 541–42.

96. Adams, "The Library in the Body."

EPILOGUE

1. Castells, *The Information Age: Economy, Society, and Culture*, vol. 1, *The Rise of the Network Society*, 460.

2. DeLillo, "The Power of History."

3. On "commodity culture," repetition, Jameson, and amnesia, see John Frow's *Time and Commodity Culture: Essays in Cultural Theory and Postmodernity* (Oxford: Oxford University Press, 1997), especially its last chapter, "*Toute la mémoire du monde:* Repetition and Forgetting," 218–46. Frow's book covers these issues more generally. It also leans on DeLillo as a prime example.

4. DeLillo, *Underworld*, 544–45.

5. Don DeLillo, "In the Ruins of the Future: Reflections on Terror and Loss in the Shadow of September," *Harper's Magazine*, December 2001, 39.

6. DeLillo, "In the Ruins of the Future," 34.

7. DeLillo, "In the Ruins of the Future," 33.

8. DeLillo, "In the Ruins of the Future," 38.

9. DeLillo, "In the Ruins of the Future," 34.

10. DeLillo, "Don DeLillo: Retour vers le futur," 80.

11. Cowart, *Don DeLillo*, 213, 215. According to critics like Lyotard, Pierre-André Taguieff, and Zaki Laïdi, time acceleration strengthens the "link between the postmodern condition and 'presentist' temporality," as Lipovetsky reminds us in *Hypermodern Times* (35). But "presentism," he adds, no longer characterizes twenty-first century culture as it used to. The future seems to be making a comeback today in "new clothes" (40), that is, in our worries about the world to come. This reflexive if tentative, "hypermodern" futurality is distinct from the one DeLillo critiques here.

12. DeLillo, *The Body Artist,* 98.

13. Toulmin, *Cosmopolis,* 2.

14. David Harvey, *The Condition of Postmodernity: An Enquiry into the Origin of Cultural Change* (Cambridge, MA: Blackwell, 1990), 298, 286.

15. See Gordon L. Clark and Kevin O'Connor, "The Informational Content of Financial Products and the Spatial Structure of the Global Finance Industry," and Meric S. Gertler, "The Spatial Construction of Capital," in Cox, *Spaces of Globalization,* 89–114 and 48–52, respectively. For Baudrillard, time, and money, see again his little essay "Global Debt and Parallel Universe." Caitlin Zaloom addresses the digital shift to no "face-to-face," electronic trading in "Trading on Numbers," in *Frontiers of Capital: Ethnographic Reflections on the New Economy,* ed. Melissa S. Fisher and Greg Downey (Durham, NC: Duke University Press, 2006), 58–85. Also in Fisher and Downey's collection, Douglas R. Holmes and George E. Marcus explore, via a reference to Ben Agger's 1989 *Fast Capitalism: A Critical Theory of Significance,* the nexus money-speed in "Fast Capitalism: Para-Ethnography and the Rise of the Symbolic Analyst," 33–57.

16. Giddens, *The Consequences of Modernity,* 24.

17. Giddens, *The Consequences of Modernity,* 25.

18. DeLillo, "The Power of History." On cybernetics and the future anterior logic in postmodernism, see Peter Lunenfeld, "Hyperaesthetics: Theorizing in Real-Time about Digital Culture," in *Postmodern Times: A Critical Guide to the Contemporary,* ed. Thomas Carmichael and Alison Lee (DeKalb: Northern Illinois University Press, 2000), 111–12.

19. Guy Debord, *The Society of the Spectacle,* trans. Donald Nicholson-Smith (New York: Zone Books, 2008), 107, 110.

20. DeLillo, "The Power of History."

21. Lash, *Another Modernity,* 11.

22. Guy Reynolds, *Apostles of Modernity: American Writers in the Age of Development* (Lincoln: University of Nebraska Press, 2008), 221.

23. Emmanuel Levinas, *Time and the Other [and Additional Essays],* trans. Richard A. Cohen (Pittsburgh: Duquesne University Press, 1987), 79.

24. Levinas, *Totalité et infini,* 47, 57.

25. Levinas, *Time and the Other,* 57.

26. DeLillo, *Underworld,* 235.

27. DeLillo, *Cosmopolis,* 91.

28. DeLillo, *Cosmopolis,* 86.

29. Edward W. Soja, *Postmodern Geographies: The Reassertion of Space in Critical Social Theory* (New York: Verso, 1989), 133, 132.

30. See Christian Moraru, *Rewriting: Postmodern Narrative and Cultural Critique in the Age of Cloning* (Albany: SUNY Press, 2001); *Memorious Discourse,* 224–34.

31. Hans Bertens and Dowe Fokkema, eds., *International Postmodernism: Theory and Practice* (Amsterdam: John Benjamins, 1997), 297–515.

32. For the "post-paranoid condition" and its treatment in Bulgarian postmodern theory, see Alexander Kiossev, ed., *Post-Theory, Games, and Discursive Resistance: The Bulgarian Case* (Albany: SUNY Press, 1995), 105–77.

33. On postmodernism as an American phenomenon in Jameson and Stuart Hall, also see, besides well-known texts by the critics, the discussion in Carmichael and Lee's introduction to *Postmodern Times,* 3–7.

34. Ihab Hassan, "From Postmodernism to Postmodernity: The Local/Global Context," https://www.ihabhassan.com/postmodernism_to_postmodernity.htm (accessed February 22, 2009); Ziauddin Sardar, *Postmodernism and the Other: The New Imperialism of Western Culture* (London: Pluto Press, 1998). Albert Borgmann is just one of the critics who define the postindustrial, highly wired world "postmodern." See his book *Crossing the Postmodern Divide* (Chicago: University of Chicago Press, 1992), 102.

35. Spivak, *A Critique of Postcolonial Reason,* 334.

36. Jameson, "Notes on Globalization as a Philosophical Issue," 65.

37. Sardar, *Postmodernism and the Other.*

38. "Although it recurs throughout the [twentieth] century, concern with difference and otherness is a distinguishing trait of thinkers who can be described as 'postmodern,'" says Mark C. Taylor in *Altarity,* xxi.

39. Spivak, *A Critique of Postcolonial Reason,* 336.

40. Lauren Berlant and Michael Warner, "Introduction to 'Critical Multiculturalism,'" in *Multiculturalism: A Critical Reader,* ed. David Theo Goldberg (Oxford: Blackwell, 1994), 112.

41. Steven Connor, introduction to Connor, *The Cambridge Companion to Postmodernism,* 15.

42. Hassan, "From Postmodernism to Postmodernity."

43. Linda Hutcheon, *The Politics of Postmodernism,* 2nd ed. (London: Routledge, 1989), 172–73.

44. Gerard Delanty, *Modernity and Postmodernity: Knowledge, Power, and the Self* (London: Sage, 2007), 155.

45. Matei Calinescu, *Five Faces of Modernity: Modernism, Avant-Garde, Decadence, Kitsch, Postmodernism* (Durham, NC: Duke University Press, 1987), 265.

46. On postmodernism, "heterology," and the ethics of their interplay, see Julian Pefanis, *Heterology and the Postmodern: Bataille, Baudrillard, and Lyotard* (Durham, NC: Duke University Press, 1991), 118.

47. Giddens, *The Consequences of Modernity,* 174–76.

48. K. Anthony Appiah, "Is the 'Post-' in 'Postcolonial' the 'Post' in 'Postmodern'?" in McClintock, Mufti, and Shohat, *Dangerous Liaisons,* 420–22.

49. Sardar, *Postmodernism and the Other,* 13–14.

50. Hardt and Negri, *Empire,* 138–39.

51. Stephen Cook, Jan Pakulski, and Malcolm Waters, *Hypermodern Times: Change in Advanced Society* (London: Sage, 1992), especially chapter 1, "Modernization and Postmodernization," 75. On the hypermodern, see Gilles Lipovetsky's *Hypermodernism Times,* trans. Andrew Brown (Cambridge: Polity, 2005). As to postmodernism's continuation of the modern(ist) project, see, among others, Matei Calinescu, "Postmodernism and Some Paradoxes of Periodization," in *Approaching Postmodernism,* ed. Dowe Fokkema and Hans Bertens (Amsterdam: John Benjamins, 1986), 239–54.

52. Hassan, "From Postmodernism to Postmodernity."

53. See, for example, Moraru, *Rewriting,* 170–73.

54. Chow, *The Age of the World Target,* 65–69.

55. Charles Jencks, "Post-Modern Architecture and Time Fusion," in Carmichael and Lee, *Postmodern Times,* 141–52.

56. Kenneth Burke, *On Symbols and Society,* ed. and with an introduction by Joseph R. Gusfield (Chicago: University of Chicago Press, 1989), 118–19.

57. On postmodernism, intertextuality, and culture as "library" and "arena" in postmodern, cosmopolitan, "geocritical," and technocritical-global scholarship, I mention here only Collins's *Uncommon Cultures*, 60–64; Scarpetta's *Éloge du cosmopolitisme*, 299–300; Westphal's *La Géocritique*, 262–65; and Finkielkraut and Soriano's *Internet, l'inquiétante extase*, 34–35.

58. On "relational reading" in postmodernism, see, among other titles, Laurie Edson's *Reading Relationally: Postmodern Perspectives on Literature and Art* (Ann Arbor: University of Michigan Press, 2000).

59. Virginia Woolf, "Mr. Bennett and Mrs. Brown," in *Modernism: An Anthology of Sources and Documents*, ed. Vassiliki Kolocotroni, Jane Goldman, and Olga Taxidou (Chicago: University of Chicago Press, 1999), 396.

60. Charles Jencks, "Postmodern vs. Late-Modern," in *Zeitgest in Babel: The Post-Modernist Controversy*, ed. Ingeborg Hoesterey (Bloomington: Indiana University Press, 1991), 5.

61. On "evolutionarism," see Jencks, "Post-Modern Architecture and Time Fusion," 151.

62. On Woolf and the "serious game" of periodization, see Brian McHale's essay "What Was Postmodernism?" *Electronic Book Review*, December 20, 2007, http://www.electronicbookreview.-com/thread/fictionspresent/tense?mode-print (accessed October 29, 2009). Regarding the disputes around postmodernism's simultaneous obsolescence and endurance, see, for instance, Frow's "What Was Postmodernism?" section of his *Time and Commodity Culture*, 13–63 (the chapter title is an allusion to Harry Levin's 1960 classical essay, "What Was Modernism?"), and, of course, McHale's own article with this title; Andrew Hoberek, John Burt, David Kadlec, Jamie Owen Daniel, Shelly Eversley, Catherine Jurca, Aparajita Sagar, and Michael Bérubé, "Twentieth-Century Literature in the New Century: A Symposium," *College English* 64, no. 1 (September 2001): 9–33; Moraru, "The Global Turn in Critical Theory"; Timothy S. Murphy, "To Have Done with Postmodernism: A Plea (or Provocation) for Globalization Studies," *symploke* 12, no. 1–2 (2004): 20–34; in the same *symploke* issue (53–68), Robert L. McLaughlin's "Post-Postmodern Discontent: Contemporary Fiction and the Social World"; Neil Brooks and Josh Toth, eds., *The Mourning After: Attending the Wake of Postmodernism* (Amsterdam: Rodopi, 2007); Alan Kirby, "The Death of Postmodernism and Beyond," *Philosophy Now* 71 (January–February 2009), http://www.philosophynow.org/issue58/58kirby.htm (accessed February 26, 2009).

63. On drastically divergent approaches to the "postmodern turn," see Ihab Hassan, *The Postmodern Turn: Essays in Postmodern Theory and Culture* (Columbus: Ohio State University Press, 1987), and Steven Best and Douglas Kellner, *The Postmodern Turn* (New York: Guilford Press, 1997).

64. Frow, *Time and Commodity Culture*, 36–38.

65. Bill Readings and Bennet Schaber, "Introduction: The Question Mark in the Midst of Modernity," in *Postmodernism across the Ages: Essays for a Postmodernity That Wasn't Born Yesterday*, ed. Bill Readings and Bennet Schaber (Syracuse, NY: Syracuse University Press, 1993), 10.

66. Woolf, "Mr. Bennett and Mrs. Brown," 396.

67. Collins, *Uncommon Cultures*, 112–16.

68. Critics who have tried, with varying degrees of enthusiasm, to update postmodernism for the late-global age include Harvey, in *The Condition of Post-*

modernity; Frederick Buell—see especially the "Postmodernism and Globalization" chapter of his book *National Culture and the New Global System*, 325–43; Michael Bérubé and the contributors to the "Postmodernism and the Globalization of English" issue of the Spring 2002 *Modern Fiction Studies* guest-edited by Bérubé; and Murphy, in his "To Have Done with Postmodernism" article. The issue is also addressed by Carmichael and Lee in the introduction to their anthology *Postmodern Times* and, in the same volume, by Lee's interview with Jencks, "Post-Modernism: A Whole Full of Holes," 245–63.

69. Albrow, *The Global Age*, 77.

70. Gibson, *Postmodernity, Ethics, and the Novel*, 27.

BIBLIOGRAPHY

Adams, Tim. "The Library in the Body." http://www.guardian.co.uk/books/2001/feb/11/fiction.-dondelillo (accessed January 22, 2009).

Agacinski, Sylviane. *Critique de l'égocentrisme: L'événement de l'autre.* Paris: Galilée, 1996.

Agamben, Giorgio. *The Coming Community.* Translated by Michael Hardt. Minneapolis: University of Minnesota Press, 1993.

Agamben, Giorgio. *The Time That Remains: A Commentary on The Letter to the Romans.* Translated by Patricia Dailey. Stanford, CA: Stanford University Press, 2005.

Albrecht, Andrea. *Kosmopolitismus.* Berlin: Gruyter, 2005.

Albrow, Martin. *The Global Age: State and Society beyond Modernity.* Stanford, CA: Stanford University Press, 1997.

Alda, Alan. *Things I Overheard while Talking to Myself.* New York: Random House, 2007.

Aldama, Frederick Luis. *Postethnic Narrative Criticism: Magicorealism in Oscar "Zeta" Acosta, Anna Castillo, Julie Dash, Hanif Kureishi, and Salman Rushdie.* Austin: University of Texas Press, 2003.

Alvarez, Julia. *How the García Girls Lost Their Accents.* New York: Penguin, 1992.

Anderson, Amanda. *The Powers of Distance: Cosmopolitanism and the Cultivation of Detachment.* Princeton, NJ: Princeton University Press, 2001.

Annesley, James. *Fictions of Globalization: Consumption, the Market, and the Contemporary American Novel.* New York: Continuum, 2006.

Aparicio, Frances R., and Susana Chávez-Silverman, eds. *Tropicalizations: Transcultural Representations of Latinidad.* Hanover, NH: University Press of New England, 1997.

Appadurai, Arjun. "Grassroots Globalization and the Research Imagination." In *Globalization,* edited by Arjun Appadurai, 1–21. Durham, NC: Duke University Press, 2001.

Appadurai, Arjun. *Modernity at Large: Cultural Dimensions of Globalization.* Minneapolis: University of Minnesota Press, 1999.

Appiah, K. Anthony. *Cosmopolitanism: Ethics in a World of Strangers.* New York: W. W. Norton, 2006.

Appiah, K. Anthony. "Cosmopolitan Reading." In Dharwadker, *Cosmopolitan Geographies,* 197–227.

Appiah, K. Anthony. "Is the 'Post-' in 'Postcolonial' the 'Post' in 'Postmodern'?" In McClintock, Mufti, and Shohat, *Dangerous Liaisons: Gender, Nation, and Postcolonial Perspectives,* 420–22.

Appiah, K. Anthony. "Thick Translation." In Venuti, *The Translation Studies Reader,* 389–401.

Appiah, Kwame Anthony, and Henry Louis Gates, Jr., eds. Michael Colin Vazquez, associate editor. *The Dictionary of Global Culture: What Every American Needs to Know as We Enter the Next Century—from Diderot to Bo Diddley*. New York: Knopf, 1997.

Apter, Emily. *Continental Drift: From National Characters to Virtual Subjects*. Chicago: University of Chicago Press, 1999.

Apter, Emily. "Taskography: Translation as Genre of Literary Labor." *PMLA* 112, no. 5 (October 2007): 1403–15.

Apter, Emily. *The Translation Zone: A New Comparative Literature*. Princeton, NJ: Princeton University Press, 2006.

Aravamudan, Srinivas. *Guru English: South Asian Religion in a Cosmopolitan Language*. Princeton, NJ: Princeton University Press, 2005.

Aravamudan, Srinivas. *Tropicopolitans: Colonialism and Agency, 1688–1804*. Durham, NC: Duke University Press, 1999.

Archibugi, Daniele. "Demos and Cosmopolis." In *Debating Cosmopolitics*, ed. Daniele Archibugi, 257–72. London: Verso, 2003.

Augustine. *The City of God against the Pagans*. Edited and Translated by R. W. Dyson. Cambridge: Cambridge University Press, 1998.

Aurelius, Marcus. *Meditations*. A new translation, with an introduction, by Gregor Hays. New York: Random House, 2002.

Auster, Paul. *The Art of Hunger: Essays, Prefaces, Interviews, and* The Red Notebook. New York: Penguin, 1993.

Badie, Bertrand, and Marc Sadoun, eds. *L'autre*. Études réunies pour Alfred Gosser. Paris: Presses de la Fondation Nationale des Sciences Politiques, 1996.

Badiou, Alain. *Saint Paul: La fondation de l'universalisme*. Paris: PUF, 2004.

Bakhtin, M. M. *Art and Answerability: Early Philosophical Essays*. Edited by Michael Holquist and Vadim Liapunov. Translation and notes by Vadim Liapunov. Supplement translated by Kenneth Brostrom. Austin: University of Texas Press, 1990.

Bakhtin, M. M. *The Dialogic Imagination: Four Essays*. Edited by Michael Holquist. Translated by Caryl Emerson and Michael Holquist. Austin: University of Texas Press, 1981.

Bakhtin, M. M. *Speech Genres and Other Late Essays*. Edited by Caryl Emerson and Michael Holquist. Translated by Vern McGee. Austin: University of Texas Press, 1986.

Barber, Benjamin. *Jihad vs. McWorld: How Globalism and Tribalism Are Reshaping the World*. New York: Ballantine Books, 1996.

Bard, Alexander, and Jan Soderqvist. *Netocracy: The Power Elite and Life after Capitalism*. London: Reuters, 2002.

Barnett, Ian. "The Translator as Hero." http://www.biblit.it/translator_hero.pdf (accessed December 2, 2007).

Barthes, Roland. "The Death of the Author." In Lodge and Wood, *Modern Criticism and Theory*, 2000 ed., 146–50.

Barthes, Roland. *The Eiffel Tower and Other Mythologies*. Translated by Richard Howard. Berkeley: University of California Press, 1997.

Barthes, Roland. *Mythologies*. Selected and translated from the French by Annette Lavers. New York: Noonday, 1993.

Bassnett, Susan. "Translation Theory." In *The Johns Hopkins Guide to Literary The-*

ory and Criticism, 2nd ed., edited by Michael Groden, Martin Kreiswirth, and Imre Szeman, 909–13. Baltimore: Johns Hopkins University Press, 2005.

Baudrillard, Jean. *America.* Translated by Chris Turner. London: Verso, 1996.

Baudrillard, Jean. *L'autre par lui-même: Habilitation.* Paris: Galilée, 1987.

Baudrillard, Jean. *Cool Memories.* Translated by Chris Turner. London: Verso, 1990.

Baudrillard, Jean. *Cool Memories II: 1997–1990.* Translated by Chris Turner. Durham, NC: Duke University Press, 1996.

Baudrillard, Jean. *Cool Memories IV: 1995–2000.* Translated by Chris Turner. London: Verso, 2003.

Baudrillard, Jean. *Fragments: Cool Memories III, 1991–1995.* Translated by Emily Agar. London: Verso, 1997.

Baudrillard, Jean. "Global Debt and Parallel Universe." In *Digital Delirium,* edited and introduced by Arthur Kroker and Marilouise Kroker, 38–40. New York: St. Martin's, 1997.

Baudrillard, Jean. *The Perfect Crime.* Translated by Chris Turner. London: Verso, 1996.

Baudrillard, Jean. *The System of Objects.* Translated by James Benedict. London: Verso, 2005.

Baudrillard, Jean. *The Vital Illusion.* Edited by Julia Witwer. New York: Columbia University Press, 2000.

Bauer, Ralph. "Hemispheric Studies." *PMLA* 124, no. 1 (January 2009): 234–50.

Bauman, Richard. *A World of Others' Words: Cross-Cultural Perspectives on Intertextuality.* Oxford: Blackwell, 2004.

Bauman, Zygmunt. *Globalization: The Human Consequences.* New York: Columbia University Press, 1998.

Beauvoir, Simone de. *The Second Sex.* Translated and edited by H. M. Parshley. Introduction to the Vintage edition by Deirdre Bair. New York: Vintage, 1989.

Beck, Ulrich. "The Cosmopolitan Perspective: Sociology in the Second Age of Modernity." In Vertovec and Cohen, *Conceiving Cosmopolitanism,* 69–85.

Beck, Ulrich. "The Cosmopolitan Society and its Enemies." *Theory, Culture, and Society* 19, no. 1–2 (2002): 17–44.

Beck, Ulrich. *Der Kosmopolitische Blick oder: Krieg ist Frieden.* Frankfurt am Main: Suhrkamp, 2004.

Beck, Ulrich. *The Reinvention of Politics: Rethinking Modernity in the Global Social Order.* Translated by Mark Ritter. Cambridge: Polity, 1997.

Beck, Ulrich. "Risk Society Revisited: Theory, Politics, and Research Programmes." In *The Risk Society and Beyond: Critical Issues for Social Theory,* edited by Barbara Adam, Ulrich Beck, and Joost Van Loon, 211–29. London: Sage, 2000.

Beck, Ulrich. *Risk Society: Towards a New Modernity.* Translated by Mark Ritter. London: Sage, 1992.

Bédier, Joseph. *The Romance of Tristan and Iseult.* Translated by Hilaire Belloc and Paul Rosenfeld. New York: Pantheon Books, 1945.

Bellow, Saul. *Herzog.* New York: Penguin, 1996.

Benda, Julien. *The Treason of the Intellectuals.* With a new introduction by Roger Kimball. Translated by Richard Aldington. New Brunswick, NJ: Transaction, 2007.

Benedict XVI. "Paul, the Apostle: Teacher for Today." http://www.ewtn.com/li brary/PAPALDOC/b16stpaul1.htm (accessed February 14, 2009).

Benhabib, Seyla. *Another Cosmopolitanism.* With commentaries by Jeremy Waldron, Bonnie Honig, and Will Kymlicka. Edited and introduced by Robert Post. Oxford: Oxford University Press, 2006.

Benhabib, Seyla. *The Claims of Culture: Equality and Diversity in the Global Era.* Princeton, NJ: Princeton University Press, 2002.

Benjamin, Walter. *Illuminations: Essays and Reflections.* Edited and with an introduction by Hannah Arendt. Translated by Harry Zohn. New York: Schocken Books, 1968.

Benso, Silvia. *The Face of Things: A Different Side of Ethics.* Albany: SUNY Press, 2000.

Bercovitch, Sacvan. "Discovering America: A Cross-Cultural Perspective." In Budick and Iser, *The Translatability of Cultures,* 147–68.

Berlant, Lauren, and Michael Warner. "Introduction to 'Critical Multiculturalism.'" In Goldberg, *Multiculturalism,* 107–13.

Berman, Jessica. *Modernist Fiction, Cosmopolitanism, and the Politics of Community.* Cambridge: Cambridge University Press, 2001.

Bernheimer, Charles. "The Bernheimer Report, 1993: Comparative Literature at the Turn of the Century." In Bernheimer, *Comparative Literature in the Age of Multiculturalism,* 39–48.

Bernheimer, Charles, ed. *Comparative Literature in the Age of Multiculturalism.* Baltimore: Johns Hopkins University Press, 1995.

Bertens, Hans. *Literary Theory: The Basics.* New York: Routledge, 2001.

Bertens, Hans, and Dowe Fokkema, eds. *International Postmodernism: Theory and Practice.* Amsterdam: John Benjamins, 1997.

Best, Steven, and Douglas Kellner. *The Postmodern Turn.* New York: Guilford Press, 1997.

Bhabha, Homi K. *The Location of Culture.* New York: Routledge, 1994.

Bhabha, Homi K. "The World and the Home." In McClintock, Mufti, and Shohat, *Dangerous Liaisons,* 445–55.

Biddle, Arthur W., and Gloria Bien. *Global Voices: Contemporary Literature from the Non-Western World.* Upper Saddle River, NJ: Prentice Hall, 1994.

Blanchot, Maurice. *The Unavowable Community.* Translated by Pierre Joris. Barrytown, NY: Station Hill Press, 1988.

Bleich, David. "What Literature Is 'Ours'?" In Schweickart and Flynn, *Reading Sites,* 286–313.

Bohman, James, and Matthias Lutz-Bachmann, eds. *Perpetual Peace: Essays on Kant's Cosmopolitan Ideal.* Cambridge, MA: MIT Press, 1997.

Bolton, Linda. *Facing the Other: Ethical Disruption and the American Mind.* Baton Rouge: Louisiana State University Press, 2004.

Borgmann, Albert. *Crossing the Postmodern Divide.* Chicago: University of Chicago Press, 1992.

Brantlinger, Patrick. *Crusoe's Footprints: Cultural Studies in Britain and America.* New York: Routledge, 1990.

Breckenridge, Carol A., Sheldon Pollock, Homi K. Bhabha, and Dipesh Chakrabarty, eds. *Cosmopolitanism.* Durham, NC: Duke University Press, 2002.

Breckenridge, Carol A., Sheldon Pollock, Homi K. Bhabha, and Dipesh Chakrabarty. "Cosmopolitanisms." In Breckenridge, Pollock, Bhabha, and Chakrabarty, *Cosmopolitanism*, 1–14.

Bremond, Claude. *Logique du recit*. Paris: Seuil, 2001.

Brennan, Timothy. *At Home in the World: Cosmopolitanism Now*. Cambridge, MA: Harvard University Press, 1997.

Brennan, Timothy. *Wars of Position: The Cultural Politics of Left and Right*. New York: Columbia University Press, 2006.

Breton, Stanislas, and Francis Guibal. *Altérités: Jacques Derrida and Pierre-Jean Labarrière*. With essays by Francis Guibal and Stanislas Breton. Paris: Osiris, 1986.

Bridgewater, P. B. "Biosphere Reserves: Special Places for People and Nature." *Environmental Science & Policy* 5 (2002): 9–12.

Brinker-Gabler, Gisela, ed. *Encountering the Others: Studies in Literature, History, and Culture*. Albany: SUNY Press, 1995.

Brooks, Neil, and Josh Toth, eds. *The Mourning After: Attending the Wake of Postmodernism*. Amsterdam: Rodopi, 2007.

Buber, Martin. *I and Thou. A New Translation with a Prologue "I and You" and Notes by Walter Kaufmann*. New York: Simon & Schuster, 1996.

Budick, Sanford. "Crises of Alterity: Cultural Untranslatability and the Experience of Secondary Otherness." In Budick and Iser, *The Translatability of Cultures*, 1–22.

Budick, Sanford, and Wolfgang Iser, eds. *The Translatability of Cultures: Figurations of the Space Between*. Stanford, CA: Stanford University Press, 1996.

Buell, Frederick. *National Culture and the New Global System*. Baltimore: Johns Hopkins University Press, 1994.

Burke, Kenneth. *On Symbols and Society*. Edited and with an introduction by Joseph R. Gusfield. Chicago: University of Chicago Press, 1989.

Butler, Judith. *Gender Trouble: Feminism and the Subversion of Identity*. New York: Routledge, 1999.

Butler, Judith. *Giving an Account of Oneself*. New York: Fordham University Press, 2005.

Calinescu, Matei. *Five Faces of Modernity: Modernism, Avant-Garde, Decadence, Kitsch, Postmodernism*. Durham, NC: Duke University Press, 1987.

Calinescu, Matei. "Modernity, Modernism, Modernization: Variations on Modern Themes." In *The Turn of the Century: Modernism and Modernity in Literature and the Arts*. Edited by Christian Berg, Frank Durieux, and Geert Lernout, 33–52. Berlin: Gruyter, 1995.

Calinescu, Matei. "Postmodernism and Some Paradoxes of Periodization." In *Approaching Postmodernism*, edited by Dowe Fokkema and Hans Bertens, 238–54. Amsterdam: John Benjamins, 1986.

Calinescu, Matei, and Ion Vianu. *Amintiri in Dialog*. Bucharest: Litera, 1994.

Campbell, Mike. "Jiro." *Behind the Name: The Etymology and History of First Names*. http://www.behindthename.com/php/view.php?name=jiro (accessed March 8, 2007).

Campbell, Mike. "Thomas." *Behind the Name: The Etymology and History of First Names*. http://www.behindthename.com/php/view.php?name=thomas (accessed March 8, 2007).

Carmichael, Thomas, and Alison Lee. "Introduction: Postmodern Life, Or What You See Is What You Get." Carmichael and Lee, *Postmodern Times*, 3–14.

Carmichael, Thomas, and Alison Lee, eds. *Postmodern Times: A Critical Guide to the Contemporary*. DeKalb: Northern Illinois University Press, 2000.

Casanova, Pascale. *The World Republic of Letters*. Translated by M. B. DeBevoise. Cambridge, MA: Harvard University Press, 2004.

Castells, Manuel. *The Information Age: Economy, Society, and Culture*. 2nd ed. Vol. 1, *The Rise of the Network Society*. Oxford: Blackwell, 2000.

Caton, Lou Freitas. *Reading American Novels and Multicultural Aesthetics: Romancing the Postmodern Novel*. New York: Palgrave Macmillan, 2008.

Caws, Mary Ann. *Surprised in Translation*. Chicago: University of Chicago Press, 2006.

Certeau, Michel de. *Culture in the Plural*. Edited and with an introduction by Luce Giard. Translated and with an afterword by Tom Conley. Minneapolis: University of Minnesota Press, 1997.

Chaunu, Pierre. *Histoire, science sociale: La durée, l'espace, et l'homme à l'époque moderne*. Paris: Société d'édition de'enseignement supérieur, 1974.

Cheah, Pheng, and Bruce Robbins, eds. *Cosmopolitics: Thinking and Feeling beyond the Nation*. Minneapolis: University of Minnesota Press, 1998.

Chen, Tina. "Impersonation and Other Disappearing Acts in *Native Speaker* by Chang-rae Lee." *Modern Fiction Studies* 48, no. 3 (Fall 2002): 637–67.

Chesnutt, Charles W. *Essays and Speeches*. Edited by Joseph R. McElrath, Jr., Robert C. Leitz III, and Jesse S. Crisler. Stanford, CA: Stanford University Press, 1999.

Chow, Rey. *The Age of World Target: Self-Referentiality in War, Theory, and Comparative Work*. Durham, NC: Duke University Press, 2006.

Chow, Rey. *Primitive Passions: Visuality, Sexuality, Ethnography, and Contemporary Chinese Cinema*. New York: Columbia University Press, 1995.

Cixous, Hélène. "Sorties." In Lodge and Wood, *Modern Criticism and Theory*, 2008 ed., 359–65.

Clark, Gordon L., and Kevin O'Connor. "The Informational Content of Financial Products and the Spatial Structure of the Global Finance Industry." In Cox, *Spaces of Globalization*, 89–114.

Clifford, James. *The Predicament of Culture: Twentieth-Century Ethnography, Literature, and Art*. Cambridge, MA: Harvard University Press, 1988.

Clifford, James. *Routes: Travel and Translation in the Late Twentieth Century*. Cambridge, MA: Harvard University Press, 1996.

Clifford, James. "Traveling Cultures." In *Cultural Studies*, edited and with an introduction by Lawrence Grossberg, Cary Nelson, and Paula Treichler, with Linda Baughman and assistance from John Macgregor, 96–112. New York: Routledge, 1992.

Clingman, Stephen. *The Grammar of Identity: Transnational Fiction and the Nature of the Boundary*. Oxford: Oxford University Press, 2009.

Codrescu, Andrei. *Wakefield*. Chapel Hill: Algonquin Books, 2004.

Coetzee, J. M. *Elizabeth Costello*. New York: Penguin, 2003.

Cohen, Daniel. *La mondialisation et ses ennemis*. Paris: Grasset, 2004.

Coldiron, A. E. B. "Toward a Comparative New Historicism: Land Tenures and

Some Fifteenth-Century Poems." *Comparative Literature* 53, no. 2 (Spring 2001): 97–116.

Collins, Jim. *Uncommon Cultures: Popular Culture and Post-Modernism.* New York: Routledge, 1989.

Connor, Steven, ed. *The Cambridge Companion to Postmodernism.* Cambridge: Cambridge University Press, 2004.

Connor, Steven. Introduction to Connor, *The Cambridge Companion to Postmodernism,* 1–19.

Cook, Stephen, Jan Pakulski, and Malcolm Waters. *Postmodernization: Change in Advanced Society.* London: Sage, 1992.

Corley, Liam. "'Just Another Ethnic Pol': Literary Citizenship in Chang-rae Lee's *Native Speaker.*" *Studies in the Literary Imagination* 37, no. 1 (Spring 2004): 61–81.

Cornis-Pope, Marcel. *Narrative Innovation and Cultural Rewriting in the Cold War Era and After.* New York: Palgrave, 2001.

Coulmas, Peter. *Les citoyens du monde: Histoire du cosmopolitisme.* Translated from the German by Jeanne Étoré. Paris: Albin Michel, 1995.

Cowart, David. "Anxieties of Obsolescence: DeLillo's *Cosmopolis.*" In *Science, Technology, and the Humanities in Recent American Fiction,* edited by Peter Freese and Charles B. Harris, 159–79. Essen, Germany: Die blaue Eule, 2004.

Cowart, David. *Don DeLillo: The Physics of Language.* Revised ed. Athens: University of Georgia Press, 2003.

Cowart, David. *Trailing Clouds: Immigrant Fiction in Contemporary America.* Ithaca, NY: Cornell University Press, 2006.

Cox, Kevin R., ed. *Spaces of Globalization: Reasserting the Power of the Local.* New York: Guilford Press, 1999.

Cronin, Michael. *Translation and Globalization.* New York: Routledge, 2003.

Cronin, Michael. *Translation and Identity.* New York: Routledge, 2006.

Culler, Jonathan. *Literary Theory: A Very Short Introduction.* Oxford: Oxford University Press, 2000.

Cutter, Martha J. *Lost and Found in Translation: Contemporary Ethnic American Writing and the Politics of Language Diversity.* Chapel Hill: University of North Carolina Press, 2005.

Dai, Sijie. *Balzac and the Little Chinese Seamstress.* Translated from the French by Ina Rilke. New York: Random House, 2001.

Dai, Sijie. *Mr. Muo's Travelling Couch.* Translated from the French by Ina Rilke. New York: Knopf, 2005.

Dai, Sijie. *Once on a Moonless Night.* Translated from the French by Adriana Hunter. New York: Knopf, 2009.

Dallmayr, Fred. "An 'Inoperative' Global Community? Reflections on Nancy." In *On Jean-Luc Nancy: The Sense of Philosophy,* edited by Darren Sheppard, Simon Sparks, and Colin Thomas, 174–96. London: Routledge, 1997.

Damrosch, David. *What Is World Literature?* Princeton, NJ: Princeton University Press, 2003.

Dante. *Literature in the Vernacular.* Translated with an introduction by Sally Purcell. Manchester, UK: Carcanet New Press, 1981.

Day, Peter, and Douglas Schuler. "Community Practice: An Alternative Vision of the Network." In *Common Practice in the Network Society,* edited by Peter Day and Douglas Schuler, 1–20. London: Routledge, 2004.

Dean, Jodi. "The Networked Empire: Communicative Capitalism and the Hope for Politics." In Passavant and Dean, *Empire's New Clothes,* 265–88.

Debord, Guy. *The Society of the Spectacle.* Translated by Donald Nicholson-Smith. New York: Zone Books, 2008.

Debray, Régis. *Transmitting Culture.* Translated by Eric Rauth. New York: Columbia University Press, 2000.

Delamarre, Bernadette. *Autrui.* Paris: Ellipses, 1996.

Delanty, Gerard. *Modernity and Postmodernity: Knowledge, Power, and the Self.* London: Sage, 2007.

Deleuze, Gilles. *Difference and Repetition.* Translated by Paul Patton. New York: Columbia University Press, 1994.

DeLillo, Don. *The Body Artist.* New York: Scribner, 2001.

DeLillo, Don. *Cosmopolis.* New York: Scribner, 2003.

DeLillo, Don. "Don DeLillo: Retour vers le futur." *Magazine littéraire* no. 425, November 2003, 80–81.

DeLillo, Don. *Falling Man.* New York: Scribner, 2007.

DeLillo, Don. *Great Jones Street.* Boston: Houghton Mifflin, 1973.

DeLillo, Don. "In the Ruins of the Future: Reflections on Terror and Loss in the Shadow of September." *Harper's Magazine,* December 2001, 33–40.

DeLillo, Don. *The Names.* New York: Random House, 1989.

DeLillo, Don. "'An Outsider in This Society': Interview with Don DeLillo." By Anthony DeCurtis. *South Atlantic Quarterly* 89, no. 2 (1990): 281–304.

DeLillo, Don. "The Power of History." *New York Times Magazine,* September 7, 1997. http://www.nytimes.com/library/books/090797article3.html (accessed May 2007).

DeLillo, Don. "That Day in Rome: Movies and Memories." *New Yorker,* October 20, 2003, 76–78.

DeLillo, Don. *Underworld.* New York: Scribner, 1997.

Demorgon, Jacques. *Critique de l'interculturel: L'horizon de la sociologie.* Paris: Anthropos, 2005.

Demorgon, Jacques. *L'interculturation du monde.* Paris: Anthropos, 2000.

Derian, James Der. "Spy versus Spy: The Intertextual Power of International Intrigue." In *International/Intertextual Relations: Postmodern Readings of World Politics,* edited by James Der Derian and Michael J. Shapiro, 162–87. Lexington, TN: Lexington Books, 1989.

Derrida, Jacques. *Adieu to Emmanuel Levinas.* Translated by Pascale-Anne Brault and Michael Naas. Stanford, CA: Stanford University Press, 1999.

Derrida, Jacques. "Autoimmunity: Real and Symbolic Suicides. A Dialogue with Jacques Derrida." In Giovanna Borradori, *Philosophy in a Time of Terror: Dialogues with Jürgen Habermas and Jacques Derrida,* 85–136. Chicago: University of Chicago Press, 2003.

Derrida, Jacques. "Des Tours de Babel." In *Difference in Translation,* edited with an introduction by Joseph F. Graham, 165–207. Ithaca, NY: Cornell University Press, 1985.

Derrida, Jacques. *The Ear of the Other: Texts and Discussions with Jacques Derrida; Otobiography. Transference. Translation.* English edition by Christie McDonald. A translation by Peggy Kamuf of the French edition edited by Claude Lévesque and Christie McDonald ("Otobiographies" translated by Avital Ronell). Lincoln: University of Nebraska Press, 1988.

Derrida, Jacques. "Letter to a Japanese Friend." In Wolfreys, *Literary Theories,* 282–87.

Derrida, Jacques. *Monolingualism of the Other; or, The Prosthesis of Origin.* Translated by Patrick Mensah. Stanford, CA: Stanford University Press, 1998.

Derrida, Jacques. *Negotiations: Interventions and Interviews, 1971–2001.* Edited, translated, and with an introduction by Elizabeth Rottenberg. Stanford, CA: Stanford University Press, 2002.

Derrida, Jacques. *Of Grammatology.* Corrected edition. Translated by Gayatri Chakravorty Spivak. Baltimore: Johns Hopkins University Press, 1998.

Derrida, Jacques. *Of Hospitality: Anne Dufourmantelle Invites Jacques Derrida to Respond.* Translated by Rachel Bowlby. Stanford, CA: Stanford University Press, 2000.

Derrida, Jacques. *On Cosmopolitanism and Forgiveness.* Translated by Mark Dooley and Michael Hughes. Preface by Simon Critchley and Richard Kearney. London: Routledge, 2001.

Derrida, Jacques. *On the Name.* Translated and edited by Thomas Dutoit. Stanford, CA: Stanford University Press, 1995.

Derrida, Jacques. *On Touching—Jean-Luc Nancy.* Translated by Christine Irizarry. Stanford, CA: Stanford University Press, 2005.

Derrida, Jacques. *The Other Heading: Reflections on Today's Europe.* Translated by Pascale-Anne Brault and Michael B. Naas. Introduction by Michael B. Naas. Bloomington: Indiana University Press, 1992.

Derrida, Jacques. *Politics of Friendship.* Translated by George Collins. London: Verso, 1997.

Derrida, Jacques. *Psyché: Inventions de l'autre.* Paris: Galilée, 1987.

Derrida, Jacques. "Structure, Sign, and Play in the Discourse of the Human Sciences." In Lodge and Wood, *Modern Criticism and Theory,* 2000 ed., 62–87.

Dewey, Joseph, Steven G. Kellman, and Irving Malin, eds. *UnderWords: Perspectives on Don DeLillo's* Underworld. Newark: University of Delaware Press, 2002.

D'haen, Theo. "Post/Modernist East." In *Re-Imagining Language and Literature for the 21st Century,* edited by Suthira Duangsamosorn, 319–30. Amsterdam: Rodopi, 2005.

Dharwadker, Vinay. *Cosmopolitan Geographies: New Locations in Literature and Culture.* New York: Routledge, 2001.

Dharwadker, Vinay. "Introduction: Cosmopolitanism in Its Time and Place." In Dharwadker, *Cosmopolitan Geographies,* 1–13.

Dillard, Annie. *For the Time Being.* New York: Knopf, 1999.

Dimock, Wai Chee. *Through Other Continents: American Literature across Deep Time.* Princeton, NJ: Princeton University Press, 2008.

Dimock, Wai Chee, and Lawrence Buell, eds. *Shades of the Planet: American Literature as World Literature.* Princeton, NJ: Princeton University Press, 2007.

Dirlik, Arif. "Globalization as the End and the Beginning of History." http://www.scribd.com/doc/2546826/Globalization-as-the-End-and-the-Beginning-of-History (accessed July 27, 2008).

Djebar, Assia. *Fantasia: An Algerian Cavalcade.* Translated by Dorothy S. Blair. Portsmouth, NH: Heinemann, 1993.

Docherty, Thomas. *Alterities: Criticism, History, Representation.* Oxford: Clarendon, 1996.

Doyle, Laura, and Laura Winkiel, eds. *Geomodernisms: Race, Modernism, Modernity.* Bloomington: Indiana University Press, 2005.

Doyle, Laura, and Laura Winkiel. "The Global Horizons of Modernism." In Doyle and Winkiel, *Geomodernisms,* 1–16.

Du Bois, W. E. B. *Color and Democracy: Colonies and Peace.* New York: Harcourt Brace, 1945.

Du Bois, W. E. B. *Writings.* New York: Library of America, 1986.

Durand, Gilbert. *Les structures anthropologiques de l'imaginaire: Introduction à l'archétypologie générale.* Paris: PUF, 1963.

Durham, Carolyn A. *Literary Globalism: Anglo-American Fiction Set in France.* Lewisburg, PA: Bucknell University Press, 2005.

During, Simon. "Postcolonialism and Globalization: Towards a Historicization of Their Inter-relation." *Cultural Studies* 14, no. 3–4 (2000): 385–404.

Duvall, John. *Don DeLillo's* Underworld: *A Reader's Guide.* New York: Continuum, 2002.

Duvall, John. "Excavating the Underworld of Race and Waste in Cold War History: Baseball, Aesthetics, and Ideology." In *Critical Essays on Don DeLillo,* edited by Hugh Ruppersburg and Tim Engles, 258–81. New York: C. K. Hall, 2000.

Eaglestone, Robert. *Ethical Criticism: Reading after Levinas.* Edinburgh: Edinburgh University Press, 1997.

Eco, Umberto. *Experiences in Translation.* Translated by Alastair McEwen. Toronto: University of Toronto Press, 2001.

Edson, Laurie. *Reading Relationally: Postmodern Perspectives on Literature and Art.* Ann Arbor: University of Michigan Press, 2000.

Ellison, Ralph. *Invisible Man.* New York: Random House, 1995.

Engles, Tim. "'Visions of me in the whitest raw light': Assimilation and Doxic Whiteness in Chang-rae Lee's *Native Speaker.*" *Hitting Critical Mass: A Journal of Asian American Cultural Studies* 4, no. 2 (Summer 1997): 27–48. http://www.ux1.eiu.edu/~cftde/hcmns.html (accessed October 10, 2005).

Eoyang, Eugene. "English as a Postcolonial Tool." *English Today* 19, no. 4 (October 2003): 23–29.

Ernout, A., and A. Meillet. *Dictionnaire étymologique de la langue latine: Histoire des mots.* Paris: Klincksieck, 1959.

Featherstone, Mike, Scott Lash, and Roland Robertson, eds. *Global Modernities.* London: Sage, 1995.

Federman, Raymond. *Aunt Rachel's Fur: A Novel Improvised in Sad Laughter; Transacted from the French by Federman and Patricia Privat-Standley.* Tallahassee: FC2, 2001.

Federman, Raymond. *Critifiction: Postmodern Essays.* Albany: SUNY Press, 1993.

Federman, Raymond. Letter to the author. November 15, 2006.

Federman, Raymond. *My Body in Nine Parts: With Three Supplements and Illustrations.* Photographs by Steve Murez. Buffalo: Starcherone Press, 2005.

Federman, Raymond. *Retour au fumier: Récit nostalgique pour mon vieux chien*

Bigleux. Translated from the English (U.S.) by Éric Giraud. Romainville, France: Éditions Al Dante, 2005.

Federman, Raymond. *Return to Manure.* Tuscaloosa: University of Alabama Press/Fiction Collective Two, 2006.

Federman, Raymond. *Take It or Leave It: An Exaggerated Second-Hand Tale to Be Read Aloud Either Standing or Sitting.* New York: Fiction Collective, 1976.

Federman, Raymond. "Le traître à la cause." http://www.montbouge.info/pip .php?article412 (accessed April 5, 2007).

Feneberg, Wolfgang. *Paulus, der Weltbürger.* Munich: Kösel, 1992.

Finkielkraut, Alain. *In the Name of Humanity: Reflections on the Twentieth Century.* Translated by Judith Friedlander. New York: Columbia University Press, 2000.

Finkielkraut, Alain, and Paul Soriano. *Internet, l'inquiétante extase.* Paris: Fayard, 2001.

Fish, Stanley. *Is There a Text in This Class? The Authority of Interpretive Communities.* Cambridge, MA: Harvard University Press, 1980.

Fish, Stanley. "Why No One's Afraid of Wolfgang Iser." *Diacritics* 11, no. 1 (1981): 2–13.

Fisher, Melissa S., and Greg Downey, eds. *Frontiers of Capital: Ethnographic Reflections on the New Economy.* Durham, NC: Duke University Press, 2006.

Fishman, Joshua A. "The New Linguistic Order." In *Globalization and the Challenges of a New Century: A Reader,* edited by Patrick O'Meara, Howard D. Mehlinger, and Matthew Crain, 435–42. Bloomington: Indiana University Press, 2000.

Flynn, Elizabeth, and Patrocinio P. Schweickart, eds. *Gender and Reading: Essays on Readers, Texts, and Contexts.* Baltimore: Johns Hopkins University Press, 1986.

Fojas, Camilla. *Cosmopolitanism in the Americas.* West Lafayette, IN: Purdue University Press, 2005.

Forster, E. M. *Howards End: Complete, Authoritative Text with Biographical and Historical Contexts, Critical History, and Essays from Five Contemporary Critical Perspectives.* Edited by Alistair M. Duckworth. Boston: Bedford/St. Martin's, 1997.

Foucault, Michel. *Technologies of the Self: A Seminar with Michel Foucault.* Edited by Luther H. Martin, Huck Gutman, and Patrick H. Hutton. Amherst: University of Massachusetts Press, 1988.

Fraser, Nancy. "Rethinking Recognition." *New Left Review* 3 (May–June 2000): 107–20.

Freud, Sigmund. "Lecture 6" of *Introductory Lectures on Psychoanalysis.* In Lodge and Wood, *Modern Criticism and Theory,* 2008 ed., 53–61.

Friedman, Thomas L. *Longitudes and Latitudes: Exploring the World after September 11.* New York: Farrar, Strauss and Giroux, 2002.

Friedman, Thomas L. *The World Is Flat: A Brief History of the Twenty-first Century.* Further updated and expanded. New York: Farrar, Strauss and Giroux, 2006.

Frow, John. *Time and Commodity Culture: Essays in Cultural Theory and Postmodernity.* Oxford: Oxford University Press, 1997.

Fukuyama, Francis. *The End of History and the Last Man.* New York: Free Press, 1992.

Gadamer, Hans-Georg. *Truth and Method*. 2nd revised edition. Translation revised by Joel Weinsheimer and Donald G. Marshall. New York: Continuum, 2004.

Geertz, Clifford. *The Interpretation of Cultures: Selected Essays*. New York: Basic Books, 1973.

Geertz, Clifford. *Local Knowledge: Further Essays in Interpretive Anthropology*. New York: Basic Books, 1983.

Geertz, Clifford. "The Uses of Diversity." *Michigan Quarterly Review* 25, no. 1 (1986): 105–23.

Gensini, Stefano. "La varietà delle lingue da Babele a Cosmopoli." In *L'idea di cosmopolitismo: Circolazione e metamorfosi*, edited by Lorenzo Bianchi, 127–58. Napoli: Liguori Editore, 2002.

Gertler, Meric S. "Between the Global and the Local: The Spatial Limits to Productive Capital." In Cox, *Spaces of Globalization*, 45–63.

Gibson, Andrew. *Postmodernity, Ethics, and the Novel: From Leavis to Levinas*. London: Routledge, 1999.

Giddens, Anthony. *The Consequences of Modernity*. Stanford, CA: Stanford University Press, 1990.

Giddens, Anthony. *Modernity and Self-Identity: Self and Society in the Late Modern Age*. Stanford, CA: Stanford University Press, 1991.

Giles, Paul. "Transnationalism and Classic American Literature." *PMLA* 118, no. 1 (January 2003): 78–89.

Gilroy, Paul. *Against Race: Imagining Political Culture beyond the Color Line*. Cambridge, MA: Belknap Press of Harvard University Press, 2000.

Gleason, Paul. "Don DeLillo, T. S. Eliot, and the Redemption of America's Atomic Waste Land." In Dewey, Kellman, and Malin, *UnderWords*, 130–43.

Goethe, Johann Wolfgang von. "Some Passages Pertaining to the Concept of World Literature." In *Comparative Literature: The Early Years. An Anthology of Essays*, edited by Hans-Joachim Schulz and Philip H. Rhein, 1–11. Chapel Hill: University of North Carolina Press, 1973.

Goldberg, David Theo. "Introduction: Multicultural Conditions." In Goldberg, *Multiculturalism*, 1–41.

Goldberg, David Theo, ed. *Multiculturalism: A Critical Reader*. Oxford: Blackwell, 1994.

Gómez-Peña, Guillermo. *Dangerous Border-Crossers: The Artist Talks Back*. New York: Routledge, 2000.

Gómez-Peña, Guillermo. *The New World Border: Prophecies, Poems, and Loqueras for the End of the Century*. San Francisco: City Lights, 1996.

Gorog, Jean-Jacques. "L'identité est 'de l'Autre.'" *La Revue de psychanalyse du Champ lacanien* 6 (March 2008): 59–65.

Goyard-Fabre, Simone. "La condition politique selon Montesquieu: Universalisme et particularisme." In Bianchi, *L'idea di cosmopolitismo*, 122–23.

Greenblatt, Stephen. "Racial Memory and Literary History." *PMLA* 116, no. 1 (January 2001): 48–63.

Greene, Roland. "Not Works but Networks: Colonial Worlds in Comparative Literature." In Saussy, *Comparative Literature in an Age of Globalization*, 212–23.

Grobman, Laurie. "Rhetorizing the Contact Zone: Multicultural Texts in Writing Classrooms." In Schweickart and Flynn, *Reading Sites*, 256–85.

Gross, Robert A. "The Transnational Turn: Rediscovering American Studies in a Wider World." *Journal of American Studies* 34, no. 3 (2000): 373–93.

Guattari, Félix. *Chaosmose.* Paris: Galilée, 1992.

Gunn, Giles. *Beyond Solidarity: Pragmatism and Difference in a Globalized World.* Chicago: University of Chicago Press, 2001.

Gupta, Suman. *Globalization and Literature.* London: Polity, 2009.

Habermas, Jürgen. *The Inclusion of the Other: Studies in Political Theory.* Edited by Ciaran Cronin and Pablo De Greiff. Cambridge, MA: MIT Press, 1999.

Habermas, Jürgen. *The Postnational Constellation: Political Essays.* Translated, edited and with an introduction by Max Pensky. Cambridge, MA: MIT Press, 2001.

Hall, Stuart. "Political Belonging in a World of Multiple Identities." In Vertovec and Cohen, *Conceiving Cosmopolitanism,* 25–31.

Hannerz, Ulf. *Transnational Connections: Culture, People, Places.* London: Routledge, 1996.

Hardt, Michael, and Antonio Negri. *Empire.* Cambridge, MA: Harvard University Press, 2000.

Hardt, Michael, and Antonio Negri. *Multitude: War and Democracy in the Age of Empire.* New York: Penguin, 2004.

Harris, Wilson. *The Womb of Space: The Cross-Cultural Imagination.* Westport, CT: Greenwood, 1983.

Harvey, David. *The Condition of Postmodernity: An Enquiry into the Origin of Cultural Change.* Cambridge, MA: Blackwell, 1990.

Hassan, Ihab. "From Postmodernism to Postmodernity: The Local/Global Context." https://www.ihabhassan.com/postmodernism_to_postmodernity.htm (accessed February 22, 2009).

Hassan, Ihab. *The Postmodern Turn: Essays in Postmodern Theory and Culture.* Columbus: Ohio State University Press, 1987.

Head, Leslie. "Cultural Ecology: The Problematic Human and the Terms of Engagement." *Progress in Human Geography* 31, no. 6 (2007): 837–46.

Heater, Derek. *World Citizenship and Government: Cosmopolitan Ideas in the History of Western Political Thought.* New York: St. Martin's Press, 1996.

Heater, Derek. *World Citizenship: Cosmopolitan Thinking and Its Opponents.* London: Continuum, 2002.

Heath, Stephen. "Difference." In Wolfreys, *Literary Theories,* 211–32.

Hedetoft, Ulf, and Mette Hjort, eds. *The Postnational Self: Belonging and Identity.* Minneapolis: University of Minnesota Press, 2002.

Hegel, G. W. F. *Phenomenology of Spirit.* Translated by A. V. Miller with analysis of the text and foreword by J. N. Findlay. Oxford: Oxford University Press, 1977.

Heidegger, Martin. *Being and Time: A Translation of Sein und Zeit.* Translated by Joan Stambaugh. Albany: SUNY Press, 1996.

Heidegger, Martin. *Poetry, Language, Thought.* Translated and with an introduction by Albert Hofstadter. New York: HarperTrade, 1981.

Heise, Ursula K. "Local Rock and Global Plastic: World Ecology and the Experience of Place." *Comparative Literary Studies* 41, no. 1 (2004): 126–52.

Heise, Ursula K. *Sense of Place and Sense of Planet: The Environmental Imagination of the Global.* Oxford: Oxford University Press, 2008.

Held, David. Afterword to *A Globalizing World? Culture, Economics, Politics,* edited by David Held, 169–77. London: Routledge in association with The Open University, 2000.

Held, David, and Anthony McGrew, eds. *Globalization Theory: Approaches and Controversies*. Cambridge: Polity, 2007.

Hirsch, E. D. "Faulty Perspectives." In Lodge and Wood, *Modern Criticism and Theory*, 2000 ed., 231–40.

Hoberek, Andrew, John Burt, David Kadlec, Jamie Owen Daniel, Shelly Eversley, Catherine Jurca, Aparajita Sagar, and Michael Bérubé. "Twentieth-Century Literature in the New Century: A Symposium." *College English* 64, no. 1 (September 2001): 9–33.

Hogue, W. Lawrence. *Postmodern American Literature and Its Other*. Champaign: University of Illinois Press, 2008.

Holland, Norman. "UNITY IDENTITY TEXT SELF." In Tompkins, *Reader-Response Criticism*, 118–33.

Hollinger, David A. *Cosmopolitanism and Solidarity: Studies in Ethnoracial, Religious, and Professional Affiliation in the United States*. Madison: University of Wisconsin Press, 2006.

Hollinger, David A. "The New Cosmopolitanism." In Vertovec and Cohen, 227–39.

Hollinger, David A. *Postethnic America: Beyond Multiculturalism*. New York: Basic Books/HarperCollins, 1995.

Holmes, Douglas R., and George E. Marcus. "Fast Capitalism: Para-Ethnography and the Rise of the Symbolic Analyst." In Fisher and Downey, *Frontiers of Capital*, 33–57.

Holmes, Martha Stoddard. "John Updike: 'Metamorphosis.'" *Literature, Arts and Medicine Database*, http://litmed.med.nyu.edu/Annnotation?action=view&annid=12403 (accessed September 24, 2007).

Holquist, Michael. "Introduction: The Architectonics of Answerability." In Bakhtin, *Art and Answerability*, ix–xlix.

Holub, Robert. *Reception Theory: A Critical Introduction*. London: Methuen, 1984.

Hopper, Paul. *Understanding Cultural Globalization*. London: Polity, 2007.

Hornstein, Lillian Herlands, ed., and G. D. Percy, coed. *The Reader's Companion to World Literature*, 2nd ed. New York: Penguin, 1984.

Hosseini, Khaled. *The Kite Runner*. New York: Penguin, 2005.

Huang, Yunte. *Transpacific Displacement: Ethnography, Translation, and Intertextual Travel in Twentieth-Century American Literature*. Berkeley: University of California Press, 2002.

Huntington, Samuel P. *The Clash of Civilizations and the Remaking of World Order*. New York: Simon & Schuster, 2003.

Hutcheon, Linda. *The Politics of Postmodernism*. 2nd ed. London: Routledge, 1989.

Iser, Wolfgang. *The Act of Reading: A Theory of Aesthetic Response*. Baltimore: Johns Hopkins University Press, 1978.

Iser, Wolfgang. "Die Appelstruktur der Texte." In *Rezeptionsästhetik*, edited by Rainer Warning, 228–52. Munich: Wilhelm Fink, 1988.

Iser, Wolfgang. "Coda to the Discussion." In Budick and Iser, *The Translatability of Cultures*, 294–302.

Iser, Wolfgang. *The Fictive and the Imaginary*. Baltimore: Johns Hopkins University Press, 1996.

Iser, Wolfgang. *The Implied Reader: Patterns of Communication in Prose Fiction from Bunyan to Beckett.* Baltimore: Johns Hopkins University Press, 1978.

Iser, Wolfgang. *The Range of Interpretation.* New York: Columbia University Press, 2000.

Iser, Wolfgang. "Talk Like Whales." *Diacritics* 11, no. 3 (1981): 82–87.

Iyer, Pico. *Abandon: A Romance.* New York: Random House, 2003.

Iyer, Pico. *The Global Soul: Jet Lag, Shopping Malls, and the Search for Home.* New York: Random House, 2000.

Iyer, Pico. "The Nowhere Man." *Prospect* 30, no. 3 (February 1997): 30–33.

Iyer, Pico. *Sun after Dark: Flights into the Foreign.* New York: Random House, 2004.

Iyer, Pico. *Video Night in Kathmandu and Other Reports from the Not-So-Far-East.* New York: Knopf, 1988.

Jacob, Margaret C. *Strangers Nowhere in the World: The Rise of Cosmopolitanism in Early Modern Europe.* Philadelphia: University of Pennsylvania Press, 2006.

Jakobson, Roman. "Linguistics and Poetics." In Lodge and Wood, *Modern Criticism and Theory,* 2000 ed., 31–55.

Jakobson, Roman. "On Linguistic Aspects of Translation." In Venuti, *The Translation Studies Reader,* 138–43.

Jameson, Fredric. *The Geopolitical Aesthetic: Cinema and Space in the World System.* Bloomington: Indiana University Press, 1995.

Jameson, Fredric. "New Literary History after the End of the New." *New Literary History* 39, no. 3 (Summer 2008): 375–87.

Jameson, Fredric. "Notes on Globalization as a Philosophical Issue." In Jameson and Miyoshi, *The Cultures of Globalization,* 54–77.

Jameson, Fredric, and Masao Miyoshi, eds. *The Cultures of Globalization.* Durham, NC: Duke University Press, 1998.

Jauss, Hans Robert. *Toward an Aesthetic of Reception.* Translated from the German by Timothy Bakhti. Introduction by Paul de Man. Minneapolis: University of Minnesota Press, 2005.

Jencks, Charles. "Post-Modern Architecture and Time Fusion." In Carmichael and Lee, *Postmodern Times,* 141–52.

Jencks, Charles. "Post-Modernism: A Whole Full of Holes." Interview by Alison Lee. In Carmichael and Lee, *Postmodern Times,* 245–63.

Jencks, Charles. "Postmodern vs. Late-Modern." In *Zeitgeist in Babel: The Post-Modernist Controversy,* edited by Ingeborg Hoesterey, 4–21. Bloomington: Indiana University Press, 1991.

Joseph, Clara A. B., and Janet Wilson. *Global Fissures: Postcolonial Fusions.* Amsterdam: Rodopi, 2006.

Jowitt, Ken. *New World Disorder: The Leninist Extinction.* Berkeley: University of California Press, 1992.

Kant, Immanuel. *Political Writings.* 2nd ed., enlarged. Edited with an introduction and notes by Hans Reiss. Translated by H. B. Nisbett. Cambridge: Cambridge University Press, 1991.

Kaplan, Caren. *Questions of Travel: Postmodern Discourses of Displacement.* Durham, NC: Duke University Press, 1996.

Kaufmann, Walter. "I and You: A Prologue." In Buber, *I and Thou,* 7–48.

Kellman, Steven G. "Don DeLillo's Logogenetic *Underworld*." In Dewey, Kellman, and Malin, *UnderWords*, 68–78.

Kellman, Steven G. *The Translingual Imagination*. Lincoln: University of Nebraska Press, 2000.

Kierkegaard, Søren. *Fear and Trembling; Repetition*. Edited and translated with introduction and notes by Howard V. Hong and Edna V. Hong. Princeton, NJ: Princeton University Press, 1983.

Kim, Daniel Y. "Do, I, Too, Sing America? Vernacular Representations and Chang-rae Lee's *Native Speaker*." *Journal of Asian American Studies* 6, no. 3 (October 2003): 231–60.

Kim, Suki. *The Interpreter*. New York: Farrar, Straus and Giroux, 2003.

Kim, Suki. "Interview with Suki Kim, author of *The Interpreter*." By Cindy Yoon. *AsiaSource*, March 24, 2003. http://www.asiasource.org/arts/sukikim.cfm (accessed July 12, 2006).

Kingston, Maxine Hong. *Tripmaster Monkey*. New York: Random House, 1990.

Kiossev, Alexander, ed. *Post-Theory, Games, and Discursive Resistance: The Bulgarian Case*. Albany: SUNY Press, 1995.

Kirby, Alan. "The Death of Postmodernism and Beyond." *Philosophy Now* 71 (January–February 2009). http://www.philosophynow.org/issue58/58kirby.htm (accessed February 26, 2009).

Knight, Peter. "Everything Is Connected: *Underworld*'s Secret History of Paranoia." *Modern Fiction Studies* 45, no. 3 (Fall 1999): 811–36.

Kollmeyer, Christopher J. "Globalization, Class Compromise, and American Exceptionalism: Political Change in 16 Advanced Capitalist Countries." *Critical Sociology* 29, no. 3 (October 2003): 369–91.

Krishnaswamy, Revathi, and John C. Hawley, eds. *The Postcolonial and the Global*. Minneapolis: University of Minnesota Press, 2007.

Kristeva, Julia. *Nations without Nationalism*. Translated by Leon S. Roudiez. New York: Columbia University Press, 1993.

Kristeva, Julia. *Polylogue*. Paris: Seuil, 1977.

Kristeva, Julia. *Strangers to Ourselves*. Translated by Leon S. Roudiez. New York: Columbia University Press, 1991.

Kumar, Amitava, ed. *World Bank Literature*. Foreword by John Berger. Afterword by Bruce Robbins. Minneapolis: University of Minnesota Press, 2003.

Kundera, Milan. *The Art of the Novel*. Translated from the French by Linda Asher. New York: Grove Press, 1988.

Kundera, Milan. *La vie est ailleurs*. Translated by François Kérel. Paris: Gallimard, 1976.

Kuorti, Joel, and Jopi Nyman, eds. *Reconstructing Hybridity: Post-Colonial Studies in Transition*. Amsterdam: Rodopi, 2007.

Kureishi, Hanif. *The Black Album*. New York: Simon & Schuster, 1996.

Lacan, Jacques, "The Insistence of the Letter in the Unconscious." In Lodge and Wood, *Modern Criticism and Theory*, 2000 ed., 62–87.

Lahiri, Jhumpa. *The Namesake*. Boston: Houghton Mifflin, 2004.

Lapierre, Nicole. *Pensons ailleurs*. Paris: Gallimard, 2006.

Lash, Scott. *Another Modernity: A Different Rationality*. Oxford: Blackwell, 1999.

Lee, Chang-rae. *Aloft*. New York: Riverhead, 2005.

Lee, Chang-rae. *A Gesture Life*. New York: Riverhead, 1999.

Lee, Chang-rae. "Mute in an English-Only World." In Muller, *The New World Reader,* 126–29.

Lee, Chang-rae. *Native Speaker.* New York: Riverhead, 1995.

Lee, Rachel C. "Reading Contests and Contesting Reading: Chang-rae Lee's *Native Speaker* and Ethnic New York." *MELUS* 29, no. 3–4 (Fall–Winter 2004): 341–52.

Lee, Young-Oak. "Gender, Race, and the Nation in *A Gesture Life,*" *Critique* 46, no. 2 (Winter 2005): 146–59.

Lefebvre, Henri. *The Production of Space.* Translated by Donald Nicholson-Smith. Oxford: Blackwell, 1991.

Levander, Caroline Field, and Robert S. Levine, eds. *Hemispheric American Studies.* Rutgers, NJ: Rutgers University Press, 2008.

Levinas, Emmanuel. *Altérité et transcendence.* Preface by Pierre Hayat. Paris: Fata Morgana, 1995.

Levinas, Emmanuel. *God, Death, and Time.* Translated by Bettina Bergo. Stanford, CA: Stanford University Press, 2000.

Levinas, Emmanuel. *Humanism of the Other.* Translated from the French by Nidra Poller. Introduction by Richard Cohen. Urbana: University of Illinois Press, 2003.

Levinas, Emmanuel. "Ideology and Idealism." In *The Levinas Reader,* edited by Seán Hand, 235–48. Oxford: Oxford University Press, 1989.

Levinas, Emmanuel. "Peace and Proximity." In Emmanuel Levinas, *Basic Philosophical Writings,* edited by Adriaan T. Peperzak, Simon Critchley, and Robert Bernasconi, 162–69. Bloomington: Indiana University Press, 1996.

Levinas, Emmanuel. *Proper Names.* Translated by Michael B. Smith. Stanford, CA: Stanford University Press, 1996.

Levinas, Emmanuel. *Time and the Other [and Additional Essays].* Translated by Richard A. Cohen. Pittsburgh: Duquesne University Press, 1987.

Levinas, Emmanuel. *Totality and Infinity: An Essay on Interiority.* Translated by Alphonso Lingis. Pittsburgh: Duquesne University Press, 1961.

Levinas, Emmanuel, and Richard Kearney. "Dialogue with Emmanuel Levinas." In *Face to Face with Levinas,* edited by Richard A. Cohen, 13–33. Albany: SUNY Press, 1986.

Lévi-Strauss, Claude. *Tristes Tropiques.* Translated from the French by John Weightman and Doreen Weightman. New York: Atheneum, 1974.

Lewis, R. W. B. *The American Adam: Innocence, Tragedy, and Tradition in the Nineteenth Century.* 1955. Chicago: University of Chicago Press, 1984.

Liddell, Henry George, and Robert Scott. *A Greek-English Lexicon.* Vol. 1. Oxford: Clarendon Press, 1940.

Liiceanu, Gabriel, ed. *Epistolar.* 2nd ed., revised and expanded. Bucharest: Humanitas, 1996.

Liiceanu, Gabriel. *The Păltiniş Diary: A Paideic Model in Humanist Culture.* Translated by James Christian Brown. Budapest: Central European University Press, 2000.

Liiceanu, Gabriel. *Uşa interzisă.* Bucharest: Humanitas, 2002.

Lipovetsky, Gilles. *Hypermodern Times.* Translated by Andrew Brown. Cambridge: Polity, 2005.

Little, G. William. *The Waste Fix: Seizures of the Sacred from Upton Sinclair to The Sopranos.* New York: Routledge, 2002.

Lodge, David, with Nigel Wood. *Modern Criticism and Theory: A Reader.* Edited by David Lodge. Revised and expanded by Nigel Wood. Harlow, UK: Longman, 2000.

Lodge, David, with Nigel Wood. *Modern Criticism and Theory: A Reader.* 3rd ed. Harlow, UK: Longman, 2008.

Long, A. A., and D. N. Sedley. *The Hellenistic Philosophers.* Vol. 1, *Translations of the Principal Sources, with Philosophical Commentary.* Cambridge: Cambridge University Press, 1987.

Longmuir, Anne. "Performing the Body in Don DeLillo's *The Body Artist.*" *Modern Fiction Studies* 53, no. 3 (Fall 2007): 527–43.

Longxi, Zhang. *Allegoresis: Reading Canonical Literature East and West.* Ithaca, NY: Cornell University Press, 2005.

Luhmann, Niklas. *Risk: A Sociological Theory.* Translated by Rhodes Barrett. New York: Aldine de Gruyter, 1992.

Luke, Timothy W. "New World Order or Neo-world Order: Power, Politics and Ideology in Informationalizing Glocalities." In Featherstone, Lash, and Robertson, *Global Modernities*, 91–107.

Lunenfeld, Peter. "Hyperaesthetics: Theorizing in Real-Time about Digital Culture." In Carmichael and Lee, *Postmodern Times*, 111–26.

Lupton, Deborah. *Risk.* London: Routledge, 1999.

Lutz, Tom. *Cosmopolitan Vistas: American Regionalism and Literary Values.* Ithaca, NY: Cornell University Press, 2004.

Maalouf, Amin. *Le dérèglement du monde.* Paris: Grasset & Fasquelle, 2009.

Maalouf, Amin. *In the Name of Identity: Violence and the Need to Belong.* Translated from the French by Barbara Bray. New York: Penguin, 2000.

MacCabe, Colin. "Broken English." In *Futures for English,* edited by Colin MacCabe, 3–14. Manchester, UK: Manchester University Press, 1988.

Macdonell, Arthur Anthony. *A Practical Sanskrit Dictionary with Transliterations, Accentuation, and Etymological Analysis Throughout.* London: Oxford University Press, 1924.

Major, René. "Names: Proper and Improper." Translated by John Forrester. In *Postmodernism: ICA Documents,* edited by Lisa Appignanesi, 185–97. London: Free Association Books, 1986.

Maltby, Paul. *Dissident Postmodernists: Barthelme, Coover, Pynchon.* Philadelphia: University of Pennsylvania Press, 1991.

Manning, Susan, and Andrew Taylor, eds. *Transatlantic Literary Studies: A Reader.* Baltimore: Johns Hopkins University Press, 2007.

Marx, Karl, and Friedrich Engels. *The Manifesto of the Communist Party.* In *The Communist Manifesto: New Interpretations,* edited by Mark Cowling. Including, in full, *The Manifesto of the Communist Party,* translated by Terrell Carver, 16–17. New York: New York University Press, 1998.

Mattelart, Armand. *Diversité culturelle et mondialisation.* Paris: La Découverte, 2005.

McCaffery, Larry, Thomas Hartl, and Doug Rice, eds. *Federman A to X: A Recyclopedic Narrative.* San Diego: San Diego State University Press, 1998.

McClintock, Anne, Aamir Mufti, and Ella Shohat, eds. *Dangerous Liaisons: Gender, Nation, and Postcolonial Perspectives.* Minneapolis: University of Minnesota Press, 1997.

McClure, John. *Late Imperial Romance*. London: Verso, 1994.

McGee, Patrick. *Telling the Other: The Question of Value in Modern and Postcolonial Writing*. Ithaca, NY: Cornell University Press, 1992.

McHale, Brian. "What Was Postmodernism?" *Electronic Book Review*, December 20, 2007. http://www.electronicbookreview.com/thread/fictionspresent/tense?mode-print (accessed October 29, 2009).

McInturff, Kate. "The Uses and Abuses of World Literature." *Journal of American Culture* 26, no. 2 (June 2003): 224–36.

McLaughlin, Robert L. "Post-Postmodern Discontent: Contemporary Fiction and the Social World." *symplokē* 12, no. 1–2 (2004): 53–68.

Messmer, Marietta. "Reading National American Literary Historiography Internationally." *Comparative Literature* 52, no. 3 (Summer 2000): 193–212.

Michaels, Walter Benn. *Our America: Nativism, Modernism, and Pluralism*. Durham, NC: Duke University Press, 1995.

Mignolo, Walter. "The Many Faces of Cosmo-polis: Border Thinking and Critical Cosmopolitanism." *Public Culture* 12, no. 3 (2000): 721–48.

Miller, J. Hillis. *Others*. Princeton, NJ: Princeton University Press, 2001.

Minh-ha, Trinh T. "Not You/Like You: Postcolonial Women and the Interlocking Questions of Identity and Difference." In McClintock, Mufti, and Shohat, *Dangerous Liaisons*, 415–19.

Miscevic, Nenad. "Close Strangers: Nationalism, Proximity, and Cosmopolitanism." *Studies in East European Thought* 51 (1999): 109–25.

Miyoshi, Masao. "'Globalization,' Culture, and the University." In Jameson and Miyoshi, *The Cultures of Globalization*, 247–70.

Miyoshi, Masao. "Turn to the Planet: Literature, Diversity, and Totality." *Comparative Literature* 53, no. 4 (Fall 2001): 283–97.

Moi, Toril. *Sexual/Textual Politics*. London: Routledge, 2001.

Moïsi, Dominique. *La Géopolitique de l'émotion*. Paris: Flammarion, 2009.

Mones, Nicole. *Lost in Translation*. New York: Random House, 1999.

Montesquieu. *Persian Letters*. Translated with an introduction and notes by C. J. Betts. New York: Penguin, 1993.

Mooney, Edward J. "*Repetition:* Getting the World Back." In *The Cambridge Companion to Kierkegaard,* edited by Alastair Hannay and Gordon D. Marino, 282–307. Cambridge: Cambridge University Press, 1998.

Moraru, Christian. "Cosmopolitics, Paroxism, Global Talk: Emerging Issues and Approaches." *symplokē* 7, no. 1–2 (1999): 197–202.

Moraru, Christian. "The Genomic Imperative: Michel Houellebecq's *The Possibility of an Island*." *Utopian Studies* 19, no. 2 (2008): 265–83.

Moraru, Christian. "The Global Turn in Critical Theory." *symplokē* 9, no. 1–2 (2001): 80–92.

Moraru, Christian. "Jurnalul de la Teheran." Translated into Romanian by Laura Savu. *Observator cultural* 257 (January 25–31, 2005), 15–16.

Moraru, Christian. *Memorious Discourse: Reprise and Representation in Postmodernism*. Madison, NJ: Fairleigh Dickinson University Press, 2005.

Moraru, Christian. "Postmodernism, Cosmopolitanism, Cosmodernism." *American Book Review* 28, no. 3 (March–April 2007): 3–4.

Moraru, Christian. *Rewriting: Postmodern Narrative and Cultural Critique in the Age of Cloning*. Albany: SUNY Press, 2001.

Moretti, Franco. *Modern Epic: The World-System from Goethe to García Márquez.* Translated by Quintin Hoare. London: Verso, 1996.

Morley, Catherine. "Don DeLillo's Transatlantic Dialogue with Sergei Eisenstein." *Journal of American Studies* 40, no. 1 (2006): 17–34.

Moses, Michael Valdez. *The Novel and the Globalization of Culture.* Oxford: Oxford University Press, 1995.

Motzkin, Gabriel. "Memory and Cultural Translation." In Budick and Iser, *The Translatability of Cultures,* 265–81.

Mukherjee, Bharati. *Desirable Daughters.* New York: Hyperion, 2002.

Mukherjee, Bharati. *Jasmine.* New York: Grove, 1989.

Mukherjee, Bharati. *The Tree Bride.* New York: Hyperion, 2004.

Muller, Gilbert H. *The New World Reader: Thinking and Writing about the Global Community.* Boston: Houghton Mifflin, 2008.

Murphet, Julian. "Postmodernism and Space." In Connor, *The Cambridge Companion to Postmodernism,* 116–35.

Murphy, Timothy S. "To Have Done with Postmodernism: A Plea (or Provocation) for Globalization Studies." *symploke* 12, no. 1–2 (2004): 20–34.

Nafisi, Azar. "Azar Nafisi: Author of *Reading Lolita in Tehran* converses with Robert Birnbaum." Interview by Robert Birnbaum. identitytheory.com: A literary website, sort of, February 5, 2004. http://www.identitytheory.com/interviews/birnbaum139.php (accessed January 14, 2005).

Nafisi, Azar. *Reading Lolita in Tehran: A Memoir in Books.* New York: Random House, 2004.

Nafisi, Azar. "The Veiled Threat." *New Republic* 220, February 22, 1999, 24–29.

Nancy, Jean-Luc. *Being Singular Plural.* Translated by Robert D. Richardson and Anne E. O'Byrne. Stanford, CA: Stanford University Press, 2000.

Nancy, Jean-Luc. *Corpus.* Paris: Métailié, 2000.

Nancy, Jean-Luc. *La création du monde* ou *la mondialisation.* Paris: Galilée, 2002.

Nancy, Jean-Luc. *The Creation of the World or Globalization.* Translated and with an introduction by François Raffoul and David Pettigrew. Albany: SUNY Press, 2007.

Nancy, Jean-Luc. *The Inoperative Community.* Edited by Peter Conor. Translated by Peter Conor, Lisa Garbus, Michael Holland, and Simona Sawhney. Foreword by Christopher Fynsk. Minneapolis: University of Minnesota Press, 1991.

Nancy, Jean-Luc. *The Sense of the World.* Translated and with a foreword by Jeffrey S. Librett. Minneapolis: University of Minnesota Press, 1997.

Nancy, Jean-Luc. *Vérité de la démocratie.* Paris: Galilée, 2008.

Nel, Philip. *The Avant-Garde and American Postmodernity: Small Incisive Shocks.* Jackson: University Press of Mississippi, 2002.

Nethersole, Reingard. "Models of Globalization." *PMLA* 116, no. 3 (May 2001): 638–49.

Newton, Adam Zachary. *The Elsewhere: On Belonging at a Near Distance; Reading Literary Memoir from Europe and the Levant.* Madison: University of Wisconsin Press, 2005.

Newton, Adam Zachary. *Narrative Ethics.* Cambridge, MA: Harvard University Press, 1995.

Nicolescu, Basarab. "The Challenge of Transdisciplinarity: From Postmodernity to Cosmodernity." Paper abstract. Centre of Transdisciplinarity. Cognitive and

State-System Sciences—Indexicals. http://indexicals.ac.at/abstractviennao5 bnicolescu.html (accessed December 31, 2006).

Nicolescu, Basarab. *L'homme et le sens de l'univers: Essay sur Jakob Boehme, suivi d'un choix de texts*. Preface by Antoine Faivre and Joscelyn Godwin. Paris: Lebeau, 1995.

Nicolescu, Basarab. *Manifesto of Transdiciplinarity*. Translated from the French by Karen-Claire Voss. Albany: SUNY Press, 2002.

Nicolescu, Basarab. *Théorèmes poétiques*. Preface by Michel Camus. Paris: Rocher, 1994.

Nicolescu, Basarab. *La transdisciplinarité: Manifeste*. Paris: Rocher, 1996.

Nicolescu, Basarab, Corin Braga, Ruxandra Cesereanu, Sanda Cordos, Anca Hatiegan, Marius Jucan, Doru Pop, Vlad Roman, Nicolae Turcan, and Mihaela Ursa. "Ce este cosmodernitatea?" Center for the Research of the Imaginary, Cluj, Romania. http://phantasma.ro/dezbateri/masa/masa14.html (accessed September 23, 2007).

Nietzsche, Friedrich. *Basic Writings of Nietzsche*. Translated and edited, with commentaries, by Walter Kaufmann. New York: Modern Library, 1992.

Nietzsche, Friedrich. *Human, All Too Human: A Book for Free Spirits*. Translated by Marion Faber with Stephen Lehmann. Introduction and notes by Marion Faber. Lincoln: University of Nebraska Press, 1984.

Nietzsche, Friedrich. *The Will to Power*. A new translation by Walter Kaufmann and R.J. Hollingdale. Edited, with commentary, by Walter Kaufmann. New York: Random House, 1968.

Niranjana, Tejaswini. *Siting Translation: History, Post-Structuralism, and the Colonial Context*. Berkeley: University of California Press, 1992.

Novalis. *Journal intime suivi des* Hymnes à la nuit *et des* Fragments inédits. Translated from the German by G. Clarette and S. Joachim-Chaigneau. Introduction by Germaine Clarette. Paris: Stock, 1927.

Ortega, Julio. "Transatlantic Translations." *PMLA* 118, no. 1 (January 2003): 25–40.

Ó Tuathail, Gearóid, Simon Dalby, and Paul Routledge, eds. *The Geopolitics Reader*. London: Routledge, 1998.

Parikh, Crystal. *An Ethics of Betrayal: The Politics of Otherness in Emergent U.S. Literatures and Culture*. New York: Fordham University Press, 2009.

Parikh, Crystal. "Ethnic America Undercover: The Intellectual and Minority Discourse." *Contemporary Literature* 43, no. 2 (Summer 2002): 249–84.

Passavant, Paul A., and Jodi Dean, eds. *Empire's New Clothes: Reading Negri and Hardt*. New York: Routledge, 2004.

Pefanis, Julian. *Heterology and the Postmodern: Bataille, Baudrillard, and Lyotard*. Durham, NC: Duke University Press, 1991.

Peyser, Thomas. "Globalization in America: The Case of Don DeLillo's *White Noise*." *CLIO* 25, no. 3 (Spring 1996): 255–71.

Peyser, Thomas. *Utopia and Cosmopolis: Globalization in the Era of American Literary Realism*. Durham, NC: Duke University Press, 1998.

Phillips, Anne. *Multiculturalism without Culture*. Princeton, NJ: Princeton University Press, 2007.

Pizer, John. "Goethe's 'World Literature' Paradigm and Contemporary Cultural Globalization." *Comparative Literature* 52, no. 3 (Summer 2000): 213–27.

Poché, Fred. *Penser avec Arendt et Lévinas: Du mal politique au respect de l'autre.* Lyon, France: Chronique Sociale, 1998.

Potkay, Adam. "Wordsworth and the Ethics of Things." *PMLA* 123, no. 2 (March 2008): 390–404.

Poulet, Georges. "Criticism and the Experience of Interiority." In Tompkins, *Reader-Response Criticism,* 41–49.

Poulet, Georges. *Entre moi and moi: Essay critiques sur la conscience de soi.* Paris: José Corti, 1977.

Pratt, Mary Louise. "Comparative Literature and Global Citizenship." In Bernheimer, *Comparative Literature in the Age of Multiculturalism,* 58–65.

Pratt, Mary Louise. *Imperial Eyes: Travel Writing and Transculturation.* London: Routledge, 1992.

Pushkin, Alexander. *The Poems, Prose, and Plays of Alexander Pushkin.* Selected and edited, with an introduction by Avrahm Yarmolinsky. New York: Random House, 1964.

Quiroga, José. *Tropics of Desire: Interventions from Queer Latino America.* New York: NYU Press, 2000.

Raffoul, François, and David Pettigrew. "Translators' Introduction." In Jean-Luc Nancy, *The Creation of the World or Globalization.* Translated and with an introduction by François Raffoul and David Pettigrew, 1–26. Albany: SUNY Press, 2007.

Randall, Alice. *Pushkin and the Queen of Spades.* Boston. New York: Houghton Mifflin, 2004.

Rauch, Molly E. "Fruit Salad." *Nation,* March 2, 1998, 28–30.

Raulet, Gérard. *Critical Cosmology: On Nations and Globalization—A Philosophical Essay.* Lanham, MD: Lexington Books, 2005.

Readings, Bill, and Bennet Schaber. "Introduction: The Question Mark in the Midst of Modernity." In *Postmodernism across the Ages: Essays for a Postmodernity That Wasn't Born Yesterday,* edited by Bill Readings and Bennet Schaber, 1–28. Syracuse, NY: Syracuse University Press, 1993.

Reichert, Klaus. "The Buber-Rosenzweig Bible Translation." In Budick and Iser, *The Translatability of Cultures,* 169–85.

Reiss, Timothy J. *Against Autonomy: Global Dialectics of Cultural Exchange.* Stanford, CA: Stanford University Press, 2002.

Reynolds, Guy. *Apostles of Modernity: American Writers in the Age of Development.* Lincoln: University of Nebraska Press, 2008.

Ricoeur, Paul. *Oneself as Another.* Translated by Kathleen Blamey. Chicago: University of Chicago Press, 1992.

Risser, James. "The Voice of the Other in Gadamer's Hermeneutics." In *The Philosophy of Hans-Georg Gadamer,* edited by Lewis Edwin Hahn, 389–402. Chicago: Open Court, 1997.

Roach, Joseph. "World Bank Drama." In Dimock and Buell, *Shades of the Planet,* 171–83.

Robbins, Bruce. *Feeling Global: Internationalism in Distress.* New York: New York University Press, 1999.

Robbins, Jill. *Altered Reading: Levinas and Literature.* Chicago: University of Chicago Press, 1999.

Robertson, Roland. *Globalization: Social Theory and Global Culture*. London: Sage, 1992.

Robertson, Roland. "Glocalization: Time-Space and Homogeneity-Heterogeneity." In Featherstone, Lash, and Robertson, *Global Modernities*, 25–44.

Robertson, Roland. "Mapping the Global Condition: Globalization as the Central Concept." In *Global Culture: Nationalism, globalization and modernity. A Theory, Culture, and Society Special Issue*, edited by Mike Featherstone, 15–30. London: Sage, 1990.

Rody, Caroline. *The Interethnic Imagination: Roots and Passages in Contemporary American Fiction*. New York: Oxford University Press, 2009.

Rønning, Anne Holding, and Lene Johannessen, eds. *Readings of the Particular: The Postcolonial and the Postnational*. Amsterdam, Rodopi: 2007.

Rorty, Richard. "Comments on Taylor's 'Paralectics.'" In Scharlemann, *On the Other*, 70–78.

Rowe, John Carlos. "Post-Nationalism, Globalism, and the New American Studies." In Rowe, *Post-Nationalist American Studies*, 23–39.

Rowe, John Carlos, ed. *Post-Nationalist American Studies*. Berkeley: University of California Press, 2000.

Rowe, John Carlos. "Reading *Reading Lolita in Tehran* in Idaho." *American Quarterly* 59, no. 2 (June 2007): 253–75.

Ruppersburg, Hugh, and Tim Engles, eds. *Critical Essays on Don DeLillo*. New York: C. K. Hall, 2000.

Rushdie, Salman. *Imaginary Homelands: Essays and Criticism 1981–1991*. London: Granta, 1991.

Rushdie, Salman. *Midnight's Children*. New York: Penguin, 1991.

Sadowski-Smith, Claudia. "The U.S.-Mexico Borderlands Write Back: Cross-Cultural Transnationalism in Contemporary U.S. Women of Color Fiction." *Arizona Quarterly* 57, no. 1 (Spring 2001): 91–112.

Salzman, Artur. "Awful Symmetries in Don DeLillo's *Underworld*." In Ruppersburg and Engles, *Critical Essays on Don DeLillo*, 302–16.

Sardar, Ziauddin. *Postmodernism and the Other: The New Imperialism of Western Culture*. London: Pluto Press, 1998.

Sartre, Jean-Paul. "*Huis clos* de Jean-Paul Sartre." http://www.alalettre.com/sartre-huisclos.htm (accessed May 20, 2006).

Sartre, Jean-Paul. No Exit *and Three Other Plays*. New York: Random House, 1973.

Saussy, Haun, ed. *Comparative Literature in an Age of Globalization*. Baltimore: Johns Hopkins University Press, 2006.

Scanlon, T. M. *What We Owe to Each Other*. Cambridge, MA: Harvard University Press, 1998.

Scarpetta, Guy. *Éloge du cosmopolitisme*. Paris: Bernard Grasset, 1981.

Scharlemann, Robert P., ed. *On the Other: Dialogue and/or Dialectics; Mark Taylor's "Paralectics."* With Roy Wagner, Michael Brint, and Richard Rorty. Lanham, MD: University Press of America, 1991.

Schedler, Christopher. *Border Modernism*. New York: Routledge, 2002.

Schleiermacher, Friedrich. "On the Different Methods of Translating." In Venuti, *The Translation Studies Reader*, 43–63.

Schlereth, Thomas J. *The Cosmopolitan Ideal in Enlightenment Thought: Its Form and Function in the Ideas of Franklin, Hume, and Voltaire, 1694–1790.* Notre Dame, IN: University of Notre Dame Press, 1977.

Schonfeld, Erick. "Analysis: Yahoo's China Problem." *Business 2.0.* http://money .cnn.com/2006/02/08/technology/yahoo_china_b20/ (accessed January 19, 2008).

Schulz, Hans-Joachim, and Phillip H. Rhein, eds. *Comparative Literature: The Early Years.* Chapel Hill: University of North Carolina Press, 1973.

Schweickart, Patrocinio P., and Elizabeth A. Flynn, eds. *Reading Sites: Social Difference and Reader Response.* New York: Modern Language Association of America, 2004.

Segalen, Martine. *L'Autre et le semblable: Regards sur l'ethnologie des sociétés contemporaines.* Gathered and introduced by Martine Segalen. Paris: CNRS, 1989.

Seidel, Michael. *Exile and the Narrative Imagination.* New Haven: Yale University Press, 1986.

Sesé, Bernard. "Pierre Teilhard de Chardin: Prophète de la mondialisation?" *Etudes* 3964 (April 2002): 483–94.

Seyhan, Azade. *Writing outside the Nation.* Princeton, NJ: Princeton University Press, 2001.

Shih, Shu-Mei. "Global Literature and the Technologies of Recognition." *PMLA* 119, no. 1 (January 2004): 16–30.

Siegel, Lee. *Love in a Dead Language: A Romance by Lee Siegel Being the* Kamasutra *of Guru Vatsyayana Mallanaga as Translated and Interpreted by Professor Leopold Roth with a Foreword and Annotation by Anang Saighal following the Commentary of Pandit Pralayananga Lilaraja.* Chicago: University of Chicago Press, 1999.

Simmel, Georg. *Simmel on Culture: Selected Writings.* Edited by David Frisby and Mike Featherstone. London: Sage, 1997.

Singer, Peter. *One World: The Ethics of Globalization.* New Haven: Yale University Press, 2002.

Singly, François de. *Les uns avec les autres: Quand l'individualisme crée du lien.* Paris: Armand Colin, 2003.

Skurnick, Lizzie. "Menace II Russian Society." *New York Times Book Review,* May 23, 2004, 8.

Smart, Barry. *Facing Modernity: Ambivalence, Reflexivity, and Modernity.* London: Sage, 1999.

Smith, Carlton. *Coyote Kills John Wayne: Postmodernism and Contemporary Fictions of the Transnational Frontier.* Hanover, NH: University Press of New England, 2000.

Smith, Zadie. *The Autograph Man.* New York: Random House, 2002.

Smith, Zadie. *On Beauty.* New York: Penguin, 2005.

Smith, Zadie. *White Teeth.* New York: Random House, 2000.

Soja, Edward W. *Postmodern Geographies: The Reassertion of Space in Critical Social Theory.* New York: Verso, 1989.

Soler, Colette. "Les noms de l'identité." *La Revue de psychanalyse du Champ lacanien* 6 (March 2008): 11–18.

Sollors, Werner. *Beyond Ethnicity: Consent and Descent in American Culture.* Oxford: Oxford University Press, 1986.

Sollors, Werner. "The Invention of Ethnicity." In *The Invention of Ethnicity*, edited by Werner Sollors, ix–xx. New York: Oxford University Press, 1991.

Sommer, Doris. *Bilingual Aesthetics: A New Sentimental Education*. Durham, NC: Duke University Press, 2004.

Spanneut, Michel. *Permanence du stoïcisme: De Zénon à Malraux*. Gembloux, Belgium: Duculot, 1973.

Spivak, Gayatri Chakravorty. *A Critique of Postcolonial Reason: Toward a History of the Vanishing Present*. Cambridge, MA: Harvard University Press, 1999.

Spivak, Gayatri Chakravorty. *Death of a Discipline*. New York: Columbia University Press, 2003.

Spivak, Gayatri Chakravorty. *Outside in the Teaching Machine*. New York: Routledge, 1993.

Squires, Claire. *Zadie Smith's* White Teeth: *A Reader's Guide*. New York: Continuum, 2002.

Stam, Robert. *Tropical Multiculturalism: A Comparative History of Race in Brazilian Cinema and Culture*. Durham, NC: Duke University Press, 1997.

Stanton, Domna. "On Linguistic Human Rights and the United States 'Foreign' Language Crisis." *Profession 2005*, 64–79.

Steger, Manfred B. *The Rise of the Global Imaginary: Political Ideologies from the French Revolution to the Global War on Terror*. Oxford: Oxford University Press, 2008.

Steiner, George. *After Babel: Aspects of Language and Translation*. 3rd ed. Oxford: Oxford University Press, 1998.

Stierle, Karlheinz. "Translatio Studii and Renaissance: From Vertical to Horizontal Translation." In Budick and Iser, *The Translatability of Cultures*, 55–67.

Sussman, Henry. *Idylls of the Wanderer: Outside in Literature and Theory*. New York: Fordham University Press, 2007.

Tabbi, Joseph, and Michael Wutz, eds. *Reading Matters: Narrative in the New Media Ecology*. Ithaca, NY: Cornell University Press, 1997.

Tan, Amy. "Mother Tongue." In Muller, *The New World Reader*, 119–25.

Taylor, Charles. *The Ethics of Authenticity*. Cambridge, MA: Harvard University Press, 1992.

Taylor, Charles. "The Politics of Recognition." In Taylor, *Multiculturalism*, 25–73.

Taylor, Charles. *Sources of the Self: The Making of Modern Identity*. Cambridge, MA: Harvard University Press, 1989.

Taylor, Charles. *Multiculturalism: Examining the Politics of Recognition*. With commentary by K. Anthony Appiah, Jürgen Habermas, Steven C. Rockefeller, Michael Walzer, and Susan Wolf. Edited and introduction by Amy Gutmann. Princeton, NJ: Princeton University Press, 1994.

Taylor, Mark C. *Altarity*. Chicago: University of Chicago Press, 1987.

Taylor, Mark C. "Introduction: System . . . Structure . . . Difference . . . Other." In *Deconstruction in Context: Literature and Philosophy*, edited by Mark C. Taylor, 1–34. Chicago: University of Chicago Press, 1986.

Taylor, Mark C. "Paralectics." Scharlemann, *On the Other*, 10–41.

Teilhard de Chardin, Pierre. *The Human Phenomenon*. A new edition and translation of *Le phénomène humain* by Sarah Appleton-Weber. With a foreword by Brian Swimme. Brighton, UK: Sussex Academic Press, 1999.

Teilhard de Chardin, Pierre. *The Letters of Teilhard de Chardin and Lucile Swan.* With a foreword by Pierre Leroy. Edited by Thomas M. King and Mary Wood Gilbert. Scranton, PA: University of Scranton Press, 2001.

Teilhard de Chardin, Pierre. *Lettres à Léontine Zanta.* Introduction by Robert Garric and Henri de Lubac. Paris: Desclée De Brouwer, 1965.

Teilhard de Chardin, Pierre. *Le Phénomène humain.* Paris: Seuil, 1955.

Terada, Rei. "Preface: Approaching Proximity." *Postmodern Culture* 15, no. 2 (2005). http://muse.jhu.edu/journals/postmodern_culture/toc/pmc15.2.html (accessed August 30, 2005).

Todorov, Tzvetan. *La conquête de l'Amérique: La question de l'autre.* Paris: Seuil, 1991.

Todorov, Tzvetan. *Nous et les autres: La réflexion française sur la diversité humaine.* Paris: Seuil, 1992.

Todorov, Tzvetan. *Le Nouveau Désordre mondial: Réflexions d'un Européen.* Preface by Stanley Hoffmann. Paris: Robert Laffont, 2003.

Todorov, Tzvetan. *La Peur des barbares: Au-delà du choc des civilisations.* Paris: Robert Laffont, 2008.

Todorov, Tzvetan. *La Vie commune: Essai d'anthropologie générale.* Paris: Seuil, 2003.

Tomlinson, John. "Globalization and Cultural Analysis." In Held and McGrew, *Globalization Theory,* 148–68.

Tomlinson, John. *Globalization and Culture.* Chicago: University of Chicago Press, 1999.

Tompkins, Jane, ed. *Reader-Response Criticism: From Formalism to Post-Structuralism.* Baltimore: Johns Hopkins University Press, 1980.

Toulmin, Stephen. *Cosmopolis: The Hidden Agenda of Modernity.* Chicago: University of Chicago Press, 1990.

Tuan, Yi-Fu. *Cosmos and Hearth: A Cosmopolite's Viewpoint.* Minneapolis: University of Minnesota Press, 1996.

Updike, John. *Bech at Bay.* New York: Knopf, 1998.

Updike, John. *Brazil.* New York: Random House, 1994.

Updike, John. *Licks of Love: Short Stories and a Sequel.* New York: Knopf, 2000.

Valdez Moses, Michael. *The Novel and the Globalization of Culture.* New York: Oxford University Press, 1995.

Valéry, Paul. *Variété II.* Paris: Gallimard, 1930.

Van der Veer, Peter. "Colonial Cosmopolitanism." In Vertovec and Cohen, *Conceiving Cosmopolitanism,* 165–79.

Vasset, Philippe. *ScriptGenerator©®™.* Translated by Jane Metter. London: Serpent's Tail, 2004.

Vattimo, Gianni. *The Transparent Society.* Baltimore: Johns Hopkins University Press, 1992.

Venuti, Lawrence. *The Scandals of Translation: Toward an Ethics of Difference.* New York: Routledge, 1998.

Venuti, Lawrence, ed. *The Translation Studies Reader.* 2nd ed. New York: Routledge, 2004.

Verdery, Katherine. *National Ideology under Socialism: Identity and Cultural Politics in Ceauşescu's Romania.* Berkeley: University of California Press, 1995.

Vertovec, Steven, and Robin Cohen, eds. *Conceiving Cosmopolitanism: Theory, Context, and Practice.* New York: Oxford University Press, 2002.

Vizenor, Gerald. *Landfill Meditation: Crossblood Stories.* Middleton, CT: Wesleyan University Press, 1991.

Walkowitz, Rebecca. *Cosmopolitan Style: Modernism beyond the Nation.* New York: Columbia University Press, 2006.

Wallace, Molly. " 'A Bizarre Ecology': The Nature of Denatured Nature." *Interdisciplinary Studies in Literature and Environment* 7, no. 2 (Summer 2000): 137–53.

Wallace, Molly. "Tropics of Globalization: Reading the New North America." *symploke* 9, no. 1–2 (2001): 145–60.

Wallerstein, Immanuel. *Geopolitics and Geoculture: Essays on the Changing World-System.* Cambridge: Cambridge University Press / Paris: Maison des Sciences de l'Homme, 1991.

Wallerstein, Immanuel. *The Modern World-System.* Vol. 1. New York: Academic Press, 1974.

Wallerstein, Immanuel. "Revolts against the System." *New Left Review,* 2nd ser., 18 (November–December 2002): 29–39.

Wallerstein, Immanuel. *Utopistics, or Historical Choices of the Twenty-first Century.* New York: New Press, 1998.

Wallerstein, Immanuel. *World-Systems Analysis: An Introduction.* Durham, NC: Duke University Press, 2004.

Warnier, Jean-Pierre. *La mondialisation de la culture.* 3rd ed. Paris: La Découverte, 2004.

Watson, Julia. "What's in a Name? Heteroglossic Naming as Multicultural Practice in American Autobiography." *Prose Studies* 17, no. 1 (April 1994): 95–119.

Westphal, Bertrand. *La Géocritique: Réel, fiction, espace.* Paris: Minuit, 2007.

Whitman, Walt. *Complete Poetry and Selected Prose.* Edited with an introduction and glossary by James E. Miller, Jr. Boston: Houghton Mifflin, 1959.

Wildiers, N. M. "Avant-propos." In Teilhard de Chardin, *Le Phénomène humain,* 11–15.

Wildiers, N. M. *An Introduction to Teilhard de Chardin.* Translation by Hubert Hoskins. Preface by Christopher F. Mooney. New York: Harper & Row, 1968.

Wilson, Rob, and Wimal Dissanayake. "Introduction: Tracing the Global/Local." In *Global/Local: Cultural Production and the Transnational Imaginary.* Edited by Rob Wilson and Wimal Dissanayake, 1–18. Durham, NC: Duke University Press, 1996.

Wolfreys, Julian, ed. *Literary Theories: A Reader and Guide.* New York: NYU Press, 1999.

Wolton, Dominique. *L'Autre mondialisation.* Paris: Flammarion, 2003.

Woolf, Virginia. "Mr. Bennett and Mrs. Brown." In *Modernism: An Anthology of Sources and Documents,* edited by Vassiliki Kolocotroni, Jane Goldman, and Olga Taxidou, 395–97. Chicago: University of Chicago Press, 1999.

Wu, Yung-Hsing. "Native Sons and Native Speakers: On the Eth(n)ics of Comparison." *PMLA* 121, no. 5 (October 2006): 1460–64.

Wutz, Michael. *Enduring Words: Literary Narrative in a Changing Media Ecology.* Tuscaloosa: University of Alabama Press, 2009.

Yamashita, Karen Tei. *Brazil-Maru.* Minneapolis: Coffee House Press, 1992.

Yamashita, Karen Tei. "An Interview with Karen Tei Yamashita." By Jean Vengua Gier and Carla Alicia Tejeda. *Jouvert* 2, no. 2 (September 2001). http://social .chass.ncsu.edu/jouvert/v2i2/yamashi.htm (accessed June 10, 2004).

Yamashita, Karen Tei. *Through the Arc of the Rain Forest.* Minneapolis: Coffee House Press, 1990.

Yamashita, Karen Tei. *Tropic of Orange.* Minneapolis: Coffee House Press, 1997.

Yarbrough, Stephen R. *Inventive Intercourse: From Rhetorical Conflict to the Ethical Creation of Novel Truth.* Carbondale: Southern Illinois University Press, 2006.

Young-Bruehl, Elisabeth, ed. *Global Cultures: A Transnational Short Fiction Reader.* Middletown, CT: Wesleyan University Press, 1994.

Zaloom, Caitlin. "Trading on Numbers." In Fisher and Downey, *Frontiers of Capital,* 58–85.

Zapf, Hubert. *Kulturökologie und Literatur: Beiträge zu einem transdisziplinären Paradigma der Literaturwissenschaft.* Heidelberg: Universitätsverlag Winter, 2008.

Zapf, Hubert. *Literatur als kulturelle Ökologie: Zur Kulturellen Funktion imaginativer Texte an Beispielen des amerikanischen Romans.* Tübingen: Max Niemeyer, 2002.

Zeller, Eduard. *The Stoics, Epicureans, and Sceptics.* Translated from the German by Oswald J. Reichel. New and revised ed. New York: Russell & Russell, 1962.

Žižek, Slavoj. "The Ideology of the Empire and Its Traps." In Passavant and Dean, *Empire's New Clothes,* 263–64.

Žižek, Slavoj. "Love Thy Neighbor? No, Thanks!" In *The Psychoanalysis of Race,* edited by Christopher Lane, 154–75. New York: Columbia University Press, 1998.

Žižek, Slavoj, Eric Satner, and Kenneth Reinhard. *The Neighbor: Three Inquiries in Political Theology.* Chicago: University of Chicago Press, 2005.

INDEX